The Best Bed & Breakfast
in England, Scotland & Wales
1993 – 94

Sigourney Welles
Jill Darbey
Joanna Mortimer

The finest Bed & Breakfast accommodations in the

British Isles

from the Scottish Hebrides to

London's Belgravia

Country Houses, Town Houses, City Apartments, Manor
Houses, Village Cottages, Farmhouses, Castles

U.K.H.M. Publishing, London, U.K.
The Globe Pequot Press, Chester, Connecticut, U.S.A.

The publishers have made every reasonable effort to ensure that the accommodations mentioned in this guide are as stated. They cannot, however, accept liability for any inaccuracies, errors, or omissions that may occur.

Library of Congress Catalog Card Number: 91-074158

U.S. ISBN 1-56440-085-9

Typeset by U.K.H.M. Publishing Ltd., London.
Printed and bound in Hong Kong

U.K.H.M. Publishing Ltd., P.O. Box 2070, London W12 8QW, England.

Stoke Cottage. Lincolnshire.

Broughton House. Cheshire.

Contents

Nab Cottage. Cumbria.

Foreword

Bed & Breakfast has suddenly become the fashionable way to travel. The secret has escaped & thousands of people are discovering for themselves that it is possible to combine high quality accommodation with friendly, personal attention at very reasonable prices. The New York Times said about us that "...after an unannounced inspection of rooms booked through The Worldwide Bed & Breakfast Association it is clear that the standards of comfort & cleanliness are exemplary ...at least as good as in a five star hotel & in most cases, better, reflecting the difference between sensitive hosts taking pride in their homes & itinerant hotel staff doing as little as they can get away with..."

Discerning travellers are turning away from the impersonal hotels with the expensive little refridgerators & microwave breakfasts in each room. How much nicer to have a real English breakfast to begin the day, enough to keep you going until evening. Many of our houses will provide dinner too - often the hostess will be a Cordon Bleu cook & the price will be within your range.

We try to provide the best accommodation possible within a wide range of prices, some as little as £9.00 per person per night, whilst others will be up to £55.00 per person per night. The choice is yours, but you can be certain that each will be the best available in that particular area of the country at that price.

Our inspectors are out & about visiting our homes to ensure that standards are maintained. We encourage everyone to use the recommendations & complaints page at the back of the book, to let us know your opinion of the accommodation or to inform us of any delightful homes you may have come across & would like to recommend for future inclusion.

In order to avoid the classification trap, which we feel is invidious, we encourage you to read about each home, what they offer & their respective price range, so that you find the one that best suits your expectations. Our hosts in turn offer hospitality in their own unique style, so each home naturally retains its individuality & interest. We have found this to be a very successful recipe which has often led to firm friendships with invitations being extended to visit each other again.

Bed & Breakfast really is a marvellous way to travel, meeting a delightful cross section of fellow travellers with whom to exchange information & maybe the address of ...that lovely little place which was discovered by chance and which serves the most delicious dinner or... the best route to take to a particular farmhouse but make sure you get there by 5 o'clock so that you're in time to watch the evening milking...

This is the fun & real pleasure that is part of Bed & Breakfasting. Once you've tried it you will be a dedicated Best Bed & Breakfaster.

How to use this Guide

To get the full benefits of staying at our Bed & Breakfast homes it is important to appreciate how they differ from hotels, so both hosts & guests know what to expect.

Arrival & Departure

These times are more important to a family than to hotel desk clerks, so your time of arrival (E.T. A.) is vital information when making a reservation either with the home directly or with one of our agencies. This becomes even more important to your reception if you intend travelling overnight & will be arriving in the early morning. So please have this information & your flight number ready when you book your rooms. Under most circumstances the usual check-in time is 6 p.m., & you will be expected to check out by 10a.m. on the morning of departure. These arrangements do vary from home to home so the secret to an enjoyable visit is to let your hosts know as much about your plans as possible & they will do their best to meet your requirements.

Other personal requests

There are a few other details that you should let your hosts know when planning your Bed & Breakfast trip that will make everyone much happier during your visit.

* Do you smoke? Would you prefer to be in a non-smoking home?

* Do you suffer from any allergies? Some families have cats, dogs, birds & other pets in the house.

* Can you make it up a flight of stairs? Would you prefer the ground floor?

* Do you have any special dietary requirements? Will you be staying for dinner?

* Do you prefer a private bathroom or are you prepared to share facilities?

* Do you prefer a shower instead of a bath?

* The ages of any children travelling

In all these cases let your host know what you need & the details can be arranged before you arrive rather than presenting a problem when you are shown to your rooms.

Prices

The prices quoted throughout the guide are the *minimum* per person per night. These prices will increase during the busy seasons. You should always confirm the prevailing rate when you make a reservation.

Facilities

The bathroom & toilet facilities effect the prices. Sharing is the cheapest, private is a little more costly & en-suite carries a premium.

Descriptions

Rooms are described as follows: Single = 1 bed (often quite small); Double = 1 large bed (sometimes King or Queen size); Twin = 2 separate single beds; Four-poster = a King or Queen size bed with a canopy above supported by four corner posts.

Bathrooms & toilets are described as follows: Shared = these facilities are shared with some other guests or perhaps the hosts; Private = for your use only, however they may occasionally be in an adjacent room; En-suite = private facilities within your bedroom suite.

Four Chimneys. Devon.

Making a Reservation

Once you have chosen where you want to stay, have all the following information ready & your reservation will go smoothly without having to run & find more travel documents or ask someone else what they think you should do. Here is a brief check list of what you will probably be asked & examples to illustrate answers:

* Dates & number of nights .... August 14-19 (6 nights).
* Estimated time of arrival at the home ....7p.m. (evening) & flight number.
* Type & number of rooms 1 Double & 2 Singles.
* Toilet & Bathroom facilities ...1 Double en-suite) & 2 singles (shared)
* Smoking or Non-smoking?
* Any allergies?
* Special dietary requests?
* Children in the party & their ages?
* Any other preferences .... Is a shower preferred to a bath?
* Maximum budget per person per night based on all the above details.

London Reservations
There is a two night minimum stay at our London Homes

These can only be made through one of the Worldwide Bed & Breakfast Agencies. A full list appears overleaf & they can be contacted by phone or fax.

All reservations must be confirmed with advance payments which are non-refundable in the event of cancellation & you simply pay the balances due after you arrive at the home. The advance payment can be made with the major credit & charge cards or by cheque. Cash is the preferred method of paying the balance & always in pounds sterling.

The advance payments confirm each night of your visit - **not just the first one**. When arriving at a later date or departing at an earlier date than those confirmed, the guest will be liable to pay only the appropriate proportion of the stated balance that is due, For example,staying three nights out of four booked means paying 3/4 of the stated balance due. A minimum of 2 nights will always apply.

Outside London
We encourage you to make use of the information in this guide & contact the homes directly. The hosts may require varying amounts of advance payments & may or may not accept credit & charge cards.

If you wish one of the agencies to make the reservations for you there will be a standard booking fee of £15 (or currency equivalent) for each location confirmed & the entire cost must be paid in advance. The scale of refunds for cancellation is shown below. This full payment can be charged to a major credit card or paid by cheque. The confirmed prices shall be those prevailing on the dates required ... as previously mentioned, *the prices shown in this guide are the minimum & will increase during the busy seasons.*

Alterations
If you wish to alter or change a previously confirmed booking though one of the agencies there will be a further fee of £15 per alteration.

Cancellations
All advance payments for London are non-refundable.
All booking fees Outside London are non-refundable.
Notice of cancellation must be given as soon as possible & the following rates shall apply **outside London only**
    50 days notice - Full refund.
    30-49 days notice - 80% refund.
    10-29 days notice - 50% refund
    0-9 days notice - No refund.
The Worldwide Bed & Breakfast Agencies reserve the right to alter your accommodation should it be necessary & will inform you of any alteration as soon as possible.

The Discount Offer

This offer is made to people who have bought this book & wish to make reservations for Bed & Breakfast in London through one of our participating agencies listed below.

The offer only applies to a minimum stay of three consecutive nights at one of our London homes between the following January 1. 1993 & April 15. 1993 then from September 15 .1993 to December 1. 1993 Only one discount per booking is allowed. Call the reservation office to make your booking in the normal way & tell the clerk that you have bought the book & wish to have the discount. After a couple of questions the discount will be deducted from the advance payment required to confirm the reservation.

Participating Agencies

In the U.K. call:

Tel: 081 742 9123 (24 Hrs.)

Fax: 081 749 7084

Outside the U.K. call:

Tel: 44 81 742 9123 (24 Hrs.)

Fax: 44 81 749 7084

In the U.S call: Toll Free 800 852 2632

Look for this symbol

Counties map

Each county has been assigned a page number where a more detailed map can be found. These maps include principal towns, major roads & the location of each Bed & Breakfast establishment.

WESTERN ISLES

SUTHERLAND

ROSS-SHIRE

HIGHLAND

ABERDEENSHIRE
431

ISLE of SKYE
448

INVERNESS
444

GRAMPIAN

SCOTLAND
419

PERTHSHIRE
449

431

ARGYLL

TAYSIDE

CENTRAL

FIFESHIRE
443

Edinburgh **436**

DUMBARTON **434**
LANARKSHIRE
AYRESHIRE **432**
STRATHCLYDE

LOTHIAN **449**

SELKIRK
PEEBLES
453 ROXBURGHSHIRE
BORDER

DUMFRIES &
GALLOWAY **434**

NORTHUMBERLAND

North Sea

TYNE AND WEAR
282

CUMBRIA
103

DURHAM

CLEVELAND

YORKSHIRE

400 HUMBERSIDE

LANCASHIRE
245

Irish Sea

MERSEYSIDE
MANCHESTER

CHESHIRE
76

127

254

LINCOLNSHIRE
260

ENGLAND

CLWYD
463

DERBYSHIRE
&
STAFFORD-
SHIRE

NOTT-
INGHAM
SHIRE
&
LEICESTER-
SHIRE

NORFOLK
267

GWYNEDD
470

SHROP-
SHIRE
304

WARWICK-
SHIRE
361

CAMBRIDGE-
SHIRE
& NORTHAMPTON-
SHIRE
67

SUFFOLK
331

479
POWYS

HEREFORD
&
WORCESTER
212

WALES
460

463
DYFED

466
GWENT
467

GLAMORGAN

182
GLOUCESTER
SHIRE

290
OXFORD
SHIRE

BEDFORDSHIRE,
BERKSHIRE,
BUCKINGHAMSHIRE
&
HERTFORDSHIRE
58

ESSEX
176

LONDON
18

36
AVON

WILTSHIRE
382

338
SURREY

KENT
214

SOMERSET
314

HAMPSHIRE
199

SUSSEX
348

164
DORSET

DEVON
139

84
CORNWALL

English Channel

Regions

To assist tourists with information during their travels, counties have been grouped together under Regional Tourist Boards that co-ordinate the various efforts of each county.

The British Tourist Authority has designated these areas in consultation with the English, Scottish & Wales Tourist Boards & we have largely adopted these areas for use in this guide

Counties are listed alphabetically throughout our guide & then have a sub heading indicating which Tourist Region they belong to.

ENGLAND
Cumbria
County of Cumbria
Northumbria.
Counties of Cleveland, Durham, Northumberland, Tyne & Wear.
North West
Counties of Cheshire, Greater Manchester, Lancashire, Merseyside, High Peaks of Derbyshire.
Yorkshire & Humberside
Counties of North Yorkshire, South Yorkshire, West Yorkshire, Humberside.
Heart of England
Counties of Gloucestershire, Herefordshire & Worcestershire, Shropshire, Staffordshire, Warwickshire, West Midlands.
East Midlands
Counties of Derbyshire, Leicestershire, Lincolnshire, Northamptonshire, Nottinghamshire.
East Anglia
Counties of Cambridgeshire, Essex, Norfolk, Suffolk.
West Country
Counties of Avon, Cornwall, Devon, Dorset (parts of), Somerset, Wiltshire, Isles of Scilly.
Southern
Counties of Hampshire, Dorset (East & North), Isle of Wight.
South East
Counties of East Sussex,Kent, Surrey West Sussex.

SCOTLAND
The subdivisions of Scottish Regions in this guide differ slightly from the current Marketing Regions of the Scottish Tourist Board.

The Borders, Dumfries & Galloway
Districts & counties of Scottish Borders, Dumfries & Galloway.
Lothian & Strathclyde
City of Edinburgh, Forth Valley, East Lothian, Kirkaldy, St. Andrews & North-East Fife, Greater Glasgow, Clyde Valley, Ayrshire & Clyde Coast, Burns Country.
Argyll & The Isles
Districts & counties of Oban & Mull, Mid Argyll, Kintyre & Islay, Dunoon, Cowal, Rothesay & Isle of Bute, Isle of Arran.
Perthshire, Loch Lommond & The Trossachs.
Districts & counties of Perthshire, Loch Lomond, Stirling & Trossachs.
The Grampians
Districts & counties of Banff & Buchan, Moray, Gordon, Angus, City of Aberdeen, Kincardine & Deeside, City of Dundee.
The Highlands & Islands
Districts & counties of Shetland, Orkney, Caithness, Sutherland, Ross & Cromarty, Western Isles, South West Ross & Isle of Skye, Inverness, Loch Ness & Nairn, Aviemore & Spey Valley, Fort William & Lochaber

WALES
The regions are defined as follows:
North Wales
Counties of Clwyd & Gwynedd (northern)
Mid Wales
Counties of Gwynedd (southern), Dyfed (northern) & Powys (northern)
South Wales
Counties of Gwent, West, South & Mid Glamorgan, Dyfed (southern) & Powys (southern).

The photographs appearing in the Introductions & Gazeteers are by courtesy of the appropriate Tourist Board for each county or W.W.B.B.A.

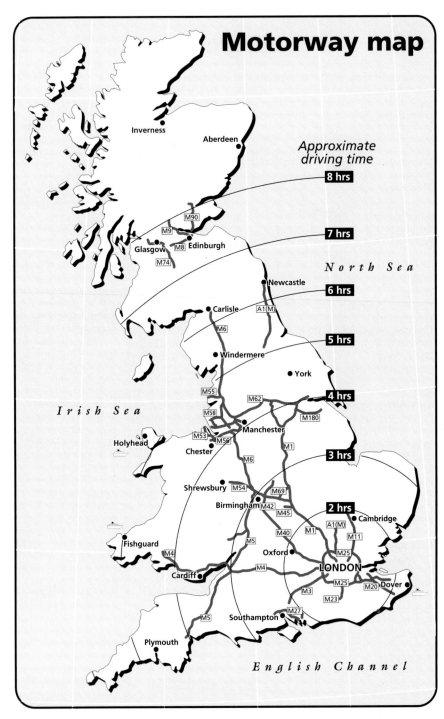

Motorway map

Approximate driving time

8 hrs

7 hrs

6 hrs

5 hrs

4 hrs

3 hrs

2 hrs

North Sea

Irish Sea

English Channel

Inverness

Aberdeen

M90

M9

Glasgow M8 Edinburgh

M74

Newcastle

Carlisle A1(M)

M6

Windermere

York

M55

M62

M58

M180

M53

M59

M51 Manchester

Holyhead

Chester

M1

M6

Shrewsbury M54

M69

Birmingham M42

M45

M40 M1 A1(M) Cambridge

M5

M11

Fishguard M4

M4

Oxford M25

M4 LONDON

Cardiff

M25 M20 Dover

M3

M23

M5 M27

Southampton

Plymouth

14

General Information

To help overseas visitors with planning their trip to Britain, we have compiled the next few pages explaining the basic requirements & customs you will find here.

Before you arrive

Documents you will have to obtain before you arrive;

Valid passports & visas. Citizens of Commonwealth countries or the U.S.A. don't need visas to enter the U.K.

Bring your local Driving Licence.

Medical Insurance.

This is strongly recommended although visitors will be able to receive free emergency treatment. If you have to stay in hospital in the U.K. you will be asked to pay unless you are a citizen of European Community Countries.

Restrictions on arrival

Immigration procedures can be lengthy & bothersome, be prepared for questions like:

a) where are you staying in the U.K.?

b) do you have a round trip ticket?

c) how long do you intend to stay?

d) how much money are you bringing in with you?

e) do you have a credit card?

Do not bring any animals with you as they are subject to 6 months quarantine & there are severe penalties for bringing in pets without appropriate licences. Do not bring any firearms, prohibited drugs or carry these things for anyone else. If you are in doubt about items in your possession, declare them by entering the Red Channel at Customs & seek the advice of an officer.

After you have arrived

You can bring in as much currency as you like. You can change your own currency or travellers cheques at many places at varying rates.

Airports tend to be the most expensive places to change money & the 'Bureau de Change" are often closed at nights. So bring enough Sterling to last you at least 2 or 3 days. Banks often charge commission for changing money. Some Cashcard machines (or A.T.M.'s) will dispense local currency using your charge card, if they are affiliated systems, & don't charge commissions to your account.

Major credit cards/charge cards are widely accepted & you may only need to carry small amounts of cash for "pocket money".

Driving

Don't forget to drive on the Left... especially the first time you get into a car... at the airport car hire parking lot... or from the front of a railway station... or straight after breakfast... old habits are hard to shake off. If you need to know the rules, get a copy of the Highway Code. You must wear a seat belt & so must any other front seat passenger. The speed limits are clearly shown in most areas - generally 30 mph. in residential areas (48 kph) & 70 mph on motorways (113 kph.). Traffic lights are at the side of the road & not hanging overhead. Car hire is relatively expensive in the U.K. & it is often a good idea to arrange this before you arrive. Mileage charges, V.A.T. (Sales Tax) & insurance are usually charged extra & you will need to be over 21 to hire a car in the U.K. Petrol (gas) is also relatively expensive & you may find petrol stations hard to find or closed at night in rural areas... so fill up often. Driving in London is not a recommended experience for newcomers & parking is also a very complex arrangement which can become a nightmare if the car gets "clamped" (immobilised) or towed away.

General Information

Buses & Coaches

If you are not driving & only want to travel 5-10 miles there are good bus services within most towns & cities, however, rural routes have seriously declined over the last few years. There are regular & fast coach services between the major towns which are very popular - so book ahead to be sure of a seat.

Trains

There is an extensive railway system throughout the U.K. which serves the major towns on a fast & frequent basis. British Rail is a relatively expensive service & like most railway systems subject to delays.

However, if you plan to do lots of rail travel the best deal is to buy a Britrail Pass before you leave home (you can't buy these once in the U.K.)

Tubes (Subways)

London is the only city with an extensive subway system although some other towns do have "Metro" trains of linked under & overground systems.

The "tube" is a very popular means of getting around London, but it can get very crowded & unpleasant at "rush hours". It is often the preferred way to get into London from say Heathrow airport in the early morning, when there are long delays on the roads that hold up both buses & taxis with increasingly expensive rides into the city centre, £25 is not unusual for this cab fare, compared with a few pounds on the "tube". The "tube" in London is operated by London Transport which also operates the London bus service ... the famous red buses. They sell tickets which allow you to travel all over London on tubes, buses & trains at very good rates, called Travelcards... a transfer system. Ask your local travel agent about these & other travel passes throughout the U.K.

Telephones - *When calling the U.K. from abroad always drop the 0 from the area code.*

In the U.K. the only free calls are the operator - 100, enquiries - 192 (international 153), emergencies - 999.

You may use your calling card to call home which is billed to your account or call collect, ask the operator to "reverse charge" the call. The famous red telephone kiosks are slowly being replaced with new glass booths & they differ in that the old boxes only take 10 & 50 pence pieces & don't give any change, whereas the new ones take many combinations of coins & do give change. Phonecards are becoming more popular as the number of boxes that only accept these cards increases. Cards can be bought at Post Offices & many newsagents & shops.

Doctors/Chemists

All local police stations have lists of chemists & doctors should you need one, at night, for instance.

Voltage

The standard voltage throughout the country is 240v AC.50Hz. If you bring small electrical appliances with you, a converter will be required.

Tipping

Is not obligatory anywhere but a general guide if you wish to leave a tip for service is between 10%-15%.

Pubs

Open between 11 a.m. & 11 p.m. on weekdays in England & Wales. On Sundays the hours are 12 noon to 3 p.m & 5 p.m. to 11p.m. In Scotland the hours are different - 11a.m. to 2.30 p.m. & 5 p.m. to 11p.m. on weekdays & 12.30 p.m. to 2.30p.m. & 6p.m to 11 p.m. on Sundays You must be over 18 years old to buy & drink alcohol in pubs .

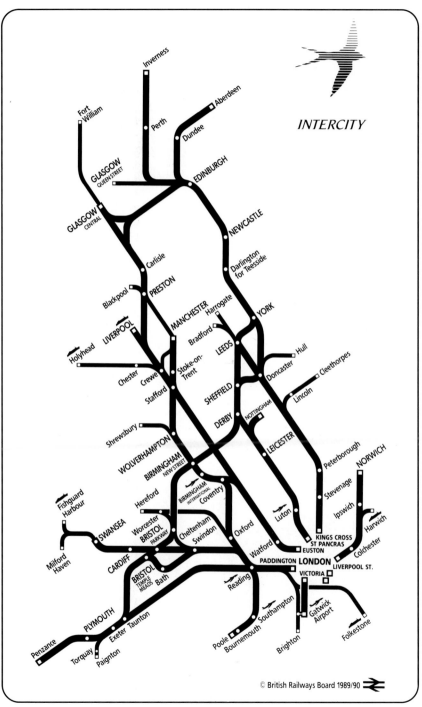

INTERCITY

© British Railways Board 1989/90

LONDON MAP

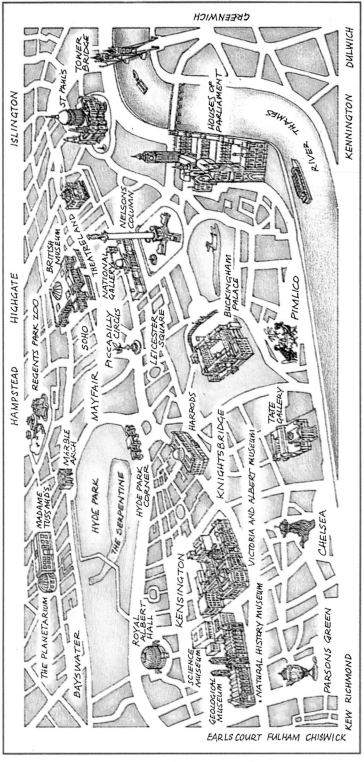

Home No. 48.   London.

London

	minimum £ per person	children taken	evening meals	animals taken

Home No. 59
W.W.B.B.A.
London
Tel:081-742-9123 (24 hrs.)
Fax: 081-749-7084
U.S. Toll Free
800-852-2632

Nearest Tube: High St. Ken. Situated just off Kensington High Street & a short stroll from Kensington Palace Gardens. This delightful apartment set in a converted Edwardian building offers 1 large double bedded room with ensuite bathroom. A choice of Continental or full English breakfast is served. A lovely home & a most charming host. Perfect for restaurants, shopping & all the sights.

£31.00 — N | N | N

Home No. 60
W.W.B.B.A.
London
Tel:081-742-9123 (24 hrs.)
Fax: 081-749-7084
U.S. Toll Free
800-852-2632

Nearest Tube: High St. Ken. A beautifully appointed home located in a quiet cul-de-sac close to Kensington Palace. A lift will take you to the 2nd floor accommodation. A delightful, spacious double room with brass bed, T.V., tea/coffee makers & biscuits are also provided. A delicious varied breakfast is also served. Knightsbridge, Kensington & the park are all just a short walk from here.

£30.00 — N | N | N

Home No. 62
W.W.B.B.A.
London
Tel:081-742-9123 (24 hrs.)
Fax: 081-749-7084
U.S. Toll Free
800-852-2632

Nearest Tube: Chalk Farm An exquisitely furnished interior designed Victorian home, very comfortable & extremely attractive. The charming hosts who really make you feel at home, offer 1 beautiful twin bedded room with ensuite bathroom. Ideally located close to Regents Park & only 5 mins. from the tube, this is a perfect base from which to exlpore London; ideal for theatreland, shopping, the British Museum & all major tourist attractions.

£25.00 — N | N | N

Home No. 69
W.W.B.B.A.
London
Tel:081-742-9123 (24 hrs.)
Fax: 081-749-7084
U.S. Toll Free
800-852-2632

Nearest Tube: Sloane Square. Centrally located, excellent for all the attractions of London including Knightsbridge, Harrods, Chelsea, Buckingham Palace, etc. This is a beautifully decorated & comfortably furnished home offering guests a choice of one double & one single room. There is also a small garden where breakfast may be served in summer. The host is very pleasant & helpful.

£30.00 — N | N | N

Home No. 75
W.W.B.B.A.
London
Tel: 081-742-9123 (24 hrs.)
Fax: 081-749-7084
U.S. Toll Free
800-852-2632

Nearest Tube: South Fields This is a most charming house in Wimbledon, only five minutes walk from the All England Tennis Club. A very pretty twin room & a single which share the same bathroom suite. Quiet & luxurious. It is like being in the heart of the country with pretty gardens & trees all around. The hostess will provide dinner if ordered in advance & will collect from the station whenever possible. A delightful home, ideal for a relaxing break.

£26.00 — N | N | N

see PHOTO over

Home No. 77 .   London.

London

		minimum £ per person	children taken	evening meals	animals taken
Home No. 86 **W.W.B.B.A.** **London** **Tel:081-742-9123 (24 hrs.)** **Fax: 081-749-7084** **U.S. Toll Free** **800-852-2632**	Nearest Tube:Earls Court. Situated on the 1st. floor of a period mansion block. This very spacious & attractive apartment with elevator access, offers 1 twin with private bathroom & 2 single bedded rooms, each very comfortable & tastefully furnished. Very friendly hosts who are well travelled & speak a variety of languages. An ideal base from which to explore London. Close to all amenities.	£27.00	N	N	N
Home No. 88 **W.W.B.B.A.** **London** **Tel:081-742-9123 (24 hrs.)** **Fax: 081-749-7084** **U.S. Toll Free** **800-852-2632**	Nearest Tube: Knightsbridge Ideal for the single traveller: this is an excellent London stop over. Located only 5 minutes walk from the famous Harrods store in Knightsbridge. The charming host offers accommodation in 1 single & a single sofa bedded room both well furnished & attractively decorated. Museums, Parks & Palaces are all easily accessed from this centrally situated home.	£32.00	N	N	N
Home No. 100 **W.W.B.B.A.** **London** **Tel:081-749-7084 (24 hrs.)** **Fax: 081-749-7084** **U.S. Toll Free** **800-852-2632**	Nearest Tube: Gloucester Rd. This is a very pleasant, large, well decorated apartment in the much sought after area of Kensington. The accommodation comprises a large en-suite double with tea/coffee making facilities. A full english breakfast is served in the attractive dining room. Ideal for sightseeing this home is just a 5 minute stroll from the Victoria & Albert museum. Many good restaurants locally.	£33.00	N	N	N
Home No. 104 **W.W.B.B.A.** **London** **Tel:081-742-9123 (24 hrs.)** **Fax: 081-749-7084** **U.S. Toll Free** **800-852-2632**	Nearest Tube: Fulham Broadway A fine Edwardian house standing in an elegant tree lined street in the Royal Borough of Kensington & Chelsea. The hosts are well travelled & enjoy the company of fellow adventurers. Accommodation is in a twin bedded room with private facilities. There are many good restaurants in the area & several popular pubs which provide excellent lunchtime meals. Good location for enjoying many of the tourist attractions.	£25.00	N	N	N
Home No. 110 **W.W.B.B.A.** **London** **Tel:081-742-9123 (24 hrs.)** **Fax: 081-749-7084** **U.S. Toll Free** **800-852-2632**	closed Sat & Sun Nearest Tube: West Brompton A warm welcome is extended to all guests at this attractively decorated Victorian terraced villa. Quietly located in a pleasant tree lined street, only a stones throw from the tube. A comfortable double with private facilities is available. Guests are given all kinds of useful hints on the best way to get around London. The comfortable lounge is always full of books & maps for guests to use at their leisure.	£25.00	N	N	N

30

Avon

During the Middle Ages the town prospered through Royal patronage & the development of the wool industry. Bath became a city of weavers, the leading industrial town in the West of England.

The 18th century gave us the superb Georgian architecture which is the city's glory. John Wood, an ambitious young architect laid out Queen Anne's Square in the grand Palladian style, & went on to produce his masterpiece, the Royal Crescent. His scheme for the city was continued by his son & a number of other fine architects, using the beautiful Bath stone. Bath was a centre of fashion, with Beau Nash the leader of a glittering society

In 1497 John & Sebastian Cabot sailed from the Bristol quayside to the land they called Ameryke, in honour of the King's agent in Bristol, Richard Ameryke. Bristol's involvement in the colonisation of the New World & the trade in sugar, tobacco & slaves that followed, made her the second city in the kingdom in the 18th century. John Cabot is commemorated by the Cabot Tower on grassy Brandon Hill - a fine vantage point from which to view the city. On the old docks below are the Bristol Industrial Museum & the SS Great Britain, Brunel's famous iron ship. Another achievement of this master engineer, the Clifton Suspension Bridge, spans Bristol's renowned beauty spot, the Clifton Gorge. For a glimpse of Bristol's elegant past, stroll through Clifton with its stately terraces & spacious Downs.

A short walk from the busy city centre & modern shopping area, the visitor in search of history will find cobbled King Street with its merchant seamens almhouses & The Theatre Royal, the oldest theatre in continuous use in England, & also Llandoger Trow, an ancient inn associated with Treasure Island & Robinson Crusoe.

Roman Baths. Bath.

Avon

Avon Gazeteer

Areas of Outstanding Natural Beauty
The Cotswolds & the Mendip Hills

Historic Houses & Castles

Badminton House - Badminton
Built in the reign of Charles II. Huge parkland where Horse Trials are held each year. Home of the Duke of Beaufort.

Clevedon Court - Clevedon
14th century manor house, 13th century hall, 12th century tower. Lovely garden with rare trees & shrubs. This is where Thackerey wrote much of 'Vanity Fair'.

Dodington House - Chipping Sodbury
Perfect 18th century house with superb staircase. Landscape by Capability Brown.

Dyrham Park - Between Bristol & Bath
17th century house - fine panelled rooms, Dutch paintings, furniture.

Horton Court - Horton
Cotswold manor house altered & restored in 19th century.

No. 1 Royal Crescent - Bath
An unaltered Georgian house built 1767.

Red Lodge - Bristol
16th century house - period furniture & panelling.

St. Vincent's Priory - Bristol
Gothic revival house, built over caves which were sanctuary for Christians.

Blaise Castle House - Henbury Nr. Bristol
18th century house - now folk museum, extensive woodlands.

Priory Park College - Bath
18th century Georgian mansion, now Roman Catholic school.

Claverton Manor - Nr. Bath
Greek revival house - furnished with 17th, 18th, 19th century American originals.

St Catherine's Court - Nr. Bath
Small Tudor house - associations with Henry VIII & Elizabeth I.

Cathedrals & Churches

Bristol Cathedral
Mediaeval. Eastern halfnave Victorian. Chapterhouse richly ornamented.

Bristol (St Mary Radcliffe)
Iron screen, 3 fonts" fairest parish church in all England".

Bristol (St. Stephens')
Perpendicular - monuments, magnificent tower.

Backwell (St. Andrew)
12th to 17th century, 15th century tower, repaired 17th century. 15th century tomb & chancel, 16th century screen, 18th century brass chandelier.

Bath Abbey
Perpendicular - monastic church, 15th century foundation. Nave finished 17th century, restorations in 1674.

Iron Acton (St. James the Less)
Perpendicular - 15th century memorial cross. 19th century mosaic floors, Laudian alter rails, Jacobean pulpit, effigies.

Wrington (All Souls)
15th century aisles & nave; font, stone pulpit, notable screens.

Yate (St. Mary)
Splendid perpendicular tower.

Museums & Galleries

American Museum in Britain - Claverton Nr. Bath
American decorative arts 17th to 19th century displayed in series of furnished rooms & galleries of special exhibits. Paintings, furniture, glass wood & metal work, textiles, folk sculpture, etc.

Holburne of Menstrie Museum - Bath
Old Master paintings, silver, glass, porcelain, furniture & miniatures in 18th century building. Work of 20th century craftworkers.

Victoria Art Gallery - Bath
Paintings, prints, drawings, glass, ceramics, watches, coins, etc. Bygones - permanent & temporary exhibitions. Geology collections.

Roman Museum - Bath
Material from remains of extensive Roman baths & other Roman sites.

Museum of Costume - Bath
Collection of fashion from 17th century to present day.

St. Nicholas Church & City Museum - Bristol
Mediaeval antiquities relating to local

Avon

history, Church plate & vestments. Altarpiece by Hogarth.

City of Bristol Museum - Bristol
Egyptology, archaeology, ethnography, geology. Bristol ships.

Bristol Industrial Museum - Bristol
Collections of transport items of land, sea & air. Many unique items.

City of Bristol Art Gallery - Bristol
Permanent & loan collections of paintings, English & Oriental ceramics.

Chatterton House - Bristol
Birth place of boy poet.
Historic Monuments

Kings Weston Roman Villa - Lawrence Weston
3rd & 4th centuries - mosaics of villa - some walls.

Hinton Priory - Hinton Charterhouse
13th century - ruins of Carthusian priory.

Temple Church - Bristol
14th & 15th century ruins.

Stoney Littleton Barrow - Nr. Bath
Neolithic burial chamber - restoration work 1858.

Roman Baths - Bath

Other things to see & do

Clifton Zoological Gardens - Bristol
Flourishing zoo with many exhibits - beautiful gardens.

Clifton Suspension Bridge - Bristol
Designed by Isambard Kingdom Brunel, opened in 1864. Viewpoint & picnic spot
Camera Obscura.

The Pump Room - Bath
18th century neo-classical interior. Spa water can be drunk here overlooking the famous hot springs.

Clifton Suspension Bridge. Bristol.

AVON

Map reference

1	Hunt	
1	Johnson	
1	Burton	
1	Addison	
1	Tovey	
1	Argyris	
1	Dodd	
1	Selby	
1	Beckett	
1	Webber	
1	Bennetts	
1	Warwick-Smith	
1	Burridge	
1	Ashman	
1	James	
1	Slape	
1	Smith	
1	King	
1	O'Flaherty	
1	Setchfield	
1	Stabbins	
1	Besley	

1	Stone
1	London
1	Archer
1	Willis
1	Kitching
2	Dore
3	Baxter
4	Graham
4	West
5	Weeks
6	Watts
7	Paz
8	Thornely
9	Rolls
9	Shellard
10	Healey

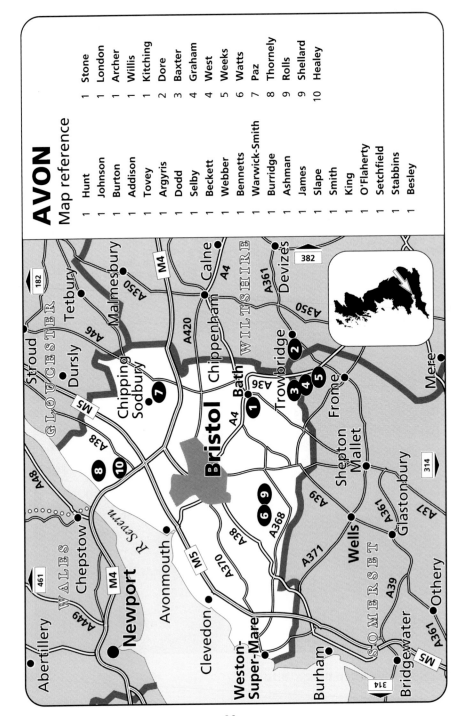

36

All the establishments mentioned in this guide
are members of the
Worldwide Bed & Breakfast Association.

If you have any comments regarding your
accommodation please send them to us
using the form at the back of the book.
We value your comments.

Avon

		minimum £ per person	children taken	evening meals	animals taken
Pat & Nigel Hunt **Armstrong House** **41 Crescent Gardens** **Upper Bristol Road** **Bath BA1 2NB** Tel: (0225) 442211 Open: ALL YEAR Map Ref No. 01	Nearest Road: A.4 A beautifully restored, Bath-city-centre Victorian house offering 4 comfortable, spacious bedrooms. All have en-suite facilities, colour T.V., hairdryers & tea/coffee making facilities. Full English breakfast is provided & the guests' sitting room is open at all times. Private parking is available. Only a short, level walk to all Bath has to offer. It is perfect for either a short break or an extended touring holiday in this lovely area.	£20.00	Y	N	N
Derek & Marjorie Dore **Arnolds Hill House** **Wingfield** **Bath** **BA14 9LB** Tel: (0225) 752025 Open: APR - OCT Map Ref No. 02	Nearest Road: A.366 This delightful Edwardian country house is set in 5 acres of attractive grounds & offers comfortable accommodation in gracious surroundings amid a relaxed & friendly atmosphere. Offering 3 double/twin bedrooms, 2 en-suite, each with colour T.V. & tea/coffee making facilities. Guests are free to relax in the sitting room or in the garden around the outdoor swimming pool. Ideally situated for visiting Bath, Bristol, Longleat, Stonehenge, Salisbury & Wells.	£17.50 (no smoking)	N	N	N
Douglas & Lynne Johnson **Astor House** **14 Oldfield Road** **Bath BA2 6SH** Tel: (0225) 429134 Open: APR - OCT Map Ref No. 01	Nearest Road: M.4, A.367 A pleasant Victorian house tastefully decorated in the style of the period. There are hot/cold basins in all bedrooms & tea making facilities, a pretty dining room & nice gardens. Quiet situation, just 10 minutes' walk from the centre of Bath. Very central for touring the Cotswolds & Wales. 3 double & 4 twin-bedded rooms. Several shower bathrooms. Children over 7 years .	£15.00	Y	N	N
John & Sue Burton **Badminton Villa** **10 Upper Oldfield Park** **Bath BA2 3JZ** Tel: (0225) 426347 Open: ALL YEAR Map Ref No. 01	Nearest Road: A.367 John & Sue welcome you to the friendly & relaxed atmosphere of Badminton Villa with its magnificent views of Bath. Conveniently situated in a quiet road just a 10 minute walk from the city centre. Bedrooms are very comfortable & are all en-suite with colour T.V. & tea/coffee facilities. Badminton Villa, with private car park, is the perfect location for visitors to Bath.	£24.00	Y	N	N
Margaret Addison **Bailbrook Lodge** **35/37 London Road West** **Bath BA1 7HZ** Tel: (0225) 859090 OpenALL YEAR (Excl.Xmas) Map Ref No. 01	Nearest Road: A.4 Bailbrook Lodge is a listed Georgian house located in pleasant surroundings on the outskirts of Bath, offering superb views across the Avon Valley. There is a choice of 13 en-suite bedrooms, all with colour T.V. & tea/coffee making facilities. Bailbrook offers full English breakfast. Evening meals are also available. This home is well located for touring the Bath area.	£25.00 (no smoking) *see PHOTO over* CREDIT CARD VISA M'CARD AMEX	Y	Y	N

38

Bailbrook Lodge. Bath.

Avon

	Description	minimum £ per person	children taken	evening meals	animals taken
Mrs Elizabeth Tovey **Bathurst Guest House** **11 Walcot Parade** **London Rd** **Bath BA1 5NF** **Tel: (0225) 421884** **Open: ALL YEAR** **Map Ref No. 01**	Nearest Road: A.4 A pretty, terraced Georgian home with 6 attractively decorated guest bedrooms, one with 4-poster bed & 2 with en-suite bathroom. All with colour T.V. & tea/coffee/chocolate making facilities. There is a comfortable lounge with piano, games table, books & puzzles. Next to Hedgemead Park, the house is a stroll from the Roman Baths & Pump Room in the city centre & the antique shops. An excellent touring base. Exclusively for non smokers. (non-smoking)	£15.50	Y	N	N
T. Argyris & J. Pascoe **Bloomfield House** **146 Bloomfield Rd** **Bath BA2 2AS** **Tel: (0225) 420105** **Fax 0225 481958** **Open: ALL YEAR** **Map Ref No. 01**	Nearest Road: A.367 A 34-room Georgian country house in sylvan setting with superb views over the city & ample parking. Antique furniture, silk curtains, French chandeliers & open fires await you. Each of the beautiful bedrooms have private bath/shower, colour T.V. & beverage making facilities. Everything from "Mrs Henshaw's" romantic 4-poster to "Master Nicholas Study" convey sheer comfort & style. A delightful home. CREDIT CARD VISA M'CARD	£17.50	Y	N	N
Marion Dodd **Brocks** **32 Brock Street** **Bath BA1 2LN** **Tel: (0225) 338374** **Open: ALL YEAR** **Map Ref No. 01**	Nearest Road: A.4 Brocks is a beautiful Georgian town house situated between the Circus & Royal Crescent. Very close to the Roman Baths, Assembly Rooms etc. This is a wonderful part of Bath. This historic house has all modern conveniences. Most of the attractive rooms have private facilities. The aim here is to offer guests the highest standards of comfort & personal attention.	£20.00	Y	N	N
David & Sue Selby **Brompton House Hotel** **St. Johns Road** **Bathwick** **Bath BA2 6PT** **Tel: (0225) 448423/420972** **OpenALL YEAR (Excl. Xmas)** **Map Ref No. 01**	Nearest Road: A.4, A.36 Brompton House is a delightful Regency residence with a country house atmosphere. Set in a peaceful central position within secluded gardens close to the main attractions only 5 minutes' walk to the city centre. A former Georgian rectory (1777) retaining the charm of a bygone age. Offering 19 en-suite rooms with T.V. Tea/coffee making facilities & 'phones. A choice of wholefood or full English breakfast is available. Licensed. Car park. (non-smoking) *see PHOTO over* CREDIT CARD VISA M'CARD	£30.00	Y	N	N
Derek & Maria Beckett **Cedar Lodge** **13 Lambridge** **London Rd** **Bath BA1 6BJ** **Tel: (0225) 423468** **Open: ALL YEAR** **Map Ref No. 01**	Nearest Road: A.4, A.46 Conveniently located for the city centre or countryside, this beautiful detached Georgian house offers period elegance, combined with home comfort. Individually designed bedrooms, one with half-tester bed, all with h&c, colour T.V. & central heating. A full English or Continental breakfast is served, using home-made preserves. Cordon Bleu dinners. Guests may relax in the lovely garden or the comfortable drawing room with open fire. Parking. Excursion-planning service available. An ideal spot for touring. (non-smoking)	£18.00	Y	Y	N

Brompton House Hotel.   Bath.

Avon

	minimum £ per person	children taken	evening meals	animals taken

Arthur & Christine Webber
Cranleigh
159 Newbridge Hill
Bath BA1 3PX
Tel: (0225) 310197
Open: ALL YEAR
Map Ref No. 01

Nearest Road: A.431
Delightful accommodation in a spacious Victorian house. Thoughtfully equipped rooms (some en-suite) have colour T.V., radio alarms, hairdryers and hospitality trays. The atmosphere is comfortable, relaxed and friendly. Parking and easy access to town centre. Generous, wholesome breakfasts to set you up for the day.

£20.00 | Y | N | N
(no smoking)
CREDIT CARD
VISA
M'CARD

Ian & Doreen Bennetts
Dorian House
One Upper Oldfield Park
Bath BA2 3JX
Tel: (0225) 426336
Open: ALL YEAR
Map Ref No. 01

Nearest Road: A.367
A warm welcome and an aura of nostalgic luxury await every guest at this gracious Victorian house. 7 charming bedrooms, all en-suite, are fully appointed with tea/coffee trays, hairdryers, telephones and colour T.V. There is a lounge, a small licensed bar, and full English breakfast menu is served. Parking available, and only a 10 minute stroll to the city centre.

£24.00 | Y | N | N
see PHOTO over
CREDIT CARD
VISA
M'CARD
AMEX

Mr & Mrs Warwick-Smith
Gainsborough Hotel
Weston Lane
Bath BA1 4AB
Tel: (0225) 311380
Fax 0225 311380
Open: ALL YEAR
Map Ref No. 01

Nearest Road: A.4
The Gainsborough is a large country house hotel, comfortably furnished & set in its own grounds near the Botanical Gardens & Victoria Park. Offering 16 attractive en-suite bedrooms with colour T.V., direct dial telephones, tea/coffee making facilities & hairdryers. The dining room & small cocktail bar overlook the lawns, where guests often relax during the summer on the sun terrace. Private parking available.

£26.00 | Y | Y | N
CREDIT CARD
VISA
M'CARD
AMEX

John & Lucille Baxter
Green Lane House
1 Green Lane
Hinton Charterhouse
Bath
BA3 6BL
Tel: (0225) 723631
Open: ALL YEAR
Map Ref No. 03

Nearest Road: A.36, B.3110
Pretty, comfortably furnished 18th century stone house in a quiet location, near the centre of a conservation village, in beautiful, wooded countryside. Green Lane House tastefully combines original features including exposed beams & working fireplaces with the comforts of modern living. 4 double/twin bedrooms, 2 en-suite, tea/coffee makers, guest lounge, dining room, parking, four-course English breakfast & friendly personal service. Convenient for Bath, Bristol, Cotswolds, Wells, Glastonbury, Stonehenge, etc.

£19.00 | Y | N | N
CREDIT CARD
VISA
M'CARD
AMEX

Roy & Rosalie Burridge
Grove Lodge Guest House
11 Lambridge
London Road
Bath BA1 6BJ
Tel: (0225) 310860
Open: ALL YEAR
Map Ref No. 01

Nearest Road: A.4, A.46
Situated in attractive gardens looking out onto the wooded hills surrounding the city; this Grade II listed Georgian house offers 8 excellent rooms with modern amenities including colour T. V. in each room. Apart from Bath's own attractions, there are numerous beauty spots, walks & places of great historic interest close by. Two golf courses, fishing & tennis are well within one & a half miles. An ideal spot for touring.

£20.00 | Y | N | N
(no smoking)

Dorian House. Bath.

Haydon House. Bath.

Avon

	Nearest Road	per person minimum £	children taken	evening meals	animals taken
Mrs Magdalene Ashman **Haydon House** **9 Bloomfield Park** **Bath BA2 2BY** **Tel: (0225) 427351/ 444919** **Fax 0225 469020** **Open: ALL YEAR** **Map Ref No. 01**	Nearest Road: A.367 A true oasis of tranquility, this elegantly furnished Edwardian house is situated in a quiet residential area. The four tastefully decorated Laura Ashley bedrooms all have private bathroom or shower en-suite, radio alarms, colour T.V., hot drink facilities, hairdryers and direct dial telephones. Imaginative breakfasts are accompanied by gentle classical music. Secluded, yet the attractions of Georgian Bath are all close by.	£26.00 *see PHOTO over* CREDIT CARD VISA M'CARD	Y	N	N
David & Davina James **Highways House** **143 Wells Road** **Bath BA2 3AL** **Tel: (0225) 421238** **Fax 0225 481169** **OpenALL YEAR (Excl.Xmas)** **Map Ref No. 01**	Nearest Road: A.367 An elegant Victorian family-run home offering superior accommodation in 7 rooms with private facilities (including 1 twin room on the ground floor) colour T.V. & tea/coffee makers. A tastefully decorated home with a lovely guest lounge. Full English breakfast is served. Located only 10 mins. from the city centre. A perfect base from which to tour the Cotswolds, Stonehenge, Salisbury & Wells. Children over 5 please. Parking.	£24.00 *see PHOTO over* CREDIT CARD VISA M'CARD	Y	N	N
David & Kathleen Slape **Leighton House** **139 Wells Road** **Bath** **BA2 3AL** **Tel: (0225) 314769** **Open: ALL YEAR** **Map Ref No. 01**	Nearest Road: A.367 Enjoy a true haven of friendliness at this delightful Victorian home, built in the 1870s, & set in its own grounds with views over the city & surrounding hills. There are 8 elegant & spacious bedrooms, all tastefully furnished & decorated. Each has en-suite facilities & is well equipped with colour T.V., radio/alarm, hospitality tray & many extras. A hearty breakfast is served & the delicious evening meals, with wine to complement, should suit the most discerning palate.	£27.00 CREDIT CARD VISA M'CARD	Y	Y	N
Mrs G. Smith **Marlborough House** **1 Marlborough Lane** **Bath BA1 2NQ** **Tel: (0225) 318175/466127** **Open: ALL YEAR** **Map Ref No. 01**	Nearest Road: A.4 Marlborough House has recently been extensively renovated, retaining many Victorian features. Situated 5 mins. level walk from the centre of Bath, Theatre Royal & Roman Baths, & only 2 mins. from the Royal Crescent & Victoria Park. All rooms have colour T.V., en-suite, & tea/coffee making facilities. A light & airy non-smoking house with a friendly atmosphere. Car parking.	£18.00	Y	N	N
Mrs L. Graham **Monmouth Lodge** **Norton St. Philip** **Bath** **BA3 6LH** **Tel: (0373) 834367** **Open: FEB-DEC** **Map Ref No. 04**	Nearest Road: A.36, B.3110 Monmouth Lodge is situated in an acre of attractive gardens, looking onto the Somerset hills, surrounding this historic village. 3 attractively furnished en-suite bedrooms with colour T.V. & tea/coffee making facilities. Guests may relax in the comfortable sitting room or enjoy the garden with views beyond. 10 mins. drive from Bath, this is an ideal base to explore the many interesting sites nearby. Private parking. Meals in 13th century pub within a short walking distance.	£23.00	Y	N	N

Highways House.   Bath.

Avon

		per person minimum £	children taken	evening meals	animals taken
Jenny King **Oakleigh House** **19 Upper Oldfield Park** **Bath** **BA2 3JX** **Tel: (0225) 315698** **Open: ALL YEAR** **Map Ref No. 01**	Nearest Road: A.367 Your comfort is assured at Oakleigh House, quietly situated only 10 minutes from the city centre. Oakleigh combines Victorian elegance with today's comforts to make your stay that extra bit special. All rooms which are tastefully furnished have en-suite bath/shower & w.c., hairdryers, colour T.V., clock radios and tea/coffee making facilities. Private car park. Oakleigh is an ideal base for beautiful Bath and beyond.	£24.00 CREDIT CARD VISA M'CARD	N	N	N
Anthony & Nicole O'Flaherty **Oldfields Guest House** **102 Wells Road** **Bath BA2 3AL** **Tel: (0225) 317984** **Fax 0225 444471** **Open: ALL YEAR** **Map Ref No. 01**	Nearest Road: A.367 A Victorian house built in Bath stone overlooking the city towards Kelson Round Hill. There are 14 delightful rooms with T. V. & tea/coffee making facilities, 8 with bath/shower en-suite. Each room has recently been restored & completely refurbished. The character remains & the Victorian elegance has been lightened by fresh Laura Ashley wallpapers & fabrics. Anthony & Nicole provide plenty of books & newspapers &....Mozart at breakfast. Parking available.	£22.50 CREDIT CARD VISA M'CARD	Y	N	N
Mrs J. Setchfield **Sheridan Guest House** **95, Wellsway** **Bath BA2 4RU** **Tel: (0225) 429562** **OpenALL YEAR (Excl.Xmas)** **Map Ref No. 01**	Nearest Road: A.367 Relax in the non-smoking comfort of this immaculate, pretty Edwardian home. 2 modern bathrooms, T.V. lounge, CH, H & C, tea/coffee making facilities in all rooms. Excellent bus service to city centre & 18 hole golf course. Easy parking. Situated on the edge of the City of Bath, Sheridan is an ideal touring centre for Wells, Salisbury, Glastonbury, Stonehenge & Bristol.	£15.00 (non-smoking)	Y	N	N
Mrs Nicky Stabbins **The Hollies** **Hatfield Road** **Wellsway** **Bath BA2 2BD** **Tel: (0225) 313366** **Open: MID JAN - MID DEC** **Map Ref No. 01**	Nearest Road: A. 367 The Hollies is a lovely old Victorian, Grade II listed house situated 1 mile from the city centre. With just 3 pretty guest rooms, 1 fully en-suite, 1 with private bathroom, personal attention and hospitality are assured. Each room has colour T.V. & beverage-making facilties. English, vegetarian or Continental breakfast is served. Private parking available and a secluded garden with apple trees and wild meadow flowers.	£16.00 (non-smoking)	Y	N	N
Chrissie Besley **The Old Red House** **37 Newbridge Road** **Bath BA1 4AB** **Tel: (0225) 330464** **Open: ALL YEAR** **Map Ref No. 01**	Nearest Road: A.4 This charming Victorian "Gingerbread House" is colourful, comfortable & warm; full of unexpected touches & intriguing little curiosities. Its leaded & stained glass windows are now double glazed to ensure a peaceful stay. The extensive breakfast menu, a delight in itself, is served in a sunny conservatory. Private parking. Special rates for 3 or more nights.	£17.50 (non-smoking) *see PHOTO over* CREDIT CARD VISA M'CARD	Y	N	Y

The Old Red House. Bath.

Avon

	minimum £ per person	children taken	evening meals	animals taken

Sonia & Rodney Stone **The Old School House** **Church Street** **Bathford** **Bath BA1 7RR** **Tel: (0225) 859593** **Open: ALL YEAR** **Map Ref No. 01**	Nearest Road: A.4, M.4. Built in 1837 The Old School House is situated within a conservation area with beautiful views over the Avon Valley & its wooded hillsides, yet only 3 miles from the Georgian city of Bath. Offering a charming country-home atmosphere with log fires on chilly evenings. 2 of the 4 double /twin rooms are on the ground floor. All have en-suite bathrooms, 'phone, colour T.V., tea/coffee, hairdryer & trouser press. A delightful home. An entirely no-smoking establishment.	£29.00 (no smoking) *see PHOTO over* CREDIT CARD VISA M'CARD	Y	Y	N
John & Olga London **The Orchard** **80 High Street** **Bathford** **Bath BA1 7TG** **Tel: (0225) 858765** **Open: MAR - OCT** **Map Ref No. 01**	Nearest Road: A.4 The Orchard is a listed Grade II Georgian country house in the hillside village of Bathford just 3 miles from Bath. The 4 spacious bedrooms have private facilities & T.V. & are individually deco-rated & furnished to a high standard of comfort. The elegant drawing and dining rooms are filled with fine pieces of period furniture. An oasis in an acre and a half of walled gardens and orchard.	£25.00 (no smoking)	N	N	N
Anita & John West **The Plaine Guest House** **Norton St. Philip** **Bath BA3 6LE** **Tel: (0373) 834723** **Fax 0373 834723** **Open: ALL YEAR** **Map Ref No. 04**	Nearest Road: A.36 The Plaine is a delightful listed building dating from the 16th Century, situated in the heart of an historic conservation village. There are three beautiful en-suite rooms, all with four-poster beds. Opposite is the famous George Inn - one of the oldest hostelries in England. Delicious break-fasts are prepared with local produce and free range eggs. Convenient location for Bath, Wells, Longleat and Cotswolds. Parking .	£19.50 (no smoking) CREDIT CARD VISA M'CARD	Y	N	N
Geoff & Avril Kitching **Wentworth House** **106 Bloomfield Road** **Bath** **BA1 7TG** **Tel: (0225) 339193** **Open: ALL YEAR** **Map Ref No. 01**	Nearest Road: A.367 Wentworth House is under the personal supervi-sion of the owners Mr & Mrs Kitching who offer thoughtfully equipped rooms, well-maintained and comfortable throughout. There is a lounge bar, and a dining room with a conservatory over-looking the outdoor swimming pool. 20 rooms, most en-suite, have tea/coffee making facilities, colour T.V. & telephones. Large car park. Abbey & Roman Baths within walking distance.	£18.00 CREDIT CARD VISA M'CARD	Y	N	N
Beryl & Leonard Willis **Villa Magdala Hotel** **Henrietta Road** **Bath BA2 6LX** **Tel: (0225) 466329** **OpenALL YEAR (Excl. Xmas)** **Map Ref No. 01**	Nearest Road: A.4 Villa Magdala is a handsome house of Italian-style architecture in attractive grounds. Inside is a fine cast-iron staircase. The 17 bedrooms are all en-suite and well appointed with telephone, radio, T.V., and tea/coffee facilities. Some rooms have four-poster beds. Extensive English break-fast menu. Private parking. Just 5 minutes' walk to the centre of Bath.	£30.00 CREDIT CARD VISA M'CARD	Y	N	N

The Old School House.   Bathford.

Avon

			per person minimum £	children taken	evening meals	animals taken
Brian & Audrey Archer **The Tasburgh Bath** **Warminster Road** **Bath** **BA2 6SH** **Tel: (0225) 425096/463842** **Fax 0225 425096** **Open: ALL YEAR** **Map Ref No. 01**	Nearest Road: A.4, A.36 Built in 1890 as a mansion for a photographer to the Royal Family, The Tasburg is set in 7 acres of lovely gardens & grounds with canal frontage & breathtaking views. Retaining many original features, it offers 13 tastefully furnished rooms (designer fabrics & Laura Ashley) with en-suite bathrooms, telephones, radio/alarms, tea/coffee facilities & colour T.V., Victorian elegance & charming decor. English/Wholefood breakfasts & ample parking. Brian & Audrey provide many extras tourist information, maps & personal care.	£22.00 *see PHOTO over* CREDIT CARD VISA M'CARD AMEX	Y	N	N
Mrs Shelley Weeks **Wheelbrook Mill** **Laverton** **Bath BA3 6QY** **Tel: (0373) 830263** **Open: ALL YEAR** **Map Ref No. 05**	Nearest Road: A.36 The Mill is set well back from a quiet lane overlooking the Wheel Brook & open fields in the picturesque hamlet of Laverton, just 15 minutes' drive from Bath. The rooms are warm, spacious & comfortably furnished with antique stripped pine & Laura Ashley fabrics. Evening meals are generally taken en famille in the large farmhouse kitchen, warmed by the Aga & woodburning stove.	£20.00	Y	Y	Y
Mary Watts **Aldwick Court Farm** **Blagdon, Wrington** **Bristol BS18 7RF** **Tel: (0934) 862305** **Fax 0934 863308** **Open: APR-OCT** **Map Ref No. 06**	Nearest Road: A.38 Aldwick Court Farm nestles in the heart of the beautiful Blagdon Valley, 10 miles south of Bristol, home to the Watts family for 4 generations. Choices of accommodation include 3 tastefully appointed bedrooms, including 17th century 4-poster bed, all furnished equally to a high standard. A fine sitting room with inglenook fireplace. A delicious traditional breakfast & home cooked suppers are prepared by the charming host.	£20.00	N	Y	N
John & Daphne Paz **Dornden Guest House** **Church Lane** **Old Sodbury** **Bristol BS17 6NB** **Tel: (0454) 313325** **Open: ALL YEAR (Excl. Xmas & New Year)** **Map Ref No. 07**	Nearest Road: A.432 Dornden, built of local Cotswold stone, stands in a beautiful garden enjoying the peace of the countryside & magnificent views to the west. There are 9 attractive rooms, 5 en-suite, overlooking the garden & open country beyond. Delicious meals are prepared, with home-grown produce where possible & free-range eggs. Grass tennis court available to guests. A delightful home with a warm, friendly atmosphere.	£20.00	Y	Y	Y
Mrs Ann Thornely **Eastcote Cottage** **Knapp Road East** **Crossways, Thornbury** **Bristol BS12 2HJ** **Tel: (0454) 413106** **Open: ALL YEAR** **Map Ref No. 08**	Nearest Road: M.4, M.5, A.38 Eastcote is a very pleasant 200 year-old stone house located in a lovely rural setting with splendid views across open countryside. Offering 3 comfortable bedrooms with modern amenities. A colour T.V. lounge is available for guests' use. Conveniently situated for the M.4/M.5 interchange for the Cotswolds, with Bristol, Bath, Cheltenham & the Wye Valley easily accessible.	£18.00	Y	N	N

The Tasburgh Bath. Bath.

Avon

		minimum £ per person	children taken	evening meals	animals taken
Elizabeth Rolls **Hillside** **Sutton Hill Road** **Bishop Sutton** **Bristol BS18 4UN** **Tel: (0275) 332208** **Open: ALL YEAR** **Map Ref No. 09**	Nearest Road: A.368 Hillside is an attractive converted stone cottage located in quiet farmland with glorious views overlooking Chew Valley Lake. Accommodation is in 2 rooms with central heating & colour T.V. & a super garden to relax in. This makes an excellent base for touring & walking. It is within easy reach of Bath, Bristol, Mendip Hills, Cheddar Gorge & Wells, & trout fishing & bird sanctuary are close by. Good pub food locally.	£13.50	Y	N	Y
Ruth Shellard **Overbrook** **Stowey Bottom** **Bishop Sutton** **Bristol BS18 4TN** **Tel: (0275) 332648** **Open: MAR - OCT** **Map Ref No. 09**	Nearest Road: A.368 Overbrook is a charming house, tastefully furnished, with a lovely garden by a brook. Situated in a quiet & peaceful lane, with a little ford by the gate, Overbrook can offer 1 twin bedded en-suite room & 1 double bedroom with private shower & WC. Both rooms have colour T.V. There is a comfortable sunny sitting room with French windows onto the garden for guests' use. Bath, Wells, Bristol & Cheddar Gorge are within easy reach & superb trout fishing on Cheddar Lake is only 5 mins. away.	£15.50	Y	Y	N
Geoff & Christine Healey **The Old Bakery** **The Street** **Olveston** **Bristol BS12 3DR** **Tel: (0454) 616437/415082** **Open: ALL YEAR** **Map Ref No. 10**	Nearest Road: A. 38 The Old Bakery is situated in the centre of the village of Olveston, just 12 miles north of Bristol. This lovely 300 year-old cottage provides comfortable accommodation in 2 attractive twin-bedded rooms. A lounge with colour T.V./video is provided exclusively for guests which overlooks a pretty walled garden. Easy access to Bath, Forest of Dean, South Cotswolds & M.4/M.5	£18.00	Y	N	N

When booking your accommodation please mention
The Best Bed & Breakfast

Beds:Berks:Bucks:Herts.

Bedfordshire
(Thames & Chilterns)

The county of Bedfordshire is an area of great natural beauty from the Dunstable Downs in the south to the great River Ouse in the north, along with many country parks & historic houses & gardens.

Two famous wildlife parks are to be found, at Woburn & Whipsnade. The Woburn Wild Animal Kingdom is Britain's largest drive-through safari park, with entrance to an exciting leisure park all included in one admission ticket.

Rose gardens. St.Albans. Herts.

Whipsnade Zoo came into existence in the 1930's as a country retreat for the animals of London Zoo, but is now very much a zoo in its own right & renowned for conservation work.

Woburn Abbey, home of the Dukes of Bedford for three centuries, is often described as one of England's finest showplaces. Rebuilt in the 8th century the Abbey houses an important art collection & is surrounded by a magnificent 3,000 acre deer park.

John Bunyan drew on local Bedfordshire features when writing the Pilgrims Progress, & the ruins of Houghton House, his "House Beautiful" still remain.

Buckinghamshire
(Thames & Chilterns)

Buckinghamshire can be divided into two distinct geographical regions: The high Chilterns with their majestic beechwoods & the Vale of Aylesbury chosen by many over the centuries as a beautiful & accessible place to build their historical homes.

The beechwoods of the Chilterns to the south of the county are crisscrossed with quiet lanes & footpaths., Ancient towns & villages like Amersham & Chesham lie tucked away in the folds of the hills & a prehistoric track; the Ichnield Way winds on its 85 mile journey through the countryside.

The Rothschild family chose the Vale of Aylesbury to create several impressive homes, & Waddesdon House & Ascott House are both open to the public. Benjamin Disraeli lived at Hughenden Manor, & Florence Nightingale, "the Lady with the Lamp", at Claydon House. Sir Francis Dashwood, the 18th century eccentric founded the bizarre Hellfire Club, which met in the man-made caves near West Wycombe House.

Berkshire
(Thames & Chilterns)

Berkshire is a compact county but one of great variety & beauty.

In the East is Windsor where the largest inhabited castle in the world stands in its majestic hilltop setting. Nine centuries of English monarchy have lived here, & it is home to the present Queen. The surrounding parkland, enormous yards, vast interior & splendour of the State Apartments make a trip to Windsor Castle an unforgettable experience.

To the West are the gently rolling Berkshire Downs where many a champion racehorse has been trained.

Beds:Berks:Bucks:Herts.

To the north of the county, the River Thames dominates the landscape - an opportunity for a river-bank stroll & a drink at a country pub.

In the south is the Kennet & Avon Canal, a peaceful waterway with horse-drawn barges.

Historically, Berkshire has occupied an important place due to its strategic position commanding roads to & from Oxford & the north, & Bath & the west. Roundheads & Cavaliers clashed twice near Newbury during the 17th century English Civil Wars. Their battles are colourfully recreated by historic societies like the Sealed Knot.

The Tudor period brought great wealth from wool-weaving. Merchants built wonderful houses & some built churches but curiously, there is no cathedral in Berkshire.

Hertfordshire
(Thames & Chilterns)

Old & new exist side by side in Hertfordshire. This attractive county includes historic sites, like the unique Roman theatre in St. Albans, as well as new additions to the landscape such as England's first Garden City at Letchworth.

The countryside varies from the chalk hills & rolling downlands of the Chilterns to rivers, lakes, canals & pretty villages. The county remains largely rural despite many large towns & cities. The Grand Union Canal, built at the end of the 18th century to link the Midlands to London, passes through some glorious scenery, particularly at Cassiobury Park in Watford.

Verulamium was a newly-built town of the Roman Empire. It was the first name of Alban, himself a Roman, who became the first Christian to be martyred for his faith in England. The great Abbey church was built by the Normans around his original church, & it was re-established under the Rule of St. Benedict & named St. Albans some 600 years after his death.

Tussauds Exhibition. Windsor. Berks.

Beds:Berks:Bucks:Herts.

Bedfordshire

Gazeteer
Area of outstanding natural beauty.
Dunstable Downs, Ivinghoe Beacon.

Historic Houses
Woburn Abbey - house & gardens, extensive art collection, deer park, antiques centre.
Luton Hoo - the Wernher collection of Old Masters, tapestries, furniture, ivories & porcelain, unique collection of Russian Faberge jewellry. Parkland landscaped by Capability Brown.

Other Things to see & do
Woburn Wildlife Park
Whipsnade Zoo-Whipsnade
Old Warden - the village houses a collection of working vintage aeroplanes with flying displays each month from April to October.

Berkshire

Gazeteer
Areas of outstanding natural beauty.
North West Downs.

Historic Houses & Castles
Windsor Castle - Royal Residence at Windsor
State apartments, house, historic treasures. The Cloisters, Windsor Chapel. Mediaeval house.
Basildon Park - Nr. Pangbourne
Overlooking the Thames. 18th century Bath stone building, massive portico & linked pavilions. Painted ceiling in Octagon Room, gilded pier glasses. Garden & wooded walks.
Cliveden - Nr. Taplow
Once the home of Nancy Astor.

Churches
Lambourn (St. Michael & All Saints)
Norman with 15th century chapel. 16th century brasses, glass & tombs.
Padworth (St. John the Baptist)
12th century Norman with plastered exterior, remains of wall paintings, 18th century monuments.

Warfield (St. Michael & All Angels)
14th century decorated style. 15th century wood screen & loft.
Henry Reitlinger Bequest - Maidenhead
Chinese, Italian, Persian & European pottery, paintings, sculpture.

Museums
Newbury Museum - Newbury
Natural History & Archaeology -
Paleolithic to Saxon & Mediaeval times.
Household Cavalry Museum - Windsor

Other Things to see & do
Racing - at Newbury, Ascot & Windsor
Highlight of the racing year is the Royal Meeting at Ascot each June, attended by the Queen & other members of the Royal Family.
Antiques - Hungerford is a famous centre for antiques.
Windsor Safari Park.

Buckinghamshire

Gazeteer
Area of outstanding natural beauty.
Burnham Beeches - 70 acres of unspoilt woodlands, inspiration to poet Thomas Gray.

Historic Houses
Waddesdon Manor & Ascott House - homes of the Rothschilds.
Chalfont St. Giles - cottage home of great English poet John Milton.
Old Jordans & the Meeting House - 17th century buildings associated with William Penn, the founder of Pennsylvania & with the Society of Friends, often called the Quakers.

Things to see & do
Buckinghamshire Railway Centre - at Quainton
Vintage steam train rides & largest private railway collection in Britain.
Chalfont Shire Horse Centre - home of the gentle giants of the horse world.

Beds:Berks:Bucks:Herts.

Hertfordshire

Gazeteer

Areas of outstanding natural beauty.
Parts of the Chilterns.

Historic Houses & Castles

Hatfield House - Hatfield
Home of the Marquess of Salisbury.
Jacobean House & Tudor Palace -
childhood home of Queen Elizabeth I.
Knebworth House - Knebworth
Family home of the Lyttons. 16th century
house transformed into Victorian High
Gothic. Furniture, portraits. Formal
gardens & unique Gertrude Jekyll herb
garden.
Shaw's Corner - Ayot St. Lawrence
Home of George Bernard Shaw.

Cathedrals & Churches

St. Albans Cathedral - St. Albans
9th century foundation, murals, painted
roof over choir, 15th century reredos,
stone rood screen

Stanstead St. Abbots (St. James)12th
century nave, 13th century chancel, 15th
century tower & porch, 16th century North
chapel, 18th century box pews & 3-decker
pulpit.
Watford (St. Mary)
13 - 15th century. Essex chapel. Tuscan
arcade. Morryson tombs

Museums

**Rhodes Memorial Museum &
Commonwealth Centre** - at Bishop
Stortford
Zoological Museum - Tring
Gardens
Gardens of the Rose - Chiswell Green
Nr. St Albans
Showgrounds of the Royal National Rose
Society
Capel Manor - extensive grounds of
horticultural college. Many fine trees,
including the largest copper beech in
the country.

Bledlow Village; Bucks.

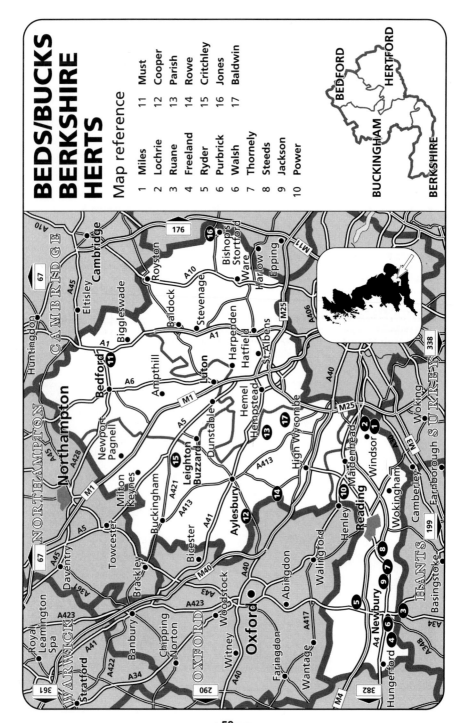

BEDS/BUCKS
BERKSHIRE
HERTS

Map reference

1 Miles	11 Must
2 Lochrie	12 Cooper
3 Ruane	13 Parish
4 Freeland	14 Rowe
5 Ryder	15 Critchley
6 Purbrick	16 Jones
6 Walsh	17 Baldwin
7 Thornely	
8 Steeds	
9 Jackson	
10 Power	

BEDFORD

HERTFORD

BUCKINGHAM

BERKSHIRE

58

Berkshire

			per person	children taken	evening meals	animals taken
Mr & Mrs J Miles **Ennis Lodge Private** **Guest House** **Winkfield Road** **Ascot SL5 7EX** **Tel: (0344) 21009** **Open: ALL YEAR** **Map Ref No. 01**	Nearest Road: A.329, A.30 Ennis Lodge is situated in central Ascot, adjacent to the racecourse. There are 4 tastefully furnished twin bedded rooms , each en-suite with colour T.V., tea/coffee making facilities, trouser press, hairdryer & radio alarm. Conveniently located within walking distance of the main line station, London is only 45 mins. by rail. Within easy reach of Windsor, Heathrow Airport, M.3, M.4 & M.25.	(no smoking) CREDIT CARD VISA M'CARD	£22.50	Y	N	Y
Mrs M. Lochrie **'Lyndrick House'** **The Avenue** **Ascot SL5 7ND** **Tel: (0344) 883520** **Fax 0344 891243** **Open: ALL YEAR** **Map Ref No. 02**	Nearest Road: A.30, M.4 'Lyndrick' is a 5-bedroom Victorian house in a quiet tree-lined avenue. All bedrooms have colour televisions & tea/coffee making facilities, most are en-suite. Breakfast is served in a pleasant conservatory. Windsor 4 miles, Ascot racecourse is 2 mins., &10 mins. to Wentworth Golf Club. Waterloo 40 mins. by train. Heathrow Airport 25 mins. Easy access to M.4, M.3, M.25, & A.30. An ideal spot for touring.	CREDIT CARD VISA M'CARD	£22.50	Y	N	Y
Paula Ruane **Adbury Holt House** **Burghclere** **Newbury RG15 9BW** **Tel: (0635) 46061** **Fax 0635 552999** **Open: ALL YEAR** **Map Ref No. 03**	Nearest Road: A.34, M.4 A delightful, secluded Victorian mansion set in its own grounds of 12 acres: of particular interest to gardening enthusiasts, for there are over 100 varieties of trees & many unusual shrubs & plants. The accommodation is very attractive with 4 lovely, well appointed bedrooms, each with its own bathroom, & radio, T.V., & tea/coffee making facilities. Excellent evening meals are available by arrangement. Parking. Non-smokers preferred.		£18.50	Y	Y	N
Mrs B Freeland **Holt Lodge** **Kintbury** **Newbury** **RG15 0SX** **Tel: (04884) 244** **Open: ALL YEAR** **Map Ref No. 04**	Nearest Road: A.4 An attractive 18th century family farmhouse set in large mature gardens surrounded by parkland. Situated south of Kintbury, halfway between River Kennet & the Hampshire Downs. A friendly welcome is assured for visitors who appreciate informality & the seclusion & comforts of a family home. A choice of bedrooms all with modern facilities are tastefully furnished.. Convenient for Berkshire, Hampshire & Wiltshire.	(no smoking)	£17.50	Y	N	Y
Jonathan & Diana Ryder **Langley Hall Farm** **Beedon** **Newbury** **RG16 8SD** **Tel: (0635) 248222** **Open: ALL YEAR** **Map Ref No. 05**	Nearest Road: M.4, A.34 A large early-Victorian manor farmhouse situated in 600 acres of unspoilt Berkshire countryside with far-reaching glorious views. Working farm with livestock. Every comfort is offered in spacious attractive bedrooms with colour T.V. & tea/coffee making facilities. Delicious farmhouse breakfast served in large dining room. Excellent base for visiting Oxford, Bath, Stratford, London. Within easy reach of Heathrow. A warm & friendly welcome is guaranteed at Langley Hall. Excellent local pubs.		£18.00	Y	N	N

Berkshire

		per person minimum £	children taken	evening meals	animals taken
Timothy & Jennifer Purbrick **Pilgrims Rest Guest House** **Oxford Road** **Newbury** **RG13 1XB** **Tel/Fax:(0635) 40694/44873** **Open: ALL YEAR** **Map Ref No. 06**	Nearest Road: M.4, A.34 A personal friendly service is always assured at the Pilgrims Rest. Conveniently located only half a mile from the town centre & railway station. Offering guests a choice of 11 comfortable & attractively furnished rooms, 2 en-suite. All have modern amenities, T.V. & tea/coffee making facilities. A guests' T.V. lounge & garden are also available. A delicious English breakfast is served & vegetarian diets can be catered for.	£18.00 CREDIT CARD VISA M'CARD	Y	Y	Y
Mrs Pamela Walsh **Speen Cottage** **Speen Lane** **Newbury RG13 1RJ** **Tel: (0635) 40859** **Open: ALL YEAR** **Map Ref No. 06**	Nearest Road: M.4, A.4 A fine Georgian house built in 1790, comfortably furnished with a blend of the modern & antique. Speen Cottage is well situated mid-way between Bath, London, Oxford & Winchester. Offering 3 comfortable rooms, 2 with private facilities, radio & tea/coffee makers. There are many pretty villages in the vicinity as well as the vale of the White Horse. Pamela is an excellent cook & dinner or supper are usually available.	£22.00	N	Y	N
Mrs Jill Thornely **Bridge Cottage** **Station Road** **Woolhampton** **Reading RG7 5SF** **Tel: (0734) 713138** **OpenALL YEAR (Excl.Xmas)** **Map Ref No. 07**	Nearest Road: A.4, M.4, M.3 A warm welcome awaits the visitor to this delightful 300 year-old riverside cottage. Offering 4 bedrooms, with beamed ceilings, including a twin bedded room with en-suite facilities. Breakfast is served in a lovely conservatory overlooking the River Kennet where old narrow boats pass by. It is surrounded by lovely countryside. Close by is the local pub which serves excellent home-cooked suppers. London with its many attractions is only 1 hour away. Ideal for Heathrow Airport.	£18.00	Y	N	N
Jane Steeds **Highwoods** **Burghfield Common** **Reading RG7 3BG** **Tel: (0734) 832320** **Fax 0734 832320** **OpenALL YEAR (Excl.Xmas)** **Map Ref No. 08**	Nearest Road: A.4, M.4 Highwoods is a fine Victorian country house set in 4 acres of attractive grounds with far reaching views. Offering 2 spacious, comfortable & attractively furnished rooms, 1 en-suite & all with modern amenities including T.V.. Guests are welcome to use the garden & hard tennis court. Also, a gallery specialising in English watercolours & prints.Easy access to London, Heathrow Airport,Windsor, Oxford & Bath.	£18.00	Y	N	N
Auriol Jackson **Hunts Cottage** **Midgham Green** **Reading** **RG7 5TT** **Tel: (0734) 712540** **Open: ALL YEAR (Excl. Xmas & New Year)** **Map Ref No. 09**	Nearest Road: M.4, A.4 Built around 1620, Hunts Cottage is a listed timber-framed house with masses of exposed beams & a pair of inglenook fireplaces. There are 3 guest rooms: a twin with en-suite bath, a double with a full tester oak four-poster bed & private bath & a single. All have colour T.V. & tea making equipment. Guests are welcome to use the sitting room, the outdoor heated pool & the large garden. This is a lovely home, conveniently located for visiting London & the many places of interest that the region has to offer.	£22.00	N	N	N

Berkshire, Bedfordshire & Buckinghamshire

		minimum £ per person	children taken	evening meals	animals taken
Michael & Joanna Power **Woodpecker Cottage** **Warren Row** **RG10 8QS** **Tel: (0628) 822772** **Fax 0628 822125** **Open: ALL YEAR** **Map Ref No. 10**	Nearest Road: A.4 Set in extensive woodland on the edge of the village west of Maidenhead, quiet house in large pretty garden; grass court & outdoor swimming pool. Lovely walks from house. Easy access M.4, M.40; 20 mins. Heathrow, Windsor; close Henley-on-Thames. 2 large ground floor twin/ double rooms, 1 with en-suite shower/WC, 1 with private bathroom. Full CH, colour T.V., radio, tea/ coffee making facilities in rooms. Children over 8; evening meals with prior notice only.	£18.00	Y	Y	N

Bedfordshire

		minimum £ per person	children taken	evening meals	animals taken
Mrs Janet Must **Church Farm** **41 High Street** **Roxton** **MK44 3EB** **Tel: (0234) 870234** **Open: ALL YEAR** **Map Ref No. 11**	Nearest Road: A.1, A.428 Church Farm is a lovely 17th century farmhouse with Georgian frontage, set in a secluded village. Furnished with a pleasant mixture of family antiques, the comfortable guest accommodation has its own staircase & bathroom, with tea/coffee making facilities in the rooms. Breakfast is served in the beamed dining room & a guest lounge is available with open fire & colour T.V.. Whether on business or a short break a warm welcome awaits you at this delightful home..	£14.00	Y	N	Y

Buckinghamshire

		minimum £ per person	children taken	evening meals	animals taken
Mrs Anita Cooper **Poletrees Farm** **Ludgershall Road** **Brill** **Aylesbury HP18 9TZ** **Tel: (0844) 238276** **Open: ALL YEAR** **Map Ref No. 12**	Nearest Road: A.41, M.40 Guests will receive a warm welcome from a friendly, helpful host at this 500 year-old farmhouse. Accommodation is in 3 rooms, sharing bathroom. Tea/coffee making facilities. There is a T.V. lounge, a delightful garden and an outdoor swimming pool available for guests' use. Buckingham Golf Course is nearby. Excellent farmhouse meals are served. Poletrees Farm is conveniently located for touring Oxford, Blenheim Palace and Waddesdon Manor.	£16.00	N	Y	N
Mrs J. M. Parish **The Old Farm** **Hog Lane** **Ashley Green** **Chesham** **HP5 3PY** **Tel: (0442) 866430** **Fax 0442 866430** **Open: MAR - DEC** **Map Ref No. 13**	Nearest Road: A.41, M.1, Old Farm is a delightful 16th century farmhouse retaining its original Tudor features including oak beams & inglenook fireplaces. Located in beautiful countryside, but with easy access to town. Accommodation is in 2 very comfortable bedrooms, 1 en-suite & 1 with private facilities, T.V./ radio & tea/coffee makers. Conveniently located for St. Albans, Windsor, Woburn & Waddesdon. London 1/2 hour. Airports easily accessible. An ideal spot for touring or visiting the many places of interest in the surrounding area.	£18.00	Y	N	N

Buckinghamshire & Hertfordshire

		per person minimum £	children taken	evening meals	animals taken
Mrs Patricia Rowe **The Elms Country House** **Radnage** **Stokenchurch** **High Wycombe** **HP14 4DW** **Tel: (0494) 482175** **Open: ALL YEAR** **Map Ref No. 14**	Nearest Road: A.40, M.40 The Elms is a delightful 17th century farmhouse standing in two acres of ground, set in an area of outstanding natural beauty. The house retains many original features including handmade roof tiles & many oak beams. There are 5 well-appointed bedrooms, each is comfortable & tastefully furnished; some have radio, T.V. & tea/coffee making facilities, 1 en-suite. A colour T.V. lounge is also available & guests may use the garden. A lovely home, ideal for touring.	£17.50	Y	Y	Y
Mrs E.M. Critchley **Partridge House** **Great Brickhill** **Milton Keynes** **MK17 9BH** **Tel: (0525) 270470** **Open ALL YEAR (Excl. Xmas)** **Map Ref No. 15**	Nearest Road: A.4146 Partridge House offers a warm welcome & wonderful views over open countryside. All rooms, which are attractive & very comfortable, have bath or shower, colour T.V., tea/coffee making facilities & shaving points. There is a bar & lounge in which guests can relax & unwind. A hearty & delicious full English breakfast is served. Partridge House has its own 9 hole golf course with free golf for guests; also lake & coarse fishing.	£30.00 CREDIT CARD VISA M'CARD	Y	N	N

Hertfordshire

		per person minimum £	children taken	evening meals	animals taken
Peter & Rosemary Jones **The Cottage** **71 Birchanger Lane** **Birchanger** **Bishops Stortford** **CM23 5QA** **Tel: (0279) 812349** **Open: ALL YEAR** **Map Ref No. 16**	Nearest Road: M.11, exit 8 Situated within a quiet village this charming 17th century listed house offers 8 comfortable en-suite bedrooms all with colour T.V. & tea/coffee makers. Oak panelled reception rooms with log burners & a conservatory/dining room looking onto mature gardens. An excellent base from which to explore the many places of interest in the region. Convenient for trips to Cambridge, London, East Anglia & within easy reach of Stanstead Airport & Bishops Stortford. Parking.	£22.50 CREDIT CARD VISA M'CARD	Y	Y	N
Mrs Lesley Baldwin **Venus Hill Farm** **Venus Hill** **Bovingdon** **HP3 0PG** **Tel: (0442) 833396** **Open: APR - OCT** **Map Ref No. 17**	Nearest Road: A.41, M.25 An absolutely delightful listed black & white 300 year-old converted farmhouse standing in 2 acres of garden & surrounded by open farmland. Guests will receive a warm welcome & very comfortable accommodation. There is a choice of 3 lovely bedrooms with modern amenities & tea/coffee makers. T.V. available. Guests may also like to use the outdoor heated swimming pool, tennis court & garden. London & Heathrow easily accessible. An ideal spot for a relaxing holiday & exploring the beautiful English countryside.	£18.00	N	N	N

Cambridge & Northants.

Cambridgeshire
(East Anglia)

A county very different from any other, this is flat, mysterious, low-lying Fenland crisscrossed by a network of waterways both natural & man-made.

The Fens were once waterlogged, misty marshes but today the rich black peat is drained & grows carrots, sugar beet, celery & the best asparagus in the world.

Drive north across the Fens & slowly you become aware of a great presence dominating the horizon. Ely cathedral, the "ship of the Fens", sails closer. The cathedral is a masterpiece with its graceful form & delicate tracery towers. Begun before the Domesday Book was written, it took the work of a full century before it was ready to have the timbered roof raised up. Norman stonemasons worked with great skill & the majestic nave is glorious in its simplicity. Their work was crowned by the addition of the Octagon in the 14th century. Despite the ravages of the Reformation, the lovely Lady Chapel survives as one of the finest examples of decorated architecture in Britain with its exquisitely fine stone carving.

To the south, the Fens give way to rolling chalk hills & fields of barley, wheat & rye, & Cambridge. Punts gliding through the broad river, between smooth, lawned banks, under willow trees, past college buildings as extravagant as wedding cakes. The names of the colleges resound through the ages - Peterhouse, Corpus Christi, Kings, Queens, Trinity, Emmanuel. A city of learning & progress, & a city of great tradition where cows graze in open spaces, just 500 yards from the market square.

Northamptonshire
(East Midlands)

Northamptonshire has many features to attract & interest the visitor, from the town of Brackley in the south with its charming buildings of mellow stone, to ancient Rockingham Forest in the north. There are lovely churches, splendid historic houses & peaceful waterways.

The Waterways Museum at Stoke Bruerne makes a popular outing, with boat trips available on the Grand Union Canal beside the museum. Horse-racing at Towcester & motor-racing at Silverstone draws the crowds, but there are quieter pleasures in visits to Canons Ashby, or to Sulgrave Manor, home of George Washington's ancestors.

In the pleasantly wooded Rockingham Forest area are delightful villages, one of which is Ashton with its thatched cottages, the scene of the World Conker Championships each October. Mary Queen of Scots was executed at Fotheringay, in the castle of which only the mound remains.

Rockingham Castle has a solid Norman gateway & an Elizabethan hall; Deene Park has family connections with the Earl of Cardigan who led the Charge of the Light Brigade & Kirby Hall is a dramatic Elizabethan ruin.

The county is noted for its parish churches, with fine Saxon examples at Brixworth & at Earl's Barton, as well as the round Church of the Holy Sepulchre in the county town itself.

Northampton has a fine tradition of shoemaking, so it is hardly surprising that boots & shoes & other leather-goods take pride of place in the town';s museums. The town has one of the country's biggest market squares, an historic Royal Theatre & a mighty Wurlitzer Organ to dance to at Turner's Musical Merry-go-round ! !

Cambridge & Northants.

Cambridgeshire Gazeteer

Areas of outstanding natural beauty
The Nene Valley

Historic Houses & Castles

Anglesy Abbey - Nr. Cambridge
Origins in the reign of Henry I. Was redesigned into Elizabethan Manor by Fokes family. Houses the Fairhaven collection of Art treasures - stands in 100 acres of Ground.
Hinchingbrooke House - Huntingdon
13th century nunnery converted mid-16th century into Tudor house. Later additions in 17th & 19th centuries.
King's School - Ely
12th & 14th centuries - original stonework & vaulting in the undercroft, original timbering 14th century gateway & monastic barn.
Kimbolton Castle - Kimbolton
Tudor Manor house - has associations with Katherine of Aragon. Remodelled by Vanbrugh 1700's - gatehouse by Robert Adam.
Longthorpe Tower - Nr. Peterborough
13th & 14th century fortification - rare wall paintings.
Peckover House - Wisbech
18th century domestic architecture - charming Victorian garden.
University of Cambridge Colleges

Peterhouse -	1284
Clare -	1326
Pembroke -	1347
Gonville & Caius -	1348
Trinity Hall -	1350
Corpus Christi -	1352
King's -	1441
Queen's -	1448
St. Catherine's -	1473
Jesus -	1496
Christ's -	1505
St. John's -	1511
Magadalene -	1542
Trinity-	1546
Emmanuel-	1584
Sidney Sussex -	1596
Downing-	1800

Wimpole Hall - Nr. Cambridge
18th & 19th century - beautiful staterooms - aristocratic house.

Cathedrals & Churches

Alconbury (St. Peter & St. Paul)
13th century chancel & 15th century roof. Broach spire.
Babraham (St. Peter)
13th century tower - 17th century monument.
Ely Catherdal
Rich arcading - west front incomplete. Remarkable interior with Octagon - unique in Gothic architecture.
Great Paxton (Holy Trinity)
12th century.
Harlton (Blessed Virgin Mary)
Perpendicular - decorated transition. 17th century monuments
Hildersham (Holy Trinity)
13th century - effigies, brasses & glass.
Lanwade (St. Nicholas)
15th century - mediaeval fittings
Peterborough Cathedral
Great Norman church fine example - little altered. Painted wooden roof to nave - remarkable west front - Galilee Porch & spires later additions.
Ramsey (St. Thomas of Canterbury)
12th century arcades - perpendicular nave. Late Norman chancel with Angevin vault.
St. Neots (St. Mary)
15th century
Sutton (St. Andrew)
14th century
Trumpington (St. Mary & St. Nicholas)
14th century. Framed brass of 1289 of Sir Roger de Trumpington.
Westley Waterless (St. Mary the Less)
Decorated. 14th century brass of Sir John & Lady Creke.
Wimpole (St. Andrew)
14th century rebuilt 1749 - splendid heraldic glass.
Yaxley (St. Peter)
15th century chancel screen, wall paintings, fine steeple.

Museums & Galleries

Cromwell Museum - Huntingdon
Exhibiting portraits, documents, etc. of the Cromwellian period.
Fitzwilliam Museum - Cambridge
Gallery of masters, old & modern, ceramics, applied arts, prints & drawing,

Cambridge & Northants.

mediaeval manuscripts, music & art library, antiquities.

Scott Polar Research Institute - Cambridge
Relics of expeditions & the equipment used. Current scientific work in Arctic & Antarctic.

University Archives - Cambridge
13th century manuscripts, Charters, Statutes, Royal letters & mandates. Wide variety of records of the University.

University Museum of Archaeology & Anthropology - Cambridge
Collections illustrative of Stone Age in Europe, Africa & Asia. Britain prehistoric to mediaeval times. Prehistoric America.

Ethnographic material from South-east Asia, Africa & America.

University Museum of Classical Archaeology - Cambridge
Casts of Greek & Roman Sculpture - representative collection.

Whipple Museum of the History of Science - Cambridge
16th, 17th & 18th century scientific instruments - historic collection.

Other Things to see & do

Nene Valley Railway
Steam railway with locomotives & carriages from many countries.

Caius College; Cambridge.

Cambridge & Northhants

Northamptonshire Gazeteer

Historic Houses & Castles

Althorp - Nr. Northampton
Family home of the Princess of Wales, with fine pictures & porcelain.
Boughton House - Nr. Kettering
Furniture, tapestries & pictures in late 17th century building modelled on Versailles, in beautiful parkland.
Canons Ashby House - Nr. Daventry
Small 16th century manor house with gardens & church.
Deene Park - Nr. Corby
Family home for over 4 centuries, surrounded by park, extensive gardens & lake.
Holdenby House - Nr. Northampton
Gardens include part of Elizabethan garden, with original entrance arches, terraces & ponds. Falconry centre. Rare breeds.
Kirby Hall - Nr. Corby
Large Elizabethan mansion with fine gardens.
Lamport Hall - Nr. Northampton
17th & 18th century house with paintings, furniture & china. One of the first garden rockeries in Britain. Programme of concerts & other special events.
Rockingham Castle - Rockingham, Nr. Market Harborough
Norman gateway & walls surrounding mainly Elizabethan house, with pictures & Rockingham china. Extensive gardens with 16th century yew hedge.
Rushton Triangular Lodge - Nr. Kettering
Symbolic of the Trinity, with 3 sides, 3 floors, trefoil windows.
Sulgrave Manor - Nr. Banbury
Early English Manor, home of George Washington's ancestors.

Museums

Abington Museum - Northampton
Domestic & social life collections in former manor house.
Museum of Leathercraft - Northampton
History of leather use, with Queen Victoria's saddle, & Samuel Pepys' wallet.

Waterways Museum - Stoke Bruerne Nr. Towcester
200 years of canal & waterway life, displayed beside the Grand Union Canal.

Cathedrals & Churches

Brixworth Church - Nr. Northampton
One of the finest Anglo-Saxon churches in the country, mostly 7th century.
Earls Barton Church - Nr. Northampton
Fine Anglo-Saxon tower & Norman arch & arcading.
Church of the Holy Sepulchre - Northampton
Largest & best preserved of four remaining round churches in England, dating from 1100.

Other Things to see & do

Billing Aquadrome - Nr. Northampton
Boating, fishing, swimming & amusements.
Wicksteed Park - Kettering
Large playground & variety of amusements for families.
Lilford Park - Nr. Oundle
Birds & farm animals in parkland setting where many special events are held.

Rushton Triangular Lodge.

CAMBRIDGESHIRE & NORTHAMPTONSHIRE

Map reference

1 Percival
1 Greening
1 Axhorn
1 Webb
2 Brash
3 Morbey
4 Bailey
5 Elbourn
7 Clarke
8 Faulkner
9 Parnell

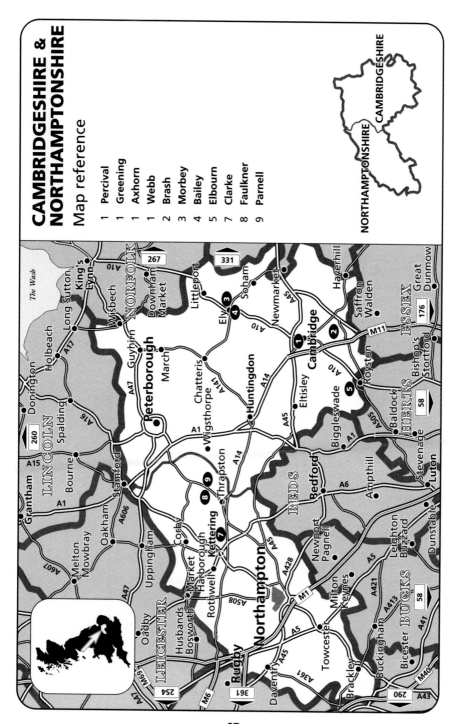

Cambridgeshire

		per person minimum £	children taken	evening meals	animals taken
Jane Greening **7 Water Street** **Cambridge** **CB4 1NZ** **Tel: (0223) 355550** **Open: ALL YEAR** **Map Ref No. 01**	Nearest Road: M.11, A.45 A warm welcome & friendly atmosphere await you at this lovely mediaeval coaching house overlooking the River Cam. Accommodation is in 3 charming rooms with tea/coffee making facilities & views across the delightful walled garden. A colour T.V. lounge is available for guests' use. A pleasant walk along the tow path leads to the many historic sights in Cambridge.	£19.00	N	N	N
Mrs Alice Percival **136 Huntingdon Road** **Cambridge** **CB3 0HL** **Tel:(0223) 65285/461142** **Open: ALL YEAR** **Map Ref No. 01**	Nearest Road: M.11 A large and attractive family house with a secluded garden and private parking, within walking distance of Magdalene College and the centre of Cambridge. Accommodation is in 2 bedrooms which are en-suite, furnished to a high standard, and equipped with tea/coffee facilities, T.V. & radio. Much thought has been put into the comfort and well-being of guests.	£25.00	Y	N	Y
Mrs A. E. Brash **Bridge House** **5 Cambridge Road** **Great Shelford** **Cambridge CB2 5JE** **Tel: (0223) 842920** **Open: ALL YEAR** **Map Ref No. 02**	Nearest Road: M.11 An old farmhouse, tastefully decorated, offering 3 attractive bedrooms furnished with antiques, in an acre of beautiful gardens with a sunny terrace where meals can be taken, & only 4 miles from the centre of the University town of Cambridge. Dinner can usually be provided if requested. John & Annie take much pleasure in entertaining their guests with a wide range of imaginative dishes. A delightful home.	£25.00	N	Y	N
Pamela Axhorn **Kirkwood House** **172 Chesterton Road** **Cambridge** **CB4 1DA** **Tel: (0223) 313874** **Open: FEB - DEC** **Map Ref No. 01**	Nearest Road: M.11, A.10 , Stay in this small Edwardian guesthouse & enjoy the comfort of its individually & tastefully decorated 5 guest bedrooms. All are centrally heated & equipped with colour T.V. & hospitality tray. Some with en-suite shower & toilet. Situated close to the river & a short walk from Cambridge city centre with its historic colleges. A lovely home & an ideal base from which to explore the many sights & attractions of the region.	£20.00	Y	N	N
Julie Webb **'Redby Lodge'** **15 Queen Edith's Way** **Cambridge** **CB1 4PH** **Tel: (0223) 242559** **Open: ALL YEAR** **Map Ref No. 01**	Nearest Road: M.11, A.10, Delightful, beautifully kept, detached cottage-style house with a large garden in a very select area of Cambridge. Exposed beams are a feature of this pleasant, quiet house. Offering 2 comfortable & newly decorated bedrooms, 1 en-suite, both with modern amenities including T.V./ radio & tea/coffee makers. Excellent meals are served in the dining room overlooking the garden. Julie & Tom are very helpful hosts. A lovely home, ideal for visiting this most historic city.	£18.00	N	Y	N

Forge Cottage. Stuntney.

Cambridgeshire & Northamptonshire

			minimum £ per person	children taken	evening meals	animals taken
Mrs Alison Morbey **Forge Cottage** **Lower Road, Stuntney** **Ely CB7 5TN** **Tel: (0353) 663275** **Mobile (0831) 833932** **Open: ALL YEAR** **Map Ref No. 03**	Nearest Road: A.142, A.10 This 17th century listed farmhouse is a Shire-horse & arable farm & is set in the centre of a quiet village in an elevated position over the Fens to Ely Cathedral. Elegantly furnished with antiques & featuring oak beams & inglenook fireplaces. Accommodation is in 2 very comfortable en-suite rooms which have colour T.V. & tea/coffee making facilities. Superbly situated for Ely, Cambridge and Newmarket.	*see PHOTO over*	£22.50	N	N	N
Mr & Mrs D. Bailey **Springfields** **Ely Road, LittleThetford** **Ely CB6 3HJ** **Tel: (0353) 663637** **Fax 0353 663130** **Open: JAN - NOV** **Map Ref No. 04**	Nearest Road: A.10 Located in a quiet area yet only 2 miles from the historic Ely Cathedral & city centre. Springfields is a lovely home set in an acre of beautiful garden. Accommodation is in 3 delightful bedrooms, 1 en-suite. All rooms have modern amenities, tea/coffee makers & T.V. A full English breakfast is served. A warm & friendly welcome awaits you at Springfields where the accent is on hospitality.	🚭	£20.00	N	N	N
Bernice & John Elbourn **Chiswick House** **Chiswick End** **Meldreth** **Royston SG8 6LZ** **Tel: (0763) 260242** **OpenALL YEAR (Excl. Xmas)** **Map Ref No. 05**	Nearest Road: A.10 A beautiful timber-framed farmhouse dating from the 16th century. The royal crest of King James I is found above the fireplace, suggesting this was his hunting lodge in the early 1600s. Jacobean panelling, oak beams & open fireplaces create a wonderful atmosphere. 6 en-suite rooms, with tea/coffee making facilities. T.V. is available. Many excellent inns nearby. An ideal base for touring Cambridge, Suffolk & Hertfordshire. A delightful home. 🚭 *see PHOTO over*	£19.00	Y	N	Y

Northamptonshire

		minimum £ per person	children taken	evening meals	animals taken
Audrey Clarke **Dairy Farm** **Cranford St. Andrews** **Kettering** **NN14 4AQ** **Tel: (053678) 273** **Open: ALL YEAR** **Map Ref No. 07**	Nearest Road: A.14 Situated in an idyllic Northamptonshire village, Dairy Farm is a charming 17th century farmhouse, featuring oak beams & inglenook fireplaces. 3 comfortable bedrooms, 2 with private bath. Families are well catered for. There is a delightful garden containing an ancient circular dovecote for guests to enjoy in a relaxed & friendly atmosphere. Delicious meals are served using farmhouse produce.	£18.00	Y	Y	Y

Chiswick House, Royston

Northamptonshire

		minimum £ per person	children taken	evening meals	animals taken
Margaret Faulkner **The Maltings** **Aldwincle** **Oundle NN14 3EP** **Tel: (08015) 233** **Fax 08015 326** **Open: All Year** **Map Ref No. 08**	Nearest Road: A.1, A.605 Since 1986, visitors have found a friendly wel- come at The Maltings, a 500 year-old former farmhouse with its inglenooks & beams & its granary close by. Furnished in antiques through- out, the accommodation is in 3 cosy, comfortable rooms with well-apppointed private bathrooms, 24 hour central heating, T.V., tea/coffee. The lovely traditional garden opened to the public twice a year is of special interest to plant lovers. Good eating places nearby. Children over 10 .	£20.00 (no smoking) CREDIT CARD VISA M'CARD	Y	N	N
Katie Parnell **Hall Farm** **Wigsthorpe** **Oundle** **Peterborough PE8 5SE** **Tel: (08015) 277** **Open: ALL YEAR** **Map Ref No. 09**	Nearest Road: A.1, A.605 A homely welcome awaits you at Hall Farm, for- merly the dower house to Lilford Hall. This is a working farm, mostly arable, set in gardens in a quiet village. Twin, double or family rooms, all with T. V. Evening meals by request. There is a games room and gymnasium in the house, and many sporting activities, walks and picnic areas close by. A good base to explore historic places in Cambridgeshire and Northamptonshire.	£17.50	Y	Y	N

All the establishments mentioned in this guide
are members of
The Worldwide Bed & Breakfast Association

When booking your accommodation please
mention
The Best Bed & Breakfast

Cheshire & Merseyside

Cheshire & Merseyside (North West)

Cheshire is located between the Peak District & the mountains of North Wales & is easily accessible from three major motorways. It has much to attract long visits but is also an ideal stopping-off point for travellers to the Lake District & Scotland, or to North Wales or Ireland. There is good access eastwards to York & the east coast & to the south to Stratford-upon-Avon & to London.

Cheshire can boast seven magnificent stately homes, the most visited zoo outside London, four of Europe's largest Garden Centres & many popular venues which feature distinctive Cheshire themes such as silk, salt, cheese, antiques & country crafts.

The Cheshire plain with Chester, its fine county town, & its pretty villages, rises up to Alderley Edge in the east from where there are panoramic views, & then climbs dramatically to meet the heights of the Peaks.

To the west is the coastline of the Wirral Peninsula with miles of sandy beaches & dunes &, of course, Liverpool.

The countryside shelters very beautiful houses. Little Moreton Hall near Congleton, is one of the most perfect imaginable. It is a black & white "magpie" house & not one of its walls is perpendicular, yet it has withstood time & weather for nearly four centuries, standing on the waterside gazing at its own reflection.

Tatton Hall is large & imposing & is splendidly furnished with many fine objects on display. The park & gardens are a delight & especially renowned for the azaleas & rhododendrons. In complete contrast is the enormous radio telescope at Jodrell Bank where visitors can be introduced to planetary astronomy in the planetarium .

Chester is a joy; a walk through its streets is like walking through living history. The old city is encircled by city walls enclosing arcaded streets with handsome black & white galleried buildings that blend well with modern life. There are many excellent shops along these "Rows". Chester Cathedral is a fine building of monastic foundation, with a peaceful cloister & outstanding wood carving in the choir stalls. Boat rides can be taken along the River Dee which flows through the city.

Manchester has first rate shopping, restaurants, sporting facilities, theatres & many museums ranging from an excellent costume museum to the fascinating Museum of Science & Industry.

Little Moreton Hall.

Liverpool grew from a tiny fishing village on the northern shores of the Mersey River, receiving its charter from King John in 1207. Commercial & slave trading with the West Indies led to massive expansion in the 17th & 18th centuries. The Liverpool of today owes much to the introduction of the steam ship in the mid 1900s, which enabled thousands of Irish to emigrate when the potatoe famine was at its height in Ireland. This is a city with a reputation for patronage of art, music & sport.

Cheshire & Merseyside

Cheshire & Merseyside Gazeteer

Area of outstanding natural beauty
Part of the Peaks National Park

Houses & Castles

Addington Hall - Macclesfield
15th century Elizabethan Black & White half timbered house.

Bishop Lloyd's House - Chester
17th century half timbered house (restored). Fine carvings. Has associations with Yale University & New Haven, USA.

Chorley Old Hall - Alderley Edge
14th century hall with 16th century Elizabethan wing.

Forfold Hall - Nantwich
17th century Jacobean country house, with fine panelling.

Gawsworth Hall - Macclesfield
Fine Tudor Half timbered Manor House. Tilting ground. Pictures, furniture, sculptures, etc.

Lyme Park - Disley
Elizabethan with Palladian exterior by Leoni. Gibbons carvings. Beautiful park with herd of red deer.

Peover Hall - Over Peover, Knutsford
16th century- stables of Tudor period; has the famous magpie ceiling.

Tatton Park - Knutsford
Beautifully decorated & furnished Georgian House with a fine collection of glass, china & paintings including Van Dyke & Canaletto. Landscaping by Humphrey Repton.

Little Moreton Hall - Nr. Congleton
15th century timbered, moated house with 16th century wall-paintings.

Cathedrals & Churches

Acton (St. Mary)
13th century with stone seating around walls. 17th century effigies.

Bunbury (St. Boniface)
14th century collegiate church - alabaster effigy.

Congleton (St. Peter)
18th century - box pews, brass candelabrum, 18th century glass.

Chester Cathedral - Chester
Subjected to restoration by Victorians - 14th century choir stalls.

Malpas (St. Oswalds)
15th century - fine screens, some old stalls, two family chapels.

Mobberley (St. Wilfred)
Mediaeval - 15th century Rood Screen, wall paintings, very old glass.

Shotwick (St. Michael)
Twin nave - box pews, 14th century quatre - foil lights, 3 deck pulpit.

Winwick (St. Oswald)
14th century - splendid roof. Pugin chancel.

Wrenbury (St. Margaret)
16th century - west gallery, monuments & hatchments. Box pews.

Liverpool Cathedral - the Anglican Cathedral was completed in 1980 after 76 years of work. It is of massive proportions, the largest in the British Isles, but containing much delicate & detailed work.

Museums & Galleries

Grosvenor Museum - Chester
Art, folk history, natural history, Roman antiquities including a special display of information about the Roman army.

Chester Heritage Centre - Chester
Interesting exhibition of the architectural heritage of Chester.

Cheshire Military Museum - Chester
The three local Regiments are commemorated here.

King Charles Tower - Chester
Chester at the time of the Civil War illustrated by dioramas.

Museum & Art Gallery - Warrington
Anthropology, geology, ethnology, botany & natural history. Pottery, porcelain, glass, collection of early English watercolours.

West Park Museum & Art Gallery - Macclesfield
Egyptian collection, oil paintings, watercolours, sketches by Landseer & Tunnicliffe.

Norton Priory Museum - Runcorn
Remains of excavated mediaeval priory. Also wildlife display.

Quarry Bank Mill - Styal
The Mill is a fine example of industrial building & houses an exhibition of the

Cheshire & Merseyside

cotton industry: the various offices retain their original furnishing, & the turbine room has the transmission systems & two turbines of 1903.

Nether Alderley Mill - Nether Alderley
15th century corn mill which was still used in 1929. Now restored.

The Albert Dock & Maritime Museum - Liverpool
Housing the Liverpool Tate Gallery, the Tate of the North.

Walker Art Gallery - Liverpool
Jodrell Bank - radio telescope & planetarium.

Historic Monuments

Chester Castle - Chester
Huge square tower remaining.

Roman Amphitheatre - Chester
12th legion site - half excavated.

Beeston Castle - Beeston
Remains of a 13th century fort.

Sandbach Crosses - Sandbach
Carved stone crosses dating from 9th century.

Gardens

Arley Hall - Northwich
Walled Gardens, topiary, shrub roses, herbaceous borders, azaleas & rhododendrons.

Cholmondeley Castle Gardens - Malpas
Gardens, lake, farm with rare breeds. Ancient chapel in park.

Ness Gardens - S. Wirral
Beautiful trees & shrubs, terraces, herbaceous borders, rose collection & herb garden.

Tatton Park - Knutsford.
Framed for azaleas & rhododendrons, an Italian terraced garden, a Japanese water garden, an orangery & a fernery.

Mersey Estuary & Ferry.

CHESHIRE MERSEYSIDE & MANCHESTER

Map reference

1 Broad
2 West
3 McGinn
4 Allwood
5 Dean
6 Sutcliffe
7 Cohen

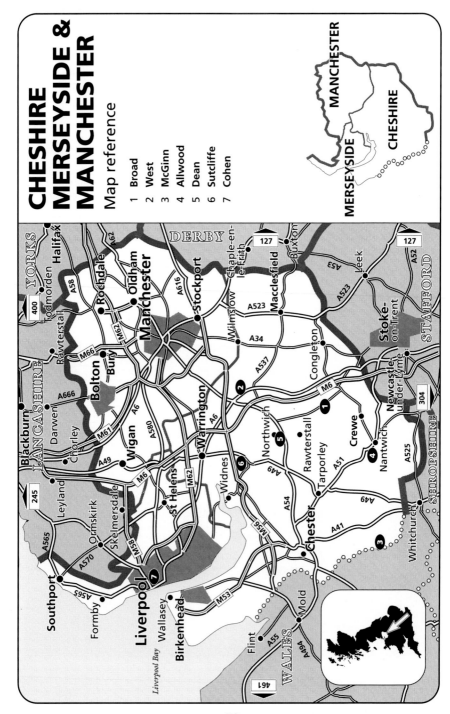

MANCHESTER

MANCHESTER

CHESHIRE

MERSEYSIDE

YORKS

Todmorden Halifax

400

Rawterstall

A62

Rochdale

A58

Oldham

A616

Manchester

Stockport

DERBY

Chaple-en-le-Frith

127

Buxton

Macclesfield

127

Leek

A53

A52

M62

M66

Bury

Wilmslow

A523

Macclesfield

A523

STAFFORD

Bolton

A666

Darwen

Blackburn

LANCASHIRE

Chorley

M61

A6

Wigan

A580

A34

A537

Congleton

Stoke-on-Trent

Newcastle-under-Lyme

M6

304

A49

Warrington

A6

2

1

Leyland

245

Ormskirk

Skelmersdale

M58

St Helens

M62

Widnes

M6

Northwich

5

Rawterstall

Tarporley

Crewe

A51

4

Nantwich

A525

SHROPSHIRE

Southport

A565

A570

Formby

A565

Liverpool

7

6

A49

A54

A41

Chester

3

Whitchurch

A49

Liverpool Bay

Wallasey

Birkenhead

M53

Mold

WALES

Flint

A55

A494

461

76

Burland Farm. Nantwich.

Cheshire

	minimum £ per person	children taken	evening meals	animals taken
Mr Bob Broad **The Folly** **Middlewich Road** **Minshull Vernon** **Crewe CW1 4RD** **Tel: (027071) 244** **Open: ALL YEAR** **Map Ref No. 01**	Nearest Road: M.6, A.530 A delightful old vicarage designed by Sir Gilbert Scott, built in 1847 on a Roman road. Accommodation is in 2 spacious double bedrooms, with modern amenities, sharing an attractive bathroom. A single room on the ground floor adjoins a shower room. All have tea/coffee making facilities & T.V. Appetising breakfasts are served in the guests' dining room overlooking one & a half acres of garden where guests may relax, play croquet or mini golf. Children over 14 years.	£18.00	Y	N	N
Pauline & Stephen West **The Longview Hotel** **55 Manchester Road** **Knutsford WA16 0LX** **Tel: (0565) 632119** **Fax 0565 652402** **Open: ALL YEAR (Excl. Xmas & New Year)** **Map Ref No. 02**	Nearest Road: M.6, A.50 Set in this pleasant Cheshire market town overlooking the common is this lovely, friendly hotel. Furnished with many antiques that reflect the elegance of this Victorian building, care has been taken to retain the character, but to provide all the comforts of the discerning traveller. All 23 en-suite bedrooms are prettily decorated, giving them that cared-for feeling which is echoed throughout the hotel. You are assured of a warm friendly welcome from the charming hosts.	£27.50 CREDIT CARD VISA M'CARD	Y	Y	Y
Valerie & John McGinn **Broughton House** **Threapwood** **Malpas SY14 7AN** **Tel: (094881) 610** **Open: ALL YEAR** **Map Ref No. 03**	Nearest Road: A.41 A friendly welcome to comfortable home within the elegant Georgian stables built for a former 17th century mansion. English breakfasts are served in the conservatory overlooking parkland with superb views to the Welsh hills & abundant wildlife. Luxurious bedrooms are all en-suite & ground floor. Large garden with croquet & tennis. 1 hour from Manchester & convenient for Chester & North Wales. Children over 10.	£20.00 *see PHOTO over*	Y	Y	N
Michael & Sandra Allwood **Burland Farm** **Wrexham Road, Burland** **Nantwich CW5 8ND** **Tel: (027074) 210** **Open: ALL YEAR (Excl. Xmas & New Year)** **Map Ref No. 04**	Nearest Road: A.534, M.6 This charming, centrally heated Victorian farmhouse is furnished with antiques & set in a lovely garden. The delightful sitting room is available to guests throughout the day, as are the 3 luxurious, en-suite, individually decorated bedrooms with colour television & hot drink facilities. Wonderful freshly prepared food is served in the dining room, from traditional breakfasts to innovative dinners. Special diets & picnics by arrangements.	£20.00 *see PHOTO over* CREDIT CARD AMEX	Y	Y	Y
Barbara Ann Dean **Ayrshire Guest House** **31 Winnington Lane** **Winnington** **Northwich CW8 4DE** **Tel: (0606) 74871** **Open: ALL YEAR** **Map Ref No. 05**	Nearest Road: A.533, A.49 A charming turn-of-the-century house, offering warmth, comfort & a friendly relaxed atmosphere. All of the 8 comfortable bedrooms, 4 en-suite, are tastefully decorated & have tea & coffee making facilities. A lounge with colour T.V. is available throughout the day, & a generous breakfast is served in the pleasant dining room. Conveniently situated for the many attractions of Cheshire & the North West.	£16.00	Y	N	N

Broughton House. Threapwood.

Cheshire & Merseyside

		minimum £ per person	children taken	evening meals	animals taken
Mr & Mrs Sutcliffe **Roughlow Farm** **Willington** **Tarporley CW6 0PG** **Tel: (0829) 51199** **Fax 0829 51199** **Open: ALL YEAR** **Map Ref No. 06**	Nearest Road: A.51, A.54 18th century sandstone farmhouse in outstanding situation with magnificent views across farmland to Shropshire & Wales. Large comfortable drawing room with T.V. 2 double/twin bedrooms, 1 with bathroom attached. 2 single bedrooms. The food here is delicious, freshly prepared with local produce where possible. Children over 6 years. Use of tennis court. Very quiet situation only 10 mins. from Chester.	£20.00	Y	Y	N

Merseyside

		minimum £ per person	children taken	evening meals	animals taken
Anna & David Cohen **Anna's** **65 Dudlow Lane** **Calderstones** **Liverpool L18 2EY** **Tel: (051) 7223708** **Fax 051 7228699** **Open: ALL YEAR** **Map Ref No. 07**	Nearest Road: M.62 Anna's is a comfortable family home where every effort is made to ensure that visitors become one of the family. Eating well is of the utmost importance here & guests may bring their own wine if they choose. Accommodation is in 4 rooms all with modern amenities, radio & tea/coffee making facilities. A resident T.V. lounge is also available as is the garden. Anna's is right in the heart of 'Beatle land'; Penny Lane & Strawberry Fields are moments away.	£15.00	Y	N	Y

When booking your accommodation please mention

The Best Bed & Breakfast

Cornwall

Cornwall
(West Country)

Cornwall is an ancient Celtic land, a narrow granite peninsula with a magnificent coastline of over 300 miles & wild stretches of moorland.

The north coast, washed by Atlantic breakers, has firm golden sands & soaring cliffs. The magnificent beaches at Bude offer excellent surfing , & a few miles to the south you can visit the picturesque harbour at Boscastle & the cliff-top castle at Tintagel with its legends of King Arthur. Newquay, with its beaches stretching for over seven miles, sheltered coves & modern hotels & shops, is the premier resort on Cornwall's Atlantic coast. St. Ives, another surfing resort, has great charm which has attracted artists for so long & is an ideal place from which to explore the Land's End peninsula.

The south coast is a complete contrast - wooded estuaries, sheltered coves, little fishing ports, & popular resorts. Penzance, with its warmth & vivid colours, is an all-the-year-round resort & has wonderful views across the bay to St. Michael's Mount. Here are excellent facilities for sailing & deep-sea fishing, as there are at Falmouth & Fowey with their superb harbours. Mevagissey, Polperro & Looe are fine examples of traditional Cornish fishing villages.

In the far west of Cornwall, you can hear about a fascinating legend: the lost land of Lyonesse - a whole country that was drowned by the sea. The legend goes that the waters cover a rich & fertile country, which had 140 parish churches. The Anglo-Saxon Chronicle records two great storms within a hundred years, which drowned many towns & innumerate people. Submerged forests are known to lie around these coasts - & in Mount's Bay beech trees have been found with the nuts still hanging on the branches, so suddenly were they swamped.

Today, St Michael's Mount & the Isles of Scilly are said to be all that remains of the vanished land. St. Michael's Mount, with its tiny fishing village & dramatic castle, can be visited on foot at low tide or by boat at high water. The Isles of Scilly, 28 miles beyond Land's End, have five inhabited islands, including Tresco with its sub-tropical gardens. Day trips to the numerous uninhabited islands are a special feature of a Scilly holiday.

Inland Cornwall also has its attractions. To the east of Bodmin, the county town, are the open uplands of Bodmin Moor, with the county's highest peaks at Rough Tor & Brown Willy. "Jamaica Inn", immortalised in the novel by Daphne du Maurier, stands on the lonely road across the moor, & "Frenchman's Creek" is on a hidden inlet of the Helford River.

There is a seemingly endless number & variety of Cornish villages in estuaries, wooded, pastoral or moorland settings, & here customs & traditions are maintained. In Helston the famous "Fleury Dance" is still performed, & at the ancient port of Padstow, May Day celebrating involves decorating the houses with green boughs & parading the Hobby Horse through the street to the tune of St. George's Song.

Helford Creek.

Cornwall

Cornwall Gazeteer

Areas of outstanding natural beauty.
Almost the entire county.

Historic Houses & Castles

Anthony House - Torpoint
18th century - beautiful & quite unspoiled Queen Anne house, excellent panelling & fine period furnishings.

Cotehele House - Calstock
15th & 16th century house, still contains the original furniture, tapestry, armour.

Ebbingford Manor - Bude
12th century Cornish manor house, with walled garden.

Godolphin House - Helston
Tudor - 17th century colonnaded front.

Lanhydrock - Bodmin
17th century - splendid plaster ceilings, picture gallery with family portraits 17th/ 20th centuries.

Mount Edgcumbe House - Plymouth
Tudor style mansion - restored after destruction in 1949. Hepplewhite furniture & portrait by Joshua Reynolds.

St. Michael's Mount - Penzance
Mediaeval castle & 17th century with 18th & 19th century additions.

Pencarrow House & Gardens - Bodmin
18th century Georgian Mansion - collection of paintings, china & furniture - mile long drive through fine woodlands & gardens.

Old Post Office - Tintagel
14th century manor house in miniature - large hall used as Post Office for a period, hence the name.

Trewithen - Probus Nr. Truro
Early Georgian house with lovely gardens.

Trerice - St. Newlyn East
16th century Elizabethan house, small with elaborate facade. Excellent fireplaces, plaster ceilings, miniature gallery & minstrels' gallery.

Cathedral & Churches

Altarnun (St. Nonna)
15th century, Norman font, 16th century bench ends, fine rood screen.

Bisland (St. Protus & St. Hyacinth)
15th century granite tower - carved wagon roofs, slate floor. Georgian wine - glass pulpit, fine screen.

Kilkhampton (St. James)
16th century with fine Norman doorway, arcades & wagon roofs.

Laneast (St. Michael or St. Sedwell)
13th century, 15th century enlargement, 16th century pulpit, some painted glass.

Lanteglos-by-Fowley (St. Willow)
14th century, refashioned 15th century, 13th century font, 15th century brasses & altar tomb, 16th century bench ends.

Launcells (St. Andrew)
Interior unrestored - old plaster & ancient roofs remaining, fine Norman font with 17th century cover, box pews, pulpit, reredos, 3 sided alter rails.

Probus (St. Probus & St. Gren)
16th century tower, splendid arcades, three great East windows.

St. Keverne (St. Keverne)
Fine tower & spire. Wall painting in 15th century interior.

St. Neot (St. Neot)
Decorated tower - 16th century exterior, buttressed & double-aisled. Many windows of mediaeval glass renewed in 19th century.

Museums & Galleries

Museum of Witchcraft - Boscastle
Relating to witches, implements & customs.

Military Museum - Bodmin
History of Duke of Cornwall's Light Infantry.

Public Library & Museum - Cambourne
Collections of mineralogy, archaeology, local antiquities & history.

Cornish Museum - East Looe
Collection of relics relating to witchcraft customs & superstitions. Folk life & culture of district.

Helston Borough Museum - Helston
Folk life & culture of area around Lizard.

Museum of Nautical Art - Penzance
Exhibition of salvaged gold & silver treasures from underwater wreck of 1700's.

Museum of Smuggling - Polperro
Activities of smugglers, past & present.

Penlee House Museum - Penlee, Penzance
Archaeology & local history & tin mining exhibits.

Cornwall

Barbara Hepworth Museum - St. Ives
Sculpture, letters, documents,
photographs, etc., exhibited in house
where Barbara Hepworth lived.
Old Mariners Church - St. Ives
St. Ives Society of Artists hold
exhibitions here.
County Museum & Art Gallery - Truro
Ceramics, art local history & antiquities,
Cornish mineralogy.

Historic Monuments

Cromwell's Castle - Tresco (Scilly Isles)
17th century castle.
King Charles' Fort - Tresco (Scilly Isles)
16th century fort.
Old Blockhouse - Tresco (Scilly Isles)
16th century coastal battery.
Harry's Wall - St. Mary's (Scilly Isles)
Tudor Coastal battery
Ballowall Barrow - St. Just
Prehistoric barrow.
Pendennis Castle - Falmouth
Fort from time of Henry VII.
Restormel Castle - Lostwithiel
13th century ruins.
St. Mawes Castle - St. Mawes
16th century fortified castle.

Tintagel Castle - Tintagel
Mediaeval ruin on wild coast, King
Arthur's legendary castle.

Things to see & do

Camel trail - Padstow to Bodmin
12 miles of recreation path along scenic
route, suitable for walkers, cyclists &
horse-riders.
Tresco Abbey Gardens - Tresco
Collection of sub-tropical flora
Trethorne Leisure Farm - Launceston
Visitors are encouraged to feed & stroke
the farm animals
Seal sanctuary - Gweek Nr. Helston
Seals, exhibition hall, nature walk,
aquarium, seal hospital, donkey paddock.
Dobwalls Theme Park - Nr. Liskeard
2 miles of scenically dramatic miniature
railway based on the American railroad.
Padstow tropical bird gardens -
Padstow
Mynack Theatre - Porthcurno

Lands End.

CORNWALL
Map reference

1	Smith	22	R. Lee
2	Lock	22	Jarratt
3	Thompson	22	Mercer
4	Knight	23	Hilder
4	Crocker	23	Wood
5	Thomas	23	Hopkins
6	Walker	24	Compton
7	Tremayne	25	Wooldridge
8	Ford	26	Richards
9	Betty	27	Barley
10	Morton	28	Studley
11	Colwill	29	Mason
12	Griffin	29	Batty
13	Spring	29	Sykes
13	Low	30	Walkley
14	Norman	30	Rayner
15	Tuckett	30	Charlick
16	Stevenson	31	Gartner
17	Owens	32	Dymond
18	Gould	33	Walker
19	Martin		
20	Sheppard		
21	Green		

Cornwall

		minimum £ per person	children taken	evening meals	animals taken
Mrs Pat Smith **Treffry Farm** **Lanhydrock** **Bodmin PL30 5AF** **Tel: (0208) 74405** **Open: APR - OCT** **Map Ref No. 01**	Nearest Road: A.30 Historic listed Georgian farmhouse which adjoins National Trust Lanhydrock with its stately home, glorious gardens and miles of country walks. You are guaranteed a warm welcome here and delicious home-cooking in generous quantities! You can enjoy relaxing in the pretty bedrooms (1 four-poster) and in the wood panelled lounge. Search out Cornwall's rugged cliffs and sandy coves from a very central location.	£18.00 (non-smoking)	N	Y	N
I.K. Lock **Whitehay** **Bodmin** **PL30 5NQ** **Tel: (0208) 831237** **Open: ALL YEAR** **Map Ref No. 02**	Nearest Road: A.30 Whitehay is really special. Totally private, surrounded by its own land of fields, orchard, woodland & river. A lovely Cornish home with a wonderfully welcoming atmosphere. Antiques, persian carpets, log fires, fresh flowers. 2 quiet & delightful double bedrooms, furnished with English chintzs & fine furniture offering guests a high standard of comfort. Both rooms have private bathrooms, colour T.V. & tea/coffee facilities. Children over 12.	£20.00 (non-smoking)	Y	N	N
Mr & Mrs B. Thompson **St. Christophers Hotel** **High Street** **Boscastle** **PL35 0BD** **Tel: (0840) 250412** **Open: MAR - OCT** **Map Ref No. 03**	Nearest Road: A.39, B.3266 A superb Georgian house retaining its original character, providing excellent, comfortable accommodation in 9 charming rooms with modern facilities, 8 en-suite. Here the welcome & standards are marvellous. The lovely harbour village is unspoilt. There is a wealth of history all around with plenty of interesting places to visit. Meals are well-prepared, delicious & personally supervised. An ideal spot for touring.	£15.50 CREDIT CARD VISA M'CARD	N	Y	Y
Mrs M. Knight **Manor Farm** **Crackington Haven** **Bude** **EX23 0JW** **Tel:(08403) 304/** **(0840) 230304** **Open: ALL YEAR** **Map Ref No. 04**	Nearest Road: A.39 A really super 11th century manor house retaining all its former charm & elegance. Mentioned in the 1086 Domesday book, it belonged to the Earl of Mortain, half-brother to William the Conqueror. Delightfully located in a beautiful & secluded position surrounded by attractive gardens & 40 acres of farmland. Guest rooms have private facilities. There is a games room for guests' use. Dining at Manor Farm is considered the highlight of the day. Only 1 mile from the beach. Non-smokers only. West Country winner of the Best Bed & Breakfast award.	£27.00 (non-smoking) *see PHOTO over*	N	Y	N
Ronald & Lucy Thomas **East Cornwall Farmhouse** **Fullaford Road** **Callington PL17 8AN** **Tel: (0579) 50018** **Open: MAR - DEC** **Map Ref No. 05**	Nearest Road: A.390 A former Count House to a silver/lead mine, East Cornwall Farmhouse is beautifully situated with views over "Silver Valley" & is ideal for touring Devon & Cornwall. It is just 2-3 miles to Cotehele House (National Trust) & St. Mellion Golf Course. Imaginative home cooking, using garden & local produce, to cater for most diets. T.V. lounge & tea/coffee facilities in bedrooms.	£14.00	Y	Y	Y

Manor Farm. Crackington Haven

Cornwall

	Nearest Road	minimum £ per person	children taken	evening meals	animals taken
Janet Crocker **Trevigue** **Crackington Haven** **Bude EX23 0LQ** **Tel: (08403) 418** **Open: ALL YEAR** **Map Ref No. 04**	Nearest Road: A.39 A delightful 16th century house built around a cobbled courtyard, on a farm mentioned in the Domesday Book. Trevigue, now a conservation-conscious dairy & stock farm, is a comfortable & welcoming home with mullioned windows, old beams, deep sofas and log fires. 4 en-suite bedrooms, 2 with T.V., all with tea-making facilities. Hearty breakfasts & excellent evening menu. Spectacular cliffs nearby. Children over 12.	£17.00 *see PHOTO over*	Y	Y	N
Mrs Jill Walker **Arrowan Common Farm** **Coverack** **TR12 6SH** **Tel: (0326) 280328** **Open: ALL YEAR** **Map Ref No. 06**	Nearest Road: A.3083, B.3293 A 150-year old traditional Cornish farmhouse, recently updated, though retaining its original character. Furnished with antiques it has a beamed lounge with granite fireplace & wood burner. A pretty sun lounge is also available, with vines & lemon trees. There are 5 very attractive & comfortable bedrooms: each with tea/coffee making facilities, & most with views across the gardens & fields to the sea. A delightful home .	£16.50	Y	N	N
Mr & Mrs T. D. Tremayne **'The Home' Country** **House Hotel** **Penjerrick** **Falmouth TR11 5EE** **Tel: (0326) 250427** **Fax 0326 250143** **Open: MAR - OCT** **Map Ref No. 07**	Nearest Road: A.39 A quiet & charming country house with views over Maenporth & Falmouth Bay. Accommodation is in 14 rooms, 7 with private bath/shower. All have tea/coffee making facilities. A colour T.V. lounge & bar are provided & guests may relax in the beautiful sheltered garden. Golf course & boating facilities nearby. A friendly host who prepares delicious meals using local produce. Special diets provided by arrangement.	£18.50	Y	Y	Y
Mrs Judy Ford **Treviades Barton** **High Cross** **Falmouth TR11 5RG** **Tel: (0326) 40524** **Open:ALL YEAR (Excl.** **Xmas & Easter)** **Map Ref No. 08**	Nearest Road: A.394 This charming 16th century listed farmhouse stands in beautiful gardens close to the Helford River. Offering 3 comfortable double bedrooms with radio & tea/coffee makers, 2 with en-suite facilities. Guests stay in a family atmosphere with a wide range of relaxing or energetic holiday opportunities available locally throughout the year. A delightful home where a warm & friendly welcome is assured.	£17.50 CREDIT CARD VISA M'CARD	Y	Y	Y
Andrea Betty **High Massetts** **Cadgwith Cove** **Helston** **TR12 7LA** **Tel: (0326) 290571** **Open: ALL YEAR** **Map Ref No. 09**	Nearest Road: A.3080 A warm welcome awaits visitors to High Massetts. Set in lovely gardens, the house is beautifully positioned with splendid views over the cove & is approached by a quaint, driveable, steep lane. 4 rooms, 1 en-suite. All have modern amenities & tea/coffee makers. Most have T.V. A guest lounge with colour T.V. is also available. The cove itself offers safe bathing, fishing, skin-diving & boating. Crab, lobster or steak suppers on request. Home grown fruit & vegetables & fresh eggs are used here. Super cliff walks, tennis, golf & riding available locally.	£15.50	Y	Y	N

Trevigue. Bude.

Cornwall

	Nearest Road	minimum £ per person	children taken	evening meals	animals taken
Mr & Mrs John Morton **Tregonning Manor** **Laddenvean** **Helston TR12 6QE** **Tel: (0326) 280222** **Open: MAR - OCT** **Map Ref No. 10**	Nearest Road: A.3083 Tregonning Manor is an old Cornish manor house, set in tranquil 10 acres with stream & mill pond, well off the beaten track on the Lizard Peninsular. Recently restored, & furnished with antiques to retain character. Only one family taken at any time in this relaxed friendly family home. One twin-bedded room with private bathroom. Also one double-bedded room available if required.	£18.00	Y	N	N
Mrs Agnes Colwill **Sutton Farm** **Boyton** **Launceston PL15 9RN** **Tel: (040927) 269** **Open: APR - OCT** **Map Ref No. 11**	Nearest Road: B.3254 A delightful 220 acre working farm. Accommodation is in 3 bedrooms, sharing 2 bathrooms. Lounge with colour T.V. available. Delicious full English breakfasts are served. T.V. snacks on request. Families are well catered for. There is a games room & cot/high chair. Guests are made very welcome & can relax in the beautiful garden. Sutton Farm is an ideal base for visiting the moors & many Cornish resorts.	£12.00	Y	N	Y
Raymond & Valerie Griffin **Wheatley Farm** **Maxworthy** **Launceston PL15 8LY** **Tel: (056681) 232** **Open: APR - SEPT** **Map Ref No. 12**	Nearest Road: A.39, A.30 You will be made very welcome at Wheatley, a spacious farmhouse built by the Duke of Bedford in 1871, which stands in landscaped gardens on a working farm in the peace of the Cornish countryside. 4 luxurious & charming en-suite bedrooms with colour T.V., tea/coffee making facilities. Tantalising & varied dinner menu. Log fires. Games room (and a secret one for children!). Pony rides. Spectacular coastline nearby.	£17.00	Y	Y	N
Brian & Lynda Spring **Allhays Country House** **Talland Bay** **Looe PL13 2JB** **Tel: (0503) 72434** **Fax 0503 72929** **OpenALL YEAR (Excl. Xmas.)** **Map Ref No. 13**	Nearest Road: A.387 Overlooking the beautiful smugglers cove of Talland Bay. House guests enjoy all the warmth & comfort of a family home complete with magnificent fireplaces & log fires. Offering 8 very comfortable bedrooms all with satellite link colour T.V., telephone, tea/coffee makers. Most are en-suite including 2 ground-floor rooms. Enjoy fine food & wine in the candlelit dining room or amidst the beautiful 'outdoor' surroundings of the elegant Victorian-style conservatory.	£28.00 *see PHOTO over* CREDIT CARD VISA M'CARD AMEX	Y	Y	Y
Pat & Bryan Norman **Fieldhead Hotel** **Portuan Road** **Looe** **PL13 2DR** **Tel: (0503) 262689** **Fax 0503 264114** **Open: FEB - DEC (Incl.Xmas)** **Map Ref No. 14**	Nearest Road: A.38 A delightful hotel with a fine reputation; guests return year after year. Set in its own grounds with panoramic views of the sea, within 200 yards of the beach. 14 most attractive & comfortable rooms with en-suite facilities. All have radio, T.V. & tea/coffee makers. An attractive residents' lounge, games room, a heated outdoor pool & lovely garden. The area is wonderful for all sports, riding, walking, fishing, sailing, golfing & the beaches are great. The Norman family make all visitors most welcome.	£27.50 CREDIT CARD VISA M'CARD	Y	Y	N

Allhays Country House. Looe

	Nearest Road / Description	minimum £ per person	children taken	evening meals	animals taken
Alexander & Sally Low **Coombe Farm** **Widegates** **Looe** **PL13 1QN** **Tel: (05034) 223** **Open: MAR - OCT** **Map Ref No. 13**	Nearest Road: B.3253, A.38 A lovely country house, beautifully furnished with antiques. Set in 10 acres of lawns, meadows, woods, streams & ponds with superb views down a wooded valley to the sea. The atmosphere is delightful with open log fires, a candlelit dining room in which to enjoy delicious home cooking & an informal licensed bar. An old barn has been converted for indoor games including snooker & table tennis. There is a croquet lawn, heated outdoor swimming pool & many birds & animals, including peacocks & horses. All rooms en-suite.	£18.50 *see PHOTO over*	Y	Y	N
Mr & Mrs A Tuckett **Trenderway Farm** **Looe** **PL13 2LY** **Tel: (0503) 72214** **Open: ALL YEAR** **Map Ref No. 15**	Nearest Road: A.387 Escape and unwind at Trenderway, 16th century listed farmhouse, heart of 400-acre working farm - off the beaten track yet 5 minutes from picturesque Polperro. Guests have the choice of 4 beautifully furnished & tastefully co-ordinated en-suite rooms with colour T.V.s, and tea/coffee making facilities. Four-course farmhouse breakfast (no need to interrupt the day for lunch!). Exceptional restaurants and inns nearby.	£22.00	N	N	N
Michael Stevenson & **Janie Flockhart** **Mixton House** **Lerryn** **Lostwithiel PL22 0QE** **Tel: (0208) 872781** **Open: APR-DEC** **Map Ref No. 16**	Nearest Road: A.390 A charming Georgian country house standing in two acres of secluded gardens, overlooking the picturesque Lerryn River Valley. Mixton offers a choice of 3 spacious, elegantly furnished bedrooms. Stylish, comfortable reception rooms, with flowers & books throughout, complete the country ambience. A tennis court & a boat & mooring are also available for guests' use. This is a delightful base from which to explore Cornwall.	£25.00	N	N	N
Mrs D. Owens **Mevagissey House** **Vicarage Hill** **Mevagissey** **PL26 6SZ** **Tel: (0726) 842427** **Open: MAR - OCT** **Map Ref No. 17**	Nearest Road: A.390, B.3273 An elegant Georgian rectory standing in 4 acres of woodland, overlooking the beautiful woodland & valley to the harbour & sea beyond. Here guests can unwind & relax in pleasant comfortable surroundings. There is a choice of 6 rooms, 4 en-suite, all with modern amenities, T.V. & tea/coffee making facilities. Snacks, morning coffee & Cornish cream teas are available on request. Evening meals are also served. Close by are fishing, beaches & golf courses. Children over 7.	£17.00 CREDIT CARD VISA M'CARD	Y	Y	N
Mrs Sarah Gould **Lusty Glaze House** **Lusty Glaze Road** **Newquay** **TR7 3AE** **Tel: (0637) 872668** **Open: EASTER - SEPT** **Map Ref No. 18**	Nearest Road: A.38, A.392 A relaxed peaceful atmosphere, friendly helpful hosts & high standards of accommodation are found here. In a unique location standing in an acre of gardens & adjoining the coastal footpath, overlooking a private beach. Lusty Glaze offers 5 comfortable rooms, all with en-suite facilities, T.V. & tea/coffee makers. Home cooking is a speciality using fresh seasonal ingredients. Vegetarians are also well catered for. Min. age of children is 6 years.	£25.00 CREDIT CARD VISA M'CARD	Y	Y	N

Coombe Farm. Widegates

Cornwall

Name / Address	Description	minimum £ per person	children taken	evening meals	animals taken
Keith & Janet Martin **Nanscawen House** **Prideaux Road** **Par PL24 2SR** **Tel: (0726) 814488** **Fax: 0726 814488** **OpenALL YEAR(Excl. Xmas)** **Map Ref No. 19**	Nearest Road: A.390 Nanscawen is a delightful country house set in an idyllic location. It stands in 5 acres of grounds & gardens in a nature conservation area. Guests have a choice of 3 luxury en-suite rooms with spa baths. The elegantly furnished drawing room leads into the conservatory where breakfast is enjoyed. Splendid, cordon bleu style dinners are available. An ideal base for touring all of Cornwall. Guests may like to use the heated swimming pool & whirlpool hot tub.	£30.00 *see PHOTO over* CREDIT CARD VISA M'CARD	Y	Y	N
C. Paul & B. Sheppard **Prospect House** **1 Church Rd** **Penryn** **TR10 8DA** **Tel: (0326) 373198** **Open: ALL YEAR** **Map Ref No. 20**	Nearest Road: A.39 Prospect House is a "gentleman's residence" built around 1830 for a local ship owner. On the edge of busy little Penryn, it is ideally situated for access to Cornwall's beauty spots, beaches, gardens, walks, National Trust properties & English Heritage monuments; but when a quiet day at home is needed, there is the walled rose garden in summer & log fires in winter... There are 3 double/twin bedrooms, all en-suite, & the house is furnished throughout with antiques.	£23.00	Y	Y	Y
David & Pamela Green **Acton Vean** **Trevean Lane** **Penzance TR20 9PF** **Tel: (0736) 762675** **Open: MAR - NOV** **Map Ref No. 21**	Nearest Road: A.394 On the edge of beyond, 6 miles from Penzance, Acton Vean is a gracious modern home of distinction on the southern coastal slope. It shares the uniquely privileged position of being adjacent to Acton Castle, with uninterrupted views of St. Michael's Mount & the bay, & access to the coastal footpath. Visitors welcomed as 'house guests'. 2 sea-facing bedrooms, barrel-ceiling sitting-room & quiet lovely gardens.	£18.00	N	N	N
Mr & Mrs R. J. Lee **Boscean Country Hotel** **Boswedden Road** **Penzance** **TR19 7QP** **Tel: (0736) 788748** **Open: MAR - OCT** **Map Ref No. 22**	Nearest Road: A.30 A warm & hospitable welcome awaits you at Boscean. A beautiful country house standing in 3 acres of walled grounds overlooking the sea & open countryside. There are 12 comfortable en-suite bedrooms each with tea/coffee making facilities. Guest lounge & bar. Delicious meals made with fresh, local or homegrown produce. Situated in an area of natural charm & beauty, an ideal place for touring the many interesting places in the Lands End peninsula.	£19.00	Y	Y	Y
Mr & Mrs R. I. Hilder **Carnson House Hotel** **East Terrace** **Penzance** **TR18 2TD** **Tel: (0736) 65589** **Open: ALL YEAR** **Map Ref No. 23**	Nearest Road: A.30 Carnson offers you a Cornish welcome & a friendly atmosphere. 8 modern bedrooms with heating, colour T.V., tea/coffee makers & some en-suite. Licensed, with a pleasant lounge. Enjoying one of Penzance's most central positions close to railway & bus stations. A variety of coach & boat trips, car hire & bus tours are available all year round & can be arranged by the hotel. Add international recommendations for food & it all makes a happy & memorable visit.	£15.00 CREDIT CARD VISA M'CARD AMEX	Y	Y	N

Nanscawen House. Par.

Cornwall

	Nearest Road	minimum £ per person	children taken	evening meals	animals taken
Mr & Mrs A. Compton **Ednovean House** **Perranuthnoe** **Penzance** **TR20 9LZ** **Tel: (0736) 711071** **Open: ALL YEAR** **Map Ref No. 24**	Nearest Road: A.30 This really is a super place to stay; a 150 year-old house offering 9 delightful, comfortable rooms, most having en-suite facilities & panoramic sea views. Situated in 1 acre of gardens & overlooking St. Michael's Mount & the entire bay. Relax in an extremely comfortable lounge, library or informal bar. Enjoy a wide selection of fine food & wines in the candlelit dining room, where vegetarians are also catered for. Ideal for coastal walks & exploring from the Lizard to Lands End.	£18.50 *see PHOTO over* CREDIT CARD VISA M'CARD AMEX	Y	Y	Y
Mr & Mrs R. Jarratt **Kenython Country** **Guest House** **Kenython Lane** **Penzance** **TR19 7PT** **Tel: (0736) 788607** **Open: APR-OCT** **Map Ref No. 22**	Nearest Road: B.3306 This attractive 90 year-old modernised farmhouse stands in 3 secluded acres of ground on the Lands End Peninsula. The comfortable surroundings, friendly atmosphere & good food ensure a delightful stay. 4 comfortable rooms, 2 with private facilities, all with modern amenities. Guests may also use the tennis court & swimming pool. The home cooking is delicious & served with guest's own wine. Well located for visiting Penzance, Lands End, St. Ives & St. Michael's Mount. Superb views over countryside.	£15.00	Y	Y	Y
Mrs F. Joan Wood **Lynwood Guest House** **41 Morrab Road** **Penzance** **TR18 4EX** **Tel: (0736) 65871** **Open: ALL YEAR** **Map Ref No. 23**	Nearest Road: A.30 A friendly relaxed atmosphere & a warm welcome await you at this Victorian house situated between promenade & town centre. Close to the sub-tropical Morrab Gardens. Offering 6 well decorated bedrooms all with modern facilities, colour T.V., tea/coffee makers. Comfortable colour T.V. lounge & large dining room offering various menus. A varied selection of restaurants within an easy walk. Ideal for visiting Lands End, Lizard, St. Michael's Mount & Isles of Scilly.	£11.00 CREDIT CARD VISA M'CARD	Y	N	Y
M. J. & C. J. Mercer **Roseudian** **Crippas Hill** **Penzance** **TR19 7RE** **Tel: (0736) 788556** **Open: MAR - OCT** **Map Ref No. 22**	Nearest Road: B.3306 Roseudian, a small quiet guest house, is ideally situated for enjoying all that the Lands End peninsula has to offer. It is a comfortably modernised, traditional Cornish cottage. 3 en-suite rooms, with tea/coffee making facilities. Lounge with colour T.V. & large garden for guests use. A warm welcome, log fire & good home-cooked meals using fresh garden produce all contribute towards a friendly & relaxing atmosphere. Children over 5. Dogs by prior arrangement only.	£15.50	Y	Y	Y
C. L. Hopkins **Woodstock Guest House** **29 Morrab Road** **Penzance** **TR18 4EZ** **Tel: (0736) 69049** **Open: ALL YEAR** **Map Ref No. 23**	Nearest Road: A.30 A warm friendly welcome awaits you at Woodstock. The sub-tropical Morrab Gardens are at the rear of the house & close to all amenities. Accommodation is in 5 charming & comfortable bedrooms, all with modern facilities including T.V. & tea/coffee makers, 1 shower en-suite. T.V. lounge. Attractive dining-room with extensive breakfast menu. An ideal base for exploring Mounts Bay & Land's End peninsula.	£11.00 CREDIT CARD VISA M'CARD AMEX	Y	N	N

Ednovean House. Perranuthnoe.

Cornwall

		minimum £ per person	children taken	evening meals	animals taken
Mr & Mrs K. Wooldridge **Beach Dunes Hotel** **Ramoth Way** **Perranporth TR6 0BY** **Tel: (0872) 572263** **Fax 0872 573824** **Open: MAR - OCT** **Map Ref No. 25**	Nearest Road: A.30, B.3285 A small friendly hotel pleasantly situated in almost an acre of grounds amidst the sand dunes adjoining the golf course & overlooking Perran Bay with its 3 miles of golden sands & Atlantic beach. Ten bedrooms, most en-suite, have tea/coffee, television/radio & private telephone. Excellent food is freshly prepared. Facilities include indoor pool, squash court, a cosy bar & residents' lounge. An excellent touring centre.	£20.50 CREDIT CARD VISA M'CARD AMEX	Y	Y	Y
Sylvia & Derek Richards **Landaviddy Manor** **Landaviddy Lane** **Polperro** **PL13 2RT** **Tel: (0503) 72210** **Open: FEB - OCT** **Map Ref No. 26**	Nearest Road: A.38 A beautiful, licensed, 18th century, small manor house built of traditional Cornish stone. Situated in lovely grounds on a hillside above the picturesque fishing village of Polperro, commanding charming views of the bay & surrounding National Trust countryside. The house retains its former character while incorporating modern comforts. All rooms are individually furnished with lovely linen, T.V. & tea/coffee makers. Many en-suite bathrooms, four-poster or Victorian beds.	£20.00 CREDIT CARD VISA M'CARD	Y	Y	Y
Mrs Marie Barley **Polmarine** **West Street** **Polruan-By-Fowey** **PL23 1PL** **Tel: (0726) 870459** **Fax 0726 870479** **Open: MAR - OCT** **Map Ref No. 27**	Nearest Road: A.390 In an idyllic situation right on the water's edge, Polmarine is a converted, early-18th Century boathouse retaining its unique character with exposed Cornish stone, oak beam fireplace and herringbone flooring. All rooms tastefully decorated and en-suite, with T.V., tea/coffee facilities. Antique four-poster available. Private quay, mooring line onto the water and direct access to the beach at low tide. Children over 10 welcome. An ideal spot for touring.	£17.50	Y	N	N
The Studley Family **Aviary Court** **Mary's Well** **Redruth TR16 4QZ** **Tel: (0209) 842256** **Open: ALL YEAR** **Map Ref No. 28**	Nearest Road: A.30 Aviary Court stands in two and a half acres of ground on the edge of Illogan Woods. This charming 300 year-old house offers guests a choice of 6 comfortable bedrooms, all with en-suite facilities, overlooking the gardens. Each has radio, colour T.V., tea/coffee making facilities & 'phone. The comfortable lounge has a bar & in winter a log fire. The restaurant serves delicious food with a selection of wine.	£27.00 CREDIT CARD VISA M'CARD AMEX	Y	Y	N
Diana & Derek Mason **Kandahar** **11 The Warren** **St. Ives TR26 2EA** **Tel: (0736) 796183** **Open: ALL YEAR (Excl.** **Xmas & New Year)** **Map Ref No. 29**	Nearest Road: A.3074 Kandahar has a unique water's-edge location lapped by the Atlantic & overlooking the harbour. The town centre, beaches, coach & railway station are all within 150 yards. 5 rooms have superb sea views, colour T.V., tea/coffee making facilities, & full central heating. There are 2 en-suite bedrooms. English & vegetarian breakfast served. There are many restaurants close by. Ideal for touring the magnificent Cornish countryside.	£16.00	Y	N	N

Cornwall

		minimum £ per person	children taken	evening meals	animals taken
Moira & Wally Batty **The Grey Mullet** **2 Bunkers Hill** **St. Ives TR26 1LJ** **Tel: (0736) 796635** **Open: ALL YEAR** **Map Ref No. 29**	Nearest Road: A.3074 The Grey Mullet, an 18th century Grade II listed building with oak beams & exposed granite walls, is situated in the old fishing & artists' quarters of St. Ives. Visitors are given a warm welcome in comfortable & homely surroundings. Some of the 7 bedrooms are en-suite & all have colour T.V. & tea/coffee making facilities. Vegetarian & low calorie diets catered for.	£16.00	Y	N	N
J. & I. Sykes **The Old Vicarage Hotel** **Parc-an-Creet** **St. Ives TR26 2ET** **Tel: (0736) 796124** **Open: APR-OCT** **Map Ref No. 29**	Nearest Road: A.30 The Old Vicarage Hotel, set in its own wooded grounds, secluded & peaceful, on the edge of the moorlands to the west of St. Ives. Accommodation is in 8 bedrooms, 6 with private bath/shower, some with colour T.V. All rooms have tea/coffee makers. Families well catered for. A delightful large garden for guests to relax in & a safe recreation area for children. Convenient for the beach & many places of interest.	£18.00 CREDIT CARD VISA M'CARD AMEX	Y	N	Y
Gillian & John Walkley **Rosebud Cottage** **Bossiney** **Tintagel** **PL34 0AX** **Tel: (0840) 770861** **Open: ALL YEAR(Excl. Nov & Xmas)** **Map Ref No. 30**	Nearest Road: A.39, B.3263 A picturesque stone Cornish cottage with secluded garden, within 10 minutes beautiful headland walk to Bossiney Cove which has a fine sandy beach & surfing. Three attractive comfortable rooms with modern facilities & tea/coffee makers. Good home cooking is the order of the day with vegetables from the garden. The evening meals are excellent value. The area has superb countryside for walking, fishing & riding & there are many ruined castles. Port Isaac, Bodwin Moor & Boscastle are a short drive away.	£14.00	Y	Y	Y
John & Christina Rayner **The Old Borough House** **Bossiney** **Tintagel** **PL34 0AY** **Tel: (0840) 770475** **Open: ALL YEAR** **Map Ref No. 30**	Nearest Road: A.39, B.3263 A delightful 17th century Cornish stone house, formerly the home of J.B. Priestley. It is located between Tintagel & Boscastle in an area of outstanding natural beauty with National Trust property nearby. The 6 comfortable bedrooms, 3 en-suite, have modern amenities & tea/coffee makers. A colour T.V. lounge & garden are also available for guests. Close by are safe bathing coves, caves & coastal walks. Delicious food & wine available. Children over 4 years.	£12.50	Y	Y	N
J Charlick & S Devlin **Trebrea Lodge** **Tintagel** **PL34 0HR** **Tel: (0840) 770410** **Open: ALL YEAR** **Map Ref No. 30**	Nearest Road: A.39 This lovely Grade II listed Georgian House set in 4 & a half acres of wooded hillside has outstanding views of the north Cornish coast. The land was originally granted by the Black Prince to the Bray family who lived here for 600 years. The bedrooms are individually decorated with antique furniture & have every comfort in mind. All have en-suite bathrooms. High quality home cooking & log fires serve to enhance the relaxed atmosphere. A truely delightful home.	£25.00 CREDIT CARD VISA M'CARD AMEX	Y	Y	Y

Cornwall

		minimum £ per person	children taken	evening meals	animals taken
Mrs Jacqueline Gartner **Laniley House** **St. Clement** **Truro TR4 9AU** **Tel: (0872) 75201** **Open:ALL YEAR (Excl. Xmas/New Year)** **Map Ref No. 31**	Nearest Road: A.3076 Laniley House, formerly a gentleman's residence, was built in 1860. It stands in 2 acres of gardens amidst beautiful unspoilt country, yet only 3 miles from the cathedral city of Truro. Offering 3 double rooms, 1 with en-suite facilities. All with T.V. & tea/coffee making facilities. A large comfortable lounge with colour T.V. & a separate breakfast/dining room is provided. A perfect location, ideal for discovering the true old Cornwall.	£15.00	N	N	N
Mr & Mrs E. Dymond **Trevispian-Vean Farm House** **Trevispian-Vean** **Truro TR4 9BL** **Tel: (0872) 79514** **Open: APR - OCT** **Map Ref No. 32**	Nearest Road: A.3076 A delightful farmhouse dating back over 300 years, offering a very warm welcome & good accommodation in 12 pleasant, comfortable guest rooms, 9 en-suite. Only 7 miles from the coast & surrounded by beautiful countryside, it is a perfect base for everyone. Families will particularly enjoy it here as children can look around the farm & there are plenty of places to visit & things to do. There's even a donkey for the children.	£16.00	Y	Y	N
Mr & Mrs M. C. Walker **The Old Mill Country House** **Little Petherick** **Wadebridge PL27 7QT** **Tel: (0841) 540388** **Open: MAR - OCT** **Map Ref No. 33**	Nearest Road: A.39, A.389 This delightful 16th century converted corn mill, complete with water wheel, stands in its own grounds at the head of Little Petherick Creek. The bedrooms are furnished with antiques, & all are en-suite with tea/coffee making facilities. Licensed with a colour T.V. available for the guests' use. There is also a terraced sun garden. All meals are traditionally cooked & offer very good value. A full 5-course evening meal is available by arrangement.	£21.00	N	Y	Y

When booking your accommodation please mention
The Best Bed & Breakfast

Cumbria

Cumbria

The Lake District National Park is deservedly famous for its magnificent scenery. Here, England's highest mountains & rugged fells surround shimmering lakes & green valleys. But there is more to Cumbria than the beauty of the Lake District. It also has a splendid coastline, easily accessible from the main lakeland centres, as well as a border region where the Pennines, the backbone of England, reach their highest point, towering over the Eden valley.

Formation of the dramatic Lakeland scenery began in the Caledonian period when earth movements raised & folded the already ancient rocks, submerging the whole mass underseas & covering it with limestone. During the ice age great glaciers ground out the lake beds & dales of todays landscape. There is tremendous variety, from the craggy outcrops of the Borrowdale Volcanics with Skiddaw at 3054 feet, to the gentle dales, the open moorlands & the lakes themselves. Each lake is distinctive, some with steep mountain sides sliding straight to the water's edge, others more open with sloping wooded hillsides. Ellerwater, the enchanting "lake of swans" is surrounded by reed & willows at the foot of Langdale. The charm of Ullswater inspired Wordsworth's famous poem "Daffodils". Whilst many lakes are deliberately left undisturbed for those seeking peace, there are others - notably Windermere - where a variety of water sports can be enjoyed. The changeable weather of the mountainous region can produce a sudden transformation in the character of a tranquil lake, raising choppy waves across the darkened surface to break along the shoreline. It is all part of the fascination of Lakeland.

Fell walking is the best way to appreciate the full beauty of the area. There are gentle walks along the dales, & the tops of the ridges are accessible to walkers with suitable footwear & an eye to the weather.

Ponytrekking is another popular way to explore the countryside & there are many centres catering even for inexperienced riders.

There are steamboats on lakes such as Coniston & Ullswater, where you can appreciate the scenery. On Windermere there are a variety of boats for hire, & facilities for water-skiing.

Traditional crafts & skills are on display widely. Craft centres at Keswick, Ambleside & Grasmere, & the annual exhibition of the Guild of Lakeland Craftsmen held in Windermere from mid-July to early September represent the widest variety of craft artistry.

Fairs & festivals flourish in Lakeland. The famous Appleby Horse Fair, held in June is the largest fair of its kind in the world & attracts a huge gypsy gathering. Traditional agriculture shows, sheep dog trials & local sporting events abound. The Grasmere Sports, held each August include gruelling fell races, Cumberland & Westmoreland wrestling, hound trails & pole-leaping.

The traditional custom of "Rushbearing" when the earth floors of the churches were strewn with rushes still survives as a procession in Ambleside & Grasmere & many other villages in the summer months

The coast of Cumbria stretches from the estuaries of Grange-over-Sands & Burrow-in-Furness by way of the beautiful beaches between Bootle & Cardurnock, to the mouth of the Solway Firth. The coastal areas, especially the estuaries, are excellent for bird-watching. The sand dunes north of the Esk are famous for the colony of black-headed gulls which can be visited by arrangement, & the colony of seabirds at St. Bees Head is the largest in Britain.

Cumbria

Cumbria

Gazeteer

Area of outstanding natural beauty.
The Lake District National Park.

House & Castles

Carlisle Castle - Carlisle
12th century. Massive Norman keep - half-moon battery - ramparts, portcullis & gatehouse.
Brough Castle - Kirby Stephen
13th century - on site of Roman Station between York & Carlisle.
Dacre Castle - Penrith
14th century - massive pele tower.
Sizergh Castle - Kendal
14th century - pele tower - 15th century great hall. English & French furniture, silver & china - Jacobean relics. 18th century gardens.
Belle Island - Boweness-on-Windermere
18th century - interior by Adams Brothers, portraits by Romney.
Swarthmoor Hall - Ulverston
Elizabethan house, mullioned windows, oak staircase, panelled rooms. Home of George Fox - birthplace of Quakerism - belongs to Society of Friends.
Lorton Hall - Cockermouth
15th century pele tower, priest holes, oak panelling, Jacobean furniture.
Muncaster Castle - Ravenglass
14th century with 15th & 19th century additions - site of Roman tower.
Rusland Hall - Ulveston
Georgian mansion with period panelling, sculpture, furniture, paintings.
Levens Hall - Kendal
Elizabethan - very fine panelling & plasterwork - famous topiary garden.
Hill Top - Sawrey
17th century farmhouse home of Beatrix Potter - contains her furniture, china & some of original drawings for her children's books.
Dove Cottage - Town End, Grasmere
William Wordsworth's cottage - still contains his furnishing & his personal effects as in his lifetime.
Brantwood
The Coniston home of John Ruskin, said to be the most beautifully situated house in the Lake District. Exhibition, gardens, bookshops & tearooms

Cathedrals & Churches

Carlisle Cathedral - Carlisle
1130. 15th century choir stalls with painted backs - carved misericords, 16th century screen, painted roof.
Cartmel Priory (St. Mary Virgin)
15th century stalls, 17th century screen, large east window, curious central tower.
Lanercost Priory (St. Mary Magdalene)
12th century - Augustinian - north aisle now forms Parish church.
Greystoke (St. Andrew)
14th/15th century. 19th century misericords. Lovely glass in chancel.
Brougham (St. Wilfred)
15th century carved altarpiece.
Furness Abbey
12th century monastery beautiful setting.
Shap Abbey
12th century with 16th century tower.

Museums & Galleries

Abbot Hall - Kendal
18th century, Georgian house with period furniture, porcelain, silver, pictures, etc. Also contains modern galleries with contemporary paintings, sculptures & ceramics. Changing exhibitions on show.
Carlisle Museum & Art Gallery - Carlisle
Archaeological & natural history collections. National centre of studies of Roman Britain. Art gallery principally exhibiting paintings & porcelain.
Hawkshead Courthouse - Kendal
Exhibition of domestic & working life housed in mediaeval building.
Helena Thompson Museum - Workington
displays Victorian family life & objects of the period.
Lakeland Motor Museum - Holker Hall - Grange-over-Sands
Exhibits cars, bicycles, tricycles, motor cycles, etc., & model cars.
Millom Folk Museum - St. George's Road, Millom
Reconstructions of drift in iron ore mine, miner's cottage kitchen, blacksmith's forge & agricultural relics.
Ravenglass Railway Museum - Ravenglass
History of railways - relics, models, etc.

Cumbria

Wordsworth Museum - Town End, Grasmere
Personal effects, first editions, manuscripts, & general exhibits from the time of William Wordsworth.

Border Regiment Museum - The Castle, Carlisle.
Collection of uniforms, weapons, trophies, documents, medals from 1702, to the present time.

Whitehaven Museum - Whitehaven
History & development of area show in geology, paleontology, archaeology, natural history, etc. Interesting maritime past.

The Beatrix Potter Gallery - Hawkshead

Fitz Park Museum & Art Gallery - Keswick
Collection of manuscripts - Wordsworth, Walpole, Coleridge, Southey.

Things to see & do

Fell Walking - there is good walking throughout Cumbria, but check weather reports, clothing & footwear before tackling the heights.

Pony-trekking - opportunities for novice & experienced riders.

Watersports - Windermere is the ideal centre for sailing, waterskiing, windsurfing, scuba-diving.

Golf - championship course to the north at Silloth.

Grasmere.

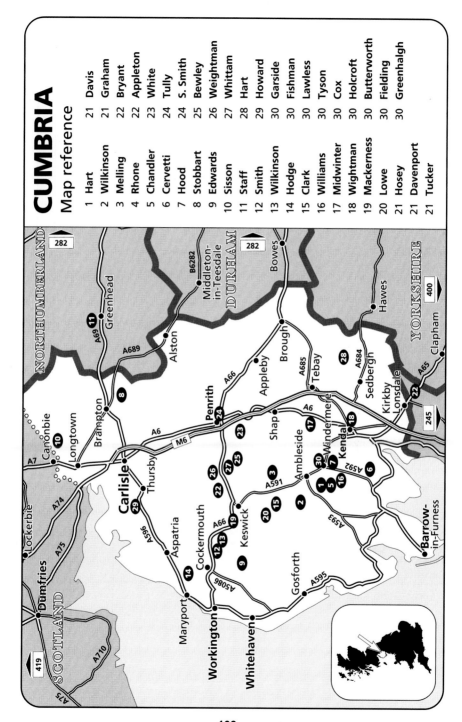

CUMBRIA
Map reference

1 Hart	21 Davis
2 Wilkinson	21 Graham
3 Melling	22 Bryant
4 Rhone	22 Appleton
5 Chandler	23 White
6 Cervetti	24 Tully
7 Hood	24 S. Smith
8 Stobbart	25 Bewley
9 Edwards	26 Weightman
10 Sisson	27 Whittam
11 Staff	28 Hart
12 Smith	29 Howard
13 Wilkinson	30 Garside
14 Hodge	30 Fishman
15 Clark	30 Lawless
16 Williams	30 Tyson
17 Midwinter	30 Cox
18 Wightman	30 Holcroft
19 Mackerness	30 Butterworth
20 Lowe	30 Fielding
21 Hosey	30 Greenhalgh
21 Davenport	
21 Tucker	

Cumbria

	Nearest Road	minimum £ per person	children taken	evening meals	animals taken
Peter & Anne Hart **Bracken Fell** Outgate Ambleside LA22 0NH Tel: (05394) 36289 Open: ALL YEAR Map Ref No. 01	Nearest Road: B.5286 Bracken Fell is situated in beautiful open countryside in the picturesque hamlet of Outgate. Located between Ambleside & Hawkshead, this makes an ideal base for exploring the Lake District. Accommodation in 6 comfortable rooms, all with tea/coffee making facilities & outstanding views. 4 have en-suite facilities. There is also a comfortable lounge & dining room. All major outdoor activities are catered for nearby, including sailing, fishing, windsurfing & pony trekking.	£16.00	Y	N	N
Mrs M. Wilkinson **Long House** Great Langdale Ambleside LA22 9JS Tel: (09667) 222 Open: FEB-NOV Map Ref No. 02	Nearest Road: B.5343 17th century lakeland cottage enjoying a peaceful position near the foot of Langdale Pikes with superb open views. There are 2 acres of orchard & garden. Beamed ceilings, stained glass windows & original slate floors. Central heating throughout. Pretty bedrooms, each with a private bathroom, full of character & very individual. Enclosed parking. Ideal walking country & centrally placed for the motorist. Home cooking, with quality food a speciality.	£21.00 CREDIT CARD VISA M'CARD	N	Y	N
Tim Melling **Nab Cottage** Rydal Ambleside LA22 9SD Tel: (05394) 35311 Fax 05394 35493 Open: ALL YEAR Map Ref No. 03	Nearest Road: A.591 A 16th century cottage in an idyllic lake-shore setting, originally owned by De Quincey & once the home of H. Coleridge. 'Nab Cottage' offers accommodation in 7 comfortable rooms, 4 with private bath/shower. A residents' lounge & beautiful garden are available for guests. Delicious breakfasts & evening meals are served. Room service available. Ideal base for walking, fishing & touring the surrounding areas of natural beauty.	£16.50	Y	Y	Y
Alan & Gillian Rhone **Riverside Lodge** **Country House** Rothay Rd Rothay Bridge Ambleside LA22 0EH Tel: (05394) 34208 Open: ALL YEAR Map Ref No. 04	Nearest Road: A.593 Riverside Lodge is an early-Georgian house superbly situated in a unique riverside setting, just a short walk from both the centre of Ambleside & Lake Windermere. The house has been refurbished to a high standard & exudes character & charm with beamed ceilings. There are also 5 very tasteful modern holiday cottages within the grounds for those who wish to cater for themselves. A beautiful home, ideal for touring the wonderful surrounding countryside.	£24.00 *see PHOTO over* CREDIT CARD VISA M'CARD	N	N	N
Wendy, Dennis & Peter **Chandler** **Walker Ground Manor** Hawkshead Ambleside LA22 0PD Tel: (05394) 36219 Open: ALL YEAR Map Ref No. 05	Nearest Road: A.591, B.5286 A genuine B & B in a 16th century house enjoyed by family & visitors alike for its charm, idyllic setting & living history. Enjoy gentle walks, easy touring, spacious gardens & glorious countryside. Return to log fires, generous hospitality & restful, pretty rooms furnished with antiques. Candlelit dinner parties are held in the spacious conservatory or in the comfortable old dining room. Books, maps & music are for general use.	£30.00	N	Y	N

Riverside Lodge Country House. Rothay Bridge.

Pickett Howe. Brackenthwaite.

Cumbria

	minimum £ per person	children taken	evening meals	animals taken
Mrs Evelyn Cervetti **'Lightwood Farmhouse'** **Cartmel Fell** **Bowland Bridge** **LA11 6NP** **Tel: (05395) 31454** **Open: JAN - NOV** **Map Ref No. 06** Nearest Road: A.592 Lightwood Farmhouse was built around 1650. Possesses all the modern amenities, whilst retaining the charm of original oak beams & staircase, standing in one & a half acres of gardens with streams running through. Only 2 miles from the southern end of Lake Windermere. Guests' private lounge with T.V. & log fire. Charming dining room facing the early morning sun serving good wholesome food. Using fresh produce wherever possible. A lovely home. CREDIT CARD VISA M'CARD	£16.50	Y	Y	N
Ray & Barbara Hood **Fairfield Country House** **Brantfell Rd** **Bowness-on-Windermere** **LA23 3AE** **Tel: (05394) 46565** **Fax 05394 47017** **Open: ALL YEAR** **Map Ref No. 07** Nearest Road: M.6 Fairfield is a small friendly 200 year-old lakeland hotel in a peaceful garden setting, 200 metres from Bowness village. Well-appointed, comfortable & tastefully furnished bedrooms all with colour T.V., welcome tray & private showers/baths. Fairfield is famous for its breakfasts. The Dales Way, an 81 mile walk from Ilkley to Bowness, ends within a short distance from the hotel. An ideal spot from which to tour this beautiful area with its many historical attractions. CREDIT CARD VISA M'CARD	£22.00	Y	Y	Y
Mrs Sheila Stobbart **'Hullerbank'** **Talkin** **Brampton CA8 1LB** **Tel: (06977) 46668** **Open: ALL YEAR (Excl.** **Xmas./New Year)** **Map Ref No. 08** Nearest Road: A.69, M.6 Georgian farmhouse dated 1635-1751, standing in its own grounds near the picturesque village of Talkin 2 1/2 miles from Brampton. Superb walking country, central for visiting Hadrian's Wall, Lake District & borders. A friendly, relaxed atmosphere awaits. 3 comfortable bedrooms with private facilities, central heating, electric underblankets & tea makers. Comfortable T.V. lounge & dining room with excellent home cooking inc. home produced lamb & fresh produce.	£17.00	Y	Y	N
David & Dani Edwards **Pickett Howe** **Brackenthwaite** **Buttermere Valley** **CA13 9UY** **Tel: (0900) 85444** **Open: MAR-NOV** **Map Ref No. 09** Nearest Road: B.5292 A listed 17th century Lakeland longhouse offering caring, friendly and relaxing hospitality. Peacefully set in 15 acres amidst stunning mountain scenery, its slate floors, oak beams and mullioned windows are enhanced by quality furnishings and antiques. Four fully en-suite bedrooms with whirlpool baths, hot drinks trays, telephones, clock radios, Victorian brass and iron bedsteads. Renowned creative cooking, meat and vegetarian; outstanding breakfast menu. *see PHOTO over* CREDIT CARD VISA M'CARD	£29.00	Y	Y	N
Jack & Margaret Sisson **Bessiestown Farm** **Catlowdy, Penton** **Carlisle CA6 5QP** **Tel: (0228) 577219** **Open: ALL YEAR** **Map Ref No. 10** Nearest Road: B.6318 off A.7 An award-winning farm overlooking the Scottish borders where a friendly relaxing atmosphere is assured. Accommodation is in 5 en-suite rooms with radio & tea/coffee making facilities. Delicious home cooking. Residential licence. Guests may also use the indoor heated pool (May-Sept). An excellent base for a holiday or touring. Restricted smoking area. *see PHOTO over*	£19.00	Y	Y	N

Bessiestown Farm. Catlowdy.

All the establishments mentioned in this guide
are members of the
Worldwide Bed & Breakfast Association.

If you have any comments regarding your
accommodation please send them to us
using the form at the back of the book.
We value your comments.

Holmhead. Greenhead.

Cumbria

	Nearest Road / Description	minimum £ per person	children taken	evening meals	animals taken
Brian & Pauline Staff 'Holmhead' Hadrian's Wall Greenhead Carlisle CA6 7HY Tel: (06977) 47402 Open:ALL YEAR (Excl. Xmas, New Year) Map Ref No. 11	Nearest Road: A.69, B.6318 Standing in 300 acres of grounds with Hadrian's Wall below. Holmhead, a 150 year-old traditional farmhouse, is an excellent base for visiting an area full of Roman history. 4 charming en-suite bedrooms with modern amenities. Longest breakfast menu in the world. All meals prepared with fresh produce. Birdswald, the highest remains of the Wall & the Roman Army Museum are close by. Host is a qualified tour guide & expert on Hadrian's Wall. Licensed.	£20.00 *see PHOTO over* CREDIT CARD VISA M'CARD	Y	Y	N
Brian & May Smith Link House Bassenthwaite Lake Cockermouth CA13 9YD Tel: (07687) 76291 Open: FEB - NOV Map Ref No. 12	Nearest Road: A.66 Link House is a small country house close to Bassenthwaite Lake. There are superb views over the lake, forest & fell. Accommodation is in 8 en-suite rooms with T.V. & tea/coffee makers. In the evenings relax in the lounge in front of the log fire surrounded by elegant furnishings, period pieces & antiques. Meals are always freshly prepared & you can enjoy a delicious 5 course dinner & good wine. Children over 7 years.	£20.00	Y	Y	N
Pauline & Bob Hodge Sundawn Carlisle Road, Bridekirk Cockermouth CA13 0PA Tel: (0900) 822384 Open: ALL YEAR Map Ref No. 14	Nearest Road: Bob & Pauline offer you a warm & friendly welcome. The emphasis here is on comfort, relaxation, personal service & imaginative home cooking. From the sunlounge view the panorama of Lakeland Fells & historic market town of Cockermouth, birthplace of William Wordsworth. Accommodation is in 4 tastefully decorated rooms, 2 en-suite, all with modern amenities & tea/coffee makers. An ideal spot for touring.	£13.50	Y	Y	Y
Angela & Martin Clark Banerigg Guest House Lake Road Grasmere LA22 9PW Tel: (05394) 35204 Open: ALL YEAR Map Ref No. 15	Nearest Road: A.591 Delightfully situated overlooking Grasmere Lake, is this small, friendly guest house. The informal hospitality & relaxing atmosphere make this a super base for a holiday. 6 comfortable rooms have modern amenities. Pleasant lounge with cosy log fire. Delicious, plentiful home-cooking is served daily. Ideally located for fell walking, sailing, canoeing & fishing. Angela & Martin ensure that guests have a memorable Lakeland holiday. Evening meals for group bookings only.	£19.00	Y	N	Y
Mr & Mrs J. Williams Ees Wyke Country House Nr. Sawrey Hawkshead LA22 0JZ Tel: (05394) 36393 Open: ALL YEAR Map Ref No. 16	Nearest Road: A.592, A.590 Beatrix Potter spent many summers at 'Ees Wyke', a charming Georgian house, standing on the shores of Esthwaite Water, surrounded by breathtaking views of lake, mountains & fells. All our 8 bedrooms have lake views, en-suite bathrooms or showers, T.V. & tea/coffee making facilities. Owners Margaret & John Williams offer a warm welcome & a guarantee of excellent food & service. An ideal base for exploring Lakeland.	£34.00	Y	Y	Y

111

Riggs Cottage. Bassenthwaite Lake

Cumbria

	minimum £ per person	children taken	evening meals taken	animals taken
Fred & Hazel Wilkinson **Riggs Cottage** **Routenbeck** **Bassenthwaite Lake** **Cockermouth CA13 9YN** **Tel: (07687) 76580** **Open: ALL YEAR** **Map Ref No. 13**	Nearest Road: A.66 Riggs Cottage is a super 17th century house, of great character & charm with many exposed oak beams, log burning inglenook fireplace & period furniture. The accommodation, in 3 rooms, is comfortable & tastefully furnished with modern amenities. The cosy lounge is available throughout the day. In the nicely furnished dining room tasty home-cooked meals are served using only the best ingredients. Oven fresh bread & home-made preserves are a speciality. *see PHOTO over*	£19.50 🚭	N	Y	N
Alison & Philip Midwinter **Low Jock Scar** **Selside** **Kendal** **LA8 9LE** **Tel: (0539) 823259** **Open: MAR - NOV** **Map Ref No. 17**	Nearest Road: A.6 Located in a wonderfully secluded, riverside setting in 6 acres of natural garden & woodland. An idyllic spot situated between the Lakes & Yorkshire Dales - en route to Scotland - perfect for a few days away from it all. 5 pleasant bedrooms, 3 en-suite with tea/coffee making facilities. Guests have their own comfortable lounge with T.V. Dinners by arrangement. Excellent home cooking using home produce. Vegetarians catered for. Residential licence. *see PHOTO over*	£18.00 🚭	N	Y	Y
Mrs Ada Wightman **The Glen** **Oxenholme** **Kendal** **LA9 7RF** **Tel: (0539) 726386** **Open: ALL YEAR** **Map Ref No. 18**	Nearest Road: M.6, A.65 A large detached house standing in its own grounds. Offering 3 rooms, all with private facilities & modern amenities including radio, colour T.V. & tea/coffee making facilities. A delicious full English breakfast is served & there is a lounge for guests to relax in. Situated only minutes from Oxenholme railway station 'The Glen' is an excellent base for touring the idyllic Lake District. Children over 12. An ideal base for touring Lakeland.	£16.00	Y	Y	N
Hilda & Geoff Mackerness **Claremont House** **Chestnut Hill** **Keswick CA12 4LT** **Tel: (07687) 72089** **Open: ALL YEAR** **Map Ref No. 19**	Nearest Road: A.591 Situated in a three quarter acre of woodland garden. This 150-year old lodge house offers accommodation in 1 single & 5 double bedrooms, all with en-suite facilities, 1 with spa bath, lace canopied beds, clock/radio & tea/coffee makers. A comfortable lounge, colour T.V. & bar licence. Delicious food, home-made bread. Vegetarians are especially welcome.	£24.00	N	Y	N
Mr & Mrs R Hosey **Derwentwater Marina** **Portinscale** **Keswick** **CA12 5RF** **Tel: (07687) 72912** **Open: ALL YEAR** **Map Ref No. 21**	Nearest Road: A.66 Derwentwater Marina, on the lake shore 1 mile from Keswick, offers affordable luxury in motel type accommodation with breakfast . En-suite rooms with patios and lake and mountain views, T.V., fridge, toaster, kettle etc. and the ingredients for you to prepare your own continental breakfast. Windsurf, sail, canoe, walk and climb, or just relax and enjoy the wonderful views - the choice is yours.	£20.00 🚭	N	N	N

Low Jock Scar. Selside

Cumbria

		minimum £ per person	children taken	evening meals	animals taken
Mr & Mrs A. Lowe **Dale Head Hall** **Lake Thirlmere** **Keswick** **CA12 4TN** **Tel: (07687) 72478** **Open: ALL YEAR** **Map Ref No. 20**	Nearest Road: A.591, A.66 Lose yourself in the ancient woodlands & mature gardens of an Elizabethan country manor, set serenely on the shores of Lake Thirlmere. Delicious dinners prepared by mother & daughter, using fresh produce from the Victorian kitchen garden, served with fine wines in the oak beamed dining room. 9 individually decorated bedrooms, some with four-posters, each with bath/shower rooms. Together with the lounge & bar there are unspoilt views across lawns, lakes & fells.	£34.50 *see PHOTO over* CREDIT CARD VISA M'CARD	Y	Y	N
David A. Davenport **Greystones** **Ambleside Road** **Keswick** **CA12 4DP** **Tel: (07687) 73108** **Open: FEB-NOV** **Map Ref No. 21**	Nearest Road: A.66 Greystones is a comfortable traditional Lakeland house where David & Eileen aim to create a friendly atmosphere for a happy relaxed holiday. Bedrooms have private facilities, most with excellent fell views. Imaginative home-made meals are served using the best quality fresh produce available. Situated in a quiet area of Keswick on Derwentwater, Greystones is only a short distance from the town centre, fells & lakeshore.	£19.50	Y	Y	N
Mr & Mrs T. J. Tucker **Rooking House** **Portinscale** **Keswick** **CA12 5RD** **Tel: (07687) 72506** **Open: MAR-DEC** **Map Ref No. 21**	Nearest Road: A.66 Tim & Heather invite you to Rooking House located in the quiet village of Portinscale, 1 mile from Keswick. Most bedrooms offer superb lake & hill views. All 6 bedrooms are non-smoking & are en-suite. All have colour T.V. & tea making facilities. Delicious home made soups & bread are included in the excellent dinners. Cumbrian breakfasts are a speciality. Private car parking. Smoking lounge available.	£21.50	Y	Y	N
Alan & Sheila Appleton **Scales Farm** **Scales** **Threlkeld** **Keswick CA12 4SY** **Tel: (07687) 79660** **Open: ALL YEAR** **Map Ref No. 22**	Nearest Road: A.66, M.6 Wonderful open views & a friendly personal welcome await you at Scales Farm, a 17th century farmhouse which has been sensitively modernised. All 5 attractively decorated bedrooms have private facilities, colour T.V. & tea/coffee makers, providing luxurious accommodation to highest standards. Guests have access to their rooms through a separate entrance at all times. Good pubs & restaurants close by & Keswick & all northern lakes within easy reach.	£17.00	Y	N	Y
Mrs J. Davis **The Mount** **Portinscale** **Keswick** **CA12 5RD** **Tel: (07687) 73070** **Open: MAR - NOV** **Map Ref No. 21**	Nearest Road: A.66 A large Victorian semi-detached house, tastefully decorated & maintaining original features, providing a friendly home-from-home atmosphere. Offering 4 bedrooms (3 with en-suite facilities) with tea/coffee makers. Lovely views over Lake Derwentwater & Skiddaw. Good walking around Keswick & Portinscale as well as boating, fishing, windsurfing & riding. An ideal base for touring the beautiful surrounding lakeside area.	£15.00	Y	Y	Y

Dale Head Hall. Lake Thirlmere

Cumbria

		minimum £ per person	children taken	evening meals	animals taken
Ron & Pauline Graham **Thornleigh** **23 Bank Street** **Keswick CA12 5JZ** **Tel: (07687) 72863** **Open: ALL YEAR** **Map Ref No. 21**	Nearest Road: A.591, A.66 A traditional Lakeland stone building situated in Keswick town, yet with magnificent views over the surrounding hills & fells. All bedrooms are en-suite with colour T.V. & tea/coffee making facilities. Thornleigh is a family run establishment with resident chef. A warm welcome is extended to all guests, old & new. An ideal spot for touring.	£18.00 CREDIT CARD VISA M'CARD	N	Y	N
Ian Bryant & Jocelyn Ruffle **Hipping Hall** **Cowan Bridge** **Kirkby Lonsdale LA6 2JJ** **Tel: (05242) 71187** **Fax 05242 72452** **Open: MAR - NOV** **Map Ref No. 22**	Nearest Road: A.65 Hipping Hall is a 17th century country house set in 4 acres of walled gardens on the edge of the Yorkshire Dales National Park, 3 miles from pretty Kirkby Lonsdale & only half an hour from Windermere. The 5 bedrooms (all en-suite) & 2 apartments are attractively furnished & fully equipped. Guests dine together in the beautiful Great Hall with a Minstrel's Gallery. All dishes are freshly prepared by Jos Ruffle from home & local produce. Children over 12 .	£34.50 *see PHOTO over* CREDIT CARD VISA M'CARD	Y	Y	Y
Mrs Lesley White **Beckfoot Country Guest House** **Helton** **Penrith CA10 2QB** **Tel: (09313) 241** **Open: MAR - NOV** **Map Ref No. 23**	Nearest Road: M.6, A fine old residence featuring a half-panelled hall, staircase, attractive panelled dining room. Set in 3 acres of grounds in the delightful Lake District, it is a quiet, peaceful retreat for a holiday base & is within easy reach of the many pleasure spots in the area. Offering 6 rooms, all with private shower/bathroom, & tea/coffee making facilities. A dining room, drawing & reading room. This is a delightful base for a touring holiday.	£22.00	Y	Y	Y
Mrs Carole Tully **Brandelhow Guest House** **1 Portland Place** **Penrith CA11 7QN** **Tel: (0768) 64470** **Open: ALL YEAR** **Map Ref No. 24**	Nearest Road: M.6, A.6, M.66 Brandelhow is a very pleasant Victorian house situated in the lovely market town of Penrith. Accommodation is in 5 tastefully decorated, bright & comfortable rooms all with modern amenities, central heating, colour T.V. & tea/coffee making facilities. Penrith is an ideal base for touring the Lake District with its beautiful scenery & enjoying the usual outdoor sporting activities. A warm & friendly welcome is assured.	£13.00	Y	N	N
Dorothy & Ian Bewley **Fair Place Wholefood Guest House** **Fair Place** **Watermillock on Ullswater** **Penrith CA11 0LR** **Tel: (07684) 86235** **Open: FEB - NOV** **Map Ref No. 25**	Nearest Road: M.6 Watermillock is a scattered hamlet on Ullswater in the English Lakes National Park. 'Fair Place', once the village school, has been modernised yet retains the original handsome rag-stone facade. 3 en-suite rooms, all with colour T.V. & tea/coffee making facilities. Delicious wholefood breakfasts are served. Lounge available throughout the day. Sailing, fishing & pony trekking nearby. Dorothy & Ian provide a caring service with every comfort & convenience. An ideal base for a relaxing Lakeland holiday.	£18.00	Y	N	Y

117

Hipping Hall. Kirkby Lonsdale

Cumbria

	Nearest Road	minimum £ per person	children taken	evening meals	animals taken
Mrs Sheila Smith **Highgate Farm** **Penrith** **CA11 0SE** **Tel: (07684) 83339** **Open: FEB - NOV** **Map Ref No. 24**	Nearest Road: M.6, A.66 A lovely stone built farmhouse dated 1730, set on a 400 acre mixed working farm. Offering a warm welcome & personal attention, full English breakfast served, tastefully decorated with old beams & brasses. Accommodation is in 5 bedrooms, 2 with king-sized old brass beds, all rooms have colour T.V. & tea/coffee making facilities. An ideal base for touring, Lake Ullswater is only 4 miles away. Children over 5 years.	£15.00	Y	N	N
Christine Weightman **Near Howe Farm Hotel** **Mungrisdale** **Penrith** **CA11 0SH** **Tel: (07687) 79678** **Open: MAR-NOV** **Map Ref No. 26**	Nearest Road: A.66 A comfortable traditional Cumbrian family house where guests receive a warm friendly welcome. Standing in 300 acres of rolling moorland, it offers a choice of 7 nice bedrooms, most with private facilities, a colour T.V. lounge, games room & a smaller lounge with a well stocked bar with log fire. In the pleasant homely dining room, freshly prepared meals are served, using local produce when possible. Close by are golf, fishing, pony trekking, boating & walking.	£16.00	Y	Y	Y
Mrs Marjorie Whittam **Netherdene Guest House** **Troutbeck** **Penrith CA11 0SJ** **Tel: (07684) 83475** **Open: FEB-NOV** **Map Ref No. 27**	Nearest Road: A.66, M.6 A traditional Lakeland house in its own quiet grounds with extensive mountain views. Offering a warm welcome & personal attention. Accommodation is in 4 very comfortable bedrooms, 1 en-suite, each with modern amenities including colour T.V. & tea/coffee making facilities. A cosy lounge with log fire & T.V. available. Delicious home cooking. An ideal base from which to explore the Lake District. Pony trekking, golf, fell walking & boating nearby.	£14.00	Y	Y	N
Frank & Lesley Hart **Cross Keys Hotel** **Cautley** **Sedbergh LA10 5NE** **Tel: (05396) 20284** **Open: APR - DEC** **Map Ref No. 28**	Nearest Road: M.6, Exit 37 A tiny 400 year-old National Trust inn within the Yorkshire Dales National Park. Magnificent mountain & views. A homely, very traditional, comfortable & relaxing atmosphere. Beautifully cooked food, all home-made & served with guests' own wine. No corkage charged. Home-baked bread & biscuits. Log fires & no T.V.'s anywhere. A place for the connoisseur.	£23.00 🚭	Y	Y	N
Ron & Mary Howard **The Royal Oak Hotel** **5 West Street** **Wigton** **CM23 5QA** **Tel: (06973) 42393** **Open: ALL YEAR** **Map Ref No. 29**	Nearest Road: A.596 Nothing is too much trouble at The Royal Oak, an attractive 17th coaching inn, with original cobbled courtyard. Accommodation is in 11 pretty,comfortable bedrooms, some en-suite, all with modern amenities, h & c, colour T.V. & tea/coffee making facilities. The restaurant is unique & the dinner menu delicious. The sole aim of Ron & Mary is to make your stay happy & memorable. An ideal spot from which to tour this beautiful area with its many attractions.	£14.50	Y	Y	Y

Cumbria

		minimum £ per person	children taken	evening meals	animals taken
Iain & Jackie Garside **Fayrer Holme Country House** **Upper Storrs Road** **Bowness** **Windermere LA23 3JP** **Tel/Fax: (05394) 88195** **Open: FEB - DEC** **Map Ref No. 30**	Nearest Road: A.5074 Iain & Jackie welcome you to their beautiful lakeland home peacefully set in 5 acres of landscaped gardens overlooking the lake & mountains. Delightful decor & tastefully furnished, spacious en-suite rooms with modern amenities. Some four poster rooms & jacuzzis. Convenient for golf club, sailing, restaurants etc. Free use of local leisure centre. Free colour brochure available. An ideal base for touring Lakeland.	£25.00	Y	N	Y
Mr & Mrs I Fishman **Fir Trees Guest House** **Lake Rd** **Windermere LA23 2EQ** **Tel: (05394) 42272** **Open: ALL YEAR** **Map Ref No. 30**	Nearest Road: A.591 Fir Trees is a charming Victorian guest house with character & is furnished with antiques throughout. Just 7 guest bedrooms, all lovely & spacious with private bath or shower rooms, provide a truely home-like atmosphere. Fir trees is well situated, being within easy walking distance of Windermere, Bowness or the lake. Simply scrumptious breakfasts . Most of all, old-fashioned hospitality. Excellent value.	£18.50 CREDIT CARD VISA M'CARD AMEX	Y	N	N
Sheila & Joe Lawless **Green Gables** **37 Broad Street** **Windermere LA23 2AB** **Tel: (05394) 43886** **Open: ALL YEAR (Excl. Xmas & New Year)** **Map Ref No. 30**	Nearest Road: A.591, A.592 Green Gables is a pleasant family-run Victorian guest house located in the centre of Windermere. The shops, restaurants, bus & railway stations close by make it a good base for touring the area. Accommodation is in 6 cosy bedrooms, some non smoking, 2 with private facilities, all with colour T.V., tea/coffee makers & hair dryers. A comfortable T.V. lounge is also available.	£12.00	Y	N	N
Barbara & Bob Tyson **Hawksmoor Guest House** **Lake Road** **Windermere** **LA23 2EQ** **Tel: (05394) 42110** **Open: JAN-NOV** **Map Ref No. 30**	Nearest Road: A.591 Hawksmoor is situated halfway between the centres of Windermere & Bowness, just 10 minutes walk from the lake. Standing in lovely grounds, this creeper-clad house has 10 charming rooms all en-suite with garden views. Some with 4-poster beds, some strictly no smoking. A most comfortable residents' lounge with colour T.V. & garden for guests' enjoyment. The house has a residential licence. Boating, golf, tennis, swimming, fishing & pony trekking all nearby. Phone for availability before booking.	£19.00 *see PHOTO over*	Y	Y	N
Mr & Mrs Cox **Kirkwood Guest House** **Prince's Road** **Windermere LA23 2DD** **Tel: (05394) 43907** **Open: ALL YEAR** **Map Ref No. 30**	Nearest Road: A.591 Kirkwood occupies a quiet spot between Windermere and Bowness, offering guests a warm and friendly atmosphere with individual, personal service. Rooms are large, mostly en-suite, and all have T.V. and tea/coffee facilities. Comfortable, quiet lounge. Guests can be met from train or coach, and your hosts will be pleased to help plan tours or walks, with maps provided. Drying facilities. Packed lunches available.	£15.00 CREDIT CARD VISA M'CARD	Y	N	Y

120

Hawksmoor Guest House.   Windermere.

Cumbria

	Nearest Road	per person minimum £	children taken	evening meals	animals taken
Frances & Brian Holcroft **Lynwood Guest House** Broad Street Windermere LA23 2AB Tel: (05394) 42550 Open: ALL YEAR Map Ref No. 30	Nearest Road: A.591 A Victorian, Lakeland stone house built in 1865; offering 9 centrally heated & very comfortable bedrooms, 4 with private bathrooms, all with modern amenities including colour T.V. & tea/coffee making facilities. Guests may relax in the T.V. lounge available throughout the day. Centrally located, only 150 yards from village shops & restaurants & only 5 mins. from the bus & railway station. Host is a lakeland tour guide, & is happy to assist in planning your stay.	£11.00	Y	N	N
Brenda Butterworth **Orrest Head House** Winderme Kendal Road Windermere LA23 IJG Tel: (05394) 44315 Open: FEB-NOV Map Ref No. 30	Nearest Road: A.591 A traditional Lakeland style house, partly 17th century, standing in 3 acres of garden. This lovely old house offers 5 rooms: 3 en-suite, 1 twin & 1 double room, all with tea/coffee making facilities. Located above Windermere village with distant views towards the Lake & mountains beyond. Guests can relax in the resident's lounge with log fires, or in the tranquil garden with its lovely surroundings. Very convenient for the railway station & bus terminal. Ample parking.	£15.00	Y	N	Y
Alan & Dorothy Fielding **Rosemount** Lake Road Windermere LA23 2EQ Tel: (05394) 43739 Open: ALL YEAR Map Ref No. 30	Nearest Road: A.591 A delightful guest house built in traditional lakeland style, ideally situated between Windermere & the lake, offering warm & comfortable accommodation. The lovely bedrooms, including 2 singles, are attractively furnished, with private facilities, colour T.V. & tea tray. Delicious English breakfasts served (or refreshing fruit alternative). Friendly & personal attention is extended from the resident owners, Alan & Dorothy Fielding. Licensed bar. Car parking. CREDIT CARD VISA M'CARD	£19.50	Y	N	N
Anthony & Aurea **Greenhalgh** **The Archway Guest House** 13 College Road Windermere LA23 1BY Tel: (05394) 45613 Open: ALL YEAR Map Ref No. 30	Nearest Road: A.591 Impeccable small Victorian guest house, quietly situated a stone's throw from Windermere village centre. Yet with marvellous, open mountain views. Beautifully furnished throughout - antiques, interesting paintings & prints, good books, fresh flowers. Accommodation is in 6 individually decorated bedrooms, mostly en-suite, all with telephone, colour T.V. & tea/coffee trays, Victorian patchwork quilts. Renowned for gourmet home cooking using fresh local produce. Home baked bread. Excellent wine list. No smoking. CREDIT CARD VISA M'CARD	£21.00	N	Y	N

When booking your accommodation please mention
The Best Bed & Breakfast

Derby & Staffs

Derbyshire
(East Midlands)

A county with everything but the sea, this was Lord Byron's opinion of Derbyshire, & the special beauty of the Peak District was recognised by its designation as Britain's first National Park.

Purple heather moors surround craggy limestone outcrops & green hills drop to sheltered meadows or to deep gorges & tumbling rivers.

Derbyshire's lovely dales have delightful names too - Dove Dale, Monk's Dale, Raven's Dale, Water-cum-Jolly-Dale, & they are perfect for walking. The more adventurous can take up the challenge of the Pennine Way, a 270 mile pathway from Edale to the Scottish border.

The grit rock faces offer good climbing, particularly at High Tor above the River Derwent, & underground there are extensive & spectacular caverns. There are show caves at the Heights of Abraham, which you reach by cable-car, & at Castleton, source of the rare Blue John mineral, & at Pole's Cavern in Buxton where there are remarkable stalactites & stalagmites.

Buxton's splendid Crescent reflects the town's spa heritage, & the Opera House is host to an International Festival each summer.

The waters at Matlock too were prized for their curative properties & a great Hydro was built there in the last century, to give treatment to the hundreds of people who came to "take the waters".

Bakewell is a lovely small town with a fascinating market, some fine buildings & the genuine Bakewell Pudding, (known elsewhere as Bakewell tart).

Well-dressing is a custom carried on throughout the summer in the villages & towns. It is a thanksgiving for the water, that predates the arrival of Christianity in Britain. Flower-petals, leaves, moss & bark are pressed in

Haddon Hall; Derby.

Derby & Staffs

intricate designs into frames of wet clay & erected over the wells, where they stay damp & fresh for days.

The mining of lead & the prosperity of the farms brought great wealth to the landowning families who were able to employ the finest of architects & craftsmen to design & build their great houses. Haddon Hall is a perfectly preserved 12th century manor house with with terraced gardens of roses & old-fashioned flowers. 17th century Chatsworth, the "Palace of the Peak", houses a splendid collection of paintings, drawings, furniture & books, & stands in gardens with elaborate fountains.

Staffordshire
(Heart of England)

Staffordshire is a contrast of town & county. Miles of moorland & dramatic landscapes lie to the north of the country, & to the south is the Vale of Trent & the greenery of Cannock Chase. But the name of Staffordshire invokes that of the Potteries, the area around Stoke-on-Trent where the world-renowned ceramics are made.

The factories that produce the Royal Doulton, Minton, Spode & Coalport china will arrange tours for visitors, & there is a purpose-built visitor centre at Barlaston displaying the famous Wedgwood tradition.

The Gladstone Pottery Museum is set in a huge Victorian potbank, & the award-winning City museum in Stoke-on-Trent has a remarkable ceramics collection.

There is lovely scenery to be found where the moorlands of Staffordshire meet the crags & valleys of the Peak District National Park. From the wild & windy valleys of The Roaches (from the French 'roche') you can look across the county to Cheshire & Wales. Drivers can take high moorland roads that are marked out as scenic routes.

The valleys of the Dove & Manifold are beautiful limestone dales & ideal for walking or for cycling. Sir Izzak Walton, author of 'The Compleat Angler', drew his inspiration, & his trout, from the waters here.

The valley of the River Churnet is both pretty & peaceful, being largely inaccessible to cars. The Caldon Canal, with its colourful narrowboats, follows the course of the river & there are canalside pubs, picnic areas, boat rides & woodland trails to enjoy. The river runs through the grounds of mock-Gothic Alton Towers, now a leisure park.

The Vale of Trent is largely rural with small market towns, villages, river & canals.

Cannock Chase covers 20 square miles of heath & woodland & is the home of the largest herd of fallow deer in England. Shugborough Hall stands in the Chase. The ancestral home of Lord Lichfeld, it also houses the Stafforshire County Museum & a farm for rare breeds including the famous Tamworth Pig.

Burton-on-Trent is known as the home of the British brewery industry & there are two museums in the town devoted to the history of beer.

Lichfield is a small & picturesque city with a cathedral which dates from the 12th century & has three graceful spires known as the 'Ladies of the Vale'. Dr. Samuel Johnson was born in the city & his house is now a museum dedicated to his life & work.

One of the Vale's villages retains its mediaeval tradition by performing the Abbot's Bromley Horn Dance every September.

Derby & Staffs

Derbyshire

Gazeteer
Areas of outstanding natural beauty.
Peak National Park. The Dales.

Houses & Castles
Chatsworth - Bakewell
17th century, built for 1st. Duke of
Devonshire. Furniture, paintings &
drawings, books, etc. Fine gardens
& parklands.
Haddon Hall - Bakewell
Mediaeval manor house - complete.
Terraced rose gardens.
Hardwick Hall - Nr. Chesterfield
16th century - said to be more glass than
wall. Fine furniture, tapestries &
furnishings. Herb garden.
Kedlestone Hall - Derby
18th century - built on site of 12th century
Manor house. Work of Robert Adam -
has world famous marble hall. Old
Master paintings. 11th century
church nearby.
Melbourne Hall - Nr. Derby
12th century origins - restored by Sir John
Coke. Fine collection of pictures & works
of art. Magnificent gardens & famous
wrought iron pergola.
Sudbury Hall - Sudbury
Has examples of work of the greatest
craftsmen of the period-Grinling
Gibbons,Pierce and Laguerre.
Winster Market House   Nr. Matlock
17th century stone built market house.

Cathedrals & Churches
Chesterfield (St. Mary & All Saints)
13th & 14th centuries. 4 chapels,
polygonal apse, mediaeval screens,
Jacobean pulpit.
Derby (All Saints)
Perpendicular tower - classical style -
17th century plate, 18th century screen.
Melbourne (St. Michael & St. Mary)
Norman with two west towers & crossing
tower. Splendid plate, 18th
century screen.
Normbury (St. Mary & St. Barloke)
14th century - perpendicular tower. Wood
carving & brasses.
Wirksworth (St. Mary)
13th century, restored & enlarged.
Norman font & 17th century font.

Brasses, mediaeval sculpture - 9th
century coffin lid.

Museums & Galleries
Buxton Museum - Buxton
Local history, geology & mineralogy,
including famous Blue John. Animal
remains from Pleistocene period onwards.
Old House Museum - Bakewell
Early Tudor house with interior walls
exposed to show wattle & daub, open-
timber chamber. Kitchen implements,
craftmen's tools, costumes.
Lecture Hall - Chesterfield
Exhibitions of photography, art, etc.
Museums & Art Gallery - Derby
Archeology, geology, local & natural
history, model rail layout.
Industrial Museum - Derby
Rolls-Royce collection of
historic aero-engines.
Regimental Museum - Derby
9th/12th Lancers.
**Elvaston Castle Working Estate
Museum** - Nr. Derby
Life on the estate re-created as it was in
1910, with cottage, craft workshops
& livestock.
Museum of Childhood - Sudbury Hall,
Nr. Derby
Life of children in the past on display in
the former servants' wing of Sudbury Hall.
National Tramway Museum - Crich,
Nr. Matlock
Rides along a one-mile scenic tramway
with a collection of tramcars from Britain
& overseas.

Other things to see & do
Caudwell's Mill - Rowsley,
19th century water-powered working flour
mill, with craft centre.
Blue John Cavern - Castleton
Stalagmites & stalactites, & source of the
rare Blue John stone.
The Heights of Abraham - Matlock Bath
Spectacular cable car ride up to wooded
landscape with two show caverns,
prospect tower & visitor centre.
Poole's Cavern - Buxton
One of the finest natural limestone
caverns, with stalactites & stalagmites.

Derby & Staffs

Speedwell Cavern - Castleton
Underground boat journey to
show cavern.
Treak Cliff Cavern - Castleton
Richest known veins of the rare Blue John
stone, stalactites & stalagmites in mainly
natural cavern.
Buxton Micrarium - Buxton
Unique exhibition of the natural world
under the microscope, with hundreds of
specimens & living creatures to see.
Dinting Railway Centre - Glossop
Famous steam locomotives & rides.

Staffordshire

Gazeteer
Houses & Castles
Ancient High House - Stafford
16th century - largest timber-framed town
house in England.
Shugborough - Nr. Stafford
Ancestral home of the Earl of Lichfield.
Mansion house, paintings, silver,
ceramics, furniture. County Museum.
Rare Breeds Farm.
Moseley Old Hall - Nr. Wolverhampton
Elizabethan house formerly half-timbered.
Stafford Castle
Large & well-preserved Norman castle in
grounds with castle trail.
Tamworth Castle
Norman motte & bailey castle with later
additions. Museum.

Cathedrals & Churches
Croxden Abbey
12th century foundation Cistercian abbey.
Ruins of 13th century church.
Ingestre (St. Mary the Virgin)
A rare Wren church built in1676.
Lichfield Cathedral
Unique triple-spired 12th century
cathedral.
Tamworth (St. Editha's)
Founded 963, rebuilt 14th century.
Unusual double spiral staircase.
Tutbury (St. Mary's)
Norman church with impressive
West front.

Museums & Galleries
City Museum & Art Gallery - Stoke-on-
Trent
Modern award-winning museum.
Ceramics, decorative arts, etc.
Dr. Johnson Birthplace Museum -
Lichfield
Gladstone Pottery Museum - Longton
Izaak Walton Cottage & Museum -
Shallowfield, Nr. Stafford
**National Brewery Museum & the Bass
Museum of Brewing**-both in Stoke-on-
Trent
Stafford Art Gallery & Craft Shop -
Stafford
Major gallery for the visual arts & centre
for quality craftsmanship.

Other things to see & do
Alton Towers - Alton
Former estate of the Earls of Shrewsbury,
now leading leisure park. Landscape
gardens, Pagoda fountain.
Dorothy Clive Garden - Willoughbridge
Rare trees, rhododendrons & azaleas.
Foxfield Steam Railway - Blythe Bridge,
Nr Stoke-on-Trent
5-mile round trip through rural
Staffordshire
Froghall - Caldon Canal
Canal boat trips Victorian-style.
Josiah Wedgwood Visitor Centre -
Barlaston
Moorlands Farm Park - Nr. Ipstones
Rare British breeds.
Natural Sciences Centre - Newchapel
Observatory, Stoke-on-Trent
Intriguing conservation site. Observatory.
Exhibitions on alternative energy.

Izaak Walton`s Cottage. Staffs.

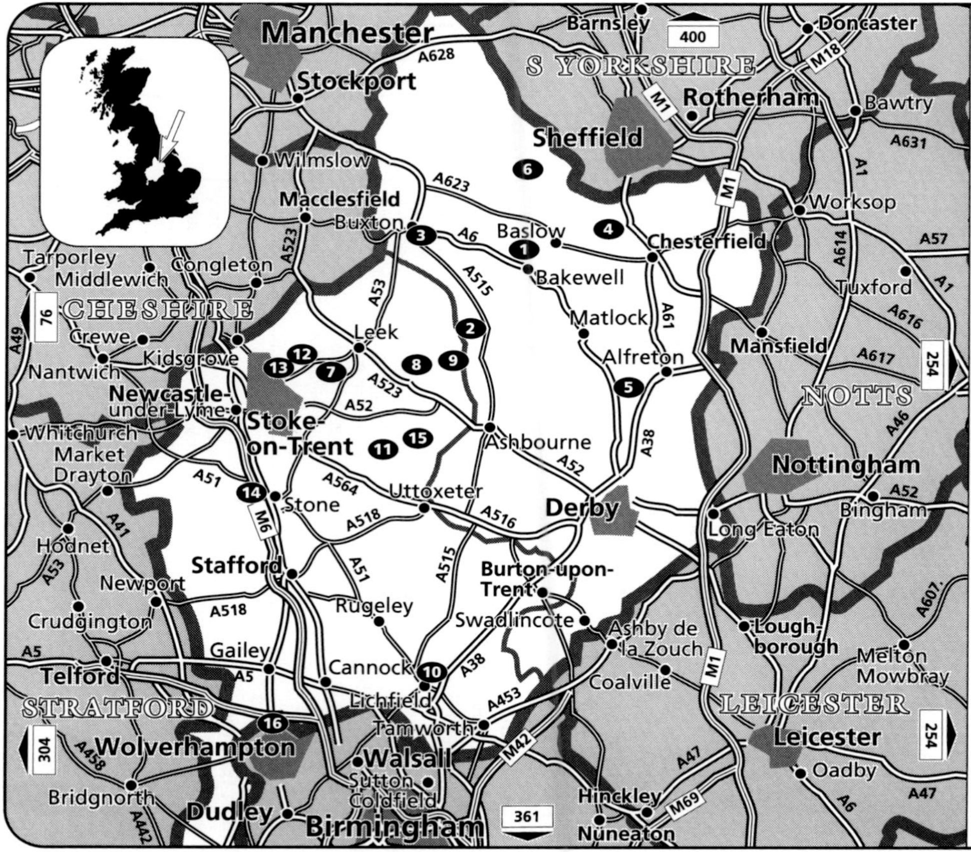

DERBYSHIRE & STAFFORDSHIRE

Map reference

1 Gilbert
2 Moffett
3 Annesley
3 Harry
3 Mackenzie
4 Ford
5 Groom
6 Bailey
7 Winterton
7 Sutcliffe
8 Martin
9 Bunce
10 Gopsill
11 Wheeler
12 White
12 Grey
13 Hodgson
14 Adams
15 Ball
16 Moreton

DERBYSHIRE

STAFFORDSHIRE

Derbyshire

	Nearest Road / Description	min £ per person	children taken	evening meals	animals taken
Mrs Sheila Gilbert **Castle Cliffe Private** **Hotel** **Monsal Head** **Bakewell DE45 1NL** **Tel: (0629) 640258** **Open: ALL YEAR** **Map Ref No. 01**	Nearest Road: A.6 A Victorian stone house built on high ground with superb views from all 9 bedrooms. 2 rooms with en-suite facilities, the others with private facilities & tea/coffee makers. The cosy lounge & bar have open fires. Home-made food with an emphasis on regional British dishes. Beautiful walks straight from the hotel into Monsal Dale & over the famous viaduct. Conveniently located for visiting Derbyshire's peaks, dales, caverns & historic houses. CREDIT CARD VISA M'CARD AMEX	£18.50	Y	Y	N
Mr & Mrs J. M. Moffett **Biggin Hall** **Biggin-by-Hartington** **Buxton SK17 0DH** **Tel: (0298) 84451** **Fax 0298 84681** **Open: ALL YEAR** **Map Ref No. 02**	Nearest Road: A.515 A really delightful 17th century stone house, completely restored, keeping all the character of its origins, massive oak beams. There are 14 beautiful rooms, all charmingly furnished, 1 with 4-poster bed, all with en-suite facilities & modern amenities. Guests have the choice of 2 sitting rooms, 1 with log fire, 1 with colour T.V. & library, & a lovely garden. The house is beautifully furnished with many antiques. Evening meals are available & are truly superb & great value. *see PHOTO over* CREDIT CARD VISA M'CARD AMEX	£20.00 🚭	N	Y	Y
Anita & John Annesley **Buxton View** **74 Corbar Rd** **Buxton SK17 6RJ** **Tel: (0298) 79222** **Fax 0298 79222** **Open: MAR-NOV** **Map Ref No. 03**	Nearest Road: A.6, A.515 A warm welcome awaits you at Buxton View. A comfortable home built of local limestone, commanding a superb view of the surrounding hills & moor. Offering 5 pleasantly decorated bedrooms each with private facilities, colour T.V. & tea/coffee makers. Delicious full English breakfasts are served. Guests can relax in the comfortable sitting room complete with maps & guide books to help plan excursions. A short walk to this elegant spa town centre.	£18.00	Y	Y	Y
Mrs Linda Harry **Coningsby Guest House** **6 Macclesfield Road** **Buxton** **SL17 9AH** **Tel: (0298) 26735** **Open: ALL YEAR** **Map Ref No. 03**	Nearest Road: A.515, A.6 John & Linda extend a warm welcome to "non-smoking" guests. At Coningsby every comfort is catered for. Accommodation is in 3 tastefully decorated comfortable rooms, each with en-suite facilities, T.V. & tea/coffee makers. There is a separate guests' lounge & an elegant dining room where breakfast & dinner are served. Coningsby is a super place to stay & explore the Peak District's beautiful places, as well as elegant Buxton itself.	£17.50 🚭	N	Y	N
Mary Mackenzie **Staden Grange** **Free Post (SK1335)** **Staden** **Buxton SK17 9YB** **Tel: (0298) 24965** **Fax 0298 72067** **Open: ALL YEAR** **Map Ref No. 03**	Nearest Road: A.515 A pleasant, spacious house set in 250 acres enjoying uninterrupted views over open farmland. Offering very attractive & comfortable en-suite rooms, with colour T.V., & tea/coffee makers. A comfortable lounge with colour T.V. & a large garden for guests' use, also riding & shooting plus a sauna & spa pool, there is also a fine golf course nearby. Only 2 miles from Buxton, this is a wonderful base for touring, walking & riding in this magnificent scenic region. CREDIT CARD VISA M'CARD AMEX	£24.00	Y	Y	Y

Biggin Hall. Biggin by Hartington.

Derbyshire & Staffordshire

	Nearest Road / Description	minimum £ per person	children taken	evening meals	animals taken
Mrs Margaret Ford **Horsleygate Hall** **Horsleygate Lane** **Holmesfield S18 5WD** **Tel: (0742) 890333** **Open: ALL YEAR** **Map Ref No. 04**	Nearest Road: B.6051 Lying on the eastern side of the Peak Park, Horsleygate Hall is an informal country house, set amongst large, secluded grounds. The accommodation is country style, comfortable & attractive, with excellent views of the surrounding countryside from all rooms. The Hall, in the peaceful & rural Cordwell Valley, is well placed for walking, riding & exploring Derbyshire. Chatsworth House & Bakewell nearby. Stabling also available.	£16.00	Y	N	N
Mrs R. A. Groom **The Manor Farmhouse** **Dethick** **Matlock DE4 5GG** **Tel: (0629) 534246** **Open: JAN - NOV** **Map Ref No. 05**	Nearest Road: M.1 Jt. 28, A.6 This part Elizabethan farmhouse stands in the peaceful unspoilt hamlet of Dethick. Accommodation is in 4 charming bedrooms, 3 en-suite, some with T.V. All comfortable & furnished with antiques. Trays of tea/coffee available on request. Delicious full English breakfasts & home cooked meals are served. Guests can relax in the lounge available throughout the day. An ideal base for touring & walking.	£16.50	Y	N	N
Mary Bailey **Carr Head Farm** **Hathersage** **Sheffield** **S30 1BR** **Tel: (0433) 650383** **Open: ALL YEAR** **Map Ref No. 06**	Nearest Road: A.625 High on the hillside above the village of Hathersage, an unusual 17th century farmhouse of outstanding character & friendly charm set in beautifully mature gardens with lawn tennis court. 3 fine bedrooms, 1 with 4-poster. Oak beamed dining room with wood burning stove & many interesting features. Adjoining drawing room for guests' use. Superbly decorated throughout & finished in period style. All rooms have magnificent views. Traditional & varied breakfast served. Set in the heart of the Peak District.	£15.00	N	N	N

Staffordshire

	Nearest Road / Description	minimum £ per person	children taken	evening meals	animals taken
Elizabeth Winterton **Brook House Farm** **Cheddleton** **Leek ST13 7DF** **Tel: (0538) 360296** **Open: ALL YEAR** **Map Ref No. 07**	Nearest Road: A.520 Brookhouse is a dairy farm in a picturesque valley 1/2 a mile from the A.520 down a private lane. Many pleasant walks locally; convenient for Peak District, Pottery Museums and Alton Towers. Comfortable rooms in farmhouse and 2 spacious family rooms with patio doors in tastefully converted cowshed. All en-suite, centrally heated, with tea/coffee facilities. Good farmhouse food served in conservatory with magnificent views. Warm welcome assured.	£15.00	Y	Y	Y
William & Elaine Sutcliffe **Choir Cottage & House** **Ostlers Lane, Cheddleton** **Leek ST13 7HS** **Tel: (0538) 360561** **Open: ALL YEAR (Excl. Xmas & New Year)** **Map Ref No. 07**	Nearest Road: A.520 This 17th century stone cottage, once the resting place for Ostlers, provides 3 beautifully appointed bedrooms with every comfort in mind. All have en-suite facilities, colour T.V., tea/coffee makers & 'phone & are completely self-contained. The "pine room" & "rose room" have 4-poster beds, 1 king-size, 1 suitable for a family suite. The ground floor "green room" has canopied double/single beds plus a private sun lounge/ patio. Ideal for the Peak District & Potteries.	£18.95 *see PHOTO over*	Y	Y	N

Choir Cottage. Cheddleton

Staffordshire

	minimum £ per person	children taken	evening meals	animals taken
Yvonne Martin **Pethills Bank Cottage** **Bottomhouse** **Leek** **ST13 7PF** **Tel:(0538) 304277/304555** **Fax 0538 304575** **Open: MAR-Mid DEC** **Map Ref No. 08**	Nearest Road: A.523 A charming 18th century former farmhouse set in 1/2 an acre of landscaped gardens amid the hilly countryside of the low Peak National Park. The picturesque beams, low ceilings, thick stone walls & fascinating nooks & crannies are complemented by charming, comfortable accommodation & detailed attention to the comfort of guests. All the rooms are fully en-suite with colour T.V. & tea/coffee tray. The garden room has its own sitting room & verandah.	£18.00 *see PHOTO over*	Y	N	N
Philomena & Jack Bunce **The White House** **Grindon** **Leek ST13 7TP** **Tel: (0538) 304250** **Open: ALL YEAR** **(Excl. Xmas/New Year)** **Map Ref No. 09**	Nearest Road: A.523 Some 1000ft. up in the Peak National Park, this 350 year-old former village inn faces south with superb views over valleys & hills. Original stone-mullioned windows & oak beams, a haven of peace, comfort & relaxation in a friendly atmosphere. Beautifully decorated bedrooms in coordinating colours, furnished for your every comfort, each with private facilities. One half tester bed with patchwork quilt. Fresh produce served with home-made bread & preserves.	£19.00	Y	N	N
Mrs Sue Gopsill **Ellfield House** **Whittington** **Lichfield WS14 9LA** **Tel: (0543) 432571** **Open: ALL YEAR** **Map Ref No. 10**	Nearest Road: A.51, A.38 This is a lovely late Georgian house set on a hill, approached along a drive of chestnut trees, standing in acres of lawns & flowers, surrounded by yew hedges. Guests are welcomed to this home as friends. The bedrooms are charming, masses of hanging space, books, plants, china & fresh flowers everywhere. Beautiful soaps & towels in abundance. The breakfasts are delicious.	£17.00	Y	N	N
Mrs Maggie Wheeler **Old Furnace Farm** **Greendale** **Oakamoor** **Stoke on Trent ST10 3AP** **Tel: (0538) 702442** **Open: ALL YEAR** **Map Ref No. 11**	Nearest Road: A.52 The farm is situated in an idyllic position, overlooking the Dimmingsdale Valley. The Victorian farmhouse, which has been tastefully renovated & furnished in keeping with the period, offers quality accommodation & friendly service. It has 3 bedrooms, each with en-suite bathroom, & colour T.V. Full central heating, log fire in visitors' lounge. An ideal location for Alton Towers (2 miles), potteries (12 miles), rambling, or just simply relaxing.	£18.00	Y	N	N
Barbara White **Micklea Farm** **Micklea Lane** **Longsdon** **Stoke-on-Trent ST9 9QA** **Tel: (0538) 385006** **Fax 0538 382882** **Open: ALL YEAR** **Map Ref No. 12**	Nearest Road: A.53 "Micklea Farm" is an 18th century cottage set in a lovely quiet garden. There are 2 twin & 2 single rooms, with cots available. There is a charming sitting room for guests, with an open fire & colour T.V. Evening meals are available, using home-grown garden produce & home baking. Choice of English or Continental breakfast, also packed lunches. Conveniently situated for the Potteries, Alton Towers & Peak District.	£14.00	Y	Y	N

Pethills Bank Cottage.   Bottomhouse.

Staffordshire

	minimum £ per person	children taken	evening meals	animals taken

Mrs Anne Hodgson
The Hollies
Clay Lake
Endon
Stoke-on-Trent ST9 9DD
Tel: (0782) 503252
Open: ALL YEAR
Map Ref No. 13

Nearest Road: A.53, B.5051
A delightful Victorian family house built in 1872, quietly situated off the B.5051 at Endon. Accommodation is in 5 delightful, comfortable rooms, 3 with en-suite facilities. All have tea/coffee makers. The T.V. lounge & dining room overlook a large secluded garden. Ample parking. Famous Royal Doulton, Wedgwood & interesting museums nearby, Alton Towers leisure park & lovely countryside. Sorry, no smoking.

£14.00 | Y | N | Y

Mrs L. Grey
The Old Vicarage
Leek Road, Endon
Stoke-on-Trent ST9 9BH
Tel: (0782) 503686
Open: ALL YEAR
Map Ref No. 12

Nearest Road: A.53
A friendly atmosphere is found at this delightful 70 year-old former vicarage. It is situated in a quiet spot in the village of Endon, between the Staffordshire moorlands & Stoke-on-Trent. Accommodation is in 3 rooms, all with modern amenities & tea/coffee making facilities. There is also a colour T.V. lounge. This makes a good base from which to visit the world famous potteries, wonderful countryside & museums.

£15.00 | Y | N | Y

Mrs G. Adams
The Boat House
71 Newcastle Road
Stone ST15 8LD
Tel:(0785) 815389/813137
OpenALL YEAR(Excl. Xmas)
Map Ref No. 14

Nearest Road: M.6, A.34
A friendly relaxed atmosphere awaits you at this renovated 18th century former inn, set in delightful gardens alongside the Trent & Mersey Canal. Traditionally furnished, it offers accommodation in 3 comfortable rooms, with T.V., tea/coffee making facilities. This is an ideal base for Wedgwood & the potteries, the Peak District & Alton Towers. Easy access to the M.6.

£17.50 | Y | N | N

Christine Ball
Manor House Farm
Prestwood
Denstone
Uttoxeter ST14 5DD
Tel: (0889) 590415
Open: ALL YEAR
Map Ref No. 15

Nearest Road: A.50
A beautiful Grade II listed farmhouse, set amid rolling hills & rivers. 2 bedrooms, both with modern amenities. 1 room with 4-poster bed. Tastefully furnished with antiques & retaining many traditional features including oak beamed ceilings & an oak panelled breakfast room. Guests may relax in the extensive gardens with grass tennis court & Victorian summer house. Ideal for visiting Alton Towers, Dovedale or the Peak District.

£16.00 | Y | N | N

see PHOTO over

CREDIT CARD
AMEX

Mrs D. E. Moreton
Moors Farm & Country Restaurant
Chillington Lane, Codsall
Wolverhampton
WV8 1QH
Tel: (0902) 842330
Fax 0902 842330
Open: ALL YEAR
Map Ref No. 16

Nearest Road: A.41, A.5
A farmhouse, standing on a 100 acre farm within a beautiful & picturesque valley bordering the countries of Staffordshire & Shropshire. This comfortably furnished home has oak-beamed rooms & a cosy residents' lounge. The 6 bedrooms have wonderful views of the surrounding countryside & all have colour T.V., tea/coffee making facilities & washbasins. 2 are en-suite. The food here is absolutely delicious. Mrs Moreton uses home-produced lamb, pork, beef, poultry, eggs & vegetables. All preserves, soups, pies & desserts are home made. Very convenient for M.6 & M.54 motorways.

£19.00 | Y | Y | N

Manor House Farm.   Prestwood.

Devon

Devon
(West Country)

Here is a county of tremendous variety. Two glorious & contrasting coastlines with miles of sandy beaches, sheltered coves & rugged cliffs. There are friendly resorts & quiet villages of cob & thatch, two historic cities, & a host of county towns & tiny hamlets as well as the wild open spaces of two national parks.

From the grandeur of Hartland Point east to Foreland Point where Exmoor reaches the sea, the north Devon coast is incomparable. At Westward Ho!, Croyde & Woolacombe the rolling surf washes the golden beaches & out to sea stands beautiful Lundy Island, ideal for bird watching, climbing & walking. The tiny village of Clovelly with its cobbled street tumbles down the cliffside to the sea. Ilfracombe is a friendly resort town & the twin towns of Lynton & Lynmouth are joined by a cliff railway.

The south coast is a colourful mixture of soaring red sandstone cliffs dropping to sheltered sandy coves & the palm trees of the English Riviera. This is one of England's great holiday coasts with a string of popular resorts; Seaton, Sidmouth, Budleigh Salterton, Exmouth, Dawlish, Teignmouth & the trio of Torquay, Paignton & Brixham that make up Torbay. To the south, beyond Berry Head are Dartmouth, rich in navy tradition, & Salcombe, a premiere sailing centre in the deep inlet of the Kingsbridge estuary. Plymouth is a happy blend of holiday resort, tourist centre, historic & modern city, & the meeting-point for the wonderful old sailing vessels for the Tall Ships Race.

Inland the magnificent wilderness of Dartmoor National Park offers miles of sweeping moorland, granite tors, clear streams & wooded valleys, ancient stone circles & clapper bridges. The tors, as the Dartmoor peaks, are called are easily climbed & the views from the tops are superb. Widecombe-in-the-Moor, with its imposing church tower, & much photographed Buckland-in-the-Moor are only two of Dartmoor's lovely villages.

The Exmoor National Park straddles the Devon/Somerset border. It is a land of wild heather moorland above deep wooded valleys & sparkling streams, the home of red deer, soaring buzzards & of legendary Lorna Doone from R.D. Blackmore's novel. The south west peninsula coastal path follows the whole of the Exmoor coastline affording dramatic scenery & spectacular views, notably from Countisbury Hill.

The seafaring traditions of Devon are well-known. Sir Walter Raleigh set sail from Plymouth to Carolina in 1584; Sir Francis Drake began his circumnavigation of the world at Plymouth in the "Golden Hind" & fought the Spanish Armada off Plymouth Sound. The Pilgrim Fathers sailed from here & it was to here that Sir Francis Chichester returned having sailed around the world in 1967.

Exeter's maritime tradition is commemorated in an excellent museum located in converted riverside warehouses but the city's chief glory is the magnificent 13th century cathedral of St. Mary & St. Peter, built in an unusual decorated Gothic style, with its west front covered in statues.

The River Dart near Dittisham.

Devon

Devon
Gazeteer
Areas of outstanding natural beauty.
North, South, East Devon.

Houses & Castles

Arlington Court - Barnstaple
Regency house, collection of shell, pewter
& model ships.
Bickleigh Castle - Nr. Tiverton
Thatched Jacobean wing. Great Hall &
armoury. Early Norman chapel, gardens
& moat.
Buckland Abbey - Nr. Plymouth
13th century Cistercian monastery - 16th
century alterations. Home of Drake -
contains his relics & folk gallery.
Bradley Manor - Newton Abbot
15th century Manor house with
perpendicular chapel.
Cadhay - Ottery St. Mary
16th century Elizabethan Manor house.
Castle Drogo - Nr.Chagford
Designed by Lutyens - built of granite,
standing over 900 feet above the gorge of
the Teign river.
Chambercombe Manor - Illfracombe
14th-15th century Manor house.
Castle Hill - Nr. Barnstaple
18th century Palladian mansion - fine
furniture of period, pictures, porcelain
& tapestries.
Hayes Barton - Nr. Otterton
16th century plaster & thatch house.
Birthplace of Walter Raleigh.
Oldway - Paignton
19th century house having rooms
designed to be replicas of rooms at
Palace of Versailles.
Powederham Castle - Nr. Exeter
14th century mediaeval castle much
damaged in Civil War. Altered in 18th &
19th centuries. Fine music room
by Wyatt.
Saltram House - Plymouth
Some remnants of Tudor house built into
George II house, with two rooms by
Robert Adam. Excellent plasterwork
& woodwork.
Shute Barn - Nr. Axminster
Interesting architecturally - built over
several centuries & finished in 16th.
Tiverton Castle - Nr. Tiverton
Fortress of Henry I. Chapel of St.
Francis. Gallery of Joan of Arc.

Torre Abbey Mansion - Torquay
Abbey ruins, tithe barn. Mansion house
with paintings & furniture.

Cathedrals & Churches

Atherington (St. Mary)
Perpendicular style - mediaeval effigies &
glass, original rood loft. Fine screens,
15th century bench ends.
Ashton (St. John the Baptist)
15th century - mediaeval screens, glass &
wall paintings. Elizabethan pulpit with
canopy, 17th century altar railing.
Bere Ferrers (St. Andrew)
14th century rebuilding - 14th century
glass, 16th century benches,
Norman font.
Bridford (St. Thomas a Becket)
Perpendicular style - mediaeval glass &
woodwork. Excellent rood screen c.1530.
Cullompton (St. Andrew)
15th century perpendicular - Jacobean
west gallery - fan tracery in roof,
exterior carvings.
Exeter Cathedral
13th century decorated - Norman towers.
Interior tierceron ribbed vault (Gothic)
carved corbets & bosses, moulded piers
& arches. Original pulpitum c.1320.
Choir stalls with earliest misericords in
England c.1260.
Haccombe (St. Blaize)
13th century effigies, 14th century glass,
17th century brasses, 19th century
screen, pulpit & reredos.
Kentisbeare (St. Mary)
Perpendicular style - checkered tower.
16th century rood screen.
Ottery St. Mary (St. Mary)
13th century, 14th century clock, fan
vaulted roof, tomb with canopy, minstrel's
gallery, gilded wooded eagle. 18th
century pulpit.
Parracombe (St. Petrock)
Unrestored Georgian - 16th century
benches, mostly perpendicular, early
English chancel.
Sutcombe (St. Andrew)
15th century - some part Norman. 16th
century bench ends, restored rood
screen, mediaeval glass & floor tiles.
Swimbrige (St. James)
14th century tower & spire - mediaeval
stone pulpit, 15th century rood screen,

Devon

font cover of Renaissance period.
Tawstock (St. Peter)
14th century, Italian plasterwork ceiling,
mediaeval glass, Renaissance memorial
pew, Bath monument.
Buckfast Abbey
Living Benedictine monastery, built on
mediaeval foundation. Famous for works
of art in church, modern stained glass,
tonic wine & bee-keeping.

Museums & Galleries

Bideford Museum - Bideford
Geology, maps, prints, shipwright's tools,
North Devon pottery.
Burton Art Gallery - Bideford
Hubert Coop collection of paintings etc.
Butterwalk Museum - Dartmouth
17th century row of half timbered
buildings, nautical museum. 140
model ships.
Newcomen Engine House - Nr.
Butterwalk Museum
Original Newcomen atmospheric/pressure
steam engine c.1725.
**Royal Albert Memorial Museum Art
Gallery** - Exeter
Collections of English watercolours,
paintings, glass & ceramics, local silver,
natural history & anthropology.
Rougemont House Museum - Exeter
Collections of archaeology & local history.
Costume & lace collection
Guildhall - Exeter
Mediaeval structure with Tudor frontage -
City regalia & silver.
Exeter Maritime Museum - Exeter
Largest collection in the world of working
boats, afloat, ashore & under cover.
The Steam & Countryside Museum -
Exmouth
Very large working layout - hundreds of
exhibits, including Victorian farmhouse -
farmyard pets for children.
Shebbear - North Devon
Alcott Farm Museum with unique
collections of agricultural implements &
photographs, etc.
The Elizabethan House - Totnes
Period costumes & furnishings, tools,
toys, domestic articles, etc.
The Elizabethan House - Plymouth
16th century house with
period furnishings.

City Museum & Art Gallery - Plymouth
Collections of pictures & porcelain,
English & Italian drawing. Reynolds'
family portraits, early printed books,
ship models.
Cookworthy Museum - Kingsbridge
Story of china clay. Local history,
shipbuilding tools, rural life.
Honiton & Allhallows Public Museum -
Honiton
Collection of Honiton lace, implements
etc. Complete Devon Kitchen.
Lyn & Exmoor Museum - Lynton
Life & history of Exmoor.
**Torquay & Natural History Society
Museum** - Torquay
Collection illustrating Kent's Cavern &
other caves - natural history & folk culture.

Historic Monuments

Okehampton Castle - Okehampton
11th -14th century chapel, keep & hall.
Totnes Castle - Totnes
13th - 14th century ruins of Castle.
Blackbury Castle - Southleigh
Hill fort - well preserved.
Dartmouth Castle - Dartmouth
15th century castle - coastal defence.
Lydford Castle - Lydford
12th century stone keep built upon site
of Saxon fortress town.
Hound Tor - Manaton
Ruins of mediaeval hamlet.

Other things to see & do

The Big Sheep - Abbotsham
Sheep-milking parlour, with gallery, dairy
& production rooms. Exhibition &
play area.
Dartington Crystal - Torrington
Watch skilled craftworkers make lead
crystalware. Glass centre & exhibition.
Dartmoor Wildlife Park - Sparkwell
Nr. Plymouth
Over 100 species, including tigers, lions,
bears, deer, birds of prey & waterfowl.
The Devon Guild of Craftsmen -
Riverside Mill, Bovey Tracey
Series of quality exhibitions throughout
the year.
**Paignton Zoological & Botanical
Gardens** - Paignton
Third largest zoo in England. Botanical
gardens, tropical house, "The Ark" family
activity centre.

DEVON

Map reference

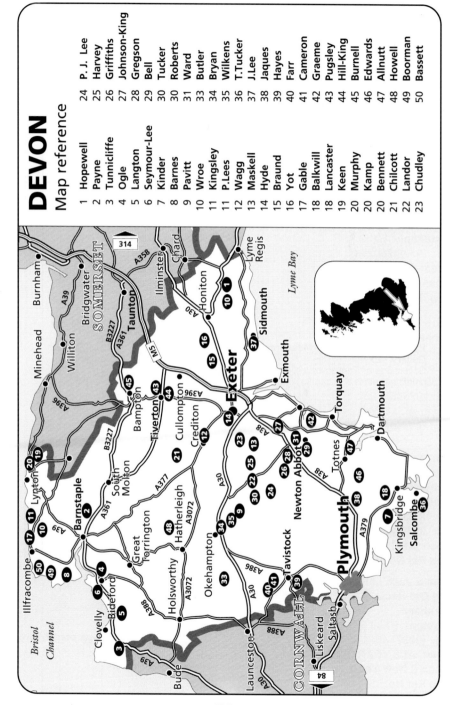

1	Hopewell	24	P. J. Lee
2	Payne	25	Harvey
3	Tunnicliffe	26	Griffiths
4	Ogle	27	Johnson-King
5	Langton	28	Gregson
6	Seymour-Lee	29	Bell
7	Kinder	30	Tucker
8	Barnes	30	Roberts
9	Pavitt	31	Ward
10	Wroe	33	Butler
11	Kingsley	34	Bryan
11	P.Lees	35	Wilkens
12	Wagg	36	T.Tucker
13	Maskell	37	J.Lee
14	Hyde	38	Jaques
15	Braund	39	Hayes
16	Yot	40	Farr
17	Gable	41	Cameron
18	Balkwill	42	Graeme
18	Lancaster	43	Pugsley
19	Keen	44	Hill-King
20	Murphy	45	Burnell
20	Kamp	46	Edwards
20	Bennett	47	Allnutt
21	Chilcott	48	Howell
22	Landor	49	Boorman
23	Chudley	50	Bassett

139

Devon

	per person minimum £	children taken	evening meals	animals taken
Mrs Helga Hopewell **Lambley Brook** **The Street** **Kilmington** **Axminster EX13 7SS** Tel: (0297) 35033 Open: FEB-DEC Map Ref No. 01	Nearest Road: A.35 — A warm & friendly atmosphere is found at this delightful, secluded 19th century converted cottage. Standing in its own grounds surrounded by open countryside & woodland on the outskirts of this picturesque village. Offering comfortable & spacious accommodation in 3 pleasant bedrooms with tea/coffee makers, lovely views. An idyllic retreat for nature lovers. Close to the Devon/Somerset, Dorset border. 7 miles from the coast. Minimum age of children is 10 years.	£15.00	Y	N	N
Mrs Jackie Payne **Huxtable Farm** **West Buckland** **Barnstaple EX32 0SR** Tel: (0598)760254 Open: ALL YEAR (Excl. Xmas & New Year) Map Ref No. 02	Nearest Road: A.361 — Relax at Huxtable Farm, a mediaeval longhouse with listed barn & round house. Carefully restored & furnished with antiques. This secluded sheep-farm (2 miles from M.5 link road) is ideally situated for Exmoor & the North Devon coast. Offering 6 rooms, most with private facilities, T.V. & tea/coffee makers. Enjoy 4-course candlelit dinners using farm/local produce served with home-made wine. Award-winning cook. Games room. Children welcome. An ideal base. CREDIT CARD AMEX	£19.00	Y	Y	N
Petre Josephine Tunnicliffe **Henaford Manor Farm** **Welcombe** **Bideford** **EX39 6HE** Tel: (028883) 252 Open: ALL YEAR Map Ref No. 03	Nearest Road: A.39 — Henaford Manor is a 13th century farmhouse set in 226 acres; retaining many traditional features including beamed ceilings & large fireplaces. Offering 3 tastefully furnished bedrooms, 1 en-suite, all with modern amenities including telephone, radio, colour T.V. & tea/coffee making facilities. Guests can relax in the spacious garden or lounge, available throughout the day. Excellent meals. Within 3 miles of Devon's Atlantic coast where there are several beaches & small coves including Clovelly & Tintagel.	£16.00	Y	Y	Y
Mrs Margaret Ogle **Lower Winsford House** **Abbotsham Road** **Bideford EX39 3QP** Tel: (0237) 475083 Fax 0237 425802 Open: APR - SEPT Map Ref No. 04	Nearest Road: A.39 — Everyone made very welcome at Lower Winsford to share our family home, tastefully furnished having a relaxing atmosphere, surrounded by lovely countryside. There are 3 rooms, 2 doubles & 1 twin, with wash basins, 2 bathrooms. Children over 5 welcome. Baby sitting arranged. Caring service at all times. Exmoor & Dartmoor within easy reach. The beach at Westward Ho! 3 miles, with lovely coastal walks.	£13.50	Y	N	N
Jean & Jack Langton **The Old Rectory** **Parkham** **Bideford EX39 5PL** Tel: (0237) 451443 Open: ALL YEAR (Excl. Xmas & New Year) Map Ref No. 05	Nearest Road: A.39 — Charming, delightfully furnished country house. Log fires, unique ambience with superb cuisine. 3 en-suite/private-facility bedrooms, very prettily decorated & furnished with every comfort in mind. Dine with your hosts & enjoy good wine with your excellent evening meal which, using fresh local produce, is home cooked by Jean to the highest of standards. Set in a designated area of outstanding beauty, it is ideally situated for the coast, picturesque Clovelly & Exmoor. *see PHOTO over*	£32.50	Y	Y	N

The Old Rectory. Parkham.

Devon

	Nearest Road	minimum £ per person	children taken	evening meals	animals taken
Penelope Seymour-Lee **Tower House** **Abbotsham Court** **Abbotsham Cliffs** **Bideford EX39 5BH** **Tel: (0237) 472418** **Open: ALL YEAR** **Map Ref No. 06**	Nearest Road: B. 3236 A unique 15th century listed building standing in a superb setting surrounded by cliffs & heaths in an area of outstanding beauty, with its own orchard with donkeys, sheep & a spring. Offering a pleasant comfortable en-suite room, with T.V. & tea/coffee making facilities. An elegant dining room where delicious meals are prepared & served by your hostess, who is an enthusiastic cook. Vegetarian & low calorie diets catered for.	£30.00 *see PHOTO over*	Y	Y	Y
David & Georgiana Kinder **Trebles Cottage Hotel** **Kingston** **Bigbury on Sea** **TQ7 4PT** **Tel: (0548) 810268/** **(0831) 558222** **Open: ALL YEAR** **Map Ref No. 07**	Nearest Road: A.379, B.3392 Originally a family cottage built in 1801, now a small hotel set in secluded grounds on the edge of an attractive unspoilt village. Trebles offers 5 bedrooms all en-suite, tastefully & individually furnished with colour T.V., radio/alarm, tea/coffee makers & hair dryers. Small cocktail bar complements the excellent restaurant. Lovely coastal walks, picturesque beach & golf nearby. David & Georgiana offer a warm welcome, personal service & a high standard of comfort & good food. A delightful home.	£23.00	N	Y	Y
Mrs Jean Barnes **Denham Farm** **North Buckland** **Braunton EX33 1HY** **Tel: (0271) 890297** **Fax 0271 890297** **OpenALL YEAR (excl.Xmas)** **Map Ref No. 08**	Nearest Road: A.361 Denham is a beautiful country house situated in the heart of the countryside with 160 acres of its own farmland. Only a short drive away are superb beaches, breathtaking scenery & lovely coastal walks. Situated only 3 miles from a championship golf course this delightful house offers 10 en-suite bedrooms with colour T.V. & tea/coffee making facilities. The inglenook fireplace & bread oven are a part of the character of this country home built in the 1700's.	£20.00	Y	Y	N
Peter & Carol Pavitt **Bly House Hotel** **Nattadon Hill** **Chagford** **TQ13 8BD** **Tel: (0647) 432404** **Open: ALL YEAR** **Map Ref No. 09**	Nearest Road: A.30 A former rectory set in 5 acres close to an old market town within the Dartmoor National Park. The house is elegantly furnished with antiques throughout. Having 6 double bedrooms, all with en-suite bathrooms, colour T.V. & tea facilities, some having 4-poster beds. The grounds & garden, with access to the moors, are a delightful feature which includes a grass tennis court & croquet lawn for guests' use.	£24.00	N	N	Y
Mrs H . S. Wroe **The Old Rectory** **Northleigh** **Colyton** **EX13 6BS** **Tel: (040487) 300** **Open: ALL YEAR** **Map Ref No. 10**	Nearest Road: A.30, A.35 Set in an idyllic south-facing situation on the slopes of a peaceful unspoilt valley with beautiful & extensive rural views. The Old Rectory offers comfortable, attractive rooms, each with T.V., washbasin & tea/coffee making facilities, some en-suite. Within 20 minutes of the sea at Seaton, Beer, Branscombe & the charming Regency resort of Sidmouth. An ideal base for exploring or just relaxing in blissful peace & quiet.	£17.00	N	N	N

Tower House. Bideford

Devon

		minimum £ per person	evening meals	children taken	animals taken
Jackie & John Kingsley **Brinscott Farmhouse** **Berry Down** **Combe Martin** **EX34 0PA** **Tel: (0271) 883146** **Open: MAR-DEC** **Map Ref No. 11**	Nearest Road: A.3123 Delightful 16th century listed longhouse with many features, garden, peaceful setting of 5 acres. Exmoor & sea 2 miles. Offering 5 comfortable rooms, 3 en-suite, all with tea/coffee making facilities & central heating. A large oak-beamed lounge has inglenook fireplace with woodburner, colour T.V. Plentiful breakfasts & an optional choice of candlelit dinners by an enthusiastic cook. Good touring centre.	£14.50	Y	Y	N
Peter & Edna Lees **Wheel Farm Country** **Guest House** **Berrydown** **Combe Martin EX34 0NT** **Tel: (027188) 2550** **Open: ALL YEAR** **Map Ref No. 11**	Nearest Road: A.39 A really delightful old farm house in beautiful grounds on the edge of Exmoor. Offering 6 spacious & comfortable rooms, 3 with bath en-suite. All have modern amenities & tea/coffee makers. Each room has wonderful views. Excellent food with home-grown produce. Wholefoods & vegetarian. Pony trekking, riding & golf arranged. Garden for guests. An ideal base from which to tour this lovely area.	£15.75	Y	Y	Y
Louisa & David Wagg **Fair Park** **Exeter Road** **Crediton EX17 3BJ** **Tel: (0363) 772686** **Open: ALL YEAR (Excl. Xmas & New Year)** **Map Ref No. 12**	Nearest Road: A.377 A comfortable Georgian family home located on the edge of town, with beautiful rural views. Decorated & furnished to a high standard with full central heating & log fires in the drawing room. All the bedrooms have private facilities & tea/coffee makers. No smoking in the bedrooms please. There is a solar-heated swimming pool & table tennis for guests' enjoyment. Delicious home cooking using garden produce. This makes an excellent touring base.	£15.00	Y	Y	N
Mr & Mrs J. H. Maskell **Bridford Guest House** **Bridford** **Exeter EX6 7HS** **Tel: (0647) 52563** **Open: Easter - DEC** **Map Ref No. 13**	Nearest Road: B.3212, B.3193 A warm welcome awaits you at this 350 year-old Guest House on Dartmoor. Accommodation is in 5 comfortable & tastefully decorated bedrooms, 2 en-suite & all with tea/coffee making facilities. Lounge with colour T.V. & large granite fireplace with log fires. Plentiful home cooking, including vegetarian, & Devon cream teas. Perfect base for long & short walks on Dartmoor. Horse riding nearby. Exeter & M.5 8 miles.	£14.00	Y	Y	Y
Richard & Susan Hyde **Raffles** **11 Blackall Road** **Exeter** **EX4 4HD** **Tel: (0392) 70200** **Open: ALL YEAR** **Map Ref No. 14**	Nearest Road: M.5 This small Victorian hotel is situated minutes from the heart of one of England's Roman cities. Accommodation in is 7 spacious & attractively furnished bedrooms, all with private facilities, colour T.V., tea/coffee making facilities & central heating. Attractively furnished in the Victorian style & retaining many original features. Home cooked 3 course meals using local produce are available with advance notice. Raffles offers an excellent standard of comfort & care.	£19.00 CREDIT CARD VISA M'CARD	Y	Y	Y

Devon

		minimum £ per person	children taken	evening meals	animals taken
Mrs L. L. Braund **Woodside** **Wood Hayes Lane** **Whimple** **Exeter EX5 2QR** **Tel: (0404) 822340** **Open: MAY-SEPT** **Map Ref No. 15**	Nearest Road: A.30 Charming accommodation in a spacious, elegantly furnished Edwardian farmhouse, delightfully situated in rural English countryside with outstanding panoramic views over Exeter to Dartmoor. Well appointed bedrooms with modern amenities. T.V. lounge, dining room, flower lounge &, outside, a garden which displays all-year colour & hosts many unusual plants. The proximity of restaurants & inns makes this an ideal base for your touring holiday of Devon.	£13.00	N	N	N
Mrs Jacqueline Yot **Colestocks House** **Colestocks** **Honiton** **EX14 0JR** **Tel: (0404) 850633** **Open: ALL YEAR** **Map Ref No. 16**	Nearest Road: A.30 Pink-washed & newly rethatched, a lovely 16th century Grade II listed country house in 2 acres of gardens. Tranquil rural situation, & well placed for touring the West Country. All rooms have en-suite bath/shower, colour T.V. & tea making facilities. Many antiques, one 4-poster, one canopied brass bed & 2 half testers. Log fires in the huge inglenook fireplace. Excellent restaurant, all home cooking. French wines personally chosen & imported by the proprietor. Children over 10. Reduced rates for 2 nights or more.	£24.50 *see PHOTO over* CREDIT CARD VISA M'CARD	Y	Y	N
Roy & Barbara Gable **Varley House** **Chambercombe Park** **Ilfracombe EX34 9QW** **Tel: (0271) 863927** **Open: MAR-OCT** **Map Ref No. 17**	Nearest Road: A.399 A spacious Victorian character house on the outskirts of Ilfracombe, having both sea & country views. The aim here is quality, comfort, courtesy & care with that extra personal touch. Accommodation is in 9 attractive rooms; all fully en-suite with C.T.V., tea/coffee making facilities. The house is elegantly furnished; the food served is imaginative & plentiful. An excellent base for exploring this lovely area.	£17.00 CREDIT CARD VISA M'CARD	Y	Y	Y
Mrs Jill Balkwill **Court Barton Farmhouse** **Aveton Gifford** **Kingsbridge** **TQ7 4LE** **Tel: (0548) 550312** **OpenALL YEAR (Excl.Xmas)** **Map Ref No. 18**	Nearest Road: A.379 An absolutely delightful 16th century, listed manor farmhouse situated on a 40-acre farm. Accommodation is in a choice of 7 comfortable & very attractive bedrooms, 6 with en-suite facilities. A comfortable, well furnished T.V. lounge with lots of books. Delicious country breakfasts are served in the sunny breakfast room. Full central heating & log fires in cooler weather. Close to moorland & beaches. An ideal base for walking, sailing, fishing & birdwatching.	£18.00	Y	Y	N
Mrs Christine Lancaster **Helliers Farm** **Ashford** **Aveton Gifford** **Kingsbridge TQ7 4ND** **Tel: (0548) 550689** **Open: ALL YEAR** **Map Ref No. 18**	Nearest Road: A.379 Set in the heart of South Hams countryside, this recently modernised farmhouse offers accommodation in 4 pleasant bedrooms with tea/coffee making facilities, a spacious dining room where good farmhouse breakfasts are served & a comfortable lounge with T.V. & games room. Close to the beaches, moors, golf courses, National Trust walks & the city of Plymouth. A non-smoking establishment.	£15.50	Y	N	N

Colestocks House.   Honiton.

Devon

	per person minimum £	children taken	evening meals	animals taken

Sybil Keen
Glen Doone
Oare
Lynton EX35 6NU
Tel: (05987) 202
Open: ALL YEAR
(Excl. Xmas)
Map Ref No. 19

Nearest Road: A.39
Glen Doone, beautifully re-furbished Victorian Rectory at Oare, tucked into a valley between Porlock & Lynmouth, with lovely Exmoor at its back. The 1000 ft. cliffs, well supplied with paths, roll down to the sea through woods, streams & waterfalls. Accommodation is in 4 bedrooms, 3 with ensuite facilities, all with modern amenities. The house is elegantly furnished, food imaginative, well presented & mostly home-produced. Children & pets welcome.

£17.00   Y   Y   Y

Brian & Dorothy Murphy
Neubia House Hotel
Lydiate Lane
Lynton
EX35 6AH
Tel: (0598) 52309
Open: FEB - NOV
Map Ref No. 20

Nearest Road: A.39
Neubia House is a delightful former 1840s farmhouse, set in own private courtyard/car park in Old Lynton. 12 very comfortable en-suite bedrooms all with colour T.V., hairdryer, telephone & tea/coffee making facilities. The restaurant offers fine cuisine & also caters for vegetarians. The snug bar has a collection of over 100 malt whiskies. Situated in hill-top village, it is an ideal base for touring this lovely region. Riding, fishing, walking & superb beaches & rocky coves are all close by.

£27.00   Y   Y   Y

CREDIT CARD
VISA
M'CARD

June & Adrian Kamp
Southcliffe
Lee Road
Lynton EX35 6BS
Tel: (0598) 53328
Open: MAR-OCT
Map Ref No. 20

Nearest Road: A.39
Charming private hotel of the Victorian era. Modernised throughout yet retaining many original features such as the natural pitch-pine staircase & doors. Beautifully appointed bedrooms - all with private bathrooms, colour T.V. & beverage makers. June & Adrian Kamp have been at Southcliffe since 1978 & have a reputation for good food, comfort, cleanliness & value for money.

£20.00   Y   Y   N

CREDIT CARD
VISA
M'CARD

Ben & Jane Bennett
Victoria Lodge
31 Lee Road
Lynton
EX35 6BS
Tel: (0598) 53203
Open: MAR - NOV
Map Ref No. 20

Nearest Road: A.39
A warm & friendly welcome awaits you at Victoria Lodge (formerly Gordon House Hotel). This gracious Victorian house provides charming period features, with modern conveniences. Accommodation is in 10 pretty bedrooms, all en-suite, with colour T.V. & tea/coffee making facilities. Dine by candlelight & enjoy delicious home cooking & good wine. Conveniently located to explore Exmoor, with secluded beaches, quaint harbours & picturesque villages close by.

£19.50   Y   Y   N

CREDIT CARD
VISA
M'CARD

Stephen Paul Chilcott
Wigham
Morchard Bishop
EX17 6RJ
Tel: (03637) 350
Open: ALL YEAR
Map Ref No. 21

Nearest Road: A.377
Wigham is a 16th century Devon longhouse with a 30 acre farm which provides fresh fruit, vegetables & dairy produce for imaginative meals. Accommodation is in 5 double rooms, including a 4-poster suite. All with colour T.V. & video & full private bathroom. There are 2 sitting rooms in which guests may relax & a snooker lounge & outdoor heated pool for pleasure. Licensed. Stabling - livery by arrangement. Minimum price includes 4 course dinner.

£40.00   N   Y   N

see PHOTO over

CREDIT CARD
VISA
M'CARD
AMEX

Wigham. Morchard Bishop.

Devon

		minimum £ per person	children taken	evening meals	animals taken
Stephen & Phyllis Landor **Cross Tree House** **Moretonhampstead** **TQ13 8NL** **Tel: (0647) 40726** **Open: MAR - DEC** **Map Ref No. 22**	Nearest Road: A.38, B.3212 Cross Tree House is a tastefully restored listed Queen Anne house located on the village edge in Dartmoor National Park. Offering guests every comfort in 3 large south-facing double bedrooms, 2 with en-suite facilities. Good English & Cordon Bleu cuisine is served. A delightful walled garden for relaxation & a nearby children's play area. An excellent base for walks & touring Devon.	£20.00	Y	Y	N
Owen & Kathleen Chudley **Great Doccombe Farm** **Doccombe** **Moretonhampstead** **TQ13 8SS** **Tel: (0647) 40694** **Open: MAR - NOV** **Map Ref No. 23**	Nearest Road: A.30, B.3212 Great Doccombe is a lovely 300 year-old farm-house, situated in a pretty village within Dartmoor National Park. 3 comfortable bedrooms, 1 en-suite, 1 on the ground floor, all with modern amenities & tea/coffee making facilities. Cosy lounge with wood-burning fire & colour T.V. In the dining room, enjoy a good farmhouse breakfast. Ideal for walking in the Teign Valley & Dartmoor.	£14.00	Y	Y	Y
P. J. & V. Lee **Barracott** **Manaton** **Newton Abbot TQ13 9XA** **Tel: (0647) 22312** **Open: APR - OCT** **Map Ref No. 24**	Nearest Road: A.382, A.38 A charming 16th century Dartmoor farmhouse set in an ancient beautiful & magical landscape with magnificent views to heatherclad granite hill tops. 2 comfortable south-facing guest rooms with private bath/shower. Colour T.V. & tea making facilities & lovely sitting room for guests' use. Situated in the National Park, Barracott is ideal for touring, riding & golf as well as marvellous walking country.	£20.00	N	N	Y
Mrs J. Harvey **Budleigh Farm** **Moretonhampstead** **Newton Abbot** **TQ13 8SB** **Tel: (0647) 40835** **Open: FEB - DEC** **Map Ref No. 25**	Nearest Road: A.382, A.38 Budleigh, a delightful old thatched farmhouse, nestles in a wooded valley in the Dartmoor National Park half a mile from Moretonhampstead. All bedrooms have tea/coffee making facilities & handbasins. Small apartments, with every comfort, are available out of season, making stays a real treat. Board games, paperbacks & magazines, maps & books are available. A delightful garden, with outdoor swimming pool, croquet & barbecue make this the perfect touring base.	£11.50	Y	N	N
Mrs Pauline Griffiths **Lower Elsford Cottage** **Bovey Tracey** **Newton Abbot** **TQ13 9NY** **Tel: (06477) 408** **Open: ALL YEAR** **Map Ref No. 26**	Nearest Road: A.38, A.382A 17th century stone cottage in magical woodland setting, with spectacular views over glorious countryside in an area of outstanding natural beauty. Complete peace and quiet, every home comfort, central heating. 1 double room with en-suite facilities, 1 single room h&c, both south-facing. Situated within the Dartmoor National Park ideal for touring, riding, golf, fishing and walking. Children over 8 welcome.	£16.00	Y	N	Y

149

Penpark. Bickington.

Devon

	Nearest Road	minimum £ per person	children taken	evening meals	animals taken
Peter & Patricia Johnson-King Oakfield Exeter Road, Chudleigh Newton Abbot TQ13 0DD Tel/Fax: (0626) 852194 Open: MAR - OCT Map Ref No. 27	Nearest Road: A.38 This lovely old family home, beautifully furnished with antiques, surrounded by 20 acres of delightfully landscaped gardens, orchards & paddocks with glorious views of the Devon countryside, offers perfect peace & tranquillity. Peter & Patricia treat their guests as friends & emphasise comfort, relaxation & excellent food. Accommodation is in 3 very attractive en-suite bedrooms. Guests may also enjoy the drawing room, billards room, library & heated swimming pool.	£25.00	Y	Y	N
Mrs Madeleine Gregson Penpark Bickington Newton Abbot TQ12 6LH Tel: (0626) 821314 Open: ALL YEAR Map Ref No. 28	Nearest Road: A.38 In the Dartmoor National Park, with secluded, beautiful woodland gardens, tennis court & glorious panoramic views, Penpark is an elegant, charming country house, a gem of its period, designed by famous architect Clough Williams Ellis. Your lovely, spacious twin room has a balcony, sofa, chairs, colour T.V., tea/coffee facilities & handbasin. Adjoining is a single room & bathroom. A warm welcome awaits you.	£20.00 see PHOTO over	Y	N	N
N. & C. Bell Sampsons Farm Restaurant Preston Newton Abbot TQ12 3PP Tel/Fax: (0626) 54913 Open: ALL YEAR Map Ref No. 29	Nearest Road: A.38, A.380 A super, relaxed, family atmosphere is found at this traditional thatched Devon longhouse. This Grade II listed building of historical importance retains much of its original charm & character with oak beams, panelling & inglenook fireplaces. All rooms have modern amenities & there are 4-poster & en-suite rooms available. Delicious breakfast served & extensive a la carte & table d'hote menu is offered in the evening. Only a short distance from coast. Riding, fishing, golf nearby.	£15.00 see PHOTO over CREDIT CARD VISA M'CARD AMEX	Y	Y	Y
Margaret & John Tucker The Gate House North Bovey Newton Abbot TQ13 8RB Tel: (0647) 40479 OpenALL YEAR (Excl. Xmas) Map Ref No. 30	Nearest Road: A.38, A.382 A listed mediaeval thatched house, with beamed ceilings, granite fireplace & bread oven. All bedrooms have en-suite/private bathrooms, colour T.V. & tea/coffee making facilities. There is a secluded garden, swimming pool & delightful views. North Bovey is a classic Dartmoor village with a green surrounded by thatched cottages. 2 miles from Moretonhampstead, there are lovely walks on Dartmoor & golf & riding nearby.	£23.00	N	N	Y
Peter & Celia Ward The Thatched Cottage Restaurant 9 Crossley Moor Rd. Kingsteignton Newton Abbot TQ12 3LE Tel: (0626) 65650 Open: ALL YEAR Map Ref No. 31	Nearest Road: A.380 A beautiful 400 year-old thatched longhouse with enclosed garden & large car park. Many original features including a wealth of oak beams & a large fireplace create a cosy, intimate atmosphere. Accommodation is in 5 bedrooms with modern amenities including T.V. & tea/coffee making facilities. Comfortable cocktail bar & restaurant with excellent cuisine. Delightful garden available for guests. A warm welcome & personal attention are guaranteed at this charming home by Peter & Celia.	£16.00 CREDIT CARD VISA	Y	Y	N

Sampsons Farm Restaurant. Newton Abbot

Devon

	Nearest Road	minimum £	children taken	evening meals	animals taken
Hilary Roberts **Willmead Farm** **Lustleigh** **Bovey Tracey** **Newton Abbot TQ13 9NP** **Tel: (06477) 214** **Open: ALL YEAR (excl.** **Xmas & New Year)** **Map Ref No. 30**	Nearest Road: A.38, A.382 Willmead Farm dates back to 1437. The hall has a minstrels gallery & there is an attractive drawing room with a large stone fireplace decked with gleaming copper & brass. A full English breakfast is served in the beamed dining room. Accommodation is in 3 attractive bedrooms, 1 with private facilities. Set in 31 acres of fields, woodland, duckpond & streams, an excellent base where peace & tranquility are guaranteed.	£20.00	Y	N	Y
Ellen Bryan **Lower Gorhuish Farm** **Northlew** **Okehampton** **EX20 3BU** **Tel: (0837) 810272** **Open: FEB - DEC** **Map Ref No. 34**	Nearest Road: A.30 A warm welcome is assured here. Accommodation is in 4 comfortable rooms, 2 en-suite, each with modern amenities, radio & tea/coffee making facilities. Plus T.V. lounge & garden. Good home cooking. Opportunities for pony trekking/riding nearby, also Okehampton 18-hole golf course. This mixed farm provides a super base for touring Devon, Cornwall, Dartmoor National Park & National Trust homes & castles.	£14.00	Y	Y	N
The Wilkens Family **Poltimore Country Hotel** **Ramsley** **South Zeal** **Okehampton EX20 2PD** **Tel: (0837) 840209** **Open: ALL YEAR** **Map Ref No. 35**	Nearest Road: A.30 Delightfully located country hotel on the fringe of Dartmoor with a warm & friendly atmosphere. Comfortable oak beamed lounge with inglenook fireplace & licensed bar. Ideally situated as a base for walking or touring. There are 7 comfortable bedrooms, 4 en-suite, each with tea/coffee making facilities & colour T.V. Home cooking using garden produce in season offering a varied menu, 4 course dinners & packed lunches.	£22.00 CREDIT CARD VISA M'CARD AMEX	N	Y	Y
Mrs Tricia Tucker **Courtenay House** **Moult Hill** **Salcombe TQ8 8LF** **Tel: (0548) 842761** **Open: ALL YEAR** **Map Ref No. 36**	Nearest Road: A.38 A beautiful Victorian house overlooking Salcombe estuary & sea. Accommodation is in 4 comfortable bedrooms with modern amenities, 3 with balcony, & T.V. On sunny days breakfast is served on the terrace looking out over the gardens to the water. Tim Tucker runs a ferry from the beach below into Salcombe, passing sandy coves & a castle ruin.	£23.00	Y	N	N
John & Diana Lee **Cheriton Guest House** **Vicarage Road** **Sidmouth EX10 8QU** **Tel: (0395) 513810** **Open: ALL YEAR** **Map Ref No. 37**	Nearest Road: M.5, A.30 This large town house stands in a secluded, prize winning garden that reaches down to the River Sid with parkland beyond, and the seafront just half a mile away. The 8 bedrooms are mostly en-suite and all have T.V. and hot drinks facilities. Cheriton is renowned for its fine cooking and varied menu. Comfortable T.V. lounge. Private parking. An ideal spot for a relaxing holiday.	£14.00	Y	Y	N

Devon

	per person minimum £	children taken	evening meals	animals taken
Mrs Josephine Butler **Four Chimneys** **Bratton Clovelly** **Okehampton** **EX20 4JF** **Tel: (083787) 409** **Open: APR - NOV** **Map Ref No. 33**	Nearest Road: A.30 Four Chimneys, originally 2 18th century cottages restored with taste & charm in one acre garden, skirts a pretty village. Guests' needs are sympathetically catered for. Special attention paid to quality, variety & presentation of meals. Homemade bread, packed lunches. Modern amenities including teasmade in warm attractive bedrooms. Guests lounge with colour T.V., piano, inglenook logfires. Private suite by arrangement. Babysitting, cots, highchairs. No smoking in bedrooms.	£17.00 *see PHOTO over*	Y	Y	Y
Allan & Bunny Jaques **Coombe House** **North Huish** **South Brent TQ10 9NJ** **Tel: (054882) 277** **Open: ALL YEAR(Excl.** **Xmas & New Year)** **Map Ref No. 38**	Nearest Road: A.38 This Country House, originally a Georgian farmhouse, offers a friendly welcome to a small number of guests. Its tranquil valley setting is home to heron, owls etc. Nearby Dartmoor offers walking, riding, fishing; several golf courses locally; quick and easy access to other parts of Devon & Cornwall. The four comfortable & tastefully furnished bedrooms have own bath and/or shower, w.c., and tea/coffee facilities. Spacious lounge with Minster fireplace. Licensed bar.	£18.50	Y	N	N
Jeanne & Martin Hayes **Colcharton** **Gulworthy** **Tavistock** **PL19 8HU** **Tel: (0822) 613047** **Open: ALL YEAR** **Map Ref No. 39**	Nearest Road: A.390 A warm welcome & an informal family atmosphere await you at this charming 16th century farmhouse. Located in a quiet valley within easy reach of the moors. Accommodation in 3 pleasant bedrooms, including a family room, with modern amenities & tea/coffee makers. This makes a good base for touring both Devon & Cornwall. A short drive away are Tavistock, Plymouth, Cotehele House, Lydford Gorge & the historic part of Morwelham.	£15.00	Y	N	Y
Gill & Andrew Farr **Moorland Hall Hotel** **Brentor Road** **Mary Tavy** **Tavistock PL19 9PY** **Tel: (0822) 810466** **Open: ALL YEAR** **Map Ref No. 40**	Nearest Road: A.386 Standing in 5 acres of gardens & paddocks, including a croquet lawn. Moorland Hall is a delightful country house with some parts over 200 years old. There are 8 en-suite bedrooms, 2 four-poster beds, all with T.V. & tea/coffee making facilities. There are 2 lounges & a small bar. The excellent menu is changed daily & includes vegetarian dishes. The coasts of Devon & Cornwall are within easy reach & the hotel is situated on the edge of the Dartmoor National Park.	£28.00 CREDIT CARD VISA M'CARD	Y	Y	Y
Mrs C.G. Cameron **Rowden House** **Brentor** **Tavistock PL19 0NG** **Tel: (0822) 810230** **Fax 0822 810230** **Open: ALL YEAR** **Map Ref No. 41**	Nearest Road: A.30 An Edwardian country residence with large, magnificent garden ideally situated on the edge of the Dartmoor National Park, with extensive views of the surrounding countryside and St. Michael's Church on the Tor. Beautiful, unspoilt rural area, noted for its peacefulness and easy access. 1 comfortable twin room with h/c, colour T.V., radio alarm, electric blankets, tea/coffee facilities. Dogs accepted by arrangement only.	£17.50	Y	N	N

154

Four Chimneys. Bratton Clovelly.

Devon

		minimum £ per person	children taken	evening meals	animals taken

Mrs Jennifer Graeme **Fonthill** **Torquay Road** **Shaldon** **Teignmouth TQ14 0AX** **Tel: (0626) 872344** **Open: FEB - DEC** **Map Ref No. 42**	Nearest Road: B.3199 Visitors are warmly welcomed to this lovely Georgian house for a peaceful holiday in charming & very comfortable accommodation. Fonthill stands in 20 acres of beautiful gardens, woodland & fields on the edge of Shaldon, a pretty village on the South Devon coast. 3 delightful rooms with every comfort. The lovely garden is for guests' enjoyment & there is also a tennis court in the grounds. Several sandy beaches nearby & an excellent 18-hole golf course.	£17.50 🚭 *see PHOTO over*	Y	N	N
Mrs Barbara Pugsley **Hornhill** **Exeter Hill** **Tiverton** **EX16 4PL** **Tel: (0884) 253352** **Open: ALL YEAR** **Map Ref No. 43**	Nearest Road: A.361 Overlooking the lovely Exe valley, 5 mins. Tiverton, 10 mins. from M.5. The friendly relaxed atmosphere is perfect for exploring Devon. 1 double (4-poster) & 1 twin bedded room, each with private bathroom. 1 ground-floor double with en-suite shower room suitable for the partially disabled. Each room is attractively furnished & has colour T.V., tea/coffee facilities & electric blankets. Comfortable drawing room with log fires & large garden available. Excellent English breakfast. Parking. Moors & coasts easily reached.	£14.00 🚭	Y	N	N
Mrs Ruth Hill-King **Little Holwell** **Collipriest** **Tiverton EX16 4PT** **Tel: (0884) 258741** **Fax 0884 258741** **OpenALL YEAR(Excl.Xmas)** **Map Ref No. 44**	Nearest Road: M.5, A.361 Little Holwell is a delightful 'olde worlde' farmhouse standing in beautiful Devon countryside, surrounded by rolling hills & woodland. This 13th century home has many oak beams, inglenook fireplace & spiral staircase. 3 rooms with tea/coffee making facilities. A lounge is also available. Home-made bread, eggs & vegetables are used whenever possible. Good for touring as Tiverton, Exeter, Exmouth & Torbay are within easy reach. Phone for directions.	£12.50 🚭 CREDIT CARD VISA M'CARD	Y	Y	N
Mrs D Burnell **The Old Mill Guest House** **Shillingford** **Tiverton EX16 9BW** **Tel: (0398) 331064** **Open: ALL YEAR** **Map Ref No. 45**	Nearest Road: B.3227 Set in a pretty riverside 'edge of village' location, The Old Mill, a former water-powered corn mill, offers superb accommodation in self-contained suites. Suite 1 is suitable for 2-4 persons & Suite 2 offers 1/2 family bedrooms; each has private or en-suite bathrooms, colour T.V. & tea/coffee making facilities. A beautiful garden & 4 large patios provide ample relaxation areas. Shooting, fishing & horse riding breaks available. Restaurant licence. An ideal spot for touring.	£18.00 🚭	Y	Y	N
Mrs Sheila Edwards **Ford Farm Guest House** **Harberton** **Totnes TQ9 7SJ** **Tel: (0803) 863539** **Open: ALL YEAR** **Map Ref No. 46**	Nearest Road: A.381 A 16th century village house, situated on the edge of a typical Devonshire village. It stands in a small, secluded 'olde worlde' garden with a stream. Accommodation is very comfortable with antique furnishings, log fires & beamed ceilings. Offering 3 bedrooms, 1 en-suite, with hairdryers, electric blankets & a bathroom courtesy chest. Tea/coffee facilities in the guest lounge. A warm, friendly atmosphere prevails at all times.	£17.00	Y	N	Y

Fonthill. Shaldon

Devon

		minimum £ per person	children taken	evening meals	animals taken
Jeannie & Peter Allnutt **The Old Forge at Totnes** **Seymour Place** **Totnes** **TQ9 5AY** **Tel: (0803) 862174** **Open: ALL YEAR** **Map Ref No. 47**	Nearest Road: A.381 - 50yds Totnes Route Centre. The Old Forge at Totnes is a delightfully converted, working, 600 year-old smithy. This family-run hotel, located in the centre of Totnes, offers visitors a choice of 10 comfortable well-equipped bedrooms, some en-suite, all with radio, colour T.V. & tea/coffee making facilities. Cottage suite also available for families. There is also a pleasant walled garden for guests' use, where delicious cream teas are served. The Old forge is ideally located for touring Torbay coast & Dartmoor. Licensed.	£19.00 *see PHOTO over* CREDIT CARD VISA M'CARD	Y	N	N
Jenny & David Howell **North Barwick** **Iddesleigh** **Winkleigh** **EX19 8BP** **Tel: (0837) 83902** **Open: APR - OCT** **Map Ref No. 48**	Nearest Road: A.377, A.3072, North Barwick is a 16th century thatched Devon long house. Originally the main farmhouse for the hamlet of Barwick, it has commanding views of the countryside, & affords tasteful accommo-dation in 3 very attractive bedrooms; with en-suite/private bathroom & tea/coffee making facili-ties, some with colour T.V. This, when accompa-nied by delicious breakfasts & fine cuisine, makes North Barwick an ideal place to stay. Convenient for Dartmoor, Exmoor & the coast.	£20.00	N	Y	N
Jean & Charles Boorman **'Sandunes' Guest House** **Beach Road** **Woolacombe** **EX34 7BT** **Tel: (0271) 870661** **Open: APR - OCT** **Map Ref No. 49**	Nearest Road: A.361 'Sandunes' is a very pleasant, most comfortable modern guest house where you are assured of a friendly welcome, relaxed atmosphere & courte-ous service. Conveniently located for Woolac-ombe Sands & village. The comfortable accom-modation is in 6 en-suite bedrooms, many with lovely sea views. The well appointed guest lounge & sun patio have marvellous panoramic views out to sea. This is an ideal base for touring with sandy beaches, Illfracombe, Lynton, Lynmouth & Exmoor within easy reach.	£14.00	N	Y	N
Mr & Mrs V. W. Bassett **Sunnycliffe Hotel** **Chapel Hill** **Mortehoe** **Woolacombe EX35 6AH** **Tel: (0271) 870597** **Open: FEB - NOV** **Map Ref No. 50**	Nearest Road: A.361 Sunnycliffe is a small, select hotel located on a hillside position with wonderful views of both coast & countryside. Accommodation is in 8 rooms, all with private facilities, T.V. & tea/coffee. All rooms have sea views. This makes a good base for any kind of holiday. Nearby are golden sands, safe swimming, surfing, riding, & walking along the coastal paths. Sea fishing & boat trips. Potteries, market towns & stately homes are within easy reach.	£23.00	N	Y	N

When booking your accommodation please mention
The Best Bed & Breakfast

The Old Forge at Totnes.   Totnes.

All the establishments mentioned in this guide are members of the Worldwide Bed & Breakfast Association.

If you have any comments regarding your accommodation please send them to us using the form at the back of the book. We value your comments.

Dorset

Dorset
(West Country)

The unspoilt nature of this gem of a county is emphasised by the designation of virtually all of the coast & much of the inland country as an Area of Outstanding Natural Beauty. Along the coast from Christchurch to Lyme Regis there are a fascinating variety of sandy beaches, towering cliffs & single banks, whilst inland is a rich mixture of downland, lonely heaths, fertile valleys, historic houses & lovely villages of thatch & mellow stone buildings.

Thomas Hardy was born here & took the Dorset countryside as a background for many of his novels. Few writers can have stamped their identity on a county more than Hardy on Dorset, forever to be known as the "Hardy Country". Fortunately most of the area that he so lovingly described remains unchanged, including Egdon Heath & the county town of Dorchester, famous as Casterbridge.

In the midst of the rolling chalk hills which stretch along the Storr Valley lies picturesque Cerne Abbas, with its late mediaeval houses & cottages & the ruins of a Benedictine Abbey. At Godmanstone is the tiny thatched "Smiths Arms" claiming to be the smallest pub in England.

The north of the county is pastoral with lovely views over broad Blackmoor Vale. Here is the ancient hilltop town of Shaftesbury, with cobbled Gold Hill, one of the most photographed streets in the country.

Coastal Dorset is spectacular. Poole harbour is an enormous, almost circular bay, an exciting mixture of 20th century activity, ships of many nations & beautiful building of the 15th, 18th & early 19th centuries.

Westwards lies the popular resort of Swanage, where the sandy beach & sheltered bay are excellent for swimming. From here to Weymouth is a marvellous stretch of coast with scenic wonders like Lulworth Cove & the arch of Durdle Door.

Chesil Beach is an extraordinary bank of graded pebbles, as perilous to shipping today as it was 1,000 years ago. It is separated from the mainland by a sheltered lagoon known as the Fleet. From here a range of giant cliffs rises to 617 feet at Golden Gap & stretches westwards to Lyme Regis, beloved by Jane Austen who wrote "Persuasion" whilst living here.

Dorset has many interesting archaeological features. Near Dorchester is Maiden Castle, huge earthwork fortifications on a site first inhabited 6,000 years ago. The Badbury rings wind round a wooded hilltop near Wimborne Minster; legend has it that King Arthur's soul, in the form of a raven, inhabited this "dread" wood. The giant of Cerne Abbas is a figure of a man 180 feet high carved into the chalk hillside. Long associated with fertility there is still speculation about the figures' origins, one theory suggesting it is a Romano-British depiction of Hercules. A Roman amphitheatre can be seen at Dorchester, & today's road still follows the Roman route to Weymouth.

Corfe Castle.

Dorset

Dorset

Gazeteer

Areas of outstanding natural beauty.
The Entire County.

Houses & Castles

Athelthampton
Mediaeval house - one of the finest in all England. Formal gardens.
Barneston Manor - Nr. Church Knowle
13th - 16th century stone built manor house.
Forde Abbey - Nr. Chard
12th century Cistercian monastery - noted Mortlake tapestries.
Manor House - Sandford Orcas
Mansion of Tudor period, furnished with period furniture, antiques, silver, china, glass, paintings.
Hardy's Cottage - Higher Bockampton
Birthplace of Thomas Hardy, author (1840-1928).
Milton Abbey - Nr. Blandford
18th century Georgian house built on original site of 15th century abbey.
Purse Caundle Manor - Purse Caundle
Mediaeval Manor - furnished in style of period.
Parnham House - Beaminster
Tudor Manor - some later work by Nash. Leaded windows & heraldic plasterwork. Home of John Makepeace & the International School for Craftsmen in Wood. House, gardens & workshops.
Sherborne Castle - Sherborne
16th century mansion - continuously occupied by Digby family.
No. 3 Trinity Street - Weymouth
Tudor cottages now converted into one house, furnished 17th century.
Smedmore - Kimmeridge
18th century manor.
Wolfeton House - Dorchester
Mediaeval & Elizabethan Manor. Fine stone work, great stair. 17th century furniture - Jacobean ceilings & fireplaces.

Cathedrals & Churches

Bere Regis (St. John the Baptist)
12th century foundation - enlarged in 13th & 15th centuries. Timber roof & nave, fine arcades, 16th century seating.

Blandford (St. Peter & St. Paul)
18th century - ashlar - Georgian design. Galleries, pulpit, box pews, font & mayoral seat.
Bradford Abbas (St. Mary)
14th century - parapets & pinnacled tower, panelled roof. 15th century bench ends, stone rood screen. 17th century pulpit.
Cerne Abbas (St. Mary)
13th century - rebuilt 15th & 16th centuries, 14th century wall paintings, 15th century tower, stone screen, pulpit possibly 11th century.
Chalbury (dedication unknown)
13th century origin - 14th century east windows, timber bellcote. Plastered walls, box pews, 3-decker pulpit, west gallery.
Christchurch (Christ Church)
Norman nave - ribbed plaster vaulting - perpendicular spire. Tudor renaissance Salisbury chantry - screen with Tree of Jesse: notable misericord seats.
Milton Abbey (Sts. Mary, Michael, Sampson & Branwaleder)
14th century pulpitum & sedilla, 15th century reredos & canopy, 16th century monument, Milton effigies 1775.
Sherborne (St. Mary)
Largely Norman but some Saxon remains - excellent fan vaulting, of nave & choir. 12th & 13th century effigies - 15th century painted glass.
Studland (St. Nicholas)
12th century - best Norman church in the country. 12th century font, 13th century east windows.
Whitchurch Canonicorum (St. Candida & Holy Cross)
12th & 13th century. 12th century font, relics of patroness in 13th century shrine, 15th century painted glass, 15th century tower.
Wimbourne Minster (St. Cuthberga)
12th century central tower & arcade, otherwise 13th-15th century. Former collegiate church. Georgian glass, some Jacobean stalls & screen. Monuments & famed clock of 14th century.
Yetminster (St. Andrew)
13th century chancel - 15th century rebuilt with embattled parapets. 16th century brasses & seating.

Dorset

Museums & Galleries

Abbey Ruins - Shaftesbury
Relics excavated from Benedictine Nunnery founded by Alfred the Great.
Russell-Cotes Art Gallery & Museum - Bournemouth
17th-20th century oil paintings, watercolours, sculptures, ceramics, miniatures, etc.
Rothesay Museum - Bournemouth
English porcelain, 17th century furniture, collection of early Italian paintings, arms & armour, ethnography, etc.
Bournemouth Natural Science Society's Museum
Archaeology & local natural history.
Brewery Farm Museum - Milton Abbas
Brewing & village bygones from Dorset.
Dorset County Museum - Dorchester
Geology, natural history, pre-history. Thomas Hardy memorabilia
Philpot Museum - Lyme Regis
Old documents & prints, fossils, lace & old fire engine.
Guildhall Museum - Poole
Social & civic life of Poole during 18th & 19th centuries displayed in two-storey Georgian market house.
Scapolen's Court - Poole
14th century house of local merchant exhibiting local & archaeological history of town, also industrial archaeology.
Sherborne Museum - Sherborne
Local history & geology - abbey of AD 705, Sherborne missal AD 1400, 18th century local silk industry.
Gallery 24 - Shaftesbury
Art exhibitions - paintings, pottery, etc.
Red House Museum & Art Gallery - Christchurch
Natural history & antiques of the region. Georgian house with herb garden.
Priest's House Museum - Wimbourne Minster
Tudor building in garden exhibiting local archaeology & history.

Other things to see & do

Abbotsbury Swannery - Abbotsbury
Unique colony of Swans established by monks in the 14th century. 16th century duck decoy, reed walk, information centre.
Dorset Rare Breeds Centre - Park Farm, Gillingham
Poole Potteries - the Quay, Poole
Sea Life Centre - Weymouth
Variety of displays, including Ocean Tunnel, sharks, living "touch" pools.

West Bay.

DORSET
Map reference

1	Du Faur	
1	Smith	
1	Farmer	
2	Walker	
3	Allan	
4	Game	
5	Jennings	
6	Rowse	
7	Willis	
8	Tomblin	
9	Hipwell	
10	Haggett	
11	Walford	
12	Collier	
13	Griffin	
14	Mayo	
15	McCallum	
16	Partridge	
17	Powell	
18	Wingate-Saul	
18	Dick	
19	Newson-Smith	
20	Gregory	
21	Rogers	
22	Spender	

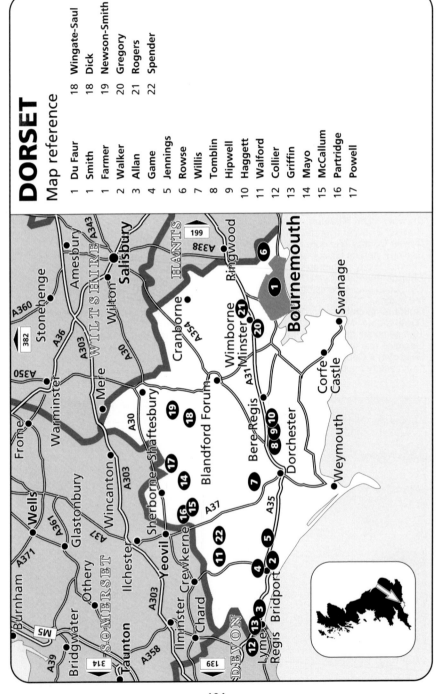

164

		minimum £ per person	children taken	evening meals	animals taken
Colin & Jean Du Faur **Sandhurst Hotel** **16 Southern Road** **Southbourne** **Bournemouth BH6 3SR** **Tel: (0202) 423748** **Open: ALL YEAR** **Map Ref No. 01**	Nearest Road: A.35 Guests' comfort is a priority at this friendly welcoming hotel. There's a choice of 9 comfortable rooms, each with colour T.V. & tea/coffee makers. Some also have large en-suite facilities, including ground floor en-suite. Good home-cooked breakfasts with evening meals available. Situated 2 mins. from the beach in a quiet suburb of Bournemouth. An ideal centre for touring, with Christchurch, Beaulieu, The New Forest, Salisbury & Dorchester a short drive. Private parking.	£15.00	Y	Y	N
Jo & Bill Smith **Silver Trees Hotel** **57 Wimborne Road** **Bournemouth BH3 7AL** **Tel: (0202) 556040** **Fax 0202 556040** **Open: ALL YEAR** **Map Ref No. 01**	Nearest Road: A.347 A charming Victorian house standing in its own wooded grounds with sweeping lawns, colourful flowers & shrubs. Offering comfortable accommodation in 8 bedrooms, 5 en-suite with colour T.V. Breakfast is cooked to order in the elegant dining room overlooking the garden. Early morning tea, evening snacks & refreshments are available on request & served in your room or in the lounge. Ideally located for visiting the New Forest & Dorset.	£19.00 CREDIT CARD VISA M'CARD	Y	N	N
Madeline & David Farmer **Wenmaur House Hotel** **14 Carysfort Road** **Boscombe** **Bournemouth BH1 4EJ** **Tel: (0202) 395081** **Open: ALL YEAR** **Map Ref No. 01**	Nearest Road: A.35, A.338 A comfortable small hotel with friendly atmosphere, offering good accommodation in 12 rooms. All rooms have T.V., tea/coffee making facilities & are fully centrally heated. Cots are provided. Centrally located for the beaches & sporting facilities are available locally. The evening meal offers a choice of menu & late night refreshments are available. Licensed.	£26.00 CREDIT CARD VISA M'CARD	Y	Y	Y
Ann & Dan Walker MHCIMA **Britmead House** **154 West Bay Road** **Bridport** **DT6 4EG** **Tel: (0308) 22941** **Open: ALL YEAR** **Map Ref No. 02**	Nearest Road: A.35 A friendly & pleasant small hotel renowned for superb facilities, delightful food & personal service. Situated between Bridport & the quaint little fishing harbour of West Bay with its beaches, golf course & the Dorset Coastal Path. 7 spacious bedrooms, 6 en-suite (1 ground floor), all with colour T.V., tea-making facilities, hair dryers & mini bar. South-facing lounge & dining room overlooking the garden. Parking. Licensed. Table d'hote dinner menu, incorporating local fish & produce. Bargain breaks.	£17.00 CREDIT CARD VISA M'CARD AMEX	Y	Y	Y
Alistair & Clemency Allan **Humbers** **Chideock** **Bridport** **DT6 6JW** **Tel: (0297) 89310** **Open: ALL YEAR** **Map Ref No. 03**	Nearest Road: A.35 This 17th century home is set in a beautiful West Dorset village. A lane leads to the sea & there is fine walking country over coastal hills with breathtaking views. A warm welcome awaits, & spacious accommodation in two rooms with modern amenities, traditional English breakfast. Information & advice on local walks & drives in Hardy country & nearby Devon & Somerset. Minimum age of children is 2 years.	£16.00	Y	N	N

Dorset

		minimum £ per person	children taken	evening meals	animals taken
Michael & Sandra Game **Riverdale** **168 St. Andrews Road** **Bridport** **DT6 3BW** **Tel: (0308) 27721** **Open: ALL YEAR** **Map Ref No. 04**	Nearest Road: A.35 Riverdale is an early Victorian house, retaining all original features & decorated & furnished in sympathetic style. Guests' breakfast in a beautiful room overlooking the traditional walled garden. The emphasis at Riverdale is on friendly family accommodation where individual needs are considered paramount. Easy flat walking to town centre, private car parking, fully adjustable central heating & tea/coffee served at any reasonable time. Breakfast is flexible & all requests catered for if possible.	£17.00	Y	N	N
Mrs C. Jennings **The Loders Arms** **Loders** **Bridport DT6 3SA** **Tel: (0308) 22431** **Open: ALL YEAR** **Map Ref No. 05**	Nearest Road: A.35 The Loders Arms is a delightful country pub set in the centre of the picturesque & tranquil village, yet only 1 mins. drive from Bridport & the sea. Accommodation is in 3 pretty, tastefully furnished & comfortable en-suite bedrooms with colour T.V.. Delicious home-cooked meals are available most evenings at the inn's restaurant. A riding establishment & golf course are close by as well as glorious country & coastal walks.	£17.50 CREDIT CARD VISA M'CARD	N	Y	Y
Michael & Jane Rowse **Monks Revel** **Winkton** **Christchurch** **BH23 7AR** **Tel: (0202) 479430** **Open: ALL YEAR** **Map Ref No. 06**	Nearest Road: B.3347 An enchanting Georgian house with grounds to the River Avon. Luxury en-suite bedrooms, delightful drawing room with comfortable sofas, log fires in Winter & French windows to sun terrace overlooking the river. Attractive dining room, serving delicious individually prepared table d'hote meals or pre-ordered local game & seafood specialities. Traditional Sunday lunch by arrangement. Close to picturesque harbour, unspoilt beaches & New Forest.	£25.00	Y	Y	Y
Mrs V. I. Willis **Lamperts Cottage** **Sydling St. Nicholas** **Cerne Abbas** **Dorchester DT2 9NU** **Tel: (0300) 341659** **Open: ALL YEAR** **Map Ref No. 07**	Nearest Road: A.37 Lamperts Cottage is a charming 16th century thatched cottage, standing in fields with streams running front & back, on the outskirts of the village. Roses climb around the windows & door. 3 bedrooms are available, equipped with tea/coffee making facilities. Full English breakfast, or Continental if preferred. Ideal for visiting Dorset's many beauty spots.	£16.00	Y	N	N
Marian Tomblin **Lower Lewell Farmhouse** **West Stafford** **Dorchester** **DT2 8AP** **Tel: (0305) 267169** **Open: ALL YEAR** **Map Ref No. 08**	Nearest Road: A.35 Lower Lewell Farmhouse dates from the 17th century & is situated in the delightful Frome Valley in the midst of Thomas Hardy country - indeed the house is reputed to be the Talbothays Dairy portrayed in Hardy's novel "Tess of the D'Urbervilles". 3 bedrooms are available, equipped with tea/coffee making facilities, & a full English breakfast is served. There is a sitting room with colour T.V. A delightful touring centre.	£15.00	Y	N	N

Rectory House.   Evershot.

Dorset

	per person minimum £	children taken	evening meals	animals taken
Mrs Anthea Hipwell **The Old Vicarage** **Affpuddle** **Dorchester BH23 7AR** **Tel: (0305) 848315** **Open: ALL YEAR (Excl.** **Xmas & New Year)** **Map Ref No. 09** Nearest Road: A.35, B.3390 The Old Vicarage is a traditional country house standing in a large mature garden in the charming Piddle Valley, at the heart of the Dorset countryside. Accommodation is in 3 comfortable & attractively furnished rooms, each with private bathroom & all facilities at hand at your request. Your hosts will be pleased to help with advice on the numerous places of interest & places to dine.	£17.50	Y	N	N
Mrs D. M. Haggett **Vartrees House** **Moreton** **Crossways** **Dorchester DT2 8BE** **Tel: (0305) 852704** **Open: ALL YEAR** **Map Ref No. 10** Nearest Road: B.3390 off A.35 A peaceful & secluded character country house set in 3 acres of picturesque woodland gardens. Built by Hermann Lea, friend of Thomas Hardy. Accommodation throughout is spacious & comfortable. Tea/coffee makers in all rooms. T.V. lounge. Situated near the pretty village of Moreton with its renowned church & burial place of Lawrence of Arabia. Coast 4 miles. Station 1/4 of mile. Excellent local pubs.	£16.00	Y	N	Y
Mrs Chris Walford **Rectory House** **Fore Street** **Evershot** **DT2 0JW** **Tel: (0935) 83273** **Open: JAN - NOV** **Map Ref No. 11** Nearest Road: A.37 Rectory House is an 18th century listed building set in the picturesque village of Evershot. 6 delightfully appointed bedrooms with en-suite bathrooms, colour T.V. & tea/coffee makers. Superb home cooking of traditional & exotic dishes. Delicious breakfasts include freshly baked bread & locally made sausages. Melbury estate adjoins the village with beautiful walks & scenery. Ideally located for visiting Bath, Bournemouth & Lyme Regis & much more. *see PHOTO over*	£25.00	N	Y	N
Mrs Ian Collier **Amherst Lodge Farm** **Uplyme** **Lyme Regis DT7 3XH** **Tel: (0297) 442773** **Open: MAR - OCT** **Map Ref No. 12** Nearest Road: A.3070 Originally a Devon long house, converted in the twenties in 'the grand manner', Amherst Lodge Farm lies in a wooded valley with trout lakes, Jacob sheep & an abundance of wildlife. The River Lyme runs through the old established & informal garden extending to 2 acres of maples, rhododendrons & orchard. There are 3 bedrooms all with en-suite bathrooms, colour T.V. & tea/coffee making facilities.	£19.00	Y	Y	Y
Geoffrey & Elizabeth Griffin **The Red House** **Sidmouth Road** **Lyme Regis** **DT7 3ES** **Tel: (0297) 442055** **Open: MAR - NOV** **Map Ref No. 13** Nearest Road: A.3052 This distinguished house, set in mature grounds, enjoys spectacular coastal views, it is only a short walk to the centre of Lyme Regis. The 3 en-suite bedrooms (1 for family use , 2 are especially spacious) are furnished with every comfort including & tea/coffee makers, colour T.V., clock-radio, desk, armchairs & drink refrigerator, central heating plus electric heaters. Fresh flowers & magazines are among the little extras. Breakfast can be taken on the garden balcony. Private parking. Minimum age children: 8 years	£19.00	Y	N	N

Almshouse Farm. Hermitage.

Dorset

	Nearest Road	per person minimum £	children taken	evening meals	animals taken
Mrs Jenny Mayo **Almshouse Farm** **Hermitage** **Sherborne DT9 6HA** **Tel: (0963) 210296** **Open: ALL YEAR** **Map Ref No. 14**	Nearest Road: A.352 This charming old farmhouse was a monastery during the 16th century, restored in 1849 & now a listed building. It is surrounded by 140 acres overlooking the Blackmore Vale. Accommodation is in 3 comfortable rooms with tea/coffee making facilities. Dining room with inglenook fireplace. The garden & lawns are available for guests' use at all times. Situated only 6 miles from Sherborne with its beautiful Abbey & Castle.	£15.00 *see PHOTO over*	Y	N	N
Mrs Vivienne Powell **'Strawberry Cottage'** **Packers Hill** **Holwell** **Sherborne DT9 5LN** **Tel: (0963) 23629** **Open: ALL YEAR** **Map Ref No. 17**	Nearest Road: A.3030, A.357 'Strawberry Cottage' is a part 16th century (listed) thatched cottage, situated in quiet countryside near Sherborne, in Hardy's Wessex & within easy reach of the coast. Guest's accommodation is in a choice of 3 bedrooms. There is a cheerful guests' T.V. lounge & the garden is also available. Children over 10 welcome. Plenty of reading material & local information provided for touring beautiful Dorset.	£16.50	Y	N	N
Ann & Jack Partridge **Manor Farmhouse** **High Street** **Yetminster** **SherborneDT9 6LF** **Tel: (0935) 872247** **Open: ALL YEAR(Excl.** **Xmas/New Year)** **Map Ref No. 16**	Nearest Road: A.37 This 17th century farmhouse with oak panelling, beams & inglenook fireplaces offers every comfort to the discerning visitor. There are 4 comfortably furnished bedrooms all with private facilities & modern amenities including T.V. & tea/coffee makers. Delicious meals served, made from traditional recipes using fresh local produce. Village described as the "best 17th century stone-built village in the south of England". An excellent centre for visiting Sherborne, Glastonbury, New Forest & Hardy's Dorset.	£23.50 🚭 *see PHOTO over* CREDIT CARD VISA M'CARD	N	Y	N
Charles & Sally Wingate-Saul **Holebrook Farm** **Lydlinch** **Sturminster Newton** **DT10 2JB** **Tel: (0258) 817348** **Open: ALL YEAR** **Map Ref No. 18**	Nearest Road: A.357 Holebrook farm is a family-run mixed farm located in the heart of Hardy Country. Accommodation is in the Georgian stone farmhouse or the delightfully converted stables with own sitting room, colour T.V., shower room & kitchen. Breakfast is served in the lovely old farmhouse kitchen with its flagstone floors, original fireplace & bread oven. A small swimming pool & games room with darts, pool table & table tennis are available for guests' use. Clay shooting can also be arranged.	£19.00	Y	Y	N
Mary Ann Newson-Smith **Lovells Court** **Marnhull** **Sturminster Newton** **DT10 1JJ** **Tel: (0258) 820652** **Open: ALL YEAR** **Map Ref No. 19**	Nearest Road: A.30, A.303 This is a rambling old house of character set in the delightful countryside with fine views across the Blackmore Vale. The market town of Sturminster Newton & abbeys of Sherborne & Milton Abbas are nearby - an ideal base for enjoying rural Dorset & its many National Trust properties. 2 en-suite rooms & 1 with private bathroom, all with colour T.V., radio & tea/coffee making facilities. Evening meals by arrangement Oct-Mar. Also excellent village inns for food all year round.	£18.50 🚭	Y	Y	N

Manor Farmhouse. Yetminster.

Dorset

		minimum £ per person	children taken	evening meals	animals taken
Ann Dick M.H.C.I.M.A. **Romaynes** **Lydlinch** **Sturminster Newton** **DT10 2HU** **Tel: (0258) 72508** **Open: ALL YEAR** **Map Ref No. 18**	Nearest Road: A.357 Romaynes is a spacious country house with an acre of garden. Ideally situated for touring beautiful Dorset. Guests from home & abroad are warmly welcomed. Double, twin, or single bedrooms all with modern amenities. Enjoy an excellent breakfast in the pleasant dining room overlooking the sun terrace & garden with views across the Dorset countryside. Children over 12 welcome. Colour brochure available.	£15.00	Y	N	N
Mrs Margaret Gregory **Ashton Lodge** **10 Oakley Hill** **Wimborne** **BH21 1QH** **Tel: (0202) 883423** **Open: ALL YEAR** **Map Ref No. 20**	Nearest Road: A.349, A.31 Detached family residence with relaxed & friendly atmosphere. The dining room overlooks an attractively laid out garden. A Full English breakfast is served, with freshly ground coffee. The 4 bedrooms are attractive, light & spacious with colour T.V. & tea/coffee making facilities & hair dryers. Ironing facilities are available on request. Ashton Lodge is conveniently situated for the coast, New Forest & Kingston Lacy House. Baby sitting service can be arranged.	£15.50	Y	N	N
Richard & Sue Rogers **The Old Oak** **Gaunts Common** **Wimborne** **BH21 4JR** **Tel: (0258) 840361** **Open: FEB - NOV** **Map Ref No. 21**	Nearest Road: A.31, A.349 You will be warmly welcomed at this charming thatched cottage, which is set in a delightful garden with heated swimming pool. 2 prettily decorated double or twin bedded rooms with private bathroom, T.V. & tea/coffee making facilities. Several attractive pubs nearby serving excellent evening meals. Situated four & a half miles from Wimborne on the edge of Cranborne chase. Within easy reach of Salisbury, Shaftesbury, New Forest & the coast.	£19.50	Y	N	N
Peter & Jane Spender **Halstock Mill** **Halstock** **Yeovil BA22 9SJ** **Tel: (0935) 891278** **Open: JAN-NOV** **Map Ref No. 22**	Nearest Road: A.37 At the end of a 1/2 mile private lane is the 17th century Halstock Mill. The 400 acres of pastureland surrounding it ensure a peaceful relaxing stay. Accommodation is in 4 spacious en-suite bedrooms with colour T.V. & tea/coffee makers. The beamed drawing room has an inglenook log fire. Jane offers a superb 4 course dinner prepared with home/local produce. An ideal base for touring Dorset, Somerset & Devon.	£22.00 *see PHOTO over* CREDIT CARD VISA M'CARD AMEX	Y	Y	N

When booking your accommodation please mention
The Best Bed & Breakfast

Halstock Mill. Halstock.

Essex

Essex
(East Anglia)

Essex is a county of commerce, busy roads & busier towns, container ports & motorways, yet it is also a landscape of mudflats & marshes, of meadows & leafy lanes, villages & duckponds. Half timbered buildings & thatched & clapboard cottages stand among rolling hills topped by orange brick windmills.

The coast on the east, now the haunt of wildfowl, sea-birds, sailors & fishermen has seen the arrival of Saxons, Romans, Danes, Vikings & Normans. The names of their settlements remain - Wivenhoe, Layer-de-la-Haye, Colchester & Saffron Walden - the original Saxon name was Walden, but the Saffron was added when the crocus used for dyes & flavouring was grown here in the 15th century.

The seaside resorts of Southend & Clacton are bright & cheery, much-loved by families for safe beaches. Harbours here are great favourites with anglers & yachtsmen.

Inland lie the watermeadows & windmills, willows & cool green water which shaped the life & work of John Constable, one of the greatest landscape painters. Scenes are instantly recognisable today as you walk from Dedham to Flatford Mill with the swift River Stour flowing by.

Colchester is England's oldest recorded town, once the Roman capital of Britain trading in corn & cattle, slaves & pearls. Roman remains are still to be seen & their original street plan is the basis of much of modern Colchester. A great feast is held here annually to celebrate the famous oyster - the "Colchester native".

South Essex, though sliced through by the M.25 motorway is still a place of woodland & little rivers. The ancient trees of Epping Forest, hunting ground for generations of monarchs, spread 6,000 acres of leafy glades & heathland into the London suburbs.

Flatford Mill.

174

Essex

Essex
Gazeteer
Areas of outstanding natural beauty.
Dedham Vale (part), Epping Forest.

Houses & Castles
Audely End House - Saffron Walden
1603 - Jacobean mansion on site of
Benedictine Abbey. State rooms & Hall.
Castle House - Dedham
Home of the late Sir A. Munnings.
President R.A. Paintings & other works.
Hedingham Castle - Castle Hedingham
Norman keep & Tudor bridge.
Layer Marney Tower - Nr. Colchester
1520 Tudor brick house. 8 storey gate
tower. Formal yew hedges & lawns.
Payecock's - Coggeshall
1500 - richly ornamented - merchant's
house - National Trust.
St. Osyth's Priory - St. Osyth
Was Augustinian Abbey for 400 years
until dissolution in 1537, 13th-18th
century buildings. 13th century chapel.
Wonderful gatehouse containing works of
art including ceramics & Chinese Jade.
Spains Hall - Finchingfield
Elizabethan Manor incorporating parts of
earlier timber structure. Paintings,
furniture & tapestries.

Cathedrals & Churches
Brightlingsea (All Saints)
15th century tower - some mediaeval
painting fragments. Brasses.
Castle Hedingham (St. Nicholas)
12th century doorways, 14th century rood
screen, 15th century stalls, 16th century
hammer beams, altar tomb.
Copford (St. Michael & All Angels)
12th century wall paints. Continuous
vaulted nave & chancel
.**Finchingfield** (St. John the Baptist)
Norman workmanship. 16th century tomb
-18th centuary tower & cupola.
Layer Marney (St. Mary)
Tudor brickwork, Renaissance
monuments, mediaeval screens,
wall paintings.
Little Maplestead (St. John the Baptist)
14th century, one of the five round
churches in England, having hexagonal
nave, circular aisle, 14th century arcade.

Newport (St. Mary the Virgin)
13th century. Interesting 13th century
altar (portable) with top which becomes
reredos when opened. 15th century
chancel screen. Pre-Reformation
Lectern. Some old glass.

Museums & Galleries
Dutch Cottage Museum - Canvey Island
17th century thatched cottage of
octagonal Dutch design. Exhibition of
models of shipping used on the Thames
through the ages.
Ingatestone Hall - Ingatestone
Documents & pictures of Essex.
The Castle - Colchester
Norman Keep now exhibiting
archeological material from Essex &
especially Roman Colchester.
Southchurch Hall - Southend-on-Sea
14th century moated & timber framed
manor house - Tudor wing, furnished as
meiaeval manor.
Thurrock - Grays
Prehistoric, Romano-British & pagan
Saxon archaeology.

Other things to see & do
Colchester Oyster Fishery - Colchester
Tour showing cultivating, harvesting,
grading & packing of oysters. Talk, tour
& sample.

Burnham on Crouch.

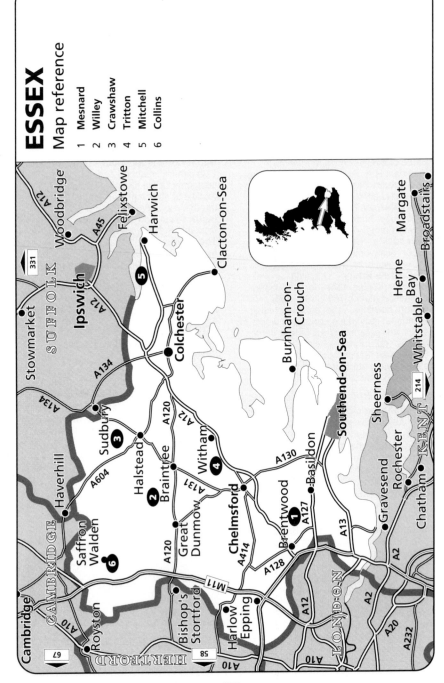

ESSEX

Map reference

1 Mesnard
2 Willey
3 Crawshaw
4 Tritton
5 Mitchell
6 Collins

Essex

		per person minimum £	children taken	evening meals	animals taken

Mrs Margaret Mesnard **Oakwood House** **126 Norsey Road** **Billericay CM11 1BH** **Tel: (0277) 655865** **Open: ALL YEAR** **Map Ref No. 01**	Nearest Road: B.1007 A detached Tudor-style house with a large rear garden backing onto 150 acre Nature Reserve. Accommodation is offered in a choice of two double en-suite bedrooms or single room with adjacent bathroom. Each room is equipped with colour T.V., hospitality tray and radio. Guests may relax in the conservatory or attractive garden. Ideal location for visiting London or touring East Anglia. Children over 5.	£18.00	Y	N	N
Helen Willey **"Corkers"** **Shalford Green** **Braintree** **CM7 5AZ** **Tel: (0371) 850376** **Open: ALL YEAR** **Map Ref No. 02**	Nearest Road: A.120 "Corkers" is a very comfortable 16th century oak beamed cottage set in a lovely 3-quarter acre garden. Offering 3 comfortable bedrooms, each with modern amenities. Restaurants, swimming, horse riding, golf & water skiing are available locally. Situated between Braintree & Saffron Walden, it is 8 miles from M.11 & Stanstead airport & is within easy reach of London. Ideal touring base for Cambridge, North Essex, rural Suffolk & Constable country.	£15.00	N	N	N
Mrs Penny Crawshaw **The Old School House** **St James Street** **Castle Hedingham** **CO9 3EW** **Tel: (0787) 61370** **Fax 0787 61605** **Open: ALL YEAR** **Map Ref No. 03**	Nearest Road: A.604, A.131 Charming terracotta-and-white Georgian house in Mediaeval village. Oak beamed, pamment-tiled hall/dining room; entrancing walled garden with many interesting plants including old-fashioned roses, and a lily pond. Bedrooms are well appointed & have private bath or shower, radio and tea/coffee facilities. 2 bedrooms are in attractive converted coach-house; one fully en-suite with sitting room & T.V. Evening meals by prior arrangement. Children over 12.	£18.50	Y	Y	N
Mrs Linda Tritton **The Wick** **Hatfield Peverel** **Chelmsford CM3 2EZ** **Tel: (0245) 380705** **Open: ALL YEAR** **Map Ref No. 04**	Nearest Road: A.12 Grade II listed 16th century farmhouse in pleasant rural setting. Large garden, duck ponds and stream. 2 attractive comfortable bedrooms, 1 single ,1 twin (own basin) sharing large bathroom. Cosy drawing-room with log fire, books, games, T.V., video. Delicious home-cooked meals served in dining room or large pine kitchen. Easy access to London and East Coast ports.	£17.50	Y	Y	N
Mrs H. P. Mitchell **New Farm House** **Spinnel's Lane** **Wix** **Manningtree CO112VJ** **Tel: (0255) 870365** **Open: ALL YEAR** **Map Ref No. 05**	Nearest Road: A.120 Modern farmhouse set in picturesque garden welcomes visitors with its warm homely atmosphere. The location offers close proximity to both Constable Country & within 10 minutes drive of Harwich Port. 12 bedrooms with modern amenities, the option of en-suite facilities & colour T.V. 2 guests' lounges incorporating well equipped kitchenette for preparing snacks. Children are especially welcome. Cot, high chair, baby sitting & play area provided.	£17.50 CREDIT CARD VISA M'CARD AMEX	Y	Y	Y

Essex

		minimum £ per person	children taken	evening meals	animals taken
Arthur & Susan Collins **The Stow** **Great Sampford** **Saffron Walden** **CB10 2RG** **Tel: (0799) 86354** **Open: ALL YEAR** **Map Ref No. 06**	Nearest Road: B.1053, A.184 The Stow is a lovely 16th century farmhouse, situated in the centre of the delightfully attractive village of Great Sampford. The house itself is a real treat, featuring beamed ceilings, buttoned chairs, Persian rugs, patchwork & embroidered cushions. The kitchen is pinewood & delicious meals are prepared on the large Aga cooker. Accommodation is in 3 rooms with modern amenities & tea/coffee making facilities. There is also a residents' colour T.V. lounge & a super garden.	£20.00	Y	Y	N

All the establishments mentioned in this guide

are members of

The Worldwide Bed & Breakfast Association

If you have any comments regarding your accommodation

please send them to us

using the form at the back of the guide.

We value your comments.

Gloucestershire

Gloucestershire
(Heart of England)

The landscape is so varied the people speak not of one Gloucestershire but of three - Cotswold, Vale & Forest. The rounded hills of the Cotswolds sweep & fold in graceful compositions to form a soft & beautiful landscape in which nestle many pretty villages. To the east there are wonderful views of the Vale of Berkeley & Severn, & across to the dark wooded slopes of the Forest of Dean on the Welsh borders.

Hill Forts, ancient trackways & long barrows of neolithic peoples can be explored, & remains of many villas from late Roman times can be seen. A local saying "Scratch Gloucester & find Rome" reveals the lasting influence of the Roman presence. Three major roads mark the path of invasion & settlement. Akeman street leads to London, Ermine street & the Fosse Way to the north east. A stretch of Roman road with its original surface can be seen at Blackpool Bridge in the Forest of Dean, & Cirencester's museum reflects its status as the second most important Roman city in the country.

Offa's Dyke, 80 miles of bank & ditch on the Welsh border was the work of the Anglo-Saxons of Mercia who invaded in the wake of the Romans. Cotswold means "hills of the sheepcotes" in the Anglo-Saxon tongue, & much of the heritage of the area has its roots in the wealth created by the wool industry here.

Fine Norman churches such as those at Tewkesbury & Bishops Cleeve were overshadowed by the development of the perpendicular style of building made possible by the growing prosperity. Handsome 15th century church towers crown many wool towns & villages as at Northleach, Chipping Camden & Cirencester, & Gloucester has a splendid 14th century cathedral. Detailing on church buildings gives recognition to the source of the wealth-cloth-workers shears are depicted on the north west buttresses of Grantham church tower & couchant rams decorate church buttresses at Compton Bedale.

Wool & cloth weaving dominated life here in the 14th & 15th centuries with most families dependent on the industry. The cottage craft of weaving was gradually overtaken by larger looms & water power. A water mill can be seen in the beautiful village of Lower Slaughter & the cottages of Arlington Row in Bibury were a weaving factory.

The Cotswold weaving industry gave way to the growing force of the Lancashire mills but a few centres survive. At Witney you can still buy the locally made blankets for which the town is famous.

From the 16th century the wealthy gentry built parks & mansions. Amongst the most notable are the Jacobean Manor house at Stanway & the contrasting Palladian style mansion at Barnsley Park. Elizabethan timber frame buildings can be seen at Didbrook, Dymock & Deerhurst but houses in the local mellow golden limestone are more common, with Chipping Camden providing excellent examples.

Cheltenham was only a village when, in 1716 a local farmer noticed a flock of pigeons pecking at grains of salt around a saline spring in his fields. He began to bottle & sell the water & in 1784 his son-in-law, Henry Skillicorne, built a pump room & the place received the name of Cheltenham Spa. Physicians published treatises on the healing qualities of the waters, visitors began to flock there & Cheltenham grew in style & elegance.

Gloucestershire

Gloucestershire Gazeteer

Areas of outstanding natural beauty
The Cotswolds, Malvern Hills & the
Wye Valley

Houses & Castles

Ashleworth Court - Ashleworth
15th century limestone Manor house.
Stone newel staircase.

Berkeley Castle - Berkeley
12th century castle - still occupied by the
Berkeley family. Magnificent collections
of furniture, paintings, tapestries & carved
timber work. Lovely terraced gardens &
deer park.

Chavenage - Tetbury
Elizabethan Cotswold Manor house,
Cromwellian associations.

Clearwell Castle - Nr. Coleford
A Georgian neo-Gothic house said to be
oldest in Britain, recently restored.

Court House - Painswick
Cotswold Manor house - has original
court room & bedchamber of Charles I.
Splendid panelling & antique furniture.

Kelmscott Manor - Nr. Lechlade
16th century country house - 17th century
additions. Examples of work of William
Morris, Rosetti & Burne-Jones.

Owlpen Manor - Nr. Dursley
Historic group of traditional Cotswold
stone buildings. Tudor Manor house with
church, barn, court house & a grist mill.
Holds a rare set of 17th century painted
cloth wall hangings.

Snowshill Manor - Broadway
Tudor house with 17th century facade.
Unique collection of musical instruments
& clocks, toys, etc. Formal garden.

Sudeley Castle - Winchcombe
12th century - home of Katherine Parr, is
rich in historical associations, contains art
treasures & relics of bygone days.

Cathedrals & Churches

Gloucester Cathedral
Birthplace of Perpendicular style in 14th
century. Fan vaulting, east windows
commemorate Battle of Crecy - Norman
Chapter House.

Prinknash Abbey - Gloucester
14th & 16th century - Benedictine Abbey.

Tewkesbury Abbey - Tewkesbury
Dates back to Norman times, contains
Romanesque & Gothic styles. 14th
century monuments.

Bishops Cleeve (St. Michael & All
Saints)
12th century with 17th century
gallery.Magnificent Norman West front &
south porch.Decorated chancel.
Fine window.

Bledington (St.Leonards)
15th century glass in this perpendicular
church--Norman bellcote.Early English
east window.

Buckland (St. Michael)
13th century nave arcades. 17th century
oak panelling, 15th century glass.

Cirencester (St. John the Baptist)
A magnificent church - remarkable
exterior, 3 storey porch, 2 storey oriel
windows, traceries & pinnacles. Wine-
glass pulpit c.1450. 15th century glass in
east window, monuments in Lady chapel.

Hailes Abbey - Winchcombe
14th century wall paintings, 15th century
tiles, glass & screen, 17th century pulpit.
Elizabethan benches.

Newland (All Saints)
13th century, restored 18th century.
Pinnacled west tower; effigies.

Museums & Galleries

Bishop Hooper's Lodgings - Gloucester
3 Tudor timber frame buildings - museum
of domestic life & agriculture in
Gloucester since 1500.

Bourton Motor Museum - Bourton-on-
the-Water
Collection of cars & motor cycles - also
vintage advertising.

Cheltenham Art Gallery - Cheltenham
Gallery of Dutch paintings, collection of
oils, watercolours, pottery, porcelain,
English & Chinese; furniture.

City Wall & Bastion - Gloucester
Roman & mediaeval city defences in an
underground exhibition room.

Stroud Museum - Cirencester
Depicts earlier settlements in the area &
has a very fine collection of
Roman antiquities.

Gloucestershire

Lower Slaughter.

Historic Monuments

Chedworth Roman Villa - Yanworth
Remains of Romano-British villa.
Belas Knap Long Barrow - Charlton
Abbots
Neolithic burial ground - three burial
chambers with external entrances.
Hailes Abbey - Stanway
Ruins of beautiful mediaeval abbey built
by son of King John, 1246.
Witcombe Roman Villa - Nr. Birdlip
Large Roman villa - Hypocaust & mosaic
pavements preserved.
Hetty Pegler's Tump - Uley
Long Barrow - fairly complete, chamber is
120 feet long.

Ashleworth Tithe Barn - Ashleworth
15th century tithe barn - 120 feet long -
stone built, interesting roof timbering.
Odda's Chapel - Deerhurst
Rare Saxon chapel dating back
to 1056.

Other things to see & do

**Cheltenham International Festival of
Music & Literature** - Annual event.
Cotswolds Farm Park - dozens of rare
breeds of farm animals
The Three Choirs Festival - music
festival staged in alternating years at
Gloucester, Hereford &
Worcester Cathedrals.
Slimbridge - Peter Scott's Wildfowl Trust.

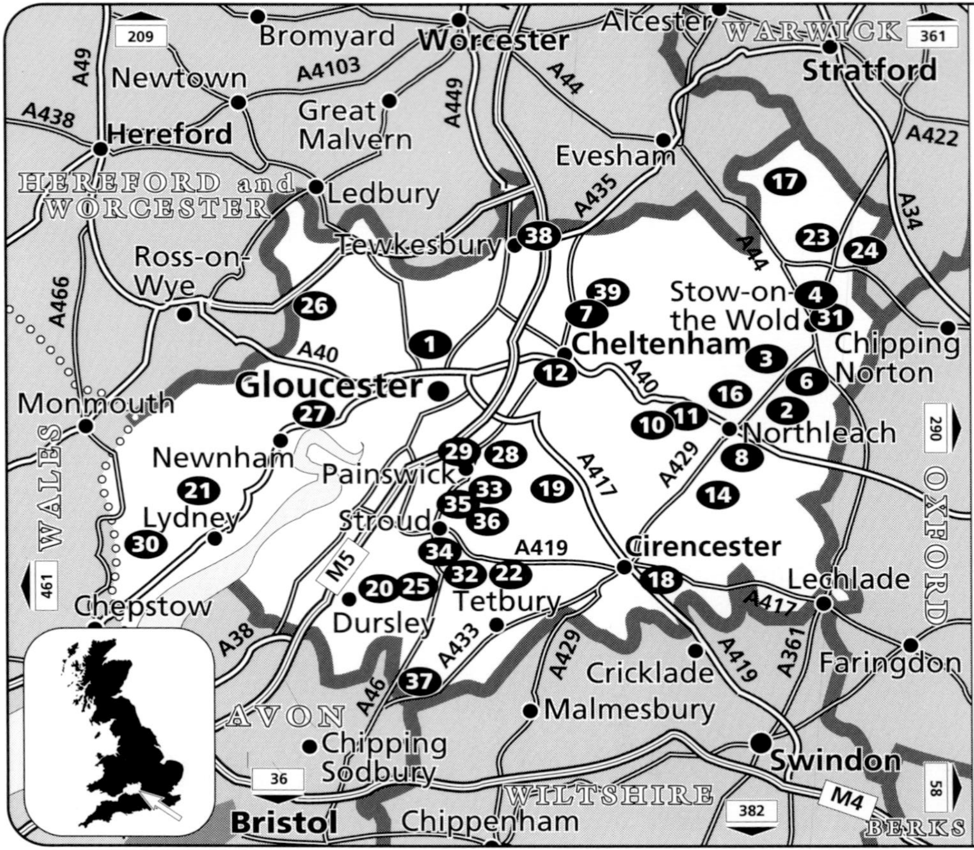

GLOUCESTERSHIRE
Map reference

1 Spiers
2 Froggatt
3 Farley
3 Minchin
3 Adams
4 Gisby
6 Leach
7 Enstone
8 Yates
8 Powell
8 Eastman
10 Carey-Wilson
11 Hudson-Evans
12 Berg
12 Milton
14 Loving
16 Burrough
17 Brown
18 Cassidy
19 Parsons
20 St. John Mildmay
21 Reid
22 Helm
23 Alderson
24 Dean
25 Williams-Allen
26 Thompson
27 Swinley
28 Wells
29 Blatchley
30 Peacock
31 Allen
31 Axon
31 Keyte
32 Hassell
33 Mills
34 Richardson
35 Mark
36 Fraser
37 Tremellen
39 Simmonds
39 Saunders

Gloucestershire

Mrs Patsy Spiers **The Green Farm** **Wainlodes Lane** **Bishops Norton** **GL2 9LN** **Tel: (0452) 730252** **Open: MAR - OCT** **Map Ref No. 01**	Nearest Road: A.38, M.5 A very attractive 300 year-old half-timbered farmhouse, standing on a 200 acre mixed farm. There are 2 charming & beautifully decorated bedrooms with modern amenities. Exposed beams, inglenook fireplaces with brasses & very comfortably furnished rooms. There are most attractive lawns with masses of flowers. Ideal for touring Gloucester, Cheltenham, Tewkesbury, the Forest of Dean & the Cotswolds.	£13.50 (no smoking)	Y	N	N
Mrs David Froggatt **Broadmoor** **Bourton-on-the-Water** **GL54 2LQ** **Tel: (0451) 820403** **Open: ALL YEAR** **Map Ref No. 02**	Nearest Road: A.40, A.429 A delightful country house in a stunning rural setting overlooking the Windrush Valley. This classic 17th century Cotswold residence, standing in 8 acres with lovely gardens, provides welcoming accommodation in a family environment. Full English breakfast is served in the elegant dining room or if weather permits on the south-facing terrace. Rooms with private bath, colour T.V. & coffee/tea making facilities.	£16.00	Y	N	N
Mrs Farley **Rooftrees** **Rissington Road** **Bourton-on-the-Water** **GL54 2EB** **Tel: (0451) 21943** **Open: ALL YEAR** **Map Ref No. 03**	Nearest Road: A.429, A.424 Warmth, comfort & hospitality are offered in the relaxed atmosphere of this detached Cotswold stone guest house, situated on the edge of the famous village of Bourton-on-the-Water. Offering 4 bedrooms, 2 have 4-poster beds & are en-suite. 2 rooms are situated on the ground floor. Traditional English home-cooking using fresh produce. An enjoyable stay is assured here while visiting the Cotswolds.	£14.00 (no smoking) CREDIT CARD VISA M'CARD	Y	Y	N
Mrs Helen Adams **Upper Farm** **Clapton-on-the-Hill** **Bourton-on-the-Water** **GL54 2LG** **Tel: (0451) 820453** **Open: MAR - NOV** **Map Ref No. 03**	Nearest Road: A.40, A.429 If peace & tranquility is what you require, then this charming undiscovered village 2 miles from Bourton is certainly the spot. Clapton enjoys one of the finest Cotswold views from its hill position. Here you will find Upper Farm with its 17th century stone farmhouse, lovingly restored & retaining a wealth of original charm. Delightful accommodation, commanding views & personal attention are complemented with fresh farmhouse fayre.	£13.50 (no smoking)	Y	N	N
Sybil Gisby **College House** **Chapel Street** **Broadwell GL56 0TW** **Tel: (0451) 832351** **Open: ALL YEAR** **(Excl. Xmas+New Year)** **Map Ref No. 04**	Nearest Road: A.429 Hidden in an enchanting & unspoilt Cotswold village, College House offers the most luxurious accommodation in lovely bedrooms with en-suite facilities. Exposed beams & ancient flagstone floors, mullioned windows with hand-painted shutters. Tranquil sitting room with massive stone fireplace. Every comfort is provided & Mrs Gisby enjoys spending time with her guests.	£17.50	N	Y	N

Gloucestershire

	Nearest Road / Description	minimum £ per person	children taken	evening meals	animals taken
Mrs Glenys Yates **Bank Villas Guest House** **West End** **Northleach** **Cheltenham** **GL54 3HG** **Tel: (0451) 860464** **Open: ALL YEAR** **Map Ref No. 08**	Nearest Road: A.40 Situated in the historic town of Northleach, in the heart of the Cotswolds. A warm & friendly welcome is assured from hosts Bob & Glenys. Bank Villas offers comfortable accommodation in 5 guest bedrooms (including 1 family room en-suite); each has modern amenities including h/c & tea/coffee making facilities. A T.V. lounge is also available. Centrally located, this is an ideal base for a relaxing holiday, or for touring & for those more energetic horseriders. Jet/water skiing & windsurfing are available nearby.	£15.00	Y	N	N
Viv & Robin Leach **Bobble Barn** **Little Rissington** **Bourton-on-the-Water** **Cheltenham GL54 2ND** **Tel: (0451) 20340** **Open: ALL YEAR** **Map Ref No. 06**	Nearest Road: A.429, A.424 Bobble Barn is a most delightful & comfortable farmhouse converted from an ancient listed Cotswold barn with magnificent views of Bourton-on-the-Water & the surrounding countryside. This lovely house offers well furnished centrally heated bedrooms with colour T.V. & tea/coffee making facilities. Some rooms have en-suite facilities. A pleasant & peaceful atmosphere at this beautiful farm. A perfect base for the Cotswolds. Children over 6 welcome.	£15.00	Y	N	N
John & Marian Enstone **Cleeve Hill Hotel** **Cleeve Hill** **Cheltenham** **GL52 3PR** **Tel: (0242) 672052** **Open: ALL YEAR** **Map Ref No. 07**	Nearest Road: A.40, B.4632 Situated in an Area of Outstanding Natural Beauty, Cleeve Hill has the friendly, relaxed atmosphere of a family home. All bedrooms have superb views, some to the Malvern Hills, & are en-suite, & equipped to the highest standards. The excellent breakfasts are generous & provide the perfect start to the day. Located in the heart of the Cotswolds, it is ideally placed for visiting Bath, Oxford, Stratford, Warwick & many charming Cotswold villages.	£27.50 *see PHOTO over* CREDIT CARD VISA M'CARD	Y	N	N
Patricia Powell **Cotteswold House** **Market Place** **Northleach** **Cheltenham GL54 3EG** **Tel: (0451) 860493** **Open: ALL YEAR** **Map Ref No. 08**	Nearest Road: A.40, A.429 This is a fine listed Costwold stone house, & having been carefully renovated to a high standard, it shows some architectural features of note. The bedrooms, of individual character, are comfortably furnished. Private facilities are available at most times. Northleach is a quiet town of historical interest & an ideal base from which to tour the surrounding area.	£15.50	Y	N	N
Mrs E.J Carey-Wilson **Halewell Close** **Withington** **Cheltenham** **GL54 4BN** **Tel: (0242) 89238** **Open: ALL YEAR** **Map Ref No. 10**	Nearest Road: A.40 Halewell is a Cotswold stone house, dating back in parts to the early 15th century. Situated on the edge of the very quiet & pretty village of Withington in a glorious setting in the hills. There are 6 superb, large, well-equipped double & twin bedded en-suite rooms of individual character. 1 twin is located at ground level, convenient for a physically disabled guest. An outstanding country home with easy access to the delights of the Cotswolds & surrounding area.	£37.50 CREDIT CARD VISA M'CARD AMEX	Y	Y	Y

Cleeve Hill Hotel. Cleeve Hill.

Gloucestershire

		minimum £ per person	children taken	evening meals	animals taken
Mr & Mrs Hudson -Evans **Hampnett Manor** **Hampnett** **Cheltenham GL54 3NW** **Tel: (0451) 860806** **OpenALL YEAR(Excl.Xmas)** **Map Ref No. 11**	Nearest Road: A.40, A.429 Hampnett Manor is a large sunny Victorian family house in a beautiful unspoilt Cotswold hamlet. A walker's paradise, there are many places of interest nearby, including the pretty old market town of Northleach. Mrs Hudson-Evans offers good home cooking - meals are served in the dining room & guests have use of the elegant drawing room. There are 2 tastefully furnished, comfortable bedrooms with tea/coffee making facilities.	£20.00	Y	Y	N
Mr & Mrs J. Berg **Hollington House Hotel** **115 Hales Road** **Cheltenham GL52 6ST** **Tel: (0242) 519718** **Fax 0242 570280** **Open: ALL YEAR** **Map Ref No. 12**	Nearest Road: A.40, M.5 An elegant late-Victorian house, 1 mile from town centre, with a large garden, croquet lawn & ample parking. Guests will enjoy the pleasant, relaxed atmosphere & personal attention of the proprietors. There are 9 spacious bedrooms with en-suite facilities, tea/coffee makers & colour T.V. A comfortable lounge with bar is also available. Good food is enjoyed here and a choice of menu is offered. An ideal base in the Cotswolds for business, holidays & short breaks.	£23.00 CREDIT CARD VISA M'CARD AMEX	Y	Y	N
Theresa & Mike Eastman **Market House** **The Square** **Northleach** **Cheltenham GL54 3EJ** **Tel: (0451) 860557** **Open: ALL YEAR** **Map Ref No. 08**	Nearest Road: A.40, A.429 A 400 year-old Cotswold stone house of 'olde worlde' charm characterised by exposed beams, inglenook fireplace & flagstone floors. Located in the centre of a quiet, unspoilt Cotswold town. Offering 3 cosy bedrooms, with handbasins, tea/coffee facilities as well as map & guide information. Full central heating throughout makes for a very comfortable stay. A choice of farmhouse breakfasts will sustain you for a day's tour in the Cotswolds, Bath & Stratford.	£15.00	N	N	N
Stephanie &St.John Milton **Milton House Hotel** **12 Royal Parade** **Bayshill Road** **Cheltenham GL50 3AY** **Tel: (0242) 582601** **Fax 0242 222326** **Open: ALL YEAR** **Map Ref No. 12**	Nearest Road: A.40, M.5 Milton House stands in a quiet tree-lined avenue of elegant Regency homes. Situated just a 4 min. stroll from the imposing promenade, restaurants & the Imperial Gardens. Guests have a choice of 9 en-suite individually styled & decorated bedrooms, colour T.V., 'phone & tea/coffee makers. A choice of healthy & generously proportioned breakfasts are available together with the morning papers. There is also a pretty sun lounge with bar & T.V. An ideal base from which to explore the lovely Cotswolds.	£23.00 CREDIT CARD VISA M'CARD AMEX	Y	Y	N
Pauline Loving **Northfield** **Cirencester Road** **Northleach** **Cheltenham GL54 3JL** **Tel: (0451) 860427** **Open: ALL YEAR** **Map Ref No. 14**	Nearest Road: A.429, A.40 Detached family house in the country with large gardens & own garden produce to complement home-cooking. Close to all local services in the small market town of Northleach. Offering 3 comfortable en-suite bedrooms. Excellent centre for visiting lovely Cotswold villages, & easily reached by car are Cheltenham, Oxford, Cirencester & Stratford.	£15.00	Y	Y	N

Gloucestershire

		minimum £ per person	children taken	evening meals	animals taken
Michael & Pamela Minchin **The Ridge** **Whiteshoots Hill** **Bourton-on-the-Water** **Cheltenham GL54 2LE** **Tel: (0451) 820660** **Open: ALL YEAR** **Map Ref No. 03**	Nearest Road: A.429, A.40 The Ridge stands in 2 acres of beautiful secluded grounds just 1 mile from the centre of Bourton-on-the-Water. A large country house with 5 individually decorated centrally heated bedrooms, most of which are en-suite; 1 is on the ground floor. This house provides an extremely pleasant & comfortable base for touring the Cotswolds. A delicious full English breakfast is served. Good restaurants & pubs nearby.	£14.00	Y	N	N
Jenny & David Burrough **Windrush Farm** **Bourton-on-the-Water** **Cheltenham** **GL54 3BY** **Tel: (0451) 820419** **Open: FEB - NOV** **Map Ref No. 16**	Nearest Road: A.436 This 150 acre farm is situated in the heart of the glorious Cotswolds renowned for its beauty & interest. The traditional, stone mullioned farmhouse has a lovely garden & commands superb views yet is only 2 miles from Bourton. Our guest rooms are tastefully furnished & comprise 1 twin-bedded & 1 double room with en-suite bathrooms & beverage making facilities. A delicious English breakfast is served. Jenny & David enjoy helping to plan your day. Children over 10 welcome.	£17.50	N	N	N
Nicholas S. Brown **The Malt House** **Broad Campden** **Chipping Campden** **GL55 6UU** **Tel: (0386) 840295** **Fax 0386 841334** **Open: ALL YEAR** **Map Ref No. 17**	Nearest Road: A.44 A personal welcome to this distinguished 17th century country house in the heart of rural England. Dinner is served on 'table d'hote' basis, the kitchen garden supplies us with fruit & vegetables in season, the cellar offers a wide choice of fine wines, spirits & liqueurs. Guests can walk in the gardens & orchards where rare breeds of poultry & Jacob sheep are kept. Croquet lawn. Children over 12 years.	£35.00 *see PHOTO over* CREDIT CARD VISA M'CARD	Y	Y	Y
Ian & Mary Cassidy **Waterton Garden Cottage** **Ampney Crucis** **Cirencester** **GL7 5RX** **Tel: (0285) 851303** **Open: FEB - NOV** **Map Ref No. 18**	Nearest Road: A.417 Set in the heart of the Cotswolds, Waterton Garden Cottage, part of a late-Victorian stable block, has been sympathetically converted, retaining many original features. A high standard of comfort & an ambience which would match many small country houses are to be found. All bedrooms are en-suite & one can expect fine cuisine, comfort & attention to detail without unnecessary formality. Every effort is made to ensure that your stay is both memorable & enjoyable.	£19.00	N	Y	N
Shaun & Susanna Parsons **Winstone Glebe** **Winstone** **Cirencester** **GL7 7JU** **Tel: (0285) 821451** **Open: ALL YEAR** **Map Ref No. 19**	Nearest Road: A.417 A small Georgian rectory overlooking a Saxon church in Domesday-listed village, enjoying spectacular rural views. Ideally situated to explore Cotswold market towns with their mediaeval churches, antique shops & rich local history. 2 delightful rooms, with private bathroom. Being an Area of Outstanding Natural Beauty, there are well-signposted walks. The more energetic can borrow a bicycle & explore further afield or just enjoy warm hospitality & good food.	£20.00	Y	Y	Y

The Malt House. Broad Campden.

Gloucestershire

Hugh & Crystal St. John **Mildmay** **Drakestone House** **Stinchcombe** **Dursley GL11 6AS** **Tel: (0453) 542140** **Open: APR - OCT** **Map Ref No. 20**	Nearest Road: A.38, B.4060 A delightful country manor house where guests receive a warm, friendly welcome & personal attention from Hugh & Crystal. The house is beautifully located on the edge of beech woods surrounded by garden, overlooking the Vale of Berkeley. This elegantly furnished & well-maintained home offers most comfortable accommodation in 3 bedrooms, each with individual charm. A cosy residents' lounge is also available. The formal Edwardian gardens are lovely & guests are welcome to use them.	£21.00 🚭	Y	Y	N
Mrs Sheila Reid **Edale House** **Folly Road, Parkend** **Lydney GL15 4JF** **Tel: (0594) 562835** **Open: ALL YEAR** **Map Ref No. 21**	Nearest Road: A.48, B.4234 Built in 1850, Edale House is a fine Georgian style residence facing the cricket green in the village of Parkend at the centre of the Royal Forest of Dean. To the rear is the RSPB Nagshead Nature Reserve, a delight for bird-watchers and walkers alike. Great care has been taken in providing all rooms with en-suite facilities and every comort for the discerning traveller. Evening meals by arrangement only.	£19.00 CREDIT CARD VISA M'CARD	Y	N	N
Margaret Helm **Hunters Lodge** **Dr. Brown's Road** **Minchinhampton** **GL6 9BT** **Tel: (0453) 883588** **Open: ALL YEAR** **Map Ref No. 22**	Nearest Road: A.419, A.46 A friendly & helpful welcome is assured for guests at this beautifully furnished Cotswold stone country house situated adjoining 600 acres of National Trust common land & golf course. Central heating throughout. Bedrooms have colour T.V., tea/coffee facilities, h/c, & private bathrooms. Visitors' lounge with colour T.V. adjoins delightful conservatory overlooking large garden. Ideal centre for Bath, Cheltenham, Cirencester and South Cotswold. (Animals by arrangement.)	£16.00	Y	N	Y
Mrs E.A. Alderson **Townend Cottage &** **Coach House** **High Street** **Moreton in Marsh** **GL56 0AD** **Tel: (0608) 50846/51621** **Open: MAR - DEC** **Map Ref No. 23**	Nearest Road: A.429 Picturesque Townend Cottage & Coach House offers comfortable accommodation with heating, colour T.V., tea/coffee facilities & en-suite or adjoining bathroom. Coffee, home-cooked lunch & tea are available in the licensed restaurant & garden, & guests may reserve an evening meal in advance or enjoy any of Moreton's excellent restaurants & pubs.	£25.00	Y	N	N
Mrs E. Dean **Treetops** **London Road** **Moreton-in-Marsh** **GL56 0HE** **Tel: (0608) 51036** **Open: ALL YEAR** **Map Ref No. 24**	Nearest Road: A.44 A beautiful family home offering traditional Bed &Breakfast. 6 attractive bedrooms, 4 with bathroom en-suite, 2 of which are on the ground floor and suitable for disabled persons or wheelchair users. All rooms have T.V., radio and tea/coffee facilities. Cots and high chairs available. Delightful secluded gardens to relax in. Ideally situated for exploring the Cotswolds. A warm and homely atmosphere awaits you here.	£14.00 🚭 CREDIT CARD VISA M'CARD	Y	Y	Y

Gloucestershire

	Nearest Road	minimum £ per person	children taken	evening meals	animals taken
Richard & Lesley Williams -Allen **The Laurels Guest House** **Inchbrook** **Nailsworth GL5 5HA** **Tel: (0453) 834021** **Fax 0453 834004** **Open: FEB - Mid DEC** **Map Ref No. 25**	Nearest Road: A.46 The Laurels is a lovely Georgian country house with a warm atmosphere. Attractive, walled garden borders a stream and fields beyond. Heated swimming pool. Older, converted buildings house family's hand-made furniture business. 3 double and 1 family room, all with en-suite or private facilities, radio alarms, T.V., tea/coffee trays. Lounge with T.V. and snooker table, conservatory, and panelled study for guests' use.	£15.00	Y	Y	Y
Mrs Anne Thompson **Orchard House** **Aston Ingham Rd** **Kilcot** **Newent** **GL18 1NP** **Tel: (0989) 82417** **Open: ALL YEAR** **Map Ref No. 26**	Nearest Road: M.50, B.4222 This beautiful Tudor-style country house is completely surrounded by 5 acres of well-tended lawns, paddocks & woodland walks. A relaxed & friendly atmosphere with every modern comfort & delicious food - traditional & vegetarian. The elegant & finely furnished rooms include 4 attractive double bedrooms overlooking the gardens, an original beamed T.V. lounge with log fires in winter & a spacious dining room. Residential licence. Well located for visiting the Wye Valley, Cotswolds & Malverns.	£17.50 *see PHOTO over* CREDIT CARD VISA M'CARD	Y	Y	N
Mrs Jenny Swinley **Broughtons** **Flaxley** **Newnham-on-Severn** **GL14 1JW** **Tel: (0452) 760328** **Open: ALL YEAR** **Map Ref No. 27**	Nearest Road: A.48 A lovely Georgian country house built by your host's ancestors 200 years ago in an idyllic pastoral setting. As a naval family, the Swinleys have enjoyed living overseas & welcome all their guests with friendly hospitality, offering 2 spacious twin bedrooms with private bathrooms & sitting room en-suite. Also, tennis, fully equipped laundry, & if required, chauffeured day trips to Bath, Cotswolds, Stratford, Wales. Good pubs & country restaurants nearby	£18.00	N	N	N
Mrs Joan Wells **Painswick Mill** **Painswick** **GL6 6SA** **Tel: (0452) 812245** **Open: ALL YEAR** **Map Ref No. 28**	Nearest Road: A.46 A beautiful Grade II listed Cotswold stone mill, dating from 1634, is set in 4 acres of lawn & natural garden - traversed by 2 streams complete with trout. Offering 2 beamed bedrooms (1 en-suite, the other private) with tea/coffee facilities & colour T.V. Lounge, garden & hard tennis court available to guests. Painswick, "the Queen of the Cotswolds", is a good base for touring & walking. Superb local pubs & restaurants serve delicious meals. Unsuitable for young children & disabled.	£19.50	Y	N	N
Barbara Blatchley **Thorne** **Friday Street** **Painswick** **GL6 6QJ** **Tel: (0452) 812476** **Open: APR-NOV** **Map Ref No. 29**	Nearest Road: B.46 Grade II Listed Tudor Cloth Merchants House in the centre of Painswick. 2 original Market Hall pillars "in situ". Perfect example of Cotswold secular architecture. 1 twin & 1 single room each with own shower & toilet. Central heating, tea making & T.V. in each room. Wonderful walking area including Cotswold Way. Within easy reach of many tourist attractions including Bath, Stratford, Slimbridge & Berkeley Castle.	£18.00	N	N	N

Orchard House, Kilcot.

Gloucestershire

Gillie Peacock **Cinderhill House** **St. Briavels** **GL15 6RH** **Tel: (0594) 530393** **Open: ALL YEAR** **Map Ref No. 30**	Nearest Road: A.466 A pretty, 14th century house tucked into the hill below the castle in St. Briavels with magnificent views across the Wye Valley to the Brecon Beacons & Black Mountains. A comfortable, lovingly restored & tastefully furnished house with 5 bedrooms (& 2 four-posters), all with private or en-suite bathroom. Host is a professional cook & takes delight in ensuring that all meals are well cooked using local produce. 3 self-catering cottages, 1 specifically for the disabled. Licensed.	£23.00	Y	Y	N
Mrs Barbara Axon **Croyde** **Evesham Road** **Stow on the Wold** **GL54 1EJ** **Tel: (0451) 831711** **Open: MAR - NOV** **Map Ref No. 31**	Nearest Road: A.429 A warm and friendly welcome awaits you at this detached Cotswold stone guest house. Ground floor accommodation, offering 2 double rooms. Just 4 minutes' walk from the centre of Stow, which makes an excellent base from which to visit the many Cotswold attractions, including Warwick Castle, Blenheim Palace, Stratford upon Avon, and the beautiful Cotswold villages. Car parking. Children over 10.	£14.00	Y	N	N
Mr B Allen **Bretton House** **Fosseway** **Stow-on-the-Wold** **GL54 1JU** **Tel: (0451) 30388** **Open: ALL YEAR** **Map Ref No. 31**	Nearest Road: A.429 Bretton House is an elegant Edwardian residence, tastefully furnished to high standards, combining good cooking with comfort & a friendly atmosphere. Set in the heart of the Cotswolds, with glorious views, there are 1 twin & 2 4-poster double rooms, each with colour T.V. & tea/coffee making facilities. Centrally situated for exploring the Cotswolds, making an ideal setting for restful breaks. Set in its own grounds of 2 acres, just a few mins' walk from Stow.	£20.00	Y	Y	Y
Mrs V. Keyte **The Limes** **Tewkesbury Road** **Stow-on-the-Wold** **GL54 1EN** **Tel: (0451) 830034** **OpenALL YEAR(Excl. Xmas)** **Map Ref No. 31**	Nearest Road: A.424 A large family house offering excellent accommodation with 3 rooms, 1 with 4-poster, all having modern facilities, 3 en-suite. Situated only 4 minutes' walk from the centre of town, it overlooks the countryside in a quiet area. Large attractive garden with ornamental pool & waterfall. A choice of good English breakfasts. From here Bourton-on-the-Water, Broadway, Burford, Chipping Campden & Moreton-in-Marsh are just a short drive.	£14.50	Y	N	Y
Queenie Mary Hassell **Burleigh Cottage** **Burleigh** **Stroud** **GL5 2PW** **Tel: (0453) 884703** **Open: ALL YEAR** **Map Ref No. 32**	Nearest Road: A.419 Situated on 600 acres of Minchinhampton Common, designated as an Area of Outstanding Natural Beauty, Burleigh Cottage offers 3 attractively decorated rooms with private bathroom, tea/coffee making facilities, colour T.V. & beautiful views. Ideal for walking, horse riding, golf or mere relaxation; wandering around the many tranquil villages nearby, stopping for refreshment in the delightful tea shops.	£15.00	Y	N	N

Gloucestershire

		per person minimum £	children taken	evening meals	animals taken
Mrs Anne Mills **Down Court** **Slad** **Stroud** **GL6 7QE** **Tel: (0452) 812427** **Open: ALL YEAR** **Map Ref No. 33**	Nearest Road: B.4070 Down Court, formerly 5 farm-labourers' cottages situated at the head of the beautiful Slad valley standing in an acre of cottage garden. Down Court still retains many of its original features, inglenook fireplaces & oak beams with modern day comforts. Uninterrupted views & an ideal centre for touring the Cotswolds, Bath, Cheltenham, Gloucester, Royal Forest of Dean & the Severn Vale. A relaxing atmosphere in homely accommodation awaits guests.	£16.50	N	Y	Y
Mrs Suzanne Richardson **Southfield Mill House** **Woodchester** **Stroud GL5 5PA** **Tel: (0453) 873437** **Fax 0453 872049** **Open: ALL YEAR** **Map Ref No. 34**	Nearest Road: A.46 Fascinating Cotswold stone house dating from 1560 with interesting historical connections. Beautifully decorated & furnished with antiques, Southfield House is situated in an area of outstanding natural beauty. 3 pubs serving good food within easy walking distance. Golf, riding, tennis & scenic walks nearby. Ideal centre for exploring the Cotswolds & shopping in Bath & Cheltenham. Sightseeing at Berkeley & Sudeley Castles & other historical sites.	£18.00	N	N	N
Albert & Audrey Mark **The Frith** **Slad** **Stroud** **GL6 7QD** **Tel: (0452) 814117** **Open: ALL YEAR** **Map Ref No. 35**	Nearest Road: A.419, A.417 A warm welcome awaits you at The Frith, a family house in beautiful Slad Valley. Panoramic views in an area of outstanding natural beauty in a peaceful country location situated on the B.4070. Ideal for walking & touring the Cotswolds. 3 double bedded rooms, 1 en-suite. All rooms with h/c & tea/coffee facilities. A good English Breakfast is served. T.V. lounge, washing/ironing facilities. Horse riding & golf nearby. Parking.	£14.00	Y	N	Y
Margaret Fraser & **Dennis Chambers** **The Old Vicarage** **167 Slad Road** **Stroud GL5 1RD** **Tel: (0453) 752315** **Open: FEB - DEC** **Map Ref No. 36**	Nearest Road: M.5, A.46 Facing south overlooking the beautiful Slad Valley in the central Cotswolds, The Old Vicarage offers elegant comfort in 3 en-suite bedrooms with colour T.V., central heating & tea/coffee making facilities. Delicious meals are served in the licensed dining room. An ideal base for visiting the Cotswolds, Berkley Vale, Bath, Cheltenham, Gloucester & the Royal Forest of Dean. Pony trekking & golf nearby.	£15.00	Y	Y	Y
Tim & Janet Tremellen **Tavern House** **Willesley** **Tetbury** **GL8 8QU** **Tel: (0666) 880444** **Open: ALL YEAR** **Map Ref No. 37**	Nearest Road: A.433 A Grade II listed, part 17th century former staging post, Tavern House has been sympathetically refurbished to provide a high standard of Bed & Breakfast accommodation. All rooms with bath & shower en-suite, direct-dial telephones, T.V., etc. Delightful gardens in which to relax. Ideally situated for the Arboretum, Badminton Horse Trials, Cheltenham Races. A genuine country house atmosphere & an excellent base from which to explore the Cotswolds. *see PHOTO over* CREDIT CARD VISA M'CARD	£22.50	Y	N	N

Tavern House.   Willesley.

Gloucestershire

		minimum £ per person	children taken	evening meals	animals taken
Mrs S. Simmonds **Gower House** **16 North Street** **Winchcombe GL54 5LH** **Tel: (0242) 602616** **OpenALL YEAR(Excl.Xmas)** **Map Ref No. 39**	Nearest Road: A.40, B.4632 Mick & Sally will welcome you to their handsome 17th century town house, situated centrally in Winchcombe, convenient for shops & restaurants. Car parking at rear of house, 3 attractive bedrooms, 1 double & 2 twin are available. Full English breakfast served with Continental alternative if requested. Pretty garden for guests' use. Baby sitting can be arranged.	£15.00	Y	N	N
Mrs J. G. Saunders **Great House** **Castle Street** **Winchcombe GL54 5JA** **Tel: (0242) 602490** **Open: ALL YEAR** **Map Ref No. 39**	Nearest Road: A.46 A superb Jacobean house offering comfortable accommodation with modern facilities. A warm welcome awaits the visitor here. It is only half a mile walking distance to Sudeley Castle, in the heart of the Cotswolds. 2 rooms are available with T.V., & 1 with 4-poster bed. There is a garden for guests' use. Ideal touring centre.	£15.00	Y	N	N

All the establishments mentioned in this guide

are members of

The Worldwide Bed & Breakfast Association

When booking your accommodation please mention
The Best Bed & Breakfast

Hampshire

Hampshire (Southern)

Hampshire is located in the centre of the south coast of England & is blessed with much beautiful & unspoilt countryside. Wide open vistas of rich downland contrast with deep woodlands. Rivers & sparkling streams run through tranquil valleys passing nestling villages. There is a splendid coastline with seaside resorts & harbours, the cathedral city of Winchester & the "jewel" of Hampshire, the Isle of Wight.

The north of the county is known as the Hampshire Borders. Part of this countryside was immortalised by Richard Adams & the rabbits of 'Watership Down'. Beacon Hill is a notable hill-top landmark. From its slopes some of the earliest aeroplane flights were made by De Haviland in 1909. Pleasure trips & tow-path walks can be taken along the restored Basingstoke Canal.

The New Forest is probably the area most frequented by visitors. It is a landscape of great character with thatched cottages, glades & streams & a romantic beauty. There are herds of deer & the New Forest ponies wander at will. To the N.W. of Beaulieu are some of the most idyllic parts of the old forest, with fewer villages & many little streams that flow into the Avon. Lyndhurst, the "capital" of the New Forest offers a range of shops & has a contentious 19th century church constructed in scarlet brickwork banded with yellow, unusual ornamental decoration, & stained glass windows by William Morris.

The Roman city of Winchester became the capital city of Saxon Wessex & is today the capital of Hampshire. It is famous for its beautiful mediaeval cathedral, built during the reign of William the Conquerer & his notorious son Rufus. It contains the great Winchester Bible.

William completed the famous Domesday Book in the city, & Richard Coeur de Lion was crowned in the cathedral in 1194.

Portsmouth & Southampton are major ports & historic maritime cities with a wealth of castles, forts & Naval attractions from battleships to museums.

The channel of the Solent guarded by Martello towers, holds not only Southampton but numerous yachting centres, such as Hamble, Lymington & Bucklers Hard where the ships for Admiral Lord Nelson's fleet were built.

The River Test.

The Isle of Wight

The Isle of Wight lies across the sheltered waters of the Solent, & is easily reached by car or passenger ferry. The chalk stacks of the Needles & the multi-coloured sand at Alum Bay are among the best known of the island's natural attractions & there are many excellent beaches & other bays to enjoy. Cowes is a famous international sailing centre with a large number of yachting events throughout the summer. Ventnor, the most southerly resort is known as the "Madeira of England" & has an exotic botanic garden. Inland is an excellent network of footpaths & trails & many castles, manors & stately homes.

Hampshire

Hampshire
Gazeteer
Areas of outstanding natural beauty.
East & South Hampshire, North Wessex
Downs & Chichester Harbour.

Houses & Castles
Avington Park - Winchester
16th century red brick house, enlarged in
17th century by the addition of two wings
& a classical portico. Stateroom, ballroom
with wonderful ceiling. Red drawing
room, library, etc.

Beaulieu Abbey & Palace House -
Beaulieu
12th century Cistercian abbey - the
original gatehouse of abbey converted to
palace house 1538. Houses historic car
museum.

Breamore House - Breamore
16th century Elizabethan Manor House,
tapestries, furniture, paintings.
Also museum.

Jane Austen's Home - Chawston
Personal effects of the famous writer.

Broadlands - Romsey
16th century - park & garden created by
Capability Brown. Home of the Earl
Mountbatten of Burma.

Mottisfont Abbey - Nr. Romsey
12th century Augustinian Priory until
Dissolution. Painting by Rex Whistler
trompe l'oeil in Gothic manner.

Stratfield Saye House - Reading
17th century house presented to the Duke
of Wellington 1817. Now contains his
possessions - also wild fowl sanctuary.

Sandham Memorial Chapel - Sandham,
Nr. Newbury
Paintings by Stanley Spencer cover
the walls.

The Vyne - Sherbourne St. John
16th century red brick chapel with
Renaissance glass & rare linenfold
panelling. Alterations made in 1654 -
classical portico. Palladian staircase
dates form 1760.

West Green House - Hartley Wintney
18th century red brick house set in
walled garden.

Appuldurcombe House - Wroxall, Isle of
Wight
The only house in the 'Grand Manner' on
the island. Beautiful English baroque east
facade. House now an empty shell
standing in fine park.

Osbourne House - East Cowes, Isle of
Wight
Queen Victoria's seaside residence.

Carisbrooke Castle - Isle of Wight
Oldest parts 12th century, but there was a
wooden castle on the mound before that.
Museum in castle.

Cathedrals & Churches
Winchester Cathedral
Largest Gothic church in Europe.
Norman & perpendicular styles, three sets
of mediaeval paintings, marble font
c.1180. Stalls c.1320 with 60 misericords.
Extensive mediaeval tiled floor.

Breamore (St. Mary) - Breamore
10th century Saxon. Double splayed
windows, stone rood.

East Meon (All Saints)
15th century rebuilding of Norman fabric.
Tournai marble front.

Idsworth (St. Hubert)
16th century chapel - 18th century bell
turret. 14th century paintings in chancel.

Pamber (dedication unknown)
Early English - Norman central tower,
15th century central pews, wooden effigy of
knight c.1270.

Romsey (St. Mary & St. Ethelfleda)
Norman - 13th century effigy of a lady -
Saxon rood & carving of crucifixion, 16th
century painted reredos.

Silchester (St. Mary)
Norman, perpendicular, 14th century
effigy of a lady, 15th century screen, Early
English chancel with painted patterns on
south window splays, Jacobean pulpit
with domed canopy.

Winchester (St. Cross)
12th century. Original chapel to Hospital.
Style changing from Norman at east to
decorated at west. Tiles, glass,
wall painting.

Hampshire

Museums & Galleries

Browning Barracks - Aldershot
Airbourne Forces Exhibition of weapons
from war, dioramas of battles, models,
equipment, medals, photographs, etc.
Bargate Guildhall Museum -
Southampton
Former Hall of Guilds - exhibition of local
history, etc.
Southsea Castle - Portsmouth
Local history & military history,
archeaology.
**Cumberland House Museum &
Aquarium** - Southsea
Natural history & geology of district.
Portsmouth Royal Naval Museum -
Portsmouth
Relics of Nelson, H.M.S. Victory, ship
models, figureheads, etc.
Dickens' Birthplace Museum -
Portsmouth
House where the author was born
in 1812.
Southampton Art Gallery - Southampton
British & French paintings, particularly
contemporary British.
Tudor House Museum - Southampton
Tudor mansion - historical
antiquarian exhibits.
Westgate Museum - Winchester
Mediaeval West Gate - exhibition
illustrating history of Winchester,
collection of weights & measures from
mediaeval time onwards.
Winchester Cathedral Treasury -
Winchester
Silver from churches & parishes, etc.
in Hampshire.
Winchester College Museum -
Winchester
English Watercolours - collections of
Greek pottery.
Museum of the Iron Age - Andover
Comprehensive view of Iron Age culture
& society

Historic Monuments

Bishop Waltham's Palace - Bishops
Waltham
12th & 15th centuries. Flint ruins of the
palace of the Bishops of Winchester.
Basing House - Nr. Basingstoke
16th century - ruined Tudor palace -

originally Saxon fortress, then
Norman Castle.
 Porchester Castle - Porchester
4th century - Saxon fort, 12th century
keep & Assheton's tower, 1368.
Netley Abbey - Nr. Hamble
13th century - remains of
Cistercian abbey.
Hurst Castle - Nr. Milford-on-Sea
Fortress built for Henry VIII - restored in
1800's.
Mary Rose Museum - Portsmouth
Almost complete Tudor Warship.
Flagship of Henry VIII. Thousands of
artifacts from the wreck including
complete ship's surgeon's implements &
the largest collection of Tudor arrows in
the world. Possibly the most important
archaeological discovery of this century.
Rockbourne Roman Villa - Nr.
Fordingbridge
Mosaics & museum.

Other things to see & do

Cholderton Rare Breeds Farm -
Cholderton
Hillier Arboretum - Nr. Romsey
World famous collection of hardy, woody
plants.
The Needles Old Battery - Isle of Wight
Former fort built 1862, 250 feet above sea
level. Tunnel to spectacular view of
the Needles.
New Forest Museum & Visitor Centre -
Lyndhurst
Displays & information
Queen Elizabeth Country Park - Nr.
Petersfield
Forest drive & walking, ponytrekking,
grass - skiing
Mid-Hants Railway - "The Watercress
Line"
Alresford station to Alton. 10 miles of
steam railway.

HAMPSHIRE
Map reference

1 Pritchard
2 Witt
3 Taylor
4 Harris
5 Cadman
6 Ratcliffe
6 Hill
6 Watts
7 Duckworth
9 Skelton
10 Poulter
11 Watling
12 Harris
13 Jenner
14 Blatter
14 Gallagher
14 Cutmore
15 Baigent

16 Nixon
17 Hughes
18 Humphryes
19 Chivers
20 Talbot
22 Farrell
23 Coombe

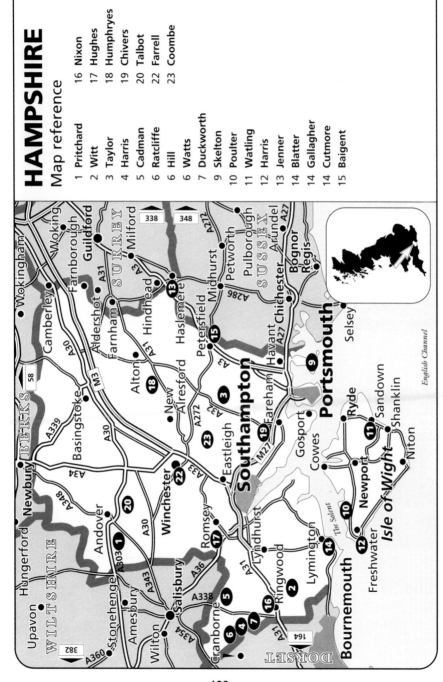

English Channel

199

Abbotts Law.   Abbotts Ann.

Hampshire

minimum £ per person / children taken / evening meals / animals taken

		minimum £ per person	children taken	evening meals	animals taken
David & Judith Pritchard **Abbotts Law** **Abbotts Ann** **Andover** **SP11 7DW** **Tel: (0264) 710350** **Open: APR-OCT** **Map Ref No. 01**	Nearest Road: A.303 A delightful country house in a picturesque village, set in 3 acres of grounds. 3 extremely attractive, large bedrooms with private facilities, colour T.V. & tea/coffee makers. 1 single room suitable for child over 10 years. Log fires & excellent cuisine. Judith is a Cordon Bleu cook & uses fresh garden produce. Heated pool, tennis court, croquet & sauna. Fishing arranged on the Test & Avon. An ideal stop on route from London to the West Country & for exploring Wessex.	£21.00 *see PHOTO over*	Y	Y	N
P. Buckley & W. Witt **Tothill House** **Forest Rd** **Bransgore** **Christchurch BH23 8DZ** **Tel: (0425) 74414** **Open: ALL YEAR** **Map Ref No. 02**	Nearest Road: A.35 Edwardian Country House set in 12 acres of woodland. An area of outstanding natural beauty noted for its flora & fauna. 5 minutes from Burley village, a popular New Forest tourist attraction. Offering good food, 3 attractive en-suite rooms individually decorated with T.V. & tea making facilities. Very secluded with peace & tranquility. Local sporting & recreational activities & a variety of places to visit.	£25.00	Y	N	N
Rosemary Taylor **Moortown Farm** **Soberton** **Droxford SO3 1QU** **Tel: (0489) 877256** **Open: ALL YEAR** **Map Ref No. 03**	Nearest Road: A.32 A friendly atmosphere is found at Moortown in the heart of the Meon Valley just by the Wayfarers Walk. Offering 2 rooms with radio, T.V. & tea & coffee making facilities. Situated in a peaceful village within easy reach of areas of outstanding beauty & historical interest such as Winchester, ancient capital of Wessex & home of King Arthur's Round Table, Portsmouth & The Mary Rose & Nelson's Flagship, Chichester & the New Forest.	£15.00	Y	N	N
Mrs Jean Harris **Colt Green** **North End** **Damerham** **Fordingbridge SP6 3HA** **Tel: (07253) 240** **Open: ALL YEAR** **Map Ref No. 04**	Nearest Road: A.354, A.338 Built by our parents for their comfort & pleasure in retirement, Colt Green blends into its peaceful surrounding acre of gardens, & looks out across its own stretch of river to meadows beyond. Rest for the traveller, peace for the soul & food for the hungry. 3 charming rooms, 1 en-suite. Also lots to see & do: the New Forest & South Coast, Salisbury, famous antiquities, great houses & gardens, 3 theatres. Sketch map showing above & more, & brochure, on request.	£16.00	Y	Y	Y
Mrs G. Cadman **Cottage Crest** **Castle Hill** **Woodgreen** **Fordingbridge SP6 2AX** **Tel: (0725) 22009** **Open: ALL YEAR** **Map Ref No. 05**	Nearest Road: A.338 Woodgreen, a typical New Forest village with cottages surrounded by thick hedges to keep out the cattle & ponies. Cottage Crest is a Victorian Drover's Cottage set high in its own 4 acres enjoying superb views of the River Avon & the valley below. Bedrooms are spacious, decorated to a very high standard, all with private bathroom/shower & w.c. An ideal base from which to tour this lovely area.	£18.00	Y	N	N

Shearings. Rockbourne.

Hampshire

		minimum £ per person	children taken	evening meals	animals taken
Mrs P.A. Ratcliffe **Hendley House** **Rockbourne** **Fordingbridge SP6 3NA** **Tel/Fax: (07253) 303** **Open: FEB - NOV** **Map Ref No. 06**	Nearest Road: A.338, A.354 Beautiful south-facing 16th century Grade II listed house with later addition, on the edge of the village overlooking a water meadow & farmland. 2 charming bedrooms, 1 twin with en-suite shower etc. & 1 double with private bathroom, in a very relaxing family home with oak beams & log fires. Spacious garden with heated swimming pool. Children over 10 .	£22.00	Y	N	N
Mrs P. H. Hill **Priory Cottage** **Rockbourne** **Fordingbridge SP6 3NA** **Tel: (07253) 246** **Open: ALL YEAR** **Map Ref No. 06**	Nearest Road: A.354, A.338 A charming house offering 3 delightful, comfortable rooms for guests. Mrs. Hill is well known for her hospitality & the house is very popular. Situated in a lovely village, it is an ideal base for visiting the numerous stately homes, museums & beauty spots in the surrounding area. Evening meals are also available, offering good cooking & home produce. Children over 12 years.	£17.00	Y	Y	N
Brigadier & Mrs A.C. Watts **Shearings** **Rockbourne** **Fordingbridge** **SP6 3NA** **Tel: (07253) 256** **Open: Mid FEB - Mid DEC** **Map Ref No. 06**	Nearest Road: A.354, A.338 Shearings is a much-photographed, warm, comfortable, exceptionally picturesque 16th century listed timber-framed thatched cottage. Located beside a stream in one of the prettiest villages in Hampshire, on the edge of the New Forest. The oak beams, some nearly 1000 years old, & inglenook fireplaces lend 'olde worlde' charm. The bedrooms have their own bath or shower & are prettily furnished every comfort in mind. A lovely sitting room is available for guests where they can relax with colour T.V. Children over 12 welcome.	£21.00 *see PHOTO over*	Y	Y	N
Mr & Mrs G Duckworth **Weir Cottage** **Bickton** **Fordingbridge** **SP6 2HA** **Tel: (0425) 655813** **Open: ALL YEAR** **Map Ref No. 07**	Nearest Road: A.338 Bickton is a tiny hamlet on the River Avon half a mile from the New Forest & 30 mins. from Salisbury, Bournemouth & Southampton. 200 year-old Weir Cottage offers 2 comfortable double rooms, each with private bathroom, & attractive views as you breakfast in the splendid upstairs beamed living room overlooking the river as it flows under the mill. The Garden Room, with colour T.V., leads out into the secluded terraced garden. 2 pianos available on request.	£18.00	Y	Y	N
David & Diane Skelton **Cockle Warren Hotel** **36 Seafront** **Hayling Island** **Havant PO11 9HL** **Tel:(0705) 464961/464838** **Open: ALL YEAR** **Map Ref No. 09**	Nearest Road: M.27, A.3 A delightful cottage hotel on Hayling seafront set in a large garden with hens & ducks & white picket fencing. Lovely en-suite bedrooms facing out to sea or overlooking the swimming pool, all with colour T.V., phones, etc. Some with 4-poster & Victorian beds. Enjoy French & English country cooking with home-made bread & French wine, & relax by the open log fire to the sound of the sea just a few yards away. National Award Winners.	£25.00 *see PHOTO over* CREDIT CARD VISA M'CARD	Y	Y	Y

203

Cockle Warren Cottage Hotel.   Hayling Island.

Hampshire

	minimum £ per person	children taken	evening meals	animals taken

Mrs Sylvia Poulter
'Quinces'
Cranmore Avenue
Yarmouth
Isle of Wight PO41 OXS
Tel: (0983) 760080
Open: ALL YEAR
Map Ref No. 10

Nearest Road: A.3054
An attractive modern house, centrally heated throughout, peacefully set between a vineyard & a dairy farm, on a private road 2 miles from Yarmouth. There are 2 delightful bedrooms with tea/coffee making facilities. Available to guests is a comfortable living room with colour T.V. & log fires in season. We offer an ideal base for exploring the lovely & varied countryside & coastline of the West Wight.

£14.00 | Y | N | Y (non-smoking)

Geraldine Watling
The Grange Country Hotel
Alverstone
Sandown
Isle of Wight PO36 0EZ
Tel: (0983) 403729
Open: FEB-NOV
Map Ref No. 11

Nearest Road: A.3056
Enjoy a peaceful stay at "The Grange". Set in a large garden beneath the Downs, it is ideally situated for all aspects of the island. A nature trail passes through the village, & sandy beaches just 2 miles away. The 7 bedrooms have en-suite facilities, the house is centrally heated & there is a comfortable lounge with log fire. Traditional English breakfast is served to start the day, & an excellent, varied menu for evening meals.

£18.50 | Y | Y | Y | CREDIT CARD AMEX

The Harris Family
The Nodes Country Hotel
Alum Bay Old Road
Totland Bay
Isle of Wight PO39 OHZ
Tel: (0983) 752859
Fax 0705 201621
Open: ALL YEAR
Map Ref No. 12

Nearest Road: B.3322
Set in two & a half acres of grounds at the foot of Tennyson Downs, this lovely old country house hotel offers 11 charming bedrooms with en-suite facilities, tea/coffee makers, radio & baby listening service. There are beautiful walks & views all around the hotel & the nearby beaches are superb. Some facilities of this delightful hotel are: Courtyard bar, T.V. lounge, log fires, badminton, table tennis, swings, etc.

£20.00 | Y | Y | Y | CREDIT CARD VISA M'CARD

Jim & Angela Jenner
The Bailiff's Cottage
Home Farm
Hollycombe
Liphook GU30 7LR
Tel: (0428) 722171
Open: ALL YEAR
Map Ref No. 13

Nearest Road: A.3
A really welcoming peaceful haven on a sheep/arable farm near the Hants/Sussex border. This 300 year-old tile-hung cottage offers 1 double/twin & 1 single room (extra child bed or cot available). Attractively furnished dining room & lounge, T.V., log fire & central heating. Lovely views & walks. 1 & a quarter hours to Gatwick or Heathrow. Chichester, Guilford, Portsmouth, Farnham & Goodwood within 25 miles.

£14.75 | Y | N | N

Mrs Ann Blatter
14 Captains Row
Lymington
SO41 9RP
Tel: (0590) 671937
Open: APR - OCT
Map Ref No. 14

Nearest Road: M.27
Built in 1790, this is a delightful Georgian property where the congenial host offers superb accommodation in 2 charming & elegantly furnished bedrooms, each with private bathroom. Both are well equipped & have tea/coffee making facilities. Guests may relax in the very pretty gardenwhich is an outstanding feature of this property. An ideal spot for touring.

£13.50 | N | N | N (non-smoking)

205

Hampshire

		minimum £ per person	children taken	evening meals	animals taken

Wendy M. Gallagher **Albany House** **Highfield** **Lymington** **BH24 1LE** **Tel: (0590) 671900** **OpenALL YEAR (Excl.Xmas)** **Map Ref No. 14**	Nearest Road: A.337 This fine Regency house built in 1842 provides a warm welcoming atmosphere in a traditionally furnished home. There are views over the town of Solent & the Isle of Wight . Accommodation is in 5 very comfortably furnished bedrooms, most with private or en-suite facilities, colour T.V. & tea/coffee makers. Delicious meals are served in the elegant dining room using freshly prepared ingredients. In season, shellfish & New Forest game will be provided.	£18.50	Y	Y	Y
Jennifer & Peter Cutmore **Wheatsheaf House** **Gosport Street** **Lymington** **SO41 9BG** **Tel: (0590) 679208** **Open: ALL YEAR** **Map Ref No. 14**	Nearest Road: A.337 A beautifully appointed early 17th century former tavern, Wheatsheaf House is close to the centre of this charming Georgian market town & only 3 minutes' walk from the historic town quay. Tea/ coffee available on request in choice of 4 large comfortable rooms with either en-suite or private facilities. Ideally placed for sailing, the New Forest & touring the whole region, you are assured of a warm welcome. Self-catering accommodation also available.	£18.00	Y	N	Y
Mrs G. W. Baigent **Trotton Farm** **Trotton, Rogate** **Petersfield GU31 5EN** **Tel: (0730) 813618** **Fax 0730 816093** **Open: ALL YEAR** **Map Ref No. 15**	Nearest Road: A.272 This charming home set in 200 acres of farmland offers comfortable accommodation in 2 twin bedded rooms with en-suite shower & 1 single room. All have modern amenities including tea/ coffee making facilities. A residents' lounge is available throughout the day. Games room & pretty garden for guests' relaxation. Ideally situated for visiting many local, historical, sporting attractions. 1 hour from Gatwick & Heathrow.	£17.50	Y	N	N
Mrs Yvonne Nixon **The Nest** **10 Middle Lane** **Ringwood** **BH24 1LE** **Tel: (0425) 476724** **Open: ALL YEAR** **Map Ref No. 16**	Nearest Road: A.31, B.3347 Charming Victorian family home, offering high standard of character accommodation. Quietly situated close to the centre of this riverside market town. Ideal base for exploring New Forest, River Avon fishing & South Coast beaches. Bournemouth, Salisbury & Southampton nearby. The "Laura Ashley" style rooms are fresh & comfortable with hand basins, tea/coffee facilities & colour T.V. Breakfast is served in delightful conservatory overlooking the garden. Parking .	£15.00	Y	N	N
Anthea Hughes **Spursholt House** **Salisbury Rd** **Romsey** **SO51 6DJ** **Tel: (0794) 512229** **Fax 0794 523142** **Open: ALL YEAR** **Map Ref No. 17**	Nearest Road: A.27 Spursholt House dates from the 17th Century, with Victorian extensions for Lord Palmerston. The gardens extend to 2 acres, with paved terraces, topiary, a parterre & roses. Rooms are furnished with antiques, & bedrooms are spacious & panelled with large beds. The sitting room, available at all times, is super, with knole sofas, T.V. & telephone in hall. Coffee/tea facilities. Excellent touring area, equidistant Winchester, Salisbury & New Forest.	£12.50	Y	N	Y

Hampshire

		per person minimum £	children taken	evening meals	animals taken
Mrs A. Humphryes **Belmont House** **Gilbert Street** **Ropley SO24 0BY** **Tel: (0962) 772344** **Open: ALL YEAR** **(Excl. Xmas/Easter)** **Map Ref No. 18**	Nearest Road: A.31 Belmont, dating back to the 19th century, is situated on a quiet country lane, set in an acre of beautiful garden with rural views from the house. Offering 1 bedroom with private facilities, T.V. & tea/coffee makers. Short walk to village with ancient church, shop & 3 pubs. Within easy reach of Petersfield, Salisbury & Winchester by car. Appox. 1 hour from London airports.	£17.00	N	N	N
Mrs Y.M. Chivers **Montrose** **Solomons Lane** **Shirrell Heath** **Wickham SO3 2HU** **Tel: (0329) 833345** **Open: ALL YEAR** **Map Ref No. 19**	Nearest Road: B.2177, A.32 Montrose offers accommodation of a high standard in tasteful surroundings. 3 delightful bedrooms, 1 en-suite. Comfort & personal attention has helped to build a superb reputation. Situated in the Meon Valley between the historical villages of Wickham & Bishops Waltham, yet close to the M.27, M.3 & continental ferry ports, thus providing an ideal base for exploring the towns of Winchester, Portsmouth & Southampton & the lovely Haampshire countryside & coastline.	£17.50	N	N	N
Mr & Mrs J. R. Talbot **Church Farm** **Barton Stacey** **Winchester SO21 3RR** **Tel: (0962) 760268** **Open: ALL YEAR** **Map Ref No. 20**	Nearest Road: A.303, A.34 Church Farm is a 15th century tythe barn, having Georgian & modern additions. Adjacent coach house & groom's cottage, recently converted, where guests may be totally self-contained or be welcomed to the log-fired family drawing room to dine on locally produced fresh food. 7 beautiful bedrooms for guests, most with en-suite, T.V., tea/coffee making facilities. Horses are kept. Swimming pool & croquet. Tennis court adjacent.	£27.00 CREDIT CARD VISA AMEX	Y	Y	Y
Ann & Tony Farrell **The Farrells** **5 Ranelagh Road** **St Cross** **Winchester SO23 9TA** **Tel: (0962) 869555** **Open: ALL YEAR** **Map Ref No. 22**	Nearest Road: A.33, M.3 A friendly atmosphere & warm welcome are found at number 5. A pleasant Victorian house retaining many of its original features. Accommodation is in 3 comfortable rooms, 1 double, 1 twin & 1 family room, with modern amenities & tea/coffee making. There is a T.V. lounge for guests to use. A lovely home, conveniently located, only 15 minutes' walk from the Cathedral. An ideal spot for touring.	£15.50	Y	N	N
Mrs M. J. Coombe **Yew Tree Cottage** **Lower Baybridge Lane** **Baybridge** **Winchester** **SO21 1JN** **Tel: (0962) 777254** **Open: ALL YEAR** **Map Ref No. 23**	Nearest Road: M.3 Charming 17th century thatched cottage with inglenook fireplace, log fires & antique furniture. There is a lovely cottage garden set in quiet countryside yet only 6 miles from Winchester. Accommodation is in 2 pretty bedrooms, 1 with private facilities, T.V., 'phone, radio & tea/coffee makers. Sitting room. Only 1 room is let unless to a family or party of friends, ensuring complete privacy. Superb dinner is served in a typical country setting. A delightful home.	£19.00	Y	Y	N

All the establishments mentioned in this guide
are members of the
Worldwide Bed & Breakfast Association.

If you have any comments regarding your
accommodation please send them to us
using the form at the back of the book.
We value your comments.

Hereford & Worcester

Hereford & Worcester
(Heart of England)

Hereford is a beautiful ancient city standing on the banks of the River Wye, almost a crossing point between England & Wales. It is a market centre for the Marches, the border area which has a very particular history of its own.

Hereford Cathedral has a massive sandstone tower & is a fitting venue for the Three Choirs festival which dates from 1727, taking place yearly in one or the other of the three great cathedrals of Hereford, Worcester & Gloucester.

The country is fortunate in having many well preserved historic buildings. Charming "black & white" villages abound here, romantically set in a soft green landscape.

The Royal Forest of Dean spreads its oak & beech trees over 22,000 acres. When people first made their homes in the woodlands it was vaster still. There are rich deposits of coal & iron mined for centuries by the foresters, & the trees have always been felled for charcoal. Ancient courts still exist where forest dwellers can & do claim their rights to use the forest's resources.

The landscape alters dramatically as the land rises to merge with the great Black Mountain range at heights of over 2,600 feet. It is not possible to take cars everywhere but a narrow mountain road, Gospel Pass, takes traffic from Hay-on-Wye to Llanthony with superb views of the upper Wye Valley.

The Pre-Cambrian Malvern Hills form a natural boundary between Herefordshire & Worcestershire & from the highest view points you can see over 14 counties. At their feet nestle pretty little villages such as Eastonor with its 19th century castle in revived Norman style that looks quite mediaeval amongst the parklands & gardens.

There are, in fact, five Malverns. The largest predictably known as Great

Malvern was a fashionable 19th century spa & is noted for the purity of the water which is bottled & sold countrywide.

The Priory at Malvern is rich in 15th century stained glass & has a fine collection of mediaeval tiles made locally. William Langland, the 14th century author of "Piers Ploughman", was educated at the Priory & is said to have been sleeping on the Malvern Hills when he had the visionary experience which led to the creation of the poem. Sir Edward Elgar was born, lived & worked here & his "Dream of Gerontius" had its first performance in Hereford Cathedral in 1902.

In Worcestershire another glorious cathedral, with what remains of its monastic buildings, founded in the 11th century, stands beside the River Severn. College Close in Worcester is a lovely group of buildings carefully preserved & very English in character.

The Severn appears to be a very lazy waterway but flood waters can reach astonshing heights, & the "Severn Bore" is a famous phenomenon.

A cruise along the river is a pleasant way to spend a day seeing villages & churches from a different perspective, possibly visiting a riverside inn. To the south of the county lie the undulating Vales of Evesham & Broadway - described as the show village of England.

The Malvern Hills.

Hereford & Worcester

Hereford & Worcester Gazeteer

Areas of outstanding natural beauty.
The Malvern Hills, The Cotswolds, The Wye Valley

Historic Houses & Castles

Berrington Hall - Leominster
18th century - painted & plastered ceilings. Landscape by Capability Brown.
Brilley - Cwmmau Farmhouse - Whitney-on-Wye
17th century timber-framed & stone tiled farmhouse.
Burton Court - Eardisland
14th century great hall. Exhibition of European & Oriental costume & curios. Model fairground.
Croft Castle - Nr. Leominster
Castle on the Welsh border - inhabited by Croft family for 900 years.
Dinmore Manor - Nr. Hereford
14th century chapel & cloister.
Eastnor Castle - Nr. Ledbury
19th century - Castellated, containing pictures & armour. Arboretum.
Eye Manor - Leominster
17th century Carolean Manor house - excellent plasterwork, paintings, costumes, books, secret passage. Collection of dolls.
Hanbury Hall - Nr. Droitwich
18th century red brick house - only two rooms & painted ceilings on exhibition.
Harvington Hall - Kidderminster
Tudor Manor house with moat, priest's hiding places.
The Greyfriars - Worcester
15th century timber-framed building adjoins Franciscan Priory.
Hellen's - Much Marcle
13th century manorial house of brick & stone. Contains the Great hall with stone table - bedroom of Queen Mary. Much of the original furnishings remain.
Kentchurch Court - Hereford
14th century fortified border Manor house. Paintings & Carvings by Grinling Gibbons.
Moccas Court - Moccas
18th century - designed by Adam - Parklands by Capability Brown - under restoration.

Pembridge Castle - Welsh Newton
17th century moated castle.
Sutton Court - Mordiford
Palladian mansion by Wyatt, watercolours, embroideries, china.

Cathedrals & Churches

Amestry (St. John the Baptist & St.Alkmund)
16th century rood screen.
Abbey Dore (St. Mary & Holy Trinity)
17th century glass & great oak screen - early English architecture.
Brinsop (St. George)
14th century, screen & glass, alabaster reredos, windows in memory of Wordsworth, carved Norman tympanum.
Bredon (St. Giles)
12th century - central tower & spire. Mediaeval heraldic tiles, tombs & early glass.
Brockhampton (St. Eadburgh)
1902. Central tower & thatched roof.
Castle Frome (St. Michael & All Angles)
12th century carved font, 17th century effigies in alabaster.
Chaddesley Corbett (St. Cassian)
14th century monuments, 12th century font.
Elmley (St. Mary)
12th century & 15th century font, tower, gargoyles, mediaeval.
Great Witley (St. Michael)
Baroque - Plasterwork, painted ceiling, painted glass, very fine example.
Hereford (All Saints)
13th-14th centuries, spire, splendid choir stalls, chained library.
Hereford Cathedral
Small cathedral - fine central tower c.1325, splendid porch, brasses, early English Lady Chapel with lancet windows. Red sandstone.
Kilpeck (St. Mary & St. David)
Romanesque style - mediaeval windows - fine carvings.
Leominster (St. Peter & St. Paul)
12th century doorway, fine Norman arches, decorated windows.
Much Marcle (St. Bartholomew)
13th century. 14th & 17th century monuments.

Hereford & Worcester

Worcester Cathedral
11th-16th century. Fine cloisters & crypt.
Tomb of King John.
Worcester (St. Swithun)
18th century - furnishings untouched.
Ceiling vaulted in plaster.

Museums & Galleries

Hereford City Museum & Art Gallery
Collections of natural history &
archeology, costumes, textiles,
embroideries, toys, agricultural bygones.
Paintings by local artists, examples of
applied art, silver, pottery & porcelain.
The Old House - Hereford
Jacobean period museum with furnishings
of time.
Churchill Gardens Museum - Hereford
Extensive costume collection, fine
furniture, work by local artists.
Almonry Museum - Evesham
Anglo-British, Roman-British, mediaeval &
monastic remains.

Avoncroft Museum of Buildings - Stoke
Heath
Open air museum showing buildings of
reconstructed iron-age dwelling to 15th
century merchant's homes.
City Museum & Art Gallery - Worcester
Local history, archaeology, natural
history, environmental studies.
**Dyson Perins Museums of Worcester
Porcelain** - Worcester
Most comprehensive collection of old
Worcester in the world.
The Commandery - Sidbury
15th century timber-framed building, was
originally a hospital. Royalist H.Q. during
Battle of Worcester 1651.

Other things to see & do

Three Choirs Festival - an annual event,
held in the cathedrals of Hereford,
Worcester & Gloucestershire, alternately.

The River Severn at Bewdley.

HEREFORD & WORCESTER

Map reference

1. Jancey
2. Lee
3. Barrell
4. Hart
5. Fothergill
6. Carter
7. Van Gelderen
7. Williams
8. Denne
10. Blunt
11. Webb
12. Meekings
13. Page
14. Chugg
15. Dean
16. Stringer
17. Teuma
18. Keel
19. Dunand
20. Neath

Herefordshire

	Nearest Road	minimum £ per person	children taken	evening meals	animals taken
Mr & Mrs W.A. Jancey **Bredwardine Hall** **Bredwardine** **Hereford** **HR3 6DB** **Tel: (0981) 500596** **Open: MAR - OCT** **Map Ref No. 01**	Nearest Road: A.438 A charming 19th century manor house with immense character and literary interest standing in secluded wooded gardens, providing elegant and well-appointed accommodation. 5 delightful bedrooms; spacious en-suite bathrooms; full central heating; tea/coffee facilities; colour T.V.s; ample parking. Excellent food and wine; relaxed, friendly atmosphere; personal service. Set in the tranquil, picturesque Wye Valley, near Hay-on-Wye and its world-famous bookshops.	£21.00	N	Y	N
Mrs Gladys W. Lee **Cwm Craig Farm** **Little Dewchurch** **Hereford HR2 6PS** **Tel: (0432) 840250** **Open: ALL YEAR** **Map Ref No. 02**	Nearest Road: A.49 Spacious Georgian farmhouse, surrounded by superb unspoilt countryside. Situated between the Cathedral city of Hereford & Ross-on-Wye, just a few minutes' drive from the Wye Valley. Ideal base for touring the Forest of Dean. All 3 bedrooms have modern amenities, shaver points & tea/coffee facilities. There is a lounge & separated dining room both with colour T.V. A full English breakfast is served.	£13.00	Y	N	N
Mrs Marjorie Barrell **Orchard Farm** **Mordiford** **Hereford HR1 4EJ** **Tel: (0432) 870253** **Open: ALL YEAR** **Map Ref No. 03**	Nearest Road: A.438, B.4224 You will be made very welcome at this delightful 17th century stone-built farmhouse, with large natural garden & superb views, in the Wye Valley Area of Outstanding Natural Beauty. Guests return for the tranquillity & the imaginative traditional & Cordon Bleu food. 3 cosy bedrooms, furnished with period furniture and antiques, have tea-trays and wash basins. 2 guest bathrooms (1 can be private). Licenced. Children over 10. CREDIT CARD AMEX	£15.00	Y	Y	N
Mrs Carol Hart **The Bowens Country House** **Fownhope** **Hereford HR1 4PS** **Tel: (0432) 860430** **Open: ALL YEAR** **Map Ref No. 04**	Nearest Road: M.50 A delightful early Georgian, 17th century farmhouse, offering accommodation in 12 well furnished rooms, 7 en-suite, 3 with super, king-size beds. 4 ground floor rooms suitable for disabled guests. Each has colour T.V. & tea trays. Good home cooking using fresh local produce. Vegetarian meals available. Grass tennis court & putting green. Set in a lovely village with lovely views & walks. Within easy reach of Iron Age hill forts, Capler Hill & Cherry Hill. CREDIT CARD VISA M'CARD	£19.50	Y	Y	Y
C & M Fothergill **'Highfield'** **Newtown** **Ivington Road** **Leominster HR6 8QD** **Tel: (0568) 613216** **Open: ALL YEAR** **Map Ref No. 05**	Nearest Road: A.44, A.49 Twins Catherine & Marguerite are eager to make you feel welcome & at home in their elegant Edwardian house in a rural tranquil location. You will be very comfortable in any of the 3 attractive bedrooms all with a bathroom (one being en-suite). There is a large garden, T.V. lounge with crackling fire & the home-made food is absolutely delicious. Residential licence.	£18.50	N	Y	N

Herefordshire

		minimum £ per person	children taken	evening meals	animals taken
Mrs Mary Carter **Kimbolton Court** **Kimbolton** **Leominster HR6 8QD** **Tel: (056887) 259** **Open: ALL YEAR** **(Excl.Xmas/ New Year)** **Map Ref No. 06**	Nearest Road: A.4112, A.49 In a tranquil rural setting, down a lane going nowhere, through a shallow ford & into an old farmyard where you can be assured of a warm welcome at this stone-built farmhouse. 2 double/ twin en-suite rooms, tea/coffee making facilities, radio & colour T.V. Large lounge with small library, T.V. & wood-burning stove. Garden room for Cordon Bleu meals & otherwise overlooks patio & lawns. Special diets. Natural springs provide the water supply.	£17.50	Y	Y	N
Renate van Gelderen **Edde Cross House** **Edde Cross Street** **Ross-on-Wye** **HR9 7BZ** **Tel: (0989) 65088** **Open: FEB - NOV** **Map Ref No. 07**	Nearest Road: A.49, A.40 Edde Cross House, once the home of Sybil the Dame of Sark, is a Georgian town house of great charm & character overlooking the river. Offering 5 beautifully decorated & comfortable furnished bedrooms. 2 en-suite, each with tea/ coffee makers, colour T.V. & hairdryer. Extensive breakfast menu including vegetarian. This is an ideal base from which to explore the Wye Valley & Forest of Dean. Children over 10.	£18.00	Y	N	N
Jeanne & Mike Denne **Peterstow Country House** **Peterstow** **Ross-on-Wye HR9 6LB** **Tel: (0989) 62826** **Fax 0989 67264** **Open: ALL YEAR** **Map Ref No. 08**	Nearest Road: A.49, M.50 Peterstow House is a magnificent Georgian rectory set in 25 acres of pastures, woodlands & paddocks. 9 bedrooms with private facilities, telephone, radio, T.V. & tea/coffee makers. Fishing, clay pigeon shooting & pony trekking in the Forest of Dean available. Within the grounds of Peterstow lies The Flann Farmhouse where the fresh produce used in the restaurant is grown. An excellent base, with Hereford, Monmouth, Gloucester & Chepstow close by. Children over 7 welcome. CREDIT CARD VISA M'CARD AMEX	£25.00	N	Y	N
Peggy & Geoff Williams **Sunnymount Hotel** **Ryefield Road** **Ross-on-Wye** **HR9 5LU** **Tel: (0989) 63880** **Open: ALL YEAR** **Map Ref No. 07**	Nearest Road: M.50, A.40 Quietly situated on the edge of the town, this attractive Edwardian house is warm & inviting. Offering 9 well appointed bedrooms, 6 en-suite, all with tea/coffee facilities. The sitting rooms (1 with colour T.V.) & dining room overlook the pretty garden. Wide choice of breakfasts using home & local produce freshly prepared for each meal. English/French cooking. Licensed. Ample private parking. An ideal base from which to explore this fascinating area. CREDIT CARD VISA M'CARD AMEX	£20.00	Y	Y	N
Val & Tony Blunt **Woodlea Hotel** **Symonds Yat West** **Ross-on-Wye** **HR9 6BL** **Tel: (0600) 890206** **Open: Mid FEB - DEC** **Map Ref No. 10**	Nearest Road: A.40 A delightful family-owned Victorian guest house, set amid glorious scenery with wonderful valley views. The house has a privileged position & overlooks the famous Wye Rapids. It offers 9 rooms, with modern amenities, telephone & radio; most have en-suite facilities. There is a T.V. lounge, reading lounge & lounge bar where guests can relax comfortably with a drink. In the spacious dining room imaginative & delicious meals are served, accompanied by fine wines. CREDIT CARD VISA M'CARD AMEX	£22.50	Y	Y	Y

Leasow House. Broadway.

Herefordshire & Worcestershire

		minimum £ per person	children taken	evening meals	animals taken
Anne & Jack Webb **Queen's House** **Wigmore** **HR6 9UN** **Tel: (056886) 451** **Open: ALL YEAR** **Map Ref No. 11**	Nearest Road: A.4110, A.4113 This 15th century Hall house has, over the years, developed into a comfortable, roomy home. Flagged breakfast hall with inglenook, T.V. lounge, bar lounge, open fires. Comfortable, attractive bedrooms. Licensed cellar restaurant. All rooms beamed. Wonderful relaxed atmosphere. Splendid food. Offa's Dyke, Welsh Border & Ludlow are only 8 miles away.	£14.00	Y	Y	Y

Worcestershire

		minimum £ per person	children taken	evening meals	animals taken
Mrs Barbara Meekings **Leasow House** **Laverton Meadows** **Broadway** **WR12 7NA** **Tel: (0386) 73526** **Fax 0386 73596** **Open: ALL YEAR** **Map Ref No. 12**	Nearest Road: A.46, B.4632 Leasow is a charming 17th century Cotswold stone farmhouse. Recently renovated, it now offers guests a choice of 9 delightful spacious bedrooms, each with shower/bath en-suite, T.V. & tea/coffee making facilities. Set in the peaceful tranquility of the open countryside, it is only two & a half miles from Broadway village. The house has wonderful panoramic views of the Cotswold escarpment. Ideally situated for touring the Cotswolds & the Vale of Evesham. A warm welcome, friendly hosts & comfortable accommodation ensure an enjoyable & memorable stay.	£25.00 *see PHOTO over* CREDIT CARD VISA M'CARD AMEX	Y	N	Y
Frances & Jim Page **Crofton Lodge** **80 New Road** **Bromsgrove B60 2LA** **Tel: (0527) 74136** **Open: ALL YEAR** **Map Ref No. 13**	Nearest Road: A.38, M.5, M.42 Crofton Lodge is an attractive Victorian town house, with a walled garden, built in 1880. 1 double & 1 twin & 1 single room, with coffee & tea making facilities, are available together with a sitting room, with colour T.V., available for guests' use. Stratford, Worcester & Birmingham are within half an hour, the Cotswolds, Malvern Hills, Shropshire & Herefordshire within 1 hrs drive. Leaflet available.	£14.50	Y	N	N

All the establishments mentioned in this guide are members of The Worldwide Bed & Breakfast Association

Church Farm. Oddingley.

Worcestershire

	minimum £ per person	children taken	evening meals	animals taken
Mrs Jacqueline Chugg **Little Lodge Farm** **Broughton Green** **Hanbury** **Droitwich WR9 7EE** **Tel: (0527) 821305** **Open: JAN - NOV** **Map Ref No. 14**	Nearest Road: A.38, B.4090 This charming Grade II listed black & white Tudor farmhouse, once a hunting lodge in the Deer Park of Feckenham Forest, is now surrounded by 330 acres of farmland. A lovely country home with exposed beams, inglenook fireplaces, dried flowers & beautiful fabrics complement the antique furniture. 3 guest bedrooms with en-suite or private bathroom. Home-made bread & preserves. An unusually quiet & scenic spot to stay. Central for Stratford, Worcester & Cotswolds.	£19.00 *see PHOTO over*	Y	N	N
Mrs Anne Dean **Church Farm** **Oddingley** **Droitwich Spa** **WR9 7NE** **Tel: (0905) 772387** **Fax 0905 772387** **Open: ALL YEAR** **Map Ref No. 15**	Nearest Road: M.5, junction 6 A secluded, attractive house set in 230 acres of grounds. Accommodation is in 3 tastefully furnished & comfortable en-suite bedrooms, each with radio & tea/coffee making facilities. Excellent breakfasts & delicious evening meals are available. Vegetarian cuisine by arrangement. Guests may relax in the pleasant lounge or pretty gardens. Conveniently situated, with easy access to the M.5 & the Midlands. Bristol 1 hour, an ideal base for touring.	£20.00 *see PHOTO over*	Y	Y	N
Sue Stringer **Cowleigh Park Farm** **Cowleigh Rd** **Malvern WR13 5HJ** **Tel: (0684) 566750** **Open: ALL YEAR** **Map Ref No. 16**	Nearest Road: A.449, B.4219 Cowleigh Park Farm is a delightful Grade II listed timber farmhouse. This beautifully restored home is peacefully situated at the foot of the Malvern Hills, creating a tranquil setting for a relaxing & friendly stay. Period furnishings throughout, & offering a choice of 3 comfortable rooms, all with en-suite shower rooms or private bathroom & colour T.V.. Guests are welcome to use the attractive gardens. Parking within the grounds.	£20.00 🚭	Y	Y	Y
Rosalind Teuma **The Nupend** **Cradley** **Malvern** **WR13 5NP** **Tel: (0886) 880881** **Open: ALL YEAR** **Map Ref No. 17**	Nearest Road: A.4103 Elegant, Georgian, former farmhouse in grounds of 2 acres in Area of Outstanding Natural Beauty. Ideal for nature lovers, walkers, painters, or as touring base for Welsh Marches, Cotswolds, Wye Valley, Shakespeare country. All 4 bedrooms have views of Malvern Hills, with en-suite bathroom, colour T.V., tea/coffee making facilities. Choice of breakfast, optional 4-course dinner, all freshly cooked in traditional manner using only finest ingredients. Vegetarians catered for.	£20.00 🚭	N	Y	N
Jane Keel **Hunthouse Farm** **Frith Common** **Tenbury Wells** **WR15 8JY** **Tel: (0299) 832277** **Open: MAR - OCT** **Map Ref No. 18**	Nearest Road: A.456, A.443 Relax and enjoy comfort, peace and hospitality in this beautiful, 16th century, timbered farmhouse ideally situated amidst 180 acre arable/sheep farm, commanding memorable views. The 3 comfortable bedrooms are all en-suite with tea-making facilities. There is a colour television in the guest sitting room where guests are welcomed with tea and home-made cake. Excellent local eating houses. Children over 8 please.	£15.00	Y	N	N

Little Lodge Farm. Hanbury.

Worcestershire

	Nearest Road	minimum £ per person	children taken	evening meals	animals taken
Mrs Carolyn Dunand **49 Britannia Square** **Worcester** **WR1 3HP** **Tel: (0905) 22756** **Open: ALL YEAR** **Map Ref No. 19**	Nearest Road: A.38, M.5 Charming home in quiet & pleasant Georgian square near the city centre. Cathedral, Theatre, Royal Worcester Porcelain & many places of historic interest in this 'Faithful City' are within walking distance. An ideal centre for touring. Spacious comfortable rooms all with tea/coffee making facilities & T.V. One double with bathroom en-suite. One twin & one single with shared bathroom. Lovely walled garden & car parking.	£20.00	Y	N	Y
Sally Neath **Church Farm** **Abberley** **Worcester WR6 6BP** **Tel: (0299) 896316** **Fax 0299 896 773** **Open: APR -OCT** **Map Ref No. 20**	Nearest Road: A.443, B.4202 You will find Church Farm 12 miles west of Worcester in a setting that delights visitors, nestling against the backdrop of the Abberley Hills. This is complemented by the attractive, individually decorated bedrooms, all en-suite. Evening meals are no problem as you can stroll from the door across the fields to the village inn. Ideally situated to visit some of England's most beautiful countryside.	£16.00	Y	N	N

All the establishments mentioned in this guide are members of
The Worldwide Bed & Breakfast Association

If you have any comments regarding your accommodation please send them to us using the form at the back of the guide.

Kent

Kent
(South East)

Kent is best known as "the garden of England". At its heart is a tranquil landscape of apple & cherry orchards, hop-fields & oast-houses, but there are also empty downs, chalk sea-cliffs, rich marshlands, sea ports, castles & the glory of Canterbury Cathedral.

The dramatic chalk ridgeway of the North Downs links the White Cliffs of Dover with the north of the county which extends into the edge of London. It was a trade route in ancient times following the high downs above the Weald, dense forest in those days. It can be followed today & it offers broad views of the now agricultural Weald.

The pilgrims who flocked to Canterbury in the 12th-15th centuries, (colourfully portrayed in Chaucer's Canterbury Tales), probably used the path of the Roman Watling Street rather than the high ridgeway.

Canterbury was the cradle of Christianity in southern England & is by tradition the seat of the Primate of All England. This site, on the River Stour, has been settled since the earliest times & became a Saxon stonghold under King Ethelbert of Kent. He established a church here, but it was in Norman times that the first great building work was carried out, to be continued in stages until the 15th century. The result is a blending of styles with early Norman work, a later Norman choir, a vaulted nave in Gothic style & a great tower of Tudor design. Thomas Becket was murdered on the steps of the Cathedral in 1170. The town retains much of its mediaeval character with half-timbered weavers' cottages, old churches & the twin towers of the west gate.

Two main styles of building give the villages of Kent their special character. The Kentish yeoman's house was the home of the wealthier farmers & is found throughout the county. It is a timber-frame building with white lath & plaster walls & a hipped roof of red tiles. Rather more modest in style is a small weatherboard house, usually painted white or cream. Rolvenden & Groombridge have the typical charm of a Kentish village whilst Tunbridge Wells is an attractive town, with a paved parade known as the Pantiles & excellent antique shops.

There are grand houses & castles throughout the county. Leeds Castle stands in a lake & dates back to the 9th century. It has beautifully landscaped parkland. Knowle House is an impressive Jacobean & Tudor Manor House with rough ragstone walls, & acres of deer-park & woodland.

Kent is easily accessible from the Channel Ports, Gatwick & London.

Ightham Mote

Kent

Kent Gazeteer

Areas of outstanding natural beauty.
Kent Downs.

Historic Houses & Castles

Aylesford, The Friars - Nr. Maidstone
13th century Friary & shrine of Our Lady,
(much restored), 14th century
cloisters - original.
Allington Castle -Nr. Maidstone
13th century. One time home of Tudor
poet Thomas Wyatt. Restored early 20th
century. Icons & Renaissance paintings.
Black Charles - Nr. Sevenoaks
14th century Hall house - Tudor
fireplaces, beautiful panelling.
Boughton Monchelsea Place - Nr.
Maidstone
Elizabethan Manor House - grey stone
battlements - 18th century landscaped
park, wonderful views of Weald of Kent.
Chartwell - Westerham
Home of Sir Winston Churchill.
Chiddingstone Castle - Nr. Edenbridge
18th century Gothic revival building
encasing old remains of original Manor
House - Royal Stuart & Jacobite
collection. Ancient Egyptian collection -
Japanese netsuke, etc.
Eyehorne Manor - Hollingbourne
15th century Manor house with 17th
century additions.
Cobham Hall - Cobham
16th century house - Gothic &
Renaissance - Wyatt interior. Now school
for girls.
Fairfield - Eastry, Sandwich
13th-14th centuries - moated castle. Was
home of Anne Boleyn. Beautiful gardens
with unique collection of
classical statuary.
Knole - Sevenoaks
15th century - splendid Jacobean interior -
17th & 18th century furniture. One of the
largest private houses in England.
 Leeds Castle- Nr. Maidstone
Built in middle of the lake, it was the home
of the mediaeval Queens of England.
Lullingstone Castle - Eynsford
14th century mansion house - frequented
by Henry VIII & Queen Anne. Still
occupied by descendants of
original owners.

Long Barn - Sevenoaks
14th century house - said to be home of
William Caxton. Restored by Edwin
Lutyens; 16th century barn added to
enlarge house. Galleried hall - fine
beaming & fireplaces. Lovely gardens
created by Sir Harold Nicholson & his wife
Vita Sackville-West.
Owletts - Cobham
Carolean house of red brick with
plasterwork ceiling & fine staircase.
Owl House - Lamberhurst
16th century cottage, tile hung; said to be
home of wool smuggler.
Charming gardens.
Penshurst Place - Tonbridge
14th century house with mediaeval Great
Hall perfectly preserved.English Gothic.
Birthplace of Elizabethan poet, Sir
Philip Sidney
Fine staterooms, splendid picture gallery,
famous toy museum. Tudor gardens
& orchards.
Saltwood Castle - Nr. Hythe
Mediaeval - very fine castle & is privately
occupied. Was lived in by Sir Ralph de
Broc, murderer of Thomas a Becket.
Squerreys Court - Westerham
Manor house of William & Mary period,
with furniture, paintings & tapestries of
time. Connections with General Wolfe.
Stoneacre - Otham
15th century yeoman's
half-timbered house.

Cathedrals & Churches

Brook (St. Mary)
11th century paintings in this unaltered
early Norman church.
Brookland (St. Augustine)
13th century & some later part. Crown-
post roofs, detached wooden belfry with
conical cap. 12th century lead font.
Canterbury Cathedral
12th century wall paintings, 12th & 13th
century stained glass. Very fine Norman
crypt. Early perpendicular nave &
cloisters which have heraldic bosses.
Wonderful central tower.
Charing (St. Peter & St. Paul)
13th & 15th century interior with 15th
century tower. 17th century restoration.

Kent

Cobham (St. Mary)
16th century carved & painted tombs - unequalled collection of brasses in county.
Elham (St. Mary the Virgin)
Norman wall with 13th century arcades, perpendicular clerestory. Restored by Eden.
Lullingstone (St. Botolph)
14th century mainly - 16th century wood screen. Painted glass monuments.
Newington-on-the-Street (St. Mary the Virgin)
13th & 14th century - fine tower. 13th century tomb. Wall paintings.
Rochester Cathedral
Norman facade & nave, otherwise early English. 12th century west door. 14th century doorway to Chapter room.
Stone (St. Mary)
13th century - decorated - paintings, 15th century brass, 16th century tomb.
Woodchurch (All Saints)
13th century, having late Norman font & priest's brass of 1320. Arcades alternating octagonal & rounded columns. Triple lancets with banded marble shafting at east end.

Museums & Galleries

Royal Museums - Canterbury
Archaeological, geological, mineralogical exhibits, natural history, pottery & porcelain. Engravings, prints & pictures.
Westgate - Canterbury
Museum of armour, etc. in 14th century gatehouse of city.
Dartford District Museum - Dartford
Roman, Saxon & natural history.
Deal Museum - Deal
Prehistoric & historic antiquities.
Dicken's House Museum - Broadstairs
Personalia of Dickens; prints, costume & Victoriana.
Down House - Downe
The home of Charles Darwin for 40 years, now his memorial & museum.
Dover Museum - Dover
Roman pottery, ceramics, coins, zoology, geology, local history, etc.
Faversham Heritage Society -
Faversham
1000 years of history & heritage.
Folkestone Museum & Art Gallery -
Folkestone
Archeology, local history & sciences.

Herne Bay Museum - Herne Bay
Stone, Bronze & Early Iron Age specimens. Roman material from Reculver excavations. Items of local & Kentish interest.
Museum & Art Gallery - Maidstone
16th century manor house exhibiting natural history & archaeolgical collections. Costume Gallery, bygones, ceramics, 17th century works by Dutch & Italian painters. Regimental museum

Historic Monuments

Eynsford Castle - Eynsford
12th century castle remains.
Rochester Castle - Rochester
Storied keep - 1126-39
Roman Fort & Anglo-Saxon Church -
Reculver
Excavated remains of 3rd century fort & Saxon church.
Little Kit's Coty House - Aylesford
Ruins of burial chambers from 2 long barrows.
Lullingstone Roman Villa - Lullingstone
Roman farmstead excavations.
Roman Fort & Town - Richborough
Roman 'Rutupiae' & fort
Tonbridge Castle - Tonbridge
12th century curtain walls, shell of keep & 14th century gatehouse.
Dover Castle - Dover
Keep built by Henry II in 1180. Outer curtain built 13th century.

Gardens

Chilham Castle Gardens - Nr. Canterbury
25 acre gardens of Jacobean house, laid out by Tradescant. Lake garden, fine trees & birds of prey. Jousting & mediaeval banquets.
Great Comp Gardens - Nr. Borough Green
Outstanding 7 acre garden with old brick walls.
Owl House Gardens - Lamberhurst
16th century smugglers cottage with beautiful gardens of roses, daffodils & rhododendrons.
Sissinghurst Castle Gardens - Sissinghurst
Famous gardens created by Vita Sackville-West around the remains of an Elizabethan mansion.

KENT
Map reference

1 Randall
2 Swatland
3 Scrivens
4 Sleigh
5 Dellaway
5 Pellay
5 Jenkins
6 Harper
6 Kirk
7 Wilton
8 Oaten
8 Stearns
9 Alexander
10 Howarth
10 Robbins
10 Oakley
11 Chesterfield
12 Latham
13 S.Coleman
14 Piper
15 Harman

16 Brooks
17 Bannock
18 L.Coleman
19 Earl
20 Dakin
21 Lindsay
22 Holdstock
23 Scott
24 Rawlinson
25 Cole
26 Emanuel
27 Godbold
28 Carrell
28 Dakin

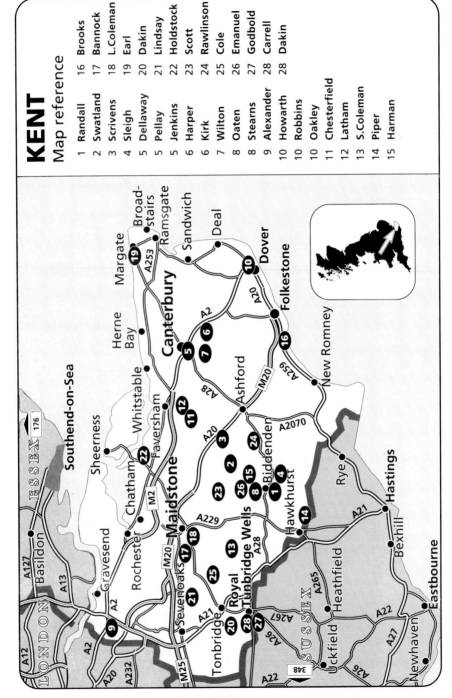

Anns House.   Canterbury.

Kent

		minimum £ per person	children taken	evening meals	animals taken
J & D Randall **Birchley** **Fosten Green Lane** **Biddenden** **Ashford TN27 8DZ** **Tel: (0580) 291413** **Fax 0580 893345** **Open: ALL YEAR** **Map Ref No. 01**	Nearest Road: A.262 Birchley, central for South East England's sights & attractions, is a 1632 timber-framed listed house in a peacefully secluded 6 acre garden with covered, heated swimming pool. There are 3 large, well-equipped en-suite bedrooms are decorated in 'Laura Ashley' style. Welcoming log fires greet you in the oak-panelled sitting room & beamed dining room where a 'very full' English breakfast is served. A 4-course evening meal is available by arrangement. 🚭 CREDIT CARD VISA M'CARD	£18.75	Y	Y	N
Mrs Anne Swatland **Groome Farm** **Newland Green** **Egerton** **Ashford TN27 9EP** **Tel: (023376) 260** **Open: APR - SEPT** **Map Ref No. 02**	Nearest Road: A.20 Groome Farm is a superb 15th century half timbered farmhouse. The rooms are quite delightful; heavily beamed with inglenook fireplaces & decorated with many lovely antiques, creating a charming 'olde worlde' atmosphere. Offering 3 rooms, each with private facilities, a residents' lounge & a fabulous garden. A plantsman's paradise beautifully tended with every kind of herb & shrub. A first class spot for a break. 🚭	£17.00	Y	N	N
Pam & Alan Scrivens **Tram Hatch** **Charing Heath** **Ashford** **TN27 0BN** **Tel: (0233) 713373** **Open: ALL YEAR** **Map Ref No. 03**	Nearest Road: A.20 Tram Hatch is a lovely 14th century manor house, standing in seven & a half acres of grounds including 2 acres of formal gardens, with the River Stour flowing through half a mile. The many original dark oak beams & inglenook fireplaces lend great charm & character to this super house. Now carefully refurbished, the accommodation offered is very spacious & comfortable, with en-suite facilities, one 4-poster bed, T.V. & radio. Guests may also like to use the swimming pool. Close by are Leeds & Chilham castles. 🚭	£19.00 *see PHOTO over*	N	Y	N
Mr & Mrs W.L. Sleigh **Crit Hall** **Cranbrook Road** **Benenden TN17 4EU** **Tel: (0580) 240609** **Fax 0580 241743** **Open: MID JAN-MID DEC** **Map Ref No. 04**	Nearest Road: A.229 Crit Hall is an elegant Georgian house in a peaceful country setting with panoramic Wealden views. Near many N.T. properties & gardens, including Sissinghurst. Lovely twin bedded rooms with either en-suite or private bathrooms. All facilities , R/C T.V., etc. Imaginative dinners/ breakfasts: local produce a feature. Fully licensed. Fine antiques throughout.	£21.50	Y	Y	N
Lisa Dellaway **Anns House** **63 London Road** **Canterbury** **CT2 8JZ** **Tel: (0227) 768767** **Open: ALL YEAR** **Map Ref No. 05**	Nearest Road: A.2 Furnished to a high standard, this delightful Victorian house offers 19 tastefully decorated bedrooms, some with 4 posters, many en-suite with colour T.V. & tea/coffee making facilities (3 on the ground floor). Delicious breakfast menu. Situated only 3 minutes' walk from the city centre, Anns House is an excellent base from which to visit Canterbury Cathedral & many other attractions. Good local pubs & restaurants. Parking. *see PHOTO over* CREDIT CARD VISA M'CARD	£18.00	Y	N	Y

Tram Hatch. Charing Heath.

Kent

	minimum £ per person	children taken	evening meals	animals taken

		minimum £ per person	children taken	evening meals	animals taken
Hilary Harper **East Bridge Country Hotel** **Bridge Hill** **Bridge** **Canterbury CT4 5AS** **Tel: (0227) 830808** **Open: ALL YEAR** **Map Ref No. 06**	Nearest Road: A.2, M.2 A friendly, elegant & comfortable Georgian house in a pretty village. 15 minutes from sea ports of Dover & Folkestone. Overlooking open country-side of outstanding beauty, the house offers accommodation in 8 rooms, 4 en-suite, all with modern amenities, T.V. & tea/coffee making facilities. Ideal for walking, riding, fishing. Close to Kent's historic castles. Tasty English break-fasts served. Licensed restaurant available to residents & non residents.	£20.00 CREDIT CARD VISA M'CARD	Y	Y	N
A. & K. Pellay **Ersham Lodge Hotel** **12 New Dover Road** **Canterbury CT1 3AP** **Tel: (0227) 463174** **Fax 0227 455 482** **Open: JAN-OCT** **Map Ref No. 05**	Nearest Road: A.2, M.2 This well established Tudor Lodge is run profes-sionally to high standards & is furnished with exquisite taste & elegance. Its delightfully ap-pointed bedrooms offer modern amenities, col-our T.V., radio, telephone, hairdryer, en-suite facilities. Public areas include a well stocked bar, a bright breakfast room & a pleasant patio. Er-sham Lodge is a leisurely 5 minute walk from the Cathedral. Parking & lock-up garage.	£23.00 CREDIT CARD VISA M'CARD AMEX	Y	N	N
David & Jill Jenkins **Thanington Hotel** **140 Wincheap** **Canterbury CT1 3RY** **Tel: (0227) 453227** **Open: ALL YEAR** **Map Ref No. 05**	Nearest Road: A.28, A.2 A lovely Georgian (1810) house with pretty walled garden & private courtyard parking. Five minutes' stroll to the city centre & restaurants. 12 mins. to the cathedral. 30 mins. drive to Channel ferry ports. All bedrooms are en-suite & newly deco-rated with modern-day conveniences. Elegant dining room, lounge & snooker room. New indoor heated swimming pool. A warm welcome & efficient service await you at Thanington Hotel.	£22.00 *see PHOTO over* CREDIT CARD VISA M'CARD AMEX	Y	N	Y
Sheila Wilton **Walnut Tree Farm** **Lynsore Bottom** **Upper Hardres** **Canterbury** **CT4 6EG** **Tel: (022787) 375** **Open: ALL YEAR** **Map Ref No. 07**	Nearest Road: A.2 Set in 6 acres of its own land, this delightful 14th century thatched farmhouse offers peace & tran-quility in unspoilt countryside. Offering family accommodation or friends wishing to share, in 2 double adjacent bedrooms with shower rooms en-suite or double en-suite, in dormer of cottage. Good farmhouse breakfast, home-made bread, marmalade, preserves & fresh eggs. Swimming pool. A delightful home, ideal as a base for walking, bird watching & en-route to Continent. Excellent pub food 2 miles away.	£17.00	Y	N	N
Barry & Pleasance Kirk **Wych Elm Guest House** **13 High Street** **Bridge** **Canterbury CT4 5JY** **Tel: (0227) 830242** **Open: ALL YEAR** **Map Ref No. 06**	Nearest Road: A.2, M.2 This pretty Regency house is delightfully situated in the small village of Bridge. Accommodation is in a choice of 3 comfortable rooms with modern amenities, 1 with private shower, all with tea making facilities. A very comfortable lounge/dining room decorated with antiques is available, as is the very attractive walled garden. The food here is delicious. Evening meals are well pre-pared & nicely served along with a complimen-tary glass of wine. Ideal as a base for touring.	£16.00	Y	Y	N

Thanington Hotel. Canterbury.

Kent

	Nearest Road	minimum £ per person	children taken	evening meals	animals taken
Mr & Mrs A.T. R. Oaten **Hancocks Farmhouse** **Tilsden Lane** **Cranbrook** **TN17 3PH** **Tel: (0580) 714645** **Open: ALL YEAR** **Map Ref No. 08**	Nearest Road: A.229. A. 262 Extended in the late 16th century, Hancocks Farmhouse is now a lovely grade II listed building, surrounded by farmland on the edge of the Wealdon town of Cranbrook. Comfortably furnished with antiques, the accommodation is in 3 beautifully decorated bedrooms, 1 with four poster, modern amenities including radio & tea/coffee making facilities. Dinner here is delicious & all the bread, rolls, cakes & jams are home made. A lounge is available & guests may relax in the pretty country garden.	£18.00	Y	Y	Y
James & Pat Stearns **Sissinghurst Castle** **Farm** **Sissinghurst** **Cranbrook TN17 2AB** **Tel: (0580) 712885** **Open: ALL YEAR** **Map Ref No. 08**	Nearest Road: A.262 This Victorian farmhouse is delightfully situated in the grounds of the famous Sissinghurst Castle. All rooms are spacious with beautiful views & have tea making facilities. One bedroom has en-suite facilities & one a private shower. A guests' colour T.V. lounge & garden are available. Evening meals provided by arrangement. Vegetarians can be catered for. This makes a good base for touring the many historic sites of Kent.	£19.50	Y	Y	Y
Mrs Sarah Alexander **Home Farm** **Riverside, Eynsford** **Dartford DA4 0AE** **Tel: (0322) 866193** **Fax 0322 868600** **Open: MAR - NOV** **Map Ref No. 09**	Nearest Road: M.25, M.20 Situated in a picturesque village within an area of outstanding natural beauty. This 18th century farmhouse set on a dairy/arable farm offers 3 attractively furnished en-suite bedrooms. Ideal for London, Gatwick & the Channel ports. Only 2 miles from the M.25/M.20 junction. Leeds Castle, Brands Hatch & many National Trust properties within easy reach. There are many places to eat in the village.	£16.00	Y	N	N
Nona Howarth **Castle Guest House** **10 Castle Hill Road** **Dover CT16 1QW** **Tel: (0304) 201656** **Fax 0304 210197** **Open:ALL YEAR (Excl.** **Xmas & New Year)** **Map Ref No. 10**	Nearest Road: A.2, M.2, A.20, Castle House is situated in the foothills of Dover Castle & is a few minutes from the town centre, ferries & hoverport. Accommodation is in 6 comfortable bedrooms, 4 with private shower, all with modern amenities, including colour T.V. & tea/coffee making facilities. A hearty English or Continental breakfast is served. Residents' lounge available throughout the day. A lovely family guest house with warm & welcoming hosts. No smoking in public rooms.	£14.00 CREDIT CARD VISA M'CARD	Y	N	N
Mr & Mrs L. Robbins **Dell Guest House** **233 Folkestone Road** **Dover CT17 9SL** **Tel: (0304) 202422** **Open: ALL YEAR** **Map Ref No. 10**	Nearest Road: A.20, M.20 A friendly welcome is extended to all guests, together with comfort & cleanliness, at this pleasant Victorian house. Offering a choice of 6 bedrooms with modern facilities. A colour T.V. lounge is also available. The Robbins' serve an English breakfast from 7 a.m.; before then it's Continental so that those catching the early-morning cross-channel ferries get a good early start. Conveniently located close to docks & station. Parking.	£13.50	Y	N	N

Frith Farm House. Otterden.

Kent

	minimum £ per person	children taken	evening meals	animals taken
Mr & Mrs C. P. Oakley **Wallett's Court Manor** **West Cliffe** **St Margarets-at-Cliffe** **Dover CT15 6EW** **Tel: (0304) 852424** **Fax 0304 853430** **OpenALL YEAR(Excl.Xmas)** **Map Ref No. 10**	Nearest Road: A.258, B.2058, A wonderful 17th century manor house, home of William Pitt the Younger, situated in countryside above the White Cliffs of Dover. 7 luxury bedrooms, all en-suite. Oak beams & inglenook fireplaces. True 17th century atmosphere. Homemade produce for breakfast & Saturday is 'Gourmet Evening' in the restaurant. Kingsdown Golf Course close by. A very warm welcome awaits all visitors to this lovely house. A good base for touring the surrounding area.	£25.00 CREDIT CARD VISA M'CARD	Y	Y	N
Mrs Susan Chesterfield **Frith Farm House** **Otterden** **Faversham ME13 0DD** **Tel: (0795) 890701** **Open: ALL YEAR** **Map Ref No. 11**	Nearest Road: A.2, A.20, M.2 A warm welcome awaits guests at this restored Georgian farmhouse, surrounded by lovely cherry trees. It stands in an area of outstanding natural beauty. Accommodation is in a choice of 3 en-suite rooms with radio, T.V. & tea/coffee making facilities. This makes a pleasant base from which to tour the whole of Kent. Leeds Castle, Rochester, Chilam & Canterbury are nearby. Children over 10 years only.	£20.00 🚭 *see PHOTO over*	N	Y	N
Prudence Latham **Tenterden House** **209 The Street** **Boughton** **Faversham ME13 9BL** **Tel: (0227) 751593** **Open: ALL YEAR** **Map Ref No. 12**	Nearest Road: A.2, M.2 Tenterden House is a listed Tudor building in the village of Boughton which is 6 miles from Canterbury, 1 mile from the M.2 & within 5 miles of the coast. The old gardener's cottage has been renovated to provide 2 comfortable bedrooms (1 double & 1 twin) with modern amenities including h&c, T.V. & tea/coffee making facilities. A full English breakfast is served in the main house. An ideal spot for touring.	£15.00	Y	N	N
Mrs S. Coleman **Crowbourne Farmhouse** **Goudhurst** **TN17 1ET** **Tel: (0580) 211226** **Open: FEB - NOV** **Map Ref No. 13**	Nearest Road: A.262 Crowbourne is a delightful 17th century farmhouse in a 125 acre fruit & sheep farm, peacefully situated with glorious views just outside the charming village of Goudhurst. Accommodation is in 3 lovely comfortable rooms with bath (1 en-suite), & sitting room with T.V. & tea/coffee making facilities. Delicious evening meals, using local produce, by arrangement only. Ideal for visiting Kent castles, especially Sissinghurst. Golf, fishing & sailing nearby. Gatwick 1 hour.	£18.00 🚭	Y	Y	N

When booking your accommodation please mention
The Best Bed & Breakfast

Lucy's. Lucy's Hill.

Kent

		minimum £ per person	children taken	evening meals	animals taken

Mrs Rosemary Piper **Conghurst Farm** **Conghurst Lane** **Hawkhurst TN18 4RW** **Tel: (0580) 753331** **Open: FEB-NOV** **Map Ref No. 14**	Nearest Road: A.268, A.229 Conghurst is a 500 acre mixed farm on the Kent/ Sussex border set in beautiful, unspoilt country- side. An excellent holiday base, there are many historic houses & gardens in area; Tunbridge Wells, Rye, Canterbury 1 hour's drive. 3 bed- rooms, all with private bathrooms, radio, tea/ coffee facilities. Separate T.V. & sitting rooms for guests' use. Outdoor swimming pool. Evening meals by prior arrangement.	£17.50	Y	Y	N
Mrs Jane Harman **Vine Farm** **Waterman Quarter** **Headcorn TN27 9JJ** **Tel: (0622) 890203** **Open: MAR - NOV** **Map Ref No. 15**	Nearest Road: A.274, M.20 Charming Kent farmhouse, beamed & full of character, dating back over 400 years. Glorious rural situation along its private drive, surrounded by farmland, ponds & garden. Attractively fur- nished with guest sitting room, T.V. & 3 bed- rooms with private bathrooms & tea/coffee making facilities. Centrally situated in Kent, it is an ideal base for visiting the county's historic sites & gardens. Every comfort & a warm welcome.	£18.50	Y	Y	N
Mrs Diana Brooks **Lucy's** **Lucy's Hill** **Hythe CT21 5ES** **Tel: (0303) 262018** **Open: ALL YEAR** **Map Ref No. 16**	Nearest Road: M.20, A.20 Lucy's, built in 1883 for Sir Henry Lucy, first editor of Punch, has panoramic sea views & lovely terraced gardens. The owners previously ran an excellent restaurant & provide a homely atmos- phere in a beautiful house. 3 bedrooms with private bathrooms, T.V., tea/coffee facilities. Children over 10 welcome. 2 golf courses, 1 mile. Under 3 miles from M.20; close to Channel Ports & Tunnel terminal. Canterbury 25 minutes' drive.	£20.00 *see PHOTO over*	Y	Y	N
Mrs Ann Earl **The Greswolde Hotel** **20 Surrey Road** **Cliftonville** **Margate CT9 2LA** **Tel: (0843) 223956** **Open: ALL YEAR** **Map Ref No. 19**	Nearest Road: M.2, A.299 The Greswolde, a 6 bedroomed Victorian Hotel retaining much of its original character & charm. All rooms have en-suite facilities, with colour T.V. & tea makers. There is a quiet, relaxing lounge/ reading room. Located 100 yds. from the prome- nade, close to championship indoor & outdoor bowling greens with many golf courses in easy reach. Pubs & eating places are nearby. Ideal for touring with Channel ports close by.	£17.00 *see PHOTO over* CREDIT CARD VISA M'CARD	Y	N	Y
Mrs Rosemarie Bannock **Court Lodge Farm** **The Street** **Teston** **Maidstone** **ME18 5AQ** **Tel: (0622) 812570** **Fax 0622 814200** **Open: ALL YEAR** **Map Ref No. 17**	Nearest Road: M.20, A.26 With lovely views overlooking the River Medway Valley with its hop gardens, orchards & sheep, this oak beamed farmhouse with inglenook fire- places & leaded windows offers warm & friendly hospitality. All 3 beautifully furnished rooms, 2 with en-suite facilities are spacious & comfort- able. Superb breakfasts. Only 4 miles from Maidstone & M.20 & convenient for visiting Leeds Castle, Ightham Mote & Chartwell, yet London, Heathrow, Gatwick, Sheerness & Dover are only 1 hour by car.	£16.00	Y	N	N

The Greswolde Hotel. Margate.

Swale Cottage. Penshurst.

Kent

		minimum £ per person	children taken	evening meals	animals taken
Mrs Lisa Coleman **Warwick House** **64 Tonbridge Road** **Maidstone ME16 8SE** **Tel: (0622) 756096** **Open: ALL YEAR** **Map Ref No. 18**	Nearest Road: A.20, M.20 A marvellous 16th century Tudor house standing in a huge garden. 4 super rooms with modern facilities. The proprietors extend a warm welcome & arrange theatres, outings, restaurants, plus a guided car tour to many interesting places. Leeds, Knowle & Hever Castles, Sissinghurst & Canterbury within driving distance. French & German spoken. No babies, please. Hostess is accredited guide to Leeds Castle & area.	£17.00	Y	N	N
Cynthia Dakin **Swale Cottage** **Old Swaylands Lane** **off Poundsbridge Lane** **Penshurst TN11 8AH** **Tel: (0892) 870738** **Open: ALL YEAR** **Map Ref No. 20**	Nearest Road: B.2176, A.26 Swale Cottage is a charmingly converted Kentish barn of architectural merit. A Grade II listed building. Formerly part of a 13th century Yeoman farm. There are 3 beautifully furnished en-suite guest rooms with T.V. & modern amenities. Four poster suite & twin bedded rooms available. Idyllic tranquil setting with views over a hilly wooded valley & rose garden. Near to Penshurst Place & Hever & Chartwell Castles. Within easy reach of both London airports.	£20.00 *see PHOTO over*	Y	N	N
Mrs Jo Lindsay A.T.D.N.D.D. **Jordans** **Sheet Hill** **Plaxtol** **Sevenoaks** **TN15 0PU** **Tel: (0732) 810379** **Open: MID MAR - MIDDEC** **Map Ref No. 21**	Nearest Road: M.25 Beautiful picture-postcard 15th century Tudor house, awarded a 'Historic Building of Kent' plaque & situated in the picturesque village of Plaxtol, among orchards & parkland. The house is beautifully furnished, has leaded windows, inglenook fireplaces, massive oak beams & an enchanting old English garden, with rambler roses & espalier trees. Within easy reach are Ightham Mote, Leeds Castle, Penshurst, Hever Castle, Chartwell & Knole. 3 lovely rooms, 2 en-suite. London 35 mins by train & easy access to airports.	£20.00 *see PHOTO over*	Y	N	N
Mrs A.J. Holdstock **Hempstead House** **London Road** **Bapchild** **Sittingbourne** **ME9 9PP** **Tel: (0795) 428020** **Open: ALL YEAR** **Map Ref No. 22**	Nearest Road: A.2 Hempstead House is a private Victorian country house situated on the main A.2 between Sittingbourne & Canterbury, set well back in 3 acres of beautifully landscaped gardens. All major towns in the area are easily accessible as well as the coastal ports. Accommodation is provided in 2 superb suites, each having private W.C. & bathroom, dressing areas, tea/coffee making & colour T.V. All food is home cooked using vegetables from the garden & local meat & fish. All guests are welcomed as friends & encouraged to enjoy the house as much as their hosts do.	£28.00	Y	Y	Y
Mrs Josephine Scott **Munk's Farm** **Smarden** **TN27 8PN** **Tel: (0233) 770265** **Open: ALL YEAR** **Map Ref No. 23**	Nearest Road: A.274, M.20 Munk's Farm is a listed 17th century, oak beamed, weatherboarded farmhouse with inglenook fireplaces; set in a large attractive garden with swimming pool, surrounded by farmland. There are 3 charming, comfortably furnished twin-bedded rooms with en-suite or private bathrooms, & guests' lounge. Sissinghurst, Leeds Castle & many other castles & gardens nearby; Canterbury, Rye & Channel Ports within easy reach.	£19.00	N	Y	N

Jordans. Plaxtol.

Kent

minimum £ per person / children taken / evening meals / animals taken

		minimum £ per person	children taken	evening meals	animals taken
Maureen Rawlinson **Brattle House** **Cranbrook Road** **Tenterden TN30 6UL** **Tel: (05806) 3565/** **(0580) 763565** **Open: FEB-DEC** **Map Ref No. 24**	Nearest Road: A.28 A handsome Georgian farmhouse dating from the 17th century, surrounded by a large garden & the Wealden countryside. Offering 3 luxuriously furnished en-suite bedrooms providing every comfort. Evening meals are served by candlelight in the elegant dining room furnished with antiques. The cooking is of a high standard & vegetarians can be catered for. Close by are Sissinghurst, Bodiam & Leeds Castles. Ideal centre for touring Kent & Sussex. Children over 12 years only.	£23.50 🚭	N	Y	N
Shirley Cole **Goldhill Mill** **Golden Green** **Tonbridge TN11 0BA** **Tel: (0732) 851626** **Fax 0732 851881** **Open: OCT - Mid JULY** **Map Ref No. 25**	Nearest Road: A.26 Goldhill Mill, as mentioned in The Doomsday Book, was a working water mill for 850 years. Peacefully set in 20 acres, the beautiful old mill house has been lovingly restored & affords superb accommodation enhanced by high quality decor & fine antique furniture. Each of the 3 attractive, well equipped, en-suite double bedrooms (1 with romantic 4-Poster, 2 with jacuzzi bath) are most charming. Breakfast is served in the splendid farmhouse kitchen with Tudor beams.	£25.00 🚭 CREDIT CARD VISA M'CARD	Y	N	N
Mrs A. Emanuel **Little Pagehurst** **Pagehurst Road** **Staplehurst** **Tonbridge TN12 OJD** **Tel: (0580) 891486** **Open: MAR-NOV** **Map Ref No. 26**	Nearest Road: M.20, A.20 Situated near Staplehurst in the Weald of Kent, this fine listed Elizabethan house set in mature grounds close to several gardens & castles. The interior combines modern & traditional furnishings. Superb breakfasts & fine English cooking. Tennis court, heated pool & croquet lawn available. A relaxed atmosphere awaits you at Little Pagehurst. An excellent base for a weekend break or an overnight stay. Children over 12.	£20.00 *see PHOTO over*	Y	N	N
Angela Jane Godbold **Danehurst House Hotel** **41 Lower Green Road** **Rusthall** **Tunbridge Wells TN4 8TW** **Tel: (0892) 527739** **Fax 0892 514804** **Open: ALL YEAR** **Map Ref No. 27**	Nearest Road: A.264 Danehurst is an attractive Victorian character house. 6 tastefully furnished bedrooms, 4 with en-suite facilities, afford you excellent accommodation. Breakfast is served in a delightful conservatory, and intimate candle-lit dinners in the elegant dining room. Your hosts welcome you most warmly to their home, and would like to feel you can relax and enjoy everything they and the area have to offer.	£27.50 🚭 CREDIT CARD VISA M'CARD AMEX	Y	Y	N
Mrs C. M. Carrell **Rowden House Farm** **Frant** **Tunbridge Wells** **TN3 9HS** **Tel: (0892) 750259** **Open: APR - OCT** **Map Ref No. 28**	Nearest Road: A.267 A delightful Elizabethan house listed as of architectural interest, standing in 20 acres with sheep, horses, dogs & chickens. Surrounded by the beautiful, rolling, wooded countryside of Sussex, it is perfectly placed for visiting the stately homes & towns of Kent & Sussex. Accommodation is in 1 twin bedded room, with private bathroom, & 2 singles with wash basins, all with tea/coffee making facilities. An attractive drawing room with colour T.V. Gatwick 1 hour, London 1 & a quarter hours. Children over 10 welcome.	£19.00	Y	N	N

Little Pagehurst.   Staplehurst.

Kent

		minimum £ per person	children taken	evening meals	animals taken

Tony & Mary Dakin
The Old Parsonage
Church Lane
Frant
Tunbridge Wells
TN3 9DX
Tel: (0892) 750773
Open: ALL YEAR
Map Ref No. 28

Nearest Road: A.267

Quietly situated in a very pretty village just 2 miles from Royal Tunbridge Wells, this classic Georgian rectory was built by Lord Abergavenny for his son in 1820. Features include beautifully furnished reception rooms & spacious Victorian conservatory, & delightful en-suite bedrooms, including 2 4-posters, all with colour T.V. There are 2 village pubs & a first-class restaurant a few minutes' walk away. Short drive to 15 historic houses & castles. Gatwick 40 mins., Heathrow 70 mins., London 40 mins. by train.

£23.00 Y N Y

see PHOTO over

All the establishments mentioned in this guide

are members of

The Worldwide Bed & Breakfast Association

When booking your accommodation please mention
The Best Bed & Breakfast

The Old Parsonage.   Frant.

Lancashire

Lancashire
(North West)

Lancashire can prove a surprisingly beautiful county. Despite its industrial history of cotton production, there is magnificent scenery & there are many fine towns & villages. Connections with the Crown & the clashes of the Houses of Lancaster & York have left a rich heritage of buildings with a variety of architecture. There are old stone cottages & farmhouses, as well as manor houses from many centuries.

For lovers of the countryside, Lancashire has the sweeping hills of Bowland, the lovely Ribble Valley, the moors of Rossendale & one mountain, mysterious Pendle Hill.

The Royal Forest of Bowland is a forest without trees, which has provided rich hunting grounds over the centuries. An old windswept pass runs over the heights of Salter Fell & High Cross Fell from Slaidburn, where the Inn, the "Hark to Bounty", was named after the noisiest hound in the squire's pack & used to be the courtroom where strict forest laws were enforced.

Further south, the Trough of Bowland provides an easier route through the hills, & here is the beautiful village of Abbeystead in Wynesdale where monks once farmed the land. The church has stained glass windows portraying shepherds & their flocks & there are pegs in the porch where shepherds hung their crooks.

Below the dramatic hills of Bowland, the green valley of the Ribble climbs from Preston to the Yorkshire Dales. Hangridge Fell, where the tales of witches are almost as numerous as those of Pendle Hill, lies at the beginning of the valley.

Pendle Hill can be reached from the pretty village of Downham which has Tudor, Jacobean & Georgian houses, village stocks & an old inn. Old Pendle rises abruptly to 1831 feet & is a strange land formation. It is shrouded in legend & stories of witchcraft.

Between Pendle Hill & the moors of Rossendale are the textile towns of Nelson, Colne, Burnley, Accrington & Blackburn. The textile industry was well established in Tudor times & the towns grew up as markets for the trading of the cloth woven in the Piece Halls.

The moors which descend to the very edges of the textile towns are wild & beautiful & have many prehistoric tumuli & earthworks. Through the towns & the countryside, winds the Liverpool & Leeds canal, providing an excellent towpath route to see the area.

Lancaster is an historic city boasting the largest castle in England, dating back to Norman times.

Lancashire's coastal resorts are legendary, & Blackpool is Queen of them all with her miles of Illuminations & millions of visitors.

Downham Village.

Lancashire

Lancashire
Gazeteer
Areas of outstanding natural beauty.
The Forest of Bowland, Parts of Arnside & Silverdale.

Historic Houses & Castles
Rufford Old Hall - Rufford
15th century screen in half-timbered hall of note. Collection of relics of Lancashire life.
Chingle Hall - Nr. Preston
13th century - small manor house with moat. Rose gardens. Haunted!
Astley Hall - Chorley
Elizabethan house reconstructed in 17th century. Houses pictures, tapestries, pottery & furniture.
Gawthorpe Hall - Padiham
17th century manor house with 19th century restoration. Moulded ceilings & some fine panelling. A collection of lace & embroidery.
Bramall Hall - Bramall
Fine example of half-timbered (black & white) manor house built in 14th century & added to in Elizabethan times. Fine grounds.
Lancaster Castle - Lancaster
Largest of English castles - dates back to Norman era.
Astley Hall - Chorley
16th century half-timbered grouped around central court. Rebuilt in the Jacobean manner with long gallery. Unique furniture.
Hoghton Tower - Nr. Preston
16th century - fortified hill-top mansion - magnificent banquet hall. Dramatic building - walled gardens & rose gardens.
Thurnham Hall - Lancaster
13th century origins. 16th century additions & 19th century facade. Beautiful plasterwork of Elizabethan period. Jacobean staircase.

Cathedrals & Churches
Lancaster (St. Mary)
15th century with 18th century tower. Restored chapel - fine stalls.
Whalley (St. Mary)
13th century with 15th century tower, clerestory & aisle windows. Fine wood carving of 15th century canopied stalls.
Halsall (St. Cuthbert)
14th century chancel, 15th century perpendicular spire. 14th century tomb. Original doors, brasses & effigies. 19th century restoration.
Tarleton (St. Mary)
18th century part 19th century.
Great Mitton (All Hallows)
15th century rood screen, 16th century font cover,
17th century pulpit.

Museums & Galleries
Blackburn Museum - Blackburn
Extensive collections relating to local history archeology, ceramics, geology & natural history. One of the finest collection of coins & fine collection of mediaeval illuminated manuscripts & early printed books.
Bury Museum & Art Gallery - Bury
Houses fine Victorian oil & watercolours. Turner, Constable, Landseer, de Wint
City Gallery - Manchester
Pre-Raphaelites, Old Masters, Impressionists, modern painters all represented in this fine gallery; also silver & pottery collections.
Higher Mill Museum - Helmshaw
One of the oldest wool textile finishing mills left in Lancashire. Spinning wheels, Hargreave's Spinning Jenny, several of Arkwrights machines, 20 foot water wheel.
Townley Hall Art Gallery & Museum, & Museum of Local Crafts & Industries - Burnley

LANCASHIRE

Map reference

1 Yeomans
2 Dodgson
3 Butler
4 Edwards
5 Townend
6 Ireland
7 Smith
8 Mitson

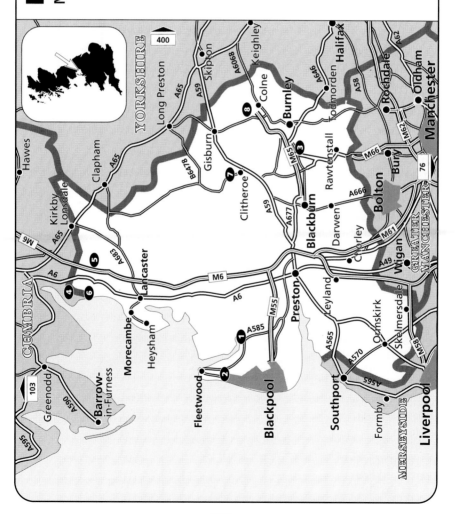

Lancashire

	Nearest Road	minimum £ per person	children taken	evening meals	animals taken
Roger & Pamela Yeomans **Mains Hall Country House** **Mains Lane** **Little Singleton** **Blackpool FY6 7LE** Tel: (0253) 885130 Fax 0253 894132 Open: ALL YEAR Map Ref No. 01	Nearest Road: A.585 A 16th century Manor House standing in 4 acres of grounds overlooking the banks of the River Wyre. Once the home of the Hesketh Family & Prince George IV. This Grade II listed house retains much of its period detail including oak panelling, open fireplaces & four-poster beds. All rooms have private facilities, colour T.V., radio, 'phone, trouser press & tea/coffee makers. Convenient for Blackpool & the Lake District.	£45.00 CREDIT CARD VISA M'CARD	Y	Y	Y
Jean & John Dodgson **Sunray Private Hotel** **42 Knowle Avenue** **Blackpool FY2 9TQ** Tel: (0253) 51937 Fax 0253 862357 Open: ALL YEAR Map Ref No. 02	Nearest Road: M.55 Situated in the seaside resort of Blackpool, Sunray Private Hotel offers attractive accommodation in 9 bedrooms, each with private bathroom, radio, colour T.V. & tea/coffee making facilities. Excellent English breakfasts & delicious evening meals served. Guests may unwind relax in the residents' lounge which is available throughout the day. An ideal base for a holiday or for visiting the many places of interest in Lancashire.	£24.00 *see PHOTO over* CREDIT CARD VISA M'CARD	Y	Y	Y
Mrs M Butler **Eaves Barn Farm** **Hapton** **Burnley** **BB12 7LP** Tel:(0282) 771591/770478 Open: ALL YEAR Map Ref No. 03	Nearest Road: M.65, A.671 Eaves Barn Farm is a mixed working farm situated in a semi-rural location. The award winning accommodation comprises a spacious cottage with 3 bedrooms, attached to the main house, offering superb facilities & fronted by attractive gardens. Quality home cooking is provided using fresh local produce. Home-made preserves a speciality. The farm is situated within close proximity of the motorway network affording easy access to all Lancashire's tourist attractions .	£18.50	Y	Y	N
Mark & Patricia Edwards **Lindeth House** **Lindeth Road** **Silverdale** **Carnforth** **LA5 0TX** Tel: (0524) 701238 Open: FEB-DEC Map Ref No. 04	Nearest Road: A.6, M.6 Ex 35 A charming country house situated in an area of outstanding natural beauty surrounded by woodland walks, yet only a few mins' from the coast. The 3 charming, individually furnished en-suite bedrooms have colour T.V., clock-radio, tea/coffee making facilities & hairdryer. 2 comfortable lounges. Enjoy an excellent candle-lit dinner, using fresh local produce, in the elegant, licensed dining room. The warm friendly atmosphere makes this an ideal base for a quiet break or touring the Lake District.	£21.00	Y	Y	N
Mrs Adelaide Ireland **Thwaite End Farm** **Bolton-le-Sands** **Carnforth** **LA5 9TN** Tel: (0524) 732551 Open: ALL YEAR Map Ref No. 06	Nearest Road: A.6, M.6 Ex 35 Guests will find a comfortable, friendly atmosphere in this delightful 17th century farmhouse. Situated on a small sheep & beef-rearing farm of 52 acres, it is conveniently located between Carnforth & Bolton-le-Sands. Accommodation is in 4 pleasant rooms, 2 with en-suite facilities & tea/coffee making facilities. There are 2 comfortable lounges, one with colour T.V. Hot drinks & biscuits are served. Breakfast is served in the attractive dining room.	£19.00	N	N	N

Sunray. Blackpool.

Lancashire

		minimum £ per person	children taken	evening meals	animals taken
Mrs Sally Townend **New Capernwray** **Farmhouse** **Capernwray** **Carnforth** **LA6 1AD** **Tel: (0524) 734284** **Open: ALL YEAR** **Map Ref No. 05**	Nearest Road: A.6, M.6 exit.35 Absolute peace & comfort are found in this enchanting 17th century house, with its many low ceilings & ancient oak beams. Enjoy the cosiness of the lounge, an excellent candle-lit dinner & retire to one of three charming fully equipped bedrooms with en-suite/private facilities & colour T.V.. 3 miles from the M.6 in superb countryside. Ideal for the Lake District/Yorkshire Dales or stopover London-Scotland. Children over 10 welcome. N.W. Regional Winner. Best Bed & Breakfast Award for Excellence.	£26.00 *see PHOTO over* CREDIT CARD VISA M'CARD	Y	Y	Y
Gordon & Jean Smith **Peter Barn** **Cross Lane** **Waddington** **Clitheroe BB7 3JH** **Tel: (0200) 28585** **Open: ALL YEAR** **Map Ref No. 07**	Nearest Road: A.59 Nestling in the Forest of Bowland, Peter Barn was a Tithe Barn that was lovingly converted by the Smith family & is surrounded by an abundance of wildlife on a lane known locally as Rabbit Lane. Furnished with antiques & family 'bric a brac', the first-floor sitting room has panoramic views, a stone fireplace & a pitched roof made of old church rafters. A delightful home where comfort & hospitality are assured.	£17.50	Y	N	N
Mrs Carole Mitson **Higher Wanless Farm** **Red Lane** **Colne BB8 7JP** **Tel: (0282) 865301** **Open: JAN - NOV** **Map Ref No. 08**	Nearest Road: M.65, A.682 Ideally situated for visiting 'Pendle Witch' country, Haworth or Yorkshire Dales - the farm nestles peacefully alongside the Leeds-Liverpool canal. Shire horses & sheep are reared on the farm, where the warmest of welcomes awaits you. Spacious & attractive bedrooms (1 en-suite) offer every comfort. Several country inns nearby offering wide range of meal facilities.	£18.00	Y	N	N

When booking your accommodation please mention
The Best Bed & Breakfast

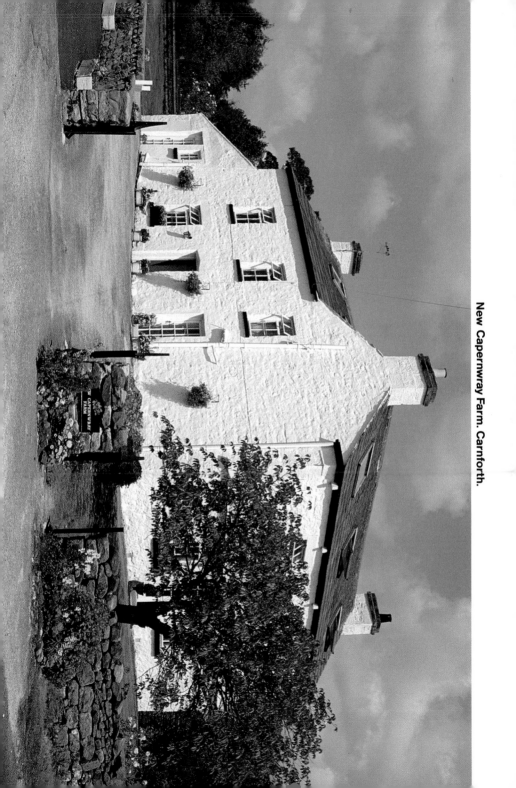

New Capernwray Farm. Carnforth.

Leicester & Notts

Leicestershire
(East Midlands)

Rural Leicestershire is rich in grazing land, a peaceful, undramatic landscape broken up by the waterways that flow through in the south of the county.

The River Avon passes on its way to Stratford, running by 17th century Stanford Hall & its motorcycle museum. The Leicester section of the Grand Union Canal was once very important for the transportation of goods from the factories of the Midlands to London Docks. It passes through a fascinating series of multiple locks at Foxton. The decorative barges, the 'narrow boats' are pleasure craft these days rather than the life-blood of the closed community of boat people who lived & worked out their lives on the canals.

Rutland was formerly England's smallest county, but was absorbed into East Leicestershire in the 1970's. Its name lives on in Rutland Water, one of Europe's largest reservoirs & an attractive setting for sailing, fishing or enjoying a trip on the pleasure cruiser. There is also the Rutland Theatre at Tolethorpe Hall, where a summer season of Shakespeare's plays is presented in the open air.

Melton Mowbray is famous for its pork pies & it is also the centre of Stilton cheese country. The "King of Cheeses" is made mainly in the Vale of Belvoir where Leicestershire meets Nottinghamshire, & the battlements & turrets of Belvoir Castle overlook the scene from its hill-top.

To the north-west the Charnwood Forest area is pleasantly wooded & the deer park at Bradgate surrounding the ruined home of Lady Jane Grey, England's nine-day queen, is a popular attraction.

Nottinghamshire
(East Midlands)

Nottinghamshire has a diversity of landscape from forest to farmland, from coal mines to industrial areas.

The north of the county is dominated by the expanse of Sherwood Forest, smaller now than in the time of legendary Robin Hood & his Merry Men, but still a lovely old woodland of Oak & Birch.

The Dukeries are so called because of the numerous ducal houses built in the area & there is beautiful parkland on these great estates that can be visited. Clumber Park, for instance has a huge lake & a double avenue of Limes.

Newstead Abbey was a mediaeval priory converted into the Byron family home in the 16th century. It houses the poet Byron's manuscripts & possessions & is set in wonderful gardens.

More modest is the terraced house in Eastwood, where D.H. Lawrence was born into the mining community on which his novels are based.

Nottingham was recorded in the Domesday Book as a thriving community & that tradition continues. It was here that Arkwright perfected his cotton-spinning machinery & went on to develop steam as a power source for industry.

Textiles, shoes, bicycles & tobacco are all famous Nottingham products, & the story of Nottingham Lace can be discovered at the Lace Hall, housed in a former church.

Nottingham Castle, high on Castle Rock, was built & destroyed & rebuilt many times during its history. It now houses the city's Art Gallery & Museum. The Castle towers over the ancient 'Trip to Jerusalem' Inn, said to be so named because crusaders stopped there for a drink on their way to fight in the Holy Land.

Leicester & Notts

Leicestershire Gazeteer

Areas of outstanding natural beauty.
Charnwood Forest, Rutland Water.

Historic Houses & Castles

Belvoir Castle - Nr. Grantham
Overlooking the Vale of Belvoir, castle rebuilt in 1816, with many special events including jousting tournaments. Home of the Duke of Rutland since Henry VIII. Paintings, furniture, historic armoury, military museums, magnificent stateroom

Belvoir Castle

Belgrave Hall - Leicester
18th century Queen Anne house - furnishing of 18th & 19th centuries.
Langton Hall - Nr. Market Harborough
Privately occupied - perfect English country house from mediaeval times - drawing rooms have 18th century Venetian lace.

Oakham Castle - Oakham
Norman banqueting hall of late 12th century
Stanford Hall - Nr Lutterworth
17th century William & Mary house - collection of Stuart relics & pictures, antiques & costumes of family from Elizabeth I onward. Motor cycle museum.
Stapleford Park - Nr. Melton Mowbray
Old wing dated 1500, restored 1663. Extended to mansion in 1670. Collection of pictures, tapestries, furniture & Balston's Staffordshire portrait figures of Victorian age.

Cathedrals & Churches

Breedon-on-the-Hill (St. Mary & St. Hardulph)
Norman & 13th century. Jacobean canopied pew, 18th century carvings.
Empingham (St. Peter)
14th century west tower, front & crocketed spire. Early English interior - double piscina, triple sedilla.
Lyddington (St. Andrew)
Perpendicular in the main - mediaeval wall paintings & brasses.
Staunton Harol (Holy Trinity)
17th century - quite unique Cromwellian church - painted ceilings.

Museums & Galleries

Bosworth Battlefield Visitor Centre - Nr Market Bosworth
Exhibitions, models, battlefield trails at site of 1485 Battle of Bosworth where Richard III lost his life & crown to Henry.
Leicestershire Museum of Technology - Leicester
Beam engines, steam shovel, knitting machinery & other aspects of the county's industrial past.
Leicester Museum & Art Gallery - Leicester
Painting collection. 18th & 19th century, watercolours & drawings, 20th century French paintings, Old Master & modern prints, English silver & ceramics, special exhibitions.
Jewry Wall Museum & Site - Leicester
Roman wall & baths site adjoining museum of archaeology.

Leicester & Notts

Melton Carnegie Museum-Melton Mobray
Displays on Stilton cheese, pork pies & other aspects of the past & present life of the area.

Rutland County Museum - Oakham
Domestic & agricultural life of Rutland, formerly England's smallest county.

Donnington Collection of Single-Seater Racing Cars - Castle Donington
Large collection of grand prix racing cars & racing motorcycles, adjoining Donington Park racing circuit..

Wygson's House Museum of Costume - Leicestershire
Costume, accessories & shop settings in late mediaeval buildings.

The Bellfoundry Museum - Loughborough
Moulding, casting, tuning & fitting of bells, with conducted tours of bellfoundry.

Historic Monuments

The Castle - Ashby-de-la-Zouch
14th century with tower added in 15th century.

Kirby Muxloe Castle - Kirby Muxloe
15th century fortified manor house with moat ruins.

Other things to see & do

Rutland Farm Park - Oakham
Rare & commercial breeds of livestock in 18 acres of park & woodland, with early 19th century farm buildings.

Stoughton Farm Park - Nr. Leicester
Shire horses, rare breeds, small animals & modern 140 dairy herd. Milking demonstrations, farm museum, woodland walks, adventure playground.

Twycross Zoo - Nr. Atherstone
Gorillas, orang-utans, chimpanzees, gibbons, elephants, giraffes, lions & many other animals.

The Battlefield Line - Nr. Market Bosworth
Steam railway & collection of railway relics, adjoining Bosworth Battlefield.

Great Central Railway - Loughborough
Steam railway over 5-mile route in Charnwood Forest area, with steam & diesel museum.

Rutland Railway Museum - Nr. Oakham
Industrial steam & diesel locomotives & wagons from quarries, mines & factories.

Nottinghamshire Gazeteer
Historic Houses & Castles

Holme Pierrepont Hall - Nr. Nottingham
Outstanding red brick Tudor manor, in continuous family ownership, with 19th century courtyard garden.

Newark Castle - Newark
Dramatic castle ruins on riverside site, once one of the most important castles of the north.

Newstead Abbey - Nr. Mansfield
Priory converted to coutry mansion, home of poet Lord Byron with many of his possessions & manuscripts on display. Beautiful parkland, lakes & gardens.

Nottingham Castle - Nottingham
17th century residence on site of mediaeval castle. Fine collections of ceramics, silver, Nottingham alabaster carvings, local historical displays. Art gallery. Special exhibitions & events.

Wollaton Hall - Nottingham
Elizabethan mansion now housing natural history exhibits. Stands in deer park, with Industrial Museum in former stables, illustrating the city's bicycle, hosiery, lace, pharmaceutical & other industries.

Cathedrals & Churches

Egmanton (St. Mary)
Magnificent interior by Comper. Norman doorway & font. Canopied rood screen, 17th century altar.

Newark (St. Mary Magdalene)
15th century. 2 painted panels of "Dance of Death". Reredos by Comper.

Southwell Cathedral
Norman nave, unvaulted, fine early English choir. Decorated pulpitum, 6 canopied stalls, fine misericords. Octagonal chapter house..

Terseval (St. Catherine)
12th century - interior 17th century unrestored

Museums & Galleries

Castlegate Museum - Nottingham
Row of Georgian terraced houses showing costume & textile collection. Lace making equipment & lace collection.

Nottingham Castle Museum - Nottingham
Collections of ceramics, glass & silver. Alabaster carvings.

Leicester & Notts

D.H. Lawrence Birthplace - Eastwood
Home of the novelist & poet, as it would
have been at time of his birth, 1885.
Millgate Museum of Social & Folk Life -
Newark
Local social & folk life, with
craft workshops.
Brewhouse Yard Museum - Nottingham
Daily life in Nottingham, displayed in 17th
century cottages & rock-cut cellars.
The Lace Hall - Nottingham
The story of Nottingham Lace audio-
visual display & exhibition with lace
shops, in fine converted church.
Museum of Costume & Textiles -
Nottingham
Costumes, lace & textiles on display in
fine Georgian buildings.
Bassetlaw Museum - Retford
Local history of north Nottinghamshire.
Canal Museum - Nottinghamshire
History of the River Trent & canal history,
in former canal warehouse.
Ruddington Framework Knitters'
Museum - Ruddington
Unique complex of early 19th-century
framework knitters' buildings with over 20
hand frames in restored workshop.

Other things to see & do

The Tales of Robin Hood - Nottingham
A 'flight to adventure' from mediaeval
Nottingham to Sherwood Forest through
the tales of the world's most
famous outlaw.
Clumber Park - Nr. Worksop
Landscaped parkland with double avenue
of limes, lake, chapel. One of the
Dukeries' estates, though the house no
longer remains.
Rufford - Nr. Ollerton
Parkland, lake & gallery with fine crafts,
around ruin of Cistercian abbey.
Sherwood Forest Visitor Centre - Nr.
Edwinstowe
Robin Hood exhibition & 450 acres of
ancient oak woodland associated with the
outlaw & his merry men.
Sherwood Forest Farm Park - Nr.
Edwinstowe
Rare breeds of cattle, sheep, pigs &
goats. Lake with wildfowl.
White Post Farm Centre - Farnsfield, Nr
Newark
Working modern farm with crops & many
animals, including cows, sheep, pigs,
hens, geese, ducks,llamas, horses.
Indoor displays & exhibits.

Newark Castle.

LEICESTERSHIRE & NOTTINGHAMSHIRE

Map reference

1 Hackney
1 Hitchen
2 Smithers
3 Ibbotson
4 Hinchley
5 Need
6 Brammer
7 Stewart-Smith

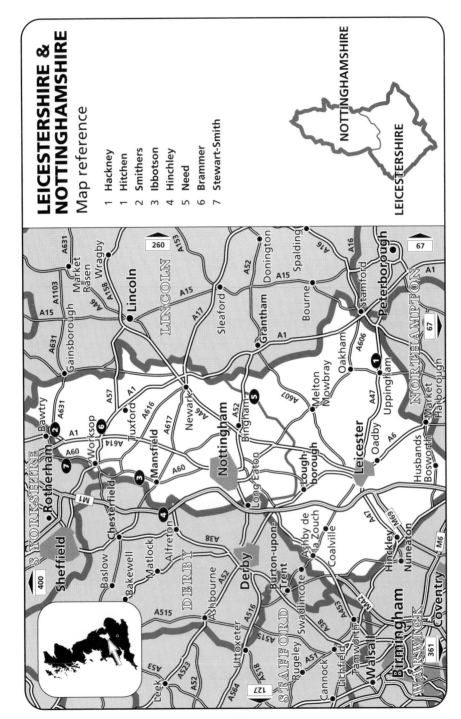

NOTTINGHAMSHIRE

LEICESTERSHIRE

Leicestershire & Nottinghamshire

		per person minimum £	children taken	evening meals	animals taken
Christine & Ian Hackney **Garden Hotel** **16 High Street West** **Uppingham LE15 9QD** **Tel: (0572) 822352** **Fax 0572 821156** **Open: ALL YEAR** **Map Ref No. 01**	Nearest Road: A.47 Regarded as Uppingham's best kept secret, this historic hotel has a reputation for friendly, homely service. All rooms en-suite with colour T.V., telephone, radio and tea/coffee facilities. Comfortable lounge and separate bar, together with large, well-tended garden, provide country-home comforts. The restaurant is renowned for traditional British home cooking. Good wine list. Summer barbecues in the garden.	£30.00 CREDIT CARD VISA M'CARD AMEX	Y	Y	Y
Mrs J. Hitchen **Rutland House** **61 High Street East** **Uppingham LE15 9PY** **Tel: (0572) 822497** **Open: ALL YEAR** **Map Ref No. 01**	Nearest Road: A.47 Rutland House offers excellent accommodation in 4 guest rooms. All rooms en-suite, central heating, colour T.V., radio/alarms & tea/coffee facilities. Being a small establishment, the rooms are quiet & homely. Full English breakfast or Continental breakfast served. Close to Rutland Water & Burghley House.	£18.50	Y	N	Y

Nottinghamshire

		per person minimum £	children taken	evening meals	animals taken
Mr & Mrs J.R. Smithers **The Old George Dragon** **Scrooby** **Doncaster DN10 6AU** **Tel: (0302) 711840** **Open: ALL YEAR** **Map Ref No. 02**	Nearest Road: A.638, A.1 M A warm welcome awaits you at this 18th century cottage. Situated in the picturesque & historic village of Scrooby. Internationally known for its links with the Pilgrim Fathers & within easy reach of Robin Hood country. Accommodation is tastefully furnished retaining many original features, offering 2 double rooms & 1 twin room all with private facilities, colour T.V. & tea/coffee making. 2 miles from A.1 M.	£18.00	Y	N	N
June M. Ibbotson **Blue Barn Farm** **Langwith** **Mansfield** **NG20 9JD** **Tel: (0623) 742248** **Open: ALL YEAR** **Map Ref No. 03**	Nearest Road: A.616, A.1, M.1 An enjoyable visit is guaranteed at this family run 250 acre farm, set in tranquil countryside on the edge of Sherwood Forest (Robin Hood country). Accommodation is in 3 guest bedrooms with modern amenities including h&c, tea/coffee making facilities & guest bathroom with shower. Colour T.V. lounge & garden are also available. Guests are very welcome to walk around the farm. Many interesting places catering for all tastes, only a short journey away.	£15.00	Y	N	Y
Mrs B. Hinchley **Titchfield House** **300/302 Chesterfield Road North** **Mansfield NG19 7QU** **Tel: (0623) 810356** **Open: ALL YEAR** **Map Ref No. 04**	Nearest Road: M.1, A.617 This is two houses, converted into one family-run guesthouse, offering 8 comfortable rooms, lounge with T.V., kitchen for guests' use, bathroom & showers. It also has an adjoining garage. Near to Mansfield, which is a busy market town. Sherwood Forest & the Peak District easily accessible. Very handy for touring this lovely area & onward travel. A warm & friendly welcome from the delightful hosts is assured here.	£15.00	Y	Y	Y

255

Nottinghamshire

		minimum £ per person	children taken	evening meals	animals taken
Peter, Marjorie & Nicky Need **Peacock Farm Guest-house & Restaurant** **Redmile NG13 0GQ** **Tel: (0949) 42475** **Open: ALL YEAR** **Map Ref No. 05**	Nearest Road: A.1, A.52 Situated within sight of Belvoir Castle, Peacock Farm is a 280 year-old farmhouse with all modern conveniences. Most rooms have unbroken views of the nearby village & Belvoir Castle set on wooded hills. A warm welcome is extended to house guests who are offered a first class service with old fashioned English hospitality. The lovely restaurant offers excellent home cooking, with local fresh produce.	£17.50 CREDIT CARD VISA M'CARD AMEX	Y	Y	Y
Roslie Brammer **'The Barns '** **Morton Farm** **Babworth** **Retford DN22 8HA** **Tel: (0777) 706336** **Open: ALL YEAR** **Map Ref No. 06**	Nearest Road: A.1, B.6420 A delightfully warm welcome & pleasant relaxed atmosphere await you at 'The Barns'. This beautifully converted 18th century barn boasts open fires & many oak beams & offers guests a choice of 6 comfortable rooms, all with en-suite facilities, radio, T.V. & tea/coffee makers. An interesting base for touring. It is located at Babworth - home of the Pilgrim Fathers - only 2 miles from Robin Hood country.	£19.00	Y	N	N
Mrs C. Stewart-Smith **Yews Farm** **Firbeck** **Worksop S81 8JW** **Tel: (0909) 731458** **Open: MAR - OCT** **Map Ref No. 07**	Nearest Road: A.1, M.1, A.634 Dating from the 16th century, this charming country house faces south with lovely views overlooking garden & fields bordered by a stream. The pretty bedrooms all have tea/coffee trays, colour T.V., radio alarm clocks & electric blankets, & with the elegant drawing & dining rooms mainly furnished with antiques. Within an hour's drive are Yorkshire & Derbyshire dales, Sherwood Forest, Lincoln & York. M.1, M.18, A.1 motorways nearby.	£22.50 CREDIT CARD VISA M'CARD	Y	Y	Y

All the establishments mentioned in this guide
are members of
The Worldwide Bed & Breakfast Association

Lincolnshire

Lincolnshire
(East Midlands)

Lincolnshire is an intriguing mixture of coast & country, of flat fens & gently rising wolds.

There are the popular resorts of Skegness & Mablethorpe as well as quieter coastal regions where flocks of wild birds take food & shelter in the dunes. Gibraltar Point & Saltfleetby are large nature reserves.

Fresh vegetables for much of Britain are produced in the rich soil of the Lincolnshire fens, & windmills punctuate the skyline. There is a unique 8-sailed windmill at Heckington. In spring the fields are ablaze with the red & yellow of tulips. The bulb industry flourishes around Spalding & Holbeach, & in early May tulip flowers in abundance decorate the huge floats of the Spalding Flower Parade.

The city of Lincoln has cobbled streets & ancient buildings & a very beautiful triple-towered Cathedral which shares its hill-top site with the Castle, both dating from the 11th century. There is a 17th century library by Wren in the Cathedral, which has amongst its treasures one of the four original copies of Magna Carta.

Boston has a huge parish church with a distincive octagonal tower which can be seen for miles across the surrounding fenland, & is commonly known as the 'Boston Stump'. The Guildhall Museum displays many aspects of the town's history, including the cells where the early Pilgrim Fathers were imprisioned after their attempt to flee to the Netherlands to find religious freedom. They eventually made the journey & hence to America.

One of England's most outstanding towns is Stamford. It has lovely churches, ancient inns & other fine buildings in a mellow stone.

Sir Isaac Newton was born at Woolsthorpe Manor & educated at nearby Grantham where there is a museum which illustrates his life & work.

The poet Tennyson was born in the village of Somersby, where his father was Rector.

Lincoln Cathedral.

Lincolnshire

Lincolnshire

Gazeteer
Areas of outstanding natural beauty.
Lincolnshire Wolds.

Historic Houses & Castles
Auborn House - Nr. Lincoln
16th century house with imposing carved staircase & panelled rooms.
Belton House - Grantham
House built 1684-88 - said to be by Christopher Wren - work by Grinling Gibbons & Wyatt also. Paintings, furniture, porcelain, tapestries, Duke of Windsor mementoes. A great English house with formal gardens & extensive grounds with orangery.
Doddington Hall - Doddington, Nr. Lincoln
16th century Elizabethan mansion with elegant Georgian rooms & gabled Tudor gatehouse. Fine furniture, paintings, porcelain, etc. Formal walled knot gardens, roses & wild gardens.
Burghley House - Stamford
Elizabethan - England's largest & grandest house of the era. Famous for its beautiful painted ceilings, silver fireplaces & art treasures.
Gumby Hall - Burgh-le-Marsh
17th century manor house.
Ancient gardens.
Harrington Hall - Spilsby
Mentioned in the Domesday Book - has mediaeval stone base - Carolinean manor house in red brick. Some alterations in 1678 to mullioned windows. Panelling, furnishings of 17th & 18th century.
Marston Hall - Grantham
16th century manor house.
Ancient gardens.
The Old Hall - Gainsborough
Fine mediaeval manor house built in 1480's with original kitchen, rebuilt after original hall destroyed during Wars of the Roses. Tower & wings, Great Hall. It was the first meeting place of the "Dissenters", later known as the Pilgrim Fathers.
Woolsthorpe Manor - Grantham
17th century house. Birthplace of Sir Isaac Newton.
Fydell House - Boston
18th century house, now Pilgrim College.

Lincoln Castle - Lincoln
William the Conqueror castle, with complete curtain wall & Norman shell keep. Towers & wall walk. Unique prisoners' chapel.
Tattershall Castle - Tattershall
100 foot high brick keep of 15th century moated castle, with fine views over surrounding country.

Cathedrals & Churches
Addlethorpe (St. Nicholas)
15th century - mediaeval stained glass - original woodwork.
Boston (St. Botolph)
14th century decorated - very large parish church. Beautiful south porch, carved stalls.
Brant Broughton (St. Helens)
13th century arcades - decorated tower & spire - perpendicular clerestory. Exterior decoration.
Ewerby (St. Andrew)
Decorated - splendid example of period - very fine spire. 14th century effigy.
Fleet (St. Mary Magdalene)
14th century - early English arcades - perpendicular windows - detached tower & spire.
Folkingham (St. Andrew)
14th century arcades - 15th century windows - perpendicular tower - early English chancel.
Gedney (St. Mary Magdalene)
Perpendicular spire (unfinished). Early English tower. 13th-14th century monuments, 14th-15th century stained glass.
Grantham (St. Wulfram)
14th century tower & spire - Norman pillars - perpendicular chantry - 14th century vaulted crypt.
Lincoln Cathedral - Lincoln
Magnificent triple-towered Gothic building on fine hill-top site. Norman west front, 13th century - some 14th century additions. Norman work from 1072. Angel choir - carved & decorated pulpitum - 13th century chapter house - 17th century library by Wren (containing one of the four original copies of Magna Carta)

Lincolnshire

St. Botolph's Church - Boston
Fine parish church, one of the largest in the country, with 272 foot octagonal tower dominating the surrounding fens.

Long Sutton (St. Mary)
15th century south porch, mediaeval brass lectern, very fine early English spire.

Louth (St. James)
Early 16th century - mediaeval Gothic - wonderful spire.

Scotter (St. Peter)
Saxon to perpendicular - early English nave - 15th century rood screen.

Stow (St. Mary)
Norman - very fine example, particularly west door. Wall painting.

Silk Willoughby (St. Denis)
14th century - tower with spire & flying buttresses. 15th-17th century pulpit.

Stainfield (St. Andrew)
Queen Anne - mediaeval armour & early needlework.

Theddlethorpe (All Saints)
14th century - 15th century & rerodos of 15th century, 16th century parcloses, 15th century brasses - some mediaeval glass.

Wrangle (St. Mary the Virgin & St. Nicholas)
Early English - decorated - perpendicular - Elizabethan pulpit. 14th century east window & glass.

Museums & Galleries

Alford Manor House - Alford
Tudor manor house - thatched - folk museum. Nearby windmill.

Boston Guildhall Museum - Boston
15th century building with mayor's parlour, court room & cells where Pilgrim Fathers were imprisoned in 1607. Local exhibits.

Lincoln Cathedral Library - Lincoln
Built by Wren housing early printed books & mediaeval manuscripts.

Lincoln Cathedral Treasury - Lincoln
Diocesan gold & silver plate.

Lincoln City & Country Museum - Lincoln
Prehistoric, Roman & mediaeval antiquities with local associations. Armour & local history.

Museum of Lincolnshire Life - Lincoln
Domestic, agricultural, industrial & social history of the county. Edwardian room

settings, shop settings, agricultural machinery.

Usher Gallery - Lincoln
Paintings, watches, miniatures, porcelain, silver, coins & medals. Temporary exhibitions. Tennyson collection. Works of English watercolourist Peter de Wint.

Grantham Museum - Grantham
Archeology, prehistoric, Saxon & Roman. Local history with special display about Sir Isaac Newton, born nearby & educated in Grantham.

Church Farm Museum - Skegness
Farmhouse & buildings with local agricultural collections & temporary exhibitions & special events.

Stamford Museum - Stamford
Local history museum, with temporary special exhibitions.

Battle of Britain Memorial Flight - Coningsby
Lancaster bomber, five Spitfires & two Hurricanes with other Battle of Britain memorabilia.

National Cycle Museum - Lincoln
Development of the cycle.

Stamford Steam Brewery Museum - Stamford
Complete Victorian steam brewery with 19th century equipment.

Other things to see & do

Springfield - Spalding
Show gardens of the British bulb industry, & home of the Spalding Flower Parade each May. Summer bedding plants & roses.

Butlins Funcoast World - Skegness
Funsplash Water World with amusements & entertainments

Castle Leisure Park - Tattershall
Windsurfing, water-skiing, sailing, fishing & other sports & leisure facilities.

Long Sutton Butterfly Park - Long Sutton
Walk-through tropical butterfly house with outdoor wildflower meadows & pets corner.

Skegness Natureland Marine Zoo - Skegness
Seal sanctuary with aquaria, tropical house, pets corner & butterfly house.

Windmills - at Lincoln (Ellis Mill - 4 sails), Boston (Maud Foster - 5 sails), Burgh-le-Marsh (5 sails), Alford (5 sails), Sibsey (6 sails), Heckington (8 sails).

LINCOLNSHIRE
Map reference

1 Foers
2 Beresford
3 Robinson
4 Standish
5 Pritchard
5 Brown
6 Wade
7 Gosse
9 Honnor

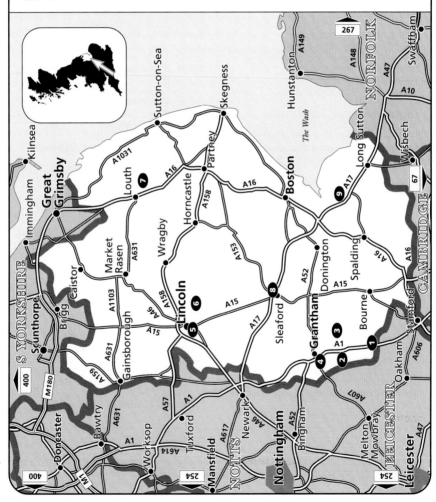

	Nearest Road / Description	Price			
(top entry — partially cut off) Map Ref No. 01	est Road: A.1 ...ifully appointed lounges, ...dded rooms with private ...ctive gardens & peaceful ...nding Bank House where ...mfort, personal service & ...This historic conservation ...rom the A.1, is ideally ... Stamford, Oakham, Rutland Water, castles, cathedrals & country houses.		🚭		
Norman & Doreen Beresford **Stoke Cottage** **Stoke Rochford** **Grantham NG33 5EP** **Tel: (0476) 83 453** **Open: JAN - NOV** Map Ref No. 02	Nearest Road: A.1 A warm welcome is extended to all guests by Doreen & Norman Beresford in this lovely thatched country house, situated in the beautiful private park of Stoke Rochford - 5 miles south of Grantham. The house is set in 4 acres of garden & woodland which guests can explore at their leisure. Adjacent is an 18 hole golf course where the first green is a "sand iron" away from the house.	£27.50 *see PHOTO over*	Y	Y	Y
Mrs Sue Robinson **Sycamore Farm** **Bassingthorpe** **Grantham** **NG33 4ED** **Tel: (047685) 274** **Open: APR - OCT** Map Ref No. 03	Nearest Road: B.6403, A.1 A warm welcome & comfortable accommodation is assured at Sycamore Farm. A large, peaceful Victorian farmhouse standing on a 450 acre mixed farm, situated approximately 4 miles from A.1 & within easy reach of Stamford, Belvoir Castle, Belton House & Lincoln. Comfortable guest lounge with open fire, colour T.V. & piano. Accommodation is in 3 comfortable, attractively decorated bedrooms, all with modern amenities & beautiful views across open countryside.	£15.00	Y	Y	N
Janice Standish **The Lanchester Guest House** **84 Harrowby Rd** **Grantham NG31 9DS** **Tel: (0476) 74169** **Open: ALL YEAR** Map Ref No. 04	Nearest Road: A.1 This well established Edwardian guest house is run professionally to high standards, & has retained its warm & friendly atmosphere. Located in a pleasant tree-lined street close to town centre. Accommodation is in 3 comfortable bedrooms, 1 with en-suite facilities, all with modern amenities, T.V. & tea/coffee makers. A T.V. lounge & separate dining room are also available. A good choice of restaurants nearby; ask for recommendations on your arrival.	£15.00	Y	N	N
Gill & John Pritchard **Carline Guest House** **1/3 Carline Road** **Lincoln** **LN1 1HW** **Tel: (0522) 530422** **Open: ALL YEAR** Map Ref No. 05	Nearest Road: A.57, A.46, A.15 Gill & John Pritchard extend a warm welcome & excellent accommodation. Offering 12 attractively furnished bedrooms, most with en-suite facilities, each with T.V., radio alarms, tea/coffee facilities & hair dryers. All public rooms & some bedrooms are totally non-smoking. The Carline is a pleasant 5 mins. walk from the historic 'uphill' area of Lincoln. There are several restaurants & public houses nearby for your lunch or evening meal. Ask for our recommendations.	£17.00 🚭	Y	N	N

See Jodors B&B 1993

261

Stoke Cottage.   Stoke Rochford.

Lincolnshire

		minimum £ per person	children taken	evening meals	animals taken
Mr Raymond H. Brown **Minster Lodge Hotel** **3 Church Lane** **Lincoln LN2 1QJ** **Tel: (0522) 513220** **Fax 0522 513220** **Open: ALL YEAR** **Map Ref No. 05**	Nearest Road: A.15 Minster Lodge is a delightful small hotel refurbished to a high standard. Offering 6 en-suite bedrooms with radio, colour T.V. & beverage facilities. Ideally situated within 50 yards of Newport Arch - the only remaining Roman Arch still in use & 5 minutes walk from Lincoln's major tourist attractions of Lincoln Cathedral & Castle & a colourful mixture of antique shops, gift shops & boutiques which are situated in the mediaeval area surrounding the cathedral & castle.	£24.50 CREDIT CARD VISA M'CARD AMEX	Y	N	N
Dr. & Mrs J. Wade **The Manor House** **Nocton Road** **Potterhanworth** **Lincoln LN4 2DN** **Tel: (0522) 791288** **Open: JAN - NOV** **Map Ref No. 06**	Nearest Road: B.1188, A.15 A peaceful 19th century Manor House clad in wisteria, honeysuckle & virginia creeper, in a pretty village 6 miles south of Lincoln. Large drawing room overlooking 8 acres of grounds, majestic trees, stream, pond & weir. Outdoor swimming pool, large summer house with table tennis, croquet & garden furniture. Cosy book-lined sitting room with T.V. In all the pretty bedrooms there are tea/coffee making facilities.	£19.00	Y	N	N
Mrs Peter Gosse **Rookery Farmhouse** **Castle Carlton** **Louth** **LN11 8JF** **Tel: (0507) 450357** **Open: ALL YEAR** **Map Ref No. 07**	Nearest Road: A.157 Rookery Farm is a delightful, traditional, late 18th century farmhouse. Restored to a high standard of comfort & convenience, while maintaining many of the original features, including low beamed ceilings & original interior brick walls. The main features outside are the old-fashioned shrub roses & herb garden. Accommodation is in 3 nice rooms with modern amenities. A residents' lounge is available. The food here is delicious, mainly wholefood with, when possible, vegetables from the garden. Home-made bread is a speciality.	£14.50	Y	Y	N
Mrs Lesley Honnor **Pipwell Manor** **Saracens Head** **Holbeach** **Spalding PE12 8AL** **Tel: (0406) 23119** **Open: ALL YEAR** **Map Ref No. 09**	Nearest Road: A.17 Pipwell Manor is a Grade II listed Georgian Manor house built around 1740 & set in paddocks & gardens in a small quiet village in the Lincolnshire Fens, just off the A.17 . Beautifully restored & decorated in English country style yet retaining many original features, Pipwell Manor is a delightful place to stay. There are 4 comfortably furnished & attractive bedrooms with tea/coffee making facilities. Guests are welcomed with tea & homemade cake. Parking available.	£17.00	Y	N	N

When booking your accommodation please mention
The Best Bed & Breakfast

Norfolk

Norfolk
(East Anglia)

One of the largest of the old counties, Norfolk is divided by rivers from neighbouring counties & pushes out into the sea on the north & east sides. This is old East Anglia.

Inland there is great concentration on agriculture where fields are hedged with hawthorn which blossoms like snow in summer. A great deal of land drainage is required & the area is crisscrossed by dykes & ditches - some of them dating back to Roman times.

Holkham Hall.

The Norfolk Broads were formed by the flooding of mediaeval peat diggings to form miles & miles of inland waterways, navigable & safe. On a bright summer's day, on a peaceful backwater bounded by reed & sedge, the Broads seem like paradise. Here are hidden treasures like the Bittern, that shyest of birds, the Swallowtail butterfly & the rare Marsh orchid.

Contrasting with the still inland waters is a lively coastline which takes in a host of towns & villages as it arcs around The Wash. Here are the joys of the seaside at its best, miles of safe & sandy golden beaches to delight children, dunes & salt marshes where birdlife flourishes, & busy ports & fishing villages with pink-washed cottages.

Cromer is a little seaside town with a pier & a prom, cream teas & candy floss, where red, white & blue fishing boats are drawn up on the beach.

Hunstanton is more decorous, with a broad green sweeping down to the cliffs. Great Yarmouth is a boisterous resort. It has a beach that runs for miles, with pony rides & almost every amusement imaginable.

It is possible to take a boat into the heart of Norwich, past warehouses, factories & new penthouses, & under stone & iron bridges. Walking along the riverbank you reach Pulls Ferry where a perfectly proportioned grey flint gateway arcs over what was once a canal dug to transport stone to the cathedral site. Norwich Cathedral is magnificent, with a sharply soaring spire, beautiful cloisters & fine 15th century carving preserved in the choir stalls. Cathedral Close is perfectly preserved, as is Elm Hill, a cobbled street from mediaeval times. There are many little shops & narrow alleys going down to the river.

Norfolk is a county much loved by the Royal family & the Queen has a home at Sandringham. It is no castle, but a solid, comfortable family home with red brick turrets & French windows opening onto the terrace.

Norfolk

Norfolk
Gazeteer

Areas of outstanding beauty.
Norfolk coast (part)

Historic Houses & Castles

Anna Sewell House - Great Yarmouth
17th century Tudor frontage. Birthplace
of writer Anna Sewell.
Blicking Hall - Aylsham
Great Jacobean house. Fine Russian
tapestry, long gallery with exceptional
ceiling. Formal garden.
Felbrigg Hall - Nr. Cromer
17th century, good Georgian interior. Set
in wooded parklands.
Holkham Hall - Wells
Fine Palladian mansion of 1734.
Paintings, statuary, tapestries, furnishings
& formal garden by Berry.
Houghton Hall - Wells
18th century mansion. Pictures, china
& staterooms.
Oxburgh Hall - Swafftham
Late 15th century moated house. Fine
gatehouse tower. Needlework by Mary
Queen of Scots.
Wolterton Hall - Nr. Norwich
Built in 1741 contains tapestries,
porcelain, furniture.
Trinity Hospital - Castle Rising
17th century, nine brick & tile
almshouses, court chapel & treasury.

Cathedrals & Churches

Attleborough (St. Mary)
Norman with late 14th century. Fine rood
screen & frescoes.
Barton Turf (St. Michael & All Angles)
Magnificent screen with painting of the
Nine Orders of Angles.
Beeston-next-Mileham (St. Mary)
14th century. Perpendicular clerestory
tower & spire. Hammer Beam roof,
parclose screens, benches, front cover.
Tracery in nave & chancel windows.
Cawston (St. Agnes)
Tower faced with freestone. Painted
screens, wall paintings, tower, screen &
gallery. 15th century angel roof.
East Harding (St. Peter & St. Paul)
14th century, some 15th century
alterations. Monuments of 15th-17th
century. Splendid mediaeval glass.

Erpingham (St. Mary)
14th century military brass to John de
Erpingham, 16th century   Rhenish glass.
Fine tower.
Gunton (St. Andrew)
18th century. Robert Adam - classical
interior in dark wood - gilded.
King's Lynn (St. Margaret)
Norman foundation. Two fine 14th
century Flemish brasses, 14th century
screens, reredos by Bodley, interesting
Georgian pulpit with sounding board.
Norwich Cathedral
Romanesque & late Gothic with 15th
century spire. Perpendicular lierne vaults
in nave, transeptsand presbytery.
Ranworth (St. Helens)
15th century screen, very fine example.
Sarum Antiphoner, 14th century
illuminated manuscript - East
Anglian work.
Salle (St. Peter & St. Paul)
15th century. Highly decorated west
tower & porches. Mediaeval glass, pulpit
with 15th century panels & Jacobean
tester. Stalls, misericords, brasses &
monuments, sacrament font.
Terrington (St. Clement)
Detached perpendicular tower. Western
front has fire-light window & canopied
niches. Georgian panelling west of nave.
17th century painted font cover.
Jacobean commandment boards.
Trunch (St. Botolph)
15th century screen with painted panels,
mediaeval glass, famous font canopy with
fine carving & painting, ringer's gallery,
Elizabethan monument.
Wiggenhall (St. Germans)
17th century pulpit, table, clerk's desk &
chair, bench ends 15th century.
Wymondham (St. Mary & St. Thomas
of Canterbury)
Norman origins including arcades &
triforium windows, 13th century font
fragments, complete 15th century font.
15th century clerestory & roof. Comper
reredos, famous Corporas Case, rare
example of 13th century
Opus Anglicanum.

Museums & Galleries

Norwich Castle Museum
Art collection, local & natural history,

Norfolk

Strangers Hall - Norwich
Mediaeval mansion furnished as museum of urban domestic life in 16th-19th centuries.
St. Peter Hungate Church Museum - Norwich
15th century church for the exhibition of ecclesiastical art & East Anglican antiquities.
Sainsbury Centre for Visual Arts - University, Norwich
Collection of modern art, ancient, classical & mediaeval art, Art Nouveau, 20th century constructivist art.
Bridewell Museum of Local Industries - Norwich
Crafts, industries & aspects of city life.
Museum of Social History - King's Lynn
Exhibition of domestic life & dress, etc., noted glass collection.
Bishop Bonner's Cottages
Restored cottages with coloured East Anglia pargetting, c. 1502, museum of archaeological discoveries, exhibition of rural crafts.
The Guildhall - Thetford
Duleep Singh Collection of Norfolk & Suffolk portraits.
Shirehall Museum - Walsingham
18th century court room having original fittings, illustrating Walsingham life.

Historic Monuments

Binham Priory & Cross - Binham
12th century ruins of Benedictine foundation.
Caister Castle - Great Yarmouth
15th century moated castle - ruins. Now motor museum.
The Castle - Burgh Castle
3rd century Saxon fort - walls - ruin.
Mannington Hall - Saxthorpe
Saxon church ruin in gardens of 15th century moated house.
Castle Rising - Castle Rising
Splendid Norman keep & earthworks.
Castle Acre Priory & Castle Gate - Swaffham

Other things to see & do

African Violet Centre - Terrington St. Clements.
60 varieties of African Violets. Talks & Tours.
Norfolk Lavender Centre - Heacham
Open to the public in July & August. Demonstrations of harvesting & distilling the oil.
Thetford Forest
Forest walks, rides & picnic places amongst conifers, oak, beech & birch.

The Broads.

NORFOLK
Map reference

1	Morfoot	23	Collins
2	Dawson	24	Garnier
3	Bartlett	25	Ford
4	Atkins	26	Whittley
5	Webb	27	Carr
6	Gillam		
7	Gent		
8	Wells		
9	Fieldsend		
10	Tweedy Smith		
10	Porter		
11	Hickey		
12	Nott		
13	Nightingale		
14	Earp		
15	Coe		
16	Wright		
16	Clarke		
17	Lovatt		
18	Parker		
19	Wace		
21	Peters		
22	Goff		

Norfolk

		minimum £ per person	children taken	evening meals	animals taken
Mrs E. M. Morfoot **Church Cottage** **Breckles** **Attleborough NR17 1EW** **Tel: (0953) 498286** **Fax 0953 498320** **Open:ALL YEAR (Excl.** **Xmas & New Year)** **Map Ref No. 01**	Nearest Road: A.11, A.1075 A friendly welcome awaits visitors to this charming 18th century house situated in beautiful Breckland overlooking typical Norfolk farmland. Centrally located for touring East Anglia . Offering 2 double & 1 twin bedroom each with modern amenities. Visitors' own sitting/dining room with colour T.V. Home made bread . Heated outdoor swimming pool. Own coarse fishing. Children over 10 years.	£15.00	Y	N	N
A. Dawson & C.Tyler **Sherbourne Country House** **Norwich Road** **Attleborough NR17 2JX** **Tel: (0953) 454363** **Fax 0953 453509** **Open: ALL YEAR** **Map Ref No. 02**	Nearest Road: A.11 Set in mature grounds, this delightful 17th century house has a friendly, family atmosphere. Accommodation is offered in 3 four-poster, en-suite rooms, 2 twins , 1 double & 2 singles. A charming lounge & lovely bar for guests. The evening meals are super & great value. The house has a fine reputation for cuisine & Australian wine list. This is an excellent base for touring Norwich & the Broads. Riding is available locally.	£22.00 CREDIT CARD VISA M'CARD AMEX	Y	Y	Y
David & Annie Bartlett **Bartles Lodge** **Church Street, Elsing** **Dereham NR20 3EA** **Tel: (0362) 637177** **Open: ALL YEAR** **Map Ref No. 03**	Nearest Road: A.47, A.1065 Beautiful fully renovated period farmhouse & converted stables with en-suite facilities & real traditional country cooking set in 5 acres of tranquil meadows with its own private fishing lake, well stocked with carp, tench, roach, etc. The village of Elsing is one of the prettiest in Norfolk, & although we are fully licensed, there is a traditional country inn only 50 metres away.	£16.00 CREDIT CARD VISA M'CARD	Y	Y	Y
Connie & Doug Atkins **Ingleneuk Lodge** **Hopton Road** **Garboldisham** **Diss IP22 2RQ** **Tel: (095381) 541** **Open: ALL YEAR** **Map Ref No. 04**	Nearest Road: A.11, A.1066 A warm welcome is extended to visitors at Ingleneuk, a large modern family-run single-storey guest house standing in 10 acres of quiet wooded countryside with riverside walks. A variety of rooms are available, most en-suite, all centrally heated, double-glazed, with colour T.V., telephone, electric blankets & hot drink facilities. Children well provided for. Residents' lounge, licensed bar, evening meals book by 1p.m. Wheelchair disabled welcome.	£17.00 CREDIT CARD VISA M'CARD AMEX	Y	Y	Y
Jill & Ian Gillam **The Old Rectory** **Gissing** **Diss** **IP22 3XB** **Tel: (037977) 575** **Fax 037977 4427** **Open: ALL YEAR** **Map Ref No. 06**	Nearest Road: A.140 This delightful Victorian house stands in grounds of mature gardens & woodland & is a haven of peace, comfort & elegance. Bedrooms are spacious with private or en-suite facilities. Every effort has been made to ensure a memorable stay - tea/coffee making facilities, colour T.V., notepaper, fresh flowers & an extensive range of toiletries. Breakfast is copious & beautifully presented. Candlelit dinner is available by prior arrangement. Amenities - croquet, indoor swimming pool (heated). Smoking restrictions.	£23.00 *see PHOTO over* CREDIT CARD VISA	Y	Y	N

The Old Rectory.   Gissing.

Norfolk

		per person minimum £	children taken	evening meals	animals taken
Ken & Brenda Webb **Strenneth Farmhouse** **Old Airfield Road** **Fersfield** **Diss IP22 2BP** **Tel: (037988) 8182** **Open: ALL YEAR** **Map Ref No. 05**	Nearest Road: A.1066 A 16th-17th century former farmhouse located close to the small market town of Diss. Renovated to a high standard. The heavily beamed house now offers guests very pleasant, comfortable accommodation in a choice of 9 bedrooms, most with en-suite facilities. A separate lounge for non-smokers. An excellent 3-course meal is available & special diets can be catered for. Children are welcome. Licensed.	£18.50 CREDIT CARD VISA M'CARD	Y	Y	Y
Tessa & Tony Gent **The Old Brick Kilns** **Little Barney** **Fakenham NR21 0NL** **Tel: (0328) 878305** **Open: Mid JAN-Mid DEC** **Map Ref No. 07**	Nearest Road: A.148 A warm welcome awaits you at these charmingly converted cottages. Situated in a quiet rural area. Yet convenient for the coast. Accommodation is in 3 rooms, all with en-suite facilities, colour T.V., radio, hair dryers & tea/coffee makers. A lounge & garden is available for guests at any time. Conveniently located as a touring base for visiting many places of local interest.	£20.50	Y	Y	N
Mrs B. Wells **'Spindrift' Private Hotel** **36 Wellesley Road** **Great Yarmouth** **NR30 1EU** **Tel: (0493) 858674** **Open: ALL YEAR** **Map Ref No. 08**	Nearest Road: A.47 Good food & comfortable accommodation are the by-words at 'Spindrift'. Attractively situated adjacent to the sea front, the Golden Mile, bowling greens, tennis courts & the water ways. Easygoing atmosphere with keys provided for access at all times. A selection of 8 bedrooms, some with excellent sea views & 5 bedrooms with en-suite facilities, all with modern amenities, colour T.V. & tea/coffee making facilities. Good on road parking, public car park at rear if space allow	£14.00 CREDIT CARD VISA M'CARD	Y	N	N
Mrs Jane Fieldsend **Windmill Guest House** **56 The Street** **Hindolveston** **Holt NR20 5DF** **Tel: (0263) 861095** **Open: ALL YEAR** **Map Ref No. 09**	Nearest Road: A.1067, B.1110. The Windmill, originally 2 farm cottages dating from 1830, has been restored & renovated & retains all its original charm & character, including an oak beamed living room with wood burning stove. Offering accommodation in the pleasantly decorated twin or double bedroom, each with tea/coffee making facilities. This is a good base for visiting rural North Norfolk's nature reserves & Blickling Hall, Holkham Hall, Mannington Hall & gardens, & Sandringham.	£16.00	Y	Y	N
Sheila Tweedy Smith **Fieldsend House** **Homefields Road** **Hunstanton** **PE36 5HL** **Tel: (0485) 532593** **Open: ALL YEAR** **Map Ref No. 10**	Nearest Road: A.149 Fieldsend is a large Carrstone house, built at the turn of the century, enjoying lovely sea views. There are canopied beds including 1 four-poster en-suite bedroom. Colour T.V. & tea/coffee makers & an oak panelled sitting room. Guests will enjoy a leisurely stay at this country house style home while being only 4 mins. from the centre of town. Delicious breakfasts served by a Cordon Bleu cook. Parking.	£17.00	Y	N	N

Norfolk

Mrs Susan Porter **Pinewood Hotel** **26 Northgate** **Hunstanton PE36 6AP** **Tel: (0485) 533068** **Open: ALL YEAR** **Map Ref No. 10**	Nearest Road: A.149 Enjoy warmth, comfort & hospitality in this friendly family run Victorian Hotel, with a natural pine look. 8 delightfully decorated bedrooms, 1 with Victorian bedstead & Laura Ashley decor. Some with sea views, 4 en-suite, all with colour T.V. & tea/coffee making facilities. Enjoy delicious home cooking & good wines, or relax in front of a log fire in our bar/lounge.	£17.50	Y	Y	Y
Linda & Martin Hickey **Corfield House** **Sporle** **Nr. Swaffham** **King's Lynn PE32 2EA** **Tel: (0760) 23636** **Open: APR - DEC** **Map Ref No. 11**	Nearest Road: A.47 This family-run country guest house is set in peaceful surroundings 3 miles from the attractive market town of Swaffham. There are 5 comfortable & well-equipped bedrooms, with en-suite bath or shower, all offer colour T.V., radio, tea/coffee making facilities & full central heating. Separate guest lounge & dining room, public telephone. Good home cooking, licensed. An ideal base for touring North Norfolk.	£18.50 CREDIT CARD VISA M'CARD	Y	Y	Y
Mr & Mrs R. E. Nott **The Mill House** **Station Road** **Snettisham** **King's Lynn PE31 7QJ** **Tel: (0485) 542180** **Open: ALL YEAR** **Map Ref No. 12**	Nearest Road: A.149 Located along a private drive, set by the millpool in a beautiful garden with waterfall, river & 18th century working watermill. The Mill House offers 3 charming bedrooms, 2 of which are en-suite/shower. Hospitality tray in each room. Breakfast is in the pine morning room which has colour T.V. & is available to guests in the evening. Guest rooms have views over the millpool & gardens. Ideally placed for Sandringham. No smoking.	£16.00	N	N	N
Dawn Nightingale **The White House** **44 Hunstanton Road** **Dersingham** **King's Lynn** **PE31 6HQ** **Tel: (0485) 541895** **Open: ALL YEAR** **Map Ref No. 13**	Nearest Road: A.149, B.1440 Comfortable detached centrally heated house built in 1901 and once owned by Edward VII & only one & a half miles from Sandringham, the Queen's Norfolk home. Accommodation is in 5 rooms all with tea/coffee making facilities. A ground-floor, double en-suite room, suitable for the disabled by arrangement. Guests lounge with colour T.V. Centrally located for many historic houses, bird reserves, museums, working windmills & beautiful beaches. Parking.	£14.00	Y	N	Y
Mrs Philippa Earp **Mornington House** **33 Church Plain** **Loddon NR14 6EX** **Tel: (0508) 28572** **Open:ALL YEAR (Excl.** **Xmas & New Year)** **Map Ref No. 14**	Nearest Road: A.146 Delightful Grade II listed character residence in market town centre. Dating back in parts to 1570, it was originally believed to be an inn and it is reputed that Charles Wesley once stayed here. Beams and inglenooks abound. 2 guest bedrooms. Both Norwich and the Heritage Coast are within easy reach. Loddon is on the river Chet, with boat hire or trips available.	£15.00	Y	N	N

Norfolk

		minimum £ per person	children taken	evening meals	animals taken
Phil & Ray Coe **Brooksbank** **Lower Street** **Salhouse** **Norwich NR13 6RW** **Tel: (0603) 720420** **Open: ALL YEAR** **Map Ref No. 15**	Nearest Road: A.1151 18th century Brooksbank stands in the centre of Salhouse village in the heart of Broadland, 2 miles from Wroxham, 7 miles from the lovely Cathedral city of Norwich. Guests have own private accommodation with T.V. lounge. Bedrooms have colour T.V., tea/coffee facilities, and all have private bathrooms. Phil & Ray Coe extend you a warm welcome to their home. Their pleasure is your comfort!	£16.00 *see PHOTO over*	Y	Y	N
D Geoffrey & S Wright **Earlham Guest House** **147 Earlham Road** **Norwich NR2 3RG** **Tel: (0603) 54169** **Open: ALL YEAR** **Map Ref No. 16**	Nearest Road: B.1108 A delightful Victorian residence on major road from city centre to the University (B.1108). All rooms have modern amenities including colour T.V. & hot drinks tray, some with private facilities, & keys are provided for freedom of access. Vegetarian foods are offered as an alternative to a generous full English breakfast, if preferred.	£16.00	Y	N	N
Eddie & Margaret Lovatt **Edmar Lodge** **64 Earlham Road** **Norwich NR2 3DF** **Tel: (0603) 615599** **Fax 0603 615515** **Open: ALL YEAR** **Map Ref No. 17**	Nearest Road: B.1108 A large corner house with parking for 6 cars, situated in a quiet area, only 10 minutes' walk from the city centre. There are 5 very attractive, comfortable rooms with every modern amenity, including tea/coffee makers & colour T.V.. 3 rooms have private facilities. Mrs Lovatt makes all her guests very welcome & serves wonderful breakfasts in a pretty dining room. Help is readily given on tour plannning & advice on Norwich City & its many gourmet restaurants.	£16.00	Y	N	N
W.R. & A.E. Parker **Elm Farm Chalet Hotel** **St. Faith** **Norwich NR10 3HH** **Tel: (0603) 898366** **Fax 0603 897129** **Open: ALL YEAR (excl. Xmas & New Year)** **Map Ref No. 18**	Nearest Road: A.140 Attractive, comfortable accommodation is offered at the 17th century farmhouse & chalet hotel. Most rooms have en-suite shower, all with tea/coffee making facilities, radio alarms, telephone & colour T.V. Large, licensed dining room & T.V. lounge. Situated in the attractive village of St. Faith, 4 miles north of Norwich & ideal for visiting the Broads & touring Norfolk & Suffolk.	£25.25 CREDIT CARD VISA M'CARD AMEX	Y	Y	N
Jean Wace **Gables Farm** **Hemblington Hall Rd** **Hemblington** **Norwich NR13 4PT** **Tel/Fax: (060549) 548** **Open: ALL YEAR** **Map Ref No. 19**	Nearest Road: A.47 This delightful 17th century thatched farmhouse stands in a large garden surrounded by a 300 acre farm. There is a twin room & a family room, each with private facilities, colour T.V. & tea makers. A traditional breakfast is served in the dining room. Guests are invited to enjoy the nearby Broads & nature reserves. Both Norwich & the beautiful coast are within easy reach.	£17.50	Y	N	N

Brooksbank. Salhouse.

Norfolk

		minimum £ per person	children taken	evening meals	animals taken
Sally Clarke **Kingsley Lodge** **3 Kingsley Road** **Norwich** **NR1 3RB** **Tel: (0603) 615819** **Open: ALL YEAR** **Map Ref No. 16**	Nearest Road: A.11, A.140 A friendly Edwardian house in the city centre yet surprisingly quiet, very close to the bus station, shops & restaurants. All 4 rooms (1 twin, 2 double, 1 single) have en-suite bathrooms, colour T.V., tea/coffee making facilities & are comfortably furnished. Traditional English breakfasts are cooked to order & served in the large lounge or in the conservatory during the summer. A lovely home & an ideal location for exploring historic Norwich & Norfolk.	£18.00 🚭	N	N	N
Carol & Donald Peters **Linden House** **557 Earlham Road** **Norwich** **NR4 7HW** **Tel: (0603) 51303** **Fax 0603 250641** **Open: ALL YEAR** **Map Ref No. 21**	Nearest Road: B.1108, A.11 Lovely house with all new facilities, ample parking & attractive gardens. University 5 minutes' walk; frequent mini-bus from house to city centre. Luxury, all-en-suite hotel accommodation at inexpensive prices. Washing machine & dryer. Fax, photocopier, metered telephone. Colour T.V., tea/coffee facilities in all rooms. Full central heating; double glazing. Reduced terms for weekends or extended visits. 4 minutes from southern bypass Exit B.1108 direction Norwich near 5-ways roundabout.	£17.00 CREDIT CARD VISA M'CARD	Y	Y	Y
Mrs Gill Goff **Rookery Farm** **Church Street** **Reepham** **Norwich NR10 4JW** **Tel: (0603) 871847** **Open: ALL YEAR** **Map Ref No. 22**	Nearest Road: A.1067 A warm welcome awaits at Rookery Farm. Situated on the edge of a small market town, this listed farmhouse, built in the 17th century, renovated in 1810 & modernised in the 20th century, retains a wealth of fascinating period features. It now offers peaceful accommodation in one of the loveliest corners of Norfolk. There are 3 very attractive & tastefully furnished guest rooms, each with en-suite facilities. In short, comfort & character with a hearty farmhouse breakfast.	£17.00 *see PHOTO over*	Y	N	Y
Mrs Christine Collins **Cedar Lodge** **West Tofts** **Thetford** **IP27 5DB** **Tel: (0842) 878281** **Open: ALL YEAR** **Map Ref No. 23**	Nearest Road: A.134 Guests receive a true country welcome at this cedar Colt house. Standing in a well kept garden it is located in the heart of Thetford Forest. Traditionally furnished & offering comfortable guest rooms, 1 with private bathroom, each with T.V. & tea/coffee making facilities. Christine is Cordon Bleu trained & loves entertaining her guests & is pleased to provide packed lunches. The North Norfolk coast, Cambridge, Norwich & Newmarket are within 45 mins. drive.	£18.00	Y	Y	Y
Lavender Garnier **College Farm** **Thompson** **Thetford** **IP24 1QG** **Tel: (053383) 318** **Open: ALL YEAR** **Map Ref No. 24**	Nearest Road: A.1075 Built 600 years ago as a College of Priests & becoming a manor house when Henry VIII dismissed the monasteries. College Farm has been modernised to provide 4 comfortable rooms all with colour T.V. & with superb views over farmland & mature trees. Delicious breakfasts are served in the panelled dining room. An excellent thatched pub in the village offers tasty meals. Norfolk coast, Norwich, Cambridge & Sandringham within easy reach by car.	£16.00	Y	N	N

Rookery Farm. Reepham.

		minimum £ per person	children taken	evening meals	animals taken
Mrs Marion Ford **Old Bottle House** **Cranwich** **Mundford** **Thetford IP26 5JL** **Tel: (0842) 878012** **Open: ALL YEAR** **Map Ref No. 25**	Nearest Road: A.134 Old Bottle House is a 275 year-old former coaching inn, on the edge of Thetford Forest. Guests have a choice of 3 spacious, colour-co-ordinated bedrooms with tea/coffee making facilities & colour T.V. Delicious meals are served in the dining room, which has an inglenook fireplace. A charming house with every comfort and a warm, friendly welcome. Children over 5 please.	£16.00	Y	Y	N
Mr & Mrs M. Whittley **The Grange** **Northwold** **Thetford IP26 5NF** **Tel: (0366) 728240** **Open: ALL YEAR** **Map Ref No. 26**	Nearest Road: A.134 Guests will enjoy the real family atmosphere at The Grange. This beautiful Regency rectory stands in 5 acres of mature garden with a stream running through the grounds. The accommodation is in 5 rooms with use of a drawing room, tea/coffee facilities & a T.V. room. There is also an outdoor heated swimming pool. Good home cooking. Centrally located for Norfolk, Suffolk & Cambridge. Children over 12 only.	£17.00 *see PHOTO over*	Y	Y	Y
Mrs D.G. Carr **White Hall** **Carbrooke** **Thetford IP25 6SG** **Tel: (0953) 885950** **Fax 0953 885950** **Open: ALL YEAR** **Map Ref No. 27**	Nearest Road: B.1108, A.1075 Elegant Georgian country house in delightful grounds of 3 acres with large natural pond. Offering 3 very attractive, comfortable & well appointed bedrooms (one en-suite), a spacious, sunny drawing room with colour T.V., traditional breakfast served in the fine dining room. Early morning tea, evening drinks, full central heating, log fires, etc., ensure your stay is enjoyable and relaxing. Ideal touring centre, lots of local interest. Good food, golf, swimming nearby.	£16.00	Y	N	N

When booking your accommodation please mention
The Best Bed & Breakfast

The Grange.   Northwold.

Northumbria

Northumbria

Mountains & moors, hills & fells ,coast & country are all to be found in this Northern region which embraces four counties - Northumberland, Durham, Cleveland & Tyne & Wear.

Saxons, Celts, Vikings, Romans & Scots all fought to control what was then a great wasteland between the Humber & Scotland.

Northumberland

Northumberland is England's Border country, a land of history, heritage & breathtaking countryside. Hadrian's Wall, stretching across the county from the mouth of the Tyne in the west to the Solway Firth, was built as the Northern frontier of the Roman Empire in 122 AD. Excavations along the Wall have brought many archaeological treasures to light. To walk along the wall is to discover the genius of Roman building & engineering skill. They left a network of roads, used to transport men & equipment in their attempts to maintain discipline among the wild tribes.

Through the following centuries the Border wars with the Scots led to famous battles such as Otterburn in 1388 & Flodden in 1513, & the construction of great castles including Bamburgh & Lindisfarne. Berwick-on-Tweed, the most northerly town, changed hands between England & Scotland 13 times.

Northumberland's superb countryside includes the Cheviot Hills in the Northumberland National Park, the unforgettable heather moorlands of the Northern Pennines to the west, Kielder Water (Western Europe's largest man-made lake), & 40 miles of glorious coastline.

Holy Island, or Lindisfarne, is reached by a narrow causeway that is covered at every incoming tide.

Here St. Aidan of Iona founded a monastery in the 7th century, & with St. Cuthbert set out to Christianise the pagan tribes. The site was destroyed by the Danes, but Lindisfarne Priory was built by the monks of Durham in the 11th century to house a Benedictine community. The ruins are hauntingly beautiful.

Durham

County Durham is the land of the Prince Bishops, who with their armies, nobility, courts & coinage controlled the area for centuries. They ruled as a virtually independent State, holding the first line of defence against the Scots.

In Durham City, the impressive Norman Castle standing proudly over the narrow mediaeval streets was the home of the Prince Bishops for 800 years.

Durham Cathedral, on a wooded peninsula high above the River Wear, was built in the early 12th century & is undoubtably one of the world's finest buildings, long a place of Christian pilgrimage.

The region's turbulent history led to the building of forts & castles. Some like Bowes & Barnard Castle are picturesque ruins whilst others, including Raby, Durham & Lumley still stand complete.

The Durham Dales of Weardale, Teesdale & the Derwent Valley cover about one third of the county & are endowed with some of the highest & wildest scenery. Here are High Force, England's highest waterfall, & the Upper Teesdale National Nature Reserve.

The Bowes Museum at Barnard Castle is a magnificent French-style chateau & houses an important art collection.

In contrast is the award-winning museum at Beamish which imaginatively recreates Northern life at the turn of the century.

Northumbria

Cleveland

Cleveland, the smallest 'shire' in England, has long been famous for its steel, chemical & shipbuilding industries but it is also an area of great beauty. The North Yorkshire National Park lies in the south, & includes the cone-shaped summit of Roseberry Topping, "Cleveland's Matterhorn".

Cleveland means 'land of cliffs', & in places along the magnificent coastline, cliffs tower more than 600 feet above the sea, providing important habitat for wild plants & sea-birds.

Pretty villages such as Hart, Elwick & Staithes are full of steep, narrow alleys. Marton was the birthplace of Captain James Cook & the museum there traces the explorer's early life & forms the start of the 'Cook Heritage Trail'.

The Tees estuary is a paradise for birdwatchers, whilst walkers can follow the Cleveland Way or the 38 miles of the Langbaurgh Loop.

There is surfing, windsurfing & sailing at Saltburn, & for the less energetic, the scenic Esk Valley Railway runs from Middlesbrough to Whitby.

Tyne & Wear

Tyne & Wear takes its name from the two rivers running through the area, & includes the large & lively city of Newcastle-on-Tyne.

Weardale lies in a beautiful valley surrounded by wild & bleak fells. Peaceful now, it was the setting for a thriving industry mining coal & silver, zinc & lead. Nature trails & recreation areas have been created among the old village & market towns.

The county was the birthplace of George Stephenson, railway engineer, who pioneered the world's first passenger railway on the Stockton to Darlington Line in 1825.

Durham Cathedral.

Northumbria

Northumbria Gazeeter

Areas of Outstanding Natural Beauty
The Heritage Coast, the Cheviot Hills, the North Pennine chain.

Historic Houses & Castles

Alnwick Castle - Alnwick
A superb mediaeval castle of the 12th century.

Bamburgh Castle-Bamburgh
A resorted 12th century castle with Norman keep.

Callaly Castle - Whittingham
A 13th century Pele tower with 17th century mansion. Georgian additions.

Durham Castle - Durham
Part of the University of Durham - a Norman castle.

Lindisfarne Castle - Holy Island
An interesting 14th century castle.

Ormesby Hall - Nr. Middlesbrough
A mid 18th century house.

Raby Castle - Staindrop, Darlington
14th century with some later alteration . Fine art & furniture. Large gardens.

Wallington Hall -Combo
A 17th century house with much alteration & addition.

Washington Old Hall-Washington
Jacobean manor house, parts of which date back to 12th century.

Cathedrals & Churches

Brancepeth (St. Brandon)
12th century with superb 17th century woodwork. Part of 2 mediaeval screens. Flemish carved chest.

Durham Cathedral
A superb Norman cathedral. A unique Galilee chapel & early 12th century vaults.

Escombe
An interesting Saxon Church with sundial.

Hartlepool (St. Hilda)
Early English with fine tower & buttresses.

Hexham (St. Andrews)
Remains of a 17th century church with Roman dressing. A unique night staircase & very early stool. Painted screens.

Jarrow (St. Pauls)
Bede worshipped here. Strange in that it was originally 2 churches until 11th century. Mediaeval chair.

Newcastle (St. Nicholas)
14th century with an interesting lantern tower. Heraldic font. Roundel of 14th century glass.

Morpeth (St. Mary the Virgin)
Fine mediaeval glass in east window - 14th century.

Pittington (St. Lawrence)
Late Norman nave with wall paintings. Carved tombstone - 13th century.

Skelton (St. Giles)
Early 13th century with notable font, gable crosses, bell-cote & buttresses.

Staindrop (St. Mary)
A fine Saxon window. Priests dwelling. Neville tombs & effigies.

Museums & Galleries

Aribea Roman Fort Museum - South Shields
Interesting objects found on site.

Berwick-on-Tweed Museum - Berwick
Special exhibition of interesting local finds.

Bowes Museum - Bernard Castle
European art from mediaeval to 19th century.

Captain Cook Birthplace Museum - Middlesbrough
Cook's life & natural history relating to his travels.

Clayton Collection - Chollerford
A collection of Roman sculpture, weapons & tools from forts.

Corbridge Roman Station - Corbridge
Roman pottery & sculpture.

Dormitory Musuem - Durham Cathedral
Relics of St. Cuthbert. Mediaeval seats & manuscripts.

Gray Art Gallery - Hartlepool
19th-20th century art & oriental antiquities.

Gulbenkian Museum of Oriental Art - University of Durham
Chinese pottery & porcelain, Chinese jade & stone carvings, Chinese ivories, Chinese textiles, Japenese & Tibetan art. Egyptian & Mesopotamian antiquities.

Jarrow Hall - Jarrow
Excavation finds of Saxon & mediaeval monastery. Fascinating information room dealing with early Christian sites in England.

Northumbria

Keep Museum - Newcastle-upon-Tyne
Mediaeval collection.
Laing Art Gallery - Newcastle-upon-Tyne
17th-19th century British arts, porcelain,
glass & silver.
National Music Hall Museum -
Sunderland
19th-20th century costume & artefacts
associated with the halls.
Preston Hall Museum - Stockton-on-
Tees
Armour & arms, toys, ivory period room
University - New Castle -Upon -Tyne
The Hatton Gallery - housing a fine
collection of Italian paintings.
Museum of Antiquities
Prehistoric, Roman & Saxon collection
with an interesting reconstruction of
a temple.
**Beamish North of England Open Air
Museum** - European Museum of the Year
Chantry Bagpipe Museum - Morpeth
Darlington Museum & Railway Centre.

Historic Monuments

Ariiea Roman Fort - South Shields
Remains which include the gateways
& headquarters.
Barnard Castle - Barnard Castle
17th century ruin with interesting keep.
Bowes Castle - Bowes
Roman Fort with Norman keep.
The Castle & Town Walls - Berwick-on-
Tweed
12th century remains, reconstructed later.
Dunstanburgh Castle - Alnwick
14th century remains.
Egglestone Abbey - Barnard Castle
Remains of a Poor House.
Finchdale Priory - Durham
13 th century church with
much remaining.
Hadrian's Wall - Housesteads
Several miles of the wall including castles
& site museum.
Mithramic Temple - Carrawbrough
Mithraic temple dating back to the
3rd century.
Norham Castle - Norham
The partial remains of a 12th
century castle.
Prudhoe Castle - Prudhoe
From the 12th century with additions.
Bailey & gatehouse well preserved.

The Roman Fort - Chesters
Extensive remains of a Roman
bath house.
Tynemouth Priory & Castle -
Tynemouth
11th century priory - ruin - with 16th
century towers & keep.
Vindolanda - Barton Mill
Roman fort dating from 3rd century.
Warkworth Castle - Warkworth
Dating from the 11th century with
additions - a great keep & gatehouse.
Warkworth Hermitage - Warkworth
An interesting 14th century Hermitage.
Lindisfarne Priory - Holy Island
(Lindisfarne)
11th century monastery. Island
accessible only at low tide.

Other things to see & do

Botanical Gardens - Durham University
Bird & Seal Colonies - Farne Islands
Conducted tours by boat
Marine Life Centre & Fishing Museum -
Seahouses
Museum of sealife, & boat trips to the
Farne Islands.
Tower Knowe Visitor Centre - Keilder
Water

Saltburn Victorian Festival.

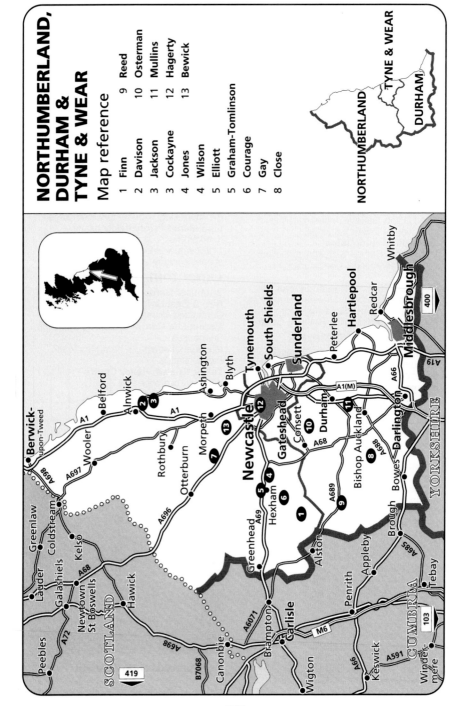

NORTHUMBERLAND, DURHAM & TYNE & WEAR

Map reference

1 Finn
2 Davison
3 Jackson
3 Cockayne
4 Jones
4 Wilson
5 Elliott
5 Graham-Tomlinson
6 Courage
7 Gay
8 Close
9 Reed
10 Osterman
11 Mullins
12 Hagerty
13 Bewick

NORTHUMBERLAND

TYNE & WEAR

DURHAM

Northumbria
Northumberland

		minimum £ per person	children taken	evening meals	animals taken
Eileen Finn **Thornley House** **Allendale** **NE47 9NH** **Tel: (0434) 683255** **Open: ALL YEAR** **Map Ref No. 01**	Nearest Road: A.69 Large country house in spacious & peaceful grounds, surrounded by fields & woods 1 mile out of Allendale village. Relaxed & comfortable accommodation here; 3 roomy & light bedrooms (1 en-suite). 2 lounges, 1 with colour T.V., 1 with Steinway Grand. Good food & home baking; unlicensed, but guests are welcome to bring their own wine. Marvellous walking country. Hadrian's Wall, Keilder Forest, & stately houses nearby.	£18.50	Y	Y	Y
Mrs Anne I. Davison **Alndyke Farmhouse** **Alnmouth Road** **Alnwick** **NE66 3PB** **Tel: (0665) 602193** **Open: MAY - OCT** **Map Ref No. 02**	Nearest Road: A.1068, A.1 Charming, listed Georgian farmhouse standing in its own grounds, commanding panoramic views. Excellent base for touring Northumberland's castles & country homes. Only 1 mile from the historical town of Alnwick & 3 miles to the coast. The farmhouse offers spacious accommodation to a high standard. All bedrooms have wash basins (1 twin room en-suite), clock/radios, hairdryers, T.V. & tea/coffee making facilities. In the elegant dining room, beautiful, traditional home-made meals served.	£17.00	N	Y	N
Dorothy Jackson **Bilton Barns Farmhouse** **Bilton Barns** **Alnmouth** **Alnwick** **NE66 2TB** **Tel: (0665) 830427** **Open: EASTER- OCT** **Map Ref No. 03**	Nearest Road: A.1 This spacious & well furnished farmhouse has beautiful, panoramic views over Alnmouth & Warkworth Bay, only 1 & a half miles away. Set in lovely countryside, ideally situated for magnificent beaches, castles, walks & recreational activities that Northumberland can offer. All rooms are centrally heated & the large bedrooms have their own washbasin, T.V. & tea/coffee making facilities. Dorothy makes many dishes with a distinctly local flavour. Brian is pleased to show any interested visitors around the farm.	£17.00	Y	Y	N
Alison Cockayne **High Buston Hall** **High Buston** **Alnmouth** **Alnwick** **NE66 3QH** **Tel: (0665) 830341** **Open: MAR-DEC** **Map Ref No. 03**	Nearest Road: A.1, B.1068 High Buston hall stands in a commanding position overlooking the Northumberland coast. It is a Grade II listed Georgian country house standing in 5 acres of mature gardens, an orchard & paddock. Downstairs there is a large drawing room with an open fire & well stocked bookshelves & separate dining room where guests share a large oak table. Furnishings are traditional & comfortable. 3 charming rooms, 1 en-suite. Excellent local produce is served & the atmosphere is one of informality & relaxation.	£22.50	Y	Y	N
Dorothy Margaret Wilson **Town Barns** **Corbridge** **NE45 5HP** **Tel: (0434) 633345** **Open: FEB - NOV** **Map Ref No. 04**	Nearest Road: A.68, A.69 A warm welcome always awaits you at Town Barns, an impressive detached stone house, once the home of authoress Catherine Cookson. Uninterrupted views over the Tyne valley, yet only 2 minutes' walk to village centre. Attractive double staircase to balcony & 3 luxurious bedrooms, 2 en-suite, all with tea/coffee making& T.V. Superb Lounge. Indoor heated pool (seasonal). Lovely walled garden. Parking.	£16.00	Y	N	Y

Northumberland

	Nearest Road	minimum £ per person	children taken	evening meals	animals taken
Tom & Sue Jones **Low Barns** **Thornbrough** **Corbridge** **NE45 5LX** **Tel: (0434) 632408** **Open: ALL YEAR** **Map Ref No. 04**	Nearest Road: A.68, A.69 Set in 2 acres of garden & paddock, this handsome 18th century farmhouse is surrounded by open countryside. It makes an ideal base for walking the Roman Wall & discovering the delights of rural Northumberland. All 3 rooms have en-suite or private facilities, tea/coffee makers & colour T.V. Evening meals are prepared using home grown produce whenever possible. Clothes washing machine & drying room available. Dogs welcome by arrangement.	£17.00 CREDIT CARD VISA M'CARD	Y	Y	Y
Eileen Elliott **Middlemarch** **Hencotes** **Hexham NE46 2EB** **Tel: (0434) 605003** **Open: ALL YEAR** **Map Ref No. 05**	Nearest Road: A.68, A.69 A beautiful Georgian house perfectly placed in this mediaeval market town. Good stop for exploring Northumberland, Roman Wall or going to & from Scotland. The well appointed, spacious bedrooms are 1 4-poster en-suite, 1 family, 1 double & 1 twin. All have W.H.B., tea/coffee facilities, remote colour T.V., radio/alarm & hairdryers. A choice of full English or Continental breakfast is offered. Private parking.	£20.00	Y	N	Y
Elizabeth Courage **Rye Hill Farm** **Slaley** **Hexham NE47 OAH** **Tel: (0434) 673259** **Open: ALL YEAR** **Map Ref No. 06**	Nearest Road: B.6306 Rye Hill Farm dates back some 300 years & is a traditional livestock unit in beautiful countryside just 5 miles south of Hexham. Recently some of the stone barns adjoining the farmhouse have been converted into superb modern guest accommodation. 6 bedrooms, all with private facilities, all have radio, colour T.V. & tea/coffee making facilities. Delicious home-cooked meals. Perfect for a "get away from it all" holiday.	£16.50	Y	Y	Y
P Graham-Tomlinson **West Close House** **Hextol Terrace** **Hexham** **NE46 2AD** **Tel: (0434) 603307** **Open: ALL YEAR** **Map Ref No. 05**	Nearest Road: B.6305, A.69 Lovingly tended secluded gardens surround this charming & immaculately maintained 1920's detached villa, situated in a peaceful, leafy cul-de-sac with private parking. 3 prettily appointed bedrooms (plus 1 super double en-suite) offer washbasins, radio/alarms& tea/coffee facilities . There is a delightful drawing room & dining/T.V. lounge for guests. Choice of Wholefood Continental or Full English Breakfasts & light suppers. A beautiful home, quality food & tasteful decor & furnishings ensure a memorable stay.	£16.00	Y	Y	Y
Stephen & Celia Gay **Shieldhall** **Wallington** **Cambo** **Morpeth** **NE61 4AQ** **Tel: (0830) 40387** **Open: MAR - NOV** **Map Ref No. 07**	Nearest Road: A.696, B.6342 Within acres of well kept gardens, offering unimpeded views & overlooking the National Trust's Wallington estate, this meticulously restored 18th century farmhouse is built around a pretty courtyard. All bedrooms are beautifully furnished & have en-suite facilities. There are very comfortable lounges & an extremely charming inglenooked dining room where home produce is often used for delicious meals which are especially prepared when booked in advance.	£16.50	Y	Y	Y

Durham

		per person minimum £	children taken	evening meals	animals taken
Helene P. Close **Grove House** **Hamsterley Forest** **Bishop Auckland** **DL13 3NL** **Tel: (038888) 203** **Open: ALL YEAR** **Map Ref No. 08**	Nearest Road: A.68 Grove House, once an aristocrats' shooting lodge, is set in 5,000 acres of woodland, moors & becks. A walker's paradise where much wildlife can be seen. If you tire of walking then simply relax & breathe the pure air. Within easy reach of England's highest waterfall, Durham City, Beamish Museum, Hadrian's Wall & Raby Castle. Golf, horseriding, bicycle hire nearby. A lovely home, conveniently located for touring.	£19.00 🚭	Y	Y	Y
Mrs B Reed **Lands Farm** **Westgate-in-Weardale** **Bishop Auckland** **DL13 1SN** **Tel: (0388) 517210** **Open: APR - OCT** **Map Ref No. 09**	Nearest Road: A.689 You will be warmly welcomed to Lands Farm, an old stone-built farmhouse within walking distance of Westgate village. Walled garden with stream meandering by. There are centrally heated double & family rooms with luxury en-suite facilities, T.V., tea/coffee making. Full English breakfast or Continental alternative served in attractive dining room. Ideal base for touring (Durham, Hadrian's Wall, Beamish Museum etc.) & for walking.	£17.00	Y	N	N
Elsie Osterman **Little Holmside Hall** **Burnhope** **DH7 0DS** **Tel: (0207) 284740** **Open: ALL YEAR** **Map Ref No. 10**	Nearest Road: A.691 Little Holmside Hall is an Elizabethan Manor House dating from 1668. Winner of a prestigious environment award for its recent restoration. 2 delightful, comfortable guest rooms, both with en-suite bathroom, T.V., & tea/coffee making facilities. The guest lounge has panoramic views of the glorious countryside. A haven of peace & tranquility is found in this easy going, friendly atmosphere. Conveniently located for Durham City, Beamish museum & the Metro Centre.	£16.00 🚭	Y	N	N
David E. Mullins **The Gables** **South View** **Middlestone Moor** **Spennymoor DL16 7DF** **Tel: (0388) 817544** **Open: ALL YEAR** **Map Ref No. 11**	Nearest Road: A.1(M) The Gables is a spacious, Victorian, detached house in a tranquil residential area, 10 mins. to A.1(M) & only 7 miles from Durham city centre & "Beamish", 1990 European Museum of the Year. Ideal touring centre for North Yorks., Moors, Teesdale, Weardale, Cumbria & Hadrian's Wall. Destinations within 30 mins. drive: Newcastle, Darlington, Sunderland, Middlesborough & Richmond Gateshead Metro centre. Colour T.V./welcome tray in each room.	£13.00 CREDIT CARD VISA M'CARD	Y	N	Y

When booking your accommodation please mention
The Best Bed & Breakfast

Tyne & Wear

		per person minimum £	children taken	evening meals	animals taken
Capt. Keith J. Hagerty **Chirton House Hotel** **46 Clifton Road** **Newcastle-upon-Tyne** **NE4 6XH** **Tel: (091) 2730407** **Open: ALL YEAR** **Map Ref No. 12**	Nearest Road: A.1, A.186 An imposing elegant house standing in its own pleasant grounds, offering 11 very comfortable rooms, 5 with private facilities, each with colour T.V. & tea/coffee making facilities available. A T.V. lounge & cocktail bar with friendly country house atmosphere. Situated within a few minutes of the city centre it is a good base for touring the countryside including Hadrian's Wall. The beaches are not far away & there are many places of great interest close by.	£18.00 CREDIT CARD VISA M'CARD	Y	Y	Y
Mrs Lyn S. Bewick **The Gables** **Ogle** **Ponteland** **Newcastle-upon-Tyne** **NE20 0AU** **Tel: (067075) 392** **Open: ALL YEAR** **Map Ref No. 13**	Nearest Road: A.696 A warm welcome awaits you at The Gables. This large, ranch-style bungalow is located in the delightful, quiet village of Ogle. Accommodation is in a choice of 4 comfortable, spacious, tastefully decorated bedrooms 2 with en-suite facilities, all with radio, T.V., tea/coffee makers, hairdryer & trouser press. Relax in the comfortable oak beamed lounge with open log fire & enjoy the country garden. Parking. A lovely home, ideal for a holiday or for touring.	£17.50	Y	N	N

All the establishments mentioned in this guide
are members of
The Worldwide Bed & Breakfast Association

Oxfordshire

Oxfordshire
(Thames & Chilterns)

Oxfordshire is a county rich in history & delightful countryside. It has prehistoric sites, early Norman churches, 15th century coaching inns, Regency residences, distinctive cottages of black & white chalk flints & lovely Oxford, the city of dreaming spires.

The countryside ranges from lush meadows with willow-edged river banks scattered with small villages of thatched cottages, to the hills of the Oxfordshire Cotswolds in the west, the wooded Chilterns in the east & the distinctive ridge of the Berkshire Downs in the south. "Old Father Thames" meanders gently across the county to Henley, home of the famous regatta.

The ancient track known as the Great Ridgeway runs across the shire, & a walk along its length reveals barrows, hill forts & stone circles. The 2,000 year old Uffington Horse cut into the chalk of the hillside below an ancient hill fort site, is some 360 feet in length & 160 feet high.

The Romans built villas in the county & the remains of one, including a magnificent mosaic can be seen at North Leigh. In later centuries lovely houses were built. Minster Lovell stands beside the Windrush; Rousham house with its William Kent gardens is situated near Steeple Aston & beside the Thames lies Elizabethan Mapledurham House with its working watermill.

At Woodstock is Blenheim Palace, the largest private house in Britain & birthplace of Sir Winston Churchill. King Alfred's statue stands at Wantage, commemorating his birth there, & Banbury has its cross, made famous in the old nursery rhyme.

Oxford is a town of immense atmosphere with fine college buildings around quiet cloisters, & narrow cobbled lanes. It was during the 12th century that Oxford became a meeting place for scholars & grew into the first established centre of learning, outside the monasteries, in England.

The earliest colleges to be founded were University College, Balliol & Merton. Further colleges were added during the reign of the Tudors, as Oxford became a power in the kingdom. There are now 35 university colleges & many other outstanding historic buildings in the city . Christ Church Chapel is now the Cathedral of Oxford, a magnificent building with a deservedly famous choir.

St. Mary's Church.

Oxfordshire

Oxfordshire Gazeteer

Areas of Oustanding Natural Beauty
The North Wessex Downs. The Chiltern Hills. The Cotswolds.

Historic Houses & Castles

Ashdown House - Nr. Lambourn
17th century, built for Elizabeth of Bohemia, now contains portraits associated with her. Mansard roof has cupola with golden ball.

Blenheim Palace - Woodstock
Sir John Vanbrugh's classical masterpiece. Garden designed by Vanbrugh & Henry Wise. Further work done by Capability Brown who created the lake. Collection of pictures & tapestries.

Broughton Castle- Banbury.
14th century mansion with moat - interesting plaster work fine panelling & fire places

Chasleton House-Morton in Marsh
17th century,fine examples of plaster work & panelling.Still has original furniture & tapestries. topiary garden from1700.

Grey Court - Henly-on-Thames
16th century house containing 18th century plasterwork & furniture. Mediaeval ruins. Tudor donkey-wheel for raising water from well.

Mapledurham House - Mapledurham
16th century Elizabethan house. Oak staircase, private chapel, paintings, original moulded ceilings. Watermill nearby.

Milton Manor House - Nr. Abingdon
17th century house designed by Inigo Jones - Georgian wings, walled garden, pleasure grounds.

Rousham House - Steeple Ashton
17th century - contains portraits & miniatures.

University of Oxford Colleges

University college,	1249
Balliol,	1263
Merton,	1264
Hertford,	1284
Oriel,	1326
New,	1379
All Souls,	1438
Brasenose,	1509
Christ Church,	1546
St. John's,	1555
Pembroke,	1624
Worcester,	1714
Nuffield,	1937
St. Edmund Hall,	1270
Exeter,	1314
The Queen's,	1340
Lincoln,	1427
Magdalen,	1458
Corpus Christi,	1516
Trinity,	1554
Jesus,	1571
Wadham,	1610
Keble,	1868

Cathedrals & Churches

Abingdon (St. Helen)
14th-16th century perpendicular. Painted roof. Georgian stained & enamelled glass.

Burford (St. John the Baptist)
15th century. Sculptured table tombs in churchyard.

Chislehampton (St. Katherine)
18th century. Unspoilt interior of Georgian period. Bellcote.

Dorchester (St. Peter & St. Paul)
13th century knight in stone effigy. Jesse window.

East Hagbourne (St. Andrew)
14th -15th century. Early glass, wooden roofs, 18th century tombs.

North Moreton (All Saints)
13th century with splendid 14th century chantry chapel - tracery.

Oxford Cathedral
Smallest of our English cathedrals. Stone spire form 1230. Norman arcade has double arches, choir vault.

Ryecote (St. Michael & All Angels)
14th century benches & screen base. 17th century altar-piece & communion rails, old clear glass, good ceiling.

Stanton Harcourt (St. Michael)
Early English - old stone & marble floor. Early screen with painting, monuments of 17th -19th century.

Yarnton (St. Bartholomew)
13th century - late perpendicular additions. Jacobean screen. 15th century alabaster reredos.

Oxfordshire

Museums & Galleries

The Ashmolean Museum of Art & Archaeology - Oxford
British ,European ,Mediterranean, Egyptian & Near Eastern archaeology. Oil paintings of Italian, Dutch, Flemish, French & English schools. Old Master watercolours, prints, drawings, ceramics, silver, bronzes & sculptures. Chinese & Japanese porcelain, lacquer & painting, Tibetan, Islamic & Indian art.

Christ Church Picture Gallery - Oxford
Old Master drawings & paintings.

Museum of Modern Art - Oxford
Exhibitiors of contemporary art.

Museum of Oxford
Many exhibits depicting the history of Oxford & its University.

The Rotunda - Oxford
Privately owned collection of dolls' houses 1700-1900, with contents such as furniture, china, silver, dolls, etc.

Oxford University Museum
Entomological, zoological, geological & mineralogical collections.

Pendon Museum of Miniature Landscape & Transport - Abingdon.
Showing in miniature the countryside & its means of transport in the thirties, with trains & thatched village. Railway relics.

Town Museum - Abingdon
17th century building exhibiting fossil, archaeological items & collection of charters & documents.

T olsey Museum - Burford
Seals, maces, charters & bygones - replica of Regency room with period furnishings & clothing.

Historic Monuments

Uffington Castle & White Horse - Uffington
White horse cut into the chalk - iron age hill fort.

Rollright Stones - Nr. Chipping Norton
77 stones placed in circle - an isolated King's stone & nearby an ancient burial chamber.

Minster Lovell House - Minster Lovell
15th century mediaeval house - ruins.

Deddington Castle - Deddington

Other things to see & do

Didcot railway centre -a large collection of locomotives etc., from Brunel's Great Western Railway.

Filkins -a working wool mill where rugs & garments are woven in traditional way.

Blenheim Palace.Woodstock.

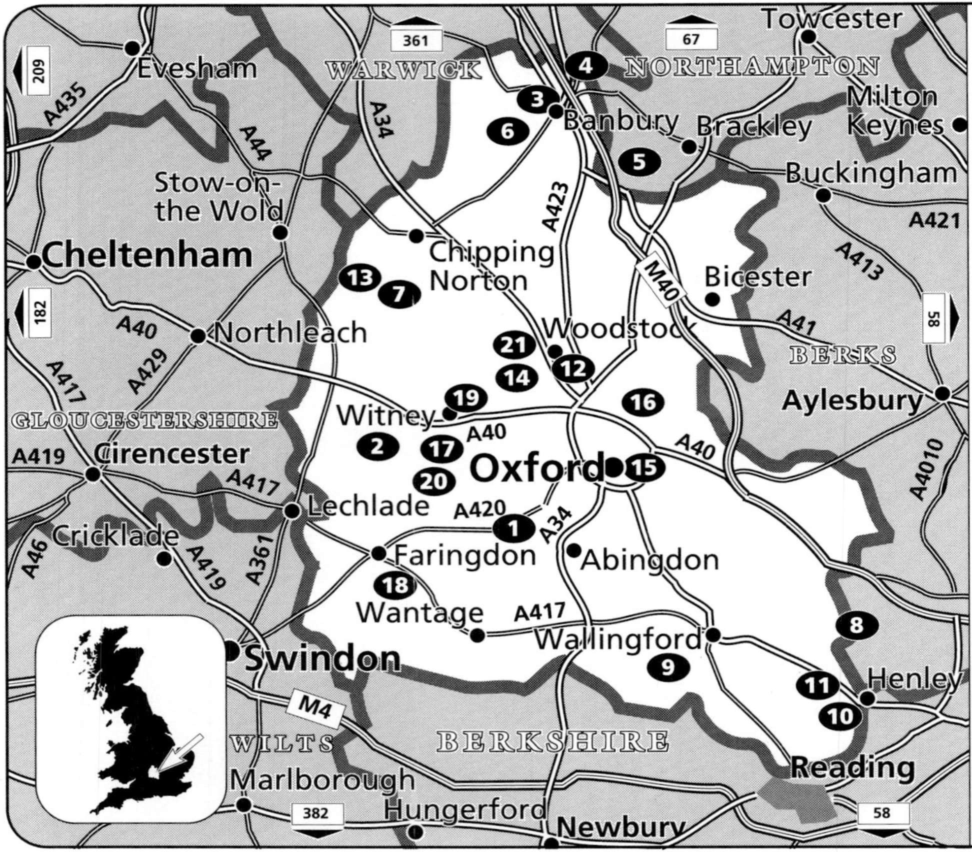

OXFORDSHIRE

Map reference

1 Crowther
2 Rouse
3 Hearne
4 Wills
5 Grove-White
6 Ritter
7 Scavuzzo
8 Wallace
9 Johnston
10 Ovey
11 Fulford-Dobson
12 Naylor
13 Sykes
14 Ellis
15 Tong
15 Edwards
15 Barrett
15 Welham
15 Morris
15 Cotmore
15 Trafford
16 Hicks
17 Peterson
18 Wadsworth
19 Simpson
20 Florey
21 Jones

Fulford House. Banbury.

Oxfordshire

		minimum £ per person	children taken	evening meals	animals taken
Mrs A. Y. Crowther **Fallowfields** **Southmoor, Bagpuize** **Abingdon** **OX13 5BH** **Tel: (0865) 820416** **Fax 0865 820629** **Open: APR - SEPT** **Map Ref No. 01**	Nearest Road: A.420 Fallowfields, the former home of Begum Aga Khan, is an absolutely delightful 300 year-old Gothic-style manor house. Beautifully furnished with the emphasis on gracious elegance. The 2 lounges are spacious & comfortable. The pleasant bedrooms have pretty linens, tea/coffee making facilities, hairdryer, radio, 'phone & valet press. The elegant dining room befits the super cuisine served. Guests are also encouraged to use the tennis court, croquet lawn & the outdoor swimming pool. Children over 10 years.	£27.00 CREDIT CARD VISA M'CARD	Y	Y	Y
Mrs M. J. Rouse **Farmhouse Hotel** **University Farm , Lew** **Bampton OX18 2AU** **Tel: (0993) 850297** **Fax 0993 850965** **Open: ALL YEAR (Excl.** **Xmas & New Year)** **Map Ref No. 02**	Nearest Road: A.40, A.4095 A charming 17th century farmhouse standing in 216 acres. Heavily beamed throughout, with a huge inglenook fireplace in the lounge. 6 prettily decorated bedooms, all with bath or shower en-suite. Honeymoon suite available. A superb timbered dining room & a most attractive lounge with colour T.V. There is a large sun terrace for guests' use. Situated in a small peaceful village, 3 miles from Witney, it is an ideal base for touring.	£25.00 CREDIT CARD VISA M'CARD	Y	Y	N
Mrs R J Grove-White **Home Farmhouse** **Charlton** **Banbury** **OX17 3DR** **Tel: (0295) 811683** **Open: ALL YEAR** **Map Ref No. 05**	Nearest Road: A.43, A.41, M.40 This charming, listed stone house dating from 1637, with its attractive, colourful, paved courtyard, provides an excellent base for visiting Oxford, Blenheim, Stratford-upon-Avon, Warwick & the beautiful Cotswold villages. Mrs Grove-White has used her expertise as a professional interior designer to ensure that the 3 double/twin bedded rooms, with en-suite or private bathroom & colour T.V., are comfortable & elegantly furnished. Evening meals by arrangement only.	£21.00 *see PHOTO over*	Y	Y	Y
Patti Ritter **La Madonette Country** **Guest House** **North Newington** **Banbury OX15 6AA** **Tel: (0295) 730212** **Open: ALL YEAR** **Map Ref No. 06**	Nearest Road: B.4035, M.40 A charming 17th century mill house situated in peaceful country surroundings. Conveniently located for the Cotswolds, Oxford, Warwick & Stratford-upon-Avon. Offering 5 comfortable & well furnished double en-suite rooms, with colour T.V. Radio, telephone & tea/coffee facilities. Delicious breakfasts served. Local pubs & restaurants offer evening meals nearby. Lounge / gardens & swimming pool for guests' use. Licensed.	£21.00 CREDIT CARD VISA M'CARD	Y	N	N
Mr & Mrs Stephen Wills **Fulford House** **The Green, Culworth** **Banbury OX17 2BB** **Tel: (0295) 760355** **Fax 0295 768304** **Open: FEB - DEC** **Map Ref No. 04**	Nearest Road: A.422, M.40 A house-party atmosphere prevails in this charming,17th century country home with its acres of grounds & beautiful terraced gardens in which to wander, play croquet or watch the training of horses & riders. Personal attention is top priority & with just 3 spacious double/twin rooms, delightfully furnished with en-suite or private facilities & T.V., there is an air of exclusivity. Dinners by arrangement. Licensed. Only 1 hr. from London/ Heathrow on the M.40.	£20.00 *see PHOTO over*	Y	Y	Y

Home Farmhouse. Charlton.

Oxfordshire

		per person minimum £	children taken	evening meals	animals taken
M & G Hearne **Easington House Hotel** **50 Oxford Road** **Banbury OX16 9AN** **Tel:(0295) 270181** **Open: ALL YEAR** **Map Ref No. 03**	Nearest Road: A.41, M.40 Easington House is a family-run, listed 16th century farmhouse located only 300 yards from Banbury Cross, the town centre shops. Accommodation is in a choice of 12 rooms, 10 en-suite, all with modern amenities, 'phone, T.V. & tea/coffee making facilities. A residents' lounge is also available. This makes a good base from which to tour Oxford & the Cotswolds. Evening meals available Monday-Friday with prior notice.	**£24.00** CREDIT CARD VISA M'CARD AMEX	Y	Y	Y
Mrs Audrey Scavuzzo **The Forge House** **Churchill** **Chipping Norton** **OX7 6NJ** **Tel: (0608) 658173** **Open: ALL YEAR** **Map Ref No. 07**	Nearest Road: A.44 The Forge House is a 150 year-old, traditional Cotswold stone cottage, with inglenook log fires & exposed beams, combining the charm of tradition with the comfort of contemporary living. 4 tastefully furnished en-suite rooms, 2 with 4-poster beds & 1 with jacuzzi. All have radio, colour T.V. & tea/coffee making facilities. Lounge & garden available for guests' use. Personal service & advice on touring the surrounding area. Convenient for Stratford-upon-Avon & the Cotswolds.	**£22.50** *see PHOTO over*	Y	N	N
W & J Wallace **Little Parmoor** **Parmoor Lane, Frieth** **Henley on Thames** **RG9 6NL** **Tel: (0494) 881447** **Open: ALL YEAR** **Map Ref No. 08**	Nearest Road: M.40, M.4 A pretty Georgian country house surrounded by farmland, situated in the beautiful Chiltern Hills between Henley & Marlow. Within easy reach of Oxford & Windsor & 40 mins. from Heathrow - a perfect & peaceful spot to begin or end a holiday. The attractively furnished bedrooms have washbasins, colour T.V. & tea making facilities. A pretty panelled drawing room. Ample parking. Evening meals served if ordered in advance.	**£18.50**	Y	Y	N
Ginnie & Peter Johnston **Chessall Shaw** **Newnham Hill, Nettlebed** **Henley-on-Thames** **RG9 5TN** **Tel: (0491) 641311** **Fax 0491 641819** **Open: ALL YEAR** **Map Ref No. 09**	Nearest Road: A.423 Delightfully located, 10 minutes from Henley-on-Thames, 40 minutes from Heathrow, Windsor & Oxford. Beautifully positioned in the peaceful idyllic Oxfordshire countryside. This welcoming house offers superb views across meadows & woodlands. 2 pretty en-suite rooms with every comfort including tea/coffee making facilities, refrigerator, T.V., radio, etc. A colour T.V. lounge, garden & swimming pool. Delicious cordon bleu cuisine using fresh, home-grown produce whenever possible. Evening meals by arrangement.	**£18.00**	Y	Y	Y
Richard & Gillian Ovey **Hernes** **Henley-on-Thames** **RG9 4NT** **Tel: (0491) 573245** **Fax 0491 574645** **Open: MID JAN - MIDDEC** **Map Ref No. 10**	Nearest Road: A.4130. Large, warm, comfortable rooms, full of the history of a family whose roots lie deep in Oxfordshire, & a welcome, traditional to Hernes for generations, await guests who visit this part 16th century house. Established gardens, with a pool & croquet lawn, overlook acres of farm & parkland. Ideal for relaxing rest or as a centre for visiting London, Windsor, Eton, Oxford, the Cotswolds, all of the Chilterns & Heathrow. Bedrooms including a 4-poster have private/en-suite bathrooms, tea/coffee facilities. Children over 13 welcomed. Evening meals by arrangement.	**£27.50**	N	Y	N

The Forge House. Chipping Norton.

Oxfordshire

		per person minimum £	children taken	evening meals	animals taken
Mrs S Fulford-Dobson **'Shepherds'** Shepherds Green Rotherfield Greys Henley-on-Thames RG9 4QL Tel: (0491) 628413 OpenALL YEAR(Excl.Xmas) Map Ref No. 11	Nearest Road: A. 423, B.481 An attractive, part 18th century house, standing on peaceful village green in its own lovely gardens & paddocks, covered in roses, wisteria, clematis & jasmine. The pretty guest bedrooms all have en-suite or private facilities. Some have T.V., all have clock-radios & tea/coffee facilities. Delightful drawing room for guests with antiques & open fire. An ideal centre for exploring Chilterns, Windsor & Oxford. Accessible to Heathrow. Children over 12 . Evening meals by prior arrangement.	£18.00	Y	Y	N
Keith & Eve Naylor **Bowood House Hotel** 238 Oxford Road Kidlington OX5 1EB Tel: (0865) 842288 Fax 0865 841858 OpenALL YEAR(Excl.Xmas) Map Ref No. 12	Nearest Road: A.4260 Situated on the A423, only 4 miles from Oxford city centre. Bowood House offers accommodation of a high standard in a warm, friendly atmosphere. There is a licensed 'a la carte' menu open to non-residents. Offering 20 en-suite rooms with colour T.V., 'phone, hairdryers & tea/coffee makers. An ideal touring centre for the Cotswolds, Stratford, Warwick, Blenheim Palace, Bladon & of course Oxford's numerous attractions. Heathrow 60 miles. CREDIT CARD VISA M'CARD	£25.00	Y	Y	N
Brian Sykes **Conygree Gate** **Country House Hotel** Church Street Kingham OX7 6YA Tel: (0608) 658389 Open: ALL YEAR Map Ref No. 13	Nearest Road: A.429, A.361 Small family run country house in Kingham village, set in heart of glorious Cotswold countryside. Converted from a farmhouse, this is a 16th century building with leaded windows, oak beams and inglenook fireplaces. Large rear garden for sitting out. 10 guest bedrooms, mostly en-suite, with colour T.V., tea/coffee facilities. 2 sitting rooms, dining room and licensed bar. Central heating and log fires throughout. Ample parking. CREDIT CARD VISA M'CARD AMEX	£24.00	Y	Y	Y
Tom & Carol Ellis **Wynford House** 79 Main Road Long Hanborough OX8 8JX Tel: (0993) 881402 Open: ALL YEAR Map Ref No. 14	Nearest Road: A.4095 Wynford House is situated in the charming village of Long Hanborough. Accommodation is in 3 guest rooms, 1 with private facilities. All have modern amenities, including colour T.V. & tea/coffee makers & are comfortably furnished. Delicious breakfasts are served with local pubs & restaurants offering tasty evening meals. Conveniently located on the doorstep of the Cotswolds, with Bladon 1 mile, Woodstock & Blenheim Palace 3 miles & Oxford 12 miles.	£16.00	Y	Y	Y
Catherine Tong **Courtfield Hotel** 367 Iffley Road Oxford OX4 4DP Tel: (0865) 242991 Open: ALL YEAR Map Ref No. 15	Nearest Road: A.423, A.4158 Courtfield Guest House has been recently refurbished to provide accommodation for guests in 6 comfortable rooms, most with en-suite facilities. A lounge & the garden are also available for visitors to relax in. Ample parking in mews-style forecourt. Situated on good bus route, one & a half miles from the centre of Oxford. Children over 3 years. No single availability. CREDIT CARD VISA M'CARD AMEX	£19.00	Y	N	N

Oxfordshire

		minimum £ per person	children taken	evening meals	animals taken
Mrs Doreen Edwards **Highfield House** **91 Rose Hill** **Oxford OX4 4HT** **Tel: (0865) 774083/** **718524** **Open: ALL YEAR** **Map Ref No. 15**	Nearest Road: A.423, A.4158 A pleasing & friendly house with good access to the city centre & Ring road. Accommodation is in 7 spacious bedrooms, 5 with en-suite bathroom. All have colour T.V. & tea/coffee making facilites. A short walk brings you to the old attractive village of Iffley, where there are good pubs & food. An excellent base for exploring the historic delights of Oxford. Evening meals by arrangement.	£16.00 CREDIT CARD VISA M'CARD	Y	Y	N
Tina & Robin Barrett **Highfield West** **188 Cumnor Hill** **Oxford OX2 9PJ** **Tel: (0865) 863007** **Open: ALL YEAR** **Map Ref No. 15**	Nearest Road: A.420, A.34 Tina & Robin invite guests to enjoy Bed & Breakfast in the comfort of their home, set in a quiet residential area of Oxford, within walking distance of Cumnor village where 2 inns both serve food. Guest rooms have excellent facilities - 1 double, 1 twin, 1 family, all en-suite, & 2 singles sharing a separate bathroom. There is a lounge, dining room, & garden with swimming pool, heated in season. Fire certificate & car parking.	£18.00	Y	N	Y
Mr & Mrs P. Welham **Norham Guest House** **16 Norham Road** **Oxford** **OX2 6SF** **Tel: (0865) 515352** **Open: ALL YEAR** **Map Ref No. 15**	Nearest Road: A.423, A.4165 A delightful Victorian house situated in a conservation area yet convenient for the many attractions of Oxford. Accommodation is in 8 tastefully furnished guest rooms, including 2 family rooms with modern amenities, h&c, T.V. & tea/coffee making facilities. Delicious breakfasts are served. Vegetarian diets provided by arrangement. Children over 5 years welcome. Convenient for the city centre. Ideal for visiting the Cotswolds & Stratford-upon-Avon.	£20.00 🚭	Y	N	N
Mr & Mrs P. Morris **Pine Castle Hotel** **290 Iffley Road** **Oxford** **OX4 4AE** **Tel: (0865) 241497** **Open ALLYEAR (Excl.Xmas)** **Map Ref No. 15**	Nearest Road: A.423, M.40 A warm welcome awaits you at this delightful Edwardian guest house which retains many of its period features. It is conveniently situated on a main bus route into the city centre. An alternative route is a short walk along the tow path beside the Thames which is both convenient & picturesque. Cots are provided, T.V. & tea/coffee making facilities in all rooms. Breakfasts vary from the healthy to the positively indulgent. Evening meals by prior arrangement.	£16.00 CREDIT CARD VISA M'CARD	Y	Y	N
Mrs Joan Hicks **Studley Farmhouse** **Arncott Rd** **Horton-cum-Studley** **Oxford OX9 1BP** **Tel: (0865) 351286** **Fax 0865 351631** **Open: ALL YEAR** **Map Ref No. 16**	Nearest Road: M.40 Studley Farmhouse has been beautifully renovated, exposing flagstone floors, timbers & inglenook fireplaces reflecting its 16th Century origins. Guests are accommodated in twin, double & single rooms with en-suite facilities available. Situated just 15 mins. from Oxford, with easy access to Blenheim, Stratford & the Cotswolds. 1 hour from London & Heathrow Airport. A super home & anideal base for a relaxing holiday.	£20.00 🚭 CREDIT CARD VISA M'CARD	N	N	N

Oxfordshire

		minimum £ per person	children taken	evening meals	animals taken
Derek &Audrey Cotmore **The Lawns** **12 Manor Road** **South Hinksey** **Oxford OX1 5AS** **Tel: (0865) 739980** **Open: ALL YEAR** **Map Ref No. 15**	Nearest Road: A.34. Situated in an 'olde worlde' village, walking distance of the city. The Lawns offers 3 bedrooms with unique views of the dreaming spires, overlooking the garden. All are attractively furnished, with modern amenities, T.V., tea/coffee making facilities, some en-suite. Garden & swimming pool for guests' enjoyment. Relax in the dining room & enjoy a varied selection of breakfast foods. Local pub serves tasty meals. Easy access to Blenheim Palace & Cotswolds.	£16.00	Y	N	N
Mr & Mrs E. E. Trafford **Tilbury Lodge Hotel** **5 Tilbury Lane** **Eynsham Rd, Botley** **Oxford OX2 9NB** **Tel: (0865) 862138** **Open: ALL YEAR** **Map Ref No. 15**	Nearest Road: B.4044 Tilbury Lodge is a pleasant, family-run private hotel situated in a quiet residential area. Offering 9 en-suite rooms with radio, T.V., 'phone, hairdryer & tea/coffee making facilities. 1 4-poster & 2 ground floor rooms. A pleasant jacuzzi bath is also available. Residents' lounge & garden. Located 2 miles west of the city centre with good pubs & restaurants a few minutes' walk away. Good bus service.	£27.50 CREDIT CARD VISA M'CARD	Y	N	N
Mrs S.D. Peterson **Hawthorn Cottage** **The Downs** **Standlake OX8 7SH** **Tel: (0865) 300588** **Open: JAN-NOV** **Map Ref No. 17**	Nearest Road: M.40 Detached house standing in 1 third of an acre. Private, well-established garden for guests' use. On the edge of a delightful Oxfordshire village noted for its leisure area. Spacious rooms elegantly furnished with private bathrooms, T.V. & tea/coffee making facilities. Large dining room with comfortable lounge area. Standlake is close to Oxford, the Cotswolds & Blenheim Palace.	£17.50	Y	N	N
Mrs C. A. Wadsworth **The Craven** **Fernham Road** **Uffington SN7 7RD** **Tel: (0367) 820449** **Open: ALL YEAR** **Map Ref No. 18**	Nearest Road: A.420 An extremely attractive 17th century thatched farmhouse with exposed beams & open log-burning fire. Accommodation is very comfortable in 7 attractive bedrooms, 1 with 4-poster bed & private bathroom. Good home cooking & fresh local produce. The Craven offers a friendly, relaxed atmosphere. The perfect base for touring this fascinating area. Within easy reach of Oxford.	£16.50 *see PHOTO over*	Y	Y	Y
Liz & John Simpson **Field View** **Wood Green** **Witney** **OX8 6DE** **Tel: (0993) 705485** **Open: ALL YEAR** **Map Ref No. 19**	Nearest Road: A.40, B.4095 Attractive Cotswold stone house set in 2 acres, situated on picturesque "Wood Green", midway between Oxford University & the Cotswolds. It is an ideal centre for touring yet only 8 minutes' walk from the centre of this lively Oxfordshire market town. A peaceful setting & a warm, friendly atmosphere await you. Accommodation is in 3 comfortable en-suite rooms with modern amenities & tea/coffee making facilities.	£18.00	Y	N	N

The Craven. Uffington.

Oxfordshire

		minimum £ per person	children taken	evening meals	animals taken
Mary Anne Florey **Rectory Farm** **Northmoor** **Witney OX8 1SX** **Tel: (0865) 300207** **Open: FEB-Mid DEC** **Map Ref No. 20**	Nearest Road: A.415 A warm welcome is assured at this listed 16th century farmhouse, situated in the centre of the quiet village of Northmoor. Both rooms are en-suite & have tea/coffee making facilities as well as superb views. There is a large dining/sitting room with colour T.V. & gardens of 1 acre for guests to enjoy. Oxford, Blenheim, Stratford & the Cotswolds are within easy reach.	£17.50	N	N	N
Mrs Barbara Jones **Gorselands Farm-** **house Auberge** **Boddington Lane** **Long Hanborough** **Woodstock OX8 6PU** **Tel: (0993) 881895** **Fax 0993 882799** **Open: ALL YEAR** **Map Ref No. 21**	Nearest Road: A.4095 A beautiful, Cotswold, stone, period farmhouse, set in an acre of grounds in idyllic countryside. Retaining much character with log fires & flag-stone floors, it offers 5 comfortable & tastefully furnished guest bedrooms, 2 en-suite. Optional French-style evening meals are served in the conservatory. Licensed. Billiards Room & grass tennis court available for guests' use. Situated near Woodstock & Oxford, convenient for visiting Blenheim Palace, North Leigh Roman Villa & many Cotswold villages.	£12.50 CREDIT CARD VISA M'CARD AMEX	Y	Y	Y

All the establishments mentioned in this guide

are members of

The Worldwide Bed & Breakfast Association

Shropshire

Shropshire
(Heart of England)

Shropshire is a borderland with a very turbulent history. Physically it straddles highlands & lowlands with border mountains to the west, glacial plains, upland, moorlands & fertile valleys & the River Severn cutting through. It has been quarrelled & fought over by rulers & kings from earliest times. The English, the Romans & the Welsh all wanted to hold Shropshire because of its unique situation. The ruined castles & fortifications dotted across the county are all reminders of its troubled life. The most impressive of these defences is Offa's Dyke, an enormous undertaking intended to be a permanent frontier between England & Wales.

Shropshire has great natural beauty, countryside where little has changed with the years. Wenlock Edge & Clun Forest, Carding Mill Valley, the Long Mynd, Caer Caradoc, Stiperstones & the trail along Offa's Dyke itself, are lovely walking areas with magnificent scenery.

Shrewsbury was & is a virtual island, almost completely encircled by the Severn River. The castle was built at the only gap, sealing off the town. In this way all comings & goings were strictly controlled. In the 18th century two bridges, the English bridge & the Welsh bridge, were built to carry the increasing traffic to the town but Shrewsbury still remains England's finest Tudor city.

Massive Ludlow Castle was a Royal residence, home of Kings & Queens through the ages, whilst the town is also noted for its Georgian houses.

As order came out of chaos, the county settled to improving itself & became the cradle of the Industrial Revolution. Here Abraham Darby discovered how to use coke (from the locally mined coal) to smelt iron. There was more iron produced here in the 18th century than in any other county. A variety of great industries sprang up as the county's wealth & ingenuity increased. In 1781 the world's first iron bridge opened to traffic.

There are many fine gardens in the county. At Hodnet Hall near Market Drayton, the grounds cover 60 acres & the landscaping includes lakes & pools, trees, shrubs & flowers in profusion. Weston Park has 1,000 acres of parkland, woodland gardens & lakes landscaped by Capability Brown.

The house is Restoration period & has a splendid collection of pictures, furniture, china & tapestries.

Shrewsbury hosts an annual poetry festival & one of England's best flower shows whilst a Festival of Art, Music & Drama is held each year in Ludlow with Shakespeare performed against the castle ruins.

Coalbrookedale Museum.

Shropshire

Shropshire Gazeteer

Areas of Outstanding Natural Beauty
The Shropshire Hills.

Historic Houses & Castles

Stokesay Castle - Craven Arms
13th century fortified manor house. Still occupied - wonderful setting - extremely well preserved. Fine timbered gatehouse.
Weston Park - Nr. Shifnal
17th century - fine example of Restoration period - landscaping by Capability Brown. Superb collection of pictures.
Shrewsbury Castle - Shrewsbury
Built in Norman era - interior decorations - painted boudoir.
Benthall Hall - Much Wenlock
16th century. Stone House - mullioned windows. Fine wooden staircase - splendid plaster ceilings.
Shipton Hall - Much Wenlock
Elizabethan. Manor House - walled garden - mediaeval dovecote.
Upton Cressett Hall - Bridgnorth
Elizabethan. Manor House & Gatehouse. Excellent plaster work. . 14th century great hall.

Cathedrals & Churches

Ludlow (St. Lawrence)
14th century nave & transepts. 15th century pinnacled tower. Restored extensively in 19th century. Carved choir stalls, perpendicular chancel - original glass. Monuments.
Shrewsbury (St. Mary)
14th, 15th, 16th century glass. Norman origins.
Stottesdon (St. Mary)
12th century carvings.Norman font.Fine decorations with columns & tracery.
Lydbury North (St. Michael)
14th century transept, 15th century nave roof, 17th century box pews and altar rails. Norman font.
Longor (St. Mary the Virgin)
13th century having an outer staircase to West gallery.
Cheswardine (St. Swithun)
13th century chapel - largely early English. 19th century glass and old brasses. Fine sculpture.

Tong (St. Mary the Virgin with St. Bartholomew)
15th century. Golden chapel of 1515, stencilled walls, remains of paintings on screens, gilt fan vaulted ceiling. Effigies, fine monuments

Museums & Galleries

Clive House - Shrewsbury
Fine Georgian House - collection of Shropshire ceramics. Regimental museum of 1st Queen's Dragoon Guards.
Rowley's House Museum - Shrewsbury
Roman material from Viroconium and prehistoric collection.
Coleham Pumping Station - Old Coleham
Preserved beam engines
Acton Scott Working Farm Museum - Nr. Church Stretton
Site showing agricultural practice before the advent of mechanization.
Ironbridge Gorge Museum - Telford
Series of industrial sites in the Severn Gorge.
CoalBrookdale Museum & Furnace Site
Showing Abraham Darby's blast furnace history. Ironbridge information centre is next to the world's first iron bridge.
Mortimer Forest Museum - Nr. Ludlow
Forest industries of today and yesterday. Ecology of the forest.
Whitehouse Museum of Buildings & Country life - Aston Munslow
4 houses together in one, drawing from every century 13th to 18th, together with utensils and implements of the time.
The Buttercross Museum - Ludlow
Geology, natural & local history of area.
Reader's House-Ludlow
Splendid example of a 16th century town house. 3 storied porch.
Much Wenlock Museum.-Much Wenlock
Geology,natural & local history.
Clun Town Museum - Clun
Pre-history earthworks, rights of way, commons & photographs.

Historic Monuments

Acton Burnell Castle - Shrewsbury
13th century fortified manor house - ruins only.

Shropshire

Boscobel House - Shifnal
17th century house.
Bear Steps - Shrewsbury
Half timbered buildings. Mediaeval.
Abbot's House - Shrewsbury
15th century half-timbered.
Buildwas Abbey - Nr. Telford
12th century - Savignac Abbey - ruins.
The church is nearly complete with 14
Norman arches.
Haughmond Abbey - Shrewsbury
12th century - remains of house of
Augustinian canons.
Wenlock Priory - Much Wenlock
13th century abbey - ruins.
Roman Town - Wroxeter
2nd century - remains of town of
Viroconium including public baths
and colonnade.
Moreton Corbet Castle - Moreton Corbet
13th century keep, Elizabethan features -
gatehouse altered 1519.

Lilleshall Abbey
12th century - completed 13th century,
West front has notable doorway.
Bridgnorth Castle - Bridgnorth
Ruins of Norman castle whose angle of
incline is greater than Pisa.
Whiteladies Priory - Boscobel
12th century cruciform church - ruins.
Old Oswestry - Oswestry
Iron age hill fort covering 68 acres; five
ramparts and having an elaborate
western portal.

Other things to see & do

Ludlow Festival of Art and Drama -
annual event
Shrewsbury Flower Show - every
August
Severn Valley Railway - the longest full
guage steam railway in the country.

Kings Head Inn. Shrewsbury.

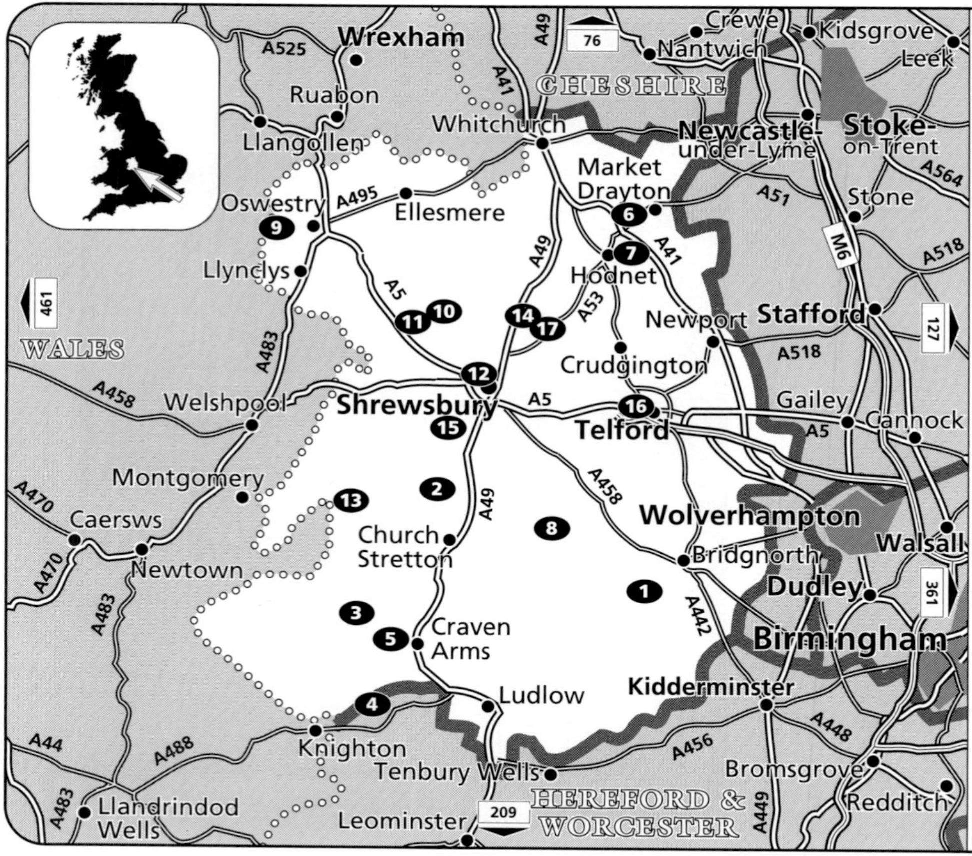

SHROPSHIRE

Map reference

1 Rowlands
2 Davies
3 Spencer
4 Lloyd
5 Royce
6 Villar
7 Thomas
8 Russell
9 Goddard
10 Baly
11 Bovill
12 Stening-Rees
12 Cox
13 Anderson
14 Grundey
15 Mitchell
16 Savage
17 Evans

Shropshire

		minimum £ per person	children taken	evening meals	animals taken
Mary Rowlands **Middleton Lodge** **Middleton Priors** **Bridgnorth WV16 6UR** **Tel: (074634) 228** **Open: ALL YEAR** **Map Ref No. 01**	Nearest Road: B.4268 Middleton Lodge is set in 20 acres of beautiful rural Shropshire countryside overlooking Brown Clee Hill. Offering 3 extremely attractive en-suite bedrooms, 1 with 4-poster. There are many places of interest within easy reach of Middleton: the scenic Severn Valley Railway, Ironbrige, Stokesay Castle, the breath-taking beauty of the Long Mynd & the picturesque Carding Mill Valley.	£20.00 (non-smoking)	N	N	N
Mrs Jeanette Davies **Rectory Farm** **Woolstaston** **Church Stretton** **SY6 6NN** **Tel: (0694) 751306** **Open: MAR - NOV** **Map Ref No. 02**	Nearest Road: A.49 An extremely attractive half-timbered farmhouse dating back to 1620, offering 3 charming rooms, all with bath en-suite. Situated on the edge of the National Trust Long Mynd Hills, it has marvellous views & superb walking right from the door. There is much for the sportsman here: golf, riding, fishing & gliding. Many historic houses & wonderful beauty spots are a short drive. Children over 12 years welcome. Restricted smoking. Best Bed & Breakfast Award Winner.	£18.00 *see PHOTO over*	N	N	N
Mr& Mrs Graham Spencer **The Old Rectory** **Hopesay** **Craven Arms** **SY7 8HD** **Tel: (05887) 245** **Open: ALL YEAR** **(Excl.Xmas)** **Map Ref No. 03**	Nearest Road: A.49, B.4368 The Old Rectory dating from the 17th century is set in beautiful landscaped gardens of one & a half acres with croquet lawn. Offering 3 spacious en-suite bedrooms, 2 with Emperor-size beds, all have radio, colour T.V. & tea/coffee makers. Comfortable drawing room & spacious dining room. Tastefully furnished throughout with antiques & many period pieces. Superb home cooking using garden produce. Unlicensed but own wine welcome. An excellent base for touring, with easy access to Ludlow, Offa's Dyke & Stokesay Castle.	£27.00 (non-smoking)	N	Y	N
Hayden & Yvonne Lloyd **Upper Buckton Farm** **Leintwardine** **Craven Arms SY7 0JU** **Tel: (05473) 634** **Open: ALL YEAR** **Map Ref No. 04**	Nearest Road: A.4113, A.4110 A delightful riverside farmhouse with spectacular views over unspoilt countryside, Upper Buckton a a lovely home furnished with many antiques & beautiful fabrics. Superb traditional & "cordon bleu" dinners are served in the dining room using fresh local produce. Excellent shower room. Pre-breakfast drink brought to your room. Electric blankets & heaters in all rooms. Log fires. A no smoking home.	£20.00 (non-smoking)	Y	Y	N
Mary & Arthur Royce **Woodville** **Clun Road** **Craven Arms** **SY7 9AA** **Tel: (0588) 672476** **Open: ALL YEAR** **Map Ref No. 05**	Nearest Road: A.49, B.4368 A restful holiday in friendly, relaxed surroundings is assured at Woodville. This large family house is set in 3/4 of an acre, surrounded by the hills & woods of the Long Mynd, Wenlock Edge, Clee Hills & Clun Forest. Accommodation is in a choice of 3 pleasant, comfortable bedrooms, 2 are en-suite (the other has private facilities) & have tea/coffee makers. This is an excellent base for touring the region, with Stokesay Castle, Ludlow & Church Stretton nearby.	£16.00 (non-smoking)	Y	Y	N

Rectory Farm. Woolstaston.

Shropshire

	minimum £ per person	children taken	evening meals	animals taken
Mr & Mrs Michael Villar **Longford Old Hall** Longford Market Drayton TF9 3PW Tel: (0603) 638279/ 638488 Open: ALL YEAR Map Ref No. 06 Nearest Road: A.41 An Elizabethan timber-frame Manor House, set in an acre of garden, with a croquet lawn & hard tennis court. 2 guest rooms are available; 1 twin bedded with private bathroom & 1 double bedded with private shower room. An adjoining sitting room has colour T.V.. Additional rooms can be made available by prior arrangement. Candlelit dinners are served & guests can enjoy open log fires, antique furniture & a baby grand piano. Ironbridge Gorge Museums, the Potteries, historic Chester & Shrewsbury within easy reach.	£20.00	Y	Y	N
Mike & Julia Thomas **Stoke Manor** Stoke-on-Tern Market Drayton TF9 2DU Tel: (063084) 222 Open: JAN-NOV Map Ref No. 07 Nearest Road: A.41, A.53 A warm welcome awaits guests at Stoke Manor, a 250-acre arable farm with farm trail & vintage tractor collection. Ironbrige & Cosford Aerospace Museums, Wedgewood Potteries, ancient towns of Shrewsbury & Chester are only a few of the many places to visit locally. Each charming bedroom has bathroom, colour T.V., tea/coffee trays. An abundance of good eating places are nearby. Residents' licence.	£20.00	Y	N	N
Mrs Julia Russell **Brockton Grange** Brockton Much Wenlock TF13 6JR Tel: (074636) 443 Open: JAN - NOV Map Ref No. 08 Nearest Road: B.4378 Idyllically set in 25 acres including private lake & woodland, this fine Country House combines the cosiness of old oak beams & log fires with later Victorian splendour. Bedrooms are en-suite with T.V., tea/coffee facilities. A friendly, relaxed atmosphere created in one of Shropshire's finest dales, where wildlife flourishes in carefully tended tranquillity. Near Ironbridge Gorge, Church Stretton, Shrewsbury. Trout & coarse fishing available.	£22.00	Y	N	N
Sheila & John Goddard **Meirion House** Llanrhaeadr ym- Mochnant Oswestry SY10 0JP Tel: (0691) 780240 Open: MAR - OCT Map Ref No. 09 Nearest Road: B.4580 Charming early 19th century stone cottage in a peaceful village. Very carefully modernised with beamed ceilings & central heating. 2 pretty bedrooms called Squirrel & Dormouse. Delicious home cooked meals by someone who loves food. Area of outstanding natural beauty, highest waterfall in Britain nearby. Plenty of walking in the hills around the village. Central for North Wales, Shropshire & Cheshire. Manchester, Liverpool & Birmingham all within easy access.	£16.00	Y	Y	N
Mrs Rosemary Baly **Fitz Manor** Bomere Heath Shrewsbury SY4 3as Tel: (0743) 850295 Open: ALL YEAR Map Ref No. 10 Nearest Road: A.5 A 15th century half timbered manor house listed Grade II with a particularly fine panelled interior of great historical interest. Although very old the house is a family home, with a relaxed atmosphere. Full central heating, large garden & farm open to all guests. Heated swimming pool. Private fishing on the River Severn available.	£16.00	Y	Y	Y

Shropshire

		per person minimum £	children taken	evening meals	animals taken
H. C. Bovill **Mytton Hall** **Montford Bridge** **Shrewsbury** **SY4 1EU** Tel: (0743) 850264 Open: ALL YEAR Map Ref No. 11	Nearest Road: A.5 An elegant white Georgian house built in 1790 with spectacular views. Accommodation is in 3 attractive & tastefully furnished en-suite rooms with tea/coffee provided on request. A delicious full English breakfast is served. Tennis court available. Private fishing rights. Set in traditional grounds & adjoining the River Perry with private fishing, there is an elegant garden for guests to relax in. A delightful home, conveniently located only 6 miles from Shrewsbury.	£20.00	N	N	N
Carol & Norman Stening **-Rees** **Roseville** **12 Berwick Road** **Shrewsbury SY1 2LN** Tel: (0743) 236470 Open: FEB - DEC Map Ref No. 12	Nearest Road: A.528, B.5067 Roseville, a late-Victorian, detached town house with own parking. 10 minutes' easy walk to town centre, rail/bus stations. Offering comfortable, centrally heated & tastefully furnished accommodation (en-suite available) in a no-smoking environment. Relaxed atmosphere encouraged. Tea, coffee, non-alcoholic drinks served on request at all reasonable times in guests' lounge. Wide choice of excellent food. Children over 12.	£15.00	Y	N	N
Roy & Sylvia Anderson **Tankerville Lodge** **Stiperstones** **Minsterley** **Shrewsbury SY5 0NB** Tel: (0743) 791401 Open: ALL YEAR Map Ref No. 13	Nearest Road: A.488 Tankerville Lodge, noted for its caring, friendly atmosphere, nestles peacefully close to the Stiperstones nature reserve & Long Mynd in the beautiful Shropshire hills. There are 4 bedrooms, all with tea/coffee making facilities, a lounge with colour T.V. & a dining room serving good home-cooked food. This is superb walking country & a good base for touring historic Shropshire & the beautiful Welsh borderland.	£14.00	Y	Y	Y
Mrs Maureen Cox **The Manse** **16 Swan Hill** **Shrewsbury** **SY1 1NL** Tel: (0743) 242659 Open: ALL YEAR Map Ref No. 12	Nearest Road: A.5, M.54 The Manse is a Georgian house set in the mediaeval town of Shrewsbury, within the loop of the River Severn. 2 comfortable bedrooms, each with modern amenities including colour T.V. & tea/coffee making facilities. 1 has a private bathroom. An attractively furnished lounge is also available. Excellent centre for sightseeing. The Manse is ideally situated for restaurants, shopping, bus & rail services. Only 2 minutes from the river & parks. Single supplement payable.	£15.00	N	N	N
Brenda & Jim Grundey **The Sett Country Hotel** **Stanton upon Hine** **Heath** **Shrewsbury SY4 4LR** Tel: (0939) 250391 Open: ALL YEAR (Excl. Xmas & New Year) Map Ref No. 14	Nearest Road: A.53 A family run country hotel in a beautiful converted barn on a small working farm in the centre of a quiet village. 6 comfortable en-suite rooms, some with hand painted window shutters, all with tea making facilities & hairdryers. Full central heating. Restful lounge with colour T.V. & separate dining rooms. Excellent food cooked on traditional A.G.A. Licensed. Special Ironbrige breaks.	£23.00 CREDIT CARD VISA M'CARD	Y	Y	Y

308

Shropshire

		minimum £ per person	children taken	evening meals	animals taken
Mike & Gill Mitchell **The White House** **Hanwood** **Shrewsbury** **SY5 8LP** **Tel: (0743) 860414** **Open: ALL YEAR** **Map Ref No. 15**	Nearest Road: A.488, A.5 Lovely 16th century black and white half-timbered guest house with nearly 2 acres of gardens and river, 3 miles south-west of mediaeval Shrewsbury. Ironbridge, Mid-Wales and the Long Mynd within half-hour drive. 6 delightful guest rooms , each with T.V., tea/coffee facilities. En-suite available. The dining room offers a fresh, varied menu supplemented by seasonal vegetables and herbs from the garden, and the house hens provide your breakfast eggs!	£20.00	N	Y	N
Mrs Jo Savage **Church Farm** **Wrockwardine** **Wellington** **Telford TF6 5DG** **Tel: (0952) 244917** **Open: ALL YEAR** **Map Ref No. 16**	Nearest Road: A.5, M.54 This listed Georgian village Farmhouse, with attractive gardens, built on the site of Wrockwardine's 12th century Manor (stonework visible), offers a warm welcome for all guests. There are delightful bedrooms, some en-suite. Oak beams, log fires & traditional breakfasts & dinners. Near Ironbridge & Shrewsbury. 1 mile M.54 & A.5 . Please ask for a brochure.	£19.00	Y	Y	Y
Mrs G. C. Evans **New Farm** **Muckleton** **Shawbury** **Telford** **TF6 6RJ** **Tel: (0939) 250358** **Open: ALL YEAR** **Map Ref No. 17**	Nearest Road: A.53 New Farm is a 70-acre farm standing in the peace & quiet of the Shropshire-Wales border. There are 4 bedrooms all with modern amenities, T.V. & tea/coffee making facilities, 3 en-suite. A comfortable guests' lounge with colour T.V. & spacious dining room is also available. Home cooked meals are available Friday, Saturday & Sunday only. New Farm is ideally located for visiting the historic towns of Shrewsbury, Chester, Ludlow, Bridgnorth & Ironbridge. The potteries are also within driving distance. Meals by arrangement. Close to Hawkstone Park Golf Course.	£16.00	Y	N	N

All the establishments mentioned in this guide are members of
The Worldwide Bed & Breakfast Association

All the establishments mentioned in this guide
are members of the
Worldwide Bed & Breakfast Association.

If you have any comments regarding your
accommodation please send them to us
using the form at the back of the book.
We value your comments.

Somerset

Somerset (West Country)

Fabulous legends, ancient customs, charming villages, beautiful churches, breathtaking scenery & a glorious cathedral, Somerset has them all, along with a distinctively rich local dialect. The essence of Somerset lies in its history & myth & particularly in the unfolding of the Arthurian tale.

Legend grows from the bringing of the Holy Grail to Glastonbury by Joseph of Arimathea, to King Arthur's castle at Camelot, held by many to be sited at Cadbury, to the image of the dead King's barge moving silently through the mists over the lake to the Isle of Avalon. Archaeological fact lends support to the conjecture that Glastonbury, with its famous Tor, was an island in an ancient lake. Another island story surrounds King Alfred, reputedly sheltering from the Danes on the Isle of Athelney & there burning his cakes.

Historically, Somerset saw the last battle fought on English soil, at Sedgemoor in 1685. The defeat of the Monmouth rebellion resulted in the wrath of James II falling on the West Country in the form of Judge Jeffreys & his "Bloody Assize".

To the west of the county lies part of the Exmoor National Park, with high moorland where deer roam & buzzards soar & a wonderful stretch of cliffs from Minehead to Devon. Dunster is a popular village with its octagonal Yarn market, & its old world cottages, dominated at one end by the castle & at the other by the tower on Conygar Hill.

To the east the woods & moors of the Quantocks are protected as an area of outstanding natural beauty. The Vale of Taunton is famous for its apple orchards & for the golden cider produced from them.

The south of the county is a land of rolling countryside & charming little towns, Chard, Crewkerne, Ilchester & Ilminster amongst others.

To the north the limestone hills of Mendip are honeycombed with spectacular caves & gorges, some with neolithic remains, as at Wookey Hole & Cheddar Gorge.

Wells is nearby, so named because of the multitude of natural springs. Hardly a city, Wells boasts a magnificent cathedral set amongst spacious lawns & trees. The west front is one of the glories of English architecture with its sculptured figures & soaring arches. A spectacular feature is the astronomical clock, the work of 14th century monk Peter Lightfoot. The intricate face tells the hours, minutes, days & phases of the moon. On the hour, four mounted knights charge forth & knock one another from their horses.

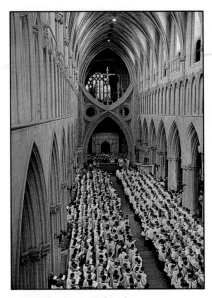

Wells Cathedral Choir.

311

Somerset

Somerset Gazeteer

Areas of Outstanding Natural Beauty
Mendip Hills. Quantock Hills. National Park - Exmoor.

Historic Houses & Castles

Abbot's Fish House - Meare
14th century house.
Barrington Court - Illminster
16th century house & gardens.
Brympton D'Evercy - Nr. Yeovil
Mansion with 17th century front & Tudor west front. Adjacent is 13th century priest's house & church. Formal gardens & vineyard.
Dodington Hall - Nether Stowey
14th & 15th century hall with minstrels' gallery.
Dunster Castle - Dunster
13th century castle with fine 17th century staircase & ceilings.
East Lambrook Manor - South Petherton
15th century house with good panelling.
Gaulden Manor - Tolland
12th century manor. Great Hall having unique plaster ceiling & oak screen. Antique furniture.
Halsway Manor - Crowcombe
14th century house with fine panelling.
Hatch Court - Hatch Beauchamp
Georgian house in the Palladian style with China room.
King John's Hunting Lodge - Axbridge
Early Tudor merchant's house.
Lytes Carry - Somerton
14th & 15th century manor house with a chapel & formal garden.
Montacute House - Yeovil
Elizabethan house with fine examples of Heraldic Glass, tapestries, panelling & furniture. Portrait gallery of Elizabethan & Jacobean paintings.
Tintinhull House - Yeovil
17th century house with beautiful gardens.

Cathedrals & Churches

Axbridge (St. John)
1636 plaster ceiling & panelled roofs.
Bishop's Lydeard (St. Mary)
15th century Notable tower, rood screen & glass.

Bruton (St. Mary)
Fine 2 towered 15th century church. Georgian chancel, tie beam roof, Georgian reredors. Jacobean screen. 15th century embroidery.
Chewton Mendip (St. Mary Magdalene)
12th century with later additions. 12th century doorway, 15th century bench ends, magnificent 16th century tower & 17th century lecturn.
Crewkerne (St. Bartholomew)
Magnificent west front & roofs, 15th & 16th century. South doorway dating from 13th century, wonderful 15th century painted glass & 18th century chandeliers.
East Brent (St. Mary)
Mainly 15th century. Plaster ceiling, painted glass & carved bench ends.
Glastonbury (St. John)
One of the finest examples of perpendicular towers. Tie beam roof, late mediaeval painted glass, mediaeval vestment & early 16th century altar tomb.
High Ham (St. Andrew)
Sumptuous roofs & vaulted rood screen. Carved bench ends. Jacobean lecturn, mediaeval painted glass. Norman font.
Kingsbury Episcopi (St. Martin)
14th-15th century. Good tower with fan vaulting. Late mediaeval painted glass.
Long Sutton (Holy Trinity)
15th century with noble tower & magnificent tie beam roof. 15th century pulpit & rood screen, tower vaulting.
Martock (All Saints)
13th century chancel. Nave with tie beam roof, outstanding of its kind. 17th century paintings of Apostles.
North Cadbury (St. Michael)
Fine chancel. 15th century roofs, parclose & portion of cope, fragments of mediaeval painted glass.
Pilton (St. John)
12th century with arcades. 15th century roofs.
Taunton (St. Mary Magdalene)
Highest towers in the county. Five nave roof, fragments of mediaeval painted glass.
Trull (All Saints)
15th century with many mediaeval art treasures & 15th century glass.

Somerset

Wells Cathedral-Wells
Magnificent west front with carved figures. Splendid tower. Early English arcade of nave & transepts. 60 fine misericords c.1330. Lady chapel with glass & star vault. Chapter House & Bishop's Palace.
Weston Zoyland (St. Mary)
15th century bench ends. 16th century heraldic glass. Jacobean pulpit.

Museums & Galleries

Admiral Blake Museum - Bridgewater
Exhibits relating to Battle of Sedgemoor, archaeology.
Burdon Manor - Washford
14th century manor house with Saxon fireplace & cockpit.
Borough Museum - Hendford Manor Hall, Yeovil
Archaeology, firearms collections & Bailward Costume Collection.
Glastonbury Lake Village Museum - Glastonbury
Late prehistoric antiquities.
Gough's Cave Museum - Cheddar
Upper Paleolithic remains, skeleton, flints, amber & engraved stones.
Wookey Hole Cave Museum - Wookey Hole
Remains from Pliocene period. Relics of Celtic & Roman civilization. Exhibition of handmade paper-making.

Historic Monuments

Cleeve Abbey - Cleeve
Ruined 13th century house, with timber roof & wall paintings.
Farleigh Castle - Farleigh Hungerford
14th century remains - museums in chapel.
Glastonbury Abbey - Glastonbury
12th & 13th century ruins of St. Joseph's chapel & Abbot's kitchen.
Muchelney Abbey - Muchelney
15th century ruins of Benedictine abbey.

Other things to see & do

Black Rock Nature Reserve - Cheddar
Circular walk through plantation woodland, downland grazing.
Cheddar Caves
Show caves at the foot of beautiful Cheddar Gorge.
Cricket St. Thomas Wildlife Park - Nr. Chard
Wildlife park, heavy horse centre, countryside museum, etc.
West Somerset Railway
Minehead to Bishop's Lydeard preserved steam railway.
Wookey Hole Caves - Wookey Hole, Nr. Wells.

Montacute House. Yeovil.

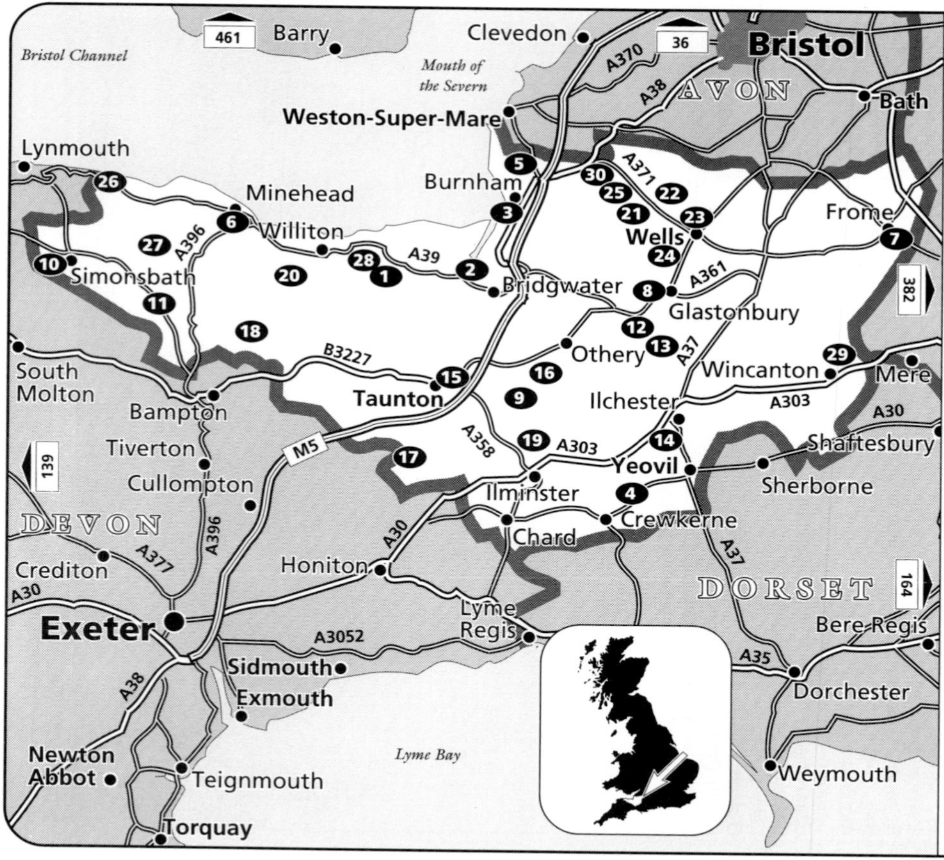

SOMERSET

Map reference

1 Laidler
2 Roe
3 Wheeler
4 Swann
5 Collins
6 Bradshaw
7 Clifford
8 Tynan
9 Carter
10 Brown
11 Young
11 Vicary
12 Middle
13 Copeland
14 Holloway
15 Clark
16 Gothard
17 Slipper
18 Garner-Richards
19 Mitchem
20 Brewer
21 White
22 Attia
23 Higgs
24 Frost
25 Thompson
26 Blue
27 Durbin
28 Criddle
29 Teague

314

Swang Farm. Cannington.

Somerset

		minimum £ per person	children taken	evening meals	animals taken
Mrs Pam Laidler **Quantock House** **Holford** **Bridgwater TA5 1RY** **Tel: (0278) 74439** **Open: ALL YEAR** **Map Ref No. 01**	Nearest Road: A.39 Quantock House is in the small picturesque village of Holford, historically connected with Wordsworth and Coleridge. Relax in this 400 year-old thatched home with cottage garden. The spacious rooms have en-suite bathrooms, T.V., & tea/coffee facilities. Sample the home cooking on offer, or enjoy nearby homely hostelries. Set near hills and the sea, a perfect centre for exploring by car or on foot.	£17.00 *see PHOTO over*	Y	Y	Y
Hilary Roe **Swang Farm** **Cannington** **Bridgwater TA5 2NJ** **Tel: (0278) 671765** **Fax 0278 671747** **Open: JAN - NOV** **Map Ref No. 02**	Nearest Road: A.39, M.5 Swang Farm, mentioned in the Doomsday Book, offers accommodation in 4 charming guest rooms, all with private facilities & modern amenities, including colour T.V. & tea/coffee makers. Residents' lounge & delightful garden for guests' use. Outdoor heated pool. Stabling available during winter. Excellent local pubs & restaurants. Close by are cottages once owned by Coleridge & Wordsworth. Ideal base for touring/walking in the Quantock Hills & surrounding area.	£25.00 *see PHOTO over*	Y	N	Y
Peter & Margaret Wheeler **The Warren Guest House** **29 Berrow Road** **Burnham-on-Sea** **TA8 2EZ** **Tel: (0278) 786726** **Open: ALL YEAR** **Map Ref No. 03**	Nearest Road: M.5, A.38 'The Warren' is an imposing Victorian house offering spacious accommodation with modern amenities including tea/coffee makers & colour T.Vs. The town centre, swimming pool & championship golf course within easy reach; the beach is 100 yds away. Guests have full use of the comfortably furnished lounge & are encouraged to browse in the attractive garden. Seedlings (in season) are available free to interested amateur gardeners. Ideally situated for touring the West Country, including Bath, Wells & Glastonbury.	£14.00 CREDIT CARD VISA M'CARD	Y	N	Y
Gillian & Robert Swann **Broadview** **43 East Street** **Crewkerne** **TA18 7AG** **Tel: (0460) 73424** **Open: ALL YEAR** **Map Ref No. 04**	Nearest Road: A.30, A.303 Secluded colonial bungalow circa 1926. Acre feature gardens, many interesting plants, lovely views. As you enter through the sun porch, which opens into the dining hall, you can sense the colonial atmosphere, which is enhanced by the hosts' personal collection of furnishings, porcelain & rugs. The guests' sitting room is extremely comfortable & relaxing. 3 en-suite/private rooms, carefully furnished with colour T.V., easy chairs, tea/coffee & C.H. Substantial quality home cooked traditional dinner. Dorset-Somerset Border.	£18.50	Y	Y	Y
Jaqui & Tony Collins **Knoll Lodge** **Church Road** **East Brent** **TA9 4HZ** **Tel: (0278) 760294** **Open: ALL YEAR** **Map Ref No. 05**	Nearest Road: M.5, A.38 Knoll Lodge is a 19th century listed Somerset house in an acre of orchard, where you are offered comfortable accommodation and quality food in friendly and peaceful rural surroundings. There are 3 spacious bedrooms - 2 double en-suite; 1 twin with private bathroom. Centrally heated, attractively decorated with antique pine furniture and hand-made American patchwork quilts. Colour T.V.s & tea/coffee facilities. Dinner available by prior arrangement.	£18.00	Y	Y	N

Quantock House. Holford.

Hillards. Curry Rivel.

Somerset

		minimum £ per person	children taken	evening meals	animals taken
Major & Mrs G.H. Bradshaw **Dollons House** **10 Church Street** **Dunster TA24 6SH** **Tel: (0643) 821880** **Open: ALL YEAR** **Map Ref No. 06**	Nearest Road: A.396 17th century Dollons House nestles beneath the castle in this delightful mediaeval village in the Exmoor National Park. Dunster is ideal for touring Exmoor & the North Devon Coast. There are 3 en-suite rooms each with its own character & special decor. 100 years ago the local pharmacist had his shop in Dollons & in the back he made marmalade for the Houses of Parliament.	£20.00 (no smoking) *see PHOTO over* CREDIT CARD VISA M'CARD AMEX	N	N	N
John & Janice Clifford **Southfield Farm** **Warminster Road** **Rodden** **Frome BA11 5LB** **Tel: (0373) 462348** **Open: APR-OCT** **Map Ref No. 07**	Nearest Road: A.362 Southfield Farm is a comfortable country guest house, 2 miles from Longleat & 13 miles from Bath. It has 6 double or twin en-suite bedrooms with colour T.V., hairdryer & hospitality tray. Children are most welcome, as are well behaved dogs by prior arrangement. Hot air ballooning & clay pigeon shoots can be arranged from the ground. Horse riding available nearby. Lots to do & see in the area close by.	£25.00 CREDIT CARD VISA M'CARD	Y	N	Y
John & Ann Tynan **No 3 Restaurant & Hotel** **3 Magdalene Street** **Glastonbury** **BA6 9EW** **Tel: (0458) 832129** **Open: FEB - DEC** **Map Ref No. 08**	Nearest Road: M.5, A.39 An attractive Grade II listed Georgian house adjoining the ruin of the once powerful Abbey. The tomb of King Arthur & Guinevere is claimed to have been discovered here in the 13th century. 6 attractive rooms, each with private facilities, telephone, radio, colour T.V. & tea/coffee makers. The restaurant produces only 'real' food with flair & innovation. Cornish lobster is a speciality. An excellent base for touring the region : Cheddar George, Wookey Hole & Wells Cathedral are all within easy reach.	£37.50 CREDIT CARD VISA M'CARD	Y	Y	N
J. Wilkins & M. Carter **Hillards** **High Street** **Curry Rivel** **Langport TA10 0EY** **Tel: (0458) 251737** **Open: ALL YEAR** **Map Ref No. 09**	Nearest Road: A.378, A.303 A charming 17th century grade II listed house of architectural & historical interest. 6 comfortable bedrooms, 3 with en-suite facilities. Dining room, oak room lounge, T.V. lounge where horse brasses adorn the cat basket hearth. Full central heating. A delightful home with a wealth of oak & elm panelled walls, beamed ceilings & large inglenook fireplaces. An excellent base from which to explore the surrounding countryside ; convenient for many West Country attractions.	£17.50 (no smoking) *see PHOTO over* CREDIT CARD AMEX	N	N	N
Mrs Julia Brown **Emmetts Grange** **Simonsbath** **Minehead** **TA24 7LD** **Tel: (064383) 282** **Open: MAR - OCT** **Map Ref No. 10**	Nearest Road: B.3223 This comfortable 19th century farmhouse is peacefully situated on a 1,200 acre farm set in the beautiful Exmoor National Park. 4 bedrooms, 2 en-suite, all with colour T.V. & tea making facilities. The lounge with open fire has a spectacular view across the garden to the moor. Delicious country cooking using local produce. Table licence. North Devon & Somerset coasts nearby. Good local walking, riding & fishing. Stabling provided. Evening meals by prior arrangement.	£20.00	Y	Y	Y

Dollons House. Dunster.

Somerset

		minimum £ per person	children taken	evening meals	animals taken
C. Alderton & J.Young **Karslake House Hotel** **Winsford** **Minehead TA24 7JE** **Tel: (064385) 242** **Open: EASTER-OCT** **Map Ref No. 11**	Nearest Road: A.396, M.5 This lovely 15th century former malt house with low beams & twisting scarlet carpeted passageways leading to 7 individual pretty bedrooms with modern comforts, welcomes a small number of guests at a time, enabling the hosts to enjoy your company & personally prepare gastronomic delights complemented by a good wine list. The very pretty village of Winsford offers excellent walking & riding in centre of National Park.	£19.00 🚭	Y	Y	Y
Mrs V. A. Vicary **Larcombe Foot** **Winsford** **Minehead** **TA24 7HS** **Tel: (064385) 306** **Open: APR - DEC** **Map Ref No. 11**	Nearest Road: A.396 Larcombe Foot, a comfortable old country house set in the beautiful & tranquil Upper Exe Valley, is an ideal base for walking, riding, fishing & touring Exmoor. Guests' comfort is paramount. There are 3 bedrooms, 2 with private bathroom & tea/coffee makers in all rooms. A comfortable sitting room with log fire & T.V. plus a pretty garden to relax in. Winsford is considered one of the prettiest villages on the moor.	£16.50	Y	N	Y
Mr & Mrs B. H. Middle **Church Farm Guest House** **School Lane** **Compton Dundon** **Somerton TA11 6PE** **Tel: (0458) 72927** **Open:ALL YEAR (Excl.** **Xmas & New Year)** **Map Ref No. 12**	Nearest Road: B.3151, A.39 A superb thatched cottage, over 400 years old, 6 delightful rooms, all with en-suite facilities, colour T.V., tea/coffee making equipment & full central heating. Most rooms in converted barn. Imaginative home cooking from fresh produce, residents' licence with choice of wines. Nestling below St. Andrew's Church in a lovely village with marvellous views in the heart of the Vale of Avalon. Walking & wildlife on the doorstep. Convenient for coast & countryside, historic houses & towns. Use of pretty garden & guests' car park.	£17.50	Y	Y	N
Roy Copeland **The Lynch Country** **House Hotel** **4 Behind Berry** **Somerton** **TA11 7PD** **Tel: (0458) 72316** **Open: ALL YEAR** **Map Ref No. 13**	Nearest Road: A.303 The Lynch is a charming small hotel, standing in acres of carefully tended, wonderfully mature grounds. Beautifully refurbished & decorated to retain all its Georgian style & elegance, it now offers accommodation in a choice of 5 attractively presented rooms, some with four-posters, others with Victorian bedsteads, all with thoughtful extras including bathrobes & magazines. Each room has en-suite facilities, 'phone, radio, T.V. & tea/coffee makers. The elegant dining room overlooks the lawns & lake.	£22.50 *see PHOTO over* CREDIT CARD VISA M'CARD	Y	N	Y
Mrs E. Holloway **Manor Farm** **Chiselborough** **Stoke-sub-Hamdon** **TR14 6TQ** **Tel: (0935) 881203** **Open: APR - OCT** **Map Ref No. 14**	Nearest Road: A.303, A.30 Manor Farm is set in the heart of rural Somerset & stands in 450 acres. A most atractive Victorian Hamstone house offering 4 charming comfortable rooms with modern amenities. A sitting room with colour T.V. for guests as well as a garden & games room. Mrs Holloway welcomes all her guests most warmly. Plenty of good pubs & restaurants within a couple of miles. A good base from which to explore this beautiful region.	£17.00	Y	N	N

The Lynch Country House Hotel.   Somerton.

Somerset

		minimum £ per person	children taken	evening meals	animals taken
Mrs C. Clark **Meryan House Hotel** **Bishops Hull** **Taunton TA1 5EG** **Tel: (0823) 337445** **Open: ALL YEAR** **Map Ref No. 15**	Nearest Road: A.38 A charming 17th century listed building of architectural & historical interest. It is set in its own grounds yet only 1 & a quarter miles from Taunton. All bedrooms are elegantly furnished with antiques, with en-suite facilities, colour T.V. (satellite & video channels) & tea/coffee making facilities. A delightful house with a wealth of beams & inglenook fireplaces. Excellent cuisine prepared from home grown produce.	£23.50 CREDIT CARD VISA M'CARD	Y	Y	Y
Mrs Sally Gothard **Slough Court** **Stoke St. Gregory** **Taunton TA3 6JQ** **Tel: (0823) 490311** **Open: FEB - NOV** **Map Ref No. 16**	Nearest Road: M.5 Delightful 14th century moated manor house situated in the heart of the nationally acclaimed Somerset Levels. The emphasis is on comfort, relaxation, personal service & good food. All rooms are elegantly furnished & have full central heating, yet they retain much of their original character with beamed ceilings, mullioned windows, inglenook fireplaces & an oak-screened hall. Tennis, swimming & croquet are available.	£20.00	Y	Y	N
Anne & Bill Slipper **Strawbridges Farm** **Guest House** **Churchstanton** **Taunton TA3 7PD** **Tel: (0823) 60591** **Open: ALL YEAR** **Map Ref No. 17**	Nearest Road: M.5, A.303 A relaxed, peaceful atmosphere, friendly hosts and high standard of accommodation in a delightful location in the Blackdown Hills. Strawbridges, now a non-working farm, offers 5 charming bedrooms (en-suite available), each with colour T.V. & tea/coffee facilities. Guests have their own comfortable lounge and separate dining room where excellent home cooking using fresh local produce is a speciality. An excellent touring base with ample parking available.	£16.00	Y	Y	N
Mrs Moira Garner-Richards **Watercombe House** **Huish Champflower** **Wiveliscombe** **Taunton TA4 2EE** **Tel: (0984) 23725** **Open: EASTER - OCT** **Map Ref No. 18**	Nearest Road: B.3227 A warm welcome awaits you at this charming Country House with river frontage in a quiet beauty spot in a fold of the Brendon Hills. Friendly personal service will ensure a happy relaxing stay. 1 double en-suite, 1 twin & 1 single room with modern amenities. The old school house retains its 'olde worlde' charm. Log fires & good home cooking. Fishing, sailing & riding available locally. An ideal spot for touring. Easy access to Exmoor & the coast. Children over 10 only.	£16.00	N	Y	N
Mrs Claire Mitchem **Whittles Farm** **Beercrocombe** **Taunton** **TA3 6AH** **Tel: (0823) 480301** **Open: FEB-NOV** **Map Ref No. 19**	Nearest Road: A.358 Guests at Whittles Farm can be sure of a high standard of accommodation & service. A superior 16th century farmhouse set in 200 acres of pastureland, it is luxuriously carpeted & furnished in traditional style. Inglenook fireplaces & log-burners. 3 bedrooms with en-suite facilities, individually furnished, T.V., tea/coffee making. Excellent farmhouse food using own meat, eggs & vegetables & local Cheddar cheese & butter. Table licence. Children over 12.	£20.00	N	Y	N

Somerset

		minimum £ per person	evening meals	children taken	animals taken
Mrs Diana Brewer **Wood Advent Farm** **Roadwater** **Watchet** **TA24 6SH** **Tel: (0984) 40920** **Open: ALL YEAR** **Map Ref No. 20**	Nearest Road: A.39 Set in the Exmoor National Park, Wood Advent Farm is a 340 acre working sheep farm with beautiful views & breathtaking parks, offering 5 relaxing en-suite bedrooms, with tea/coffee facilities. A chintz lounge with log fire, available at all times, & an inglenook woodburner heats the dining room, where country dishes are served, most of the produce being home produced on the farm or locally. Grass tennis court, outdoor heated pool. Ideal base for the West Country.	£17.50	Y	Y	Y
Doug & Carolyn White **Box Tree House** **Westbury-sub-Mendip** **Wells BA5 1HA** **Tel: (0749) 870777** **Open: ALL YEAR** **Map Ref No. 21**	Nearest Road: A.371 A warm welcome is assured at this delightful, converted 17th century farmhouse located right in the heart of the village. Accommodation is in 3 comfortable en-suite bedrooms with tea/coffee making facilities. A charming T.V. lounge is also available. Full English breakfast is served with local preserves, croissants & homemade muffins. Also workshops for stained glass & picture framing with many unique items for sale.	£15.00	Y	N	N
Mrs M. J. Attia **Glencot House** **Glencot Lane** **Wookey Hole** **Wells BA5 1BH** **Tel: (0749) 677160** **Fax 0749 670210** **Open: ALL YEAR** **Map Ref No. 22**	Nearest Road: M.5, A.371 Set in 18 acres of garden & parkland with river frontage, Glencot House is a Grade II listed Victorian mansion, which over the past few years has been restored to its former glory to provide comfortable country house accommodation with friendly service & homely atmosphere. It is elegantly furnished & offers peace & tranquility, yet is only one & a half miles from Wells & a quarter of a mile from Wookey Hole. An ideal base for the tourist who wishes to appreciate the beauty of Somerset.	£30.00 CREDIT CARD VISA M'CARD	Y	Y	Y
Mrs Pat Higgs **Home Farm** **Stoppers Lane** **Upper Coxley** **Wells BA5 1QS** **Tel: (0749) 672434** **Open:ALL YEAR (Excl. Xmas & New Year)** **Map Ref No. 23**	Nearest Road: A.39 Home Farm is set in the peace & quiet of the Somerset countryside where guests can enjoy a relaxing holiday. Offering accommodation in a choice of 7 rooms, some with private/en-suite bathroom, all with modern amenities & most with lovely views of the Mendip Hills. A colour T.V. lounge & garden are also available. Nearby are Wells, Bath, Cheddar Gorge & Wookey Hole Caves making this an ideal spot for touring. Plenty of good pubs & restaurants nearby.	£15.50	Y	N	Y
Chris & Anita Frost **Southway Farm** **Polsham** **Wells BA5 1RW** **Tel: (0749) 673396** **Open: FEB-OCT** **Map Ref No. 24**	Nearest Road: A.39 Southway Farm is a Grade II listed Georgian farmhouse, situated half way between Glastonbury & Wells. 3 comfortable & attractively furnished bedrooms, 2 en-suite. A delicious full English breakfast is served, although vegetarians are catered for. Guests may relax in the cosy lounge with colour T.V. or in the pretty, tranquil garden. An ideal location for a restful holiday or for touring the glorious West Country.	£15.00	Y	N	N

Cutthorne. Luckwell Bridge.

Somerset

		per person minimum £	children taken	evening meals	animals taken
Mrs A.W. Thompson **Stoneleigh House** **Westbury-sub-Mendip** **Wells BA5 1HF** **Tel: (0749) 870668** Open: ALL YEAR Map Ref No. 25	Nearest Road: A.371 Stoneleigh House is a delightful 18th century farmhouse on the edge of a picturesque village which lies on the southern slopes of the Mendip Hills between Cheddar, with its spectacular Gorge, and Wells with its beautiful cathedral. The house has a large garden with lovely views and its own Country Life Museum. Excellent accommodation in 2 en-suite rooms with colour T.V.& tea and coffee facilities. Children over 10 please.	£16.00 🚭	Y	N	N
Stephen Blue **Bales Mead** **West Porlock** **TA24 8NX** **Tel: (0643) 862565** Open: ALL YEAR Map Ref No. 26	Nearest Road: A.39 A small, elegant Edwardian country house offering superb accommodation. An outstanding, peaceful setting, with panoramic views towards both sea & rolling countryside of Exmoor. All 3 double bedrooms are exquisitely furnished, offering colour T.V., clock/radio, hairdryer & hot beverage tray. Breakfast is served in the elegant dining room or 'al fresco' in the Summer, weather permitting. An excellent base for walking/touring Exmoor & the North Devon Coast.	£20.00 🚭	N	N	N
Ann & Philip Durbin **Cutthorne** **Luckwell Bridge** **Wheddon Cross** **TA24 7EW** **Tel: (064383) 255** Open: FEB - NOV Map Ref No. 27	Nearest Road: B.3224, A.396. An 18th century Yeomans farmhouse totally secluded in the heart of Exmoor National Park. Spacious & comfortable accommodation with log fires & central heating. The 4 bedrooms have lovely views of the countryside. 3 luxury en-suite bathrooms. Four-poster bed. Candlelit dinners & delicious home cooking. For extra privacy, beautifully appointed medieval stone cottages on side of farmhouse overlooking pond & cobbled yard. Stabling provided. Ideal base for touring.	£17.50 *see PHOTO over*	Y	Y	Y
Richard & Daphne Criddle **Curdon Mill** **Lower Vellow** **Williton** **TA4 4LS** **Tel: (0984) 56522** **Fax 0984 56197** Open: ALL YEAR Map Ref No. 28	Nearest Road: A.358 Curdon Mill is a lovely working water mill situated on 200 acres of farmland at the foot of the beautiful Quantock Hills. Offering 6 pretty en-suite bedrooms with T.V. & tea/coffee making facilities. Lounge available for guests' use. Meals are delicious. Real country cuisine using local or home-produced meat & fish with fresh fruit, vegetables & herbs from the garden. A lovely base for touring the region. Heated outdoor pool in spacious relaxing garden, stabling for horses available. Children over 8 only.	£20.50 *see PHOTO over* CREDIT CARD VISA	Y	Y	Y
Mrs Alicia Teague **Lower Church Farm** **Rectory Lane** **Charlton Musgrove** **Wincanton BA9 8ES** **Tel: (0963) 32307** Open: ALL YEAR Map Ref No. 29	Nearest Road: A.303 Lovely countryside surrounds this 18th century farmhouse & its 60 acres of dairy pasture. A pleasant, homely atmosphere prevails in the house with its beams & inglenooks. 3 bedrooms are available to guests with modern amenities & tea/coffee making facilities. There is a lounge with colour T.V. & guests have the use of cottage garden & patio. On the borders of Wiltshire, Dorset, central for touring.	£12.00	Y	N	Y

Curdon Mill. Williton.

Suffolk

Suffolk
(East Anglia)

In July, the lower reaches of the River Orwell hold the essence of Suffolk. Broad fields of green and gold with wooded horizons sweep down to the quiet water. Orwell Bridge spans the wide river where yach tsand tan-sailed barges share the water with ocean-going container ships out of Ipswich. Downstream the saltmarshes echo to the cry of the Curlew. The small towns and villages of Suffolk are typical of an area with long seafairing traditions. This is the county of men of vision; like Constable and Gainsborough, Admiral Lord Nelson and Benjamin Britten.

The land is green and fertile and highly productive. The hedgerows shelter some of our prettiest wild flowers, & the narrow country lanes are a pure delight. Most memorable is the ever-changing sky, appearing higher and wider here than elsewhere in England. There is a great deal of heathland, probably the best known being Newmarket where horses have been trained and raced for some hundreds of years. Gorse-covered heath meets sandy cliffs on Suffolks Heritage Coast. Here are bird reserves and the remains of the great mediaeval city of Dunwich, sliding into the sea.

West Suffolk was famous for its wool trade in the Middle Ages, & the merchants gave thanks for their good fortune by building magnificent "Wool Churches". Much-photographed Lavenham has the most perfect black & white timbered houses in Britain, built by the merchants of Tudor times. Ipswich was granted the first charter by King John in 1200, but had long been a trading community of seafarers. Its history can be read from the names of the streets - Buttermarket, Friars Street, Cornhill, Dial Lane & Tavern Street. The latter holds the Great White Horse Hotel mentioned by Charles Dickens in Pickwick Papers. Sadly not many ancient buildings remain, but the mediaeval street pattern and the churches make an interesting trail to follow. The Market town of Bury St. Edmunds is charming, with much of its architectural heritage still surviving, from the Norman Cornhill to a fine Queen Anne House. The great Abbey, now in ruins, was the meeting place of the Barons of England for the creation of the Magna Carta, enshrining the principals of individual freedom, parliamentary democracy and the supremacy of the law. Suffolk has some very fine churches, notably at Mildenhall, Lakenheath, Framlingham, Lavenham & Stoke-by-Nayland, & also a large number of wonderful houses & great halls, evidence of the county's prosperity.

Lavenham.

328

Suffolk

Suffolk
Gazeteer

Areas of Outstanding Natural Beauty
Suffolk Coast. Heathlands.
Dedham Vale.

Historic Houses & Castles

Euston Hall - Thetford
18th century house with fine collection of pictures. Gardens & 17th century Parish Church nearby.

Christchurch Mansion - Ipswich
16th century mansion built on site of 12th century Augustinian Priory. Gables & dormers added in 17th century & other alteration & additions made in 17th & 18th centuries.

Gainsborough's House - Sudbury
Birthplace of Gainsborough, well furnished, collection of paintings.

The Guildhall - Hadleigh
15th century.

Glemham Hall - Nr Woodbridge
Elizabethan house of red brick - 18th century alterations. Fine stair, panelled rooms with Queen Anne furniture.

Haughley Park - Nr. Stowmarket
Jacobean manor house.

Heveningham Hall - Nr. Halesworth
Georgian mansion - English Palladian - Interior in Neo-Classical style. Garden by Capability Brown.

Ickworth - Nr. Bury St. Edmunds
Mixed architectural styles - late Regency & 18th century. French furniture, pictures & superb silver. Gardens with orangery.

Kentwell Hall - Long Melford
Elizabethan mansion in red brick, built in E plan, surrounded by moat.

Little Hall - Lavenham
15th century hall house, collection of furniture, pictures, china, etc.

Melford Hall - Nr. Sudbury
16th century - fine pictures, Chinese porcelain, furniture. Garden with gazebo.

Somerleyton Hall - Nr. Lowestoft
Dating from 16th century - additional work in 19th century. Carving by Grinling Gibbons. Tapestries, library, pictures.

Cathedrals & Churches

Bury St. Edmunds (St. Mary)
15th century. Hammer Beam roof in nave, wagon roof in chancel. Boret monument 1467.

Bramfield (St. Andrew)
Early circular tower. Fine screen & vaulting. Renaissance effigy.

Bacton (St. Mary)
15th century timbered roof. East Anglian stone & flintwork.

Dennington (St. Mary)
15th century alabaster monuments & bench ends. Aisle & Parclose screens with lofts & parapets.

Earl Stonhay (St. Mary)
14th century - rebuilt with fine hammer roof & 17th century pulpit with four hour-glasses.

Euston (St. Genevieve)
17th century. Fine panelling, reredos may be Grinling Gibbons.

Framlingham (St. Michael)
15th century nave & west tower, hammer beam roof in false vaulting. Chancel was rebuilt in 16th century for the tombs of the Howard family, monumental art treasures. Thamar organ. 1674.

Fressingfield (St. Peter & St. Paul)
15th century woodwork - very fine.

Lavenham (St. Peter & St. Paul)
15th century. Perpendicular. Fine towers. 14th century chancel screen. 17th century monument in alabaster.

Long Melford (Holy Trinity)
15th century Lady Chapel, splendid brasses. 15th century glass of note. Chantry chapel with fine roof. Like cathedral in proportions.

Stoke-by-Nayland (St. Mary)
16th-17th century library, great tower. Fine nave & arcades. Good brasses & monuments.

Ufford (St. Mary)
Mediaeval font cover - glorious.

Museums & Galleries

Christchurch Mansion - Ipswich
Country house, collection of furniture, pictures, bygones, ceramics of 18th century. Paintings by Gainsborough, Constable & modern artists.

Ipswich Museum - Ipswich
Natural History; prehistory, geology & archaeology to mediaeval period.

Suffolk

Moyse's Hall Musuem - Bury St. Edmunds
12th century dwelling house with local antiquities & natural history.
Abbot's Hall Museum of Rural Life - Stowmarket
Collections describing agriculture, crafts & domestic utensils.
Gershom-Parkington Collection - Bury St. Edmunds
Queen Anne House containing collection of watches & clocks.
Dunwich Musuem - Dunwich
Flora & fauna; local history.

Historic Monuments

The Abbey - Bury St. Edmunds
Only west end now standing.

Framlingham Castle
12th & 13th centuries - Tudor almshouses.
Bungay Castle - Bungay
12th century. Restored 13th century drawbridge & gatehouse.
Burgh Castle Roman Fort - Burgh
Coastal defences - 3rd century.
Herringfleet Priory - Herringfleet
13th century - remains of small Augustinian priory.
Leiston Abbey - Leiston
14th century - remains of cloisters, choir & trancepts.
Orford Castle - Orford
12th century - 18-sided keep - three towers.

The House in the Clouds. Thorpeness.

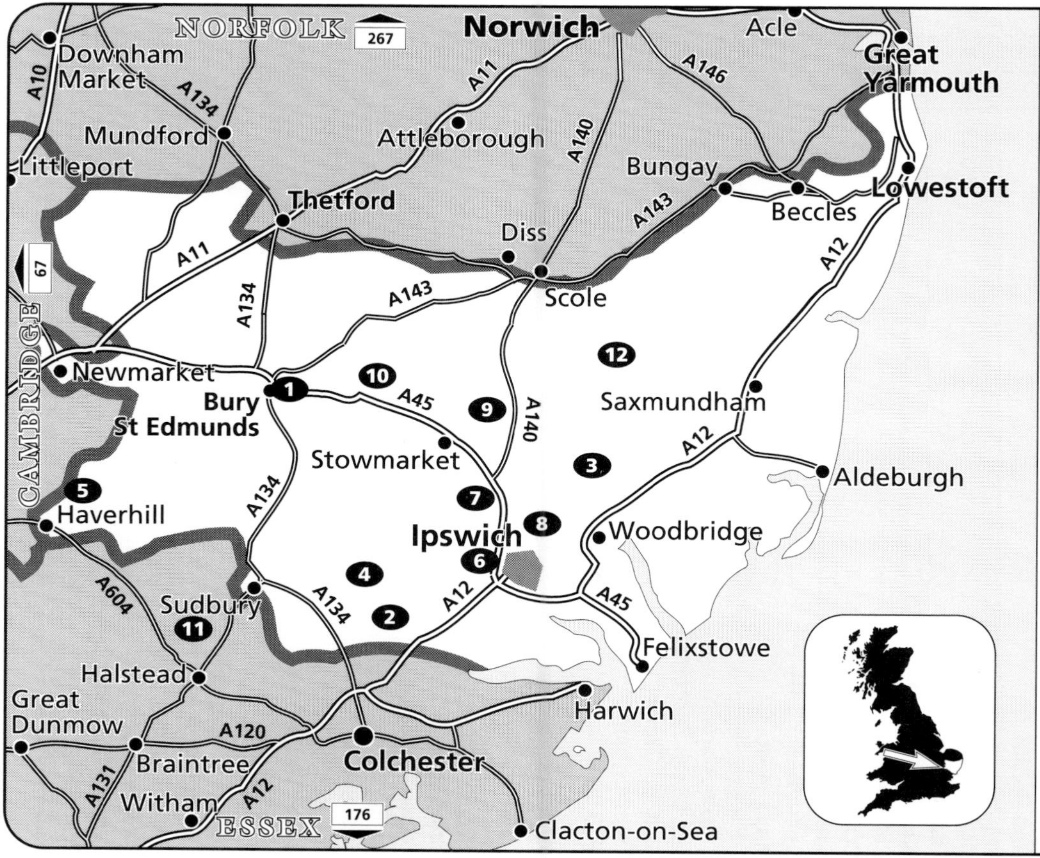

SUFFOLK
Map reference

1 Dakin
2 Watkins
3 Albrecht
4 Rolfe
5 Sheppard
6 Debenham
7 Hackett-Jones
8 Hilton
9 Ridsdale
10 Bowden
11 Morse
12 Bagnall

331

Suffolk

		minimum £ per person	children taken	evening meals	animals taken
Ann & Roy Dakin 'Dunston Guest House/Hotel' 8 Springfield Road Bury St. Edmunds IP33 3AN Tel: (0284) 767981 Open: ALL YEAR Map Ref No. 01	Nearest Road: A.45 A 19th century house, full of character, with a warm, friendly atmosphere. There are 16 pleasant & tastefully furnished rooms, many with en-suite facilities, all very comfortable, each with colour T.V., tea/coffee & ironing facilities. T.V. lounge, sun lounge & garden for guests' use. A ground floor room is available for handicapped guests. Licenced. Situated in the centre of East Anglia, it is an ideal base for touring the region, with lovely towns & villages plus coastline.	£18.00	Y	Y	N
Mrs Penny Watkins The Bauble Higham Colchester CO7 6LA Tel: (0206) 37254 Open: ALL YEAR Map Ref No. 02	Nearest Road: A.12 The Bauble is a delightful house offering accommodation in 3 attractively furnished bedrooms with modern amenities including T.V. & tea/coffee making facilities. A full English breakfast is served. Lounge, garden, heated pool & tennis court available for guests' use. Higham lies in the heart of Constable country & is within easy reach of many wool villages with their churches, antiques shops & National Trust properties. Children over 12 years welcome.	£17.50	Y	N	N
Carole Albrecht The Limes Farm House Saxtead Green Framlingham IP13 9QH Tel: (0728) 685303 Fax 0728 685825 Open: ALL YEAR Map Ref No. 03	Nearest Road: A.12 The Limes is a large listed Grade II farmhouse, dating from 1490, with large garden, 2 meadows, pond, chickens, ducks, dogs & cats. Every comfort is offered to guests & excellent food - vegetarians catered for. Cooked with home grown & local fresh produce. Situated on Saxtead Green, close to historical Framlingham - 25 mins. drive from coast; Aldeburgh Festival, etc. An ideal spot from which to visit the many places places of interest in the region.	£18.00	Y	Y	Y
Mrs Angela Rolfe Edgehill Hotel 2 High Street Hadleigh IP7 5AP Tel: (0473) 822458 Open: ALL YEAR Map Ref No. 04	Nearest Road: A.12, A.45 Edgehill is a family-run Georgian house in central Hadleigh. Beautifully restored & tastefully modernised, the hotel offers delightful accommodation. Particular attention is paid to friendly service & traditional home cooking with organic vegetables. Situated in the most picturesque part of Suffolk, it is a good base from which to visit the surrounding towns & villages of East Anglia.	£18.25	Y	Y	Y
Mrs Jane Sheppard The Old Vicarage Great Thurlow Haverhill CB9 7LE Tel: (044083) 209 Open: ALL YEAR Map Ref No. 05	Nearest Road: A.604 The Old Vicarage is set in the quiet of the Suffolk countryside, with wonderful views. On the edge of Constable country, with Newmarket 10 miles, Cambridge and Saffron Walden 18 miles away. The 2 guest bedrooms have en-suite or private facilities. (No smoking in bedrooms) Evening meals with prior notice or reservations will gladly be made at good nearby Pubs. Children over 7 please. Pets by arrangement.	£18.00	Y	Y	Y

Suffolk

		per person minimum £	children taken	evening meals	animals taken
Mrs P. A. Debenham **Mulberry Hall** **Burstall** **Ipswich** **IP8 3DP** **Tel: (047387) 348** **Open: ALL YEAR** **Map Ref No. 06**	Nearest Road: A.12, A.45 A lovely 16th century timber-framed farmhouse, once owned by Cardinal Wolsey, standing in one & a half acres of garden. Accommodation is in a choice of 3 bedrooms with modern amenities, hair dryer & ironing facilities available. The house is comfortably & prettily furnished & guests may use the lounge with log-burning inglenook fireplace. Plenty of games & reading matter plus information on local events. Tennis, badminton & croquet available. A delightful home.	£16.00	Y	Y	N
Raewyn Hackett-Jones **Pipps Ford** **Norwich Road** **Needham Market** **Ipswich IP6 8LJ** **Tel: (044979) 208** **Fax 044979 561** **Open:ALL YEAR (Excl.** **Xmas & New Year)** **Map Ref No. 07**	Nearest Road: A.45, A.140 A beautiful Tudor, beamed guest house in a pretty, old fashioned garden by the River Gipping. Accommodation is in 6 well-appointed & very attractive bedrooms each with private bathroom & tea/coffee making facilities. A very extensive breakfast menu & delicious 4 course evening meals are served in the delightful conservatory. Licensed. Colour T.V., tennis court & swimming pool. Winner of The Best Bed & Breakfast award for East Anglia. A good central position for touring all of East Anglia.	£22.00 *see PHOTO over* CREDIT CARD VISA	Y	Y	N
Lise & Michael Hilton **Otley House** **Otley** **IP6 9NR** **Tel: (0473) 890253** **Open: MAR-NOV** **Map Ref No. 08**	Nearest Road: A.12, A.140 A magnificent 17th century house standing in its own spacious grounds, surrounded by mature trees with 2 small lakes, croquet lawn & putting green. Offering 4 luxuriously furnished en-suite bedrooms, some with colour T.V. Evening meals are a delight & served in the Regency dining room. Billiard room, T.V. & drawing room for guests' use. Ideally located for visiting Woodbridge, Oxford, Southwold, Norfolk & Cambridge. No smoking in the bedrooms.	£22.00	Y	Y	N
Martin & Diana Ridsdale **Cherry Tree Farm** **Mendlesham Green** **Stowmarket** **IP14 5RQ** **Tel: (0449) 766376** **Open: FEB-NOV** **Map Ref No. 09**	Nearest Road: A.140 Traditional timber-framed farmhouse, standing in three quarters of an acre of garden with orchard & duck ponds in a peaceful Suffolk village. 3 bedrooms, 2 with en-suite facilities. A spacious & comfortable lounge, inglenook fireplaces with log fire. Hearty English breakfast served in the oak-beamed dining room. Home-baked bread, own preserves & honey. Imaginative evening meals, with garden & local produce, good cheeses & fine English wines. Children over 10 yrs.	£19.00	Y	Y	N
Mrs J. Bowden **The Old Rectory** **Wetherden** **Stowmarket IP14 3LS** **Tel: (0359) 40144** **Open: MAR - NOV** **Map Ref No. 10**	Nearest Road: A.45 Situated on a hill overlooking the village of Wetherden, just off the A.45 between Bury St. Edmunds & Stowmarket, this beautiful Georgian house is set in 13 acres. 3 bedrooms, 2 with own bathroom. Sitting room with log fire & coloured T.V. Large garden with croquet lawn. Ideally placed for touring the lovely region of East Anglia.	£17.50	N	N	N

Pipps Ford.   Needham Market.

Suffolk

		minimum £ per person	children taken	evening meals	animals taken
Catherine & David Morse **St. Mary Hall** **Belchamp Walter** **Sudbury** **CO10 7BB** **Tel: (0787) 237202** **Open: ALL YEAR** **Map Ref No. 11**	Nearest Road: A.604, A.134 Fine example of mediaeval Suffolk manor house in lovely 4-acre garden, 1 mile south of the village of Belchamp Walter (guests advised to obtain directions in advance). On arrival, you will be warmly welcomed. There are two twin/double and one single room, each with private bathroom. Book-lined library with T.V. Pretty dining room. Large outdoor pool, tennis court, croquet. Catherine, a gourmet cook, will provide dinner at 24 hr. notice. Children over 12.	£20.00	Y	Y	Y
Sue Bagnall **Abbey House** **Monk Soham** **Woodbridge** **IP13 7EN** **Tel: (0728) 685225** **Open: JAN - NOV** **Map Ref No. 12**	Nearest Road: A.1120 Abbey House is a Victorian Rectory set in 10 acres of peaceful Suffolk countryside. The house is surrounded by secluded gardens, with mature trees & several large ponds. The remainder of the grounds are occupied by Jersey cows. A flock of sheep & an assorted collection of chickens & waterfowl. 3 attractive double bedrooms. Private bathrooms, tea making facilities, imaginative evening meals using home produced meat & vegetables. Outdoor swimming pool.	£17.00	N	Y	N

All the establishments mentioned in this guide
are members of
The Worldwide Bed & Breakfast Association

Surrey

Surrey
(South East)

One of the Home Counties, Surrey includes a large area of London, south of the Thames. Communications are good in all directions so it is easy to stay in Surrey & travel either into central London or out to enjoy the lovely countryside which, despite urban development, survives thanks to the 'Green Belt' policy. The county is also very accessible from Gatwick Airport.

The land geographically, is chalk sandwiched in clay, & probably the lack of handy building material was responsible for the area remaining largely uninhabited for centuries. The North Downs were a considerable barrier to cross, but gradually settlements grew along the rivers which were the main routes through. The Romans used the gap created by the River Mole to build Stane Street between London & Chichester, this encouraged the development of small towns. The gap cut by the passage of the River Wey allows the Pilgrims Way to cross the foot of the Downs. Dorking, Reigate & Farnham are small towns along this route, all with attracitve main streets & interesting shops & buildings.

Surrey has very little mention in the Domesday Book, &, although the patronage of the church & of wealthy families established manors which developed over the years, little happened to disturb the rural tranquility of the region. As a county it made little history but rather reflected passing times, although Magna Carta was signed at Egham in 1215.

The heathlands of Surrey were a Royal playground for centuries. The Norman Kings hunted here & horses became part of the landscape & life of the people, as they are today on Epsom Downs.

Nearness to London & Royal patronage began to influence the area, & the buildings of the Tudor period reflect this. Royal palaces were built at Hampton Court & Richmond, & great houses such as Loseley near Guildford often using stone from the monasteries emptied during the Reformation. Huge deer parks were enclosed & stocked. Richmond, described as the "finest village in the British Dominions", is now beset by 20th century traffic but still has a wonderful park with deer, lakes & woodland that was enclosed by Charles I. The terraces & gardens of such buildings as Trumpeters House & Asgill House on the slopes of Richmond overlooking the Thames, have an air of spaciousness & elegance & there are lovely & interesting riverside walks at Richmond.

Polesden Lacey.

Surrey

Surrey
Gazeteer
Historic Houses & Castles

Albury Park - Albury, Nr. Guildford
A delightful country mansion designed by Pugin.
Clandon Park - Guildford
A fine house in the Palladian style by Leoni. A good collection of furniture & pictures. The house boasts some fine plasterwork.
Claremont - Esher
A superb Palladian house with interesting interior.
Detillens - Limpsfield
A fine 15th century house with inglenook fireplaces & mediaeval furniture. A large, pleasant garden.
Greathed Manor- Lingfield
An imposing Victorian manor house.
Hatchlands - East Clandon
A National Trust property of the 18th century with a fine Adam interior
Loseley House - Guildford
A very fine Elizabethan mansion with superb panelling, furniture & paintings.
Polesden Lacy - Dorking
A Regency villa housing the Grevill collection of tapestries, pictures & furnishings. Extensive gardens.

Cathedrals & Churches

Compton (St. Nicholas)
The only surviving 2-storey sanctuary in the country. A fine 17th century pulpit.
Esher (St. George)
A fine altar-piece & marble monument.
Hascombe (St. Peter)
A rich interior with much gilding & painted reredos & roofs.
Lingfield (St. Peter & St. Paul)
15th century. Holding a chained bible.
Ockham (St. Mary & All Saints)
Early church with 13th century east window.
Stoke D'Abernon (St. Mary)
Dating back to Pre-conquest time with additions from the 12th-15th centuries. A fine 13th century painting. Early brasses.

Museums & Galleries

Charterhouse School Museum - Godalming
Peruvian pottery, Greek pottery, archaeology & natural history.
Chertsey Museum - Chertsey
18th-19th century costume & furnishing displayed & local history.
Guildford House - Guildford
The house is 17th century & of architectural interest housing monthly exhibitions.
Guildford Museum - Guildford
A fine needlework collection & plenty on local history.
Old Kiln Agricultural - Tilford
A very interesting collection of old farm implements.
Watermill Museum - Haxted
A restored 17th century mill with working water wheels & machinery.
Weybridge Museum - Weybridge
Good archaeological exhibition plus costume & local history.

The Gardens. Wisley

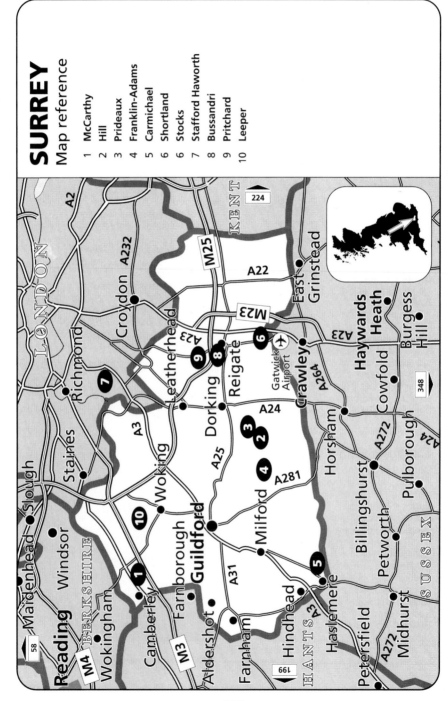

SURREY
Map reference

1 McCarthy
2 Hill
3 Prideaux
4 Franklin-Adams
5 Carmichael
6 Shortland
6 Stocks
7 Stafford Haworth
8 Bussandri
9 Pritchard
10 Leeper

Surrey

		minimum £ per person	children taken	evening meals taken	animals taken
Tommy & Ann McCarthy **Pineleigh** **10 Castle Road (off** **Waverley Drive)** **Camberley GU15 2DS** **Tel: (0276) 64787** **Open: ALL YEAR** **Map Ref No. 01**	Nearest Road: M.3, A.325 Pineleigh is a spacious Edwardian house built in 1906, set in half an acre of mature garden in a very quiet area. Accommodation is in 3 comfortable guest rooms, all en-suite with telephone, T.V. & hospitality tray. Attractively furnished in Victorian style with many old prints & pictures. A full English breakfast is served, evening meals by arrangement. Conveniently located, with easy access to Heathrow Airport & London.	£20.00	N	Y	N
Mrs Gill Hill **Bulmer Farm** **Holmbury St. Mary** **Dorking RH5 6LG** **Tel: (0306) 730210** **Open: ALL YEAR** **Map Ref No. 02**	Nearest Road: A.25, B.2126 Enjoy a warm welcome at this delightful 17th century farmhouse complete with many beams & an inglenook fireplace. Offering 3 charming rooms all with h&c & tea/coffee making facilities. Adjoining the house around a courtyard are 5 attractive barn conversion en-suite bedrooms for non smokers. Farm produce & home-made preserves are provided. Situated in a picturesque village, it is convenient for London airports.	£15.00	N	N	Y
Mrs D V Prideaux **Mark Ash** **Abinger Common** **Dorking** **RH5 6JA** **Tel: (0306) 731326** **Open: MAR - NOV** **Map Ref No. 03**	Nearest Road: A.25 A pleasant Victorian house standing in its own delightful garden, located in an area of 'outstanding natural beauty'. Accommodation is in a choice of 2 comfortable rooms, 1 with private facilities. Both have modern amenities, radio & tea/coffee making facilities. A residents' drawing room is also available. Full English or Continental breakfast. Packed lunches can be provided with prior notice. There is also a heated outdoor swimming pool & tennis court. 35 mins. to Gatwick & Heathrow. London under 1 hour's drive.	£25.00	Y	N	N
Mrs Carol Franklin Adams **High Edser** **Shere Road** **Ewhurst GU6 7PQ** **Tel: (0483) 278214** **Open: ALL YEAR** **Map Ref No. 04**	Nearest Road: A.25 A large, handsome Grade II listed home, the earliest part built in the 14th century, situated in an Area of Outstanding Natural Beauty. There are two rooms available; one double and one twin with private facilities. Residents lounge and T.V. Tennis court in grounds and golf nearby. 35 minutes to Gatwick and London Airports. Approximately an hour's drive to London.	£18.00	Y	N	Y
Mrs Elizabeth Carmichael **Deerfell** **Blackdown Park** **Fernden Lane** **Haslemere** **GU27 3LA** **Tel: (0428) 653409** **Open: FEB-NOV** **Map Ref No. 05**	Nearest Road: A.286 A warm welcome in a spacious & comfortable family home set in downland countryside, with breathtaking views to the hills & valleys of Sussex. Stone built at the turn of the century on a sunny gorse-clad slope, it was the coach house to Blackdown House. Offering 3 comfortable rooms, 2 with private facilities. Close by, Haslemere station (4 miles), London three quarters of an hour, Midhurst, Petworth, Goodwood & Chichester. Walking & riding. Children & pets welcome. Gatwick/Heathrow - 1 hour.	£18.00	Y	N	Y

Chase Lodge. Kingston.

Surrey

		per person minimum £	children taken	evening meals	animals taken
Mrs Daphne Shortland **Chalet Guest House** **77 Massetts Road** **Horley RH6 7EB** **Tel: (0293) 821666** **Fax 0293 821619** **Open: ALL YEAR** **Map Ref No. 06**	Nearest Road: A.23, M.23 A family run guest house offering accommodation with modern facilities in a bright and friendly atmosphere. 7 bedrooms, mostly en-suite, with T.V., tea/coffee trays. Single availability. Garden and ample parking. Local interests include the Six Bells Pub, circa 827. Lovely Sussex countryside adjacent. Gatwick airport 5 minutes. London or the South Coast 30 minutes by train.	£22.00 CREDIT CARD VISA M'CARD	Y	N	N
Mr & Mrs K.C. Stocks **The Lawn Guest House** **30 Massetts Road** **Horley RH6 7DE** **Tel: (0293) 775751** **Open: ALL YEAR** **Map Ref No. 06**	Nearest Road: A.23, M.23 A well appointed Victorian house 4 minutes from Gatwick, 25 miles to London or Brighton. Very useful as a base for travelling, it is close to the rail station & town centre. There are 7 bedrooms 4 with en-suite facilities, very comfortable & well decorated, with colour T.V. A pleasant breakfast room & a garden for guests' use. There is a supplement payable for single use of rooms.	£17.50 (no smoking) *see PHOTO over* CREDIT CARD VISA M'CARD AMEX	Y	N	Y
Denise & Nigel Stafford Haworth **Chase Lodge** **10 Park Road** **Hampton Wick** **Kingston KT1 4AS** **Tel: (081) 9431862** **Fax 081 9439363** **Open: ALL YEAR** **Map Ref No. 07**	Nearest Road: M.25, M.4, M.3 Built in 1870, Chase Lodge, boarded by Royal Bushey Park, offers 5 attractively decorated, comfortably furnished bedrooms, 1 with a four-poster; each has tea/coffee making facilities, refrigerator & T.V.. Guests may also relax in the colourful patio garden. To the rear, a gate leads directly into Hampton Court Palace. An excellent location, near to Kew Gardens. Central London only half an hour away. Courtesy car to & from the airport for guests staying 3 nights or more.	£18.50 *see PHOTO over* CREDIT CARD VISA M'CARD AMEX	Y	Y	Y
Mr & Mrs G. Bussandri **Cranleigh Hotel** **41 West Street** **Reigate RH2 9BL** **Tel:(0737) 240600/223417** **Fax 0737 223734** **Open: ALL YEAR** **Map Ref No. 08**	Nearest Road: A.25, M.25 The Cranleigh Hotel has a reputation for comfort, cleanliness & hospitality. Its modern facilities include hairdryers, T.V. & a pleasant bar & lounge etc. Comfortable accommodation in pleasant rooms. Three quarters of an hour from London & a few minutes from Gatwick airport, the hotel stands in lovely gardens which provide flowers & fresh food for the table. Very convenient for travellers to the South West. Ideal for first or last night of travel.	£40.00 CREDIT CARD VISA M'CARD AMEX	Y	Y	N
Mrs Brenda Pritchard **Field House** **Babylon Lane** **Lower Kingswood** **Tadworth KT20 6XE** **Tel: (0737) 221745** **Open: ALL YEAR** **Map Ref No. 09**	Nearest Road: M.25, A.217 Enjoy your stay in this elegant country home; farmland views from all windows. 2 minutes to A.217 & M.25. Gatwick 15 minutes. Accommodation is in 3 attractive rooms each with T.V. & tea/coffee facilities. Double with bathroom, twin with basin & single. Large bathroom close by. A friendly & warm welcome awaits you at this delightful home. Close to Walton Heath & Kingswood golf clubs & allergy clinic.	£22.00	Y	N	N

The Lawn Guest House. Horley.

Surrey

Kevin & Teresa Leeper **Knaphill Manor** **Carthouse Lane** **Woking** **GU21 4XT** **Tel: (0276) 857962** **Open: ALL YEAR** **Map Ref No. 10**	Nearest Road: M.25, exit 11 A delightful, large family home dating back to the 1700's, set in 6 acres of grounds with tennis court & croquet lawn. Located in a farming area, the house is quiet & secluded yet Heathrow & Gatwick are only a 35 minute drive. Accommodation is very comfortable with en-suite or private facilities, plus T.V. & tea/coffee makers. A guests' colour T.V. lounge is also available. Early morning arrivals are welcome. London 25 mins. Ascot, Windsor & Oxford are easily reached.	**£27.50** *see PHOTO over* CREDIT CARD VISA M'CARD	Y	Y	N

All the establishments mentioned in this guide

are members of

The Worldwide Bed & Breakfast Association

If you have any comments regarding your accommodation please send them to us using the form at the back of the guide. We value your comments

Knaphill Manor. Knaphill.

Sussex

Sussex
(South East)

The South Downs of Sussex stretch along the coast, reflecting the expanse of the North Downs of Kent, over the vast stretches of the Weald.

The South Downs extend from dramatic Beachy Head along the coast to Chichester & like the North Downs, they are crossed by an ancient trackway. There is much evidence of prehistoric settlement on the Downs. Mount Caburn, near Lewes, is crowned by an iron age fort, & Cissbury Ring is one of the most important archaeological sites in England. This large earthwork covers 80 acres & must have held a strategic defensive position. Hollingbury Fort carved into the hillside above Brighton, & the Trundle (meaning circle) date from 300-250 B.C., & were constructed on an existing neolithic settlement. The Long Man of Wilmington stands 226 feet high & is believed to be Nordic, possibly representing Woden, the God of War.

Only two towns are located on the Downs but both are of considerable interest. Lewes retains much of its mediaeval past & there is a folk museum in Ann of Cleves' house, which itself is partly 16th century. Arundel has a fascinating mixture of architectural styles, a castle & a superb park with a lake, magnificent beech trees & an unrivalled view of the Arun valley.

The landscape of the inland Weald ranges from bracken-covered heathlands where deer roam, to the deep woodland stretches of the Ashdown Forest, eventually giving way to soft undulating hills & valleys, patterned with hop-fields, meadows, oast houses, windmills & fruit orchards. Originally the whole Weald was dense with forest. Villages like Midhurst & Wadhurst hold the Saxon suffix "hurst" which means wood. As the forests were cleared for agriculture the names of the villages changed & we find Boscham & Stedham whoe suffix "ham" means homestead or farm.

Battle, above Hastings, is the site of the famous Norman victory & 16th century Bodiam Castle, built as defence against the French in later times, has a beautiful setting encircled by a lily-covered moat.

Sussex has an extensive coastline, with cliffs near Eastbourne at Beachy Head, & at Hastings. Further east, the great flat Romney Marshes stretch out to sea, & there is considerable variety in the coastal towns.

Chichester has a magnificent cathedral & a harbour reaching deep into the coastal plain that is rich in archaeological remains. The creeks & mudflats make it an excellent place for birdwatching.

Brighton is the most famous of the Sussex resorts with its Pier, the Promenade above the beaches, the oriental folly of George IV's Royal Pavilion & its Regency architecture. "The Lanes" are a maze of alleys & small squares full of fascinating shops, a thriving antique trade, & many good pubs & eating places. Hastings to the east preserves its "Old Town" where timbered houses nestle beneath the cliffs & the fishing boats are drawn up on the shingle whilst the nets are hung up to dry in curious tall, thin net stores. Winchelsea stands on a hill where it was rebuilt in the 13th century by Edward I when the original town was engulfed by the sea. It is a beautiful town with a fine Norman church, an excellent museum in the Town Hall, & many pretty houses. Across the Romney Marshes on the next hill stands Rye, its profile dominated by its church. It is a fascinating town with timbered houses & cobbled streets.

Sussex

Sussex Gazeteer

Areas of Outstanding Natural Beauty
The Sussex Downs. Chichester Harbour.

Historic Houses & Castles

Arundel Castle - Arundel
18th century rebuilding of ancient castle, fine portraits, 15th century furniture.
Cuckfield Park - Cuckfield
Elizabethan manor house, gatehouse. Very fine panelling & ceilings.
Danny - Hurstpierpoint
16th century - Elizabethan .
Goodwood House - Chichester
18th century - Jacobean house - Fine Sussex flintwork, paintings by Van Dyck, Canaletto & Stubbs, English & French furniture, tapestries & porcelain.
Newtimber Place - Newtimber
Moated house - Etruscan style wall paintings.
Purham - Pulborough
Elizabethan house containing important collection of Elizabethan, Jacobean & Georgian portraits, also fine furniture.
Petworth House - Petworth
17th century - landscaped by Capability Brown - important paintings - 14th century chapel.
St. Mary's - Bramber
15th century timber framed house - rare panelling.
Tanyard - Sharpthorne
Mediaeval tannery - 16th & 17th century additions.
The Thatched Cottage - Lindfield
Close-studded weald house - reputedly Henry VII hunting lodge.
Uppark - Petersfield
17th century - 18th century interior decorations remain unaltered.
Alfriston Clergy House - Nr. Seaford
14th century parish priest's house - pre-reformation.
Battle Abbey - Battle
Founded by William the Conqueror.
Charleston Manor - Westdean
Norman, Tudor & Georgian architectural styles - Romanesque window in the Norman wing.
Bull House - Lewes
15th century half-timbered house - was home of Tom Paine.

Bateman's - Burwash
17th century - watermill - home of Rudyard Kipling.
Bodiam Castle - Nr. Hawkshurst
14th century - noted example of mediaeval moated military architecture.
Great Dixter - Northiam
15th century half-timbered manor house - great hall - Lutyens gardens
Glynde Place - Nr. Lewes
16th century flint & brick - built around courtyard-collection of paintings by Rubens, Hoppner, Kneller, Lely, Zoffany.
Michelham Priory - Upper Dicker, Nr. Hailsham
13th century Augustinian Priory - became Tudor farmhouse - working watermill, ancient stained glass, etc., enclosed by moat.
Royal Pavilion - Brighton
Built for Prince Regent by Nash upon classical villa by Holland. Exotic Building - has superb original works of art lent by H.M. The Queen. Collections of Regency furniture also Art Nouveau & Art Deco in the Art Gallery & Museum.
Sheffield Park - Nr. Uckfield
Beautiful Tudor House - 18th century alterations - splendid staircase.

Cathedrals & Churches

Alfriston (St. Andrew)
14th century - transition from decorated style to perpendicular, Easter sepulchre.
Boxgrove (St. Mary & St. Blaise)
13th century choir with 16th century painted decoration on vaulting. Relic of Benedictine priory. 16th century chantry. Much decoration.
Chichester Cathedral
Norman & earliest Gothic. Large Romanesque relief sculptures in south choir aisle.
Etchingham (St. Mary & St. Nicholas)
14th century. Old glass, brasses, screen, carved stalls.
Hardham (St. Botolph)
11th century - 12th century wall paintings.
Rotherfield (St. Denys)
16th century font cover, 17th century canopied pulpit, glass by Burne-Jones, wall paintings, Georgian Royal Arms.

Sussex

Sompting (St. Mary)
11th century Saxon tower - Rhenish Helm
Spire - quite unique.
Worth (St. Nicholas)
10th century - chancel arch is the largest
Saxon arch in England. German carved
pulpit c.1500 together with altar rails.
Winchelsea (St. Thomas the Apostle)
14th century - choir & aisles only.
Canopied sedilia & piscina.

Museums & Galleries

Barbican House Museum - Lewes
Collection relating to pre-historic,
Romano-British & ,mediaeval   antiquities
of the area.Prints & water colours of the
area.
Battle Museum-Battle
 Remains from archeological sites in area.
Diorama of Battle of Hastings.
Bignor Roman Villa Collection - Bignor
4th century mosaics, Samian pottery,
hypocaust, etc.
Brighton Museum & Art Gallery -
Brighton
Old Master Paintings, watercolours,
ceramics, furniture. Surrealist paintings,
Art Nouveau & Art Deco applied art,
musical instruments & many
other exhibits.

Marlipins Museum - Shoreham
12th century building housing collections
of ship models, photographs, old maps,
geological specimens, etc.
**Royal National Lifeboat Institution
Museum** - Eastbourne
Lifeboats of all types used from earliest
times to present.
Tower 73 - Eastbourne
Martello tower restored to display the
history of these forts. Exhibition of
equipment, uniforms & weapons of
the times.
The Toy Museum - Rottingdean,
Brighton
Toys & playthings from many countries -
children's delight.

Other things to see & do

Bewl Water - Nr. Wadhurst
Boat trips, walks, adventure playground
Chichester Festival Theatre -
Chichester
Summer season of plays from May to
September.
Goodwood Racecourse

The Royal Pavilion. Brighton.

SUSSEX
Map reference

English Channel

Sussex

		per person minimum £	children taken	evening meals	animals taken
Peter & Sarah Fuente **Mill Lane House** **Slindon** **Arundel PL27 7QT** **Tel: (0243) 65440/814440** **Open: ALL YEAR** **Map Ref No. 01**	Nearest Road: A.27, A.29 Magnificent views to the coast. Situated in a beautiful downland village with many miles of footpaths. Superb bird watching locally. All 7 comfortable rooms are en-suite & have T.V.s. Within easy reach are Pagham & Chichester Harbour, Arundel Castle, Fishbourne Roman Palace, Goodwood, Chichester, cathedral & Festival Theatre. Beaches 6 miles. Excellent pubs within easy walking distance.	£16.00	Y	Y	Y
Mrs J. Cowpland **Powdermills** **Powdermill Lane** **Battle TN33 0SP** **Tel: (04246) 5511** **Fax 04246 4540** **Open: ALL YEAR** **Map Ref No. 02**	Nearest Road: A.21 This large, impressive Georgian house is set in 150 acres of woodlands with pleasant walks with three fishing lakes. It was originally part of the Battle Abbey Estate. The house is furnished with antiques. All the bedrooms are stylish, comfortable & en-suite. A new restaurant, The Orangery, is the latest addition to the hotel. Large Georgian style windows overlook the pool & terrace which may be enjoyed by the guests..	£30.00 CREDIT CARD VISA M'CARD AMEX	Y	Y	Y
Mrs Mai Hashfield **Taplow Cottage** **81 Nyewood Lane** **Bognor Regis PO21 2UE** **Tel: (0243) 821398** **Open: FEB - NOV** **Map Ref No. 03**	Nearest Road: B.2166 A warm welcome is offered in this charming cottage style house, which has 3 most pleasant, cosy bedrooms with modern amenities including tea/coffee makers & colour T.V. in each room. A comfortable T.V. lounge is also available. Conveniently situated for visiting the South Downs, the coast, Arundel Castle, Goodwood Racecourse & Portsmouth. Within a few mins. walking distance of the beach, shops & restaurants.	£13.00	Y	N	Y
Geoffrey & Sally Earlam **Timbers Edge** **Spronketts Lane** **Warninglid** **Bolney RH17 5TE** **Tel: (0444) 461456** **Open: ALL YEAR** **Map Ref No. 04**	Nearest Road: M.23, A.272 Beautiful Sussex Country House set in over 2 acres of formal garden with swimming pool & surrounded by woodlands. There are 4 attractive bedrooms each with colour T.V. & beverage making facilities; some have private bathroom. Located within easy reach of Gatwick (20 mins.), Hickstead , Ardingly, Nymans & Leonardslee Gardens & Brighton. This makes an ideal base for touring the lovely Sussex countryside.	£20.00	Y	N	N
Mrs C. B. Gregory **Braemar Guest House** **Steyning Road** **Rottingdean** **Brighton BN2 7GA** **Tel: (0273) 304263** **Open: ALL YEAR** **Map Ref No. 05**	Nearest Road: A.259 A charming house, family-run, offering 14 pleasant, comfortable rooms with modern facilities. The proprietors really go out of their way to make their guests' stay a memorable one. From here Rudyard Kipling's house is only 2 minutes' walk. The town is a famous smuggling place with many ancient buildings & a Saxon church. There is a multitude of places to discover in the area. A friendly welcome awaits all guests at Braemar.	£14.00	Y	N	Y

Sussex

		minimum £ per person	children taken	evening meals	animals taken
Mr & Mrs J.P. Hansell **Trouville Hotel** **11 New Steine** **Brighton BN2 1PB** **Tel: (0273) 697384** **Open: FEB-DEC** **Map Ref No. 06**	Nearest Road: A.23 The Trouville is a Regency Grade II listed townhouse, tastefully restored & furnished. Accommodation is in 9 attractive rooms, each with colour T.V. & tea/coffee making facilities. En-suite & 4-poster rooms available. Situated in a charming seafront square, the Trouville is convenient for shopping, the Pavilion, the Lanes, Marina, Conference Centre & the many restaurants which are all within walking distance. CREDIT CARD VISA M'CARD AMEX	£18.00	Y	N	N
Mrs Jeannette Dridge **Chichester Lodge** **Oakwood** **Chichester PO18 9AL** **Tel: (0243) 786560** **Open: JAN - DEC** **Map Ref No. 07**	Nearest Road: B.2178 A picturesque, Grade II listed 1840's Gothic Lodge set in very quiet country surroundings, yet only 4 minutes' drive from the city centre and the Festival Theatre. Two tastefully furnished bedrooms with 4-poster beds, and en-suite bathrooms. Adjoining garden room has tea making facilities and a cosy log burning fire. You are assured of a warm and friendly welcome.	£17.50	N	N	N
Ron & Pam Foden **'Crouchers Bottom'** **Birdham Road** **Apuldram** **Chichester PO20 7EH** **Tel: (0243) 784995** **Fax 0243 539797** **Open: ALL YEAR** **Map Ref No. 08**	Nearest Road: A.286, A.27 'Crouchers Bottom' is a converted 1920's farmhouse standing in its own grounds. Offering 6 tastefully furnished & comfortable en-suite rooms, colour T.V., clock radio, tea making facilities, hair dryer, direct-dial phones, etc. A brick-laid patio overlooks a 'sunken' lawn & small pond with waterfowl. Lovely countryside & views of Chichester Cathedral, & Halnaker Mill with the South Downs. The proprietors are keen sailors, providing guests with a unique opportunity to sample a day's sailing. Delicious evening meals available. CREDIT CARD VISA M'CARD AMEX	£29.50	Y	Y	N
Susan & Antony Trotman **White Barn** **Crede Lane** **Bosham** **Chichester PO18 8NX** **Tel: (0243) 573113** **Open: ALL YEAR** **Map Ref No. 09**	Nearest Road: A.259 An outstanding modern, open plan house with heavily timbered interior. Located in the attractive Saxon harbour village of Bosham. 3 delightful en-suite bedrooms with tea/coffee making facilities & radio. A charming sitting room with colour T.V. & log fire on chilly evenings. Breakfast is served overlooking the pleasant, colourful garden. Meals are memorable using only the freshest ingredients whenever possible. Every care is taken to ensure your comfort. CREDIT CARD VISA M'CARD AMEX	£25.00	Y	Y	N
Mr & Mrs P. Blencowe **The Old Rectory** **Cot Lane** **Chidham** **Chichester** **PO18 8TA** **Tel: (0243) 572088** **Open: ALL YEAR** **Map Ref No. 10**	Nearest Road: A.259 The Old Rectory is a large, comfortable period house, set in a country lane in the quiet village of Chidham. 3 charming bedrooms all with private facilities, colour T.V., tea making facilities & electric underblankets. There is a delightful lounge with colour T.V. & grand piano & a large garden with swimming pool. Opposite the Saxon church & close to the village pub serving excellent meals. Chichester Harbour is nearby.	£19.00	Y	N	N

Sussex

		minimum £ per person	children taken	evening meals	animals taken
Mrs Mary Waller **Hatpins** **Bosham Lane** **Old Bosham** **Chichester PO18 8HG** **Tel: (0243) 572644** **Open: ALL YEAR** **Map Ref No. 09**	Nearest Road: A.259 Situated in the charming picturesque harbour village of Old Bosham. 3 miles west of Chichester & near to Goodwood House, H.M.S. Victory & the Mary Rose. This elegant property offers luxurious & inviting interior designed decor & antiques, including a half-tester & Victorian brass beds & sauna. Suitable & welcoming for honeymoon couples. All rooms have private bathrooms.	£22.50 🚭 *see PHOTO over*	N	N	N
Mrs Marjorie Setchfield **Chimneys** **Ifield Wood** **Crawley RH11 0LE** **Tel: (0293) 521312** **Open: ALL YEAR** **Map Ref No. 12**	Nearest Road: A.23 A charming Georgian country cottage dating back over 200 years, situated in a peaceful rural area. 2 pleasant & comfortable rooms with modern amenities. Rooms have T.V. & radio. Tea/coffee facilities are downstairs. Guests may use the garden. Very conveniently situated for Gatwick Airport - only 10 mins. away. Brighton, Redhill, Reigate are all easily accessible from here. Free transport to Gatwick airport.	£18.50	Y	N	N
K & M Hambleton **Southcroft Private Hotel** **15 South Cliff Avenue** **Meads** **Eastbourne BN20 7AH** **Tel: (0323) 29071** **Open: JAN - NOV** **Map Ref No. 13**	Nearest Road: A.22 A pleasant hotel offering 7 comfortable rooms, all with en-suite facilities. Situated in a quiet residential area within easy reach of the beach, shopping centre & theatres. The area offers lovely walks through Friston Forest & the Cuckmere Valley. Plenty for everyone around here. Tea/coffee making facilities in all rooms. Licensed. A friendly atmosphere is assured.	£20.00	N	Y	N
Mrs Susan Tyrie **Findon Manor** **High Street** **Findon** **BN14 0TA** **Tel: (0903) 872733** **Open: ALL YEAR** **Map Ref No. 14**	Nearest Road: A.24 Set in the picturesque village of Findon, in a delightful garden with splendid trees & colourful shrubs. Findon Manor offers accommodation in 10 en-suite bedrooms with telephone, colour T.V. & tea/coffee making facilities, some with 4-poster bed. Though completely refurbished, the original features remain, amongst elegant & attractive furnishings. Excellent meals are served in the spacious dining room & afterwards guests may relax in the charming lounge or bar.	£45.00 CREDIT CARD VISA M'CARD AMEX	Y	Y	Y
Denis & Jean Lloyd **Racehorse Cottage** **Nepcote** **Findon** **BN14 0SN** **Tel: (0903) 873783** **Open: ALL YEAR** **(Excl.Xmas)** **Map Ref No. 14**	Nearest Road: A.24, A.27 Comfortable cottage in historic & peaceful downland village sheltering under Cissbury Ring. An excellent base for exploring. 4 miles from the South Coast & easily accessible by car, train or bus from Gatwick, Brighton, Arundel, Chichester & London. 2 twin-bedded rooms with downland views, tea/coffee making facilities & a guests' own bathroom. Visitors have full use of house, sun room, garden & T.V. Evening meals with home baking & garden produce by arrangement. Children over 8 years welcome.	£13.00	Y	Y	Y

Hatpins. Old Bosham.

Sussex

Mrs L. Pengilley
Blackstock Farm
Grove Hill, Hellingly
Hailsham BN27 4HF
Tel: (0323) 844453
Open: APRIL - SEPT
Map Ref No. 15

Nearest Road: A.22, A.267
This friendly family warmly welcome guests to their 240 acre working farm. The large rambling Victorian farmhouse is located in lovely countryside yet only 3 miles from Hailsham. Guests have a choice of 2 very comfortable rooms with T.V. & tea/coffee making facilities. There are a number of excellent local pubs where delicious evening meals can be obtained.

£14.00 | N | N | N

CREDIT CARD
VISA
M'CARD

Douglas & Sally Simpson
Cleavers Lyng
Church Road
Herstmonceux
Hailsham BN27 1QJ
Tel: (0323) 833131
Fax 0323 833617
Open: ALL YEAR
Map Ref No. 15

Nearest Road: A.271
A delightful 16th century country hotel offering 8 pleasant, comfortable rooms for visitors. Here one finds age-blackened beams, inglenook fireplaces & a warm welcome. Situated adjacent to Herstmonceux Castle, it is an ideal base for touring the country as there are many historic sites & houses, museums & galleries plus superb villages within a short drive. An ideal base from which to tour this lovely area.

£19.75 | Y | Y | Y

Christine & David Cooper
Bolebroke Watermill
Perry Hill
Edenbridge Road
Hartfield TN7 4JP
Tel: (0892)770425
Open: MAR - NOV
Map Ref No. 16

Nearest Road: A.264
Magical Watermill, first recorded in 1086A.D., & Elizabethan Miller's Barn offer 5 en-suite rooms of genuine, unspoilt rustic charm, set amid woodland, water & pasture. The mill is complete with machinery, trap doors & very steep stairs. The barn has low doors & ceilings & includes the enchanting honeymooners hayloft with a four-poster bed. Delicious country cooking including Sussex suppers & award winning breakfasts are served in the adjoining house.

£24.00 | Y | Y | N

see PHOTO over

CREDIT CARD
VISA
M'CARD
AMEX

Roy & Carol Pontifex
Old Cudwells Barn
Lewes Road, Scaynes Hill
Haywards Heath
RH17 7NA
Tel: (0444) 831406
Open: ALL YEAR
Map Ref No. 17

Nearest Road: A.272, B.2111
Old Cudwells Barn is part of a larger house in an attractive courtyard setting. Roy has renovated this unique barn using original materials in keeping with the period featuring the original character including inglenook fireplaces & beams. Guests can choose from 2 very pretty, comfortable rooms with private facilities. Roy & Carol welcome you as friends. Good food, bonhomie & a warm happy atmosphere awaits you. Convenient for Gatwick Airport & touring.

£19.00 | Y | Y | N

Mrs Sylvia Fowler
Frylands
Wineham
Henfield BN5 9BP
Tel: (0403) 710214
Fax 0403 711449
OpenALL YEAR (Excl.Xmas)
Map Ref No. 18

Nearest Road: A.272, A.23,
Frylands is a timber framed Tudor farmhouse in a quiet setting of farmland, woods & river. 3 lovely bedrooms, 1 with private facilities, all with colour T.V., radio & tea/coffee tray with home made biscuits. Traditional breakfast cooked to order with a selection of home made preserves & local honey. Large garden with heated swimming pool. Good pubs & food nearby. 20 mins. Gatwick & Brighton.

£16.00 | Y | N | N

Bolebroke Watermill.   Hartfield.

Sussex

		minimum £ per person	children taken	evening meals	animals taken
Mrs M. Wilkin **Great Wapses Farm** **Wineham** **Albourne** **Henfield BN5 9BJ** **Tel: (0273) 492544** **Open: ALL YEAR** **Map Ref No. 19**	Nearest Road: A.23, B.2116 An attractive Tudor/Georgian farmhouse set in rural & peaceful surroundings with horses, calves, chickens, etc. Offering 3 rooms, all en-suite, 1 with 4-poster bed. T.V. & tea/coffee making facilities. Locally there are plenty of nice pubs & restaurants serving good food. Within easy reach of Brighton, Gatwick, Goodwood & Hickstead. Tennis court available.	**£17.50** CREDIT CARD AMEX	Y	N	Y
Michael & Mary Chick **The Tithe Barn** **Brighton Road** **Woodmancote** **Henfield BN5 9ST** **Tel: (0273) 492267** **Open: ALL YEAR** **Map Ref No. 20**	Nearest Road: A.281 The Tithe Barn is a lovely old house converted from a flint barn, set in 2 acres of gardens enjoying panoramic views to the South Downs. The cottage-style bedrooms are newly decorated in an appropriate style & are extremely comfortable & well-equipped. Breakfast is served in the spacious conservatory in summer & in the beamed, log fired dining room in winter. The Tithe Barn is conveniently situated for the coast, NT properties, the Downs & Gatwick Airport.	**£16.00**	Y	N	N
Mrs Elizabeth Cox **Glebe End** **Church Street** **Warnham** **Horsham** **RH12 3QW** **Tel: (0403) 61711** **Open: ALL YEAR** **Map Ref No. 21**	Nearest Road: A.24 Glebe End is a fascinating tile, wood & stone, part mediaeval house standing in its own beautifully tended walled garden. Located in a pretty Sussex village in the rolling countryside. 4 pleasant bedrooms with their own bathrooms, radio, T.V. & tea/coffee making facilities. A colour T.V. lounge with open fireplace & delightful Tudor dining room with log-burning stove. Mrs Cox is an excellent cook & meals are delicious. Tennis & golf nearby. Health centre/gymnasium/sauna next door. 20 mins. from Gatwick.	**£18.00**	Y	Y	Y
Mrs K. M. Ticktum **Westlands Guest House** **Brighton Road** **Monks Gate** **Horsham RH13 6JD** **Tel: (0403) 891383** **Open: ALL YEAR** **Map Ref No. 21**	Nearest Road: A.281 Westlands is an elegant Victorian country house offering superb accommodation. It is set in an acre of beautifully tended garden with terrace & fish pond (floodlit at night). Bedrooms are large & tastefully decorated, with private facilities & T.V. A comfortable guest lounge also, with T.V., where you can relax with tea or coffee. Village pubs/restaurants, golf course & public gardens nearby. Gatwick 20 mins., coast 30 mins.	**£18.75**	Y	N	N
Roland & Brenda Gough **Ousedale House** **Offham** **Lewes** **BN7 3QF** **Tel: (0273) 478680** **Open: ALL YEAR** **Map Ref No. 22**	Nearest Road: A.275, A.27 Ousedale House is a spacious Victorian country house set on a hillside plateau in three & a half acres of garden & woodland overlooking the River Ouse Valley. There are 3 attractive bedrooms, 2 en-suite, 1 with private bathroom, each with radio, T.V. & tea/coffee making facilities. Guest lounge. Delicious country cooking. Centrally located for touring Sussex, with easy access to Gatwick, Newhaven, Brighton & Glyndebourne (hampers provided). Ample parking.	**£20.00** CREDIT CARD VISA M'CARD AMEX	Y	Y	N

355

Jeake's House.   Rye.

Sussex

		per person minimum £	children taken	evening meals	animals taken
Gillian & John Mulcare **Huggetts Furnace Farm** **Stonehurst Lane** **Five Ashes** **Mayfield TN20 6LL** **Tel: (0825) 830220** **Fax 0435 866610** **Open: ALL YEAR** **Map Ref No. 23**	Nearest Road: A.272 A beautiful mediaeval farmhouse (Grade II listed), set well off the beaten track in tranquil countryside. 3 attractive bedrooms all with ensuite/ private facilities, radio & tea/coffee trays. The oak beamed sitting/dining room for guests has an inglenook fireplace with log fires on chilly evenings & colour T.V. Excellent & creatively cooked dinners & breakfasts using home grown & local produce. Heated outdoor swimming pool & 12 acres of grounds. Gatwick 45 mins., coast 30 mins. & nearby many N.T. properties.	£20.00	Y	Y	N
Mr & Mrs J. R. Field **Mill Farm** **Trotton, Petersfield** **Midhurst GU31 5EL** **Tel: (0730) 813080** **Open: ALL YEAR** **Map Ref No. 24**	Nearest Road: A.272 A Sussex country house set in 15 acres of pasture & large garden with grass tennis court. Delightful accommodation in 4 pleasant rooms with superb views over the South Downs. Colour T.V.s & tea making facilities. Log fires in hall & drawing room. Lovely walks & excellent pubs. Chichester, Goodwood & Petworth Houses, Arundel Castle, Heathrow, Gatwick & the coast within easy reach. Ideal as a holiday base.	£13.00	Y	N	Y
Mrs J.C. Francis **Mizzards Farm** **Rogate** **Petersfield GU31 5HS** **Tel: (0730) 821656** **Open ALL YEAR (Excl.Xmas)** **Map Ref No. 25**	Nearest Road: A.3, A.272 This beautifully modernized farmhouse is set in gardens & farmland by the River Rother. All rooms have en-suite facilities & colour T.V. . There is an elegant drawing room & breakfast is served in a magnificent vaulted hall dating from the 16th century. There is a covered swimming pool for guests' use & beautiful gardens. Situated close to the South Downs, the coast & several National Trust houses.	£20.00	Y	N	N
Alma Steele **New House Farm** **Broadford Bridge Road** **West Chiltington** **Pulborough RH20 2LA** **Tel: (0798) 812215** **Open: JAN - NOV** **Map Ref No. 26**	Nearest Road: A.29 A lovely 15th century house with oak beams & inglenook fireplaces. Situated in the village with a 12th century church. 3 delightful rooms, 2 with en-suite facilities. T.V. & tea/coffee makers. A pleasant lounge with T.V. & a lovely garden. Gatwick Airport is easily reached. Parham Gardens, W. Sussex golf course, Amberley Wild Brooks, Arundel Castle, Petworth House. Polo at Cowdray Park. Good evening meals available at local inns nearby. Golf nearby. Children over 10.	£18.00	Y	N	N
Francis & Jenny Hadfield **Jeake's House** **Mermaid Street** **Rye** **TN31 7ET** **Tel: (0797) 222828** **Fax 0797 222623** **Open: ALL YEAR** **Map Ref No. 27**	Nearest Road: A.259, A.268 Jeakes House is an outstanding 17th century listed building. Retaining original features including oak beams, wood panelling & decorated throughout with antiques. 12 comfortable & well decorated bedrooms overlook the peaceful gardens, with either en-suite or private facilities, T.V. & tea/coffee making facilities. 4-poster available. Guests dine in the galleried former Baptist chapel, where a choice of full English, wholefood vegetarian or Continental breakfast is served. Located in one of Britain's most picturesque mediaeval streets, a delightful base for touring.	£19.50 *see PHOTO over* CREDIT CARD VISA M'CARD AMEX	Y	N	Y

Sussex

Mrs Sheila Luck **Green Hedges** **Hillyfields** **Rye Hill** **Rye TN31 7NH** **Tel: (0797) 222185** **Open: JAN - NOV** **Map Ref No. 27**	Nearest Road: A.268 Green Hedges is a large Edwardian House within easy 10 minute walk of the beautiful mediaeval town of Rye. Set in 1 & a half acres of lovely gardens with heated outdoor pool (May to Sept., weather permitting). 3 delightful en-suite rooms, each with colour T.V. & tea/coffee making facilities. Breakfast prepared from best local produce. Home-made preserves, fruit from garden, (seasonal) local fish, home-made waffles & free range eggs. Wonderful countryside for touring.	£23.00	Y	N	N
Sara Brinkhurst **Little Orchard House** **West Street** **Rye** **TN31 7ES** **Tel: (0797) 223831** **Open: ALL YEAR** **Map Ref No. 27**	Nearest Road: A.259, A.268 This charming Georgian townhouse with traditional walled garden, is a delightful surprise at the heart of ancient Rye. Whilst a perfect base for visiting the beautiful castles, gardens and country houses of the region, the house itself has many original features, open fires, antique furnishings and books, to ensure a peaceful, relaxed atmosphere. 3 lovely en-suite bedrooms. Generous country breakfasts feature organic and free-range local produce.	£28.00 CREDIT CARD VISA M'CARD	N	N	N
Mrs Susan Renshaw **High Noon Cottage** **Blackboys** **Uckfield TN22 5HD** **Tel: (0825) 890398** **Open: MAY - AUG** **Map Ref No. 28**	Nearest Road: A.22 A traditional Sussex-style, 15th century, tile-hung property offering accommodation in 1 charming & elegantly furnished twin-bedded room with an adjacent private bathroom. Excellent breakfasts are served. An attractive drawing room with inglenook fireplace & French doors, opening out onto a pretty garden, is available to guests. Parking available. Ideally placed for touring the region, convenient for Glyndebourne.	£20.00	N	N	N
Dorene & John Taylor **Aspen House** **13 Winchester Road** **Worthing** **BN11 4DJ** **Tel: (0903) 230584** **Open: ALL YEAR** **Map Ref No. 30**	Nearest Road: A.27 Situated in a quiet location, this elegant Edwardian house is ideally sited to discover West Sussex. Goodwood, Arundel, Chichester & Brighton are all a short drive away & Gatwick 40 mins. 2 doubles, 1 twin & 1 single bedroom, all beautifully furnished, have colour T.V., en-suite & tea/coffee making facilities. Traditional full English or Continental breakfast is served in the attractive period dining room.	£19.00	N	N	N
John & Doreen Carver **Bonchurch House** **1 Winchester Road** **Worthing** **BN11 4DJ** **Tel: (0903) 202492** **Open: ALL YEAR** **Map Ref No. 30**	Nearest Road: A.259 Bonchurch is a home-from-home guest house where a warm welcome is extended to all guests. There are 7 bedrooms, all with shaver points & H & C washbasins. Some rooms have en-suite shower/bathroom, all have T.V. & tea/coffee making facilities. There is, for the convenience of guests, a comfortable lounge with colour T.V. Home cooking is a speciality. Ideally situated in a picturesque setting, yet close to the sea front, shops & entertainment.	£15.00	Y	Y	N

Warwickshire

Warwickshire
(Heart of England)

Warwickshire contains much that is thought of as traditional rural England, but it is a county of contradictions. Rural tranquillity surrounds industrial towns, working canals run along with meandering rivers, the mediaeval splendour of Warwick Castle vies with the handsome Regency grace of Leamington Spa.

Of course, Warwickshire is Shakespeare's county, with his birthplace, Stratford-upon-Avon standing at the northern edge of the Cotswolds. You can visit any of half a dozen houses with Shakespearian associations, see his tomb in the lovely Parish church or enjoy a performance by the world famous Royal Shakespeare Company in their theatre on the banks of the River Avon.

Warwickshire was created as the Kingdom of Mercia after the departure of the Romans. King Offa of Mercia left us his own particular mark - a coin which bore the imprint of his likeness known as his "pen" & this became our penny. Lady Godiva was the wife of an Earl of Mercia who pleaded with her husband to lessen the taxation burden on his people. He challenged her to ride naked through the streets of Coventry as the price of her request. She did this knowing that her long hair would cover her nakedness, & the people, who loved her, stayed indoors out of respect. Only Peeping Tom found the temptation irresistible.

The 15th, 16th, & 17th centuries were the heyday of fine building in the county, when many gracious homes were built. Exceptional Compton Wynyates has rosy pink bricks, twisted chimney stacks, battlements & moats & presents an unforgettably romantic picture of a perfect Tudor House.

Coventry has long enjoyed the reputation of a thriving city, noted for its weaving of silks and ribbons, learned from the refugee Huguenots. When progress brought industry, watches, bicycles & cars became the mainstay of the city. Coventry suffered grievously from aerial bombardment in the war & innumerable ancient & treasured buildings were lost.

A magnificent new Cathedral stands besides the shell of the old. Mystery plays enacting the life of Christ are performed in the haunting ruin.

Warwick Castle.

Warwickshire

Warwickshire
Gazeteer
Areas of Outstanding Natural Beauty
The Edge Hills

Historic Houses & Castles
Arbury Hall - Nuneaton
18th century Gothic mansion - made
famous by George Elliot as Cheverel
Manor - paintings, period furnishings, etc.
Compton Wynyates
15th century - famous Tudor house - pink
brick, twisted chimneys, battlemented
walls. Interior almost untouched -
period furnishing.
Coughton Court - Alcester
15th century - Elizabethan half-timbered
wings. Holds Jacobite relics.
Harvard House - Stratford-upon-Avon
16th century - home of mother of John
Harvard, University founder.
Homington Hall - Shipston-on-Stour
17th century with fine 18th century
plasterwork.
Packwood House - Hockley Heath
Tudor timber framed house - with 17th
century additions. Famous yew garden.
Ragley Hall - Alcester
17th century Palladian - magnificent
house with fine collection of porcelain,
paintings, furniture, etc. & a
valuable library.
**Shakespeare's Birthplace Trust
Properties** - Stratford-upon-Avon
Anne Hathaway's Cottage - Shottery
The thatched cottage home of
Anne Hathaway.
Hall's Croft - Old Town
Tudor house where Shakespeare's
daughter Susanna lived.
Mary Arden's House - Wilmcote
Tudor farmhouse with dovecote. Home of
Shakespeare's mother.
New Place - Chapel Street
Shakespeare's last home - the
foundations of his house are preserved in
Elizabethan garden.
Birthplace of Shakespeare - Henley
Street
Many rare Shakespeare relics exhibited in
this half-timbered house.
Lord Leycester Hospital - Warwick
16th century timber framed group around
courtyard - hospital for poor persons in
the mediaeval guilds.

Upton House - Edge Hill
Dating from James II reign - contains
Brussels tapestries, Sevres porcelain,
Chelsea figurines, 18th century furniture &
other works of art, including Old Masters.
Warwick Castle - Warwick
Splendid mediaeval castle - site was
originally fortified more than a thousand
years ago. Present castle 14th century.
Armoury.

Cathedrals & Churches
Astley (St. Mary the Virgin)
17th century - has remains of 14th
century collegiate church. 15th century
painted stalls.
Beaudesert (St. Nicholas)
Norman with fine arches in chancel.
Brailes (St. George)
15th century - decorated nave & aisles -
14th century carved oak chest.
Crompton Wynyates
Church of Restoration period having
painted ceiling.
Lapworth (St. Mary)
13th & 14th century - steeple & north aisle
connected by passage.
Preston-on-Stour (The Blessed Virgin
Mary)
18th century. Gilded ceiling,
17th century glass
Tredington (St. Gregory)
Saxon walls in nave - largely14th century,
17th century pulpit. Fine spire.
Warwick (St. Mary)
15th century Beauchamp Chapel, vaulted
choir, some 17th century Gothic.
Wooten Wawen (St. Peter)
Saxon, with remnants of mediaeval wall
painting, 15th century screens & pulpit:
small 17th century chained library.

Museums & Galleries
**The Royal Shakespeare Theatre
Picture Gallery** - Stratford-upon-Avon
Original designs & paintings, portraits of
famous actors, etc.
Motor Museum - Stratford-upon-Avon
Collection of cars, racing, vintage, exotic,
replica of 1930 garage. Fashions, etc. of
1920's era.

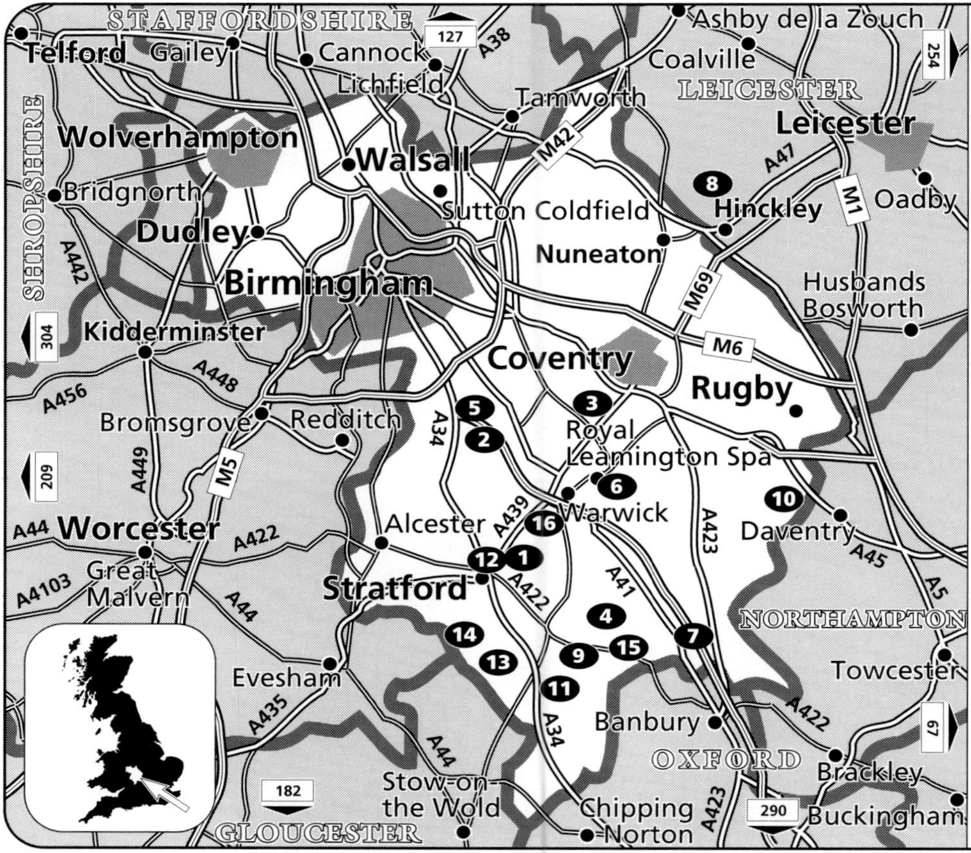

WARWICKSHIRE
Map reference

1 Waterworth
2 Jamouse
3 Wilson
4 Howard
5 Staite
6 Lawson
7 Lea
8 Walliker
9 Hutsby
10 Mills
11 Mawle
12 Evans
12 Pettitt
12 Workman
12 Castelli
12 Short
12 Evans
12 Coulson
12 Everitt
12 Andrews
12 Evans
12 Palmer
12 Hallworth
12 Morton
12 Walters
12 Tozer
12 Mander
13 Vernon Miller
14 Lyon
15 Trought
16 Greenwood

8 Clarendon Crescent. Leamington Spa.

Warwickshire

		per person minimum £	children taken	evening meals	animals taken
Mrs H.P. Waterworth **Sandbarn Farm** **Hampton Lucy** **CV35 8AU** **Tel: (0789) 842280** **Open: ALL YEAR** **Map Ref No. 01**	Nearest Road: M.40, A.46 Seventeenth century farmhouse in charming village offering luxury bed and breakfast accommodation. Tranquil setting with lovely views, only 3 miles from Stratford-upon-Avon. Warwick and Kenilworth Castles are nearby, also many National Trust houses and parks. Of the 4 guest bedrooms, 3 are en-suite and 1 private. Single availability. Residents lounge and T.V. Children over 5 please. A delightful home.	£20.00	Y	N	N
H.A. Jamouse **Ashleigh House** **Whitley Hill** **Henley-in-Arden** **B95 5DL** **Tel: (0564) 792315** **Fax 0564 794133** **Open: ALL YEAR** **Map Ref No. 02**	Nearest Road: A.34, M.40 A spacious & elegant Edwardian house set in its own lovely grounds with magnificent views towards the Cotswold Hills. Beautifully decorated with many antiques. There are 10 delightful rooms, each with en-suite facilities & T.V. An attractive lounge with colour T.V. & a garden for guests to enjoy. Excellent breakfast. Very convenient for Stratford-upon-Avon only 7 miles, the National Exhibition Centre, Stoneleigh Agricultural Centre & Warwick University.	£25.00 CREDIT CARD VISA M'CARD	N	Y	N
Mrs Joan Wilson **Ferndale Guest House** **45 Priory Road** **Kenilworth** **CV8 1LL** **Tel: (0926) 53214** **Open: ALL YEAR** **Map Ref No. 03**	Nearest Road: A.46 You are assured of a warm welcome in this family-run spacious Victorian house situated in a quiet tree-lined avenue only 5 mins. walk from town centre. There are 8 comfortablebedrooms, all are en-suite & tastefully decorated with colour T.V. & coffee/tea making facilities. A guests' T.V. lounge is available throughout the day. Ideally located for Warwick, Coventry, Leamington Spa, National Exhibition Centre, Stoneleigh Agricultural Centre & Warwick University.	£17.00	Y	N	Y
Carolyn Howard **Willowbrook House** **Lighthorne Road** **Kineton CV35 0JL** **Tel: (0926) 640475** **Fax 0926 641747** **OpenALL YEAR (Excl. Xmas)** **Map Ref No. 04**	Nearest Road: B.4100, M.40 Willowbrook is a very comfortable house in gardens & paddocks in rolling countryside, handy for Stratford-upon-Avon, Warwick & the Cotswolds. Twin & double rooms, some en-suite, all with tea trays & lovely views. Guests' large sitting room, dining room, log fires, central heating & antiques. Enjoy watching lambs & rare breeds of poultry, or sit on the terrace by the garden pool on summer evenings. Friendly, attentive service. M.40 (ex.12) only 3 & a half miles.	£13.50 🚭	Y	N	Y
Christine & David Lawson **8 Clarendon Crescent** **Leamington Spa** **CV32 5NR** **Tel: (0926) 429840** **Fax 0926 451660** **Open: ALL YEAR** **Map Ref No. 06**	Nearest Road: A.452 A Grade II listed Regency house overlooking a private dell. Situated in a quiet backwater of Leamington. Elegantly furnished with antiques & offering accommodation in 4 tastefully furnished bedrooms, 3 en-suite. A delicious full English breakfast is served. Located only 5 minutes from the town centre. Very convenient for Warwick, Stratford, Stoneleigh Agricultural Centre, Warwick University & the National Exhibition Centre.	£25.00 *see PHOTO over*	Y	N	N

363

Ambion Court Hotel. Dadlington.

Warwickshire

	minimum £ per person	children taken	evening meals	animals taken

D. Staite & G. Boucher **Lapworth Lodge** **Bushwood Lane** **Lapworth B94 5PJ** **Tel: (0564) 783038** **Fax 0564 783635** **Open: ALL YEAR** **Map Ref No. 05**	Nearest Road: A.3400, M.40 This imposing Georgian house enjoys outstand- ing views over the glorious Warwickshire coun- tryside. All 8 lovely bedrooms are exceptionally large, with en-suite facilities, co-ordinated decor, colour T.V., tea/coffee makers & central heating. The 4-course breakfast is renowned. This is a guest house for those who prefer superior com- forts combined with the warmest of welcomes. Convenient for Stratford, Warwick & the N.E.C. CREDIT CARD VISA M'CARD	£20.00	Y	N	N
Deborah Lea **Crandon House** **Avon Dassett** **Leamington Spa** **CV33 0AA** **Tel: (0295) 770652** **OpenALL YEAR(Excl. Xmas)** **Map Ref No. 07**	Nearest Road: B.4100, M.40 Guests receive a specially warm welcome at Crandon House offering a high standard of ac- commodation & comfort. Set in 20 acres. Beau- tiful views over unspoilt countryside. Small work- ing farm. Own produce. Excellent food. 3 attractive rooms with private facilities, T.V., tea/ coffee tray. Large garden. Full C.H. & log fire. Peaceful & quiet yet within easy reach of Strat- ford, Warwick, Oxford & the Cotswolds. Located between M.40 junctions 11 & 12 (4 miles). CREDIT CARD VISA	£17.00	Y	Y	Y
John Walliker **Ambion Court Hotel** **The Green, Dadlington** **Nuneaton CV13 6JB** **Tel: (0455) 212292** **Fax 0455 213141** **Open: ALL YEAR** **Map Ref No. 08**	Nearest Road: A.5, M.69. A charming, modernised Victorian farmhouse overlooking Dadlington's village green, 2 miles north of Hinckley. Each room iscomfortably fur- nished with en-suite bathroom, T.V., radio, tele- phone & hospitality tray. The lovely Pine Room is available for honeymoons, etc. There is a delightful lounge, cocktail bar & restaurant offer- ing delicious, tradtional fare. Ambion Court pro- vides comfort, hospitality & exceptional tranquil- ity for those seeking complete relaxation. *see PHOTO over* CREDIT CARD VISA M'CARD	£25.00	Y	Y	Y
Sue Hutsby **Nolands Farm & Country** **Restaurant** **Oxhill** **CV35 0RJ** **Tel: (0926) 640309** **Fax 0926 640309** **Open: ALL YEAR** **Map Ref No. 09**	Nearest Road: A.422 Nolands Farm is situated in a tranquil valley surrounded by fields, woods & a lake for fishing. 9 bedrooms are annexed to the house in con- verted stables, with some ground floor bedrooms, some with a romantic 4-poster, all are en-suite with central heating, tea/coffee makers & T.V. Dine in the beautiful granary-style restaurant which is licensed & serves the freshest produce & fine cuisine. Everything for the discerning country lover. Clay pigeon shooting, bicycles for hire & riding nearby. *see PHOTO over* CREDIT CARD VISA M'CARD	£15.00	Y	Y	N
Alison Mills **Tibbits Farm** **Nethercote** **Flecknoe** **Rugby CV23 8AS** **Tel: (0788) 890239** **Open: ALL YEAR** **Map Ref No. 10**	Nearest Road: A.425, A.45 Retreat from the trials of life to the tranquility of this 17th century house hidden in acres of coun- tryside. Tibbits is beamed, spacious & beautifully furnished; the pretty bedrooms have C.H., colour T.V., tea/coffee facilities & lovely views. In the Winter, take tea beside huge log fires & in Sum- mer sit in the old gardens. Many interesting & historic places within a short drive. It is a place to find peace in the heart of the countryside.	£20.00	Y	N	Y

Nolands Farm & Country Restaurant.   Oxhill.

Warwickshire

		per person minimum £	children taken	evening meals	animals taken
Rebecca Mawle **Lower Farm Barn** **Great Wolford** **Shipston-on-Stour** CV36 5NQ **Tel: (0608) 74435** **Open: ALL YEAR** **Map Ref No. 11**	Nearest Road: A.44, A.3400 This lovely 100 year-old converted barn stands in the small, peaceful Warwickshire village of Great Wolford. The property retains much of its original form including exposed beams & ancient stone work. Now tastefully modernised, it makes a very comfortable home. The accommodation is in 2 beautifully furnished double rooms with en-suite facilities. An ideal spot for touring.	£13.50	Y	N	Y
Mrs Liz Vernon Miller **Blackwell Grange Farm** **Blackwell** **Shipston-on-Stour** **Stratford-upon-Avon** **CV36 4PF** **Tel: (0608)82357/682357** **Open: ALL YEAR** **Map Ref No. 13**	Nearest Road: A.3400, A.429 Blackwell Grange is a Grade II listed farmhouse, part of which dates from 1603. It is situated 2 miles from Shipston-on-Stour & 7 miles from Stratford-upon-Avon, found on the edge of the village with fine views of the Ilmington Hills & surrounding countryside. A peaceful haven with a warm welcome & log fires. 2 ground-floor en-suite rooms, suitable for the disabled. Ideal for touring the Cotswolds & Shakespeare country. Children over 10 years.	£20.00 *see PHOTO over*	Y	Y	N
Mrs Marian J. Walters **Church Farm** **Dorsington** **Stratford-upon-Avon** **CV37 8AX** **Tel: (0789) 720471** **Open: ALL YEAR** **Map Ref No. 12**	Nearest Road: B.439 A warm welcome awaits you at this mixed working farm with lakes, equestrian course & woodlands to explore. Situated on the edge of a quiet pretty village, yet close to Stratford, Warwick, Cotswolds & NEC. Accommodation is in 7 delightful rooms, some en-suite. Stabling & fishing available. An excellent base from which to explore the many sights & attractions of the region.	£13.00	Y	N	N
Margaret Everitt **Eastnor House Hotel** **33 Shipston Road** **Stratford-upon-Avon** **CV37 7LN** **Tel: (0789) 268115** **Fax 0789 266516** **Open: ALL YEAR** **Map Ref No. 12**	Nearest Road: A.34, A.3400 By the River Avon, 125 metres from Clopton Bridge, with private parking & just a stroll from theatres & Shakespeares birthplace. This large Victorian townhouse built for a wealthy draper offers super accommodation with oak panelling, central open staircases, pleasant breakfast room & elegant lounge. The tastefully furnished bedrooms have private bathrooms, colour T.V. & welcome tray. Breakfast is individually prepared, completing a comfortable & restful stay.	£19.00 CREDIT CARD VISA M'CARD AMEX	Y	N	Y
Meg & Bob Morton **Grove Farm** **Ettington** **Stratford-upon-Avon** **CV37 7NX** **Tel: (0789) 740228** **Open: ALL YEAR** **Map Ref No. 12**	Nearest Road: A.422, A.429 A warm & friendly welcome awaits you at this beautiful old farmhouse set on a 500-acre working farm. Superb views. Log fires, antiques, a friendly labrador dog & old horses. Private bathrooms. Guests are welcome to ramble through the fields & woods. Peace & tranquility in lovely surroundings very near to Stratford-upon-Avon, Warwick Castle & the Cotswolds. Delicious dinners are available nearby.	£14.50	Y	N	N

Blackwell Grange. Shipston-on-Stour.

All the establishments mentioned in this guide
are members of the
Worldwide Bed & Breakfast Association.

If you have any comments regarding your
accommodation please send them to us
using the form at the back of the book.
We value your comments.

Kawartha House.   Stratford-upon-Avon.

Warwickshire

	Nearest Road / Description	per person minimum £	children taken	evening meals	animals taken
Jill & Ernie Coulson 'Hardwick House' 1 Avenue Road Stratford-upon-Avon CV37 6UY Tel: (0789) 204307 Fax 0789 296760 OpenALL YEAR(Excl. Xmas) Map Ref No. 12	Nearest Road: A.439, A.34, You will be welcomed to 'Hardwick House', an impressive Victorian home in a quiet area, yet just 5 mins. walk to the town centre & the theatre. A choice of 14 spacious, tastefully furnished & comfortable bedrooms, many with private facilities, all with T.V. & tea/coffee making facilities. Residents' lounge, parking space. Enjoy its friendly atmosphere & home-cooked breakfasts. An ideal base from which to explore the region with its many historic attractions. CREDIT CARD VISA M'CARD AMEX	£18.00	Y	N	N
Mrs M. Evans Kawartha House 39 Grove Road Stratford-upon-Avon CV37 6PB Tel: (0789) 204469 Open: ALL YEAR Map Ref No. 12	Nearest Road: A.439 Kawartha House is a well appointed town house with a friendly atmosphere overlooking the 'old town' park. It is located just a few minutes' walk from the town centre & is ideal for visiting the many places of historic interest. Private parking is available. With pretty en-suite bedrooms & quality food, these are the ingredients for a memorable stay. A very pleasant home & an ideal base for touring. *see PHOTO over*	£13.00	Y	N	Y
Mr & Mrs I. Castelli Minola Guest House 25 Evesham Place Stratford-upon-Avon CV37 6HT Tel: (0789) 293573 Open: ALL YEAR Map Ref No. 12	Nearest Road: A.439 A comfortable house with a relaxed atmosphere offering good accommodation in 5 rooms, 2 with private shower, 1 en-suite; all have colour T.V. & tea/coffee makers. Stratford offers a myriad of delights for the visitor including the Royal Shakespeare Theatre. Set by the River Avon, this makes a lovely place for a picnic lunch or early evening meal before the performance. Cots are provided. Italian & French spoken.	£16.00	Y	N	N
Pat & Peter Short Nando's 18-20 Evesham Place Stratford-upon-Avon CV37 6HT Tel/Fax: (0789) 204907 Open: ALL YEAR Map Ref No. 12	Nearest Road: A.34 A.4390 Pat & Peter extend the warmest of welcomes to their guests. The friendly hosts pride themelves on the quality of food & high standard of hygiene. Nando's is conveniently located only minutes away from the Royal Shakespeare Theatre. Offering 21 rooms, 7 with en-suite facilities, all with colour T.V. A residents' T.V. lounge is also available. Nando's makes the perfect base for visiting the many places of interest in the town & in the surrounding area. CREDIT CARD VISA M'CARD AMEX	£13.00	Y	Y	Y
Richard & Susan Evans Oxstalls Farm Warwick Road Stratford-upon-Avon CV37 4NR Tel: (0789) 205277 Open: ALL YEAR Map Ref No. 12	Nearest Road: A.439 This charming thoroughbred stud farm overlooks the beautiful Welcombe Hill & golf course. It provides excellent accommodation for touring or relaxing in peaceful surroundings. There are 20 tastefully furnished bedrooms many with en-suite facilities, T.V. & tea/coffee makers. For the keen fisherman there is a well stocked trout pond. A guided tour of the farm to see the animals is also available. 1 mile from Stratford town centre & the Royal Shakespeare Theatre.	£14.00	Y	N	N

Melita Hotel. Stratford-upon-Avon.

Warwickshire

	minimum £ per person	children taken	evening meals	animals taken
Patricia Ann Andrews **Melita Private Hotel** **37 Shipston Road** **Stratford-upon-Avon** **CV37 7LN** **Tel: (0789) 292432** **Open: ALL YEAR** **Map Ref No. 12** Nearest Road: A.3400 An extremely friendly family-run hotel. Offering pleasant service, good food & accommodation in 12 excellent bedrooms, all with private facilities, colour T.V., tea/coffee & direct-dial telephones. Comfortable lounge/bar & pretty, award-winning garden for guests' use. Ample car parking. A pleasant 5 minute walk to Shakespearian properties/theatres, shopping centre & beautiful riverside gardens. Superbly situated for Warwick Castle, Coventry & the Cotswolds.	£20.00 *see PHOTO over* CREDIT CARD VISA M'CARD AMEX	Y	N	Y
Jo & Roger Pettitt **Parkfield Guest House** **3 Broad Walk** **Stratford-upon-Avon** **CV37 6HS** **Tel: (0789) 293313** **Open: ALL YEAR** **Map Ref No. 12** Nearest Road: A.439, A.34. A delightful Victorian house, in a quiet location in Old Town just 5 minutes' walk to town centre & the Royal Shakespeare Theatre. Ideally situated for touring the Cotswolds, Warwick Castle, etc. 7 spacious & comfortable rooms, 5 en-suite, all with full central heating, colour T.V. & tea/coffee making facilities. Excellent breakfast. Private parking. Lots of tourist information. Guests can be collected from the station.	£15.00 CREDIT CARD VISA M'CARD	N	N	Y
Mrs Margaret Mander **Pear Tree Cottage** **7 Church Road** **Wilmcote** **Stratford-upon-Avon** **CV37 9UX** **Tel: (0789) 205889** **Open: ALL YEAR** **Map Ref No. 12** Nearest Road: A.46, A.3400, A delightful half-timbered 16th century house located in the Shakespeare village of Wilmcote. It retains all its original charm & character with oak beams, flagstone floors, inglenook fireplaces, thick stone walls with deep-set windows, decorated with antiques. Offering 7 very comfortable en-suite rooms, all with tea/coffee making facilities & colour T.V. A delicious breakfast is served each morning in the dining room. A comfortable lounge is also provided. A lovely base from which to tour the whole region.	£19.00 *see PHOTO over*	Y	N	Y
Richard Workman **Ravenhurst** **2 Broad Walk** **Stratford-upon-Avon** **CV37 6HS** **Tel: (0789) 292515** **Open: ALL YEAR** **Map Ref No. 12** Nearest Road: A.439, A.4390 A Victorian town house with a warm & friendly atmosphere. Ideally situated on the edge of the old town & only a few minutes' walk from the Shakespeare Theatre, town centre & places of historical interest. Enjoy the comfort & quiet of this family run guest house where all bedrooms have colour T.V. & tea/coffee making facilities. Special double en-suite rooms available with 4-poster beds. The Workmans are Stratfordians, therefore local knowledge a speciality.	£16.00 CREDIT CARD VISA M'CARD AMEX	Y	N	N
Philip & Jean Evans **Sequoia House Hotel** **51/53 Shipston Road** **Stratford-upon-Avon** **CV37 7LN** **Tel: (0789) 268852** **Fax 0789 414559** **Open: ALL YEAR** **Map Ref No. 12** Nearest Road: A.3400 A beautifully appointed private hotel situated across the River Avon from the Royal Shakespeare Theatre. Offering 24 bedrooms (many en-suite), cocktail bar, cottage annex & garden restaurant. The hotel is comfortably furnished & decorated in a warm & restful style with many extra thoughtful touches. The garden overlooks the town cricket ground & the old tramway. Pleasant walks along the banks of the River Avon opposite the Theatre & Holy Trinity Church.	£18.50 CREDIT CARD VISA M'CARD AMEX	Y	N	N

Pear Tree Cottage. Wilmcote.

Warwickshire

Kevin & Jeanne Hallworth **The Croft Guest House** **49 Shipston Road** **Stratford-upon-Avon** **CV377LN** **Tel: (0789) 293419** **Open: ALL YEAR** **Map Ref No. 12**	Nearest Road: A.3400 The Croft is a friendly family-run Victorian guest house only 200 yards from the River Avon. Accommodation is in 9 pleasant rooms, 6 with en-suite facilities. All with colour T.V. & tea/coffee making facilities. Residents' lounge & garden. 5 minutes from theatre, river boats & town. Ideal base for touring the Cotswolds, Warwick & many local places of interest.	**£16.50** CREDIT CARD VISA M'CARD	Y	Y	Y
Paul & Dreen Tozer **Victoria Spa Lodge** **Bishopton Lane** **Stratford-upo Avon** **CV379QY** **Tel: (0789) 267985** **Fax 0789 204728** **Open: ALL YEAR** **Map Ref No. 12**	Nearest Road: A.3400, A.46 Victoria Spa is a very large Victorian house originally opened in 1830 as a health spa. Today Paul & Dreen offer guests comfortable accommodation in 7 tatefully furnished rooms, 4 en-suite, each with colour T.V. & tea/coffee makers. Situated only one & a half miles from Stratford Theatre. Your hosts are happy to prepare pre-theatre dinner with prior notice. Ideally placed for visiting Warwick Castle, the Cotswolds or the National Exhibition Centre.	**£19.50** *see PHOTO over* CREDIT CARD VISA M'CARD	Y	N	N
Terry & Margarita Palmer **Craig Cleeve House** **67-69 Shipston Road** **Stratford-upon-Avon** **CV37 7LW** **Tel: (0789) 296573** **Fax 0789 299452** **OpenALL YEAR (Excl. Xmas)** **Map Ref No. 12**	Nearest Road: A.34 A warm welcome & a most hospitable house, offering 15 excellent rooms with comfortable accommodation & modern amenities. All have radio, T.V. & tea/coffee makers, 9 are en-suite. A very good base for visiting this most historic town with its superb theatre & Shakespeare connections. Many museums & galleries in the area & lovely countryside. Cots & highchairs provided. Mr Palmer can collect you from the station. A convenient spot for touring the region.	**£19.50** CREDIT CARD VISA M'CARD AMEX	Y	N	Y
Mrs G Lyon **Winton House** **The Green, Upper Quinton** **Stratford-upon-Avon** **CV37 8SX** **Tel: (0789) 720500** **Open: ALL YEAR** **Map Ref No. 14**	Nearest Road: B.4632 Historic Victorian farmhouse situated in tranquil, rural area of outstanding natural beauty 6 miles from Stratford. En-suite bedrooms feature antique wrought iron half tester & Irish box bed, old pine, lace, quilts & tea/coffee facilities. Delicious choice of breakfasts served with homemade jam & fruit from our orchard, log fires. Colour T.V. in guest lounge. Children welcome. Cycles included in price. Special winter walking holidays.	**£20.00**	Y	N	N
Mrs Topsy Trought **Brookland** **Peacock Lane** **Tysoe** **Warwick CV35 0SG** **Tel: (0295) 680202** **Open: ALL YEAR** **Map Ref No. 15**	Nearest Road: A.422 Dating from 1634, Brookland is situated in the pretty village of Tysoe, resting in the Vale of the Red Horse. 3 prettily furnished bedrooms. Lounge with an open fire & T.V. Topsy provides excellent cuisine, using fresh home-grown produce, served in the 17th century dining room with an inglenook fireplace & wooden beams. Tysoe, a conservation area is well placed for visiting Shakespeare's country, the Cotswolds & the South Midlands. Only 20 mins. from Stratford.	**£14.50**	Y	Y	N

Victoria Spa Lodge. Stratford-upon-Avon.

Warwickshire

		minimum £ per person	children taken	evening meals	animals taken
M. J. & C. Greenwood	Nearest Road: A.46, M.40	£19.50	Y	Y	Y
The Old Rectory	A licensed Georgian country house rich in beams, flagstones & inglenooks. Situated in a gem of an				
Vicarage Lane	English village, 1 third of a mile from M.40,				
Sherbourne	junction 15. Accommodation is in 14 elegantly	*see PHOTO over*			
Warwick CV35 8AB	appointed en-suite bedrooms which thoughtfully provide all possible comforts, many antique brass				
Tel: (0926) 624562	beds & some wonderful, Victorian-style bath-	CREDIT CARD			
Open:ALL YEAR (Excl.Xmas)	rooms. Hearty breakfasts served amid antique	VISA			
Map Ref No. 16	oak. A delightful home & an ideal base from which to tour the area.	M'CARD			

All the establishments mentioned in this guide
are members of
The Worldwide Bed & Breakfast Association

When booking your accommodation please
mention
The Best Bed & Breakfast

The Old Rectory. Sherbourne.

Wiltshire

Wiltshire
(West Country)

Wiltshire is a county of rolling chalk downs, small towns, delightful villages, fine churches & great country houses. The expanse of Salisbury Plain is divided by the beautiful valleys of Nadder, Wylye, Ebble & Avon. In a county of open landscapes, Savernake Forest, with its stately avenues of trees strikes a note of contrast. In the north west the Cotswolds spill over into Wiltshire from neighbouring Gloucestershire.

No other county is so rich in archaeological sites. Long barrows and ancient hill forts stand on the skylines as evidence of the early habitation of the chalk uplands. Many of these prehistoric sites are at once magnificent and mysterious. The massive stone arches and monoliths of Stonehenge were built over a period of 500 years with stones transported over great distances. At Avebury the small village is completely encircled by standing stones and a massive bank and ditch earthwork. Silbury Hill is a huge, enigmatic man-made mound. England's largest chambered tomb is West Kennet Long Barrow and at Bush Barrow, finds have included fine bronze and gold daggers and a stone sceptre-head similar to one found at Mycenae in Greece.

Some of England's greatest historic houses are in Wiltshire. Longleat is an Elizabethan mansion with priceless collections of paintings, books & furniture. The surrounding park was landscaped by Capability Brown and its great fame in recent years has been its Safari Park, particularly the lions which roam freely around the visiting cars. Stourhead has celebrated 18th century landscaped gardens which are exceptional in spring when rhododendrons bloom.

Two delightful villages are Castle Combe, nestling in a Cotswold valley, & Lacock where the twisting streets hold examples of buildings ranging from mediaeval half-timbered, to Tudor & Georgian. 13th century Lacock Abbey, converted to a house in the 16th century, was the home of Fox Talbot, pioneer of photography.

There are many notable churches in Wiltshire. In Bradford-on-Avon, a fascinating old town, is the church of St. Lawrence, a rare example of an almost perfect Saxon church from around 900. Farley has an unusual brick church thought to have been designed by Sir Christopher Wren, & there is stained glass by William Morris in the church at Rodbourne.

Devizes Castle.

Salisbury stands where three rivers join, on a plain of luxuriant water-meadows, where the focal point of the landscape is the soaring spire of the Cathedral; at 404 feet, it is the tallest in England. The 13th century cathedral has a marvellous & rare visual unity. The body of the building was completed in just 38 years, although the spire was added in the next century. Salisbury, or "New Sarum" was founded in 1220 when the Bishop abandoned the original cathedral at Old Sarum, to start the present edifice two miles to the south. At Old Sarum you can see the foundation of the old city including the outline of the first cathedral.

Wiltshire

Gazeteer

Area of Outstanding Natural Beauty
The Costwolds & the North Wessex
Downs.

Historic Houses & Castles

Corsham Court - Chippenham
16th & 17th centuries from Elizabethan &
Georgian periods. 18th century furniture,
British, Flemish & Italian Old Masters.
Gardens by Capability Brown.
Great Chalfield Manor - Melksham
15th century manor house - moated.
Church House - Salisbury
15th century house.
Chalcot House - Westbury
17th century small house in
Palladian manner.
Lacock Abbey - Nr. Chippenham
13th century abbey. In 1540 converted
into house - 18th century alterations.
Mediaeval cloisters & brewery.
Longleat House - Warminster
16th century - early Renaissance,
alterations in early 1800's.
Italian Renaissance decorations.
Splendid state rooms, pictures, books,
furniture. Victorian kitchens.
Game reserve.
Littlecote - Nr. Hungerford
15th century Tudor manor. Panelled
rooms, moulded plaster ceilings.
Luckington Court - Luckington
Queen Anne for the most part - fine
ancient buildings.
Malmesbury House - Salisbury
Queen Anne house - part 14th century.
Rococo plasterwork.
Newhouse - Redlynch
17th century brick Jacobean trinity house
- two Georgian wings,
Philips House - Dinton
1816 Classical house.
Sheldon Manor - Chippenham
13th century porch & 15th century chapel
in this Plantagenet manor.
Stourhead - Stourton
18th century Palladian house with framed
landscape gardens.
Westwood Manor - Bradford-on-Avon
15th century manor house - alterations in
16th & 17th centuries.
Wardour Castle - Tisbury
18th century house in Palladian manner.

Wilton House - Salisbury
17th century - work of Inigo Jones & later
of James Wyatt in 1810. Paintings, Kent
& Chippendale furniture.
Avebury Manor - Nr Malborough
Elizabethan manor house - beautiful
plasterwork, panelling & furniture.
Gardens with topiary.
Bowood - Calne
18th century - work of several famous
architects. Gardens by Capability Brown -
famous beechwoods.
Mompesson House - Salisbury
Queen Anne town house - Georgian
plasterwork.

Cathedrals & Churches

Salisbury Cathedral
13th century - decorated tower with stone
spire. Part of original stone pulpitum is
preserved. Beautiful large decorated
cloister. Exterior mostly early English.
Salisbury (St. Thomas of Canterbury)
15th century rebuilding - 12th century
font, 14th & 15th century glass, 17th
century monuments. 'Doom' painting
over chancel & murals in south chapel
Amesbury (St. Mary & St. Melor)
13th century - refashioned 15th &
restored in 19th century. Splendid timber
roofs, stone vaulting over chapel of north
trancept, mediaeval painted glass, 15th
century screen, Norman font.
Bishops Cannings (St. Mary the Virgin)
13th-15th centuries. Fine arcading in
transept - fine porch doorway - 17th
century almsbox, Jacobean Holy table.
Bradford-on-Avon (St. Lawrence)
Best known of all Saxon churches
in England.
Cricklade (St. Sampson)
12th -16th century. Tudor central tower
vault, 15th century chapel.
Inglesham (St. John the Baptist)
Mediaeval wall paintings, high pews, clear
glass, remains of painted screens.
Malmesbury (St. Mary)
Norman - 12th century arcades,
refashioning in 14th century with
clerestory, 15th century stone
pulpitum added.
Fine sculpture.

Wiltshire

Tisbury (St. John the Baptist)
14th-15th centuries. 15th-17th century
roofing to nave & aisles. Two storeyed
porch & chancel.
Potterne (St. Mary)
13th,14th,15th centuries. Inscribed
Norman tub font. Wooden pulpit.

Museums & Galleries

Salisbury & South Wiltshire Museum -
Salisbury
Collections showing history of the area in
all periods. Models of Stonehenge & Old
Sarum - archaeologically
important collection.
Devizes Museum - Devizes
Unique archaeological & geological
collections, including Sir Richard Colt-
Hoare's Stourhead collection of
prehistoric material.
Alexander Keiller Museum - Avebury
Collection of items from the Neolithic &
Bronze ages & from excavations
in district.
Athelstan Museum - Malmesbury
Collection of articles referring to the town
- household, coin, etc.
Bedwyn Stone Museum - Great Bedwyn
Open-air museum showing where
Stonehenge was carved.
Lydiard Park - Lydiard Tregoze
Parish church of St. Mary & a splendid
Georgian mansion standing in park -
memorials - also permanent &
travelling exhibitions.

**Borough of Thamesdown Museum &
Art Gallery** - Swindon
Natural History & Geology of Wiltshire,
Bygones, coins, etc. 20th century British
art & ceramic collection.
Great Western Railway Museum -
Swindon
Historic locomotives.

Historic Monuments

Stonehenge - Nr. Amesbury
Prehistoric monument - encircling bank &
ditch & Augrey holes are Neolithic.
Stone circles possibly early Bronze age.
Avebury
Relics of enormous circular gathering
place B.C. 2700-1700.
Old Sarum - Nr. Salisbury
Possibly first Iron Age camp, later
Roman area, then Norman castle.
Silbury Hill - Nr. Avebury
Mound - conical in shape - probably a
memorial c.3000-2000 B.C.
Windmill Hill - Nr. Avebury
Causewayed camp c.3000-2300 B.C.
Bratton Camp & White Horse - Bratton
Hill fort standing above White Horse.
West Kennet Long Barrow
Burial place c.4000-2500 B.C.
Ludgershall Castle - Lugershall
Motte & bailey of Norman castle,
earthworks, also flint walling from
later castle.

Castle Combe.

WILTSHIRE
Map reference

1	Threlfall	19	Ross
1	Hartland	20	Tucker
2	Roberts	20	Bone
2	Chapman	20	Arthey
2	Price	20	Rodwell
3	Denning	21	Johnson
4	Cooper	22	Gifford-Mead
5	Lippiatt	23	Bruges
6	Steed	24	Singer
7	Addison	25	Cottle
8	Stafford		
9	Richmond		
9	Fletcher		
10	Quinlan		
10	Horton		
11	Firth		
13	Eavis		
14	Edwards		
15	Francis		
16	Davies		
17	Couzens		
18	Cornelius		

Burghope Manor. Bradford-on-Avon.

Wiltshire

			per person minimum £	children taken	evening meals	animals taken

Mrs Valerie Threlfall
1 Cove House
Ashton Keynes
SN6 6NS
Tel: (0285) 861226
Open: ALL YEAR
Map Ref No. 01

Nearest Road: A.419
Southern half of a beautiful 17th century manor house in a pretty Cotswold village. 2 double & 1 twin bedded room all elegantly decorated, 2 with en-suite facilities. Guests' sitting room is located in the beamed attic whose interior reflects the hosts' joint hobbies of vintage car & costume collection. A walled garden is reached via a recently renovated ballroom. 3 local hostelries offering meals within easy walking distance.

£19.00 — Y N Y (non-smoking)

Peter & Elizabeth Hartland
Cove House
2 Cove House
Ashton Keynes
SN6 6NS
Tel: (0285) 861221
Open: APR - NOV
Map Ref No. 01

Nearest Road: A.419
Peter & Elizabeth will welcome you warmly to their historic Cotswold manor house containing many antiques & interesting paintings. The charming old house stands in a secluded garden & offers 3 spacious bedrooms, with bath/shower en-suite. Dinner 'en famille' is ideal for planning the next day's excursions & guests will enjoy good home cooking, using garden produce when in season. Bath, Oxford, Avebury & the delightful Cotswold villages are within easy reach. Tennis, squash, golf, fishing & riding can be arranged.

£18.00 — Y Y Y

Priscilla & Peter Roberts
Bradford Old Windmill
4 Masons Lane
Bradford-on-Avon
BA15 1QN
Tel: (0225) 866842
Open: ALL YEAR
Map Ref No. 02

Nearest Road: M.4, A.363
A cosy, relaxed atmosphere greets you at this converted windmill high on the hill above the town. The old stone tower overflows with character & with the many "finds" picked up by Peter & Priscilla on their back-packing trips around the world. Most of the unusually shaped bedrooms have their own distinctive en-suite bathrooms. Imaginative breakfasts are served beneath the massive grain weighing scales. 5 minutes' walk from the town centre.

£24.50 — Y Y N (non-smoking)
CREDIT CARD
VISA
M'CARD

Elizabeth & John Denning
Burghope Manor
Winsley
Bradford-on-Avon
BA15 2LA
Tel: (0225) 723557
Fax 0225 723113
OpenALL YEAR (Excl.Xmas)
Map Ref No. 03

Nearest Road: A.36
This historic 13th century family home is set in beautiful countryside on the edge of the village of Winsley - overlooking the Avon Valley - 5 miles from the centre of Bath & 1 & a half miles Bradford-on-Avon. Although steeped in history, Burghope Manor is first & foremost a living family home, which has been carefully modernised so that the wealth of historical features complement the present day comforts which include central heating & en-suite bathrooms. Village pub & restaurant within short walking distance.

£30.00 — Y N N
see PHOTO over
CREDIT CARD
VISA
M'CARD
AMEX

Carey & Diana Chapman
Priory Steps
Newtown
Bradford-on-Avon
BA15 1NQ
Tel: (0225) 862230
Fax 0225 866248
Open: ALL YEAR
Map Ref No. 02

Nearest Road: A.363
A warm & friendly welcome awaits you at this delightful, mellow, stone-built, 17th century, former clothiers house. Tastefully renovated & furnished with antiques, Priory Steps offers 5 individually decorated en-suite bedrooms with tea/coffee making facilities & colour T.V. All rooms have super views over the town towards Westbury Hills. A wide choice of delicious breakfasts is available -these are served in the elegant dining room- & Diana's delicious evening meals are not to be missed.

£28.00 — Y Y N
CREDIT CARD
VISA
M'CARD

Fosse Farmhouse Country Hotel. Nettleton.

Wiltshire

	minimum £ per person	children taken	evening meals	animals taken

John & Pauline Price **Widbrook Grange** **Trowbridge Road** **Widbrook** **Bradford-on-Avon** BA15 1UH **Tel: (02216) 4750 /3173** **Fax 02216 2890** **Open: ALL YEAR** **Map Ref No. 02**	Nearest Road: A.363 Widbrook Grange is a Georgian grade II listed house set in 11 acres & only 8 miles from the fascinating Georgian city of Bath. The house has been lovingly restored by John & Pauline, with elegant rooms offering en-suite facilities & some 4-poster beds in both the house & the courtyard 'cottages'. Peaceful comfort & a warm welcome await you. Restaurant within walking distance. An ideal base from which to tour the beautiful Wiltshire countryside.	£30.00 CREDIT CARD VISA M'CARD AMEX	Y	Y	N
Caron Cooper **Fosse Farmhouse** **Nettleton Shrub** **Nettleton** **Chippenham SN14 7NJ** **Tel: (0249) 782286** **Fax 0249 783066** **Open: ALL YEAR** **Map Ref No. 04**	Nearest Road: B.4039, M.4 This 18th century Farmhouse is situated midway between Bath, Bristol & The Cotswolds. Castle Combe, one of the prettiest villages in England, lies just across the valley. A warm welcome & excellent en-suite accommodation awaits every guest. The beautiful original interiors were re- cently featured in the 'American Country Living' magazine. The newly converted stable buildings house a tea room, antique shop & gourmet res- taurant. A delightful home.	£30.00 *see PHOTO over* CREDIT CARD VISA M'CARD AMEX	Y	Y	Y
Mrs Victoria Lippiatt **Manor Farm** **Alderton** **Chippenham SN14 6NL** **Tel: (0666) 840271** **Open: ALL YEAR** **Map Ref No. 05**	Nearest Road: B.4040, M.4 This beautiful 17th century family home, in pictur- esque Alderton, welcomes small numbers of guests to warm hospitality. Each lovely bedroom has en-suite facilities with colour T.V. The sur- rounding area is steeped in interest, & boasts an excellent variety of places to wine & dine. Guests are most welcome to enjoy the garden & the interest of this working farm. Write ahead for touring details. Children over 12 years.	£20.00 *see PHOTO over*	Y	N	N
Gloria Steed **The Cottage** **Westbrook** **Bromham** **Chippenham SN15 2EE** **Tel: (0380) 850255** **Open: ALL YEAR** **Map Ref No. 06**	Nearest Road: A.3102, M.4 This delightful cottage is reputed to have been a coaching inn & dates back to 1450. There are 3 charming bedrooms all with private shower, T.V. & tea/coffee makers, in a beautifully converted barn. Many exposed beams that were ships' timbers. Breakfast is served in the old beamed dining room. There is a lovely garden & paddock for guests' use. This lovely house is an ideal centre for visiting Bath, Bristol, Devizes, Marle- borough, Avebury, Stonehenge & Longleat.	£19.00	Y	N	N
Margaret Addison **The Old Rectory** **Cantax Hill, Lacock** **Chippenham SN15 2JZ** **Tel: (0249) 730335** **Open: ALL YEAR** **Map Ref No. 07**	Nearest Road: A.350, A.4 Situated in the mediaeval village of Lacock, the Old Rectory, built in 1866, is a fine example of Victorian gothic architecture with creeper-clad walls & mullioned windows. It stands in 12 acres of its own carefully tended grounds which include a tennis court & croquet lawn. It offers 5 comfort- able bedrooms, all with private bath.	£15.00	Y	N	N

Manor Farm. Alderton.

Devizes Castle. Devizes.

Wiltshire

		per person minimum £	children taken	evening meals	animals taken
Mrs Gill Stafford **Pickwick Lodge Farm** **Corsham** **SN13 0PS** **Tel: (0249) 712207** **Fax 0249 715975** **Open: MAR - NOV** **Map Ref No. 08**	Nearest Road: M.4, A.4 A delightful 17th century Cotswold stone farmhouse, set in peaceful surroundings. Accommodation is in 3 well-appointed & tastefully furnished bedrooms, each with private bathroom, radio, T.V. & tea/coffee making facilities. Hearty & delicious breakfasts are served. Ideally situated for visiting many sites of historical interest, such as the Wiltshire White Horses, Avebury & Stonehenge; many stately homes & National Trust properties within easy reach. Ample car parking.	£15.00 🚭	Y	N	Y
Mrs S Quinlan **Blackwells Farm** **Chandlers Lane** **Bishops Cannings** **Devizes** **SN10 2JZ** **Tel: (0380) 860438** **Open: ALL YEAR** **Map Ref No. 10**	Nearest Road: A.4361 Blackwells Farm is an early-17th century, Grade II listed thatched cottage, settled in the Wiltshire countryside between open downland & the Kennet & Avon Canal, yet only 3 miles from the market town of Devizes. Retaining much of its original character with oak beams & inglenook fireplaces, it offers attractive accommodation in 3 comfortable bedrooms, each with tea/coffee making facilities. Guests may use the swimming pool, sauna & pleasant garden. Within easy reach of Stonehenge, Bath, Salisbury & Oxford.	£16.00 🚭	Y	N	Y
Sigourney Richmond **Devizes Castle** **Devizes** **SN10 1HL** **Tel: (0380) 726632** **Fax 0380 727113** **Open: ALL YEAR** **Map Ref No. 09**	The Lord & Lady of the Manor of Willoughby upon the Wolds welcome you to their home. Romantic Devizes castle, situated between Stongehenge & Bath dates back to the 12th century. Offering 3 luxurious rooms with private facilities in the fabulous south tower. Guests have their own magnificent circular drawing room, overlooking the battlement gardens. Modern comfort combines with romantic,circular rooms, spiral staircases, tranquil & secluded setting yet only 2 mins. from Devizes. Avebury, Lacock Abbey & Bath easily accessible. Minimum 2 night stay. Advance bookings only.	£45.00 🚭 *see PHOTO over* CREDIT CARD VISA M'CARD AMEX	N	N	N
Malcolm & Janet Firth **Eastcott Manor** **Easterton** **Devizes SN10 4PL** **Tel: (0380) 813313** **OpenALL YEAR(Excl.Xmas)** **Map Ref No. 11**	Nearest Road: B.3098 Eastcott is a Grade II listed Elizabethan manor house set in its own grounds & gardens of 20 acres, in a quiet and tranquil setting on the edge of Salisbury Plain. The interior is furnished with antiques, & the bedrooms are fully modernised & comfortable. Ideal centre for Bath, Salisbury, Stonehenge, Longleat etc. Excellent walking and riding on the Ridgeway with fine views.	£18.00	Y	Y	Y
Mrs Ann Horton **Easton Farmhouse** **Bishops Cannings** **Devizes** **SN10 2LR** **Tel: (0380) 860228** **Open: ALL YEAR** **Map Ref No. 10**	Nearest Road: A.361 Easton Farmhouse is situated in the pretty village of Bishops Cannings. Accommodation is in 2 rooms with washbasins, which share 1 bathroom. Both have tea/coffee making facilities. Tennis court & garden available for guests' use. Excellent evening meals served in local pub/restaurant. Ideal place for walking along the Kennet & Avon Canal which borders the farm. An excellent base, conveniently located for Bowood, Bath, Salisbury & Stonehenge.	£16.00	Y	N	N

Rathlin Guest House   Devizes.

Wiltshire

		minimum £ per person	children taken	evening meals	animals taken
Peter & Barbara Fletcher **Rathlin Guest House** **Wick Lane** **Devizes** **SN10 5DP** **Tel: (0380) 721999** **Open: ALL YEAR** **Map Ref No. 09**	Nearest Road: A.360 A beautiful detached Edwardian house set in tranquil gardens, with ample car parking space, situated in a quiet residential area only a short walk from the town centre. Tastefully furnished with antiques, the house has great period charm. An elegant staircase leads to individually furnished en-suite bedrooms, all with colour televisions & hospitality tray. Ideal touring base for Bath, Stonehenge, Avebury, Longleat & Bowood.	£18.50 *see PHOTO over*	Y	N	N
Mrs Ross Eavis **Manor Farm** **Corston** **Malmesbury** **SN16 0HF** **Tel: (0666) 822148** **Open: ALL YEAR** **Map Ref No. 13**	Nearest Road: A.429 Relax & unwind in a charming 17th century Grade II listed farmhouse standing in 436 acres. There are 5 spacious comfortable rooms, some en-suite, all with tea/coffee makers, radio & T.V. on request. Lounge with T.V. & secluded garden available for guests' relaxation. Excellent meals served in the local pub within walking distance. Corston makes a marvellous base for exploring the Cotswolds, Bath & Tetbury.	£16.00 CREDIT CARD VISA M'CARD AMEX	Y	N	N
Mrs Edna Edwards **Stone Hill Farm** **Charlton** **Malmesbury SN16 9DY** **Tel: (0666) 823310** **Open: ALL YEAR** **Map Ref No. 14**	Nearest Road: B.4040, M.4 A warm welcome is yours at Stonehill, a 500 year-old Cotswold stone farmhouse on 200 acres of dairy & sheep farm. In a quiet location, but only 15 mins. from the M.4 (junctions 16 & 17), it is ideally situated for days out in Bath, the Cotswolds, Stratford, Salisbury & Stonehenge. 3 bedrooms available, 1 with en-suite facilities. Children (& dogs) are welcome & will enjoy the homely atmosphere.	£15.00	Y	N	Y
A & G Francis **Laurel Cottage** **Southend** **Ogbourne St. George** **Marlborough SN8 1SG** **Tel: (067284) 288** **Open: APRIL - OCT** **Map Ref No. 15**	Nearest Road: A.345 Nestling in a fold of the Marlborough Downs, this 16th century thatched cottage has been fully modernised whilst retaining its unique 'olde worlde' charm. Low beamed ceilings, inglenook fireplace & bread oven are characteristic of these properties. 4 attractive bedrooms, 1 with en-suite facilities. Situated 30-40 miles from Bath, Oxford & Salisbury. Stonehenge & Avebury close by. An ideal base for touring.	£16.00	Y	Y	N
Mrs Judy Davies **Marridge Hill** **Ramsbury** **Marlborough SN8 2HG** **Tel: (0672) 20237** **Fax 0672 20053** **Open: ALL YEAR** **Map Ref No. 16**	Nearest Road: M.4, B.4192 A mainly Victorian family home set in glorious countryside above the Kennet Valley, yet only 1 hours drive from Heathrow Airport. You will be warmly welcomed into a relaxed informal atmosphere. There are 3 comfortable twin bedded rooms, with many extras, a pleasant lounge & dining room with log fires & an acre of attractive garden. An ideal base for touring, within easy reach of Avebury, Marlborough, Hungerford, Bath, Salisbury, Oxford & the Cotswolds.	£15.00	Y	N	Y

The Old Vicarage. Burbage.

Wiltshire

	Description	minimum £ per person	children taken	evening meals	animals taken
Barbara Couzens **Sunrise Farm** **Manton** **Marlborough SN8 4HL** Tel: (0672) 512878 Open: JAN - NOV Map Ref No. 17	Nearest Road: A.4 A warm welcome awaits you at Sunrise, peacefully situated on the outskirts of Manton village, 1 mile from Marlborough, with panoramic views over the Marlborough Downs. Sunrise has 1 double & 2 twin rooms. 1 twin on the ground floor with private bathroom. Large guest lounge has T.V., tea/coffee making facilities. Ideal base for Bath, Salisbury, Stonehenge, Avebury, Ridgeway & surrounding area.	£14.00 🚭	N	N	N
Mrs Jane Cornelius **The Old Vicarage** **Burbage** **Marlborough SN8 3AG** Tel: (0672) 810495 Open:ALL YEAR (Excl. Xmas & New Year) Map Ref No. 18	Nearest Road: A.4, A.346 A large Victorian vicarage on the village green, next to the church, surrounded by thatched cottages. This pleasant country house offers guests 3 large, pretty rooms, decorated & furnished to a very high standard, with en-suite bathrooms. A most attractive lounge where guests can relax, giving out onto 2 acres of mature gardens. Within easy reach is Stonehenge, Avebury & Savernake Forest. An ideal base from which to visit Bath, Oxford & Salisbury.	£30.00 🚭 *see PHOTO over* CREDIT CARD VISA M'CARD AMEX	N	Y	N
Colin & Susan Ross **Chetcombe House Hotel** **Chetcombe Road** **Mere** **BA12 6AZ** Tel: (0747) 860219 Open: ALL YEAR Map Ref No. 19	Nearest Road: A.303 Chetcombe is a country house hotel set in an acre of lovely garden in the picturesque little town of Mere. Accommodation is in 5 attractively furnished rooms with private facilities & modern amenities including T.V. & tea/coffee makers. Delicious meals are served. Guests may relax in the comfortable lounge or enjoy the pretty garden. Ideal as a stopover en-route to the West Country, or as a centre to explore the delights of Wiltshire. No smoking in bedrooms.	£24.00 CREDIT CARD VISA M'CARD	Y	Y	Y
Mary Tucker **1 Riverside Close** **Laverstock** **Salisbury SP1 1QW** Tel: (0722) 320287 Fax 0722 320287 Open: ALL YEAR Map Ref No. 20	Nearest Road: A.30 An executive's home in a quiet area 1 & a half miles from Salisbury Cathedral. A tastefully furnished ground-floor suite comprising private shower room, a double & single room with patio door, opening onto a beautiful, flower arranger's garden. In addition guests have their own colour T.V. & tea/coffee making facilities. An excellent base for those visiting this historic city. Guests will receive every consideration here.	£18.00 🚭	Y	N	N
Chris & Sandie Bone **Avon Lodge Guest House** **28 Castle Road** **Salisbury** **SP1 3RJ** Tel: (0722) 331359 Open: ALL YEAR Map Ref No. 20	Nearest Road: A.345 Avon Lodge is a Victorian house conveniently situated on the main Stonehenge road, within a few minutes walk of the city centre with its famous cathedral & many other historical buildings. Accommodation is in 3 attractive rooms with modern amenities including colour T.V. & tea/coffee making facilities. Lounge & garden available for guests' relaxation. Friendly & personal attention is assured in a homely & comfortable atmosphere. An ideal base for touring.	£14.00	Y	N	N

Wiltshire

		per person minimum £	children taken	evening meals	animals taken
Ann & Peter Arthey **Byways Guest House** **31 Fowlers Road** **Salisbury SP1 2QP** **Tel: (0722) 328364** **Fax 0722 322146** **Open: ALL YEAR** **Map Ref No. 20**	Nearest Road: A.30, A.36 Attractive family-run Victorian house close to cathedral in a quiet residential area of city centre. Leaving your car in the car park enables you to walk to Salisbury's magnificent cathedral. Comfortable bedrooms are with en-suite bathroom facilities & colour T.V.'s. Traditional English breakfasts together with vegetarian menus are included. An ideal place to stay for visiting Salisbury, Stonehenge, Avebury & the New Forest.	£17.50 CREDIT CARD VISA M'CARD	Y	Y	Y
Mrs G. Rodwell **Farthings** **9 Swaynes Close** **Salisbury SN10 5DP** **Tel: (0722) 330749** **Open: ALL YEAR** **Map Ref No. 20**	Nearest Road: A.30 Farthings is a comfortable old house in a very quiet tree-lined street conveniently close to Salisbury's market square & its many excellent restaurants. There are 4 bedrooms, 2 single, 2 double / twin en-suite, each with tea/coffee makers. Residents' lounge with colour T.V. & an interesting collection of old photos. A delicious choice of breakfast is available.	£15.00 🚭	Y	N	N
Jill Johnson **Newcourt Lodge** **Nunton Drive** **Nunton** **Salisbury** **SP5 4HZ** **Tel: (0722) 335877** **Open: ALL YEAR** **Map Ref No. 21**	Nearest Road: A.338 An attractive house, with a friendly atmosphere, situated in a quiet village 3 miles from Salisbury. Newcourt Lodge incorporates original old bricks & timber features, with a large, mature garden giving extensive views over the rolling Wiltshire countryside. Each bedroom furnished to a high standard. Including T.V., H&C, C.H. & tea/coffee making facilities. A delightful home ideal for visiting Salisbury, Stonehenge, New Forest & the West Country. Nearby are attractive country pubs serving evening meals.	£15.00 🚭	Y	N	N
Diana Gifford-Mead **The Mill House** **Berwick St. James** **Salisbury** **SP3 4TS** **Tel: (0722) 790331** **Open: ALL YEAR** **Map Ref No. 22**	Nearest Road: A.303, A.36 The lovely rooms of Mill House, built in 1785, view the River Till running through beautiful old-fashioned rose gardens & acres of water-meadows, rich with birds & wild flowers. Tea making facilities & T.V. in rooms on request. The old mill, still working, straddles a quarter of a mile of dry fly-fishing. Stonehenge is within walking distance. Numerous stately homes & historic sites. Pubs & eating places are nearby. Diana offers the warmest of welcomes. Children over 5 only.	£18.00	Y	N	N
Mrs Michael Bruges **Brook House** **Semington** **Trowbridge** **BA14 6JR** **Tel: (0380) 870232** **Open: FEB-NOV** **Map Ref No. 23**	Nearest Road: A.350 This Georgian listed house is set in its own grounds, with tennis & croquet lawns, swimming pool & a brook bordering the orchard, where kingfishers can be seen. Offering 2 comfortable twin bedded rooms, with wash basins & tea/coffee facilities. The drawing room & conservatory can be made available for guests' use. Conveniently located for Bath, Longleat, Stourhead & Badminton horse trials.	£17.00 *see PHOTO over*	Y	N	Y

Brook House. Semington.

Wiltshire

		minimum £ per person	children taken	evening meals	animals taken
Colin & Rachel Singer **Springfield** **Crockerton** **Warminster** **BA12 8AU** **Tel: (0985) 213696** **Open: ALL YEAR** **Map Ref No. 24**	Nearest Road: A.350, A.36 Situated in the beautiful Wylye Valley, on the edge of the famous Longleat Estate, Springfield is a charming village house dating from the 17th century. Rachel & Colin welcome you to their home with its beams, open fires, fresh flowers, & sunny, south facing rooms, private or en-suite, overlooking the garden & grass tennis court. Marvellous base for touring, walking or just relaxing. Bath, Salisbury, Wells, Glastonbury, Stonehenge, Stourhead easily reached.	£17.00	Y	Y	N
Margaret Cottle **Sturford Mead Farm** **Corsley** **Warminster** **BA12 7QU** **Tel: (0373) 832213** **Open: ALL YEAR** **Map Ref No. 25**	Nearest Road: A.362 Sturford Mead is conveniently located between Frome & Warminster opposite Longleat with its Safari Park, lake & grounds. Offering comfortable accommodation in a choice of 4 rooms, 1 with private facilities, 3 en-suite, all with radio, tea/coffee makers & T.V. There is also a T.V. lounge & garden for guests' use. This is an ideal base for visiting the ancient cities of Wells & Bath. Cheddar Gorge & Wookey Hole are close by.	£16.00	Y	N	N

All the establishments mentioned in this guide
are members of
The Worldwide Bed & Breakfast Association

When booking your accommodation please mention
The Best Bed & Breakfast

Yorkshire

Yorkshire & Humberside

England's largest county is a region of beautiful landscapes, of hills, peaks, fells, dales & forests with many square miles of National Park. It is a vast area taking in big industrial cities, interesting towns & delightful villages. Yorkshires broad rivers sweep through the countryside & are an angler's paradise. Cascading waterfalls pour down from hillside & moorland.

The North sea coast can be thrilling, with wild seas & cliff-top walks, or just fun, as at the many resorts where the waves break on long beaches & trickle into green rock-pools. Staithes & Robin Hoods Bay are fascinating old fishing villages. Whitby is an attractive port where, below the Abbey, the small town tumbles in red-roofed tiers down to the busy harbour from which Captain Cook sailed.

The Yorkshire Dales form one of the finest landscapes in England. From windswept moors to wide green valleys the scenery is incomparable. James Herriot tells of of the effect that the broad vista of Swaledale had on him. "I was captivated", he wrote, "completely spell-bound....". A network of dry stone walls covers the land; some are as old as the stone-built villages but those which climb the valley sides to the high moors are the product of the 18th century enclosures, when a good wall builder would cover seven meters a day.

Each of the Dales has a distinctive character; from the remote upper reaches of Swaledale & Wensleydale, where the air sings with the sound of wind, sheep, & curlew, over to Airedale & the spectacular limestone gorges of Malham Cove & Gordale Scar, & down to the soft meadows & woods of Wharfedale where the ruins of Bolton Priory stands beside the river.

To the east towards Hull with its mighty River Humber crossed by the worlds largest single-span suspension bridge, lie the Yorkshire Wolds. This is lovely countryside where villages have unusual names like Fridaythorpe & Wetwang. Beverley is a picture-postcard town with a fine 13th century Minster.

The North Yorks National Park, where the moors are ablaze with purple fire of heather in the late summer, is exhilarating country. There is moorland to the east also, on the Pennine chain; famous Ilkley Moor with its stone circle known as the twelve apostles, & the Haworth Moors around the plain Yorkshire village where the Bronte sisters lived; "the distant dreamy, dim blue chain of mountains circling every side", which Emily Bronte describes in Wuthering Heights.

The Yorkshire Pennines industrial heritage is being celebrated in fascinating museums, often based in the original Woolen Mills & warehouses, which also provide workshop space for skilled craftspeople.

Yorkshires Monastic past is revealed in the ruins of its once great Abbeys. Rievaulx, Jervaux & Fountains, retain their tranquil beauty in their pastoral settings. The wealth of the county is displayed in many historic houses with glorious gardens, from stately 18th Century Castle Howard of 'Brideshead Revisited' fame to Tudor Shibden Hall, portrayed in Wuthering Heights.

York is the finest mediaeval city in England. It is encircled by its limestone city walls with four Great Gates. Within the walls are the jumbled roof line, dog-leg streets & sudden courtyards of a mediaeval town. Half timbered buildings with over-sailing upper storeys jostle with Georgian brick houses along the network of narrow streets around The Shambles & King Edward Square.

Yorkshire

Yorkshire Gazeteer

Areas of Outstanding Natural Beauty.
The North Yorkshire Moors & The Yorkshire Dales.

Historic Houses & Castles.

Carlton Towers
17th century, remodelled in later centuries. paintings, silver, furniture, pictures. Carved woodwork, painted decorations, examples of Victorian craftmanship.

Castle Howard - Nr. York
18th century - celebrated architect, Sir John Vanbrugh - paintings, costumes, furniture by Chippendale, Sheraton, Adam. Not to be missed.

East Riddlesden Hall - Keighley
17th century manor house with fishponds & historic barns, one of which is regarded as very fine example of mediaeval tithe barn.

Newby Hall - Ripon
17th century Wren style extended by Robert Adam. Gobelins tapestry, Chippendale furniture, sculpture galleries with Roman rotunda, statuary. Award-winning gardens.

Nostell Priory - Wakefield
18th century, Georgian mansion, Chippendale furniture, paintings.

Burton Constable Hall - Hull
16th century, Elizabethan, remodelled in Georgian period. Stained glass, Hepplewhite furniture, gardens by Capability Brown.

Ripley Castle - Harrogate
14th century, parts dating during 16th & 18th centuries. Priest hole, armour & weapons, beautiful ceilings.

The Treasurer's House - York
17th & 18th centuries, splendid interiors, furniture, pictures.

Harewood House - Leeds
18th century - Robert Adam design, Chippendale furniture, Italian & English paintings. Sevres & Chinese porcelain.

Benningbrough Hall - York
18th century. Highly decorative woodwork, oak staircase, friezes etc. Splendid hall.

Markenfield Hall - Ripon
14th to 16th century - fine Manor house surrounded by moat.

Heath Hall - Wakefield
18th century, palladian. Fine woodwork & plasterwork, rococo ceilings, excellent furniture, paintings & porcelain

Bishops House - Sheffield
16th century. Only complete timber framed yeoman farmhouse surviving. Vernacular architecture. Superb

Skipton Castle- Skipton
One of the most complete & well preserved mediaeval castles in England.

Cathedral & Churches

York Minster
13th century. Greatest Gothic Cathedral north of the Alps. Imposing grandeur - superb Chapter house, contains half of the mediaeval stained glass of England. Outstandingly beautiful.

York (All Saints, North Street)
15th century roofing in parts - 18th century pulpit wonderful mediaeval glass.

Ripon Cathedral
12th century - though in some parts Saxon in origin. Decorated choir stalls - gables buttresses. Church of 672 preserved in crypt, , Caxton Book, ecclesiastic treasures.

Bolton Percy (All Saints)
15th century. Maintains original glass in east window. Jacobean font cover. Georgian pulpit. Interesting monuments.

Rievaulx Abbey
12th century, masterpiece of Early English architecture. One of three great Cistercian Abbeys built in Yorkshire. Impressive ruins.

Campsall (St. Mary Magdalene)
Fine Norman tower - 15th century rood screen, carved & painted stone altar.

Fountains Abbey - Ripon
Ruins of England's greatest mediaeval abbey - surrounded by wonderful landscaped gardens. Enormous tower, vaulted cellar 300 feet long.

Whitby (St. Mary)
12th century tower & doorway, 18th century remodelling - box pews much interior woodwork painted - galleries. High pulpit. Table tombs.

Yorkshire

Whitby Abbey - Whitby (St. Hilda)
7th century superb ruin - venue of Synod
of 664. Destroyed by Vikings, restored
1078 - magnificent north trancept.
Halifax (St. John the Baptist)
12th century origins, showing work from
each succeeding century - heraldic
ceilings. Cromwell glass.
Beverley Minster - Beverley
14th century. Fine Gothic Minster -
remarkable mediaeval effigies of
musicians playing instruments. Founded
as monastery in 700.
Bolton Priory - Nr. Skipton
Nave of Augustinian Priory, now Bolton's
Parish Church, amidst ruins of choir &
transepts, in beautiful riverside setting.
Selby Abbey - Selby
11th century Benedictine abbey of which
the huge church remains. Roof &
furnishings are modern after a fire of
1906, but the stonework is intact.

Museums & Galleries

Aldborough Roman Museum -
Boroughbridge
Remnants of Roman period of the town -
coins, glass, pottery, etc.
Great Ayton
Home of Captain Cook, explorer &
seaman. Exhibits of maps, etc.
Art Gallery - City of York
Modern paintings, Old Masters,
watercolours, prints, ceramics.
Lotherton Hall - Nr. Leeds
Museum with furniture, paintings, silver,
works of art from the Leeds collection &
oriental art gallery.
National Railway Museum - York
Devoted to railway engineering & its
development.
York Castle Museum
The Kirk Collection of bygones including
cobbled streets, shops, costumes, toys,
household & farm equipment -
fascinating collection.
Cannon Hall Art Gallery - Barnsley
18th century house with fine furniture &
glass, etc. Flemish & Dutch paintings.
Also houses museum of the 13/18
Royal Hussars.
Mappin Art Gallery - Sheffield
Works from 18th,19th & 20th century.

Graves Art gallery-Sheffield.
British portraiture. European works, &
examples of Asian & African art. Loan
exhibitions are held there.
Royal Pump Room Museum - Harrogate
Original sulphur well used in the Victorian
Spa. Local history costume & pottery.
Bolling Hall - Bradford
A period house with mixture of styles -
collections of 17th century oak furniture,
domestic utensils, toys & bygones.
Georgian Theatre - Richmond
Oldest theatre in the country - interesting
theatrical memorabilia.
Jorvik Viking Centre - York
Recently excavated site in the centre of
York showing hundreds of artifacts dating
from the Viking period. One of the most
important archaeological discoveries
this century.
Abbey House Museum - Kirkstall, Leeds
Illustrated past 300 years of Yorkshire life.
Shows 3 full streets from 19th century
with houses, shops & workplaces.
Piece Hall - Halifax
Remarkable building - constructed around
huge quadrangle - now Textile Industrial
Museum, Art Gallery & has craft &
antique shops.
**National Museum of Photography, Film
& Television** - Bradford
Displays look at art & science of
photography, film & T.V. Britain's only
IMAX arena.
The Colour Museum - Bradford
Award-winning interactive museum,which
allows visitors to explore the world of
colour & discover the story of dyeing &
textile printing.
Calderdale Industrial Museum - Halifax
Social & industrial Museum of the
year 1987
Shibden Hall & Folk Museum of Halifax
Half-timbered house with folk museum,
farmland, miniature train & boating lake.
**Leeds City Art Gallery & Henry Moore
Sculpture Gallery**
Yorkshire Sculpture Park - Wakefield
Yorkshire Museum of Farming - Murton
Award-winning museum of farming &
the countryside.

YORKSHIRE & HUMBERSIDE

Map reference

1 Lillie
2 Thomas
3 Young
4 Berry
5 Armstrong
6 Tanner-Smith
6 Broad
7 Popplewell
8 Bloom
9 Eccles
10 Bateson
10 Black
10 Bendtson
10 Young
10 Thomson
10 Drake
10 Greenhalgh
10 Simmons
11 King
12 Macdonald
13 Nelson
14 Maughan
15 Scott
16 Thompson

17 Sugars
18 Whitworth
19 Van Der Horst
20 Feather
21 Scott
22 Watson
23 Shepherd
24 Chamberlain
25 Sutton
26 Rathmell
27 Gloag
28 Atkinson
29 Williamson
30 Buckle
31 Beaufoy
31 McClure
31 Moreland
31 Thompson
31 Greaves
31 Wood
31 Jackman
31 Brown
31 Robinson
31 Miller
31 Gramellini
31 Tree
31 Whitbourn-Hammond
31 Nixon
31 Calder
31 Cox
32 White
33 Hepworth
33 Moverley
35 Ritchie
36 Jackson

YORKSHIRE

HUMBERSIDE

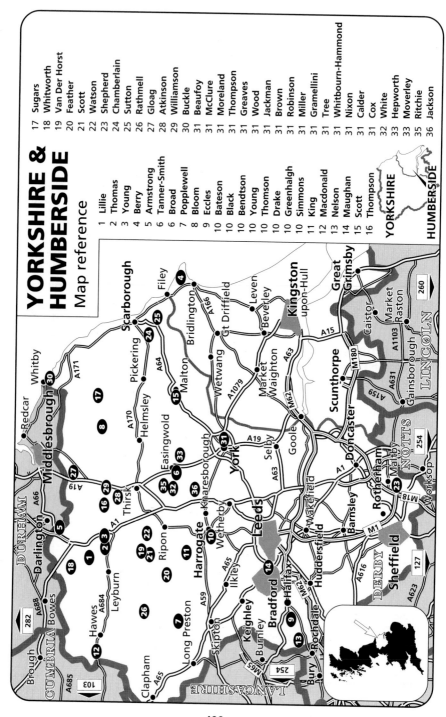

Yorkshire

		per person minimum £	children taken	evening meals	animals taken
Edith & Jim Lillie **Elmfield Country House** Arrathorne Bedale DL8 1NE Tel: (0677) 50558/50557 Open: ALL YEAR Map Ref No. 01	Nearest Road: A.1 Located in its own grounds in the country. Enjoy a relaxed, friendly atmosphere in spacious surroundings with a high standard of furnishings. Centrally heated with 9 en-suite bedrooms comprising twin bedded, double & family rooms. 2 rooms have been adapted for disabled guests, another has a four-poster bed. All rooms have satellite colour T.V., 'phone, radio/alarm & tea/coffee makers. Games room & solarium. Excellent farmhouse cooking. Residential licence.	£19.00 CREDIT CARD VISA	Y	Y	N
David & Felicity Thomas **The Old Rectory** Patrick Brompton Bedale DL8 1JN Tel: (0677) 50343 Open: FEB - NOV Map Ref No. 02	Nearest Road: A.684, A.1 The Old Rectory is a Grade II listed Georgian house set in a charming village in beautiful North Yorkshire. Tastefully furnished in keeping with its period. 3 spacious bedrooms, each with private facilities, some overlooking a walled garden with lawns beyond. Excellent meals are prepared by Felicity & served in the well appointed dining room. Nearby are small market towns, great medieval abbeys, cathedral cities & spa towns.	£19.00 🚭	N	Y	Y
Mrs Jane Young **The Old Vicarage** Crake Hall Bedale DL8 1HE Tel: (0677) 422967 Open: ALL YEAR Map Ref No. 03	Nearest Road: A.1 The Old Vicarage is a delightful Victorian house built in 1842, set in an acre of garden with fabulous views of the countryside. The atmosphere is friendly & informal, & the hosts enjoy sharing their home with their guests. 5 attractive rooms are offered; some have en-suite bathroom, each has colour T.V., tea/coffee making facilities, & more. Situated in the heart of Herriot country, this is an ideal base for exploring the Dales & Moors. York, Ripon, Skipton, Durham, Harrogate, etc., within easy reach.	£18.00 🚭	Y	N	N
Lesley Berry **The Manor House** Flamborough Bridlington YO15 1PD Tel: (0262) 850943 OpenALL YEAR (Excl. Xmas) Map Ref No. 04	Nearest Road: A.165, A.166 A manor of Flamborough is recorded in the Domesday Book. The current Georgian house is a handsomely proportioned family home offering spacious & comfortable accommodation in well appointed rooms. Historic Flamborough head is designated a Heritage Coast, with interesting walks & nearby bird reserve. Ideal for exploring North & East Yorkshire. Dinner, by prior arrangement, features local seafood when available.	£24.00 CREDIT CARD VISA M'CARD	Y	Y	N
David & Heather Armstrong **Clow Beck House** Monk End Farm Croft-on-Tees Darlington DL2 2SW Tel: (0325) 721075 Open: ALL YEAR Map Ref No. 05	Nearest Road: A.1, A.167 A modern well appointed farmhouse, set in tranquil countryside offering attractive accommodation in 3 bedrooms with modern amenities & tea/coffee making facilities. All rooms are tastefully furnished, one has a tented ceiling & Laura Ashley decor. The elegant dining room features handcrafted furniture. A charming home with hosts who extend hospitality in true Yorkshire style. Convenient for exploring 'Herriot Country', Durham, York & the East Coast.	£18.00	Y	N	N

Yorkshire

	Nearest Road	minimum £ per person	children taken	evening meals	animals taken
Joan & Geoffrey Broad **The Old Vicarage** **Market Place** **Easingwold** **YO6 3AL** **Tel: (0347) 21015** **Open: APR-OCT** **Map Ref No. 06**	Nearest Road: A.19 A listed property of immense character, built in the 18th century & thoughtfully brought up to modern standards, yet still retaining many delightful features. Now offering 7 en-suite rooms with T.V. & tea/coffee makers. Standing in extensive lawned gardens, overlooking the market square, with croquet lawn & walled rose garden, it is an ideal touring centre for York, the Dales, the Yorkshire Moors & 'Herriot' countryside.	£19.00	Y	Y	Y
Mike & Jill Popplewell **Greenways Guest House** **Wharfeside Avenue** **Threshfield** **Grassington BD23 5BS** **Tel: (0756) 752598** **Open: APR-OCT** **Map Ref No. 07**	Nearest Road: B.6265 Greenways is situated half a mile off the main Skipton to Grassington road & is set overlooking the River Wharfe. The accent is on homely comfort throughout & Jill aims to produce meals prepared from local produce which are satisfying & attractive. Greenways is a good centre to explore from - Bronte Parsonage at Haworth, Fountains Abbey, York, Settle to Carlisle Railway & the lovely Yorkshire Dales within easy access.	£20.00	Y	Y	Y
Dr & Mrs M Bloom **Manor House Farm** **Ingleby** **Greenhow** **Great Ayton TS9 6RB** **Tel: (0642) 722384** **Open: JAN - NOV** **Map Ref No. 08**	Nearest Road: A.19, B.1257 A charming old farm in idyllic surroundings at the foot of the Cleveland Hills in the North York Moors National Park. Set in park & woodland, this lovely house with beams & open fires has 3 delightful rooms with en-suite/private facilities. A pretty lounge with T.V. for guests & also a garden. Very friendly, personal service. Hosts are proud of their reputation for fine cooking. Wine & dine by candlelight. Horse riding & golf locally, plus stabling if you can bring your own mount.	£21.00	N	Y	N
Valerie Eccles **Wood End** **(off Lighthazels Road)** **Soyland, SowerbyBridge** **Halifax HX6 4NP** **Tel: (0422) 824397** **Open: ALL YEAR** **Map Ref No. 09**	Nearest Road: A.58, M.62 A 17th century converted weaver's cottage with beamed ceiling offering comfortable accommodation, excellent cuisine, a friendly, relaxed atmosphere in a peaceful, secluded setting with superb views over the beautiful Ryburn Valley. Located on the edge of a conservation village, it is 7 miles from the M.62 midway between Leeds & Manchester. Ideal for walking or touring with Bronte Country & the Yorkshire Dales within easy reach. A delightful home.	£17.50 *see PHOTO over*	Y	Y	Y
Mr & Mrs P.J. Bateson **Acacia Lodge** **21 Ripon Road** **Harrogate** **HG1 2JL** **Tel: (0423) 560752** **Open: ALL YEAR** **Map Ref No. 10**	Nearest Road: A.61 Acacia Lodge offers six luxurious, en-suite rooms in a warm, beautifully furnished Victorian house in a select area with pretty gardens and ample private parking. The breakfasts are 'award winning' and the personal attentions of the owner and his wife - Peter and Dee - contribute to a homely atmosphere. The town centre, with its varied attractions, is two minutes away. An ideal base from which to explore North Yorkshire with its many attractions & beautiful scenery.	£21.00	Y	N	N

Wood End. Sowerby Bridge.

Yorkshire

	Nearest Road / Description	per person minimum £	children taken	evening meals	animals taken
John & Roberta Black **Alexa House & Stable Cottages** **26 Ripon Road** **Harrogate HG2 2JJ** Tel: (0423) 501988 Fax 0423 504086 Open: ALL YEAR Map Ref No. 10	Nearest Road: A.61 Built in 1830 for Baron de Ferrier & now a welcoming small hotel. Offering 13 comfortable en-suite bedrooms each with 'phone, colour T.V., clock/radio alarms & tea/coffee makers. There is a friendly atmosphere, nurtured by staff who 'belong' & guests who regularly return. The breakfasts are superb. Harrogate's many restaurants are only a stroll away so you may leave your car in Alexa's car park. Convenient for touring this most historic region withs many attractions.	£23.00 CREDIT CARD VISA M'CARD	Y	Y	N
Mrs Gill Bendtson **Ashwood House** **7 Spring Grove** **Harrogate HG1 2HS** Tel: (0423) 560081 Open: ALL YEAR (Excl. Xmas & New Year) Map Ref No. 10	Nearest Road: A.61 An elegant 10 bedroomed Edwardian house, situated in a quiet residential cul-de-sac, minutes from the town centre. Charmingly decorated, it offers attractive bedrooms, some with 4-poster beds & en-suite bathrooms. All with tea/coffee making facilities, hair dryers, radio & colour T.V. A high standard of service, a warm welcome & an ample & delicious breakfast is assured. An attractive home & an ideal spot for touring.	£20.00	Y	N	N
Mrs E.J. Young **Daryl House** **42 Dragon Parade** **Harrogate HG1 5DA** Tel: (0423) 502775 Open: ALL YEAR (excl. Xmas & New Year) Map Ref No. 10	Nearest Road: A.59 A small, friendly, family-run house offering excellent accommodation in 6 most pleasant rooms with every modern comfort. Tea/coffee makers & T.V. in all rooms. An attractive lounge with colour T.V. & garden for guests' enjoyment. Home-cooked food & personal attention are the hallmarks of Daryl House. Close to the town centre with its conference facilities. A very warm welcome awaits all visitors.	£14.00	Y	Y	N
C.S. & G.A. King **High Winsley Cottage** **Burnt Yates** **Harrogate** **HG3 3EP** Tel: (0423) 770662 Open: MAR - DEC Map Ref No. 11	Nearest Road: A.61 Traditional Dales cottage in Nidderdale, situated well off the road in peaceful countryside with lovely views all around & ideally placed for both town & country. Well appointed 3 twin & 2 double rooms all with en-suite facilities. 2 large sitting rooms with guide books, games, T.V., etc. Imaginative home cooking using produce from the extensive kitchen garden, complemented by wines from an interesting list.	£19.00	Y	Y	N
Peter & Marion Thomson **Knox Mill House** **Knox Mill Lane** **Harrogate HG3 2AE** Tel: (0423) 560650 Open: ALL YEAR (Excl. Xmas & New Year) Map Ref No. 10	Nearest Road: A.61 Built in 1785, this lovely old millhouse stands on the banks of a stream in a quiet rural setting, yet only one & a half miles from the centre of Harrogate. Beautifully renovated, it still retains all its original features: oak beams, inglenook fireplace & stone arches. There are 3 delightful rooms attractively & comfortably furnished, 2 en-suite, each with tea/coffee makers, & views over the stream & fields. A delightful lounge with colour T.V. & garden for guests' enjoyment.	£16.00	Y	N	N

Yorkshire

		minimum £ per person	children taken	evening meals	animals taken
M. Bateson & A. Drake **The Duchy Hotel** **51 Valley Drive** **Harrogate** **HG2 0JH** **Tel: (0423) 565818** **Open: ALL YEAR** **Map Ref No. 10**	Nearest Road: A.1, A.61 The Duchy Hotel on Valley Drive overlooks the famous Valley Gardens, yet this beautiful Parkland setting is only 5 mins. from the town centre shops, theatres & restaurants. This warm & welcoming small hotel offers 9 en-suite bedrooms with colour T.V., tea/coffee facilities, telephones & easy chairs. Delicious home-cooked food is the pride of the house & the warmth & hospitality of Marilyn & Alan assure their valued guests of a most pleasant & memorable stay.	£24.00 CREDIT CARD VISA M'CARD	Y	Y	N
Susan Greenhalgh **The Rosedale** **86 Kings Road** **Harrogate HG1 5JX** **Tel: (0423) 566630** **Open: ALL YEAR** **Map Ref No. 10**	Nearest Road: A.1 The Rosedale is a pleasant Victorian villa which has been recently refurbished in keeping with the period. Panelled staircase & open fireplaces create a warm & cosy atmosphere. Accommodation in 8 comfortable bedrooms, 7 en-suite, each with colour T.V. & tea/coffee makers, hairdryer & complimentary toiletries. A guests' lounge & bar are also available. A very comfortable base for touring Yorkshire. Children over 5 years.	£23.50 CREDIT CARD VISA M'CARD	Y	Y	N
Mr & Mrs J. Simmons **The Ruskin Hotel** **1 Swan Road** **Harrogate HG1 2SS** **Tel: (0423) 502045** **Open: ALL YEAR** **Map Ref No. 10**	Nearest Road: A.1, A.61 A most charming Victorian hotel, set in beautiful grounds with car park, offers 6 lovely en-suite bedrooms with pretty antique furniture & every facility. Delightful bar lounge, restaurant/tea rooms with Victorian balcony, serving delicious traditional English food. Situated in conservation area, yet only 150 yards from conference & exhibition halls, town centre & valley gardens. Ideal base for excursions to the Dales, etc.	£34.00 CREDIT CARD VISA M'CARD	Y	Y	N
Gail Ainley & **Ann Macdonald** **Brandymires** **Muker Road** **Hawes DL8 3PR** **Tel: (0969) 667482** **Open: APR - OCT** **Map Ref No. 12**	Nearest Road: A.684 A warm welcome awaits you in this comfortable mid-19th century stone house in a tranquil rural setting. Every room has a splendid view over the fells. 4 spacious double bedrooms, 2 with 4-poster beds, full central heating. Good home cooking is an important feature & dinner is available with prior notice except on Thursdays. Brandymires is an ideal centre for exploring the glorious countryside of the Yorkshire Dales & historic surrounding towns. No T.V.. Ample parking.	£16.00	N	Y	Y
Mrs N.W. Nelson **'Springfield'** **Cragg Road** **Cragg Vale** **Hebden Bridge** **HX7 5SR** **Tel: (0422) 882029** **Open: ALL YEAR** **Map Ref No. 13**	Nearest Road: A.646, B.6138 A warm Yorkshire welcome awaits visitors at Springfield. Standing in an acre of garden in a picturesque wooded valley in the South Pennines with open views of woods & moorland. Guests may choose from 4 comfortably furnished, centrally heated rooms with adjacent bath/shower, 1 with en-suite facilities. All rooms have modern amenities including T.V., radio & tea/coffee makers. Sauna available. Mrs Nelson's breakfasts have won a "Best Yorkshire Breakfast Award". An ideal spot for touring.	£15.00	Y	N	N

Yorkshire

	minimum £ per person	children taken	evening meals	animals taken
Mr & Mrs D. Maughan **Lynnwood House** **18 Alexandra Road** **Uppermoor, Pudsey** **Leeds LS28 8BY** **Tel: (0532) 571117** **Open: ALL YEAR** **Map Ref No. 14**	Nearest Road: A.647, B.6154 This comfortable centrally heated home has a friendly atmosphere. Only 15 minutes from Leeds/Bradford Airport & the city centre, with rail station & buses nearby. Good shopping & theatre as well as stately homes, castles & the industrial heritage of Northern England. Cricket club, leisure centre & good park within easy reach. Visitors welcome at local golf club. Marjorie is a creative cook & welcomes vegetarians.	£30.00	Y	Y	N
Richard & Stella Scott **Red House** **Wharram-le-Street** **Malton** **YO17 9TL** **Tel: (09446) 455** **Open: JAN-Mid DEC** **Map Ref No. 15**	Nearest Road: A.64 Stella & Richard warmly welcome everyone to their elegant 19th century home. Standing in an acre of garden in the heart of the Yorkshire Wolds, it offers 4 very comfortable bedrooms with private facilities, T.V. & tea/coffee makers & guests' lounge with lovely log fires. Good home cooking using their own produce. Special diets catered for. Licensed dining rooms. Nearby are Castle Howard, Sledmere House, Nunnington Hall. York 23 miles. Grass tennis facility.	£23.00	Y	Y	Y
Peter & Shirley Thompson **Porch House** **68 High Street** **Northallerton** **DL7 8EG** **Tel: (0609) 779831** **Open: ALL YEAR** **Map Ref No. 16**	Nearest Road: A.1, A.19 A charming family house in the centre of this busy & picturesque market town. Built in 1584, the house has many historical connections - Charles I stayed here when in the region. Offering 5 bedrooms with excellent facilities, the present owners have continued the tradition of making improvements yet have retained many of the original features. Dinner by arrangement. Ample parking. York, Durham & Newcastle within 1 hour's drive. An ideal spot for touring.	£20.25 CREDIT CARD VISA M'CARD	Y	Y	Y
Linda Sugars **'Sevenford House'** **Thorgill** **Rosedale Abbey** **Pickering YO18 8SE** **Tel: (07515) 283** **Open: ALL YEAR** **Map Ref No. 17**	Nearest Road: A.170 Originally a vicarage & built from the stones of Rosedale Abbey. 'Sevenford House' stands in 4 acres in the heart of the Yorkshire Moors National Park. 3 well decorated, comfortable rooms with modern amenities & lovely views. Garden for guests' use. This beautiful country house is an excellent base for exploring the region. Riding & golf locally. Ryedale Folk Museum, ruined abbeys, Roman roads, steam railways, the beautiful coastline & pretty fishing towns.	£15.00	Y	N	N
Ian & Angela Whitworth **The White House** **Arkle Town** **Arkengarthdale** **Richmond DL11 6RB** **Tel: (0748) 84203** **Open: JAN - NOV** **Map Ref No. 18**	Nearest Road: A.66 18th century former farmhouse, modernised, tastefully decorated and furnished to a high standard. Three rooms offer modern amenities (2 en-suite). Cosy visitors' lounge with open fire. Only the best ingredients used in tasty, home-cooked meals. In the heart of Herriot country, and set above the road with superb uninterrupted views, the ideal centre for exploring the Yorkshire Dales. Children over 10 please.	£15.00	Y	Y	N

406

Yorkshire

	Description	minimum £ per person	children taken	evening meals	animals taken
Phillip Gill & Anton Van Der Horst Bank Villa, Masham Ripon HG4 4DB Tel: (0765) 689605 Open: Easter - OCT Map Ref No. 19	Nearest Road: A.6108 A fine Georgian house overlooking the River Ure in large terraced gardens, offering delightful accommodation in 7 comfortable double rooms with modern amenities. It is a super base for visiting the Druids Temple, Jervaulx Abbey, Middleham Castle, Fountains Abbey & the wonderful 'James Herriot Country'. Dutch is spoken. Meals are excellent value. Children over 5 welcome.	£16.75	Y	Y	Y
Mrs Angela Feather Dales Flora Barn Low Missise Farm Laverton Ripon HG4 3SY Tel: (0765) 658653 Open: ALL YEAR Map Ref No. 20	Nearest Road: A.1 Lovely new barn conversion adjoining main house in idyllic surroundings. A perfect place to relax & unwind. Large sitting room with beams, log fire T.V./video & French windows opening onto the garden. 3 bedrooms all with en-suite/private facilities (1 located in main house) & hairdryer, towelling robes, toiletries & tea making facilities. Within walking distance of Dales & Moors but convenient for York, Harrogate & Richmond. Evening meals by arrangement only.	£22.50 CREDIT CARD M'CARD	Y	Y	N
Avril Scott Pasture House Healey Masham Ripon HG4 4LJ Tel: (0765) 689149 Open: ALL YEAR Map Ref No. 21	Nearest Road: A.6108 Pasture House is a large, comfortable house providing guests with pleasant accommodation in the quiet of the lovely Yorkshire Dales. A perfect centre for walkers & horse racing enthusiasts with several courses & Middleham training gallops nearby. There are 4 attractive & comfortable rooms with T.V. & tea/coffee makers, a residents' lounge & large garden are also available. Pony trekking, golf & fishing locally. Children & pets welcome. Facilities for babies.	£12.00	Y	Y	Y
Elaine M. Watson Sleningford Grange North Stainley Ripon HG4 3HX Tel: (0765) 635252 Open: ALL YEAR Map Ref No. 22	Nearest Road: A.1 A delightful listed manor house dating from the 15th century. Sleningford Grange stands in lovely & extensive gardens on the verge of the Yorkshire Dales. The interior is elegant & furnished with antiques. 3 comfortable & spacious en-suite bedrooms & views across rolling countryside. An ideal base for exploring the Dales/Moors & wealth of historic towns & abbeys - or overnight break midway London-Edinburgh.	£22.00 (no smoking)	Y	N	N
Mr & Mrs M. Shepherd Stonecroft Hotel Main Street Bramley Rotherham S66 0SF Tel: (0709) 540922 Open: ALL YEAR Map Ref No. 23	Nearest Road: M.18 ex. 1 Stonecroft is a Grade II listed building with a homely atmosphere. The main building is 300 years old with a profusion of oak beams & open fireplaces. Accommodation is in 9 tastefully furnished rooms, 7 with private bathroom, all with modern amenities including colour T.V., radio & tea/coffee making facilities. Residents' lounge & delightful garden available for guests to relax in. Ideally situated for visiting the many sights & attractions in Yorkshire & Derbyshire.	£21.15 CREDIT CARD VISA M'CARD	Y	Y	Y

Yorkshire

		minimum £ per person	children taken	evening meals	animals taken
Mrs Sally Chamberlain **Church Farmhouse** **3 Main Street** **East Ayton** **Scarborough YO13 9HL** **Tel: (0723) 862102** **Open: ALL YEAR** **Map Ref No. 24**	Nearest Road: A.170 Listed 18th century farmhouse, now a charming, cosy village hotel retaining many original features. A warm welcome, personal service and good home cooking come naturally here. 3 attractive en-suite rooms plus 1 single with private bathroom; all with radio, T.V., tea/coffee facilities. (No smoking in bedrooms). Children welcome. Large games room. Residential licence. National Park village at entrance to beautiful Forge Valley & North Yorkshire Moors.	£21.00	Y	Y	Y
Virginia S. Sutton **Willerby Wold Farm** **Staxton** **Scarborough YO12 4TF** **Tel: (0944) 70747** **OpenALL YEAR (Excl. Xmas)** **Map Ref No. 25**	Nearest Road: A.64 Peacefully situated on an 800-acre farm, this lovely spacious house is ideally located for exploring the East coast, North Yorkshire Moors & York. The attractive bedrooms are elegant & well equipped. There are beautiful walks, an all weather tennis court & some excellent local pubs. Ganton Golf Club is 2 miles away. Evening meals by prior arrangement.	£15.00	Y	Y	N
Tim & Marie Rathmell **Hilltop Country Guest House** **Starbotton** **Skipton BD23 5HY** **Tel: (0756) 760321** **Open: MAR-NOV** **Map Ref No. 26**	Nearest Road: A.59, B.6160 Hilltop Country Guest House is a 17th century listed house in 4 acres of beckside gardens overlooking an unspoilt village in the heart of the Yorkshire Dales. Excellent centre for fell & riverside walks or for touring. Spacious & immaculate bedrooms, all en-suite. Fine food & wine served in oak beamed dining room. This delightful house offers the warmth & hospitality of a house party. Ideal spot for touring this lovely region.	£25.00	Y	Y	N
Mrs Anne Gloag **Busby House** **Stokesley** **TS9 5LB** **Tel: (0642) 710425** **Open: All Year (Excl. Xmas & New Year)** **Map Ref No. 27**	Nearest Road: A.1, A.19 This is a lovely old farmhouse situated 2 & a half miles south of Stokesley, off the A.172. The principal rooms look south over the garden & fields to the hills beyond. The atmosphere is peaceful & relaxed, & exudes warmth & friendliness. Perfect base for exploring the Moors, Dales & coast, & within easy reach of York, Durham & many places of historic interest. Only 25 mins. from the A.1. Children over 12.	£22.50	Y	Y (no smoking)	N
Mrs Shirley Atkinson **Mill Cottage** **Stockton Rd** **South Kilvington** **Thirsk** **YO7 2NL** **Tel: (0845) 522796** **Open: APR - OCT** **Map Ref No. 28**	Nearest Road: A.19 Delightful, large, period cottage with oak beams, just 1 mile north of Thirsk, overlooking the Cleveland Hills. 3 comfortable rooms with tea trays & wash basins, & separate guest bathroom. Lovely large garden & attractive sitting room with colour T.V., in which guests may relax. Log fire. Delicious Yorkshire home cooking. Private parking. Easy access to A.1 & A.19 for touring the Dales, York, Harrogate, Moors & resorts of Scarborough & Whitby. A lovely home, ideal for exploring this beautiful & scenic region.	£13.00	Y	Y (no smoking)	N

Yorkshire

	Nearest Road / Description	per person minimum £	children taken	evening meals	animals taken
Mrs Tess Williamson **Thornborough House** **Farm** **South Kilvington** **Thirsk YO7 2NP** Tel: (0845) 522103 Open: ALL YEAR Map Ref No. 29	Nearest Road: A.19 A warm welcome awaits you at this 200 year old farmhouse, set in lovely countryside. Only one & a half miles north of Thirsk, this working farm is situated in the town made famous by James Herriot. 3 warm & comfortable rooms, 1 en-suite, all with tea/coffee making facilities. Guests have their own sitting/dining room with colour T.V. & open fire. Good home cooking a speciality. Conveniently located for York, Ripon, Pennine Dales & East Coast.	£12.00 CREDIT CARD VISA M'CARD	Y	Y	Y
Mike & Ann Beaufoy **18 St. Paul's Square** **York** **YO2 4BD** Tel: (0904) 629884 OpenALL YEAR(Excl. Xmas) Map Ref No. 31	Nearest Road: A.59 A delightful Victorian house located in a pleasant Victorian garden square in the centre of York. Skilfully restored & furnished with period antiques, it now offers 3 very comfortable en-suite bedrooms, a guests' colour T.V. lounge & garden. Mike & Ann enjoy sharing their home & knowledge of York with their guests & are happy to give advice on where to go & what to see locally. An ideal spot for touring.	£28.00	Y	N	N
Daphne Tanner-Smith **Alderside** **Thirsk Road** **Easingwold** **York YO6 3HJ** Tel: (0347) 22132 Open: MAR - NOV Map Ref No. 06	Nearest Road: A.19 Alderside is a comfortable Edwardian former school house set in large private gardens. 2 comfortable double bedrooms, each with private bathroom, colour T.V., radio & tea/coffee facilities. 1 single bedroom is available for an accompanying relative. A full English Breakfast is served using local produce & homemade preserves. A pleasant walk to Easingwold market place with its variety of shops, pubs, etc. Easy access to York & surrounding countryside.	£15.00	N	N	N
Bob & Marilyn Moreland **Annjoa House** **34/36 Millfield Road** **Scarcroft Road** **York YO2 1NQ** Tel: (0904) 653731 Open: ALL YEAR Map Ref No. 31	Nearest Road: A.64 Small family-run licensed hotel, quietly located close to railway station. Offering guests a choice of 12 rooms, 6 en-suite, all with modern amenities, tea/coffee & some with T.V. There's a residents' colour T.V. lounge & a comfortable bar to relax in. Conveniently located for city centre & race course, making this a good base from which to explore the historic city of York with its fine Minster & many interesting museums & ancient Roman & Viking sites.	£13.00 CREDIT CARD VISA M'CARD	Y	Y	Y
John & Sue White **Brafferton Hall** **Brafferton** **Helperby** **York YO6 2NZ** Tel/Fax: (0423) 360352 Open: ALL YEAR Map Ref No. 32	Nearest Road: A.1 Brafferton Hall is a comfortable family home set in a quiet village near the River Swale in the heart of North Yorkshire, yet only 4 miles from the A.1. Offering 5 comfortable & attractively furnished bedrooms each with either en-suite or private facilities, T.V., radio & tea/coffee making facilities. Ideally placed for exploring York, the National Parks & Herriot country, all within an easy 30 minute drive. Informality accompanied by excellent fare is to be enjoyed at Brafferton Hall.	£20.00 CREDIT CARD VISA	Y	Y	Y

Yorkshire

Name & Address	Description	minimum £ per person	children taken	evening meals	animals taken
Ian & Rosalie Buckle **Dunsley Hall** **Dunsley** **Whitby** **YO21 3TL** **Tel: (0947) 83437** **Open: ALL YEAR** **Map Ref No. 30**	Nearest Road: A.171 Peaceful & elegant Country Hall in 4 acres of secluded grounds, providing a truely relaxed atmosphere. Oak panelled rooms, including superb carved Billiard Room with stained glass window. 7 en-suite bedrooms with full facilities & central heating. Within North York Moors National Park, 3 miles outside Whitby (Captain Cook country) & ideal for Heritage Coast, Castle Howard & York. Indoor heated swimming pool, fitness room, tennis, putting & croquet.	£35.00 *see PHOTO over* CREDIT CARD VISA M'CARD	Y	Y	Y
Mrs Yvonne Thompson **Brentwood Cottage** **Main Street** **Shipton-by-Beningbrough** **York YO6 1AB** **Tel: (0904) 470111** **Open: ALL YEAR** **Map Ref No. 31**	Nearest Road: A.19 A warm & friendly welcome awaits all guests at Brentwood Cottage. Located 5 miles outside the historic city of York, it offers guests a choice of 4 pleasant bedrooms, all with private facilities, amenities & tea/coffee makers. There is also a residents' lounge & garden available. This makes a good spot for touring York & the beautiful surrounding countryside. A lovely home, convenient for many attractions . Large car park.	£13.00	Y	N	N
Mr & Mrs M. Greaves **Carlton House Hotel** **134 The Mount** **York** **YO2 2AS** **Tel: (0904) 622265** **Open ALL YEAR (Excl. Xmas)** **Map Ref No. 31**	Nearest Road: A.1036, A.64 Each & every guest will receive a warm & friendly welcome from proprietors Liz & Malcolm Greaves. This pleasant family-run hotel offers guests a choice of 14 rooms, all with colour T.V., radio & tea/coffee makers. Some have private facilities. The spacious lounges are comfortable & pleasantly furnished. A traditional English breakfast cooked to order. Light refreshments are available at most times throughout the day. Nearby are York race course & the Minster.	£18.00	Y	N	N
Keith Jackman **Dairy Wholefood Guest House** **3 Scarcroft Road** **York YO2 1ND** **Tel: (0904) 639367** **Open: ALL YEAR** **Map Ref No. 31**	Nearest Road: A.59, A.64 The Dairy is a tastefully renovated Victorian house within walking distance of the city centre & just 200 yards from the mediaeval city walls. Decorated & furnished in the styles of Habitat, Sanderson's & Laura Ashley, with the emphasis on pine & plants. 5 bedrooms with modern amenities, colour T.V., hot drink facilities & extensive information on York & Yorkshire. There is a lovely enclosed courtyard. Breakfast choices are from English to wholefood vegetarian.	£15.00	Y	N	N
Adrian & Julie Brown **Four Seasons Hotel** **7 St. Peters Grove** **Clifton** **York YO3 6AQ** **Tel: (0904) 622621** **Fax 0904 430565** **Open ALL YEAR (Excl.Xmas)** **Map Ref No. 31**	Nearest Road: A.19 An elegant, detached Victorian residence with much character & appeal. Ideally situated in a peaceful cul-de-sac yet only 5 mins. walk from York Minster & the city's many historic attractions. Offering pleasant, comfortable accommodation with modern facilities tastefully incorporated into the fine original surroundings. Full English breakfast. Residential licence. A warm & friendly welcome awaits you from Julie & Adrian. Private car park. CREDIT CARD VISA M'CARD	£18.00	Y	N	Y

Frommers Budget Guide

*Fodors - B.J.B 's
q2.*

Dunsley Hall. Whitby.

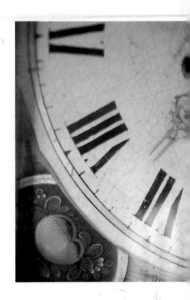

Yorkshire

	per person minimum £	children taken	evening meals	animals taken
Robin & Anne McClure **4 South Parade** York YO2 2BA Tel: (0904) 628229 Open: ALL YEAR Map Ref No. 31 Nearest Road: A.1036, A.64 An elegant Grade II listed Georgian townhouse in private cobbled street. Beautifully decorated and furnished with antiques. 3 lovely guest rooms each with its own individual character, en-suite facilities in Edwardian style, original fireplaces with working cast iron hob grates, fresh flowers, bowls of fruit, Teletext remote control T.V., and direct dial telephones. Be pampered with old fashioned hospitality, service & delicious food.	£30.00 *see PHOTO over*	N	Y	N
Jenny Robinson **Grange Lodge** **52 Bootham Crescent** **Bootham** York YO3 7AH Tel: (0904) 621137 Open: ALL YEAR Map Ref No. 31 Nearest Road: A.19 The Grange Lodge guest house offers a warm & friendly welcome to every guest. Accommodation is in a choice of 7 comfortable & attractively furnished bedrooms, 4 with en-suite facilities, colour T.V. & tea/coffee makers. A residents' lounge available throughout the day. Conveniently located for all York's attractions. Only a 10 min. stroll from York Minster. An ideal spot for touring this most beautiful region.	£12.50	Y	Y	N
Belle & Peter Hepworth **Halfway House** **Crayke** **York** YO6 4TJ Tel: (0347) 22614 Fax 0347 22942 Open ALL YEAR (Excl. Xmas) Map Ref No. 33 Nearest Road: A.19 Halfway House stands in an acre of mature garden with pleasant views across open farmland to the Dales. Accommodation is in a choice of 3 very comfortable, attractively furnished rooms. The converted granary offers a four-poster bedoom with private facilities, & a games room etc. The twin is located within the house itself & offers en-suite facilities. Each has radio, colour T.V. & tea/coffee makers. Delicious food is served in the oak panelled dining room where evening meals are sometimes provided. Guests may use the hard tennis court. CREDIT CARD VISA M'CARD	£20.00	Y	Y	Y
Mrs Rosemary Miller **Hobbits Hotel** **9 St. Peter's Grove** **Clifton** York YO3 6AQ Tel: (0904) 624538 Open ALL YEAR (Excl. Xmas) Map Ref No. 31 Nearest Road: A.19 Hobbits Hotel is an elegant Edwardian House in a quiet cul-de-sac, just 10 minutes' walk from York Minster. Guests will receive a warm welcome in this small, family-run hotel. All rooms are en-suite with facilities including mini-bars, T.V., radio, tea & coffee making. A comfortable stay & a good breakfast await all who stay at Hobbits. A lovely spot from which to tour this spendid region with its many interesting attractions. CREDIT CARD VISA M'CARD	£25.00	Y	N	Y
Joan Tree **Inglewood Guest House** **7 Clifton Green** **Clifton** York YO3 6LH Tel: (0904) 653523 Open: ALL YEAR Map Ref No. 31 Nearest Road: A.19 In this charming Victorian house guests will instantly feel completely at home. The friendliness & warmth of your host will ensure an enjoyable & relaxing stay. Accommodation is in 9 comfortable bedrooms, some with en-suite facilities, all with colour T.V. & modern amenities. The first class breakfast is served in the attractive dining room. An ideal base from which to visit the many attractions of York.	£15.00	Y	N	N

4 South Parade. York.

Yorkshire

Richard & Wendy Wood **Curzon Lodge & Stable** **Cottages** **23 Tadcaster Road** **Dringhouses** **York YO2 2QG** Tel: (0904) 703157 **Open: ALL YEAR** **Map Ref No. 31**	Nearest Road: A.64, A.1036 A charming 17th century Grade II listed house & delightful stables conversion with original oak beams, in a conservation area overlooking the racecourse. Once a home of the Terry family, the renowned York chocolate makers. Guests are invited to share the unique atmosphere, in 10 comfortably furnished rooms. All have en-suite, colour T.V., telephone, radio, hairdryer & tea/coffee facilities. Some 4-posters & brass beds. Many antiques, pretty lounge & "farmhouse kitchen" breakfast room. Large walled car park.	£22.00 *see PHOTO over* CREDIT CARD VISA M'CARD	Y	N	N
Russell & Cherry **Whitbourn-Hammond** **Nunmill House** **85 Bishopthorpe Road** **York YO2 1NX** Tel: (0904) 634047 **Open: MAR-OCT** **Map Ref No. 31**	Nearest Road: A.64, A.59 A warm friendly welcome awaits you at Nunmill House, a delightful late Victorian house, tastefully restored throughout with Laura Ashley furnishings to enhance the original architectural features. Offering a choice of 9 delightful bedrooms, some with en-suite facilities. Ideally situated just outside the mediaeval walls & a 10 minute walk to all the historic attractions of the city. Complimentary tea & coffee are available & special diets can be catered for by arrangement.	£14.00	Y	N	N
Donald Nixon **The Abbingdon** **60 Bootham Cresent** **Bootham** **York YO3 7AH** Tel: (0904) 621761 **Open: ALL YEAR** **Map Ref No. 31**	Nearest Road: A.1237 , A.19 Friendly service & all the comforts expected of a small hotel will be found at The Abbingdon. Beautifully appointed throughout, the house offers a choice of 9 rooms, most with en-suite bathroom facilities. Remote control T.V., hair dryers & courtesy trays. A hearty English or Continental breakfast is served. Residents' lounge. Within easy walking distance of the Minster. If driving, take the outer ring road onto the A.1237 onto the A.19.	£15.00	Y	N	N
Diana Calder **The Dower House** **143 Main Street, Fulford** **York YO1 4PP** Tel: (0904) 633508 **Open: ALL YEAR** **Map Ref No. 31**	Nearest Road: On A.19, A.64 This lovely converted Georgian farmhouse stands on the A.19 in the attractive village of Fulford, just 2 miles south of York city centre. Each of the 3 bedrooms has a private bathroom & tea/coffee making facilities. Whenever weather permits, breakfast is served in the pretty enclosed garden at the rear. A convenient bus service reaches the sights & museums of the city in 7 minutes.	£28.00	Y	Y	Y
Joy & Peter Cox **The Hazelwood** **24/25 Portland Street** **Gillygate** **York YO3 7EH** Tel: (0904) 626548 Fax 0904 628032 **OpenALL YEAR (Excl. Xmas)** **Map Ref No. 31**	Nearest Road: A.19 The Hazelwood is a city-centre town house built in 1862, offering guests warm & attractive accommodation in 16 rooms, many with en-suite facilities, all with radio, colour T.V. & tea/coffee making facilities.. Personal attention is paramount here serving to complement your visit to this lovely city. Ideally situated to explore the reality of York's history: only 4 minutes from the Minster. Convenient for touring this beautiful region.	£16.65 CREDIT CARD VISA M'CARD	Y	N	N

Fodors

Curzon Lodge. York.

Yorkshire

		per person minimum £	children taken	evening meals	animals taken
C. & R. Gramellini **Holmwood House** **Hotel** **114 Holgate Road** **York YO2 4BB** **Tel: (0904) 626183** **Fax 0904 670899** **Open: ALL YEAR** **Map Ref No. 31**	Nearest Road: A.59, A.64 The conversion of 2 listed early-Victorian town houses has created an elegant hotel, offering guests a feeling of home with a touch of luxury. All rooms, which have en-suite facilities, are different both in size & decoration, & there are now 2 honeymoon rooms, 1 with 4 poster bed, a suite on the ground floor with spa bathroom & a guest sitting room with open fire & bar. A large proportion of rooms are set aside for non-smokers. As always, the aim is to offer guests a magic mix of friendliness & professionalism.	£25.00 *see PHOTO over* CREDIT CARD VISA M'CARD	Y	Y	Y
Mrs Dorothy Moverley **The Hermitage** **Crayke** **York** **YO6 4TB** **Tel: (0347) 21635** **Open: JAN - NOV** **Map Ref No. 33**	Nearest Road: A.19 Set in a large garden on the edge of the picturesque village of Crayke with panoramic views of the Howardian Hills. The Hermitage, an attractive farmhouse, offers accommodation in 2 comfortable & attractively furnished rooms, 1 en-suite. Guests may relax in the pleasant sitting room with colour T.V. & log fires in season. Delicious breakfasts served in the conservatory. A good base for York, the Moors & the Dales; with a warm & friendly host.	£18.00	Y	N	N
Rachel Ritchie **The Old Rectory** **Thornmanby** **Easingwold** **York YO6 3NN** **Tel: (0845) 401417** **Open: ALL YEAR** **Map Ref No. 35**	Nearest Road: A.19 Thormanby is a small village between Easingwood & Thirsk. The Old Rectory built in 1737 retains many of its original features & is furnished with antiques. 3 spacious bedrooms with modern amenities, 1 has a four-poster bed. Charming lounge with colour T.V. & open fire. Large mature garden available. Delightful inns & restaurants nearby. Situated in James Herriot country, convenient for visiting the Dales, Moors, York & historic abbeys & houses.	£14.00	Y	N	Y
Kathleen Jackson **Townend Farm** **Great Ouseburn** **York** **YO5 9RG** **Tel: (0423) 330200** **Open: FEB - NOV** **Map Ref No. 36**	Nearest Road: A.1, A.59 A 300 year-old famhouse with open fires in an original inglenook fireplace, situated on an arable farm with livestock. Offering 3 well furnished & comfortable rooms with modern amenities, including tea/coffee making facilities. A lovely secluded garden available for guests to enjoy. Tasty breakfasts served using free-range eggs & freshly baked produce. Good evening meals available locally. Only a short drive from York, Castle Howard & Herriot Country.	£14.00	Y	N	Y

When booking your accommodation please mention
The Best Bed & Breakfast

Holmwood House Hotel.   York.

All the establishments mentioned in this guide
are members of the
Worldwide Bed & Breakfast Association.

If you have any comments regarding your
accommodation please send them to us
using the form at the back of the book.
We value your comments.

Scotland

Scotland

Scotland's culture & traditions, history & literature, languages & accents, its landscape & architecture, even its wildlife set it apart from the rest of Britain. Much of Scotland's history is concerned with the struggle to retain independence from England.

The Romans never conquered the Scottish tribes, but preferred to keep them at bay with Hadrian's Wall, stretching across the Border country from Tynemouth to the Solway Firth.

Time lends glamour to events, but from the massacre of Glencoe to the Highland Clearances, much of Scotland's fate has been a harsh one. Robert the Bruce did rout the English enemy at Bannockburn after scaling the heights of Edinburgh Castle to take the city, but in later years Mary, Queen of Scots was to spend much of her life imprisoned by her sister Elizabeth I of England. Bonnie Prince Charlie (Charles Edward Stuart) led the Jacobite rebellion which ended in defeat at Culloden.

These events are recorded in the folklore & songs of Scotland. The Border & Highland Gatherings & the Common Ridings are more than a chance to wear the Tartan, they are reminders of national pride.

Highland Games are held throughout the country where local & national champions compete in events like tossing the caber & in piping contests. There are sword dances & Highland flings, the speciality of young men & boys wearing the full dress tartan of their clan.

Scotland's landscape is rich in variety from the lush green lowlands to the handsome splendour of the mountainous Highlands, from the rounded hills of the Borders to the far-flung islands of the Hebrides, Orkney & Shetland where the sea is ever-present.

There are glens & beautiful lochs deep in the mountains, a spectacular coastline of high cliffs & white sandy beaches, expanses of purple heather moorland where the sparkling water in the burns runs brown with peat, & huge skies bright with cloud & gorgeous sunsets.

Argyll & The Islands

This area has ocean & sea lochs, forests & mountains, 3000 miles of coastline, about 30 inhabited islands, the warming influence of the Gulf Stream & the tallest tree in Britain (in Strone Gardens, near Loch Fyne).

Sites both historic & prehistoric are to be found in plenty. There is a hilltop fort at Dunadd, near Crinan with curious cup-&-ring carvings, & numerous ancient sites surround Kilmartin, from burial cairns to grave slabs.

Kilchurn Castle is a magnificent ruin in contrast to the opulence of Inveraray. Both are associated with the once-powerful Clan Campbell. There are remains of fortresses built by the Lords of the Isles, the proud chieftains who ruled the west after driving out the Norse invaders in the 12th century.

Oban is a small harbour town accessible by road & rail & the point of departure for many of the islands including Mull.

Tobermory. Isle of Mull.

Scotland

Mull is a peaceful island with rugged seascapes, lovely walks & villages, a miniature railway & the famous Mull Little Theatre. It is a short hop from here to the tiny island of Iona & St. Columba's Abbey, cradle of Christianity in Scotland.

Coll & Tiree have lovely beaches & fields of waving barley. The grain grown here was once supplied to the Lords of the Isles but today most goes to Islay & into the whisky. Tiree has superb windsurfing.

Jura is a wilder island famous for its red deer. The Isles of Colonsay & Oronsay are joined at low water.

Gigha, 'God's Isle', is a fertile area of gardens with rare & semitropical plants. The Island of Staffa has Fingal's Cave.

The Borders, Dumfries & Galloway

The borderland with England is a landscape of subtle colours & contours from the round foothills of the Cheviots, purple with heather, to the dark green valley of the Tweed.

The Lammermuir Hills sweep eastwards to a coastline of small harbours & the spectacular cliffs at St. Abbs Head where colonies of seabirds thrive.

The Border towns, set in fine countryside, have distinctive personalities. Hawick, Galashiels, Selkirk & Melrose all played their parts in the various Border skirmishes of this historically turbulent region & then prospered with a textile industry which survives today. They celebrate their traditions in the Common Riding ceremonies.

The years of destructive border warfare have left towers & castles throughout the country. Roxburgh was once a Royal castle & James II was killed here during a seige. Now there are only the shattered remains of the massive stone walls. Hermitage Castle is set amid wild scenery near Hawick & impressive Floors Castle stands above Kelso.

At Jedburgh the Augustine abbey is remarkably complete, & a visitors centre here tells the story of the four great Border Abbeys; Jedburgh itself, Kelso, Dryburgh & Melrose.

The lovely estate of Abbotsford where Sir Walter Scott lived & worked is near Melrose. A prolific poet & novelist, his most famous works are the Waverley novels written around 1800. His house holds many of his possessions, including a collection of armour. Scott's View is one of the best vantage points in the borderlands with a prospect of the silvery Tweed & the three distinctive summits of the Eildon Hills.

Eildon Hills.

There are many gracious stately homes. Manderston is a classical house of great luxury, & Mellerstain is the work of the Adam family. Traquair was originally a Royal hunting lodge. Its main gates were locked in 1745 after a visit from Bonnie Prince Charlie, never to be opened until a Stuart King takes the throne.

Dumfries & Galloway to the southwest is an area of rolling hills with a fine coastline.

Plants flourish in the mild air here & there are palm trees at Ardwell House & the Logan Botanic Garden.

Scotland

The gardens at Castle Kennedy have rhododendrons, azaleas & magnolias & Threave Gardens near Castle Douglas are the National Trust for Scotland's School of gardening.

The Galloway Forest Park covers a vast area of lochs & hills & has views across to offshore Ailsa Craig. At Caerlaveroch Castle, an early Renaissance building near the coast of Dumfries, there is a national nature reserve.

The first church in Scotland was built by St. Ninian at Whithorn in 400 on a site now occupied by the 13th century priory. The spread of Christianity is marked by early memorial stones like the Latinus stone at Whithorn, & the abbeys of Dundrennan, Crossraguel, Glenluce & Sweetheart, named after its founder who carried her husband's heart in a casket & is buried with it in the abbey.

At Dumfries is the poet Burns' house, his mausoleum & the Burns Heritage Centre overlooking the River Nith.

In Upper Nithsdale the Mennock Pass leads to Wanlockhead & Leadhills, once centres of the lead-mining industry. There is a fascinating museum here & the opportunity of an underground trip.

Lothian & Strathclyde

The Firth of Clyde & Glasgow in the west, & the Firth of Forth with Edinburgh in the east are both areas of rich history, tradition & culture.

Edinburgh is the capital of Scotland & amongst the most visually exciting cities in the world. The New Town is a treasure trove of inspired neo-classical architecture, & below Edinburgh Castle high on the Rock, is the Old Town, a network of courts, closes, wynds & gaunt tenements around the Royal Mile.

The Palace of Holyrood House, home of Mary, Queen of Scots for several years overlooks Holyrood Park & nearby Arthur's Seat, is a popular landmark.

The City's varied Art Galleries include The Royal Scottish Academy, The National Gallery, Portrait Gallery, Gallery of Modern Art & many other civic & private collections.

The Royal Museum of Scotland displays superb historical & scientific material. The Royal Botanic Gardens are world famous.

Cultural life in Edinburgh peaks at Festival time in August. The official Festival, the Fringe, the Book Festival, Jazz Festival & Film Festival bring together artistes of international reputation.

The gentle hills around the city

Inverary Castle.

offer many opportunities for walking. The Pentland Hills are easily reached, with the Lammermuir Hills a little further south. There are fine beaches at Gullane, Yellowcraigs, North Berwick & at Dunbar.

Tantallon Castle, a 14th century stronghold, stands on the rocky Firth of Forth, & 17th century Hopetoun House, on the outskirts of the city is only one of a number of great houses in the area.

North of Edinburgh across the Firth of Forth lies the ancient Kingdom

Scotland

of Fife. Here is St. Andrews, a pleasant town on the seafront, an old university town & Scotland's ecclesiastical capital, but famous primarily for golf.

Glasgow is the industrial & business capital of Scotland. John Betjeman called it the 'finest Victorian city in Britain' & many buildings are remarkable examples of Victorian splendour, notably the City Chambers.

Many buildings are associated with the architect Charles Rennie MacKintosh; the Glasgow School of Art is one of them. Glasgow Cathedral is a perfect example of pre-Reformation Gothic architecture.

Glasgow is Scotland's largest city with the greatest number of parks & fine Botanic Garden. It is home to both the Scottish Opera & the Scottish Ballet, & has a strong & diverse cultural tradition from theatre to jazz. Its museums include the matchless Burrell Collection, & the Kelvingrove Museum & Art Gallery, which houses one of the best civic collections of paintings in Britain, as well as reflecting the city's engineering & shipbuilding heritage.

The coastal waters of the Clyde are world famous for cruising & sailing, with many harbours & marinas. The long coastline offers many opportunities for sea-angling from Largs to Troon & Prestwick, & right around to Luce Bay on the Solway.

There are many places for birdwatching on the Estuary, whilst the Clyde Valley is famous for its garden centres & nurseries.

Paisley has a mediaeval abbey, an observatory & a museum with a fine display of the famous 'Paisley' pattern shawls.

Further south, Ayr is a large seaside resort with sandy beach, safe bathing & a racecourse. In the Ayrshire valleys there is traditional weaving & lace & bonnet making, & Sorn, in the rolling countryside boasts its 'Best Kept Village' award.

Culzean Castle is one of the finest Adam houses in Scotland & stands in spacious grounds on the Ayrshire cliffs.

Robert Burns is Scotland's best loved poet, & 'Burns night is widely celebrated. The region of Strathclyde shares with Dumfries & Galloway the title of 'Burns Country' The son of a peasant farmer, Burns lived in poverty for much of his life. The simple house where he was born is in the village of Alloway. In the town of Ayr is the Auld Kirk where he was baptised & the footbridge of 'The Brigs of Ayr' is still in use. The Tam O'Shanter Inn is now a Burns museum & retains its thatched roof & simple fittings. The Burns Trail leads on to Mauchline where Possie Nansie's Inn remains. At Tarbolton the National Trust now care for the old house where Burns founded the 'Batchelors Club' debating society.

Perthshire, Loch Lomond & The Trossachs

By a happy accident of geology, the Highland Boundary fault which separates the Highlands from the Lowlands runs through Loch Lomond, close to the Trossachs & on through Perthshire, giving rise to marvellous scenery.

In former times Highlanders & Lowlanders raided & fought here. Great castles like Stirling, Huntingtower & Doune were built to protect the routes between the two different cultures.

Stirling was once the seat of Scotland's monarchs & the great Royal castle is set high on a basalt rock. The Guildhall & the Kirk of the Holy Rude are also interesting buildings in the town, with Cambuskenneth Abbey & the Bannockburn Heritage Centre close by.

Perth 'fair city' on the River Tay,

Scotland

has excellent shops & its own repertory theatre. Close by are the Black Watch Museum at Balhousie Castle, & the Branklyn Gardens, which are superb in May & June.

Scone Palace, to the north of Perth was home to the Stone or Scone of Destiny for nearly 500 years until its removal to Westminster. 40 kings of Scotland were crowned here.

Pitlochry sits amid beautiful Highland scenery with forest & hill walks, two nearby distilleries, the famous Festival theatre, Loch Faskally & the Dam Visitor Centre & Fish Ladder.

In the Pass of Killiecrankie, a short drive away, a simple stone marks the spot where the Highlanders charged barefoot to overwhelm the redcoat soldiers of General MacKay.

Queens View.

Famous Queen's View overlooks Loch Tummel beyond Pitlochry with the graceful peak of Schiehallion completing a perfect picture.

Other lochs are picturesque too; Loch Earn, Loch Katrine & bonnie Loch Lomond itself, & they can be enjoyed from a boat on the water. Ospreys nest at the Loch of the Lowes near Dunkeld.

Mountain trails lead through Ben Lawers & the 'Arrocher Alps' beyond Loch Lomond. The Ochils & the Campsie Fells have grassy slopes for walking. Near Callander are the Bracklinn Falls, the Callander Crags & the Falls of Leny.

Wooded areas include the Queen Elizabeth Forest Park & the Black Wood of Rannoch which is a fragment of an ancient Caledonian forest. There are some very tall old trees around Killiecrankie, & the world's tallest beech hedge - 26 metres high - grows at Meikleour near Blairgowrie.

Creiff & Blairgowrie have excellent golf courses set in magnificent scenery.

The Grampians

This is spacious countryside with glacier-scarred mountains & deep glens cut through by tumbling rivers. The Grampian Highlands make for fine mountaineering & walking.

There is excellent skiing at Glenshee, & a centre at the Lecht for the less experienced, whilst the broad tops of the giant mountains are ideal for cross-country skiing. The chair-lift at Glenshee is worth a visit at any season.

The Dee, The Spey & The Don flow down to the coastal plain from the heights. Some of the world's finest trout & salmon beats are on these rivers.

Speyside is dotted with famous distilleries from Grantown-on-Spey to Aberdeen, & the unique Malt Whisky Trail can be followed.

Royal Deeside & Donside hold a number of notable castles. Balmoral is the present Royal family's holiday home, & Kildrummy is a romantic ruin in a lovely garden. Fyvie Castle has five dramatic towers & stands in peaceful parkland. nearby Haddo House, by contrast, is an elegant Georgian home.

There is a 17th century castle at Braemar, but more famous here is the Royal Highland Gathering. There are wonderful walks in the vicinity - Morrone Hill, Glen Quoich & the Linn O'Dee are just a few.

The city of Aberdeen is famed for its sparkling granite buildings, its uni-

Scotland

versity, its harbour & fish market & for North Sea Oil. It also has long sandy beaches & lovely year-round flower displays, of roses in particular.

Around the coast are fishing towns & villages. Crovie & Pennan sit below impressive cliffs. Buckie is a typical small port along the picturesque coastline of the Moray Firth.

The Auld Kirk at Cullen has fine architectural features & elegant Elgin has beautiful cathedral ruins. Pluscarden Abbey, Spynie Palace & Duffus Castle are all nearby.

Nairn has a long stretch of sandy beach & a golf course with an international reputation. Inland are Cawdor Castle & Culloden Battlefield.

Dunnottar Castle.

The Highlands & Islands

The Northern Highlands are divided from the rest of Scotland by the dramatic valley of the Great Glen. From Fort William to Inverness sea lochs, canals & the depths of Loch Ness form a chain of waterways linking both coasts.

Here are some of the wildest & most beautiful landscapes in Britain. Far Western Knoydart, the Glens of Cannich & Affric, the mysterious lochs, including Loch Morar, deeper than the North Sea, & the marvellous coastline, all are exceptional.

The glens were once the home of crofting communities, & of the clansmen who supported the Jacobite cause. The wild scenery of Glencoe is a favourite with walkers & climbers, but it has a tragic history. Its name means 'the glen of weeping' & refers to the massacre of the MacDonald clan in 1692, when the Royal troops who had been received as guests treacherously attacked their hosts at dawn.

The valleys are empty today largely as a result of the infamous Highland Clearances in the 19th century when the landowners turned the tenant crofters off the land in order to introduce the more profitable Cheviot sheep. The emigration of many Scots to the U.S.A. & the British Colonies resulted from these events.

South of Inverness lie the majestic Cairngorms. The Aviemore centre provides both summer & winter sports facilities here.

To the north of Loch Ness are the remains of the ancient Caledonian forest where red deer & stags are a common sight on the hills. Rarer are sightings of the Peregrine Falcon, the osprey, the Golden Eagle & the Scottish wildcat. Kincraig has excellent wildlife parks.

Inverness is the last large town in the north, & a natural gateway to the Highlands & to Moray, the Black Isle & the north-east.

The east coast is characterised by the Firths of Moray, Cromarty & Dornoch & by its changing scenery from gentle pastureland, wooded hillsides to sweeping coastal cliffs.

On the Black Isle, which is not a true island but has a causeway & bridge links with the mainland, Fortrose & Rosemarkie in particular have lovely beaches, caves & coastal walks. There is golf on the headland at Rosemarkie & a 13th century cathedral of rosy pink

Scotland

sandstone stands in Fortrose.

Golspie, further north is a pleasant resort with a golf course & the fairytale turrets of Dunrobin Castle nearby.

Helmsdale is at the foot of Strath Kildonan, scene of the Gold Rush of 1868, & it still attracts amateur gold prospectors.

At the western end of the Great Glen & north of Fort William, the landscape is at its most majestic. Nearby Ben Nevis is Britain's highest peak, & hills with dramatic contours - Canisp, Quinag & Cul Mor add grandeur to the skyline of Wester Ross & Sutherland. Countless hill lochs lie in the hollows of this breathtaking landscape. Otters hunt along the tideline & seals swim in the clear waters.

The railway from Fort William to Mallaig is beautiful, & runs a steam-hauled service in summer. A car ferry crosses from Mallaig to Ardvasar on Skye, whilst the more northerly connection to the Isle is at Kyle of Lochalsh.

The matchless Cuillins of Skye work their hill magic on visitors year after year. The island is a charmed landscape of mountain, sea & sky, small towns & crofting communities.

Sailings from Uig go to Harris & North Uist in the Outer Hebrides where the Gaelic culture & language remains strong. Harris is famous for its tweed cloth, & traditional knitters can be seen at work in Lewis & South Uist.

The standing stones of Callanish on Harris form the most elaborate & complete prehistoric site in Britain, & the beaches beneath the wild southern mountains are spectacular.

Returning to the mainland, Applecross is a charming coastal village reached by a fine shoreline drive or by dramatic 'Bealach na Ba' - the Pass of the Cattle - climbing to 2100 feet.

Lochinver is a small village near the Inverpolly Nature Reserve. Canisp & Suilven are nearby, as are some of the most scenic roads in Scotland, notable through Drumbeg & Inverkirkaig.

Plockton, a crofting village is famous for its colourful cottages, gardens & palm trees.

On the north coast the white sands & high rolling waves at Bettyhill are a delight. Puffins float on the winds above the cliffs at Dunnet Head where the lighthouse is open to visitors. Nearby Scrabster ferry port is the departure point for the Orkney Isles.

Orkney is one of the richest historical & archaeological sites in Britain & also a haven for thousands of seabirds.

Neolithic Scara Brae is a Stone Age village that was covered by sand in 2500 B.C. & uncovered by another storm in 1850.

The standing stones at Stenness & the Ring of Brodgar are awesome & there are many burial mounds (Maes Howe is a fine example), & brochs.

Kirkwall & Stromness are fascinating towns with busy harbours. In Kirwall, the Cathedral was built as a memorial to the gentle Earl Magnus who was put to death in the 12th century.

In Orkney & Shetland the Scandinavian influence is strong. The islands were not a part of Scotland until the 15th century when they formed part of the dowry of a Scandinavian princess.

The Norse festival of Up Helly Aa is celebrated annually & with great enthusiasm in Shetland.

Nature abounds in this mosaic of 100 islands with teeming seabird colonies, porpoises, otters & seals. Jarlshof is a remarkable site with extensive remains of Bronze Age, Viking & mediaeval settlements.

Summer nights are magical in these northern parts, where the sun is reluctant to leave the sky.

Scotland

Scotland Gazeteer

Areas of outstanding natural beauty

It would be invidious, not to say almost impossible, to choose any particular area of Scotland as having a more beautiful aspect than another - the entire country is a joy to the traveller. The Rugged Highlands, the great glens, tumbling waters, tranquil lochs - the deep countryside or the wild coastline - simply come & choose your own piece of paradise.

Historic Houses & Castles

Bowhill - Nr. Selkirk
18th-19th century - home of the Duke of Bucceleugh & Queensberry. Has an outstanding collection of pictures by Canaletto,Claude, Gainsborough, Reynolds & Leonardo da Vinci,,Superb silver, porcelain & furniture.16th & 17th century miniatures. -

Traquair House - Innerleithen
A unique & ancient house being the oldest inhabited home in Scotland. It is rich in associations with every form of political history & after Bonnie Prince Charlie passed through its main gates in 1745 no other visitor has been allowed to use them. There are treasures in the house dating from 12th century, & it has an 18th century library & a priest's room with secret stairs.

Linlithgow Palace - Linlithgow
The birthplace of Mary, Queen of Scots.

Sirling Castle - Stirling
Royal Castle.

Drumlanrigg Castle - Nr. Thornhill
17th century castle of pale pink stone - romantic & historic - wonderful art treasures including a magnificent Rembrandt & a huge silver chandelier. Beautiful garden setting.

Braemar Castle - Braemar
17th century castle of great historic interest. Has round central tower with spiral staircase giving it a fairy-tale appearance.

Drum Castle - Nr. Aberdeen
Dating in part from 13th century, it has a great square tower.

Cawdor Castle - Nairn
14th century fortress - like castle - has always been the home of the Thanes of Cawdor - background to Shakespeare's Macbeth.

Dunvegan Castle - Isle of Skye
13th century - has always been the home of the Chiefs of McLeod.

Hopetoun House - South Queensferry
Very fine example of Adam architecture & has a fine collection of pictures & furniture. Splendid landscaped grounds.

Inverary Castle - Argyll
Home of the Dukes of Argyll. 18th century - Headquarters of Clan Campbell.

Burn's Cottage - Alloway
Birthplace of Robert Burns - 1659 - thatched cottage - museum of Burns' relics.

Bachelors' Club - Tarbolton
17th century house - thatched - where Burns & friends formed their club - 1780.

Blair Castle - Blair Atholl
Home of the Duke of Atholl, 13th century Baronial mansion - collection of Jacobite relics, armour, paintings, china & many other items.

Glamis Castle - Angus
17th century remodelling in Chateau style - home of the Earl of Strathmore & Kinghorne. Very attractive castle - lovely grounds by Capability Brown.

Scone Palace - Perth
has always been associated with seat of Government of Scotland from earliest times. The Stone of Destiny was removed from the Palace in 1296 & taken to Westminster Abbey. Present palace rebuilt in early 1800's still incorporating parts of the old. Lovely gardens.

Edinburgh Castle
Fortress standing high over the town - famous for military tattoo.

Culzean Castle & Country Park - Maybole
Fine Adam house & spacious gardens perched on Ayrshire cliff.

Dunrobin Castle - Golspie
Ancient seat of the Earls & Dukes of Sutherland.

Eilean Donan Castle - Wester Ross
13th century castle, Jacobite relics.

Manderston - Duns
Great classical house with only silver staircase in the world. Stables, marble diary, formal gardens.

Scotland

Cathedrals & Churches

Dunfermline Abbey - Dunfermline
Norman remains of beautiful church.
Modern east end & tower.
Edinburgh (Church of the Holy Rood)
15th century - was divided into two in 17th
century & re-united 1938. Here Mary,
Queen of Scots was crowned.
Glasgow (St. Mungo)
12th-15th century cathedral - 19th century
interior. Central tower with spire.
Kirkwall (St. Magnus)
12th century cathedral with very
fine nave.
Falkirk Old Parish Church - Falkirk
The spotted appearance (faw) of the
church (kirk) gave the town its name. The
site of the church has veen used since 7th
century, with succesive churches built
upon it. The present church was much
rebuilt in 19th century. Interesting
historically.
St Columba's Abbey - Iona

Museums & Galleries

Agnus Folk Museum - Glamis
17th century cottages with stone slab
roofs, restored by the National Trust for
Scotland & houses a fine folk collection.
Mary, Queen of Scots' House -
Jedburgh
Life & times of the Queen along with
paintings, etc.
Andrew Carnegie Birthplace -
Dunfermline
The cottage where he was born is now
part of a museum showing his life's work.
Aberdeen Art Gallery & Museum -
Aberdeen
Sculpture, paintings, watercolours, prints
& drawings. Applied arts. Maritime
museum exhibits.
Provost Skene's House - Aberdeen
17th century house now exhibiting local
domestic life, etc.
Highland Folk Museum - Kingussie
Examples of craft work & tools - furnished
cottage with mill.
West Highland Museum - Fort William
Natural & local hsitory. Relics of
Jacobites & exhibition of the '45 Rising.
Clan Macpherson House - Newtonmore
Relics of the Clan.

Glasgow Art Gallery & Museum -
Glasgow
Archaeology, technology, local & natural
history. Old Masters, tapestries,
porcelain, glass & silver, etc. Sculpture.
Scottish National Gallery - Edinburgh
20th century collection - paintings &
sculpture - Arp, Leger, Giacometti,
Matisse, Picasso.
Modern Scottish painting.
**National Museum of Antiquities in
Scotland** - Edinburgh
Collection from Stone Age to modern
times - Relics of Celtic Church, Stuart
relics, Highland weapons, etc.
Gladstone Court - Biggar
Small indoor street of shops, a bank,
schoolroom, library, etc.
Burns' Cottage & Museum - Alloway
Relics of Robert Burns - National Poet.
Inverness Museum & Art Gallery -
Inverness
Social history, archaeology & cultural life
of the Highlands. Display of the Life of
the Clans - good Highland silver -
crafts, etc.
Kirkintilloch - Nr. Glasgow
Auld Kirk Museum. Local history,
including archaeological specimens from
the Antonine Wall (Roman). Local
industries, exhibitions, etc
Pollock House & Park - Glasgow
18th century house with collection of
paintings, etc. The park is the home of
the award-winning Burrell Collection
The foregoing are but a few of the many
museums & galleries in Scotland - further
information is always freely available from
the Tourist Information

Historic Monuments

Aberdour Castle - Aberdour
14th century fortification - part still roofed.
Balvenie Castle - Duffton
15th century castle ruins.
Cambuskenneth Abbey - Nr. Stirling
12th century abbey - seat of Bruce's
Parliament in 1326. Ruins.
Dryburgh Abbey - Dryburgh
Remains of monastery.
Loch Leven Castle - Port Glasgow
15th century ruined stronghold - once
lived in by Mary, Queen of Scots.

Scotland

Newark Castle - Port Glasgow
16th century turreted castle.
Rothesay Castle - Rothesay
13th century moated castle.
Elgin Cathedral - Elgin
13th century cathedral with fine Chapter
House - now ruins.
Rosslyn Castle - Rosslyn
14th century castle - ruins.
Tolquhon Castle - Taves
15th century tower - 16th century
mansion, now roofless.
Hagga Castle - Glasgow
16th century castle now museum
for children.
Jedburgh Abbey
Remarkably well-preserved ruins of
Augustinian priory.
Sweetheart Abbey
Cistercian Abbey founded by
Lady Dervogilla
Melrose Abbey
Red sandstone ruins of Cistercian Abbey
founded by David 1st.

Other things to see & do

Inverewe Gardens - Poolewe
Rare & Sub-tropical plants in remarkable
garden sheltered by the mountains of
Wester Ross.
Royal Botanic Gardens - Edinburgh
Founded 17th century. Plant houses,
rock gardens, arboretum, panoramic view
over the city.
Botanic Gardens - Glasgow
40 acres of extensive collection of plants.
Lochwinnoch - Strathclyde
R.S.P.B. Visitor Centre.
New Lanark
18th century industrial village restored &
nominated as World Heritage Site.
Scara Brae - Orkney
Stone Age village uncovered in the
19th century.
 Mellerstain House- Gordon
Adam house,fineinterior,paintings,
furniture,library.

Castle Stalker

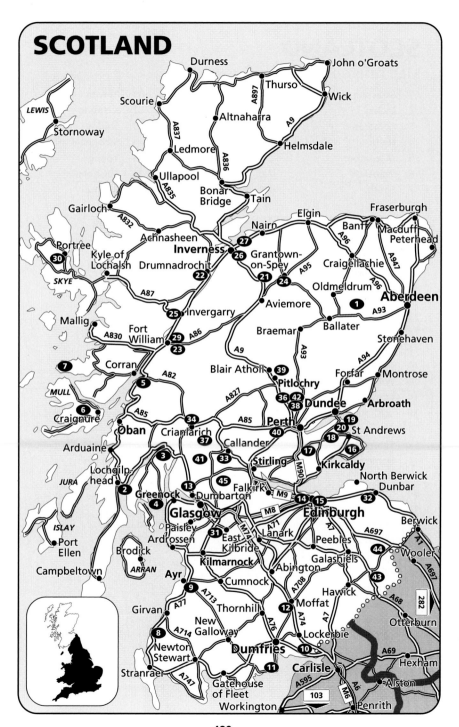

SCOTLAND

LEWIS

Durness
John o'Groats
Thurso
Scourie
A897
Wick
Stornoway
Altnaharra
A9
Ledmore
A836
Helmsdale
A837
Ullapool
A835
Bonar
Bridge
Tain
Gairloch
A832
Nairn
Elgin
Fraserburgh
Banff
Macduff
Peterhead
Achnasheen
A96
Craigellachie
A947
Portree
Inverness
27
Grantown-
on-Spey
30
Kyle of
Lochalsh
Drumnadrochit
26
A95
A96
Oldmeldrum
Aberdeen
SKYE
22
21
24
A93
A87
Aviemore
1
Invergarry
25
Ballater
Mallig
Braemar
Stonehaven
A830
Fort
William
29
A86
A93
A94
23
A9
7
Corran
5
A82
Blair Atholl
39
Forfar
Montrose
MULL
Pitlochry
A827
36 42
6
A85
38
Dundee
Arbroath
Craignure
34
A85
Perth
19
Oban
Crianlarich
37
40
20
St Andrews
Arduaine
41
33
Callander
18
3
17
16
Stirling
Lochgilp-
head
JURA
2
13
45
Falkirk
Kirkcaldy
Greenock
Dumbarton
M9
North Berwick
4
14 15
Dunbar
ISLAY
Glasgow
M8
Edinburgh
32
Port
Ellen
Paisley
31
East
Lanark
A7
Berwick
Ardrossen
Kilbride
A697
Wooler
Brodick
Peebles
44
A697
Campbeltown
ARRAN
Kilmarnock
Galashiels
A68
Ayr
Abington
43
282
9
Cumnock
A708
Girvan
A713
Thornhill
Hawick
A7
Otterburn
A77
Moffat
A69
8
A714
New
Galloway
12
A74
A68
Hexham
Newton
Stewart
A76
Lockerbie
10
A69
Stranraer
Dumfries
Carlisle
Alston
A747
11
A595
103
M6
A6
Gatehouse
of Fleet
Workington
Penrith

SCOTLAND
Map references

1	Strachan	17	Steven	31	Bewick
2	McKay	18	Grant	32	J. Young
3	Cameron	19	Scott	33	Shirley
4	Nairn	20	Black	34	McDonald
5	MacArthur	21	Rawson	34	Young
6	Wagstaff	22	MacDonald-Haig	34	Chisholm
7	Smith	23	Waugh	36	Buxton
8	Beale	24	Casey	37	Lewis
8	Crosthwaite	24	Paterson	38	Parke
9	Taylor	24	Elder	39	Collier
10	Airey	25	King	40	Niven
11	Jeffries	26	Young	41	Dalziel-Williams
12	Daniel	26	Reid	42	Pearman
13	MacDonald	26	Baillie	43	Irvine
14	Deacon	27	Pottie	44	Smith
14	Baird	29	Cairns	45	Haslam
14	Hinnrichs	30	Kemp		
14	Telfer				
14	Wilson				
14	Conway				
14	Leishman				
14	Clark				
14	Simpson				
14	Daniel				
14	Hogg				
14	Stuart				
14	Thomas				
14	Welch				
14	Gallo				
14	Vidler				
14	Wright				
14	Robins				
14	Stuart				
14	Coville				
14	Logan				
15	Dewar				
15	More Nisbett				
15	Hall				
16	MacGeachy				

Scotland
Aberdeenshire

		minimum £ per person	children taken	evening meals	animals taken
Anne & Eddie Strachan **Hazlehurst Lodge** **Ballater Road** **Aboyne** **AB34 5HY** **Tel: (03398) 86921** **Open: FEB - DEC** **Map Ref No. 01**	Nearest Road: A.93 Charming Victorian coachman's lodge to Aboyne Castle, set in wooded garden. Reflecting the owners' artistic background, accommodation is in 3 beautifully designed bedrooms, all with en-suite facilities. Anne Strachan is a fine chef with a growing reputation for imaginative cooking, using the best of Scottish produce. Her superb meals are served with friendly informality in the small licensed restaurant. Aboyne is an ideal centre for a truly relaxing stay on Royal Deeside, an area of outstanding natural beauty.	£25.00 CREDIT CARD VISA M'CARD AMEX	Y	Y	Y

Argyll

		minimum £ per person	children taken	evening meals	animals taken
Margaret & Harvey McKay **'Allt-na-Craig'** **Tarbert Road** **Ardrishaig** **PA30 8EP** **Tel: (0546) 603245** **Open: ALL YEAR (Excl. Xmas & New Year)** **Map Ref No. 02**	Nearest Road: A.83 The McKays warmly welcome all their guests to 'Allt-na-Craig', a lovely old Victorian mansion set in picturesque grounds overlooking Loch Fyne. Accommodation in 6 comfortable en-suite bed-rooms with tea/coffee makers. A guests' lounge with open fire & dining room is also available. This is a perfect base for outdoor activities, like hill-walking, fishing, golf, riding & windsurfing, or for visiting the islands. Delicious evening meals by prior arrangement.	£28.00	Y	Y	Y
Mrs Sandra Cameron **Thistle House** **St Catherines** **Cairndow** **PA25 8AZ** **Tel: (0499) 2209** **Open: APR - OCT** **Map Ref No. 03**	Nearest Road: A.815 Spacious Victorian house superbly situated in large garden looking over Loch Fyne to Inveraray and its famous castle. Five comfortable bed-rooms, three en-suite, all with tea and coffee facilities & electric blankets. Full Scottish break-fast. Several good eating places nearby for eve-ning meals. The Cowal peninsula is well located for touring Argyll and Loch Lomond areas. Only one hour from Glasgow Airport. Children over 7.	£19.00	Y	N	Y
Duncan & Carole Nairn **Abbot's Brae Hotel** **West Bay** **Dunoon** **PA23 7QJ** **Tel: (0369) 5021** **Open: MAR - OCT** **Map Ref No. 04**	Nearest Road: A.815 Elegant Victorian country house hotel set in 2-acre, secluded woodland glen with breathtaking views of the sea & hills. 7 tastefully furnished, spacious bedrooms all en-suite with colour T.V., radio, direct-dial telephone & tea/coffee facilities. Unwind with a drink by the fire in our comfortable lounge, & dine in our cosy dining room with its delicious menu & select wine list. The perfect base to explore Argyll.	£20.00 CREDIT CARD VISA M'CARD	Y	Y	Y

Scotland
Argyll

		minimum £ per person	children taken	evening meals	animals taken
Flavia MacArthur **Ardsheal Home Farm** **Kentallen** **Duror in Appin** **PA38 4BZ** **Tel: (0631) 74229** **Open: APR - OCT** **Map Ref No. 05**	Nearest Road: A.828 A charming Scottish hill farm of 1000 acres, surrounded by breathtaking scenery on the shores of Loch Linnhe, overlooking the Morvern Hills. A warm welcome is assured from the most friendly hosts, who offer 3 attractive bedrooms, comfortable & well furnished with tea/coffee making facilities, electric blankets, etc. Delicious evening meals served. Convenient for touring & sailing to the inner Isles. An idyllic holiday retreat, there is even a mile of private beach.	£13.00	Y	Y	Y
John & Eleanor Wagstaff **Red Bay Cottage** **Deargphort** **Fionnphort** **Isle of Mull PA66 6BP** **Tel: (06817) 396** **Open: ALL YEAR** **Map Ref No. 06**	Nearest Road: A really warm welcome awaits the visitor to this charming modern house offering 3 very comfortable rooms with modern facilities. Situated only 20 metres from the sea & overlooking Iona Sound & the white sandy beaches on the Isle of Iona, this surely must be the ideal base. Mr. Wagstaff offers superb food. Half board rates are excellent. A lovely home.	£14.50	Y	Y	Y
Roy & Janet Smith **'Meall Mo Chridhe'** **Kilchoan** **West Ardnamurchan** **PH36 4LH** **Tel: (09723) 238** **Open: MAR-NOV** **Map Ref No. 07**	Nearest Road: A.861 Meall Mo Chridhe ("Little Hill of my Heart") is an elegant former manse c. 1790, situated on the most westerly point of the U.K. mainland in 45 acres, on water's edge. A high standard of en-suite accommodation, cosy log fire in sitting room & character dining room. Imaginative menus include boneless quail, king scallops & venison. Janet makes her own bread, jams, mustards & chutneys. Unbeatable hospitality.	£26.50	Y	Y	Y

Ayrshire

		minimum £ per person	children taken	evening meals	animals taken
Janet & Adrian Beale **Balkissock Lodge** **Ballantrae** **KA26 0LP** **Tel: (0465) 83537** **Open: ALL YEAR** **Map Ref No. 08**	Nearest Road: A.77 Janet & Adrian have converted this lovely, rambling, 200 yr. old former shooting lodge into a luxurious & welcoming guest house. Convenient & quiet for travellers; wonderful for longer stays. All of the comfortable rooms have central heating, private facilities, colour T.V., hospitality trays & room service menus. The cuisine is of a high standard. Guests are offered interesting & imaginative menus for breakfast & dinner - at realistic prices. Local fish & game are featured & vegetarians are welcomed. An ideal spot from which tour this interesting region.	£20.00 CREDIT CARD VISA M'CARD	Y	Y	N

Brenalder Lodge.   Doonfoot.

Scotland
Ayrshire

		minimum £ per person	children taken	evening meals	animals taken
Mr & Mrs R Crosthwaite **Cosses** **Ballantrae** **KA26 0LR** **Tel: (046583) 363** **Open: ALL YEAR** **Map Ref No. 08**	Nearest Road: A.77 Delightfully converted farmhouse in a secluded valley of woodland & garden. The house contains treasures from Robin & Susan's 10 years in the Middle & Far East. The kitchen garden supplements local produce for delicious Cordon Bleu meals. This undiscovered part of Scotland offers many castles, gardens, Burn's birthplace, walking, golfing, river & loch fishing, mountain bikes & ponies. Irish ferry terminal 30 mins. drive.	£26.00	Y	Y	Y
Brenda & Bert Taylor **Brenalder Lodge** **39 Dunure Road** **Doonfoot** **KA7 4HR** **Tel: (0292) 43939** **Open: ALL YEAR** **Map Ref No. 09**	Nearest Road: A.77 Brenda & Bert Taylor welcome you to Brenalder Lodge. There are panoramic views of the Carrick Hills & overlooking the Firth of Clyde. Easy access to Prestwick airport & the world famous Turnberry & Royal Troon golf courses. The Lodge is an ideal base for touring the Burns country. All rooms have en-suite facilities, colour T.V. & tea/coffee makers. A delicious 4 course Scottish breakfast is served in the new conservatory style dining room. All day access to the Lodge & ample parking. A 4 course dinner is served at 6 p.m. if 24 hrs' notice is given.	£25.00 *see PHOTO over*	Y	Y	Y

Dumbartonshire

		minimum £ per person	children taken	evening meals	animals taken
S. & G. MacDonald **Kirkton House** **Darleith Road** **Cardross PA25 8AZ** **Tel: (0389) 841951** **Fax (0389) 841 868** **Open:ALL YEAR (Excl.** **Xmas & New Year)** **Map Ref No. 13**	Nearest Road: A.814 Loch Lomond, the Trossachs, Glasgow Airport & most Highland routes are easily reached from this 19th century converted farmhouse, which commands superb views from a tranquil rural setting above Cardross village north of the Clyde. The well appointed accommodation has an informal & unpretentious ambience. All bedrooms are en-suite, each has T.V., phone, hair-dryer & tea/coffee tray. A wide range of reading matter is available in the guest lounge, & you may wine & dine by oil lamplight.	£24.50 CREDIT CARD VISA M'CARD	Y	Y	Y

Dumfriesshire

		minimum £ per person	children taken	evening meals	animals taken
James & Mary Airey **Northfield House** **Annan** **DG12 5LL** **Tel: (0461) 202851** **Open:ALL YEAR (Excl.** **Xmas & New Year)** **Map Ref No. 10**	Nearest Road: A.75 This unique country residence with many antiques stands in 12 acres of mature gardens overlooking the River Annan with private fishing. 3 beautifully appointed en-suite bedrooms with every facility & the delightful drawing room with log fire provide a particularly peaceful & relaxing atmosphere. Enjoy outstanding cuisine in the candlelit dining room. No smoking in bedrooms & dining room. Children over 12. An ideal spot from which to tour this interesting region.	£32.00 *see PHOTO over*	N	Y	N

Northfield House. Annan.

Scotland
Dumfrieshire

		minimum £ per person	children taken	evening meals	animals taken
Mr & Mrs F.D. Jeffries **Cavens House** **Kirkbean-by-Dumfries** **DG2 8AA** **Tel: (0387) 88234** **Open: ALL YEAR** **Map Ref No. 11**	Nearest Road: A.710 Formerly an old mansion, this charming guest house offers 6 comfortable rooms with modern facilities, including private bath or shower. Tea making facilities & colour T.V. in each room. Standing in 11 acres of mature gardens & woodland, it makes a perfect base for those wishing to explore the joys of the Solway Coast with its beautiful scenery & excellent beaches. Sailing, fishing, walking, golfing & riding all local. Excellent cuisine. Friendly atmosphere & good value.	£22.00 *see PHOTO over* CREDIT CARD VISA M'CARD	Y	Y	Y
Alan & Andrea Daniel **Hartfell House Hotel** **Hartfell Crescent** **Moffat DG10 9AL** **Tel: (0683) 20153** **Open: MAR - NOV** **Map Ref No. 12**	Nearest Road: A.74 Hartfell House is a splendid Victorian manor house located in a rural setting overlooking the hills, yet only a few mins. walk from the town. A listed building known locally for its fine interior woodwork. Offering 9 spacious bedrooms, 5 with en-suite facilities. Standing in landscaped gardens of approximately 2 acres of lawns & trees providing an atmosphere of peaceful relaxation.	£18.00	Y	Y	Y

Edinburgh

		minimum £ per person	children taken	evening meals	animals taken
Mrs Helen Baird **64 Glasgow Road** **Corstorphine** **EH12 8LN** **Tel: (031) 3342610** **Open: APR-OCT** **Map Ref No. 14**	Nearest Road: M.8, M.9. A warm Scottish welcome awaits you here at this very pleasant & comfortable detached bungalow, situated only 3 miles from the city centre, excellent bus service. There are 3 lovely bedrooms all with modern amenities, all kept to a very high standard. Tea/coffee making & en-suite facilities available. Parking. An ideal base from which to explore this lovely city with its many places of historical interest.	£15.00	Y	N	N
Annie Deacon **53 Eskside West** **Musselburgh** **Edinburgh** **EH21 6RB** **Tel: (031) 6652875** **Open: ALL YEAR** **Map Ref No. 14**	Nearest Road: A.1 A warm, friendly & helpful hostess awaits you at this very pleasant stone-built terraced house located right on the banks of the River Esk. Charmingly decorated & furnished throughout to a high standard, it offers 2 delightful bedrooms with fresh flowers, radio, T.V., tea/coffee making facilities & luxurious guests' bathrooms. Annie Deacon is a professional cook & breakfast is excellent, beautifully prepared & served with grace & charm. This makes a really super base. 15 minutes by car from Holyrood Palace & 20 minutes from Edinburgh.	£12.50	Y	Y	N

Cavens House. Kirkbean-by-Dumfries.

Scotland
Edinburgh

		minimum £ per person	children taken	evening meals	animals taken
Mr & Mrs D. Hinnrichs **Allison House Hotel** **15-17 Mayfield Gardens** **Edinburgh EH9 2AX** **Tel: (031) 6678049** **Fax 031 667 5001** **Open: ALL YEAR** **Map Ref No. 14**	Nearest Road: A.7 Elegant Georgian-style listed building in a residential area on A.7 route. 24 comfortable rooms with private facilities, colour T.V., central heating, double glazing & tea/coffee making facilities & direct dial telephones. On main bus route within 1 mile of Princes Street. A warm welcome awaits all guests at the Allison. Parking available for 12 cars. An ideal spot from which to tour this historic city with its many places of interest & attractions.	£20.00 CREDIT CARD VISA M'CARD	Y	Y	Y
Mrs A.H. Telfer **'Ard-Thor'** **10 Mentone Terrace** **Newington** **Edinburgh EH9 2DG** **Tel: (031) 6671647** **Open: APR - OCT** **Map Ref No. 14**	Nearest Road: A.1, A.68, A.7, A charming, 19th century Victorian guest house only 10 minutes from the city centre, castle & Princes Street by good local bus service. The Ard-Thor is quiet & friendly & your comfort is ensured by the personal attention of your host. Guests are offered a choice of 3 rooms which are comfortable & tastefully furnished, all have T.V., tea/coffee making facilities. Queens Park & Commonwealth Pool are nearby.	£14.50	Y	N	N
Mrs Jenny Wilson **Camus House** **4 Seaview Terrace** **Edinburgh EH15 2HD** **Tel: (031) 6572003** **Open: ALL YEAR** **Map Ref No. 14**	Nearest Road: A.1 A Victorian terraced Villa overlooking the Firth of Forth, Camus House enjoys the peace of the seaside along with an excellent bus service to the city centre with its cultural, historical and leisure interests. The 3 guest rooms are comfortably furnished and have washbasins, colour T.V., radio alarms & tea/coffee facilities. A genuine and friendly welcome is assured.	£14.00	Y	N	Y
Mrs Moira Conway **Crannoch But and Ben** **467 Queensferry Road** **Edinburgh** **EH4 7ND** **Tel: (031) 3365688** **Open: ALL YEAR** **Map Ref No. 14**	Nearest Road: A.90, A.8 Warm Scottish hospitality at this very pleasant private house. The two ground-floor guest rooms have private facilities and tea/coffee making. Guest lounge has T.V., and evening tea or coffee is served whilst you digest the available information on all there is to do in Edinburgh. Private parking on site and excellent bus service to the heart of the city (just 3 miles to Princes Street). A warm & friendly welcome Is assured.	£18.00	Y	N	N
Cecilia Leishman **Ellesmere House** **11 Glengyle Terrace** **Edinburgh** **EH3 9LN** **Tel: (031) 229 4823** **Open: ALL YEAR** **Map Ref No. 14**	Nearest Road: A.702 A warm welcome is extended to all visitors at this attractive & comfortable Victorian house overlooking the park. The spacious bedrooms are decorated & furnished to a high standard & well equipped with every comfort in mind. Delicious breakfasts are served, with special diets provided by arrangement. Good local restaurants. Conveniently situated for the Castle, Princes St, The Royal Mile, shops & theatres.	£15.00	Y	N	N

Scotland
Edinburgh

		minimum £ per person	children taken	evening meals	animals taken
Sheila & Bob Clark **Galloway Guest House** **22 Dean Park Crescent** **Edinburgh** **EH4 1PH** **Tel: (031) 332 3672** **Open: ALL YEAR** **Map Ref No. 14**	Nearest Road: A.9, A.90 A warm welcome, delightful atmosphere & superb breakfasts combine to make quality the hall mark of this well known Victorian town house. Located half a mile from Princes Street with free street parking. It offers accommodation in 10 comfortable rooms, 6 en-suite, all with colour T.V. & tea/coffee makers. Visitors have the whole of Edinburgh on their doorstep from this central vantage point. 7 nights for the price of 6.	£16.00	Y	N	N
Dorothy & David Simpson **Greenside Hotel** **9 Royal Terrace** **Edinburgh** **EH7 5AB** **Tel: (031) 5570022** **Open: JAN - NOV** **Map Ref No. 14**	Nearest Road: A.1 The Greenside, a really delightful hotel, is situated in a Georgian terrace, about 15 minutes' walk from Edinburgh city centre. Offering 12 spacious, comfortable rooms, 6 with en-suite facilities, with private facilities & is fully centrally heated. A large lounge with T.V. A hearty breakfast is served between 8 & 9 a.m., & coffee is served in the lounge each evening around 9.30p.m. The Simpsons' will make you most welcome.	£22.50	Y	N	Y
Wilma & Bill Hogg **Kingsley Guest House** **30 Craigmillar Park** **Newington** **Edinburgh EH16 5PS** **Tel: (031) 6678439** **Open: ALL YEAR** **Map Ref No. 14**	Nearest Road: A.701 You are assured of a warm welcome & personal attention at this family run guest house. The pleasant Victorian terraced villa offers 6 comfortable rooms, 4 en-suite. All rooms are well equipped with colour T.V., tea/coffee making facilities & central heating. It is conveniently situated on the south side of the city centre in the residential university area. A really good base for everyone, with an excellent bus service from the door & a private car park.	£14.00 CREDIT CARD VISA M'CARD	Y	N	N
Jon & Gloria Stuart **Meadows Guest House** **17 Glengyle Terrace** **Edinburgh EH3 9LN** **Tel: (031) 2299559** **Fax 031 557 0563** **Open: ALL YEAR** **Map Ref No. 14**	Nearest Road: A.702 Quietly situated overlooking a park, Meadows is warm, comfortable & spacious with a friendly atmosphere. 7 attractive rooms, with colour T.V. & tea/coffee making facilities, some with private bathroom. Jon & Gloria will welcome you & help you with where to go, what to do & where to eat. Bookings of 3 nights or more taken in advance. Centrally located within easy reach of the Castle, Princes St., shops, theatres & restaurants.	£19.00 CREDIT CARD VISA M'CARD	Y	N	Y
Catherine & Ian Thomas **"Pearlview"** **2 Seaview Terrace** **Joppa, Portobello** **Edinburgh EH15 2HD** **Tel: (031) 6698516** **Open: ALL YEAR** **Map Ref No. 14**	Nearest Road: A.1 "Pearlview" is a Victorian terraced villa with panoramic views over the Firth of Fourth. Offering guests a choice of 3 attractive bedrooms. All with modern amenities, including radio, colour T.V. & tea/coffee making facilities. Conveniently located, frequent bus service to the city centre & many sporting facilities nearby. "Pearlview" welcomes all guests with a warm & friendly atmosphere. Free parking.	£13.50	Y	N	N

Scotland
Edinburgh

	Nearest Road	minimum £ per person	children taken	evening meals	animals taken
Len & Sue Welch **Ravensdown Guest House** **248 Ferry Road** **Edinburgh** **EH5 3AN** **Tel: (031) 5525438** **Open: ALL YEAR** **Map Ref No. 14**	Nearest Road: A.1 Built at the beginning of the 1900s, Ravensdown offers unsurpassed panoramic views of the Edinburgh skyline. Each of the 7 spacious well decorated bedrooms have modern amenities, colour T.V. & tea/coffee making facilities. A warm lounge enables guests to socialise, with bar service on the premises. Your friendly hosts are always available to offer assistance with tours, etc. A delicious breakfast gets you off to a good start each morning. Private parking available. Only 3 kilometres from the city centre.	£13.00	Y	N	N
Mr & Mrs A. Gallo **Rosedene Guest House** **4 Queen's Crescent** **Edinburgh EH9 2AZ** **Tel: (031) 6675806** **Open: MAR - NOV** **Map Ref No. 14**	Nearest Road: A.68, A.7 A fine detached Victorian villa with beautiful garden - situated in a select residential area just off the main road. Queen's Crescent lies between the A.7/701 & the A.68 main roads into the city from the south & is only one & a half miles from Princes Street. Private parking available. 8 guest bedrooms, 3 with en-suite facilities, each with tea/coffee makers.	£13.00	Y	N	N
Alan & Angela Vidler **Rowan Guest House** **13 Glenorchy Terrace** **Newington** **Edinburgh EH9 2DQ** **Tel: (031) 6672463** **Open: ALL YEAR** **Map Ref No. 14**	Nearest Road: A.7, A.701 Quietly located in one of Edinburgh's loveliest areas, Rowan House, built in 1880, retains the character of a bygone age with present day comfort. Bedrooms are tastefully furnished, some with private facilities. Complimentary tea, coffee & biscuits available. Unrestricted parking. City centre only 10 minutes by bus. Breakfast includes traditional porridge & freshly baked scones. A warm welcome & attentive service is assured.	£15.00	Y	N	N
Mr & Mrs William Wright **Salisbury Hotel** **45 Salisbury Road** **Edinburgh EH16 5AA** **Tel: (031) 6671264** **Open: ALL YEAR** **Map Ref No. 14**	Nearest Road: A.7, A.68 Enjoy real Scottish hospitality in the comfort of this Georgian house. The Wright family offer you tastefully decorated, comfortable bedrooms, all with private facilities, colour T.V. tea/coffee makers. Their home has been carefully refurbished during their 12 year ownership. Central heating throughout. Secluded garden to the rear. 10 mins. by bus to the city centre, railway station & tourist attractions. Private car park.	£18.00	Y	N	N
Mr & Mrs D.R. Robins **Sonas Guest House** **3 East Mayfield** **Edinburgh** **EH9 1SD** **Tel: (031) 6672781** **Open: ALL YEAR** **Map Ref No. 14**	Nearest Road: A.7, A.68 Guests are assured of a warm welcome & a memorable stay at Sonas (the old Gaelic word for peace & happiness). Built in 1876 & recently refurbished it now provides 7 tastefully decorated bedrooms with en-suite facilities. It retains many of its original features including a lovely sweeping staircase & ornate cornices. A delicious Scottish breakfast is served each morning. Private parking. Excellent bus service.	£17.00	Y	N	Y

Scotland
Edinburgh

	minimum £ per person	children taken	evening meals	animals taken

Gloria Stuart
Stuart House
12 East Claremont Street
Edinburgh EH7 4JP
Tel: (031) 5579030
Fax 031 5570563
Open: ALL YEAR
Map Ref No. 14

Nearest Road: A.1
Stay in this lovingly restored & beautifully decorated Georgian-style town house. Only 15 minutes' easy walk from the city centre, it is in a very quiet location with free street parking. The 6 guest bedrooms, all en-suite, have been fully & thoughtfully equipped to a very high standard for your comfort. Totally no smoking. Light suppers available. An ideal spot from which to tour this beautiful historic city with its many attractions.

£26.00 | Y | Y | N

CREDIT CARD
VISA
M'CARD

Mrs Jane Coville
Teviotdale House
53 Grange Loan
Edinburgh EH9 2ER
Tel: (031) 6674376
Fax 031 6674376
Open: MID JAN - MIDDEC
Map Ref No. 14

Nearest Road: A.7, A.702
Tastefully restored, elegant, Victorian gentleman's town house. Located in a quiet residential conservation area. Lovely original woodwork. All 7 spacious rooms have every modern facility with private or en-suite bath rooms, colour T.V., radio & tea/coffee makers. Some rooms have refrigerator. Breakfast is a banquet. Home baked scones, jams & bread. Guaranteed to delight the most travelled of guests. Parking. 10 mins. to town centre. A lovely home.

£20.00 | Y | N | Y

CREDIT CARD
VISA
M'CARD
AMEX

Ritchie & Linda Logan
The Buchan
3 Coates Gardens
Edinburgh
EH12 5LG
Tel: (031) 3371045/8047
Open: ALL YEAR
Map Ref No. 14

Nearest Road: A.8
A small, happy family-run hotel, very centrally situated, where the emphasis is on making guests comfortable. 11 pleasant rooms, all with modern amenities, 5 en-suite each with colour T.V. & tea/coffee makers. A comfortable lounge is also available. Vegetarian & special diets catered for at breakfast. Only mins. away from Princes Street, the Castle & many wonderful antique shops. A warm welcome awaits all visitors.

£18.00 | Y | N | Y

CREDIT CARD
VISA
M'CARD
AMEX

Alan & Patrea More Nisbett
The Drum
Gilmerton
Edinburgh EH17 8RX
Tel: (031) 664 7215
Fax 031 6581944
Open: ALL YEAR
Map Ref No. 15

Nearest Road: A.7, A.68,
If you have never stayed in a stately home, this is your opportunity. The Drum is Edinburgh's largest (some say finest) private house, a Grade I listed 15th century castle with extensions (& world famous plasterwork) by William Adam (1726), yet only 4 miles (15 mins.) from Princes Street & half a mile north of the Edinburgh bypass. Ghosts, snooker, tennis, croquet, games room etc., haunted State Room with 4-poster, antiques & private bathrooms.

£39.50 | Y | N | N

CREDIT CARD
VISA
M'CARD
AMEX

Mrs Helen Hall
'Woodlands'
55 Barnton Avenue
Davidsons Mains
Edinburgh EH4 6JJ
Tel: (031) 3361685
Open: ALL YEAR
Map Ref No. 15

Nearest Road: A.90
A small mansion house set in 2 acres of garden & woodlands, overlooking the Royal Burgess Golf Course. 3 miles from west end of Princes Street. All bedrooms are equipped with tea/coffee making facilities, hair dryers, electric blankets, radios & colour T.V. Whilst the city itself holds a wealth of interest, the surrounding countryside should not be overlooked. Regional Winner of the Best Bed & Breakfast Award.

£16.00 | Y | N | Y

441

Scotland
Edinburgh

		minimum £ per person	children taken	evening meals	animals taken
Mrs Mairi Dewar **Glenesk** **Delta Place** **Smeaton Grove** **Inveresk** **EH21 7TP** **Tel: (031) 6653217** **Open: MAR - OCT** **Map Ref No. 15**	Nearest Road: A.1 Quietly situated in the picturesque village of Inveresk, 'Glenesk' is a spacious detached villa. It is convenient for all the scenic beauties, beaches & sporting activities of the east coast, while only 7 miles from the centre of Edinburgh, 1 mile from the busy shopping centre of Musselburgh. All 3 bedrooms have private shower rooms or bathrooms, colour T.V. & tea/coffee making facilities. Comfortable lounge. Parking space. No signs displayed - conservation area.	£16.00	N	N	N

Fifeshire

		minimum £ per person	children taken	evening meals	animals taken
Mrs Ella MacGeachy **'The Dykes'** **69 Pittenweem Road** **Anstruther KY10 3DT** **Tel: (0333) 310537** **Open: MAR - SEPT** **Map Ref No. 16**	Nearest Road: A.917 A delightful modern bungalow offering 2 comfortable guest rooms, 1 family room, with modern facilities. Situated overlooking the golf course & the sea, this is an ideal base for families & tourists to this lovely region. There are many historic houses & golf courses locally & the walking & riding are excellent. Only 9 miles from St. Andrews. An ideal base for touring.	£14.00	Y	N	N
Donald & Isobel Steven **Ardchoille Farmhouse** **Dunshalt** **Auchtermuchty** **KY14 7EY** **Tel: (0337) 28414** **Fax 0337 28414** **Open: ALL YEAR** **Map Ref No. 17**	Nearest Road: A.91, B.936 Relax & enjoy the warm comfort, delicious "Taste of Scotland" food & excellent hospitality at Ardchoille Farmhouse. 3 en-suite twin bedded rooms, tastefully furnished with colour T.V. & tea/coffee trays with homemade butter shortbread. Large comfortable lounge, elegant dining room with fine china & crystal. Dinner is 4 Courses. Situated close to the Royal Palace of Falkland, historic home of Mary Queen of Scots. 20 mins. from St. Andrews & 1 hr. from Edinburgh. Ideal base for golfing & touring.	£20.00	Y	Y	N
Mrs May Grant **Greigston Farm** **Peat Inn** **Cupar** **KY15 5LF** **Tel: (033484) 284** **Open: MAY-OCT** **Map Ref No. 18**	Nearest Road: B.941, B.940, A Scottish Laird's house dating from the 17th-18th century, offering 3 absolutely charming, comfortable guest rooms, 2 with private facilities. Here the welcome is very warm & the cooking is superb. Standing in a sheltered position with lawns, there are marvellous beaches, wildlife reserves, superb golf at Carnoustie & Gleneagles with St. Andrews only 6 miles away. Evening meal by prior arrangement only. This is a working farm. A delightful home.	£15.00	Y	N	Y

Scotland
Fifeshire

		minimum £ per person	evening meals children taken	animals taken
Mrs Patricia Scott **Forgan House** **Newport-on-Tay** **DD6 8RB** **Tel: (0382) 542760** **Open: ALL YEAR** **Map Ref No. 19**	Nearest Road: A.92 Forgan House, the former manse of the area, is a listed Georgian country house situated in 2 acres of grounds in the tranquil & rural setting of north-east Fife. The emphasis is on quality & comfort & the spacious rooms provide panoramic views & private facilities. The surrounding area offers world famous golf courses, outstanding beaches, horse riding, bird watching & much more. A delightful home.	£18.50	Y	Y	N
Mrs Helen Black **Milton Farm** **Milton of Leuchars** **St. Andrews** **KY16 0AB** **Tel: (0334) 839281** **Open: ALL YEAR** **Map Ref No. 20**	Nearest Road: A.92, A.919, A warm & friendly welcome awaits you at Milton Farm. A spacious, tastefully modernised & peaceful Georgian farmhouse. Accommodation is in 3 stylish & elegantly furnished bedrooms with very pretty linen. A full English breakfast is served including home made bread, preserves & fresh farm eggs. Packed lunches are provided on request. Guest lounge with colour T.V. & delightful garden. Many excellent golf courses nearby. St. Andrews 5 miles.	£15.00	Y	N	N

All the establishments mentioned in this guide
are members of
The Worldwide Bed & Breakfast Association

When booking your accommodation please
mention
The Best Bed & Breakfast

443

Scotland
Inverness-shire

		per person minimum £	children taken	evening meals	animals taken
Peter & Penny Rawson **Feith Mhor Country House** **Station Road, Beananach** **Carrbridge** **PH23 3AP** **Tel: (047984) 621** **Open: ALL YEAR** **Map Ref No. 21**	Nearest Road: A.9 A warm friendly atmosphere is found at this charming 19th century house set in 1 & a half acres of delightful garden, surrounded by peaceful unspoilt countryside. Tastefully furnished & full of character. Offering 6 comfortable en-suite bedrooms with tea/coffee makers & colour T.V.. Excellent views from each room. Pleasant dining room & spacious lounge are also available. Super home cooking with fresh produce in season. Vegetarian dishes provided with prior notice.	£19.00	Y	Y	Y
Vera G. Waugh **Cabana House** **Union Road** **Fort William** **PH33 6RB** **Tel: (0397) 705991** **Open: ALL YEAR** **Map Ref No. 23**	Nearest Road: A.82 This elegant Victorian house has been renovated to an exceptional standard. 3 designer-decorated bedrooms, 2 en-suite, all with every modern amenity. T.V. lounge/dining room. Excellent home cooking, tastefully presented with true Scottish hospitality. Situated in a prime position close to Fort William town centre, with private parking & garden. An ideal holiday base for touring the spectacular Highlands & islands. Open for winter skiing holidays.	£16.00	N	N	Y
Barbara & Jim Casey **Ardconnel Guest House** **Woodlands Terrace** **Grantown-on-Spey** **PH26 3JU** **Tel: (0479) 2104** **Open: ALL YEAR** **Map Ref No. 24**	Nearest Road: A.95 A warm, friendly Scottish welcome awaits you at this beautiful Victorian country house overlooking forest, lochan & hills. Quality accommodation with 7 well-appointed bedrooms, all en-suite with colour T.V., hairdryers & welcome trays. 1 superb 4-poster bedroom. Relax in the tastefully furnished sitting room, or practise your skill on the croquet lawn. An ideal base for touring the spectacular Highlands. Children over 10 years.	£16.50	Y 🚭	Y	N
Joyce Paterson **Dunstaffnage House** **Woodside Avenue** **Grantown-on-Spey** **PH26 3JR** **Tel: (0479) 2000** **Open: ALL YEAR (Excl. Xmas & New Year)** **Map Ref No. 24**	Nearest Road: A.9, A.95 Dunstaffnage is a spacious, warm & friendly country house of character, set in an acre of garden located next to a pine forest & lake. Conveniently situated within 2 minutes' walk of both the town centre & River Spey, it offers most attractive & restful accommodation. All rooms have private facilities, tea/coffee makers, colour T.V., etc. Ideally situated for highland touring. Fishing, golf, walking or birdwatching are available nearby. A delightful base from which to explore this lovely region.	£22.50 *see PHOTO over*	Y 🚭	N	N
David & Katherine Elder **Kinross House** **Woodside Avenue** **Grantown-on-Spey** **PH26 3JR** **Tel: (0479) 2042** **Open: MAR - NOV** **Map Ref No. 24**	Nearest Road: A.9 Peacefully situated Victorian villa in delightful country town. Bedrooms, all with T.V. & tea/coffee trays, are warm restful & spacious. 4 are en-suite. Delicious traditional dinner (7 p.m.) is served by David in his MacIntosh kilt. Table licence. Sorry, no dinner on Wednesdays nor children under 7. Special spring & autumn breaks. Send for a brochure. True hospitality from your Scottish hosts.	£17.00 🚭	Y	Y	N

Dunstaffnage House.   Grantown-on-Spey.

Scotland
Inverness-shire

		Minimum £ per person	Children taken	Evening meals	Animals taken
Mr & Mrs Macdonald-Haig **Borlum Farmhouse** **Drumnadrochit** **IV3 6XN** **Tel/Fax: (04562) 358** **Open: ALL YEAR** **Map Ref No. 22**	Nearest Road: A.82 This 180 year-old farmhouse has a unique position overlooking Loch Ness. each year visitors world-wide are delighted with the fresh, tastefully furnished rooms, good food & friendly atmosphere. Borlum is an historic working hill farm, dating back to its service to Urquhart Castle in the16th century. The farm also has its own BHS approved riding centre, making it the ideal place to spend a riding holiday. 🚭 *see PHOTO over* CREDIT CARD VISA M'CARD	£15.50	Y	N	N
Barry & Lorna King **Lundieview Guest House** **By Invergarry** **PH35 4HN** **Tel: (08093) 291** **Open: ALL YEAR** **Map Ref No. 25**	Nearest Road: A.82 Lundieview is a converted gamekeeper's/crofter's cottage (But n' Ben), set amidst beautiful scenery. Situated in the heart of the Great Glen, it is ideal for touring, walking, fishing, boating, golf, etc. 6 charming bedrooms, with en-suite/private bathrooms & tea/coffee making facilities. Hearty breakfasts & delicious evening meals available. Within easy reach of Loch Ness, Fort William, the Western Isles, Inverness, Speyside & Oban. CREDIT CARD VISA M'CARD	£15.00	N	Y	Y
J. Young **Crownleigh** **6 Midmills Road** **Inverness 1V2 3NX** **Tel: (0463) 220316** **Open: ALL YEAR** **Map Ref No. 26**	Nearest Road: A.9 Situated only 5 minutes' walk from the town centre & rail/coach stations, in the old historic part of Inverness. Crownleigh offers comfortable accommodation in 5 bedrooms with tea/coffee making facilities. A full English or Continental breakfast is served. Packed lunches available on request. Guests may relax after a weary day in the cosy lounge with colour T.V. Unlimited parking. A lovely spot for touring.	£15.00	Y	N	Y
Mrs Margaret Pottie **Easter Dalziel Farm-** **house** **Dalcross** **Inverness IV1 2JL** **Tel: (0667) 462213** **Open: MAR - NOV** **Map Ref No. 27**	Nearest Road: A.96, B.9039 This Scottish farming family offer the visitor a friendly Highland welcome on their 200 acre stock/arable farm. 3 charming bedrooms are available in the delightful early Victorian farmhouse. Lounge has log fire & colour T.V. Delicious home cooking & baking served, including a choice of breakfasts. Ideal base for exploring the scenic Highlands. Local attractions are Cawdor Castle, Culloden, Fort George, Loch Ness & nearby Castle Stuart.	£15.00	Y	Y	Y
Jim & Geraldine Reid **The Old Royal Guest** **House** **10 Union Street** **Inverness IV1 1PL** **Tel: (0463) 230551** **Fax 0463 230551** **Open: JAN - NOV** **Map Ref No. 26**	Nearest Road: A.9 Personally managed by the resident proprietors Jim & Geraldine. The Old Royal is conveniently situated in the centre of town opposite the railway station. Accommodation is in 10 comfortable guest bedrooms, 5 with en-suite facilities. All have colour T.V. & tea/coffee makers. The Old Royal has "a home from home" atmosphere & provides visitors with a comfortable holiday base from which to tour the locality. CREDIT CARD VISA M'CARD	£17.50	Y	N	N

Borlum Farmhouse. Drumnadrochit.

Scotland
Inverness-shire

	minimum £ per person	children taken	evening meals	animals taken
Mrs C. Baillie **Victoria Guest House** **1 Victoria Terrace** **Inverness IV2 3QA** **Tel: (0463) 237682** **Open: APR - OCT** **Map Ref No. 26** Nearest Road: A.9 A pleasant Victorian terraced house offering 1 family, 1 double & 1 twin room, each with private showers. Situated near the site of King Duncan's Castle, it is a good base for touring the region. Clava Stones, a Druid burial ground, is well worth visiting. Delicious & hearty breakfasts served.Cots & highchairs provided for.	£15.00	Y	N	N
Mrs Margaret Cairns **Invergloy House** **Spean Bridge** **PH34 4DY** **Tel: (039781) 681** **Open: ALL YEAR** **Map Ref No. 29** Nearest Road: A.82 A really interesting Scottish coach house dating back 110 years, offering 3 charming comfortable twin bedded rooms with modern facilities; 2 bathrooms. Situated 5 miles north of the village of Spean Bridge towards Inverness, it is sign-posted on the left along a wooded drive. Guests have use of own sitting room, overlooking Loch Lochy in 50 acres of superb woodland of rhodo-dendron & azaleas. Fishing from the private beach & rowing boats, hard tennis court. Children over 12 welcome. Non-smokers only please.	£15.00	Y	Y	N

Isle of Skye

	minimum £ per person	children taken	evening meals	animals taken
Mr & Mrs D.D. Kemp **Craiglockhart Guest House** **Beaumont Crescent** **Portree IV51 9DF** **Tel: (0478) 2233** **Open: FEB - DEC** **Map Ref No. 30** Nearest Road: A.850, A.87 A house of great architectural interest - a listed building - which has been tastefully modernised, offering 9 comfortable guest rooms with modern facilities. Everyone will love the area as there is much to discover here. Beaches, fishing, swim-ming, sea trips & riding all locally available. A warm welcome awaits the visitor here. Children over 3 only. A lovely home, an ideal base from which to explore the island.	£16.00	Y	N	N

Lanarkshire

	minimum £ per person	children taken	evening meals	animals taken
Mrs Kate Bewick **Six Fathoms** **6 Polnoon Street** **Eaglesham** **Renfrewshire by** **Glasgow G76 0BH** **Tel: (03553) 2321** **Open: ALL YEAR** **Map Ref No. 31** Nearest Road: A.77, M.74, Set in the picturesque Village of Eaglesham, 10 miles from Glasgow. Guests can be sure of a warm, Scottish welcome at this delightful home, with a choice of twin room with sitting room & private facilities & 2 single rooms, 1 spacious, 1 cosy - all rooms with colour T.V. 3 pubs/restau-rants, excellent & varied, within 5 minutes' walk. Convenient for Glasgow & Prestwick Interna-tional Airports, M.74, Loch Lomond, Burns Coun-try & the Burrell Collection.	£18.50	N	N	N

Scotland
Lothian

	minimum £ per person	children taken	evening meals	animals taken
Mrs J Young **Redheugh Hotel** **Bayswell Park** **Dunbar EH42 1AE** **Tel: (0368) 62793** **Fax 0368 62793** **Open: ALL YEAR** **Map Ref No. 32**	Nearest Road: A.1 Family run licensed hotel with a quiet cliff top location & panoramic views of the Firth of Forth, yet only 5 minutes' walk from town centre & 30 mins. from Edinburgh & 16 golf courses. All bedrooms are en-suite with bath/shower, central heating, tea/coffee making facilities, 'phones, mini bar & colour T.V. Excellent restaurant where the chef specialises in meals prepared from local fresh produce. **£27.50** CREDIT CARD VISA M'CARD AMEX	N	Y	Y

Perthshire

	minimum £ per person	children taken	evening meals	animals taken
Dee & David Shirley **Highland House Hotel** **South Church Street** **Callander** **FK17 8BN** **Tel: (0877) 30269** **Open: MAR - NOV** **Map Ref No. 33**	Nearest Road: A.84 A delightful Georgian house offering 9 comfortably furnished bedrooms, some with private shower & w.c. en-suite. There is a T.V. lounge & bar with informal atmosphere where guests can relax before dining. The bar has an extensive range of malt whisky. A carefully selected wine list is offered to complement your meal. A warm welcome & personal attention from your hosts is assured. A real taste of Scotland. **£19.00** CREDIT CARD VISA M'CARD AMEX	Y	Y	Y
Jean & Jimmy Young **The Lodge House** **Crianlarich** **FK20 8RU** **Tel: (08383) 276** **Open: MAR - NOV** **Map Ref No. 34**	Nearest Road: A.82 Situated atop an acre of trees & heather, this home enjoys uninterrupted views of mountains, glens & salmon river. 6 well-appointed en-suite bedrooms (non smoking), all with tea/coffee facilities & colour T.V. (incl. satelite). Bar & separate T.V. lounge (non smoking). Experience renowned home cooking, quality wines & malt whisky bar in a relaxed, informal atmosphere. An ideal base for a touring holiday. **£24.00** CREDIT CARD VISA	Y	Y	N
Mr & Mrs S. Chisholm **Tigh Na Struith Guest House** **Crianlarich** **FK20 8RU** **Tel: (08383) 235** **Open: APR - OCT** **Map Ref No. 34**	Nearest Road: A.82 Voted the best house in Britain by the Guild of Travel Writers in 1984, this superbly situated guest house comprises 6 luxurious bedrooms, each with unrestricted views of the surrounding hills & glens. A feature remarked upon by many of the guests is the abundance of oil paintings on the walls, & the comforts of T.V. & tea/coffee making facilities in every bedroom. Personally supervised by the owners, Janica & Sandy Chisholm. Tigh na Struith gives visitors a unique opportunity to relax & enjoy rural Scotland at its best. No single occupancy. **£16.00**	Y	N	Y

Scotland
Perthshire

		minimum £ per person	children taken	evening meals	animals taken
Roger McDonald **Allt-Chaorain Country House** **Crianlarich FK20 8RU** Tel: (08383) 283 Fax 08383 238 Open: MAR-NOV Map Ref No. 34	Nearest Road: A.82 Allt-Chaorain House is a small family hotel situated in an elevated position with commanding views of Ben More & Strathfillian from the south-facing sun lounge. 9 comfortable bedrooms, all with private facilities. 'Taste of Scotland' home cooking & packed lunches available on request. The friendly & relaxing atmosphere will unwind you as you sit by the log fire after walking, fishing or touring the central Highlands.	£27.00 *see PHOTO over* CREDIT CARD VISA M'CARD	Y	Y	Y
Mrs Patricia W. Buxton **Bheinne Mhor Guest House** **Perth Road** **Birnam** **Dunkeld PH8 0DH** Tel: (0350) 727779 Open: ALL YEAR Map Ref No. 36	Nearest Road: A.9 A warm welcome awaits you at this comfortable Victorian detached house with turret & private garden, ideally situated for lovely walks in Macbeth's Birnam Woods & alongside the rivers Tay & Braan. Many places of historic interest & beauty nearby including Dunkeld Cathedral, Scottish National Trust's 'The Hermitage' & Loch of Lowes Wildlife Reserve. Boundless opportunities for anglers & golfers. Selection of 4 bedrooms, 2 with en-suite facilities, all with modern amenities, tea/coffee making.	£18.00	Y	N	N
Robert & Jean Lewis **Monachyle Mhor** **Balquhidder** **Lochearnhead** **FK19 8PQ** Tel: (08774) 622 Open: ALL YEAR Map Ref No. 37	Nearest Road: A.84 Monachyle Mhor is a small, 18th century, award-winning farmhouse/hotel set in its own 2000 acres with magnificent views over 2 lochs. The house is furnished with period furniture & fine pictures. All rooms have wonderful outlooks & all guest bedrooms are en-suite; the dining room & conservatory restaurant allow you to wine & dine on the very finest of Scottish food including game from our own estate. Walking & fishing in season.	£19.50 CREDIT CARD VISA M'CARD	N	Y	N
Mura E. Parke **Tay Farmhouse** **Meikleour** **Perth** **PH2 6EE** Tel: (0250) 883345 Open: ALL YEAR Map Ref No. 38	Nearest Road: A.93, A.9 Tay Farmhouse is situated on the Marquis of Lansdowne's estate, just off the A.984 between Dunkeld & the Beech Hedge at Meikleour. Within easy reach of Blairgowrie, Perth, Glamis Castle & Balmoral, it is in a beautiful touring area with castles, gardens, distilleries & sporting facilities in abundance. There are many opportunities for birdwatching & hill walking. Tay Farm itself is an ideal base, offering excellent comfort in 3 delightful en-suite rooms & delicious food.	£16.00	N	Y	Y
Mae & Bob Collier **Dundarave House** **Strathview Terrace** **Pitlochry** **PH16 5AT** Tel: (0796) 473109 Open: ALL YEAR Map Ref No. 39	Nearest Road: A.9 A charming Victorian house, specialising in bed & breakfast. Set in formal terraced gardens in a secluded location of approx. half an acre. Quality accommodation with 7 well-appointed bedrooms, 5 en-suite, with T.V. & tea/coffee makers. Comfortable, period lounge. A hearty Scottish breakfast served in the tastefully decorated dining room. The owners aim to provide a personal & friendly atmosphere in relaxing surroundings.	£22.00	Y	Y	Y

Allt-Chaorain House Hotel. Crianlarich.

Scotland
Perthshire

		minimum £ per person	children taken	evening meals	animals taken
Mr & Mrs I. A. Niven **Gloagburn Farm** **Tibbermore by Perth** **PH1 1QL** **Tel: (0738) 840228** **Open: ALL YEAR** **Map Ref No. 40**	Nearest Road: A.9 A charming family home with outstanding views of open countryside. Accommodation is in 2 very comfortable, attractive rooms. Delicious full English or Continental breakfasts served. An excellent base for golfing - Gleneagles is within easy reach; fishing, touring or visiting the city of Perth with its many attractions.	£15.00	Y	N	N
Morna Dalziel-Williams **Dundarroch House** **Brig O'Turk** **Trossachs-by-Callander** **FK17 8HT** **Tel: (08776) 200** **Fax 08776 200** **Open: APR - OCT** **Map Ref No. 41**	Nearest Road: A.821, A.84 Enjoy award-winning hospitality in this delightful Victorian country house, set in 14 acres, in the heart of the Trossachs. 3 lovely bedrooms, each with en-suite facilities, colour T.V., refrigerator, radio & tea/coffee maker. Residents' lounge & dining room, furnished with paintings & fine antiques, have superb views to the river & mountains. Wonderful breakfasts. Delicious dinners served in 'Byre' restaurant with quaint bar set in the grounds of Dundarrock.	£23.00	Y	Y	N

Roxburghshire

		minimum £ per person	children taken	evening meals	animals taken
Mrs C Pearman **The Old Bank House** **Brown Street** **Blairgowrie PH10 6EX** **Tel: (0250) 872902** **Open: ALL YEAR** **Map Ref No. 42**	Nearest Road: A.93 Old Bank House is Georgian elegance converted to offer 9 en-suite bedrooms. Situated at the foot of the Highlands not far from Glamis Castle & Slone Palace. Loch Tay, the Angus Glens & Royal Deeside are all within easy reach. Golf at Rosemont, ski at Glenshee or birdwatch at Osprey & Capercaille. In the evening fine food & wines served in front of roaring fires. CREDIT CARD VISA M'CARD	£19.50	Y	Y	Y
Mrs H. Irvine **'Froylehurst'** **Friars** **Jedburgh TD8 6BN** **Tel: (0835) 62477** **Fax 0835 62477** **Open: MAR - OCT** **Map Ref No. 43**	Nearest Road: A.68 An attractive late Victorian house offering 4 comfortable guest rooms & residents' lounge. H/C, tea/coffee making facilities & colour T.V. in all bedrooms. Situated in a large garden overlooking the town in a quiet residential area. Edinburgh only 1 hour by car. Golf, pony trekking, fishing & sports centre all local. An ideal base from which to explore this beautiful region.	£13.50	Y	N	N
Mrs Betty Smith **Whitehill Farm** **Nenthorn** **Kelso TD5 7RZ** **Tel: (0573) 470203** **Open:ALL YEAR (Excl. Xmas & New Year)** **Map Ref No. 44**	Nearest Road: A.6089 A comfortable & peaceful farmhouse with large garden standing on a 455-acre mixed farm, 4 miles from Kelso. 4 attractive bedrooms, 2 single & 2 twin, 1 with en-suite shower room, have superb views over rolling countryside. All have central heating & washbasins. A pleasant sitting room with log fire is available to guests. An ideal base for touring, maps available. Good home cooking. Dinner by arrangement.	£15.00	Y	Y	Y

Scotland
Stirlingshire

		per person	minimum £	children taken	evening meals	animals taken
Laird Andrew Haslam Culcreuch Castle Fintry Loch Lomond Stirling G63 0LW Tel: (036086) 555 Fax 0532 390093 Open: ALL YEAR Map Ref No. 45	Nearest Road: A.811 Retreat to 700 years of history at magical Culcreuch, ancestral fortalice and Clan Castle of the Galbraiths, home of the Barons of Culcreuch, now a country house hotel where the Laird and his family extend an hospitable welcome. Set in 1600 spectacular acres, yet only 19 miles from central Glasgow, 17 from Stirling. Eight handsome, well-appointed bedrooms with en-suite or private facilities, 4-poster bedroom supplement £8 per person per night. Elegant period-style decor and antiques, log fires, the romance of dining by candlelight. Prices £41.00 Apr & Oct, £44.00 May-Sept p.p.p.n.	£37.00	Y	Y	Y
		see PHOTO over				
		CREDIT CARD VISA M'CARD AMEX				

All the establishments mentioned in this guide
are members of
The Worldwide Bed & Breakfast Association

When booking your accommodation please
mention
The Best Bed & Breakfast

Culcreuch Castle.   Fintry.

Wales

Wales

Wales is a small country with landscapes of intense beauty. In the north are the massive mountains of the Snowdonia National Park, split by chasms & narrow passes, & bounded by quiet vales & moorland. The Lleyn peninsula & the Isle of Anglesey have lovely remote coastlines.

Forests, hills & lakeland form the scenery of Mid Wales, with the great arc of Cardigan Bay in the west.

To the south there is fertile farming land in the Vale of Glamorgan, mountains & high plateaux in the Brecon Beacons, & also the industrial valleys. The coastline forms two peninsulas, around Pembroke & the Gower.

Welsh, the oldest living language of Europe is spoken & used, most obviously in the north, & is enjoying a resurgence in the number of its speakers.

From Taliesin, the 6th century Celtic poet, to Dylan Thomas, Wales has inspired poetry & song. Every August, at the Royal National Eisteddfod, thousands gather to compete as singers, musicians & poets, or to listen & learn. In the small town of Llangollen, there is an International Music Eisteddfod for a week every July

North Wales.

North Wales is chiefly renowned for the 850 miles of the Snowdonia National Park. It is a land of mountains & lakes, rivers & waterfalls & deep glacier valleys. The scenery is justly popular with walkers & pony-trekkers, but the Snowdon Mountain Railway provides easy access to the summit of the highest mountain in the range with views over the "roof of Wales".

Within miles of this wild highland landscape is a coastline of smooth beaches & little fishing villages.

Barmouth has mountain scenery on its doorstep & miles of golden sands & estuary walks. Bangor & Llandudno are popular resort towns.

The Lleyn peninsula reaches west & is an area of great charm. Abersoch is a dinghy & windsurfing centre with safe sandy beaches. In the Middle Ages pilgrims would come to visit Bardsey, the Isle of 20,000 saints, just off Aberdaron, at the tip of the peninsula.

The Isle of Anglesey is linked to the mainland by the handsome Menai Straits Suspension Bridge. Beaumaris has a 13th century castle & many other fine buildings in its historic town centre.

Historically North Wales is a fiercely independent land where powerful local lords resisted first the Romans & later the armies of the English Kings.

The coastline is studded with 13th century castles. Dramatically sited Harlech Castle, famed in fable & song, commands the town, & wide sweep of the coastline.

The great citadel of Edward I at Caernarfon comprises the castle & the encircling town walls. In 1969 it was the scene of the investiture of His Royal Highness Prince Charles as Prince of Wales.

There are elegant stately homes like Plas Newydd in Anglesey & Eriddig House near Wrexham, but it is the variety of domestic architecture that is most charming. The timber-frame buildings of the Border country are seen at their best in historic Ruthin set in the beauti-

The Snowdon Mountain Railway.

Wales

ful Vale of Clwyd. Further west, the stone cottages of Snowdonia are built of large stones & roofed with the distinctive blue & green local slate. The low, snow-white cottages of Anglesey & the Lleyn Peninsula are typical of the "Atlantic Coast" architecture that can be found on all the western coasts of Europe. The houses are constructed of huge boulders with tiny windows & doors.

By contrast there is the marvellous fantasy of Portmeirion village. On a wooded peninsula between Harlech & Porthmadog, Sir Clough Williams Ellis created a perfect Italianate village with pastel coloured buildings, a town hall & luxury hotel.

Mid Wales

Mid Wales is farming country where people are outnumbered three to one by sheep. A flock of ewes, a lone shepherd & a Border Collie are a common sight on these green hills. Country towns like Old Radnor, Knighton & Montgomery with its castle ruin, have a timeless quality. The market towns of Rhyader, Lampeter & Dolgellau have their weekly livestock sales & annual agricultural festivals, the largest of which is the Royal Welsh Show at Builth Wells in July.

This is the background to the craft of weaving practised here for centuries. In the valley of the River Tefi & on an upper tributary of the Wye & the Irfon, there are tiny riverbank mills which produce the colourful Welsh plaid cloth.

Towards the Snowdonia National Park in the North, the land rises to the scale of true mountains. Mighty Cader Idris & the expanses of Plynlimon, once inaccessible to all but the shepherd & the mountaineer, are now popular centres for walking & pony trekking with well-signposted trails.

The line of the border with England is followed by a huge earth work of bank & ditch. This is Offa's Dyke, built by the King of Mercia around 750 A.D. to deter the Welsh from their incessant raids into his kingdom. Later the border was guarded by the castles at Hay-on-Wye, Builth Wells, Welshpool, & Chirk which date from mediaeval times.

North from Rhayader, lies the Dovey estuary & the historic town of Machynlleth. This is where Owain Glyndwr's parliament is thought to have met in 1404, & there is an exhibition about the Welsh leader in the building, believed to have been Parliament House.

Wales lost many fine religious houses during the Dissolution of the Monasteries under Henry VIII. The ruins at Cymer near Dolgellau & at Strata Florida were abbeys of the Cistercian order. However, many remote Parish Churches show evidence of the skills of mediaeval craftsmen with soaring columns & fine rood screens.

The Cambrian Coast (Cardigan Bay) has sand dunes to the north & cliffs to the south with sandy coves & miles of cliff walks.

Llangrannog Headland.

Aberystwyth is the main town of the region with two beaches & a yachting harbour, a Camera Obscura on the cliff top & some fine walks in the area. Water-skiing, windsurfing &

Wales

sailing are popular at Aberdovey, Aberaeron, New Quay, Tywyn & Barmouth & there are delightful little beaches further south at Aberporth, Tresaith or Llangrannog.

South Wales

South Wales is a region of scenic variety. The Pembrokeshire coastline has sheer cliffs, little coves & lovely beaches. Most of the area is National Park with an 80 mile foot path running along its length, passing pretty harbour villages like Solva & Broad Haven.

A great circle of Norman Castles stands guard over South Pembrokeshire, Roch, Haverfordwest, Tenby, Carew, Pembroke & Manorbier.

Tenby.

The northern headland of Saint Brides Bay is the most westerly point in the country & at the centre of a tiny village stands the Cathedral of Saint David, the Patron Saint of Wales. At Bosherton near Saint Govans Head, there is a tiny chapel hidden in a cleft in the massive limestone cliffs.

The Preseli Hills hold the vast prehistoric burial chambers of Pentre Ifan, & the same mountains provided the great blue stones used at faraway Stonehenge.

Laugharne is the village where Dylan Thomas lived & worked in what was a boat-house & is now a museum.

In the valleys, towns like Merthyr Tydfil, Ebbw Vale & Treorchy were in the forefront of the boom years of the Industrial Revolution. Now the heavy industries are fast declining & the ravages of the indiscriminate mining & belching smoke of the blast furnaces are disappearing. The famous Male Voice Choirs & the love of rugby football survives.

The Vale of Glamorgan is a rural area with pretty villages. Beyond here the land rises steeply to the high wild moorlands & hill farms of the Brecon Beacons National Park & the Black Mountains, lovely areas for walking & pony trekking.

The Wye Valley leads down to Chepstow & here set amidst the beautiful woodlands is the ruin of the Great Abbey of Tintern, founded in 1131 by the Cistercian Order.

Swansea has a strong sea-faring tradition maintained by its new Marine Quarter - marina, waterfront village, restaurants, art gallery & theatre.

Cardiff, the capital of Wales, is a pleasant city with acres of parkland, the lovely River Taff, & a great castle, as well as a new civic centre, two theatres & the ultra-modern St. David's Concert Hall. It is the home of the Welsh National Opera & here also is the National Stadium where the singing of the rugby crowd on a Saturday afternoon is a treat.

Pony Trekking

Wales

Wales

Gazeteer

Areas of Outstanding Natural Beauty
The Pembrokeshire Coast. The Brecon Beacons. Snowdonia. Gower.'

Historic Houses & Castles

Cardiff Castle - Cardiff
Built on a Roman site in the 11th century.
Caerphilly Castle - Caerphilly
13th century fortress.
Chirk Castle - Nr. Wrexham
14th century Border Castle. Lovely gardens.
Coity Castle - Coity
Mediaeval stronghold - three storied round tower.
Gwydir Castle - Nr. Lanrwst
Royal residence in past days - wonderful Tudor furnishings. Gardens with peacocks.
Penrhyn Castle - Bangor
Neo-Norman architecture 19th century - large grounds with museum & exhibitions. Victorian garden.
Picton Castle - Haverfordwest
12th century - lived in by the same family continuously. Fine gardens.
Caernarfon Castle - Caernarfon
13th century - castle of great importance to Edward I.
Conway Castle - Conwy
13th century - one of Edward I's chain of castles.
Powis Castle - Welshpool
14th century - reconstruction work in 17th century. Murals, furnishings, tapestries & paintings, terraced gardens.
Pembroke Castle - Pembroke
12th century Norman castle with huge keep & immense walls. Birthplace of Henry VII.
Plas Newydd - Isle of Anglesey
18th century Gothic style house, home of the Marquis of Anglesey. Stands on the edge of the Menai Strait looking across to the Snowdonia Range. Famous for the Rex Whistler murals.
The Tudor Merchant's House - Tenby
Built in 15th century.
Tretower Court & Castle - Crickhowell
Mediaeval - finest example in Wales.

Cathedrals & Churches

St. Asaph Cathedral
13th century - 19th century restoration. Smallest of Cathedrals in England & Wales.
Holywell (St. Winifred)
15th century well chapel & chamber - fine example.
St. Davids (St. David)
12th century Cathedral - splendid tower - oak roof to nave.
Gwent (St. Woolos)
Norman Cathedral - Gothic additions - 19th century restoration.
Abergavenny (St. Mary)
14th century church of 12th cventury Benedictine priory.
Llanengan (St. Engan)
Mediaeval church - very large with original roof & stalls 16th century tower.
Esyronen
17th century chapel, much original interior remaining.
Llangdegley (St. Tegla)
18th century Quaker meeting house - thatched roof - simple structure divided into schoolroom & meeting room.
Llandaff Cathedral (St. Peter & St. Paul)
Founded in 6th century - present building began in 12th century. Great damage suffered in bombing during war, now restored with Epstein's famous figure of Christ.

Museums & Galleries

National Museum of Wales - Cardiff
(also Turner House)
Geology, archaeology, zoology, botany, industry, & art exhibitions.
Welsh Folk Museum - St. Fagans Castle - Cardiff
13th century walls curtaining a 16th century house - now a most interesting & comprehensive folk museum.
County Museum - Carmarthen
Roman jewellery, gold, etc. Romano-British & Stone Age relics.
National Library of Wales - Aberystwyth
Records of Wales & Celtic areas. Great historical interest.
University College of Wales Gallery - Aberystwyth
Travelling exhibitions of painting & sculpture.

Wales

Newport Museum & Art Gallery - Newport
Specialist collection of English watercolours - natural history, Roman remains, etc.
Legionary Museum - Caerleon
Roman relics found on the site of legionary fortress at Risca.
Nelson Museum - Monmouth
Interesting relics of Admiral Lord Nelson & Lady Hamilton.
Bangor Art Gallery - Bangor
Exhibitions of contemporary paintings & sculpture.
Bangor Museum of Welsh Antiquities - Bangor
History of North Wales is shown. Splendid exhibits of furniture, clothing, domestic objects, etc.
Also Roman antiquities.
Narrow Gauge Railway Museum - Tywyn
Rolling stock & exhibitions of narrow gauge railways of U.K.

Museum of Childhood - Menai Bridge
Charming museum of dolls & toys & children's things.
Brecknock Museum - Brecon
Natural history, archaeology, agriculture, local history, etc.
Glynn Vivian Art Gallery & Museum - Swansea
Ceramics, old & contemporary, British paintings & drawings, sculpture, loan exhibitions.
Stone Museum - Margam
Carved stones & crosses from pre-historic times.
Plas Mawr - Conwy
A beautiful Elizabethan town mansion house in its original condition. Now holds the Royal Cambrain Academy of Art.

Historic Monuments

Rhuddlan Castle - Rhuddlan
13th century castle - interesting diamond plan.
Valle Crucis Abbey - Llangollen
13th century Cistercian Abbey Church.

Cader Idris.

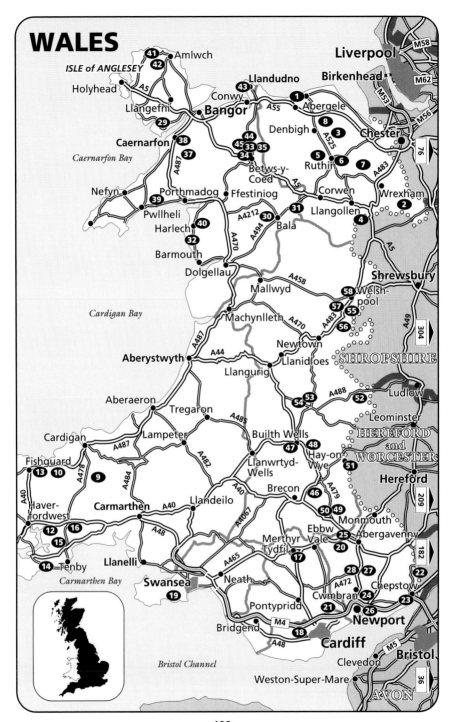

WALES

ISLE of ANGLESEY

Amlwch 41 42

Holyhead
Llangefni
Conwy
Bangor 29

A5

Liverpool M58
Birkenhead M62
Llandudno 43
Abergele 1
M53 M56

Denbigh 8 3
Chester

Caernarfon 38
Caernarfon Bay
A487 37
44 45 33 35 34
Betws-y-Coed
Ruthin 5 6 7 A483
A525

76

Nefyn
Porthmadog 39
Pwllheli 40
Harlech
Barmouth 32
Dolgellau

Ffestiniog
A4212 30 31
Bala
A494

Corwen
Llangollen 4
Wrexham 2

A5

Mallwyd
A458
Welsh-pool 58
57 55 A483 56
Machynlleth A470

Shrewsbury

A49 304

Cardigan Bay

Aberystwyth
Llangurig
Newtown
Llanidloes

A44
A485

SHROPSHIRE

Aberaeron
Tregaron
Lampeter
Cardigan A487
A482 A484
Fishguard 13 10 9

54 53 A488 52
Ludlow
Leominster

Builth Wells 47 48
Llanwrtyd-Wells
Hay-on-Wye 51

HEREFORD and WORCESTER

Hereford 209

Haver-fordwest
Carmarthen A40
Llandeilo
Brecon 46
50 49 Monmouth
Ebbw Vale 25 Abergavenny
20

12 16 15
14 Tenby
Llanelli
Carmarthen Bay
Swansea 19
Neath
A48
A465
Merthyr Tydfil 17
Pontypridd
Cwmbran 24
21 26
Newport

28 27
Chepstow 23
22

182

Bridgend
M4
18
Cardiff
A48

Clevedon
Bristol M5
Weston-Super-Mare
AVON 36

Bristol Channel

460

WALES
Map references

1	Webb	35	Pitman	47	Hammond
2	Williams-Lee	37	Pinnock	48	M. Jones
3	Evans	38	Bayles	49	Usborne
4	Pashen	39	Murray	50	Cracroft
5	J. Jones	39	Clayton	51	Roberts
6	Spencer	40	Roberts	52	Hood
7	Parry	40	Newton Davies	53	Millan
8	Roberts	41	Hirst	54	Knott
9	Vaughton	42	M. Hughes	55	Bright
10	Heard	43	Rigby	56	Richards
12	Barlow	44	Stephens	57	Marriott
13	Moore	45	Barker	58	S. Jones
14	McHugh	46	Cole		
15	Fielder				
16	Gilder				
17	Hurley				
18	Renwick				
19	Wearing				
20	Weatherill				
21	L. Price				
22	Stubbs				
23	Hunter				
24	Watkins				
25	Harris				
26	Park				
27	Bradley				
28	Armitage				
29	Roberts				
30	Cunningham				
31	Fullard				
32	Thompson				
33	Gibson				
34	Fakhri				
34	Whittingham				
34	Valadini				
34	Howard				
34	Ratcliffe				
34	Muskus				

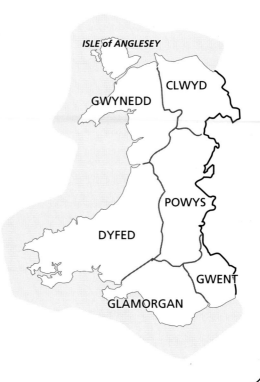

ISLE of ANGLESEY

GWYNEDD

CLWYD

POWYS

DYFED

GWENT

GLAMORGAN

Wales
Clwyd

		minimum £ per person	children taken	evening meals	animals taken
Mrs Gwyneth Webb **Plas Newydd Farm** **Llanddulas** **Abergele LL22 8HH** **Tel: (0492) 516038** **Open: APR - OCT** **Map Ref No. 01**	Nearest Road: A.55 A lovely 400 year-old Welsh farmhouse retaining its original character including lots of oak beams. Accommodation is in 2 pleasant bedrooms with modern amenities. An ideal base for touring as Snowdonia, Conway & Anglesey are within easy reach; also conveniently placed for the local beaches & outdoor activities.	£14.50	Y	N	N
Francis Williams-Lee & **Cedric B Sumner** **Buck Farm** **Hanmer** **SY14 7LX** **Tel: (094874) 339** **Open: ALL YEAR** **Map Ref No. 02**	Nearest Road: On A.525 between Wrexham/Whitchurch Warm hospitality in an unspoilt, half timbered 16th century farmhouse. A 1 acre woodland lovely with changing drifts of wildflowers from Spring to mid-Summer. A wild garden alive with butterflies. Ideal for touring North Wales, Cheshire, Shropshire & Staffordshire. Excellent wholefood country cooking using fresh local produce, organic when possible. Wholemeal breads, granola, vegetable soups (no M.S.G.). Vegetarian, vegan, meat meals. Special diets on request.	£16.00	Y	Y	N
Neil & Susan Evans **The Old Mill Guest House** **Melin-y-Wern** **Denbigh Road, Nannerch** **Mold CH7 5RH** **Tel: (0352) 741542** **Open: MAR-JAN** **Map Ref No. 03**	Nearest Road: A.541 This family owned private hotel features en-suite bedrooms equipped & furnished to excellent standards. Delightfully located within a complex of restored watermill buildings. Extensive table d'hote evening menu & wine list. Central for the walled Roman cathedral city of Chester, stately homes & gardens, Welsh castles & mountains, coast & golfing. Landscaped gardens. Fire certificate. A delightful home.	£22.50 **CREDIT CARD** VISA M'CARD AMEX	Y	Y	Y
Lorraine Pashen **Bron Heulog** **Waterfall Road** **Llanrhaeadr-Y-M** **Oswestry SY10 0JX** **Tel: (0691) 780521** **Open: ALL YEAR** **Map Ref No. 04**	Nearest Road: A.5, B.4396 Bron Heulog is a large Victorian home with a mixture of antique & traditional furnishings, & where good food & a warm welcome awaits. Although not en-suite, the 3 bedrooms are very comfortable, with washbasins, radio, colour T.V. & tea/coffee facilities. Guests may play the grand piano or relax with one of the many books. Area of Natural Beauty with Pistyll Rhaeadr waterfall; ideal for walking, birdwatching, or just getting away from it all!	£13.50	Y	Y	Y
Beryl J. Jones **Bryn Awel Farm** **Brynawel** **Bontuchel** **Ruthin** **LL15 2DE** **Tel: (0824) 702481** **OpenALL YEAR (Excl. Xmas)** **Map Ref No. 05**	Nearest Road: A.5105, A.5 This 35-acre working farm is situated in the beautiful hamlet of Bontuchel, where you can relax in perfect peace & tranquility & enjoy a wealth of wonderful walks, wild flowers & wildlife. Beryl has many cooking awards to her credit & can oblige most requests for special diets. Tea making facilities in all rooms. Heating throughout. A warm welcome & good food is top priority at this delightful farmhouse. Ideal for a relaxing holiday or for touring.	£15.00	Y	Y	N

Wales
Clwyd & Dyfed

		minimum £ per person	children taken	evening meals	animals taken
Mrs Jen Spencer **Eyarth Station** **Llanfair D.C.** **Ruthin** **LL15 2EE** **Tel: (0824) 703643** **Open: ALL YEAR** **Map Ref No. 06**	Nearest Road: A.525 A warm & friendly reception awaits the visitor to Eyarth Station. A super converted former railway station located in the beautiful countryside of the Vale of Clwyd. 6 bedrooms, all with private shower. Comfortable colour T.V. lounge & guests are welcome to use the garden, sun patio & outdoor heated pool. Conveniently located for the many historic towns in the region including Conwy, Caernarfon & Ruthin Castles with mediaeval banquet 2 minutes drive. The Roman town of Chester is also within driving distance. 1987 winner of Best Bed & Breakfast Award.	£19.00 *see PHOTO over* CREDIT CARD VISA M'CARD	Y	Y	Y
Mrs E A Parry **Llainwen Ucha** **Pentre Celyn** **Ruthin** **LL15 2HL** **Tel: (097888) 253** **Open: ALL YEAR** **Map Ref No. 07**	Nearest Road: A.525 A working farm set in 130 acres overlooking the beautiful Vale of Clwyd. Offering 2 pleasantly decorated rooms with modern amenities, accommodating up to 5 persons. All rooms are centrally heated. Good home cooking made with fresh local produce. Offa's Dyke, fishing & pony riding nearby. Conveniently situated for visiting Chester, Llangollen, Snowdonia & the Coast. A home from home atmosphere with a warm & friendly welcome is assured.	£12.00	Y	Y	N
Anwen Roberts **Bach-y-Graig Farm** **Bach-y-Graig** **Tremeirchion** **St. Asaph** **LL17 0UH** **Tel: (0745) 730627** **Open: ALL YEAR** **Map Ref No. 08**	Nearest Road: A.55, A.541 A super 16th century farmhouse nestling at the foot of the Clwydian range with undisturbed views of the surrounding countryside. Walk a 40 acre mediaeval woodland trail on the farm where the royal Black Prince once hunted, & enjoy the wealth of rare plants & flowers. All rooms ensuite/private, with tea/coffee, radio alarms & colour T.V. A large lounge with colour T.V., inglenook with roaring log fires during colder part of season, central heating. Central for Chester, Snowdonia & coastal resorts.	£16.00 🚭	Y	N	N

Dyfed

Mrs C.M. Vaughton **Awel-Y-Grug** **Boncath** **SA37 0JP** **Tel: (0239) 841260** **Open: ALL YEAR** **Map Ref No. 09**	Nearest Road: B.4332 Awel-Y-Grug is a small family-run guest house where guests are welcome to a relaxed homely atmosphere. Good & plentiful home-cooked food is served using home grown fruit & vegetables when available & vegetarian meals are a speciality. Licensed. 4 bedrooms, 2 with en-suite facilities. Dining room, T.V. lounge with log fires, games room & a large & pleasant garden. Children welcome. Laundry facilities & cots & highchairs available. Credit cards accepted.	£15.00 CREDIT CARD VISA M'CARD	Y	Y	Y

Eyarth Station.   Llanfair D.C.

		minimum £ per person	children taken	evening meals	animals taken
Peter & Jane Heard **Tregynon Country** **Farmhouse Hotel** **Gwaun Valley** **Fishguard SA65 9TU** **Tel: (0239) 820531** **Fax 0239 820808** **Open: ALL YEAR** **Map Ref No. 10**	Nearest Road: B.4313, B.4329 A traditional beamed, award winning 16th century family-run farmhouse, standing in acres of grounds by ancient oak woodlands, overlooking the glorious Gwaun Valley in the Pembrokeshire Coast National Park. It is unique & of great natural beauty & still quite unspoiled. Accommodation is in 8 rooms, all en-suite & on the ground floor. Traditional & special diets, wholefood & vegetarian specialities, using fresh local produce when possible. A good range of wine is also available. Own trout ponds, 200ft waterfall & Iron Age fort, abundant wildlife. CREDIT CARD VISA M'CARD	£22.00	Y	Y	N
P. Barlow **Rosehill Farm** **Slebech** **Haverfordwest SA62 4AY** **Tel: (0437) 751204** **Fax 0437 751204** **Open: ALL YEAR** **Map Ref No. 12**	Nearest Road: A.40 Large Georgian farmhouse within the Pembrokeshire National Park. Formerly the home farm for the Slebech Estate. Beautifully situated in the centre of its own land with extensive views over surrounding countryside & woodland. Fully modernised to a very high standard whilst retaining its character & comfortably furnished with antiques. Cleddau Estuary & Picton Castle 2 minutes' drive. Coast 20 mins. Fishguard & Pembroke ferries 35 minutes.	£15.00	Y	N	Y
Mr & Mrs M.J. Moore **Hotel Plas Glyn-y-Mel** **Lower Fishguard** **SA65 9LY** **Tel: (0348) 872296** **Open: ALL YEAR** **Map Ref No. 13**	Nearest Road: A.40, A.487. An imposing Georgian country house hotel, splendidly located in the shelter of the Gwann Valley, 2 mins from Lower Fishguard Harbour. In 20 acres of mature wooded grounds with beautiful views across the garden & meadows to the River Gwann. Elegant accommodation is furnished with family antiques, each bedroom has private bathroom & tea/coffee maker. Magnificent indoor heated swimming pool . Chef/proprietor takes great pride in his excellent cuisine.	£33.00	Y	Y	Y
Mrs Jill McHugh **The Old Vicarage** **Manorbier** **SA70 7TN** **Tel: (0834) 871452** **Open: ALL YEAR** **Map Ref No. 14**	Nearest Road: A.4139 Overlooking the coastal villages of Manorbier with its 11th century castle. The Old Vicarage is set in its own mature grounds of 2 & a half acres & offers the perfect stepping off point for exploring the magnificent scenery of Pembrokeshire. There are 2 spacious bedrooms with views across Barafundle Bay. The renowned Pembrokeshire coastal path passes through the village. A non-smoking establishment. Beaches a 5 mins. walk.	£17.50	Y	N	N
L.E. & J.M. Fielder **Old Stable Cottage** **Carew** **Tenby** **SA70 8SL** **Tel: (0646) 651889** **Open: APR - OCT** **Map Ref No. 15**	Nearest Road: A.477 At one time a carthouse and stables for Carew Castle, Old Stable Cottage (Grade II listed), with its inglenook fireplace and original bread oven, is full of charm. The stable is now a games room, and a spiral staircase leads to the 3 well-appointed, en-suite bedrooms. Delicious food is prepared in the farmhouse kitchen with Aga cooker. A conservatory overlooks the walled garden and barbecue area. Children over 5 please.	£22.50	Y	Y	N

Wales
Dyfed & Glamorgan

		per person minimum £	children taken	evening meals	animals taken
P.G. & M.J. Gilder **Llangwm House** **Whitland** **SA34 0RB** **Tel: (0994) 240621** **Open: ALL YEAR** **Map Ref No. 16**	Nearest Road: A.40 Llangwm House is a large, fully modernised farmhouse with panoramic views, ideally situated for the Pembrokeshire Coast with its beautiful beaches, walks & abundant wildlife. The spacious bedrooms, 2 of which have private bathrooms, are tastefully furnished with comfort in mind. All have tea/coffee making facilities. Guests are assured of a welcome & may find it interesting to watch Peter train his sheepdogs. Children over 5. Evening meals by prior arrangement.	£15.00	Y	Y	Y

Glamorgan

		per person minimum £	children taken	evening meals	animals taken
Michael & Kathleen Hurley **Tregenna Hotel** **Park Terrace** **Merthyr Tydfil CF47 8RF** **Tel:(0685) 723627/82055** **Fax 0685 721951** **Open: ALL YEAR** **Map Ref No. 17**	Nearest Road: A.470, M.4 Family-run hotel with high degree of comfort & class. 23 bedrooms with bathroom, 7 of which are designated for tourists & family use at special rates (50% reduction for children sharing). Telephone, tea/coffee service tray, colour T.V. in all rooms. Lunch, afternoon tea & dinner served 7 days a week. Brecon Beacons National Park 8 minutes drive. 45 minutes Cardiff/Wales Airport. Two & a quarter hours London Heathrow Airport.	£23.00 CREDIT CARD VISA M'CARD AMEX	Y	Y	Y
Paul & Monica Renwick **Sant-Y-Nyll House** **St. Brides-Super-Ely** **CF5 6EZ** **Tel: (0446) 760209** **Open: ALL YEAR** **Map Ref No. 18**	Nearest Road: M.4 You can be assured of a friendly welcome to Sant-Y-Nyll, a charming Georgian country residence in its own extensive grounds with spectacular views over the Vale of Glamorgan. 6 guest rooms with modern facilities, T.V., tea/coffee making. Comfortable, warm & relaxing. Licensed. Children welcome. Cardiff just 7 miles. St. Fagans Welsh Folk Museum 2 miles. Paul & Monica look forward to meeting you.	£20.00 CREDIT CARD AMEX	Y	N	Y
Bruce & Heather Wearing **Parkway Hotel** **253 Gower Road** **Sketty** **Swansea SA2 9JL** **Tel: (0792) 201632** **Fax 0792 201839** **Open: ALL YEAR** **Map Ref No. 19**	Nearest Road: A.4118 A small mansion-style house in its own grounds offering 15 pleasant, comfortable en-suite rooms with tea making facilities. This is an ideal base for touring the lovely Gower Peninsula & Swansea Bay. The city centre is easily accessible & is full of interest, as are the many historic sites which are found in this region. Personal service & warm welcome await all visitors in a friendly & relaxed atmosphere. A delightful home.	£22.50 CREDIT CARD VISA M'CARD AMEX	Y	Y	Y

466

Wales
Gwent

		minimum £ per person	children taken	evening meals	animals taken
Mr & Mrs Bruce Weatherill **Llanwenarth House** **Govilon** **Abergavenny** **NP7 9SF** **Tel: (0873) 830289** **Open: MAR - Mid JAN** **Map Ref No. 20**	Nearest Road: A.465 A truly delightful 16th century manor house, standing in its own beautiful grounds & surrounded by the tranquil scenic hills of the Brecon Beacons National Park. Elegantly furnished, tastefully decorated & with superb views, this house is a real pleasure to visit. Dinner prepared by Amanda, a Cordon Bleu cook, is a delight. It is served by candlelight in the lovely dining room. Accommodation is in 5 rooms, all with en-suite facilities. Fishing, golf, climbing, walking & shooting nearby. Children over 10 yrs please.	£34.00	Y	Y	Y
Mrs Dinah L. Price **'Great House'** **Isca Road** **Old Village** **Caerleon** **NP6 1QG** **Tel: (0633) 420216/312** **Open: ALL YEAR** **Map Ref No. 21**	Nearest Road: M.4 ex.25 'Great House' is an attractive 16th century home located on the banks of the River Usk. Retaining much of its original character, including beams & inglenook fireplaces, this delightful home offers 4 very pretty rooms with T.V. & tea/coffee making facilites. An attractive T.V. lounge & pretty garden are also available for guests' use. Within easy reach are riding, golf, fishing & forest trails. Roman amphitheatre, museums & the ancient village of Caerleon. Ideal as a stop-over for those on the way through Wales.	£18.00	Y	N	N
Dereck & Vickie Stubbs **Parva Farmhouse Hotel** **& Restaurant** **Tintern Parva, Tintern** **Chepstow NP6 6SQ** **Tel: (0291) 689411** **Open: ALL YEAR** **Map Ref No. 22**	Nearest Road: A.466, M.4, M.5 A delightful 17th century stone farmhouse situated 50 yards from the River Wye. The quaint bedrooms with their designer fabrics are gorgeous, some offering breathtaking views over the River Wye & woodland. The beamed lounge with log fires, leather Chesterfields & 'Honesty Bar' is a tranquil haven in which to unwind. Mouth-watering dishes served in the intimate, candlelit Inglenook Restaurant reflects the owner's love of cooking. An ideal spot for touring.	£24.00 *see PHOTO over* CREDIT CARD VISA M'CARD	Y	Y	Y
Mrs Julia Hunter **Spring Farm** **Brockweir** **Chepstow** **NP6 7NU** **Tel: (0291) 689439** **Open: MAR-NOV** **Map Ref No. 23**	Nearest Road: A.466 Spring Farm is located in an area of outstanding beauty with breathtaking views across the Wye Valley. This lovely old stone farmhouse stands in an idyllic, peaceful setting, nestled into the hillside overlooking the River Wye. Beautifully furnished, with 3 lovely bedrooms, 2 with en-suite bathrooms. In addition to the traditional English breakfast a 4-course dinner is available. Close to Tintern Abbey & many Welsh border castles. Riding, fishing, pony trekking & golf nearby.	£26.00	N	Y	N
Beryl Watkins **The Glebe** **Croes-Y-Ceiliog** **Cwmbran NP44 2DE** **Tel: (063349) 251/242** **Open: ALL YEAR** **Map Ref No. 24**	Nearest Road: A.4042, M.4 A friendly & helpful host awaits you at Glebe Farm. A spacious, modern farmhouse overlooking a lovely corner of rural Wales where the family have farmed for generations. Offering 3 attractive & comfortable rooms with modern amenities. A substantial breakfast is served in the morning & in the evening good pub fare can be found a pleasant walk away. Ideal for a relaxing break. Convenient for the M.4./M.5.	£15.00	Y	N	N

Parva Farmhouse and Restaurant. Tintern.

Wales
Gwent

Mr & Mrs B. L. Harris **The Wenallt** **Abergavenny** **Gilwern NP7 0HP** **Tel: (0873) 830694** **Open: ALL YEAR** **Map Ref No. 25**	Nearest Road: A.465 A 16th century Welsh longhouse set in 50 acres of farmland in the Brecon Beacons National Park commanding magnificent views over the Usk Valley. Retaining all its old charm with oak beams, inglenook fireplace, yet offering a high standard of accommodation with en-suite bedrooms, good food & a warm welcome. An ideal base from which to see & explore Wales & the surrounding areas. Licensed.	£15.00	Y	Y	Y
Mrs C.T. Park **Brick House Country** **Guest House** **Redwick** **Newport NP6 3DX** **Tel: (0633) 880230** **Open: ALL YEAR** **Map Ref No. 26**	Nearest Road: M.4 Brick House Farm is a listed Grade II Georgian farmhouse dating from about 1765, but with up-to-date conveniences. All double bedrooms have en-suite bathroom& are very comfortable. A pleasant T.V. lounge, dinning room & bar. Full central heating. There is a delightful garden where guests may take cream teas, weather permitting. Brick House is ideally placed for touring South Wales & the Wye Valley, or as a stopping-off point just over the Severn Bridge.	£19.50	Y	Y	N
Ann Bradley **Pentwyn Farm** **Little Mill** **Pontypool** **NP4 0HQ** **Tel: (049528) 249** **Open: FEB-NOV** **Map Ref No. 27**	Nearest Road: A.472 Pentwyn is a 120 acre farm situated on the edge of the Brecon Beacons National Park, where good food and hospitality are of prime importance. The 16th century pink-washed longhouse has the comforts of the 20th century without losing its charm. Large garden with swimming pool. There are 4 pretty bedrooms (2 en-suite), with tea making facilities. Attractive sitting room with open fire, piano & books. Restaurant licence. Rough shooting available.	£13.00	Y	Y	N
Mrs S.D. Armitage **Ty'r-Ywen Farm** **Lasgarn Lane** **Mamhilad via Trevethin** **Pontypool NP4 8TT** **Tel: (049528) 200** **Fax 049528 200** **Open: ALL YEAR** **Map Ref No. 28**	Nearest Road: A.472, M.4 A remote & secluded 16th century Welsh longhouse high on the Gwent Ridgeway in the Brecon Beacons National Park with 30 mile views down the Usk Valley. Spacious bedrooms including 1 twin & 2 four-poster rooms. One delightful four-poster room with jacuzzi. All have colour T.V.'s, radio & luxury en-suite bathrooms. An ideal centre for walking. Dinner available with advance notice only. A lovely home where a warm welcome is assured. 'Phone for directions. CREDIT CARD VISA M'CARD	£16.00	N	Y	Y

When booking your accommodation please mention
The Best Bed & Breakfast

Wales
Gwynedd

		per person minimum £	children taken	evening meals	animals taken
Mr & Mrs B Cunningham **Abercelyn** **Llanycil** **Bala LL23 7YF** **Tel: (0678) 521109** **Open: MAR - NOV** **Map Ref No. 30**	Nearest Road: A.494 1724-built Welsh country house standing in attractive grounds within Snowdonia National Park. The 3 bedrooms are bright & spacious, with views over the lake. A relaxing sitting room warmed by open log fire, & dining room overlooking the mountain stream splashing through the garden. Charming stone cottage annexe for extra privacy - or families. Traditional cooking, home-baked bread & spring water.	£16.50	Y	N	N
Richard & Beryl Fullard **Melin Meloch** **Llanfor** **Bala LL23 7DP** **Tel: (0678) 520101** **Open: ALL YEAR** **Map Ref No. 31**	Nearest Road: A.494 Close to the River Dee, just outside Bala, stands this interesting old water mill & miller's house. Set in 3 acres of lovely landscaped watergardens with trout stream, fish from which may be served at the table for dinner. Offering accommodation in 3 pretty rooms, all with en-suite facilities. Relax in the hospitable atmosphere of very comfortable spacious lounges filled with interesting bygones. Self-contained suites available.	£15.00	Y	Y	Y
Paula & Peter Thompson **Llwyndu Farmhouse** **Llwyndu** **Llanaber** **Barmouth LL42 1RR** **Tel: (0341) 280144** **OpenALL YEAR (Excl. Xmas)** **Map Ref No. 32**	Nearest Road: A.496 Enjoy a relaxed, friendly stay in this 17th century farmhouse & converted granary. Wonderfully situated over Cardigan Bay. All 7 bedrooms have great charm & are en-suite, some with T.V.. Savour imaginative dishes, including vegetarian, in a superb atmosphere of oak beams & inglenooks. Dinner by candlelight. Licensed. Log fires in Winter. Children very welcome. Beaches nearby. Peacefully secluded yet convenient for Barmouth. A beautiful region to explore.	£19.00	Y	Y	Y
Michael & Anne Gibson **Bron Eirian Guest House** **Town Hill** **Llanrwst** **Betws-y-Coed LL26 0NF** **Tel: (0492) 641741** **Open: ALL YEAR** **Map Ref No. 33**	Nearest Road: A.5, A.55 A lovely Victorian house in a peaceful spot, set on an hill overlooking the market town of Llanrwst, the Conway Valley & the mountains of Snowdonia. 3 en-suite guest rooms, with colour T.V., tea trays, hairdryers & central heating, all very tastefully furnished. Pretty lounge & dining room where guests can relax & enjoy a hearty breakfast. An ideal base from which to explore Snowdonia, walk, fish or pony trek. Whatever your choice, a warm welcome is assured.	£16.00	Y	Y	Y
Maureen & Clive Muskus **Ty'n-Y-Celyn House** **Llanrwst Road** **Betws-Y-Coed** **LL24 0HD** **Tel: (0690) 710202** **Fax 0690 710800** **Open: ALL YEAR** **Map Ref No. 34**	Nearest Road: A.470 A high standard of comfort & friendly, helpful hosts await you at Ty'n-Y-Celyn. This large Victorian home, located in a lovely position above the picturesque village of Betws-Y-Coed, has panoramic views of the Llugney Valley, mountains & Conway river. Accommodation is in a choice of 8 very comfortable en-suite bedrooms with T.V. & tea/coffee makers. Most also have wonderful views. A residents' T.V. lounge & garden are also available. This is an ideal centre for touring, walking, fishing & golf.	£18.00	Y	N	Y

see PHOTO over

Ty'n-Y-Celyn House.   Betws-Y-Coed.

Wales
Gwynedd

	minimum £ per person	children taken	evening meals	animals taken

Jean & Peter Whittingham
Fron Heulog
Betws-y-Coed
LL24 0BL
Tel: (0690) 710736
Open: ALL YEAR
Map Ref No. 34

Nearest Road: A.5, A.470
You will enjoy real hospitality at Fron Heulog - "The Country House in the Village" - a pleasant Victorian stone-built house, in quiet peaceful riverside wooded scenery, which offers superb accommodation, with full-facility bedrooms, spacious lounges & pleasant dining room. Highly recommended for friendly atmosphere, warmth, comfort & hostess home cooking. Set in the heart of picturesque Snowdonia - with so much to see & do - Fron Heulog is more home than hotel.

£16.00 — N — N — N — (no smoking)

R.T & B.M. Valadini
Henllys (Old Court) Hotel
Old Church Road
Betws-Y-Coed
LL24 OAL
Tel: (0690) 710534
Open: ALL YEAR
Map Ref No. 34

Nearest Road: A.5
No wonder guests return time after time to this beautifully converted Victorian magistrates court, set in peaceful riverside gardens. Choose from judges chambers to convicted felons single cell, each individually designed bedroom is fully equipped for your comfort. The police station houses the fireside bar, the magistrates court the dining room, where superb food is imaginatively prepared from freshly grown produce.

£21.50 — Y — Y — N — (no smoking)
CREDIT CARD
VISA
M'CARD

Ann Howard
Tan Dinas Guest House
Coed Cynhelier Road
Betws-Y-Coed
LL24 0BL
Tel: (0690) 710635
Open: ALL YEAR
Map Ref No. 34

Nearest Road: A.5
A warm welcome awaits you at this lovely Victorian country home, situated in 3 acres of woodland gardens, offering peace & seclusion, & only 500 yards from village centre. Guests may choose from 6 spacious, centrally heated rooms, with lovely views. All rooms have h&c & tea/coffee making facilities. 4 rooms en-suite. Log fires in winter. Forest walks from house. Golf & fishing nearby. Ideal touring centre. Ample parking. Evening meals available. Licensed. Video library.

£14.50 — Y — Y — N — (no smoking)

Peter & Janet Pitman
Tan-y-Foel Country House
Capel Garmon
Betws-y-Coed LL26 0RE
Tel: (0690) 710507
Fax 0690 710681
Open: ALL YEAR
Map Ref No. 35

Nearest Road: A.470, A.5
Tan-y-Foel is a country house, set in the Snowdonia National Park with wonderful views across the Conwy Valley. The characterful stone-built house, dating from the 16th century, has been tastefully refurbished & hosts, Peter & Janet, go out of their way to provide a personal style of service which many would find hard to emulate. Bedrooms (some with 4-posters) are individually decorated & fresh flowers are in abundance. Superb cuisine. Children over 12 years.

£36.00 — Y — Y — N — (no smoking)
see PHOTO over
CREDIT CARD
VISA
M'CARD
AMEX

James & Shelagh Ratcliffe
Ty Gwyn Hotel
Betws-Y-Coed
LL24 0SG
Tel: (0690) 710383/710787
Open: ALL YEAR
Map Ref No. 34

Nearest Road: A.5
Open fire, beamed ceilings & antique furniture all help to recall the days when this small, friendly, family hotel was a coaching inn. Each pretty bedroom (some with 4-poster beds) has its own tasteful colour scheme & interesting "bric a brac" to add a homely touch. Ty Gwyn offers food which is a tribute to the local area & is an ideal base for exploring the Snowdonia range, coastal towns & Lleyn Peninsula.

£18.00 — Y — Y — Y
CREDIT CARD
VISA
M'CARD

Tan-y-Foel Country House.   Capel Garmon.

Wales
Gwynedd

	Nearest Road / Description	per person minimum £	children taken	evening meals	animals taken
M. & R.E. Fakhri **Bryn Bella Guest House** **Llanrwst Road** **Betws-Y-Coed** **LL24 0HD** **Tel: (0690) 710627** **Open: ALL YEAR** **Map Ref No. 34**	Nearest Road: A.5, A.470 Nestling in a quiet wooded hillside in the Snowdonia National Park, Bryn Bella is a small Victorian guest house overlooking the picturesque village of Betws-Y-Coed, standing at the junction between the Conwy, Llugwy & Lledr Rivers & their valleys. 6 comfortably furnished rooms with washbasins, tea/coffee making facilities & colour T.V. Some rooms have shower/w.c. en-suite. Betws-Y-Coed is an ideal base for touring, climbing, riding, fishing, golf & other outdoor activities.	£13.50	Y	N	N
Mr & Mrs J Pinnock **Cae Cyd** **Groeslon** **Caernarfon LL54 7DP** **Tel: (0286) 880253** **Open: APR - OCT** **Map Ref No. 37**	Nearest Road: A.487 For a peaceful bed and breakfast stay in Cae Cyd, a small Welsh stone cottage with character, set in 3 acres of garden on the edge of Snowdonia National Park. Delight in the views of Caernarfon Bay and Anglesey, walk in the fields, watch the sunsets over the sea. Accommodation is in two guest bedrooms, a double and a twin-bedded room. A delightful home.	£14.00	N	N	Y
Mr & Mrs R Bayles **The White House** **Llanfaglan** **Caernarfon** **LL54 5RA** **Tel: (0286) 673003** **Open: ALL YEAR** **Map Ref No. 38**	Nearest Road: A.487 The White House is a large detached house in its own grounds, overlooking Foryd Bay with the Snowdonia mountains behind. There are 5 tastefully decorated bedrooms all with bath or shower, tea/coffee making facilities & colour T.V. Guests are welcome to use the residents' lounge, outdoor pool & gardens. Ideally situated for bird-watching, walking, windsurfing, golf & visiting the historic Welsh castles.	£16.00	Y	N	Y
Mrs Rita Murray **Min-Y-Gaer Hotel** **Porthmadog Road** **Criccieth LL52 0HP** **Tel: (0766) 522151** **Fax 0766 522151** **Open: MAR - OCT** **Map Ref No. 39**	Nearest Road: A.497 A pleasant, licensed house in a quiet residential area, offering very good accommodation in 10 comfortable rooms, of which most have a bathroom en-suite. All have a colour T.V. & tea/coffee making facilities. The hotel enjoys commanding views of Criccieth Castle & the scenic Cardigan Bay coastline, & is only 2 minutes' walk from the safe, sandy beach. Car parking on the premises. An ideal base for touring Snowdonia. CREDIT CARD VISA M'CARD AMEX	£16.25	Y	N	N
Patricia Clayton **Trefaes Guest House** **Y Maes** **Criccieth** **LL52 0AE** **Tel: (0766) 523204** **Fax 0766 523013** **Open: ALL YEAR** **Map Ref No. 39**	Nearest Road: A.497 An elegant Edwardian house on the edge of Criccieth Green, with views of the sea and Castle. The 4 comfortable bedrooms have en-suite facilities, T.V., tea/coffee tray, central heating. Quiet lounge for reading, writing, cards. Delicious breakfasts. Guests may relax in the garden with a Welsh tea. Evening meals are fish and vegetarian cuisine only. Parking in grounds. Excellent base for historic sites, sea and walking holidays. Children over 5 please. An ideal spot for touring.	£16.50	Y	Y	N

Wales
Gwynedd

	per person minimum £	children taken	evening meals	animals taken

Mr & Mrs G.H. Roberts **Castle Cottage Hotel** **Pen Llech** **Harlech** **LL46 2YL** Tel: (0766) 780479 Open: ALL YEAR Map Ref No. 40	Nearest Road: A.496, A.470 Castle Cottage is a comfortable family-run hotel & restaurant. This delightful house, dating back at least 200 years, has many exposed beams & offers 6 rooms of great character which are comfortable & have modern amenities. The restaurant is known for its good food. Only 200 yards from Harlech Castle. The beach & nature reserve are within 5 miles. An ideal base for touring this lovely region. Golf arrangements at Royal St. Davids. Garden for guests' use.	£20.00 CREDIT CARD VISA M'CARD AMEX	Y	Y	Y
Gillian & Eric Newton **Davies** **Noddfa Hotel** **Lower Road** **Harlech LL46 2UB** Tel: (0766) 780043 Open: ALL YEAR Map Ref No. 40	Nearest Road: A.496 A Victorian country house situated within the National Park with superb views of Snowdon, Tremadog Bay & Harlech Castle. 4 comfortable rooms (2 en-suite, T.V.). Extensive menu, licensed. Gillian & Eric will be delighted to explain the Medieval weaponry displayed in the bar, the history of Harlech Castle & give archery lessons in the hotel grounds. Very close to the Castle, beach, indoor swimming pool & theatre.	£15.50 CREDIT CARD VISA M'CARD	Y	Y	N
Tony & Gina Hirst **Hafod Country House** **Cemaes Bay** **Isle of Anglesey** **LL67 0DS** Tel: (0407) 710500 Open: MAR - OCT Map Ref No. 41	Nearest Road: A.5025 A spacious Edwardian house standing in an acre of garden. Set in peaceful surroundings with superb sea & mountain views. Only a 10 min. walk to the village with its picturesque harbour & sandy beach. Offering 3 comfortable bedrooms, 2 en-suite, with beverage facilities. A large, elegant lounge with colour T.V. & dining room are also available. Garden with tennis & croquet. Renowned for excellent food. Licensed. Nearby is golf, bird sanctuary, lake & sea fishing.	£16.50	Y	Y	N
Mrs Margaret Hughes **Llwydiarth Fawr Farm** **Llanerchymedd** **Isle of Anglesey** **LL71 8DF** Tel:(0248) 470321/470540 Open: ALL YEAR Map Ref No. 42	Nearest Road: A.5 Secluded Georgian mansion set in 800 acres of woodland & farmland with lovely open views. Ideal touring base for the island's coastline, Snowdonia & North Wales Coast. 4 delightfully furnished bedrooms with en-suite facilities & T.V. Full central heating, log fires. Enjoy a taste of Wales with delicious country cooking using farm & local produce. Personal attention & a warm Welsh welcome to guests, who will enjoy the scenic walks & private fishing. Convenient for Holyhead to Ireland crossings.	£18.50 *see PHOTO over*	Y	Y	N
Marian Roberts **Plas Trefarthen** **Brynsiencyn** **Isle of Anglesey** **LL61 6SZ** Tel: (0248) 430379 Open: ALL YEAR Map Ref No. 29	Nearest Road: A.5, A.4080 Plas Trefarthen is a large Georgian house standing in 200 acres of land on the shores of the Menai Straits, with uninterrupted views of Caernarfon Castle & the Snowdonia mountain range. Ideal touring base, close to Plas Newydd, Penrhyn Castle National Trust & Sea Zoo. Elegant rooms with en-suite bathrooms, colour T.V. & tea/coffee facilities. A warm Welsh welcome awaits you from Marian Roberts.	£16.00	Y	Y	N

Llwydiarth Fawr Farm. Anglesey.

Wales
Gwynedd

		per person minimum £	children taken	evening meals	animals taken
Eileen & Peter Rigby **White Lodge Hotel** **9 Neville Crescent** **Central Promenade** **Llandudno LL30 1AT** **Tel: (0492) 877713** **Open: APR - OCT** **Map Ref No. 43**	Nearest Road: A.5, A.55 Situated on the promenade of this beautiful Victorian holiday resort; all bedrooms are comfortable & en-suite & have tea/coffee making facilities & colour T.V.'s. There is a small bar & pleasant lounge facing the sea for guests' use. 'White Lodge' offers an ideal touring centre for those day trips to Conway Castle, Caernarfon Castle, Chester or the mountains & valleys of Snowdonia. An excellent spot for touring.	£19.50 CREDIT CARD AMEX	Y	Y	Y
Brian Stephens **Cae'r Berllan** **Betws Road** **Nr. Betws-y-Coed** **Llanrwst LL26 0PP** **Tel: (0492) 640027** **Open: ALL YEAR** **Map Ref No. 44**	Nearest Road: A.5, B.470 Tranquility reigns in this magnificent 16th century country house with massive oak beams and family antiques, set in beautiful private gardens in the Conwy Valley near Betws-y-Coed. Ideal base for Snowdonia and North Wales. Luxurious beamed bedrooms, private facilities, T.V., etc. Wonderful views from every window. Renowned for high standards of international cuisine served in the relaxed atmosphere of the inglenook dining room. The warmest of welcomes awaits you.	£22.00 CREDIT CARD VISA M'CARD	Y	Y	Y
Norman T. Barker **Hafod House Hotel** **Trefriw** **LL27 0RQ** **Tel: (0492) 640029** **Fax 0492 641351** **Open: ALL YEAR** **Map Ref No. 45**	Nearest Road: A.5 A most attractive 17th century traditional Welsh stone farmhouse in a peaceful setting on the edge of Trefriw in the beautiful Conway Valley, inside Snowdonia National Park. All 8 guest rooms are very well appointed, 2 having luxury status with designer decor, 4-poster beds & whirlpool baths. Your host is your chef serving first class dishes. Children over 11 years welcome. Centrally located for touring all North Wales.	£16.50 *see PHOTO over* CREDIT CARD VISA M'CARD AMEX	N	Y	N

All the establishments mentioned in this guide
are members of
The Worldwide Bed & Breakfast Association

Hafod House, Trefriw.

Wales
Powys

		minimum £ per person	children taken	evening meals	animals taken
Mrs Mary Cole **'Dolycoed'** **Talyllyn** **Brecon** **LD3 7SY** **Tel: (0874) 84666** **Open: ALL YEAR** **Map Ref No. 46**	Nearest Road: A.40 Dolycoed, built at the turn of the century, retains many of its interesting original features. Standing in a sheltered position in Brecon Beacons National Park, it offers a warm, friendly, homely welcome to all. 2 comfortable guest bedrooms with radio & tea/coffee makers & a guests' lounge with colour T.V. Many outdoor activities nearby: pony trekking, riding, fishing, watersports & walking. A lovely home.	£14.00	Y	N	Y
C.H. Hammond **Querida** **43 Garth Road** **Builth Wells** **LD2 3AR** **Tel: (0982) 553642** **Open: ALL YEAR** **Map Ref No. 47**	Nearest Road: A.483 A pleasant stone-built guest house within easy reach of the town centre. Accommodation is in 2 rooms with modern amenities. 1 double & 1 twin room with tea/coffee making facilities. A guests lounge with colour T.V. is also available. Golf, fishing & 2 sports halls are nearby. There are excellent walks along the River Wye. The Brecon Beacons, Black Mountains & the Elan Valley are easily reached. Convenient for touring.	£12.00	Y	N	Y
Nancy M. Jones **Ty-Isaf Farm** **Erwood** **Builth Wells LD2 3SZ** **Tel: (0982) 560607** **Open: ALL YEAR** **Map Ref No. 48**	Nearest Road: A.470 Ty-Isaf Farm, situated in the attractive village of Erwood, offers accommodation in 3 comfortably furnished rooms with modern amenities & tea/coffee making facilities. Plentiful English or Continental breakfasts are served. Special diets, packed lunches provided by arrangement. Guests may relax in the cosy lounge with T.V. throughout the day. An ideal base for touring.	£12.00	Y	Y	Y
Mr & Mrs J.H. Usborne **Glan-Nant** **Brecon Road** **Crickhowell** **NP8 1DL** **Tel: (0873) 810631** **Open: APR - OCT** **Map Ref No. 49**	Nearest Road: A.40 A substantial country family house, part Georgian, part Regency, with an attractive verandah, standing in peaceful grounds with superb views over the mountains & countryside. Accommodation is in 3 attractive rooms with modern facilities, 1 with bath en-suite. Tea/coffee makers provided. Situated in a marvellous area for touring & walking. Pony trekking & fishing locally. Excellent pub opposite for evening meals. Children over 8 years welcome.	£14.00	Y	N	N
Mrs P.K. Cracroft **Tretower House** **Tretower** **Crickhowell** **NP8 1RF** **Tel: (0874) 730225** **Open: ALL YEAR** **Map Ref No. 50**	Nearest Road: A.40 Charming old family house set in the beautiful Usk Valley with views of the Black Mountains. A warm welcome awaits at Tretower House where there are 2 very comfortable & attractively furnished rooms, 1 en-suite & 1 with private bathroom. Each has tea/coffee making facilities. Beautiful garden & plenty of walks, pony trekking, fishing & golf locally. A delightful home, ideal for a relaxing holiday or for touring. Excellent first stop as you enter Wales.	£16.00	Y	N	N

Wales
Powys

	minimum £ per person	children taken	evening meals	animals taken
Peter & Olwen Roberts **York House** **Hardwicke Road, Cusop** **Hay-on-Wye HR3 5QX** **Tel: (0497) 820705** **Open: ALL YEAR** **Map Ref No. 51**	Nearest Road: A.438 Peter and Olwen Roberts welcome you to their traditional Victorian guest house quietly situated in beautiful gardens on the edge of Hay. Sunny mountain views are enjoyed by the well-appointed rooms, mostly en-suite. Ideal for a relaxing holiday browsing the world famous bookshops, exploring the National Park and Kilvert country, or just enjoying the freshly prepared home cooking. Private parking. Children over 8 please. CREDIT CARD VISA M'CARD	£16.50	Y	Y	Y
Mrs C.H. Hood **Pilleth Court** **Whitton** **Knighton LD7 1NP** **Tel: (05476) 272** **Open:ALL YEAR (Excl.** **Xmas & New Year)** **Map Ref No. 52**	Nearest Road: A.488 An Elizabethan house with all the character & atmosphere retained. 3 delightful guest rooms, 1 en-suite, with radio & tea/coffee making facilities. Set in 600 acres it is surrounded by marvellous unspoilt countryside. The site of the Battle of Pilleth & a 12th century church are close by. A wonderful base for walking or touring. Evening meals cooked with 'flair' are available by arrangement. Children over 9 welcome.	£15.00	Y	Y	N
Anne & Tony Millan **Guidfa House** **Crossgates** **Llandrindod Wells** **LD1 6RF** **Tel: (0597) 851241** **Fax 0597 851875** **Open: ALL YEAR** **Map Ref No. 53**	Nearest Road: A.483, A.44 Licensed Georgian guest house, situated in an ideal location for touring lakes, mountains, national parks & the coast. The bedrooms are all comfortable & spacious, most en-suite, all with colour T.V. & tea/coffee making facilities. A ground floor room is also available. Meals are prepared by Anne, who is Cordon Bleu trained. Dinner is a set menu but special diets/requests can always be catered for with a little prior notice. A lovely home, conveniently located for touring. CREDIT CARD VISA M'CARD	£22.00	N	Y	N
Leslie & Sylvia Knott **The Ffaldau Country** **House** **Llandegley** **Llandrindod Wells** **LD1 5UD** **Tel: (0597851) 421** **Open: ALL YEAR** **Map Ref No. 54**	Nearest Road: A.44 Nestling in the lee of the Radnor Hills, this charming Welsh stone 'cruck' built long-house, c.1500, set in 1 & a half acres of garden, enjoys uninterrupted views of beautiful countryside. Pretty bedrooms are furnished with extra little touches. Guests may enjoy the library of approximately 400 books. Oak beamed dining room with log fire, excellent country produce cooked to Cordon Bleu standards. A la carte menu, good wine list. Excellent centre for outdoor pursuits. Children over 10 welcome. CREDIT CARD M'CARD	£18.00	Y	Y	N
Mrs Gaynor Bright **Little Brompton Farm** **Montgomery** **SY15 6HY** **Tel: (0686) 668371** **Open: ALL YEAR** **Map Ref No. 55**	Nearest Road: B.4385, A.489 Little Brompton Farm is a 17th century farmhouse standing on a 100 acre mixed working farm, including geese & peacocks. Retaining much of its original character with oak beams & inglenook fireplace. Furnished with period pieces & antiques. Offering 3 comfortable bedrooms, 2 en-suite, all with modern amenities & tea/coffee making facilities. Good home-cooked food is served. A good base for touring & walking. Offa's Dyke actually runs through the farm.	£14.50	Y	Y	Y

Wales
Powys

		minimum £ per person	children taken	evening meals	animals taken
Mrs Ceinwen Richards **The Drewin Farm** **Churchstoke** **Montgomery** **SY15 6TW** **Tel: (0588) 620325** **Open: APR - NOV** **Map Ref No. 56**	Nearest Road: A.489, B.4385 A warm Welsh welcome awaits you at Drewin, a delightful 17th century farmhouse retaining much of its original character with oak beams & inglenook fireplace. It has panoramic views overlooking beautiful unspoilt countryside. 2 pleasant bedrooms with tea/coffee making facilities, T.V. if required. Good home cooking is a feature with vegetarian dishes available. Games room with snooker table for guests' use. Offa's Dyke footpath runs through this 104 acre mixed farm.	£14.00	Y	Y	Y
Paul & Maureen Marriott **A Country Manor** **Dysserth Hall** **Powis Castle** **Welshpool** **SY21 8RQ** **Tel: (0938) 552153** **Open: MAR-DEC** **Map Ref No. 57**	Nearest Road: A.483, A.458 Dysserth Hall is a delightful Georgian house standing in the beautiful countryside of mid-Wales, a short walk from Powis Castle. The accommodation is very comfortable, with antique furnishings. 4 bedrooms are individually decorated, 1 with antique mahogany & 1 twin with Victorian brass beds. All have views of the Severn Valley & Long Mountain or woodlands. Excellent 3-course dinner available by arrangement. Paul & Maureen are most helpful hosts, & arrange short breaks for golf, fishing, etc.	£15.00	Y	Y	N
Mrs Sue Jones **Lower Trelydan Farm** **Guilsfield** **Welshpool** **SY21 9PH** **Tel: (0938) 553105** **Open: ALL YEAR** **Map Ref No. 58**	Nearest Road: A.483, A.490 Graham & Sue welcome you to this wonderful old black & white farmhouse on this working farm, listed for its history & beauty. Bedrooms are tastefully furnished with en-suite facilities & colour T.V. on request. Oak beamed lounge & dining room where home cooking is a speciality & is served every night. Licensed bar & tea/coffee tray. Powis Castle & many beauty spots nearby, also many leisure activities & walks. A wonderful base for a holiday. Relax in this lovely home & capture the atmosphere of 4 centuries of history in this outstanding house.	£14.50	Y	Y	N *see PHOTO over*

When booking your accommodation please mention
The Best Bed & Breakfast

Lower Trelydan Farm. Guilsfield.

Towns & Counties Index

Towns & Counties Index

Towns & Counties Index

Town	County	Country
Knighton	Powys	Wales
Langport	Somerset	England
Lapworth	Warwickshire	England
Launceston	Cornwall	England
Leamington Spa	Warwickshire	England
Leeds	Yorkshire	England
Leek	Staffordshire	England
Leominster	Herefordshire	England
Lewes	Sussex	England
Lichfield	Staffordshire	England
Lincoln	Lincolnshire	England
Liverpool	Merseyside	England
Llandrindod Wells	Powys	Wales
Llandudno	Gwynedd	Wales
Llanrwst	Gwynedd	Wales
Llansilin	Clwyd	Wales
Loch Lomond	Stirlingshire	Scotland
Lochearnhead	Perthshire	Scotland
Loddon	Norfolk	England
Long Hanborough	Oxfordshire	England
Looe	Cornwall	England
Lostwithiel	Cornwall	England
Louth	Lincolnshire	England
Lower Fishguard	Dyfed	Wales
Lydney	Gloucestershire	England
Lyme Regis	Dorset	England
Lymington	Hampshire	England
Lynton	Devon	England
Malmesbury	Wiltshire	England
Malton	Yorkshire	England
Malvern	Worcestershire	England
Manningtree	Essex	England
Manorbier	Dyfed	Wales
Mansfield	Nottinghamshire	England
Margate	Kent	England
Market Drayton	Shropshire	England
Marlborough	Wiltshire	England
Masham	Yorkshire	England
Matlock	Derbyshire	England
Mayfield	Sussex	England
Mere	Wiltshire	England
Merthyr Tydfil	Glamorgan	Wales
Mevagissey	Cornwall	England
Midhurst	Sussex	England
Minchinhampton	Gloucestershire	England
Minehead	Somerset	England
Moffat	Dumfriesshire	Scotland
Montgomery	Powys	Wales
Morchard Bishop	Devon	England
Moreton-in-Marsh	Gloucestershire	England
Moretonhampsted	Devon	England
Morpeth	Northumberland	England
Mortehoe	Devon	England

Town	County	Country
Much Wenlock	Shropshire	England
Mundford	Norfolk	England
Nailsworth	Gloucestershire	England
Newark	Nottinghamshire	England
Newbury	Berkshire	England
Newcastle-upon-Tyne	Tyne & Weir	England
Newent	Gloucestershire	England
Newnham-on-Severn	Gloucestershire	England
Newport	Gwent	Wales
Newport-on-Tay	Fifeshire	Scotland
Newquay	Cornwall	England
Newton Abbot	Devon	England
Northallerton	Yorkshire	England
Northwich	Cheshire	England
Norton	Gloucestershire	England
Norwich	Norfolk	England
Nuneaton	Warwickshire	England
Okehampton	Devon	England
Ongar	Essex	England
Otley	Suffolk	England
Oswestry	Shropshire	England
Oundle	Northamptonshire	England
Oxford	Oxfordshire	England
Oxhill	Warwickshire	England
Painswick	Gloucestershire	England
Par	Cornwall	England
Penrith	Cumbria	England
Penryn	Cornwall	England
Penshurst	Kent	England
Penzance	Cornwall	England
Perranporth	Cornwall	England
Perth	Perthshire	Scotland
Peterborough	Northamptonshire	England
Petersfield	Hampshire	England
Pickering	Yorkshire	England
Pitlochry	Perthshire	scotland
Polperro	Cornwall	England
Polruan-By Fowey	Cornwall	England
Pontypool	Gwent	Wales
Portree	Isle of Skye	Scotland
Pulborough	Sussex	England
Reading	Berkshire	England
Redmile	Nottinghamshire	England
Redruth	Cornwall	England
Reigate	Surrey	England
Renfrewshire by Glasgow	Lanarkshire	Scotland
Retford	Nottinghamshire	England
Richmond	Yorkshire	England
Ringwood	Hampshire	England
Ripon	Yorkshire	England
Ropley	Hampshire	England
Ross-on-Wye	Herefordshire	England
Rotherham	Yorkshire	England

Towns & Counties Index